Japan under the DPJ:
The Politics of Transition and Governance

JAPAN

UNDER

THE DPJ

The Politics of Transition

and Governance

Edited by Kenji E. Kushida and Phillip Y. Lipscy

THE WALTER H. SHORENSTEIN
ASIA-PACIFIC RESEARCH CENTER

THE WALTER H. SHORENSTEIN ASIA-PACIFIC RESEARCH CENTER (Shorenstein APARC) is a unique Stanford University institution focused on the interdisciplinary study of contemporary Asia. Shorenstein APARC's mission is to produce and publish outstanding interdisciplinary, Asia-Pacific–focused research; educate students, scholars, and corporate and governmental affiliates; promote constructive interaction to influence U.S. policy toward the Asia-Pacific; and guide Asian nations on key issues of societal transition, development, U.S.-Asia relations, and regional cooperation.

The Walter H. Shorenstein Asia-Pacific Research Center
Freeman Spogli Institute for International Studies
Stanford University
Encina Hall
Stanford, CA 94305-6055
tel. 650-723-9741
fax 650-723-6530
http://aparc.stanford.edu

Japan under the DPJ: The Politics of Transition and Governance
may be ordered from:
The Brookings Institution
c/o DFS, P.O. Box 50370, Baltimore, MD, USA
tel. 1-800-537-5487 or 410-516-6956
fax 410-516-6998
http://www.brookings.edu/press

Library of Congress Control Number: 2013944293

ISBN 978-1-931368-33-9

First printing, 2013.

Typeset by Classic Typography in 10½/13 Sabon MT Pro

Contents

Tables and Figures

Tables

Figures

Contributors

ALISA GAUNDER is professor of political science at Southwestern University in Georgetown, Texas. Gaunder received her PhD from the University of California, Berkeley, in 2001. Her research interests include comparative political leadership, campaign finance reform in Japan and the United States, and women and politics. She is the author of *Political Reform in Japan: Leadership Looming Large* (2007) and the editor of *The Routledge Handbook of Japanese Politics* (2011).

LINDA HASUNUMA received her PhD in comparative politics from UCLA in 2010. She is assistant professor of government at Franklin and Marshall College. Her dissertation analyzes changes to Japan's central-local relations since the electoral reform and the politics of decentralization. She also co-authored a book chapter on the Kōmeitō's policy influence while in coalition with the LDP from 1999–2009. Her current projects investigate Japan's relations with South Korea, and issues related to local politics and gender and politics in these two countries. Hasunuma is a US-Japan Network for the Future, Maureen and Mike Mansfield Fellow (Cohort II).

CHRISTOPHER W. HUGHES (BA Oxford University; MA Rochester University; PhD Sheffield University) is professor of international politics and Japanese studies, chair of the Department of Politics and International Studies, and chair of the Faculty of Social Sciences, at the University of Warwick, UK. He was formerly a research associate at the University of Hiroshima; *Asahi Shimbun* Visiting Professor of Mass Media and Politics, University of Tokyo; and Edwin O. Reischauer Visiting Professor of Japanese Studies,

Department of Government, Harvard University. His most recent book is *Japan's Remilitarisation* (2009). He is currently president of the British Association of Japanese Studies, and joint editor of *The Pacific Review.*

ELLIS S. KRAUSS is professor at the School of International Relations and Pacific Studies, University of California, San Diego. He received his PhD from Stanford University (1973). An expert on postwar Japanese politics and U.S.-Japan relations, he has coauthored a book with Robert Pekkanen (University of Washington) about the development of Japan's long-time ruling party, *The Rise and Fall of Japan's LDP: Political Party Organizations as Historical Institutions* (Cornell University Press, 2010). He and Pekkanen have now begun a book project on political leadership in postwar Japan. He has published articles in numerous journals, including the *American Political Science Review*, *American Journal of Political Science*, *Journal of Japanese Studies*, and *Journal of East Asian Studies.*

KENJI E. KUSHIDA is the Takahashi Research Associate in Japanese Studies at the Walter H. Shorenstein Asia-Pacific Research Center at Stanford University. He holds a PhD in political science from the University of California, Berkeley. Kushida's research focuses on comparative political economy, particularly in the areas of information technology and comparative capitalist systems. His streams of research include commoditization in information technology sectors around the world, cloud computing, Japan-Korea comparisons in the broadband and wireless industries, Japan's "Galapagos" IT sector, the Fukushima nuclear disaster, systemic change in Japan's financial sector, the effects of multinational corporations in Japan, and Silicon Valley–Japan relationships.

PHILLIP Y. LIPSCY is assistant professor of political science at Stanford University and Thomas Rohlen Center Fellow at the Walter H. Shorenstein Asia-Pacific Research Center. His research focuses on international and comparative political economy with an emphasis on East Asia, particularly Japan.

YUKIO MAEDA is associate professor of political science at the Institute of Social Science at the University of Tokyo, Japan. His research interests lie in the areas of public opinion, electoral behavior, and survey research. He has published mainly on Japan's public opinion and party politics. Maeda is currently researching the impact of public opinion polling and cabinet approval ratings in Japanese politics.

KENNETH MORI MCELWAIN is assistant professor of political science at the University of Michigan, Ann Arbor. His research focuses on the politics of institutional design, including the manipulation of electoral rules, the democratization of political parties, and the formation of national constitutions. His current project examines why Japanese governments are short-lived. He is a coeditor of *Political Change in Japan: Electoral Behavior, Party Realignment, and the Koizumi Reforms* (2009).

ROBERT J. PEKKANEN is associate professor at the University of Washington. He received his PhD in political science from Harvard University in 2002. In addition to numerous articles in journals including the *American Political Science Review* and *Comparative Political Studies*, he has coauthored or coedited six books on topics ranging from Japan's LDP (with Ellis S. Krauss) to U.S. nonprofit advocacy (with Steven Rathgeb Smith and Yutaka Tsujinaka). His first book, *Japan's Dual Civil Society* (Stanford 2006) won the Masayoshi Ohira Prize. His most recent book, *Japan Decides 2012* (Palgrave, 2013, coedited with Steven R. Reed and Ethan Scheiner) is on Japan's House of Representatives election of December 2012.

STEVEN R. REED is professor of modern government at Chuo University in Japan, where all of his classes are taught in Japanese. His major areas of research are parties, elections, electoral systems, and Japanese politics. He recently coedited with Robert Pekkanen and Ethan Scheiner *Japan Decides: The Japanese General Election of 2012*. His current research interests include religion and politics and political corruption.

ETHAN SCHEINER is professor of political science at the University of California, Davis. He has published articles in a number of political science and Japanese studies journals, and he is the author of the Cambridge University Press books *Democracy without Competition in Japan* (2006) and *Electoral Systems and Political Context* (2012), and coeditor of *Japan Decides 2012*, which analyzes the recent lower-house election in Japan.

KAY SHIMIZU is assistant professor in the Department of Political Science and the Weatherhead East Asian Institute at Columbia University. Her research concerns the political economy of Japan and Greater China, with a focus on central-local government relations, fiscal politics, and financial institutions. She has published in the *Socio-Economic Review*, the *Journal of East Asian Studies*, and the *Journal of Social Science Japan* and is a coeditor of and contributor to *Political Change in Japan: Electoral Behavior, Party Realignment, and the Koizumi Reforms* (2009).

DANIEL M. SMITH is assistant professor in the Department of Government at Harvard University. He earned his PhD in political science from the University of California, San Diego, in 2012. He has conducted research in Japan as a Ministry of Education, Culture, Sports, Science, and Technology research scholar at Chuo University, and as a Fulbright dissertation research fellow at the University of Tokyo. Most recently, he was a postdoctoral fellow at the Walter H. Shorenstein Asia-Pacific Research Center at Stanford University.

DANIEL SNEIDER is the associate director for research at the Walter H. Shorenstein Asia-Pacific Research Center at Stanford University. His research focuses on Asian regional issues, on wartime historical memory in Asia, on U.S. foreign and security policy toward East Asia, and on Korean and Japanese foreign policy. Sneider is a former foreign correspondent who served in Japan, India, and the Soviet Union.

Acknowledgments

We would like to extend our sincerest thanks to everybody who made this volume possible. The Walter H. Shorenstein Asia-Pacific Research Center (Shorenstein APARC) at Stanford University, under the leadership of Director Gi-Wook Shin, generously supported its publication. Generous funding was also provided by the Japan Fund at the Freeman Spogli Institute of International Studies, Stanford University. Initial papers that form the basis of this volume were submitted by participants at the "Political Change in Japan: One Step Forward, One Step Back?" conference held at Shorenstein APARC in February 2011. We thank presenters and discussants for the lively and rigorous interactions that led to many of the chapters in this volume. They include Michael Armacost, Amy Catalinac, Gary Cox, Leif-Eric Easley, Robert Eberhart, Thomas Fingar, Tobias Harris, Shigeo Hirano, Llewlyn Hughes, Ellis Krauss, Gene Park, T.J. Pempel, Benjamin Self, Gi-Wook Shin, David Straub, Michael Thies, Steven Vogel, and Robert Weiner. We also thank the many current and former politicians, policymakers, and others in the academic and media community who were generous with their time and insights as this project moved forward. We are also grateful to the anonymous reviewers for their valuable insights.

Several of the papers presented at the conference became a special issue of the *Journal of East Asian Studies*, coedited by Phillip Lipscy and Ethan Scheiner. We thank Stephan Haggard and Lynne Rienner Publishers for allowing us to reprint the articles, some with minor edits and revisions, for this volume. The *Journal of Japanese Studies* kindly gave permission to reprint the chapter by Christopher Hughes.

We would also like to recognize Daniel Sneider, associate director of research at Shorenstein APARC, for supporting the conference and this volume in a tightly packed publishing pipeline. Finally, we thank George Krompacky, publications manager at Shorenstein APARC, for his tireless and meticulous efforts to push forward with the innumerable tasks on the road to this publication.

Kenji E. Kushida
Phillip Y. Lipscy
Stanford University

Japan under the DPJ:
The Politics of Transition and Governance

Introduction

1 The Rise and Fall of the Democratic Party of Japan

Kenji E. Kushida and Phillip Y. Lipscy

The Democratic Party of Japan (DPJ) came to power in 2009 in a land-slide electoral victory, ending the Liberal Democratic Party's (LDP's) nearly continuous rule of over half a century. This was widely heralded as Japan's most significant political transformation since the LDP's formation and assumption of power in 1955.[1] For the first time in over fifty years, the LDP was no longer the largest party in the House of Representatives (lower house) of the Japanese Diet. The DPJ came to power with a strong hand; in combination with its coalition partners, it already controlled the House of Councillors (upper house), and the party now commanded 64 percent of lower-house seats. However, in 2012, just over three years later, the DPJ fell from power in an equally stunning landslide loss to the LDP.

The DPJ ran on a platform of change, promising a decisive break from LDP rule and a wide range of political and policy reforms. However, the DPJ was unable or unwilling to carry out most of its reform promises. Furthermore, DPJ rule was characterized by unstable leadership—three prime ministers in just over three years in power. Public enthusiasm for the

---

[1] For examples, see Iinuma (2009); Arase (2010); Green (2010); Reed, Scheiner, and Thies (2012); and Reed, Scheiner, and Thies (2009). An extensive list of media quotes can be found in Rosenbluth and Thies (2010, 186).

We thank Ethan Scheiner, Dan Smith, and participants at the 2011 conference "Political Change in Japan," at Stanford University, for valuable feedback. We also thank Trevor Incerti for excellent research assistance and the Japan Fund at the Freeman Spogli Institute at Stanford University and the Walter H. Shorenstein Asia-Pacific Research Center for their generosity and support.

DPJ quickly faded and turned to disillusionment. Although approval ratings for the DPJ recovered briefly with each new prime minister, public support eroded rapidly, culminating in a crushing electoral defeat that left many wondering whether the party would survive.

The brief reign of the DPJ raises two core puzzles. The first is the party's remarkable ascendance and equally dramatic fall from power. The DPJ's coming to power necessitates a reassessment of many of the central questions of Japanese party politics. Japan was long described as an "uncommon democracy" (Pempel 1990), a political system characterized by LDP dominance and fragmented, weak opposition parties (Scheiner 2006). The DPJ's landslide victory of 2009 clearly signaled that it was no longer appropriate to characterize Japanese politics in these terms. However, the DPJ's assumption of power raises equally compelling questions: Why are electoral outcomes in Japan now so volatile? Has Japan become a true two-party system? What factors enabled the DPJ to grow so quickly from a small party to a governing party with an overwhelming majority in the Diet? And, why did the party fall from grace so decisively in just a few years?

The second core puzzle concerns policymaking under the DPJ government. The DPJ came to power in 2009 with an ambitious reform agenda, promising fundamental transformations across the spectrum—among other areas, social policy, education, fiscal policy, transportation policy, foreign policy, relations between central and local governments, and the relationship between politicians and bureaucrats. However, the DPJ achieved remarkably little while in power. Most of the party's policy platform was scaled back or abandoned. Legislative activity under the DPJ government stagnated, falling to levels comparable to or below the waning years of LDP rule. This is doubly puzzling, because when it assumed power in 2009, the DPJ controlled both houses of the Diet in combination with minor coalition partners. Traditional explanations for constraints on policy change, such as divided government (Kelly 1993; Quirk and Nesmith 1995; Cameron et al. 1997; Edwards, Barrett, and Peake 1997; Binder 1999) and veto players (Tsebelis 1995, 2011, 1999) do not appear to offer compelling explanations for policy stasis under the DPJ. Why was the DPJ unable to deliver on the promises that brought it to power?

This volume represents one of the first comprehensive examinations of the DPJ's rise as a political party and its policies in power. The chapters make important contributions to the study of Japanese politics but also draw on and advance academic work on a wider range of issues of interest to political scientists. Foremost among these is the role of electoral institutions and their impact on political organization and policymaking (Duverger 1954;

Downs 1957; Rae 1971; Lijphart 1994; Cox 1997; Bawn and Thies 2003). We show that some aspects of Japanese politics have evolved as predicted by this literature—in particular, increasing convergence toward two-party politics, greater electoral volatility, and broader policy appeals designed to attract the median voter. However, we also observe important anomalies, particularly the continuing influence of rural regions and the absence of policy differentiation between the two major parties. Beyond electoral issues, individual chapters also address salient issues with broad relevance, such as the politics of redistribution, fiscal decentralization, environmental politics, gender and politics, and the politics of disaster response.

In this chapter, we begin by providing an overview of the DPJ as a political party, tracing its history from its founding through its ascent to power. Then, through references to the chapters in this volume, we discuss the political conditions and changes that contributed to the DPJ's rise. Primary among them is the 1994 reform of Japan's electoral institutions. The new electoral system generates strong incentives for political consolidation in the direction of a two-party system, and it has nationalized elections, reducing the importance of local factors and increasing the volatility of outcomes. This made it possible for the DPJ to ascend rapidly as a credible alternative to the LDP and to take over power in the decisive election of 2009. In addition, the DPJ benefited from effective organization and strategy, particularly in the recruitment of credible candidates and the targeting of rural regions, which still remain influential in Japanese politics. The media also portrayed the DPJ in a favorable light despite the fact that it was a newcomer to the political scene. Finally, there was an element of chance: The 2009 election came on the heels of the 2008 global financial crisis, which plunged Japan into its worst economic recession since the end of World War II.

We then consider governance under the DPJ. We provide an overview of the reforms proposed by the DPJ in its campaign manifesto of 2009, and then examine the extent to which these reforms were realized. For the most part, the DPJ failed to implement its reform agenda. Time-series data indicate that the DPJ government was characterized by anomalously low levels of legislative activity compared to previous LDP-led governments; not only did the DPJ implement few of its promised reforms, but it implemented very little of anything. We describe how the contributions to this volume shed light on this puzzling lack of action—what accounts for political change without policy change under the DPJ?

The chapters in this volume point to six crucial factors. First, electoral incentives, which facilitated the DPJ's rapid rise, also ironically constrained its ability to implement ambitious reforms once it was in power. As local interpersonal networks became less critical to winning elections, electoral volatility increased, shortening the time horizons of politicians. Far-reaching reforms, particularly those with short-term pain, became all the more unattractive. Second, the continuing influence of rural regions, particularly in local politics and in the upper house of the Diet, places an important constraint on reform for both major political parties. Third, the DPJ was paralyzed by internecine conflict for many of the same reasons that the LDP has fragmented in recent years. Fourth, the DPJ's promises to reduce the power of the bureaucracy ironically deprived it of administrative capacity, reducing its ability to formulate and execute policy. Fifth, economic constraints, particularly Japan's large and growing public debt, constrained the scope for several of the DPJ's signature programs, such as the child allowance and elimination of highway tolls. This was further compounded by the March 11, 2011, Great East Japan Earthquake, tsunami, and Fukushima nuclear disaster, which necessitated additional fiscal outlays for emergency response and reconstruction. Sixth, in foreign policy, international structural constraints—particularly regional threats and Japan's continuing reliance on the United States for security—forced the DPJ to quickly abandon its plans to differentiate itself from the LDP.

The struggles of the DPJ government illustrate several important features of Japanese politics today. There are common structural constraints facing any Japanese party in power, including the dire state of public finances, demographic challenges of an aging and shrinking population, and geopolitical realities. One of the contributions of this volume is to illustrate how electoral incentives have also impeded major reforms.

However, these structural constraints do not necessarily doom prospects for future parties, or for reform. The DPJ clearly suffered from several party-specific problems that made it difficult to govern effectively. The party's awkward power structure and upheavals in party leadership surely owe something to the personalities of key politicians, particularly Ozawa Ichiro. Moreover, there were also important, avoidable blunders, such as Hatoyama's declaration, made without consultation with the United States, that the Futenma base would be "at minimum" relocated out of Okinawa, and Kan's mishandling of the consumption tax issue before the 2010 upperhouse elections. The DPJ also overpromised in its 2009 campaign manifesto, for example by proposing large increases in government outlays and reductions in taxes and fees that were unrealistic given the state of Japan's public finances. Furthermore, the DPJ's policy to undercut the bureaucracy was ultimately reversed, but only after depriving the party of administrative capacity during its early days in power. The DPJ's record of governance therefore provides important lessons for future governing parties.

In 2010, and to a far greater extent in 2012, many of the same factors that aided the DPJ's rise contributed to its dramatic fall from power. In both elections, the LDP reversed the DPJ's gains in still-influential rural regions. In the 2010 upper-house election, this was enough to swing the result in the LDP's favor thanks to malapportionment—the LDP won seven more seats than the DPJ despite receiving seven million fewer votes. In 2012, floating voters abandoned the DPJ in droves, abstaining or gravitating toward other parties. Low turnout amplified the LDP's advantage among reliable, rural voters. The volatile electoral system delivered another extreme outcome, lifting the LDP from 118 to 294 seats and diminishing the DPJ from 230 to 57. The DPJ lost public support and fell from power in much the same way the LDP had only three years earlier—a ruling party beset with infighting, widely perceived as out of touch with the general public, and unable to implement meaningful reform.

The DPJ: Origins and Ascent to Power

What are the origins of the DPJ, and how did it develop as a credible political party, capable of assuming a majority of the lower house in 2009? For most of Japan's postwar history, the political system was dominated by the LDP, with a weak or fragmented opposition. During the Cold War, the primary opposition party was the Socialist Party of Japan (SPJ), which relied heavily on organized labor and focused on ideological issues such as opposition to the Self-Defense Forces and the U.S.-Japan security alliance. The LDP's primary support base was large business, small business, and agriculture, sometimes characterized as "Corporatism without Labor" (Pempel and Tsunekawa 1979). Other small opposition parties were fragmented or marginal, although the Kōmeitō, which could rely on intense support from a religious organization, the *Sōka Gakkai*, later became an important coalition partner of the LDP.

The LDP utilized the advantages of incumbency to shape the political system and sustain its grip on power (Pempel 1990). Japan's multimember district, single nontransferable vote (MMD-SNTV) electoral system encouraged intraparty competition within the LDP and disadvantaged opposition parties that lacked dense, local ties and access to central government funds.[2] Malapportionment further magnified the influence of rural voters, who overwhelmingly supported the LDP. The LDP funneled public works funds into local areas, with personalistic patronage (pork-barrel) ties to localities; parties that were not in power, with no realistic chances to gain power, were unable to

---

2 For overviews, see Rosenbluth and Thies (2010); Pempel (1998); and Kabashima and Steel (2011).

offer these resources to local voters and small and medium-sized businesses, further entrenching the LDP's incumbent position (Scheiner 2006).

In 1993, for the first time since 1955, the LDP lost its lower-house majority when Ozawa Ichiro bolted from the party along with a large group of defectors. A coalition of nine parties formed a government, putting the LDP out of power. The coalition broke apart in a year, however, and the LDP returned to power in 1994 by forming an unlikely coalition with its historical opposition party, the SPJ, and the small New Party Sakigake. This ushered in a second period of LDP rule, albeit through reliance on various coalition partners. The SPJ shifted many of its long-held policy positions in order to govern alongside the LDP. It abandoned core principles, such as opposition to the U.S.-Japan security alliance, leading many members to desert the party. The party, renamed the Japan Socialist Party (JSP), was decimated in the 1996 lower-house election and became increasingly irrelevant.

The DPJ itself was founded in 1996 through a merger of several parties, including former members of the Socialist Party and defectors from the incumbent LDP. Hatoyama Yukio, a fourth-generation LDP politician, and Kan Naoto, from the Democratic Social Federation, were the two founders. They had been part of the New Party Sakigake, consisting mostly of reform-minded LDP politicians who had left the party and had joined the non-LDP government in 1993–94. In the 1996 lower-house election, the DPJ's success was limited, and it won only 52 seats—the same number it held before (Smith, Pekkanen, and Krauss chapter in this volume).

In 1998, the DPJ absorbed six small opposition parties, transforming itself into a "new" DPJ. The New Frontier Party (Shinshinto, NFP), the primary opposition party after the 1996 election, had splintered apart, precipitating a major realignment of opposition party members. The "new" DPJ emerged as the primary beneficiary. As shown in figure 1.1, beginning from the 2000 lower-house election, the DPJ quickly established itself as the dominant opposition party. In 2003, the Liberal Party merged with the DPJ, further consolidating the DPJ's position as the primary opposition party. The Liberal Party was led by Ozawa Ichiro, a former LDP strongman. Ozawa joined the ranks of Hatoyama and Kan as a leader of the new DPJ. Until the 1990s, Japan's political opposition was defined by the JSP and its ideological defiance to LDP rule. In contrast, by the 2000 election, there were fewer former socialists among DPJ ranks than candidates who were former LDP or Sakigake politicians.

The 2005 election marked a major setback for the DPJ. The LDP's Prime Minister Koizumi Junichiro ran a highly successful campaign by framing his postal privatization plan as a litmus test for reform. By ejecting many

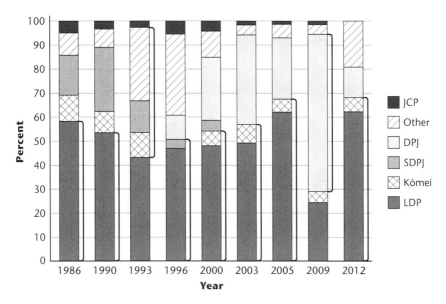

FIGURE 1.1 Japan's House of Representatives (Lower-House) Strength, 1986–2012
Source: National Diet.
Note: Brackets indicate majority party or coalition after election.

of his detractors from his own party, Koizumi was able to focus the election on an internecine struggle within the LDP. DPJ members were split over the postal reforms, further sidelining the party during the election. After Koizumi stepped down in 2006 of his own accord, however, the LDP could not maintain its popularity. The party cycled through three prime ministers in as many years. The LDP seemed to retrench from its reform agenda. Abe Shinzo, Koizumi's successor, allowed recently expelled postal rebels back into the party in 2006. LDP leaders increasingly criticized Koizumi's reforms as going too far in the direction of American-style, cutthroat capitalism.

In elections for the less powerful House of Councillors (upper house), in which half of the 242 seats are elected every three years, the DPJ's growth began in 1998, as seen in figure 1.2. It grew steadily in each election, and in 2007 the DPJ became the largest party in the upper house as Abe's government rapidly lost the public support that Koizumi had so effectively harnessed. This created a so-called twisted Diet, in which the lower house was controlled by the LDP and the upper house by opposition parties. The LDP retained a two-thirds majority in the lower house, which technically allowed the party to overturn upper-house decisions. However, this was considered an extraordinary option and was exercised in moderation.

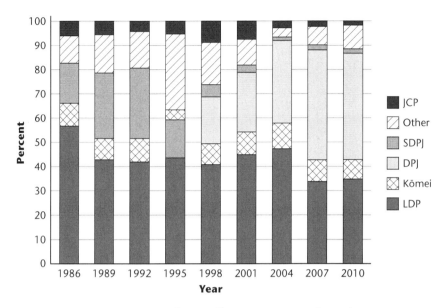

FIGURE 1.2 Japan's House of Councillors (Upper-House) Strength, 1986–2010
Source: National Diet.

In the 2009 lower-house election, as we described earlier, the DPJ won in a landslide, the first lower-house election that the LDP had lost outright since the party's formation in 1955.

Explaining the DPJ's Rise and Fall

How did the DPJ ascend so rapidly to power? Why did it fall so dramatically only three years later?[3] The chapters in this volume emphasize changes in electoral institutions, the continuing influence of local politics in rural regions, the DPJ's success in recruiting new candidates, and media coverage.

Several authors in this volume argue that electoral institutions were a crucial factor that facilitated the DPJ's rise to power. In 1994, Japan's electoral system underwent the most significant change in postwar history. The multimember district, single nontransferable vote system for lower-house elections was replaced with a combination of single-member districts (SMD, 300 seats) and proportional representation (PR, 200 seats in 1996, reduced to 180 from 2000). These changes profoundly altered the incentive structures confronted by politicians and voters.

3 The DPJ's fall from power is analyzed in greater detail in a forthcoming volume that focuses on the 2012 election (Pekkanen, Reed, and Scheiner 2013).

The electoral reforms of the 1990s weakened one-party rule by mitigating incumbency advantage and the malapportionment of districts that had long tilted electoral outcomes in favor of the LDP. In his contribution to the volume, McElwain shows that reelection of candidates has been increasingly determined by partisan swings rather than by past performance or the strength of local networks. This has contributed to greater electoral volatility; even powerful, well-established politicians are now routinely expelled from office in Japanese national elections. This new electoral reality has made it more feasible for opposition parties like the DPJ to assume power in a "wave election" that tilts districts uniformly in favor of one party. On the flip side, volatility implies that the pendulum can swing back equally decisively, as the 2012 electoral defeat of the DPJ illustrates. Scheiner similarly argues that electoral incentives have promoted a two-party system in Japan, much as the theoretical literature on electoral politics predicts. This means that SMD seats are increasingly contested by only two competitive candidates.[4]

Despite the general trend toward consolidation under a two-party system, some third parties, such as the Kōmeitō, have survived and exercised important influence over Japanese politics in recent years. The DPJ government in 2009 was also formed as a coalition with two minor parties, the People's New Party and the Social Democratic Party, primarily in order to maintain a majority in the upper house. What allows some third parties to retain influence in the Japanese political system? Reed finds that the key factor for third-party survival is party organization rooted within civil society and the capacity to elect significant numbers of candidates to local assemblies. Failed third parties had little organization of their own and depended upon candidates' own local support networks *(kōenkai)*, a less effective organizational structure under the new electoral system.

Despite lower-house electoral changes that have shifted the focus of politicians toward urban voters, local politics and rural regions retain outsized influence over Japanese politics. One reason for this is malapportionment in the upper house, in which rural regions still receive disproportionate representation. Shimizu highlights another reason in her contribution to this volume: the increasing independence of local politicians. The LDP's dominance was long buttressed by a strong support base in rural areas led by local politicians who worked on behalf of national LDP candidates. In recent years, municipal mergers drastically weakened the LDP's support base by reducing the number of local politicians and redrawing electoral

---

4 This trend was partially reversed in 2012, and it remains to be seen whether the pattern will hold in future elections.

district boundaries. Shimizu finds, however, that the DPJ was not able to take full advantage of the new institutional arrangements, with local politicians becoming more independent of both major parties. While Ozawa was able to capture many rural votes with promises of subsidies in 2007 and 2009, these votes were not as loyal as they once were to the LDP, and they reverted to the LDP during subsequent elections. This has contributed to a broader phenomenon: an increase in "floating voters," who have no allegiance to any major party. Although rural regions still tilt in the direction of the LDP, neither of Japan's major parties can now take for granted a reliable, local support base. To succeed, parties must pay attention to the changing needs of increasingly independent—and very often still rural—localities. Hasunuma similarly points to the DPJ's promise of rural decentralization as a factor that enabled the DPJ to gain seats after rural voters felt abandoned by the LDP, particularly following reforms enacted under Prime Minister Koizumi that decreased funding flows from the national to local governments.

A key factor in the DPJ's rise was its success in candidate recruitment—the ability to field credible candidates across a large number of electoral districts. This challenge, which is often a difficult one for opposition parties, is examined by Smith, Pekkanen, and Krauss. They find that the *kōbo* (literally translated as "public recruitment") system of candidate recruitment effectively grew the DPJ's candidate pool by adding credible candidates where the local party organization was otherwise weak. Remarkably, candidates recruited through *kōbo* performed no worse than other, more well-established DPJ candidates. This enabled the DPJ to rapidly field candidates against the LDP across the nation. Reed also points out that the DPJ's merger with Ozawa's Liberal Party before the 2003 election strengthened the party by allowing it to field more credible candidates nationwide. For example, before the merger, the DPJ was virtually irrelevant in Ozawa's stronghold in Iwate Prefecture.

Finally, the DPJ's electoral fortunes were buttressed by favorable media coverage. Maeda analyzes an intriguing advantage that the DPJ has enjoyed: the rise of public support for the party even while it was in opposition. Maeda notes that in democracies around the world, increased media coverage tends to increase public support for parties. Opposition parties usually fail to gain significant media attention, leading to difficulties in gaining public support. The DPJ, however, enjoyed increasing news coverage from 2003 on, as it gained recognition as a serious contender in an emerging two-party system against the LDP, and then again after the 2007 upper-house election, when it won a majority of upper-house seats. Maeda argues that this unusual level of media coverage for an opposition party increased the DPJ's support in opinion polls and helped propel the party to power.

The DPJ in Power

Following its rapid ascent and landslide victory, the DPJ government quickly fell out of favor with the public. Figure 1.3 shows cabinet approval and disapproval ratings from 1998 until 2012. The shaded areas indicate periods when disapproval rates exceeded approval rates. The LDP's Mori government was highly unpopular, with record-low approval rates and a surging disapproval rate. This situation was reversed almost completely under Koizumi, who consistently saw net-positive approval ratings during his five years in office. Koizumi's successors, however, followed a predictable pattern of initially high approval ratings followed by a rapid decline and exit from office within about a year. Figure 1.3 shows that this pattern—high initial approval followed by rapid decline—largely continued under successive DPJ governments.

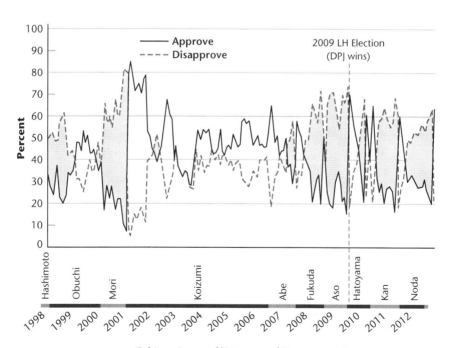

FIGURE 1.3 Cabinet Approval/Disapproval Ratings, 1998–2012
Source: NHK (http://www.nhk.or.jp/bunken/yoron/political/index.html).

After the DPJ came to power, Prime Minister Hatoyama Yukio's term began with high approval ratings, reflecting the public's high hopes for the DPJ administration. By early spring 2010, internal political strife, mishandling of the Futenma U.S. military base relocation issue,[5] and DPJ party president Ozawa Ichiro's campaign financing scandals contributed to lower approval ratings. Kan Naoto and Noda Yoshihiko came to office with successively lower initial approval ratings, a pattern mirroring the approval ratings of Abe, Fukuda, and Aso. Public disapproval dominated the tenure of the Kan and Noda cabinets. The Japanese public had become quickly disillusioned with DPJ government.

Figure 1.4 depicts party identification from 1998 to 2012, focusing on the LDP and DPJ. In the initial years since its founding, only a very small share of the Japanese population supported the DPJ, with support generally hovering in the single digits. Support increased to the 10-to-15 percent range during the Koizumi years, as the DPJ established itself as the main opposition party. Support continued to increase during the governments of Koizumi's successors, with a spike in 2007 when the DPJ became the largest party in the upper house. Public support for the DPJ decisively overtook that of the LDP only in 2009, which coincided with the party's landslide victory in the lower-house elections. However, support for the DPJ dropped below that of the LDP during the Kan government and continued to fall under Noda. The LDP's approval rating shot up dramatically in late 2012 after its landslide victory in the lower house, while support for the DPJ declined to lows not observed since the early years of the party's founding.

5 The location of U.S. military bases in Okinawa, particularly those in the middle of densely populated areas, is a contentious issue in local politics. In 1996, the LDP government reached an agreement with the United States to reduce the U.S. military presence in the more populous regions of southern Okinawa, following an incident in which U.S. servicemen raped a local 14-year-old girl, which sparked widespread local protests. Futenma airbase, located in the middle of Ginowan City, was a focal point of local protests particularly after an incident in which a helicopter crashed into the neighboring area during a U.S. military exercise. In 2006, Washington signed a pact with the LDP to relocate Futenma airbase from Ginowan City to a new offshore location in Henoko Bay of northern Okinawa. The DPJ opposed these arrangements from its inception, and shortly before taking office in 2009, Hatoyama promised to move the airbase "at least" outside of Okinawa Prefecture and signaled a personal desire to relocate the base to Guam. The United States opposed this, and in 2009, Secretary of State Hillary Clinton visited Japan to ensure that the original agreement, along with Japanese financial support to relocate a number of troops to Guam, was maintained. Under U.S. pressure and domestic criticism for his handling of the issue, Hatoyama reneged on his promise to move Futenma in May 2010, and formally apologized to the governor of Okinawa. One month later, he resigned from office.

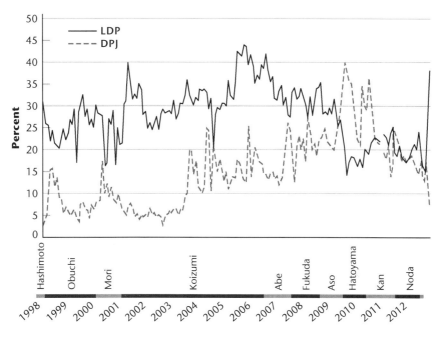

FIGURE 1.4 Party Identification, 1998–2012
Source: NHK (http://www.nhk.or.jp/bunken/yoron/political/index.html).

To provide context and reference, table 1.1 shows a timeline of the major events during the DPJ's rule.

Policymaking under the DPJ: Party Change without Policy Change

An important reason for the sharply declining popular support of the DPJ while it was in power was the perceived failure of the DPJ to govern effectively and enact its proposed legislative agenda. How much did the DPJ actually achieve while it was in power? What did the DPJ's policymaking track record look like?

It is useful to begin by placing the DPJ government in historical comparative perspective. To do so, we examine time-series data on the total number of laws submitted and passed under various governments in Japan since 1980. Figure 1.5 shows that legislative activity increased sharply in Japan between the mid-1990s and mid-2000s, a period associated with administrative reforms enacted by the Hashimoto and Koizumi governments. A large body of scholarship has documented how these reforms affected many of Japan's governing institutions (Schaede 2008; Vogel 2006; Kushida and

TABLE 1.1

Timeline of Major Events during DPJ Rule

PM	Year	Date	Major event
Hatoyama	2009	8/30	DPJ wins 308 seats in the House of Representatives.
		9/16	Hatoyama cabinet is formed.
		9/22	Hatoyama pledges to cut greenhouse gas emissions 25 percent by 2020.
		11/11	Budget screening begins.
		12/15	Hatoyama announces reconsideration of Futenma relocation site.
	2010	1/15	Ozawa Ichiro's secretaries arrested for misreporting funds in Tokyo land deal.
		3/9	Report submitted to the Ministry of Foreign Affairs regarding a confidential agreement reached between Japan and the United States in the 1960s on the introduction of nuclear weapons into Japan.
		5/4	Hatoyama reneges on his Futenma relocation promise.
		5/30	SDP leaves DPJ-led coalition over Futenma issue.
		6/2	Hatoyama resigns.
Kan		6/8	Kan cabinet is formed.
		7/11	DPJ loses majority in upper-house elections.
		9/7	Chinese fishing trawler collides with Japanese Coast Guard patrol boat near the disputed Senkaku Islands.
		9/11	Kan reshuffles the cabinet.
		11/27– 11/28	Censure motions passed against Chief Cabinet Secretary Sengoku Yoshito and MLIT Minister Mabuchi Sumio.
	2011	1/14	Kan reshuffles cabinet a second time.
		1/31	Ozawa indicted for alleged violation of the Political Funds Control Law.
		3/7	Foreign Minister Machara Seiji resigns after it is revealed that he received an illegal donation from a foreigner.
		3/11	The Great East Japan Earthquake.
		3/19	LDP President Tanigaki Sadakazu rejects DPJ proposal for a grand coalition.
		5/6	Kan orders the decommissioning of the Hamaoka nuclear power plant, due to high likelihood of an above–magnitude 8 earthquake occurring in the next 30 years.

		6/2	A no-confidence motion against PM Kan is defeated, 293 to 152.
Noda		7/13	Kan calls for a gradual phase-out of nuclear power.
		8/26	Kan passes bills authorizing a ¥2 million supplementary budget for Tohoku reconstruction, the authorization of new bond issuance to finance reconstruction, and increased government investment in renewable energy.
		8/30	Kan resigns.
		9/2	Noda cabinet is formed.
		9/10	METI Minister Hachiro resigns over radiation jest.
		11/11	Noda declares Japan's intention to join Trans-Pacific Partnership talks.
		12/9	Censure motions adopted against Defense Minister Yasuo Ichikawa and Minister of Consumer Affairs Yamaoka Kenji.
	2012	1/13	Noda reshuffles the cabinet.
		2/10	Reconstruction Agency is formed.
		3/30	Consumption tax increase bill submitted to the Diet.
		4/20	Censure motions adopted against Defense Minister Tanaka Naoki and Transportation Minister Maeda Takeshi.
		6/4	Noda reshuffles cabinet a second time.
		6/8	Ōi nuclear power plant is restarted.
		6/26	Consumption tax hike bill passes the lower house; Ozawa leaves the DPJ.
		8/8	Consumption tax hike bill passes the upper house.
		8/10	South Korean President Lee Myung-bak visits the disputed Takeshima Islands.
		8/29	Censure motion passed by LDP and Kōmeitō against PM Noda.
		9/10	Minister of Financial Services Matsushita Tadahiro commits suicide.
		9/11	Senkaku Islands are nationalized.
		10/1	Noda reshuffles cabinet a third time.
		10/23	Justice Minister Tanaka Keishu resigns over criminal yakuza connections.
		11/14	Noda calls for December 16 lower-house election.
		11/16	Lower house is dissolved for December election.

Source: Based on "Minshutō seiken yureta 3 nen" [Three rocky years of DPJ rule]. 2012. *Nihon Keizai Shimbun.* November 18, 4.

Note: MLIT: Ministry of Land, Infrastructure, Transport, and Tourism

METI: Ministry of Economy, Trade, and Industry

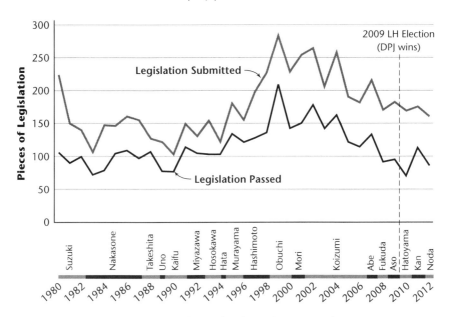

FIGURE 1.5 Legislation Submitted and Legislation Passed, 1980–2012
Source: Cabinet Office.

Shimizu, 2013). The decline of legislative activity during the LDP governments following Koizumi is consistent with the conventional wisdom that
reforms had stalled.

What is perhaps most striking from figure 1.5, however, is what occurs
after the DPJ assumed power in 2009. Already in control of the upper house
alongside its coalition partners, the DPJ won the lower house in a landslide
on a platform of reform and change. Yet, under the Hatoyama government,
legislation proposed and enacted did not noticeably increase, and in fact *declined* compared to the already low levels during the late stages of LDP rule.
The spike during the Kan administration consists largely of reconstruction
bills related to the March 11, 2011, Great East Japan Earthquake. After
those were passed, the Noda government reverted to a low level of legislative
activity. Thus, despite coming to office with an aggressive reform agenda,
the DPJ government was characterized by limited overall legislative activity.

Figure 1.6 disaggregates the data from figure 1.5 according to Diet sessions. Bold dates on the *x* axis are Regular Diet sessions, and others are
Extraordinary and Special sessions. The figure also depicts several key events,
such as the 2009 lower-house election (which brought the DPJ to power), the
3/11 disaster, and periods of divided government or "twisted Diets," during which the party in control of the lower house did not control the upper

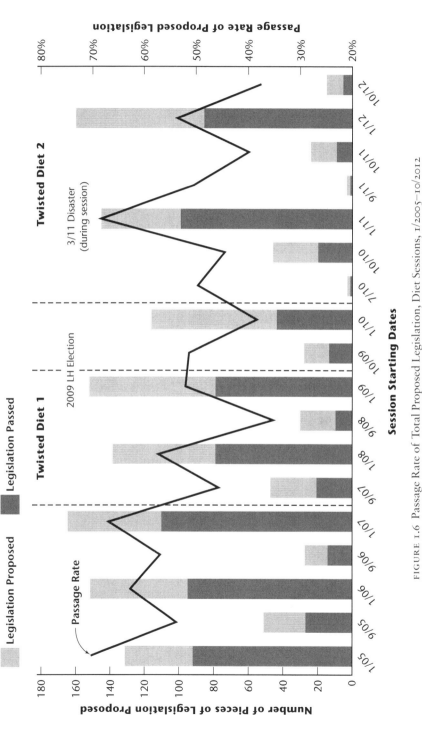

FIGURE 1.6 Passage Rate of Total Proposed Legislation, Diet Sessions, 1/2005–10/2012

Source: Cabinet Office.

Note: Regular Diet sessions are in bold. The Extraordinary session from 9/16/2009 to 9/19/2009 and Special session from 8/7/2007 to 8/10/2007 are absent, since no legislation was proposed.

house. The first twisted Diet in the figure, which lasted from September 2007 to October 2009, was associated with a lower average passage rate compared to that of the preceding period. This is intuitive; legislation is more difficult to pass when the opposition controls one house of the legislature. LDP Prime Minister Fukuda cited the difficulty of operating under a twisted Diet as one reason for his resignation in September 2008. However, figure 1.7 also shows that the passage rate was extremely low immediately after the DPJ came to power with a majority in both houses, with only about 40 percent of proposed legislation passed during the Regular Diet session of 2010.

Figure 1.7 reveals perhaps the most remarkable feature of legislative patterns under the DPJ. The figure depicts the absolute numbers and percentage of cabinet-submitted legislation passed according to calendar year. After the DPJ came to power, not only did the overall passage rate of legislation decline, but the passage rate of cabinet-submitted legislation dropped sharply to historically unprecedented low levels. Under LDP rule, about 70 to 100 percent of legislation submitted by the cabinet was passed. Under the DPJ, this rate fell to a low of 55 percent in 2010 and averaged 66 percent. With the ruling coalition in control of both houses of the Diet for most of 2010, it is astonishing that legislation submitted by the cabinet would have such a low rate of passage.

The sharp drop in passage of cabinet-submitted legislation was due in large measure to the DPJ's internal discord.[6] For example, an early tussle developed between Maehara Seiji (then minister of Land, Infrastructure, Transport, and Tourism) and Ozawa Ichiro (then secretary general of the party). Ozawa, following the traditional LDP playbook, intended to use transportation policy to reward the trucking industry and peel off its support from the LDP. Maehara refused, seeing such pork-barrel politics as antithetical to the DPJ's reform agenda. In retaliation, the chairman of the Land, Infrastructure, and Transport Committee of the lower house, a member of the Ozawa group, blocked consideration of all Ministry of Land, Infrastructure, Transport, and Tourism (MLIT)-submitted legislation.[7] After the DPJ lost control of the upper house in 2010, lack of cooperation from opposition parties, particularly from the LDP, further impeded the DPJ's legislative agenda.[8]

6 It is worth noting that the literature on veto players generally predicts that party cohesion tends to increase policy stability (Tsebelis 1995). Contrary to these expectations, in this case, the lack of cohesion acted as an impediment to policy change. We will return to this theme later in the chapter.

7 For more detail on transportation policy under the DPJ, see the Lipscy chapter in this volume.

8 For an overview of the LDP's role as an opposition party, see Endo, Pekkanen, and Reed (2013).

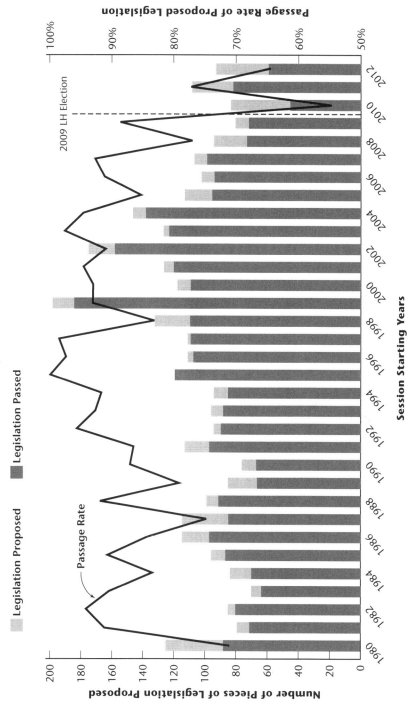

FIGURE 1.7 Passage Rate of Cabinet-Submitted Legislation, 1980–2012

Source: Cabinet Office.

We now consider the substance of DPJ policymaking. The DPJ initiated the practice of publishing campaign manifestos during the 2003 lower-house election. The LDP was forced to respond by producing its own manifesto, and the word *manifesuto* (the Japanese pronunciation of manifesto) became a mainstay in election campaigns thereafter. The DPJ also came to power in 2009 campaigning on a manifesto that sought to introduce major reforms touching on several important areas of governance and policy. We examine the extent to which these campaign pledges were implemented during DPJ rule.

Table 1.2 shows the DPJ's policy promises in its manifesto for the 2009 lower-house election, after which the party ascended to power. The manifesto pledged to change Japanese society in five distinct ways: (1) End wasteful spending, (2) reduce the costs of child-rearing and education, (3) reform pensions and medical care, (4) increase regional sovereignty, and (5) reinvigorate the economy. The table also shows the status of the promised reforms as the party exited from power at the end of 2012. Table 1.3 shows

TABLE 1.2

DPJ's 2009 Manifesto Pledges and Outcomes as of 2012

2009 manifesto pledge	Status as of 2012
Ending wasteful spending	
Completely rework 207 trillion yen state budget, and find an additional 16.8 trillion yen per year	Public works spending reduced, but overall spending reductions did not reach goals
Eliminate *amakudari*	Not implemented
Ban hereditary Diet seats	Implemented as DPJ party policy (no legislation passed)
Ban donations by corporations	Not implemented
Eliminate 80 PR lower-house seats	Not implemented
Reduce civil service personnel costs by 20 percent	Civil service salaries reduced by 7.8 percent
Child-rearing and education	
Pay lump-sum childbirth benefit of 550,000 yen	Increased from 380,000 yen to 420,000 yen
Pay 26,000 yen/month "child allowance" for all children through junior high school	Currently, monthly allowance of 13,000 yen increased to 15,000 for children under 3, and decreased to 10,000 yen for children ages 3–12
Free high school education	Successfully implemented
Greater number of university scholarships	Tuition waivers increased. Number of students eligible for scholarship loans increased
Revive supplement for unemployed single mothers and fathers	Revived in December 2009
Eliminate day care waiting lists	Not completely eliminated, but additional child care centers added

TABLE I.2 (CONTINUED)

2009 manifesto pledge	Status as of 2012
Pensions and medical care	
Issue "pension passbooks"	Restored 13 million pension records and established online pension record tracking
Create unified pension system	Not implemented
Establish "minimum guaranteed pension" of at least 70,000 yen/month	No change. Concession to LDP for consumption tax increase
Abolish Health Insurance Scheme for People Aged 75 and Over	Not abolished. Concession to LDP for consumption tax increase
Increase the capacity of medical schools and number of doctors by 50 percent	Enrollment limit increased for medical schools; 7,793 students in 2008 to 8,991 in 2012
Cancel planned social security spending cuts of 220 billion yen	Partially accomplished. Spending cuts reduced
Regional sovereignty	
Increase funds under local governments' independent control	Largely accomplished
Create a household income support system for farming households	Implemented
Eliminate highway tolls	Plans abandoned after March 11
Abolish provincial gasoline tax	Implemented, but replaced with higher de facto gasoline tax rate
Abolish earmarked subsidies to local governments, and replace with grants whose use can be freely determined	Implemented
Income compensation for livestock and dairy farmers, fisheries, and foresters	Implemented
Increase food self-sufficiency ratio	Remained essentially flat, and fell for wheat, fruits, and meats in 2009 and 2010, according to the Ministry of Agriculture (MOA)
Employment and economy	
Reduce corporate tax rate for small and medium-sized enterprises from 18 to 11 percent	Reduced to 15 percent
100,000 yen monthly allowance to job-seekers during training	"Hello Work" gives 40,000 yen/month for employers to "test" new employees
Foster green industry and green jobs	Encouraged through green subsidies.
Ban dispatch of temporary workers to manufacturing jobs	Ban on temporary contract of 30 days or less implemented. Ban on temporary dispatch to manufacturing sector not implemented
Establish national average minimum wage of 1,000 yen/hr	Remained at 749 yen/hr by end of 2012
Equal treatment and wages regardless of gender	Not accomplished
Establish cap-and-trade system	Indefinitely postponed in December 2010
Subsidize purchases of solar panels, "green" vehicles, and energy-saving appliances	Solar subsidies and feed-in-tariffs implemented. Subsidies for electric cars and efficient appliances

Sources: DPJ, MLIT, METI, *Nihon Keizai Shimbun, Yomiuri Shimbun.*

TABLE 1.3

*DPJ's Nonmanifesto Policy Pledges
and Outcomes as of 2012*

Item	Status
Consumption tax increase	Enacted
Futenma relocation	Advocated
Income tax increase for highest earners	Enacted
Inheritance tax base broadened	Enacted
Relaxation of arms export ban	Enacted
Trans-Pacific Partnership (TPP) ratification	Advocated
Zero nuclear energy by 2030	Advocated

Source: Authors.

the most notable policies and pledges undertaken by the DPJ that were not included in the manifesto. On most counts, the DPJ was unsuccessful in implementing its policy proposals. According to the *Yomiuri Shimbun* ("Minshūtō Seiken Sōkatsu" 2012), one month prior to the 2012 House of Representatives election, only 30 percent of the DPJ's 170 original proposals had been implemented.

On ending wasteful spending, the DPJ pledged to go through every budget item to find approximately 17 trillion yen ($188 billion at 1$ = 90 yen) in savings, eliminate *amakudari* (postretirement bureaucrats taking private-sector jobs in the industries they oversaw), ban hereditary Diet seats, ban corporate donations, eliminate 80 proportional representation lower-house seats, and reduce civil service personnel costs by 20 percent. While the DPJ did draw media attention to its public *shiwake* process of cutting government expenditures, it did not implement the rest. It should be noted that public works spending did fall to its lowest levels since 1978 following the 2009 election, a trend that began in the early 2000s (Noble 2010; Mulgan 2010). However, the decrease was largely offset by increases in supplemental funding from the central government to the localities that was not earmarked for public works but could be used for that purpose.

In child care and education, the DPJ achieved mixed success. The DPJ implemented free high school education and tuition waivers, and the total number of students eligible for scholarships was increased at the university level. The childbirth benefit was increased slightly. However, the DPJ's signature initiative, the child allowance (*kodomo teate*), encountered considerable headwinds due to its high price tag. The child allowance was implemented in April 2010 at half of the amount proposed in the manifesto. However, the policy was scaled back dramatically after April 2012 and was replaced with a modestly expanded version of the child allowance, *jido teate*, which had existed prior to DPJ rule.

Pension and medical care reform was limited. The DPJ successfully restored 13 million of the 50 million pension records that had been lost before it came to power,[9] and launched an online database for tracking and viewing pension records. The number of students in medical school increased moderately, and the magnitude of planned social security spending cuts was reduced. However, as a concession to the LDP to ensure the success of the consumption tax hike bill in 2012, the DPJ abandoned its goal of establishing a minimum guaranteed pension of 70,000 yen per month (approximately $780 at $1 = 90 yen) and abolishing the current Health Insurance Scheme for people aged 75 and over.

The DPJ's promise to increase regional sovereignty largely consisted of payouts to rural voters. Taking a page out of the LDP playbook, the DPJ created a household income support system for farming households and established income compensation for livestock and dairy farmers, fisheries, and foresters. However, the DPJ's plan to eliminate highway tolls—a major campaign promise—was repeatedly scaled back and ultimately abandoned after the March 11 Tohoku earthquake. Plans to abolish the provisional gasoline tax rate were also abandoned in all but name (for details, see the Lipscy chapter in this volume). There was no meaningful increase in the food self-sufficiency ratio.

The employment and economy manifesto pledges were also implemented to only a limited extent. The DPJ could not rewrite the 207 trillion yen ($2.30 billion) budget and identify 16.8 trillion yen in new revenue per year—a promise that was at the heart of the party's 2009 campaign. While the DPJ did slightly reduce the corporate tax rate for small and medium-sized enterprises (SMEs), it was by a smaller margin than originally intended. Efforts to aid the livelihood of temporary workers were only moderately successful, with a ban on the dispatch of temporary workers to manufacturing jobs never implemented. By the end of 2012, the national average minimum wage[10] was still closer to 700 yen than 1000 yen, the DPJ goal (MHLW 2012). Gender equality in the workplace was far from realized;

---

9 During the Abe administration, a major scandal erupted in which it was discovered that the government had lost the pension records of 50 million citizens during the migration process to a computer-based system. The DPJ claims that it investigated 28.6 million of the 50 million pension records lost prior to the 2009 election and that it fully restored the records of 13 million people, reaching a total value of 1.7 trillion yen in restored funds. http://www.dpj.or.jp/article/101716/.

10 Japan's minimum wage is set at the regional and industry level—with the higher of the two applying to any specific company.

Gaunder's contribution to this volume provides greater detail and contends that the lack of female representation in the DPJ overall, as well as in the senior leadership of the DPJ, contributed to a lack of support for measures to increase gender equality. In environmental economic policy, the DPJ implemented a number of green subsidies for efficient cars and appliances, solar subsidies, and feed-in-tariffs, but indefinitely postponed the establishment of a cap-and-trade system in 2010.

Energy policy is one area where a departure from initial promises would have been understandable. The massive Tohoku earthquake and tsunami of 2011 and attendant nuclear disaster at the Fukushima Dai-Ichi power plant were transformative events. When the disaster struck, the Kan government had just passed an energy bill upon coming to power in 2010, which included increasing the ratio of nuclear power–generated electricity to 50 percent by 2030. However, after the Fukushima nuclear disaster, Kan called for halting all of Japan's operating nuclear reactors until "stress tests" were conducted to determine their safety. He called for a new energy policy that would eventually phase out nuclear power all together, relying instead on a new array of investments into sustainable energy. This was a bold policy change stemming from the magnitude of the disaster, Kan's background,[11] and his personal involvement in the crisis. However, Kan's successor, Noda, quickly moved to restart the nuclear reactors that had stopped and called for another overhaul of the long-term energy plan that did not involve a complete phase-out of nuclear power. As Kushida explains in his chapter, the DPJ's policy instability over the nuclear issue, along with delays in implementing a new nuclear safety organization, further undermined its credibility as a governing party.

Ironically, the DPJ's major policy achievement was one that seemingly contradicted its campaign manifesto and was deeply unpopular—doubling the consumption tax. The DPJ's 2009 manifesto explicitly stated that no rise in the consumption tax would occur within four years after the DPJ's election. However, less than a year later, and immediately after coming to office in June, Prime Minister Kan announced his inttention to double the consumption tax rate to 10 percent by 2015. This announcement came before

---

11 Kan, while minister of Health in the non-LDP coalition government in power in 1993–94, became famous for uncovering a major scandal involving bureaucracy-industry collusion in covering up HIV-tainted blood used on patients. Deeply suspicious of large power companies colluding with the Ministry of Economy, Trade, and Industry (METI) in formulating Japan's energy policy, and having been highly frustrated at Tokyo Electric Power Company's (TEPCO) seeming incompetence in dealing with the nuclear crisis, he had few reservations in reversing their policy. (See Kushida, "The DPJ's Response to the Fukushima Nuclear Disaster," in this volume.)

the 2010 upper-house election, and the DPJ was punished in the polls.[12] Kan dropped the issue and focused most of his tenure on the passage of a set of bills to fund reconstruction of the Tohoku region.

Prime Minister Noda, from very early in his premiership, publicly stated that he was staking his political career on passing the consumption tax bill. In June 2012, Noda introduced a bill to raise the consumption tax to 8 percent in 2014 and to 10 percent in 2015. The bill caused a split within the DPJ, necessitating cooperation and coordination with the opposition LDP. Noda was forced to make concessions to the LDP, shelving pension and welfare reform until a later date to gain support for the tax hike. Noda was widely criticized for trading away core pledges in the DPJ manifesto in order to secure a tax increase that was not part of the party's campaign platform.

Noda's "Comprehensive Reform of Social Security and Tax Systems" led to an irreparable split within the ranks of the DPJ. Ozawa was adamantly opposed and threatened to walk away from the party. The bill passed with support from most of the DPJ, LDP, and Kōmeitō. In response, Ozawa and 49 of his followers—33 of whom were first-term members with grim reelection prospects—left the DPJ to form a new party, the People's Life First Party.[13]

Explaining Party Change without Policy Change

Why did the DPJ enact so little legislation while in power and implement so few of the reform proposals it had promised?[14] The chapters in this volume propose several factors that account for policy stasis under the DPJ: electoral incentives, the continuing influence of rural regions, policy incoherence and infighting, strained relations with the bureaucracy, and economic and international constraints. Ironically, some of these are the very factors that facilitated the DPJ's rise to power.

12 Gerald Curtis has suggested that Kan made this announcement because he felt that repercussions would be small due to the fact that the LDP also endorsed a tax hike (Akagawa 2010).

13 Ozawa's new party then joined forces with the Kizuna Party of DPJ defectors who also opposed the consumption tax increase. (People's Life First then combined with another small opposition party, but it was decimated in the 2012 lower-house election, declining to 9 seats from its previous 61.

14 Much of the material in this section is drawn from the introductory chapter in a *Journal of East Asian Studies* special issue (Lipscy and Scheiner 2012), which was published earlier and assembled articles from this volume that focus on electoral issues.

Electoral Incentives

Previous sections outlined how Japan's electoral system contributed to the rapid rise and fall of the DPJ. Electoral incentives also constrained the DPJ's ability to implement policy reforms once in power. McElwain's chapter shows how electoral reforms in the 1990s made it more difficult for any party to enact fundamental policy reforms. Since electoral reforms weakened incumbency advantage and reduced the malapportionment of districts that had long supported the LDP, reelection of candidates has been increasingly determined by partisan swings rather than by past performance or the strength of local networks. Greater electoral volatility under this new system has reduced the ability of young, reformist politicians to establish themselves politically. The point is highlighted in Gaunder's chapter, which shows how female candidates, who are the most likely instigators of reform on gender issues, were swept from office quickly in both major parties. Volatility also thinned out the ranks of experienced politicians familiar with the policymaking process.

Japan's new electoral system may also reduce the scope for policy differentiation among the major parties. The lack of a major policy cleavage is largely consistent with the predictions of the literature on party competition under majoritarian electoral rules; as both parties attempt to court the median voter, policy positions have converged and dramatic policy shifts have become less likely (Downs 1957). As Scheiner highlights, candidates from both the LDP and DPJ have converged toward one another in their policy appeals. Lipscy provides one example of how this limited the scope of DPJ reforms: Several of the DPJ's popular initiatives in the transportation sector were co-opted by the LDP government, eliminating some low-hanging fruit before the DPJ assumed power.

Moreover, as Scheiner shows—and as expected by Downs (1957)—as the LDP's and DPJ's policy positions have become more similar, voters have increasingly cast ballots based on "valence" (that is, nonpolicy) evaluations of the parties. Previously, voters had given great weight to the political experience of candidates, but as the party system became nationalized, elections were decided by voters' images of the LDP and DPJ as agents of change (Reed, Scheiner, and Thies 2012). With elections increasingly determined by party image and not by differences in policy, it has become less likely that a new party will come to power with a clear mandate to implement significant, specific change. For example, as Gaunder highlights, rather than proposing and implementing meaningful policies favoring women, both parties have turned to "female assassin" candidates to demonstrate their reform bona fides and therefore appeal to fickle popular sentiment.

In addition, as Lipscy discusses, Japan's current electoral system, which places emphasis on broad appeal to the median voter, makes it risky to enact policy reforms that impose diffuse costs on the general public. This has had an adverse impact on Japan's ability to deal with several important policy issues. On energy efficiency and climate change, Japan has struggled to enact and maintain policies that encourage conservation by elevating energy costs for the general consumer. Similarly, it has been excruciatingly difficult for the Japanese government to address lingering budget deficits by increasing revenues. Noda managed to raise the consumption tax in 2012, but much like his predecessors who sought to do the same, he was met with a powerful electoral backlash.

Continuing Influence of Rural Regions

Japan's new electoral incentives in and of themselves do not imply policy stasis; countries governed by majoritarian electoral systems frequently engage in major policy reforms, as seen in the United States and Great Britain during the 1930s and 1980s. Another factor that has limited policy change in Japan, and more specifically under the DPJ, is the fact that Japanese policymakers have not been able to fully cater to the median voter, due to the continuing influence of rural regions in Japan's political system.

For sure, the influence of rural regions has declined compared to the heyday of LDP rule. Malapportionment in the lower house has been substantially reduced, and rural subsidies have been cut substantially over the past two decades, particularly with the Koizumi reforms. However, as Hasunuma points out, rural areas still exercise outsized influence over Japanese politics.[15] Despite their declining overall representation, rural residents have acted as swing voters in recent elections (Lipscy and Scheiner 2012). Moreover, as Shimizu argues, redistricting and local autonomy have cut against lower-house electoral incentives by increasing the leverage of rural politicians vis-à-vis central politicians. Finally, although Japan's new electoral rules have placed greater emphasis on urban voters, rural voters tend to turn out more reliably. Because overall turnout itself is volatile, cultivating the rural vote has remained an important electoral strategy for both political parties as an insurance policy against low-turnout elections.

Recognizing these realities, Ozawa, the DPJ's electoral mastermind, pursued what became known as a *kawakami* (upstream) strategy, which placed great emphasis on appealing to rural voters who lived near the upper reaches of Japanese rivers. The DPJ manifesto incorporated benefits specifically

15 See also Reed, Scheiner, and Thies (2012).

targeted toward such voters, such as household income support for farmers, and Ozawa sought to cultivate support from interest groups more traditionally associated with the LDP. As Hasunuma points out, spending cuts to rural areas were difficult for the DPJ precisely because its electoral strategy depended on appealing to those constituencies. This strategy was a critical element of the DPJ's electoral success, particularly during the 2007 upper-house election. However, the DPJ's rural strategy also split the party between reformers such as Okada and Maehara and traditional politicians exemplified by Ozawa. This mirrors a similar split in the LDP in recent years, which was particularly salient under Koizumi. The DPJ achieved considerable success in the 2004 and 2007 upper-house and 2009 lower-house elections by following Ozawa's *kawakami* strategy, but the LDP turned the tide in the 2010 upper-house election primarily by winning back rural single-member districts.

Internecine Conflict

Japanese political parties face strong electoral incentives to cater to urban, floating voters, who are generally enamored with reformist politicians promising sweeping change. At the same time, the influence of rural regions remains strong. This raises a natural question: Why has the Japanese political system not split along something resembling an urban-rural cleavage, with the DPJ catering to reform-minded urban voters and the LDP to conservative rural voters? Such a split has been predicted by much of the recent work on electoral politics in Japan (Rosenbluth and Thies 2010). Instead, the primary expression of the urban-rural cleavage in recent years has occurred within the two major parties, with both the LDP and DPJ split between reformist and traditionalist politicians.

Several chapters in this volume shed light on this intriguing outcome. As Hasunuma points out, although the electoral overrepresentation of rural interests has diminished considerably in recent years, they are still overrepresented in the upper-house prefectural districts, and the nearly coequal status of the two houses makes it imperative to secure double majorities. Both parties must therefore craft political platforms that appeal not only to urban floating voters but also to local, rural constituencies. This makes it less feasible for either of the two major parties to ignore one constituency or the other.

This dynamic has been exacerbated by lower-house electoral volatility in recent years. The lower house has delivered extreme outcomes in three consecutive elections, particularly in single-member districts: The LDP captured 73 percent of single-member district seats in 2005, the DPJ 74 percent (2009), and the LDP 79 percent (2012). As a consequence, the LDP and

DPJ in recent years have represented much broader constituencies in power than as opposition parties. This reduced internal cohesion and legislative productivity within the governing parties, as party leaders struggled to reconcile constituents with diverse and conflicting interests. A similar pattern has been observed in American politics, where legislative productivity under unified government is often no higher than during periods of divided government (Mayhew 1991). Newly minted politicians from outside each party's traditional base of support (the so-called Koizumi and Ozawa "Children") became major sources of internal discord.

In addition, the electoral system creates disincentives for partisan realignment that would promote greater policy coherence within parties and differentiation between parties, a point Scheiner makes in his chapter. The dynamics of two-party competition have ironically acted as a constraint on partisan reorganization; despite internal policy disagreements, legislators have strong incentives to remain inside their current parties. Examining transportation policy, Lipscy shows how intraparty divisions between reformists and traditionalist politicians in both the LDP and DPJ have complicated policymaking and often resulted in incoherent policy outcomes.

Aside from these electoral incentives, the depth of the internecine struggles that stymied the DPJ also surely owed something to the personalities of key party leaders and the particular circumstances that prevailed as the party ascended to power. The DPJ came to power with an uncomfortable power structure. Ozawa had been the party president of the DPJ from March 2006 until May 2009, when he resigned due to a financial scandal. While Hatoyama became prime minister under the first DPJ government, Ozawa remained a major power broker within the party, with significant influence particularly over newly elected party members who had secured victory in traditionally LDP-leaning areas. Yet, Ozawa was not part of the cabinet, due to the repercussions of the ongoing financing scandal. This created a dual power structure within the DPJ government, which came to be split between the cabinet, initially led by Hatoyama, and the party, led by Ozawa.

As shown by Kushida in his chapter on IT policy, the fall from power by Ozawa and Hatoyama within the DPJ created significant policy incoherence when the Kan administration rejected many of the longer-term trajectories put in place by the Hatoyama/Ozawa appointees. Then, as shown by Kushida in his chapter on the Fukushima nuclear disaster, Ozawa supporters within the DPJ aggressively mounted a campaign to remove Kan from power, going so far as to join forces with the LDP to threaten supporting a vote of no confidence. As Reed puts it in his chapter, Ozawa acted "as an independent entrepreneur within the party, using the candidates he had recruited . . . as a weapon against the leadership." In summer 2009, Ozawa did in fact bolt from the party, but, despite his seemingly large base of support within the party, in the end only roughly three dozen members of the lower house, mostly facing a relatively low likelihood of reelection, left with Ozawa.

Relations with the Bureaucracy

The DPJ came to power with a mantra of empowering politicians against the elite bureaucracy, which had fallen from grace through numerous scandals and perceived mismanagement of the economy and many aspects of society. Ironically, this acted as a constraint on the DPJ's ability to implement its reform agenda. The DPJ initially planned to centralize control of budgets and personnel at the level of the prime minister's office by creating a National Strategy Bureau and Cabinet Personnel Bureau within the prime minister's office. However, this required legal changes, so the Hatoyama administration began by creating a National Strategy Office, installing Kan, then vice minister, as its head. However, there was disagreement within the party about how much power to give this new National Strategy Bureau, with Kan seeing it as more of a think tank without authority over the budget. When Hatoyama fell from power within the DPJ and the party lost its upper-house majority under Kan's leadership, the idea of a centralized bureau to control ministry personnel disappeared.

The other major initiative of the DPJ in attempting to curtail the influence of the bureaucracy was to make bureaucrats subservient to politicians in the decision-making process. The role of political appointees was expanded, with the top three levels of bureaucratic leadership occupied by politicians. The DPJ initially removed bureaucrats from the decision-making processes and restricted the flow of information to the bureaucracy. However, because the DPJ was beset by internal discord and did not have an effective mechanism to coordinate policy within the party, the outcome was widespread confusion and uncertainty about the government's objectives and policy goals. For example, Foreign Ministry officials lamented that they did not know what Japan's official stance was on major policy issues. Foreign counterparts grew frustrated as they received contradictory messages. Policymaking stagnated as the appointed political leadership of each ministry ended up overseeing minute details of policy themselves. By the time Kan came to power, the DPJ had reverted to allowing bureaucratic management of everyday policy, leading to some critiques that they ended up more dependent on bureaucrats than the LDP (*Nikkei* 2012). Moreover, as Kushida (IT chapter) points out, the increased political control vis-à-vis bureaucrats magnified policy volatility when political infighting within the party led to new political leadership that wanted to focus on removing the influence of the previous government.

Economic Constraints

It is also clear that ruling governments in Japan in recent years have been constrained by economic realities prevailing since the burst of the bubble in 1991. For the past two decades, the Japanese economy has stagnated, the primary exception being during the period of sustained growth from 2003 to 2007, which exceeded the performance of the United States and major European economies according to some measures, such as GDP per capita. Weak growth meant weak revenues and high expenditures on countercyclical economic measures. Japan also has the most rapidly aging population in the developed world, which has put enormous pressure on the pension and health system. Combined with Japan's high level of preexisting public debt, these factors limit the scope for new, expensive policy measures.

The DPJ was clearly hampered by this budgetary reality as it sought to enact its core campaign promises. As Lipscy documents, the elimination of highway tolls and other transportation taxes engendered fierce opposition not only from the Ministry of Finance but also from budget hawks, such as Fujii Hirohisa, within the DPJ. The child allowance was also widely criticized as a throwaway of public money and was ultimately scaled back as the party struggled to secure adequate resources to fund the measure. The March 11, 2011, Tohoku earthquake and tsunami put further pressure on the budget, as expensive reconstruction and nuclear safety measures were prioritized. The earthquake contributed directly to the cancellation of several central DPJ campaign promises, most importantly the elimination of highway tolls, which was scrapped to raise revenues for reconstruction.

The nuclear meltdown at Fukushima Dai-Ichi has not only compounded Japan's budgetary problems, but it also constrains Japan's ability to pursue further reform in the area of energy policy, because the country is forced to rely on fossil fuels for its short-term and medium-term energy needs. The Japanese government had already made it clear that the 25 percent CO_2 reductions target advocated by Hatoyama would need to be abandoned. The disaster solidified Japan's decision to abandon the Kyoto Protocol.

International Structural Constraints

The DPJ's foreign-policy record illustrates the international structural constraints that limit the scope for major policy change. The DPJ came to office promising better relations with Japan's Asian neighbors and a somewhat tougher approach toward the United States. Relations with the United States were indeed strained early on, as Hatoyama attempted to re-negotiate the Futenma base relocation issue. However, the DPJ's foreign policy came to be defined by rapidly deteriorating relations with China over the Senkaku/Diaoyu territorial dispute and policies closely mirroring the LDP on U.S.-Japan relations. In this instance, the structural constraints on international relations proposed by realist scholars such as Kenneth Waltz and John Mearsheimer appear to have considerable credence: The geopolitical realities of East Asia, with a volatile North Korea and rapidly rising China, necessitate ever closer ties with the United States and limit Japan's maneuverability in the realm of foreign policy.

As Hughes argues in this volume, the DPJ's foreign policy was constrained by domestic and international structural factors, which led the party to pursue a trajectory similar to that of the LDP despite coming to office with an ambitious grand-strategy vision. As Hughes notes, Hatoyama's blunders in dealing with the Futenma relocation issue, by promising a move before negotiating with the United States or a new target location, was not dissimilar to what the LDP had done over the past several decades. However, it ended up sparking the controversy that led to his downfall. Territorial disputes between China and South Korea led to a precipitous decline in support for Kan in late 2010, and an attempt to ease restrictions on weapons sales abroad was thwarted by the Social Democratic Party during the 2010 budget negotiations. Consequently, the DPJ defaulted back into a strategy in the style of the LDP, characterized not by "reluctant realism" but by a "resentful realism." Sneider similarly notes that on both sides of the Pacific, policymakers perceived a return to the LDP-era postwar consensus, particularly regarding the U.S.-Japan security relationship, which became strongly evident by the time of the Noda government.

Organization of the Book

We conclude by providing an overview of the volume and brief descriptions of the chapters. The book is divided into five sections: electoral structure, the DPJ, domestic policy, foreign policy, and disaster response.

Electoral Structure

The first four chapters focus on electoral structure and the transformed political logic following the electoral institutional change in 1994, and the continuing influence of local politics.

Kenneth Mori McElwain shows that the postwar electoral dominance of the LDP was founded upon two primary factors: a strong incumbency advantage, which insulated its legislators from declining party popularity, and the malapportionment of districts, which overvalued the electoral clout of the party's rural base. He contends that the LDP's demise in 2009 was due to the reversal of both factors, each of which was related to the electoral reforms in the 1990s. McElwain demonstrates that elections are becoming more "nationalized," due to the growing weight that voters attach to the attractiveness of party leaders. Past performance has become a less reliable predictor of incumbent reelection, giving way to large partisan swings that are increasingly correlated across districts. Also, malapportionment was reduced almost by one-half in 1994, meaning that rural votes are now worth fewer seats. As a result, parties that can attract swing voters nationally are better positioned for victory than those with a narrow regional base.

Ethan Scheiner argues that Japan's electoral system, which emphasizes first-past-the-post, single-member district rules, has led the country's party system to become consolidated around the LDP and DPJ. At the same time, Japan's electoral rules also make it likely that the two parties do not differ markedly in their policy positions, as well as hinder the emergence of new partisan alignments that could offer more clearly distinct policy options. Put differently, Japan's electoral rules have encouraged the development of what is essentially a two-party system, but one in which party alternation in power need not produce sharp policy change.

Steven R. Reed analyzes the resources and strategies of Japan's third parties, since the introduction of the mixed-member electoral system in 1994, in an effort to explain why some have failed while others have survived. He examines the policy profile, electoral strategy, and resource bases of small parties in order to determine what distinguishes the survivors from the failures. Reed finds that the key factor for third-party survival in Japan is party organization rooted within civil society, with the capacity to elect significant numbers to local assemblies. Third parties that fail primarily have little organization of their own and depend upon candidate *kōenkai*, a less effective organizational structure under the new mixed electoral system.

Kay Shimizu contends that neither the DPJ nor the LDP currently has a stable local voter base across the country. The dominance of the LDP was long buttressed by the existence of a strong political support base in the rural areas led by local politicians who worked on behalf of national LDP politicians seeking reelection. In recent years, municipal mergers have drastically weakened the LDP's support base by reducing the number of local politicians and redrawing electoral district boundaries. Surprisingly, the main opposition party, the DPJ, could not take full advantage of the new institutional arrangements. Instead, local politicians became more independent of both major parties. As a result, at a time of increasing numbers of floating voters, neither of Japan's two major parties has a reliable local base across the country. To succeed, both parties must pay attention to the changing needs of the increasingly independent—and very often still rural—localities.

The DPJ

The next two chapters analyze aspects of the DPJ as a political party, including new candidate recruitment and media coverage.

Daniel M. Smith, Robert J. Pekkanen, and Ellis S. Krauss examine the recruitment of new candidates within the DPJ, finding that the background of DPJ candidates has changed over time and that the vast majority of DPJ candidates today do not have political experience prior to DPJ membership. They examine how the party has evolved in character and grown over time, based on an extensive data set of the recruitment methods, personal backgrounds, and electoral and legislative careers of DPJ candidates to the House of Representatives from 1996 to 2012, as well as personal interviews with DPJ politicians and party staff. They find that the DPJ has been largely successful at using innovations in candidate recruitment to diversify its candidate pool and gradually build the party from weak beginnings. However, they also find that members who started their careers in the LDP and other founding parties continue to dominate the DPJ leadership.

Yukio Maeda points out that new political parties rarely succeed in gaining the support of a majority of respondents in opinion polls. Established political parties control a large share of partisan supporters, so new parties face an uphill struggle in convincing independents and supporters of other parties to support them. Indeed, in advanced industrial democracies, it is not common for a new party to cultivate a majority within its first several years of activity. However, the DPJ is a rare example of such a party, having achieved majority status just ten years after its founding. Previous research on aggregate partisanship focuses primarily on stable party systems, and provides few clues to understanding the process that a new political party follows to develop support among the electorate. Thus, it is worthwhile to analyze how DPJ partisanship has grown since the party was first formed in 1996. Maeda empirically examines the growth of DPJ partisanship, using a time-series statistical analysis of *Mainichi Shimbun* monthly opinion polls from the party's founding to December 2011. He also examines the quantity of news reports about the DPJ in the mass media, which changed as a function of the electoral fortunes of the party over the years. Maeda shows that an increase in DPJ partisanship is a consequence of electoral victory, rather than a prerequisite for it, and that a government party has an advantage over opposition parties in attracting the attention of the mass media, and consequently, the attention of the electorate.

Domestic Policy

This volume includes four chapters on domestic policy in the areas of energy efficiency and transportation, information technology, decentralization, and women.

Phillip Lipscy demonstrates that although the DPJ came to power in 2009 promising significant transportation-sector reform, it struggled to implement its proposals. He argues that the DPJ's initiatives faltered due to the legacy of "efficiency clientelism." Historically, Japanese transportation policy combined two imperatives: (1) to encourage efficiency by raising the cost of energy-inefficient transportation, and (2) to redistribute benefits to supporters of the incumbent LDP. Because of the legacy of efficiency clientelism, DPJ campaign pledges—designed to appeal broadly to the general public by reducing transportation costs—ran up against the prospect of sharp declines in revenues and energy efficiency. Efficiency clientelism was well suited to the political realities in Japan prior to the 1990s, but recent developments have undercut its viability. This raises profound questions about the sustainability of Japan's energy-efficiency achievements.

Kenji E. Kushida finds that Japan's information and communications technology (ICT) policy, which straddled the two logics of Japan's political economy—strategic or developmental, and clientelistic or distributive—continued to be pulled in both directions after the DPJ came to power. The DPJ's campaign promises had suggested it would curtail the distributive elements of politics while focusing on bold reforms. In ICT, bold reforms were initially promulgated, but they contained a surprising degree of seemingly distributive regional infrastructure projects. Moreover, policy volatility was high, because the bold reform proposal itself was retracted as personnel were reshuffled in an internal DPJ political upheaval. This chapter shows how politicians leading the policymaking process over bureaucrats, the DPJ's mantra, can pave the way for bold reform initiatives, but that the very nature of having political leadership responsible for policy can lead to greater policy volatility and politicized policy.

Linda Hasunuma contends that the LDP-Kōmeitō coalition accelerated decentralization reforms and transformed the geographical, political, and financial structure of Japan's local governments. Because these reforms were blamed for deepening regional inequalities, the DPJ was able to capitalize on this issue and win majorities in both houses by pledging to restore "people's livelihoods." Once in power, however, the DPJ faced incentives to restore resources to rural areas because rural voters were still pivotal in the upper house and had switched their support from the LDP to the DPJ. Electoral incentives forced the DPJ to not only put the brakes on decentralization but also to reverse some of those policies in order to provide a cushion to groups that had been made worse off by the previous government's reforms to local governments. The party that had once championed decentralization while in opposition was restoring resources to rural areas—much like the old LDP.

Alisa Gaunder points out that although the DPJ successfully elected a large number female candidates to the Diet, the DPJ's victory did not have a substantive policy impact for women. The DPJ saw 40 of its 46 female candidates elected in the 2009 lower-house election; 26 were first-time candidates. Recently, both the LDP and the DPJ have supported more women as "change" candidates in response to changing electoral incentives that favor broad appeals. The DPJ's victory, however, did not have a large impact on women in terms of governance or policy. An exploration of child allowance, day care provision, and dual-surname legislation under the DPJ reveals that low seniority and the lack of a critical mass prevented DPJ women from overcoming significant veto points. The electoral incentives of the emerging two-party system have resulted in a larger number of women in office, but the volatility of the system has sustained a weak voice for women in policymaking.

Foreign Policy

The next two chapters focus on foreign policy. Christopher W. Hughes challenges the dominant negative critiques of the foreign policy of the DPJ. He contends that the DPJ possesses a coherent grand-strategy vision, capable of securing Japan's national interests in an age of multipolarity and centered on a less dependent and more proactive role in the U.S.-Japan alliance, strengthened Sino-Japanese ties, and enhanced East Asian regionalism. However, the DPJ has failed to implement its policy, due to domestic and international structural pressures. Consequently, the DPJ is defaulting back to a strategy in the style of the LDP. Hughes suggests that Japanese and U.S. policymakers should recognize the risks of a strategy characterized not by "reluctant realism" but by the more-destabilizing "resentful realism."

Daniel Sneider provides an account of the DPJ's mandate to alter Japan's foreign-policy position, shifting away from dependence on the U.S.-Japan security alliance and toward realignment with Asia. Instead of domestic reform and a rebalancing of the U.S.-Japan security alliance, a series of foreign policy and security-policy blunders ensued following the DPJ's electoral victory. Sneider argues that these blunders were shaped by a combination of uncertainty of purpose and the DPJ's inability to quickly transition from the rhetoric of opposition politics to the realities of governance. As a result of these missteps, Prime Minister Noda attempted to restore the centrality of the U.S.-Japan security alliance after assuming office. However, Sneider argues that this should not be interpreted as a simple reversion to LDP-era policy. The DPJ still attempted to shift away from a policy of absolute dependence and subordination to U.S. policy, and Japanese political discourse now embraces trilateral cooperation between the United States, Japan, and Asia in an effort to manage the rise of China.

Disaster Response

In the final chapter, Kenji E. Kushida explores the political dynamics following Japan's March 11, 2011, triple disaster of earthquake, tsunami, and nuclear catastrophe. The DPJ was widely blamed for a chaotic initial response to the nuclear accident at the Fukushima Dai-Ichi nuclear power plant. Prime Minister Kan was even accused of severely worsening the crisis by intervening personally in the rescue effort. In the medium term, the DPJ's stance toward nuclear power was volatile and controversial, oscillating from Kan's move to completely end Japan's dependence on nuclear power to Prime Minister Noda Yoshihiko's call to restart existing reactors even before a new nuclear governance structure was in place. Kushida shows how the DPJ's initial chaotic response stemmed from a combination of the government's inadequate contingency planning and problematic organizational structures inherited from the LDP era. Kan's own leadership style and negative predisposition toward industry and government bureaucracies, shaped by his previous experiences, led to his personal interventions, which did not substantially worsen the crisis. The DPJ's medium-term policy volatility toward nuclear power stemmed from structural and organizational tensions within the DPJ itself, and opportunistic politicking by the opposition LDP in the context of a "twisted Diet."

References

Akagawa, Roy K. 2010. "Curtis: Responsible Leadership Elusive." *Asahi Shimbun Digital*. http://www.asahi.com/english/TKY201006290383.html.

Arase, D. 2010. "Japan in 2009: A Historic Election Year." *Asian Survey* 50 (1): 40–55.

Bawn, Kathleen, and Michael F. Thies. 2003. "A Comparative Theory of Electoral Incentives Representing the Unorganized under PR, Plurality and Mixed-Member Electoral Systems." *Journal of Theoretical Politics* 15 (1): 5–32.

Binder, Sarah A. 1999. "The Dynamics of Legislative Gridlock, 1947–96." *American Political Science Review* 93 (3): 519–33.

Cameron, Charles, William Howell, Scott Adler, and Charles Riemann. 1997. "Divided Government and the Legislative Productivity of Congress, 1945–1994." Paper presented at the annual meeting of the American Political Science Association, Washington, DC.

Cox, Gary W. 1997. *Making Votes Count: Srategic Coordination in the World's Electoral Systems*. Vol. 7. New York: Cambridge University Press.

Downs, Anthony. 1957. *An Economic Theory of Democracy*. New York: Harper & Row.

Duverger, Maurice. 1954. *Political Parties: Their Organization and Activity in the Modern State*. London, New York: Methuen; Wiley.

Edwards, George, Andrew Barrett, and Jeffrey Peake. 1997. "The Legislative Impact of Divided Government." *American Journal of Political Science* 41 (2): 545–63.

Endo, Masahisa, Robert Pekkanen, and Steven R. Reed. 2013. "The LDP's Path Back to Power." In *Japan Decides: The Japanese General Election of 2012*, edited by Robert Pekkanen, Steven R. Reed, and Ethan Scheiner. New York: Palgrave.

Green, M.J. 2010. "Japan's Confused Revolution." *The Washington Quarterly* 33 (1): 3–19.

Iinuma, Yoshisuke. 2009. "Koizumi Says DPJ is Party of Reform; Hatoyama: I'm No Puppet." *Oriental Economist* 77 (10): 6–7.

Kabashima, Ikuo, and Gill Steel. 2011. *Changing Politics in Japan*. Ithaca, NY: Cornell University Press.

Kelly, Sean Q. 1993. "Divided We Govern? A Reassessment." *Polity* 25 (3): 475–84.

Kushida, Kenji E., and Kay Shimizu. 2013. "Syncretism: The Politics of Japan's Financial Reforms." *Socio-Economic Review* 11 (2): 337–69.

Lijphart, Arend. 1994. *Electoral Systems and Party Systems: A Study of Twenty-Seven Democracies, 1945–1990*. Comparative European Politics. Oxford, New York: Oxford University Press.

Lipscy, P.Y., and Ethan Scheiner. 2012. "Japan under the DPJ: The Paradox of Political Change without Policy Change." *Journal of East Asian Studies* 12 (3): 311–22.

Mayhew, David. 1991. *Divided We Govern*. New Haven: Yale University Press.

MHLW (Ministry of Health, Labor, and Welfare). 2012. *Chiikibetsu Saitei Chingin no Zenkoku Ichiran* [Minimum wage by prefecture]. Tokyo:

MHLW. http://www.mhlw.go.jp/seisakunitsuite/bunya/koyou_roudou/roudoukijun/minimumichiran/.

"Minshūtō Seiken Sōkatsu, Seiji no Rekka o Maneita Datsukanryō" [Recapping the DPJ administration, debureaucratization fostered political decay]. 2012. *Yomiuri Shimbun*, morning edition, November 18.

Mulgan, Aurelia George. 2010. "What Has Japan's DPJ Government Actually Done with Public Works Spending?" *East Asia Forum*, May 14.

Nihon Keizai Shimbun. 2012. "Shūinsen Minshutō Seiken no Kōzai (jō), Seiji Shudō Kakegoedaore. Keikenbusoku de Konran, Kanryō Fukken" [The merits and demerits of DPJ rule: calls for politician-led control failed; inexperience led to chaos, and bureaucrats retook control]. November 25, 4.

Noble, Gregory W. 2010. "The Decline of Particularism in Japanese Politics." *Journal of East Asian Studies* 10 (2): 239–73.

Pekkanen, Robert, Steven R. Reed, and Ethan Scheiner. 2013. *Japan Decides: The Japanese General Election of 2012*. New York: Palgrave.

Pempel, T. J. 1990. *Uncommon Democracies: The One-Party Dominant Regimes*. Ithaca, NY: Cornell University Press.

———. 1998. *Regime Shift: Comparative Dynamics of the Japanese Political Economy*. Cornell Studies in Political Economy. Ithaca, NY: Cornell University Press.

Pempel, T. J., and K. Tsunekawa. 1979. "Corporatism without Labor? The Japanese Anomaly." In *Trends Toward Corporatist Intermediation*, edited by Phillippe Schmitter and Gerhard Lehmbruch, 231–70. London: Sage.

Quirk, Paul J., and Bruce Nesmith. 1995. "Divided Government and Policy Making: Negotiating the Laws." In *The Presidency and the Political System*, edited by Michael Nelson, 4th ed. Washington, DC: CQ Press.

Rae, Douglas W. 1971. *The Political Consequences of Electoral Laws*. New Haven: Yale University Press.

Reed, Steven R., Ethan Scheiner, and Michael F. Thies. 2009. "New Ballgame in Politics." *The Oriental Economist* 77 (10): 8–9.

———. 2012. "The End of LDP Dominance and the Rise of Party-Oriented Politics in Japan." *Journal of Japanese Studies* 38 (2): 353–76.

Rosenbluth, Frances McCall, and Michael F. Thies. 2010. *Japan Transformed: Political Change and Economic Restructuring*. Princeton, NJ: Princeton University Press.

Schaede, Ulrike. 2008. *Choose and Focus: Japanese Business Strategies for the 21st Century*. Ithaca, NY: Cornell University Press.

Scheiner, Ethan. 2006. *Democracy without Competition in Japan: Opposition Failure in a One-Party Dominant State*. New York: Cambridge University Press.

Tsebelis, George. 1995. "Decision Making in Political Systems: Veto Players in Presidentialism, Parliamentarism, Multicameralism and Multipartyism." *British Journal of Political Science* 25 (3): 289–325.

———. 1999. "Veto Players and Law Production in Parliamentary Democracies: An Empirical Analysis." *American Political Science Review* 93 (3): 591–608.

———. 2011. *Veto Players: How Political Institutions Work*. Princeton, NJ: Princeton University Press.

Vogel, Steven K. 2006. *Japan Remodeled: How Government and Industry Are Reforming Japanese Capitalism*. Ithaca, NY: Cornell University Press.

Electoral Structure

2 The Nationalization of Japanese Elections

Kenneth Mori McElwain

The postwar electoral dominance of the Liberal Democratic Party (LDP) was founded on (1) a strong incumbency advantage, which insulated its legislators from declining party popularity, and (2) the malapportionment of districts, which overvalued the electoral clout of the party's rural base. The LDP's demise in 2009 was due to the reversal of both factors, each of which was related to the electoral reforms in the 1990s. First, I demonstrate that elections are becoming more "nationalized," due to the growing weight that voters attach to the attractiveness of party leaders. Past performance has become a poorer predictor of incumbent reelection, giving way to large partisan swings that are increasingly correlated across districts. Second, malapportionment was reduced by almost one-half in 1994, meaning that rural votes are now worth fewer seats. As a result, parties that can attract swing voters nationally are better positioned for victory than those with a narrow regional base.

Japanese politics has traditionally hinged on personalistic linkages between legislators and their constituents. Politicians attracted support through their individual accomplishments, ties to local organizations, and the promise of particularistic benefits. These linkages were especially strong in rural areas, where social networks were denser and local businesses relied heavily on government contracts and subsidies. This type of personalism produced high levels of incumbency advantage and low electoral turnover,

This chapter was originally published in the *Journal of East Asian Studies*, Vol. 12, #3. Copyright © 2012 by the East Asia Institute. Used with permission by Lynne Rienner Publishers, Inc.

especially for the long-ruling Liberal Democratic Party (LDP), which leveraged its access to fiscal resources and higher-quality candidates to dominate the Japanese Diet from 1955 to 2009.

Recent election outcomes, however, suggest a fundamental transformation in this political nexus. Steven Reed, Ethan Scheiner, and Michael Thies (2012) find that in 2005 and 2009, party affiliation supplanted candidate characteristics as the strongest predictor of electoral victory. As voters' preferences became unmoored from personalistic ties to specific candidates, a large number of incumbents lost their seats. This instability in voter preferences manifested as a landslide victory for the LDP in 2005 and, more consequentially, as a massive swing in favor of the Democratic Party of Japan (DPJ) in 2009. This last reversal of fortunes was particularly striking in rural regions such as Kyushu and Shikoku, where the LDP had long enjoyed an electoral monopoly.

In this chapter, I investigate one overarching question regarding current and future trends in Japan: Do parties have a better shot at winning a majority if they diversify their support base nationally to attract swing voters than if they cultivate a narrower, stable clientele in particular regions? This question is of particular relevance to the LDP, whose supporters have historically been concentrated in rural Japan. Although the DPJ won in 2009 by increasing its vote share nationally, should the LDP mimic this approach or, instead, double-down on its rural base? Is the urban-rural cleavage in voter preferences, which has long influenced patterns of fiscal redistribution, still salient today?

To answer this question, I analyze two separate factors before and after the electoral reform in 1994: (1) the magnitude of incumbency advantage, and (2) the relative weight of rural votes. First, I demonstrate that elections are becoming more "nationalized," meaning that personalistic support no longer insulates incumbents from national shifts in voter sentiment. Nationalization is a result of greater voter attention to the attractiveness of party leaders than to individual candidate qualities. Its extent can be estimated through the magnitude of electoral volatility (fluctuations in vote share over time) and cohesiveness (covariance of vote shares across districts). Adapting techniques from the study of U.S. elections, I test whether the victory or loss of individual incumbents is better predicted by their past performance or by national vote swings experienced by their party. I find that for both the LDP and the main opposition parties, the salience of partisan vote swings has increased almost fivefold since the 1990s, reducing the reelection chances of incumbents significantly. Crucially, there is strong evidence that the LDP has relinquished its dominance of rural districts, leaving it fewer safe havens.

Second, I argue that this decline in incumbency advantage harms the LDP disproportionately because of the reduction in malapportionment in 1994. The party's support base has been clustered in rural areas, and as Reed, Scheiner, and Thies (2012) and Ko Maeda (2010) show, this continues to be true today. The LDP's lock in rural areas was founded on decades of fiscal redistribution and favorable subsidies for declining industries. This was a viable strategy in the past, because rural districts were consistently apportioned more legislators per capita than their urban counterparts. However, this approach has begun to backfire following the substantial equalization of seat apportionment. Although the LDP continues to experience a higher vote share in rural areas, those votes do not yield as many legislative seats. As a result, the LDP would do better nationally if it were to cultivate a broader electoral base instead of investing further in rural dominance.

At the moment, disaffection with the LDP's policies has produced more floating voters that are up for grabs, allowing the DPJ to make inroads into the LDP's rural bailiwicks. With fewer "safe" districts, the LDP and DPJ now face similar incentives to make programmatic appeals to the median voter instead of consolidating their respective bases through clientelistic redistribution. Electoral victory today relies on national trends, not local factors, and parties that are more diversified should perform better in the long run.

From Localized to Nationalized Elections

Through much of postwar history, the primary determinant of Japanese electoral outcomes has been candidate- and district-specific characteristics. Scheiner (2005) demonstrates that the LDP's postwar dominance was built on its ability to recruit better candidates, especially former local politicians and well-known celebrities. Because Japanese laws restrict election campaigning to a short time period, candidates who can marshal votes quickly through preexisting support networks and name recognition have been better positioned to win (McElwain 2008). The party's close linkages to rural districts further contributed to its longevity. The dependence of rural economies on fiscal transfers, especially in the agricultural and construction sectors, made them a reliable voting bloc for the LDP. By contrast, voter partisanship was more volatile in urban regions, where social networks are less dense and the private-sector economy is more self-sufficient. However, because district boundaries and seat apportionments were updated infrequently, rural votes counted relatively more than urban ballots, placing a primacy on winning in the former (Christensen 2002; Curtis 1999; Horiuchi and Saito 2003; Ohmiya 1992).

These two factors—candidate quality and geography of partisanship—have produced election outcomes that have varied district by district based on local conditions. Empirically, this lack of a unified, national trend in voter preferences has resulted in low levels of electoral volatility and cohesiveness. Volatility refers to fluctuations in each party's vote share across time, while cohesiveness is the spatial correlation in party vote share across districts. Descriptive analysis of elections between 1958 and 1990—the LDP's heyday—gives us a flavor of these trends.[1] The correlation in LDP vote share in a given district between two consecutive elections is a robust 0.91, suggesting low levels of volatility. By contrast, the correlation between the LDP's vote share in a given district and the party's mean vote share across all other districts in the same year is only 0.26, denoting low levels of spatial cohesiveness.

The backdrop to district-level stability is the electoral system itself. For most of the postwar period, Japanese elections were fought under the multi-member district, single nontransferable vote (MMD-SNTV) system. District magnitudes (M)—the number of seats per district—typically ranged from three to five, with the top M vote-getters winning representation to the House of Representatives. Parties seeking a parliamentary majority needed to win at least half the seats in each district, which meant that copartisan candidates frequently fought over the same ideological subset of voters. This incentivized copartisans to differentiate themselves based on personal qualifications, such as their ability to bring central government funds back to the district (Curtis 1971; Ramseyer and Rosenbluth 1993). The explicit focus on the "personal vote" meant that campaigns—at least within the LDP—downplayed political ideology or broad programmatic appeals, making contests highly localized and lowering the spatial cohesiveness of elections. Furthermore, because the LDP based its internal promotion ladder and policy influence on seniority norms (Krauss and Pekkanen 2011; Sato and Matsuzaki 1986), incumbents could credibly claim greater political clout than challengers, cementing their reelection chances and reducing diachronic electoral volatility.

1 I tabulate the LDP's total vote share by district year between 1958 and 1990 (inclusive). In estimating district vote share, I include not only LDP-endorsed candidates, but also LDP-affiliated independents and ex-LDP candidates of the New Liberal Club, who coordinated their electoral efforts with the LDP. While it is not strictly necessary to include these "unofficial" LDP candidates, other studies have found this method to be a better proxy for the total conservative vote share at the district level. I further restrict the analysis to constituencies whose district magnitude was between three and five seats. During the time period under observation, a small number of districts had one, two, or six seats (less than 1.5 percent of the total districts). These were relatively idiosyncratic cases and so were excluded from the analysis to focus on modal patterns of LDP support.

Personalistic electoral competition, however, also generated negative political externalities. Close linkages between incumbents and interest groups, based on quid pro quo exchanges of policy benefits for campaign contributions and votes, resulted in recurring corruption scandals (Nyblade and Reed 2008). Political observers pressed for electoral reform to elevate ideological competition over personalism and to encourage more frequent government turnover (Christensen 1994; Curtis 1999; Reed and Thies 2001). Following the watershed 1993 election, an eight-party coalition ousted the LDP and instituted a new mixed-member majoritarian (MMM) electoral system that is still in operation today. Multimember districts were replaced with 300 single-member districts (SMDs), wherein the plurality vote-getter wins the seat. In addition, 180 separate proportional representation (PR) seats (200 in 1996) are now distributed among 11 regional blocs. In the PR tier, parties rank-order their candidates on a preordained "closed" list, with seats given to candidates in order of their ranking. However, candidates can be nominated in both the SMD and PR tiers, and these dual candidates can also be ranked equally on their party's list (e.g., multiple candidates can be ranked as number 1). In this latter scenario, SMD losers who have the highest *sekihai-ritsu* (losing ratio), defined as their SMD vote share relative to the winner, are allocated seats first.

The dual candidacy system places a premium on maximizing votes in the SMD tier, since even SMD losers can increase their odds of winning a PR insurance seat by waging a competitive race (McKean and Scheiner 2000). As Ethan Scheiner demonstrates in chapter 3 of this book, there has been a Duvergerian convergence to two competitive candidates per SMD seat. The rise of the DPJ as a viable alternative to the LDP has made it easier for voters to make an explicit choice between dueling government options. Prior to 2003, an array of various parties challenged the LDP, but the implementation of a predominantly first-past-the-post electoral system encouraged opposition groups to coalesce. Now, instead of anti-LDP votes being spread among numerous challengers, they are more easily funneled to the DPJ. Ko Maeda (2010) echoes this idea, demonstrating that the DPJ benefited greatly from the decision of minor progressive parties, especially the Communist Party, to forgo nominating competing candidates, thereby minimizing the vote fragmentation that had historically plagued the opposition. At the national level, we have seen the emergence of a stable two-party system, led by the LDP on the center-right and the DPJ on the center-left.

The purpose of electoral reform, however, was not only to establish a two-party system but also to transform elections from localized, personalistic contests to nationalized, party-oriented ones. To the extent that the old MMD-SNTV system contributed to low levels of electoral volatility and cohesiveness, we would expect institutional reform to shake up these two indicators. With only one winner per SMD, parties no longer have incentives to run multiple candidates, eliminating copartisan competition and deemphasizing personalistic campaigns. In addition, parliamentary reforms in the last two decades, particularly the growing policy capacity and autonomy of the prime minister (Estévez-Abe 2006), have heightened the electoral salience of party leaders (Kabashima and Imai 2002; McElwain 2009). As voters and the media pay increasing attention to party leaders (Krauss and Nyblade 2005), electoral volatility has increased, because the popularity of leaders fluctuates much more than does voter affinity to their parties (McElwain and Umeda 2011). Kay Shimizu, in chapter 5 of this book, also points to underlying changes in local politics. Municipal mergers since 2003 have reduced the absolute number of local politicians, who play an important role in attracting and mobilizing supporters for national-level contests. Accordingly, the salience of local networks has decreased substantially, making elections less subject to personalistic or district-specific factors.

Of course, swing voters with relatively independent partisanship have always comprised a sizable bloc of urban constituents. Attracting their allegiance has been crucial to capturing a parliamentary majority, as rural voters have been less persuadable in their ballot preferences. As Scheiner (2005) argues, Japan has had a "parallel party system": the LDP monopolizes rural regions, but there is competitive bipartyism in urban areas. Because of the disproportionate allocation of seats, however, the LDP could rely on rural dominance to cushion against temporary setbacks in its popularity among urban independents. If, however, rural voters are increasingly up for grabs, then we should observe opposition parties making inroads in rural districts as well.

The growing nationalization of elections, especially the weakening of incumbency advantage, has enormous ramifications for policymaking in the Diet. Incumbents are, by definition, sitting legislators who can directly influence government policy. If voters are turning their focus from local to national factors, then incumbent legislators will be incentivized to prioritize common programmatic policies, such as social welfare or government deficit reduction, over local goods. At the same time, it will also shift the most important voter bloc from rural districts, where incumbency advantage was strongest, to swing votes in urban areas.

Before ascertaining whether this policy shift will occur, we must determine the magnitude of electoral "nationalization." This will allow us to estimate the relative value of cultivating a narrow but reliable core of rural voters versus a broader but less stable national coalition of swing voters. I do this by examining the extent to which the incumbency advantage has eroded over time. Historically, high reelection rates were anchored by low levels of electoral volatility and cohesiveness; that is, the vote shares of incumbent candidates were fairly stable over time and uncorrelated with one another. Figure 2.1 displays changes in the reelection rate of incumbents from the LDP and the main opposition party—the Japan Socialist Party (JSP) until 1994, the New Frontier Party in 1996, and the DPJ thereafter. We can see that incumbents survived elections at an 80 percent rate until 1993, after which electoral reform and the resulting party realignment produced a temporary decline. Although this rate rebounded in 2000, we can observe an unprecedented drop in 2009, due to the sudden national swing in favor of the DPJ. Another point is that the reelection rates of LDP and non-LDP candidates diverged in 2005. Prior to reform, the incumbency survival rates of the LDP and the opposition were negatively correlated, but not excessively so. In the 2005 and 2009 elections, however, we see a much sharper deviation in their relative performance, reflecting the growing size of partisan vote swings. The implication here is that party affiliation may be driving electoral outcomes more than individual characteristics.

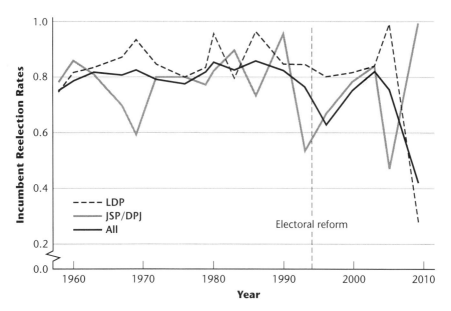

FIGURE 2.1 Incumbent Reelection Rates Dropping
Source: Author.

This drop in the incumbency advantage is likely driven by the rise in independent, nonpartisan voters, not only in urban Japan but also in rural regions. Figure 2.2 shows the ratio of voters who claim no party preference in the *Asahi* newspaper's preelection polls. These polls, which are taken in the two weeks leading up to a lower-house election, conduct separate surveys for each prefecture, allowing us to observe geographic variation. The horizontal axis in figure 2.2 is the prefectural average of the densely inhabited districts (DID) measure, where higher values indicate greater urbanization. If tradition holds, partisanship should be stronger in rural areas. While the correlation between urbanization and the ratio of floating voters is indeed positive (0.39), the graphs suggest that intertemporal variation is substantially greater than cross-district variation, especially when comparing the vastly different intercepts for the 2005 and 2009 surveys. This poses a challenge for any party trying to establish a stable support base in rural regions.

If these "floating" voters make ballot choices based on their (fluctuating) evaluations of political parties, not candidates, then we should observe greater volatility in vote shares over time. At the same time, electoral cohesiveness across constituencies should also increase. With two viable candidates per district—typically representing the two dominant parties—voters are effectively choosing between two competing policy platforms and/or

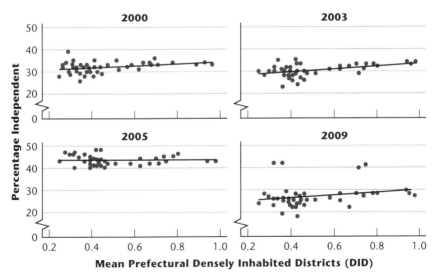

• = Percent of independents

FIGURE 2.2 Ratio of Floating Voters Varying by Year, Not Urbanization

Source: Survey data shared by *Asahi Shimbun.*

Note: Percentage of respondents in a prefecture who report no party affinity in *Asahi Shimbun*'s preelection poll.

prime ministerial candidates. As the voters' gaze shifts from political control of their resident district to the national parliament, we should expect a
reduction in the electoral salience of local factors. In other words, elections
should be transformed from narrow contests between specific incumbents
and challengers to a more unified, national contest between parties.

Incumbency Advantage Giving Way to Partisan Swings

As shown in figure 2.1, the reelection rate of incumbents was over 80
percent under MMD-SNTV, for both the LDP and its main rival, the JSP.
This reelection rate held even as the popularity of the LDP itself steadily
dropped through the 1970s and 1980s. The resilience of the LDP speaks to
institutional advantages that insulate incumbents, such as access to pork-
barrel funds and restrictive electioneering laws that benefit better-known
candidates (McElwain 2008). Unsurprisingly, the incumbency advantage
produced low levels of electoral volatility and cohesiveness.

Has this incumbency advantage waned since electoral reform? Is there
continuing variance in the survivability of urban versus rural candidates? I
test these questions by analyzing the "partisan swing" (Tufte 1973), or the
extent to which a candidate's electoral prospects are affected by national
swings in his or her party's popularity. In the case of a "weak" partisan
swing, changes in the vote share of copartisan candidates do not correlate
with an incumbent's own reelection probability. This would suggest that
electoral cohesiveness is lacking; national trends do not greatly affect individual candidate performance. We can contrast the explanatory power of
the national partisan swing with that of a candidate's own vote share in past
years. This latter measure captures electoral volatility, or the propensity of
local voters to pick the same candidate in successive elections. Weak partisan swings are associated with low volatility; previous vote share should be
a better predictor of incumbent reelection than national trends.

Methodology: National Partisan Swings vs. District-Level Factors

There are a number of ways to estimate the size of the partisan swing,
varying in methodology and the number of control variables. Here, I utilize
a basic logistic regression model that replicates and expands on an earlier
analysis of the pre-1993 period by Gary Cox and Frances Rosenbluth (1995).
Cox and Rosenbluth focus on electoral cohesiveness, defined as the extent to
which the reelection rates of same-party incumbents are intertwined. They
first run a probit model, using a dichotomous dependent variable for whether
an incumbent was reelected or defeated. As explanatory factors, they include
the incumbent's margin of victory in the preceding election (*Last Margin*)

and the average vote swing to all other incumbents from the same party that year (*Party Swing*). Using the coefficients from the probit model, they then simulate the expected probability decrement suffered by a typical incumbent when *Party Swing* changes from zero to average. Comparing incumbents in Japan, the United States, and the United Kingdom, they find that the impact of the party swing is smallest in Japan and largest in the UK. This finding reflects conventional wisdom that voter partisanship is very strong in the UK, while candidate quality matters most in Japan.

I replicate Cox and Rosenbluth's study, albeit with two wrinkles. First, I incorporate data from the single-member district tier after the introduction of MMM, spanning five elections from 1996 to 2009.[2] Second, I include a district-specific measure of population density, *Urban*. One recurring finding in Japanese elections is that vote volatility tends to be higher in more urban districts. If urbanization has weaker partisan effects today, meaning that it no longer influences the LDP and the opposition parties differently, then it provides an important clue as to the geographical causes of recent volatility. My statistical model takes this form:

$$Win_i = B_o + B_1(Last\ Margin_i) + B_2(Party\ Swing_j) + B_3(Urban_k) + e$$

- Each incumbent is denoted by i, who belongs to Party j and competes in District k. My analysis is restricted to incumbents from the two major parties. Under the MMD-SNTV system, these are the LDP and JSP; under MMM, these are the LDP and DPJ.
- The dependent variable, Win_i, takes the value "1" when a given Incumbent i wins reelection, and "0" when Incumbent i loses.
- *Last Margin* is the difference between the vote shares of Incumbent i and the losing candidate with the highest vote share (i.e., the "first loser") in District k in the preceding election. Under MMD-SNTV (before 1993), *Last Margin* is the vote difference between i and the candidate with M+1 highest vote share, where M is the number of seats allocated to that district. In a four-seat district, for example, *Last Margin* is the difference between the vote shares of each incumbent and the fifth-highest vote-getter. Under MMM (1994 and after), the first loser is the candidate with the second-highest district vote share.
- *Party Swing* is the mean vote change of all other incumbents from Party j that Incumbent i belongs to, from the last to the current elections.

2 Here, and in the rest of this chapter, I gratefully use data shared by Steven Reed.

- *Urban* is the population density of each District *k*. Under MMD-SNTV, *Urban* is a four-part ordinal variable where "1" is rural and "4" is metropolitan districts. Under MMM, *Urban* is a continuous variable ranging from 0 to 1, measuring the percentage of the district's population that lives in densely inhabited districts (DID), as defined by the national census.

- In terms of scope, the sample is restricted as follows. Under MMD-SNTV, I omit incumbents from districts where the number of seats is one, two, or six, which are rare and idiosyncratic. I also include only the 13 elections between 1958 and 1993, because 1958 was the first year that the LDP competed in elections. Under MMM, I look only at incumbents from the four elections between 2000 and 2009, in order to focus on candidates who had previously won an SMD contest. This omits the 1996 election, which was the first under MMM.

Findings

Table 2.1 shows the regression coefficients and standard errors for four models. Model 1 is restricted to LDP incumbents under MMD-SNTV, while Model 2 is restricted to JSP incumbents under the same. Model 3 is restricted to LDP incumbents under MMM, while Model 4 is restricted to DPJ incumbents under the same. I use separate models for the SNTV and MMM periods because of differences in the operationalization and implication of key independent variables, especially *Urban* and *Last Margin*.

In every model, the two key variables—*Last Margin* and *Party Swing*—are statistically significant at conventional levels. The positive coefficients indicate that the probability of incumbent victory increases when previous vote margins are higher and the party's national vote share is trending upward. *Urban*, in contrast, shows different results by party. Substantively, LDP incumbents have higher reelection probabilities in more rural districts (as seen by the negative coefficients in Models 1 and 3), as do DPJ incumbents in the postreform era. The JSP, however, tended to do better in more urban districts.

To interpret the actual substantive predictions of these models, we need to transform the logistic regression coefficients in table 2.1, which give us log-odds ratios, into predicted probabilities. I do this by first setting all independent variables at their median levels and then examining marginal changes in reelection probability when we let the IVs vary. Figure 2.3 shows these marginal changes for the LDP, JSP, and DPJ before and after electoral reform. The descriptive statistics used for the analysis are located at the bottom of table 2.1. Predictions for the LDP are denoted by the symbol ×, while those for the JSP/DPJ are denoted by ○. Confidence intervals at the 95 percent level

TABLE 2.1

Partisan Swings in Japanese Elections

	1 LDP (–1993)	2 JSP (–1993)	3 LDP (2000–)	4 DPJ (2000–)
Last Margin	14.54	10.73	13.14	15.26
	(1.50)**	(1.91)**	(2.219)**	(3.111)**
Party Swing	27.05	27.72	33.66	23.95
	(4.80)**	(3.00)**	(3.373)**	(3.489)**
Urban	–0.13	0.12	–1.72	–1.99
	(–0.05)*	(0.06)*	(0.442)**	(0.990)*
Constant	1.49	0.75	0.96	1.14
	(0.15)**	(0.19)**	(0.384)*	(–0.84)
Proportional reduction in errors	–0.6%	+1.2%	+57.9%	+40.5%
Pseudo-R^2	0.06	0.07	0.46	0.33
N	3,308	1,431	631	253

Notes: DV = Win versus Loss (1, 0) for incumbent candidates. Robust standard errors in parentheses; * significant at 5%; ** significant at 1%.

Proportional reduction in errors is calculated relative to the modal outcome. For Models 1, 2, and 3, the default prediction is that *Win* = 1. For Model 4, the model prediction is that *Win* = 0.

Descriptive Statistics (Median)			
	LDP1	JSP	LDP2	DPJ
Last margin	0.041	0.035	0.149	0.071
Party swing	–0.004	–0.007	0.014	0.030
Urban[a]	2	3	0.510	0.860

[a] Under MMD-SNTV, *Urban* ranges from 1 to 4, where 4 is the most urban. Under MMM, *Urban* ranges from 0 to 1, where 1 is the most urban.

are depicted as bars (solid = SNTV elections, dotted = MMM elections). For *Last Margin*, I examine the marginal change in incumbent reelection chances when the last election's vote margin increases from the median rate to the median +1 percent. Under MMD-SNTV, a 1 percent increase in the past performance improved the victory rate of LDP incumbents by 2.2 percent and of JSP incumbents by 1.8 percent. After electoral reform, DPJ incumbents improved their prospects similarly (+2.5 percent), but LDP incumbents fared less well (only +0.9 percent). Indeed, this is a statistically significant drop in the substantive effects of *Last Margin* for the LDP, albeit not for the JSP/DPJ.

The most striking change is the uniform increase in the significance of *Party Swing* after electoral reform. The standard econometric practice is to examine changes in reelection probability when the partisan swing to one's party is changed from zero to the absolute value of the median level. Figure 2.3 shows that the probability shift in reelection chances due to partisan swings almost quintupled from before to after reform. One reason is that the magnitude of the party swings themselves has almost tripled over time (see the descriptive statistics in table 2.1). This is an interesting trend in itself and has been documented by Maeda (2010) and Reed, Scheiner, and Thies (2012). The larger significance for this chapter is that the partisan swing plays a greater role in election outcomes today.

The rising influence of the partisan swing is due in part to the competitiveness of the DPJ, which has broader geographical popularity than the urbanite JSP. The *Urban* coefficient shows that LDP incumbents who compete in the median DPJ district (which is quite urban) see their reelection probability drop by 5.4 percent. By contrast, DPJ incumbents would improve their prospects by 10 percent even if they were in a typical LDP district. That the DPJ is catching up in rural areas is a radical departure from past elections. The LDP's 50-year control over the government allowed it to use a broad range of fiscal and regulatory tools to establish a stable electoral

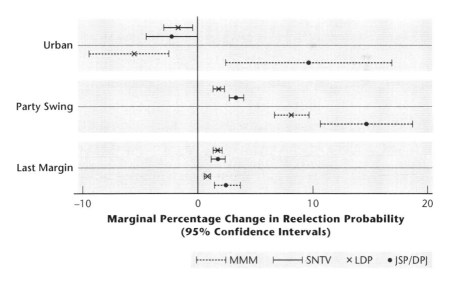

FIGURE 2.3 Party Swing Increases after Electoral Reform

Source: Author.

Note: Urban = switch from LDP to Opposition median and vice versa; Party swing = change from 0 to party median; Last margin = 1% change from median.

base, especially in poorer, rural districts that depended on budgetary lar-gesse. The DPJ's encroachment into LDP strongholds is reflected in its in-creasing electoral viability in rural areas. This means that there are no more regional bailiwicks that consistently benefit particular parties, suggesting that the urban-rural partisan divide characterizing the "1955 system" has lost salience. I return to this point in the next section.

A number of methodological caveats are in order here, because the re-sults under SNTV and MMM are not perfectly comparable. First, there were multiple seats per district up for grabs under SNTV (3–5), meaning that more candidates and parties entered each race. The proliferation of candidates meant that the margins of victory also tended to be smaller, lead-ing to systematic variation across electoral systems in the observed empirical range of the *Last Margin* variable. Second, even after electoral reform, it is not so easy to compare LDP and DPJ candidates. This is most obvious in the case of the *Urbanization* variable. Given the LDP's stronghold in rural dis-tricts, there are very few actual DPJ incumbents in rural areas. This means that our predictions of how well a typical DPJ candidate would do in a normal (i.e., rural) LDP district are subject to greater error. This is reflected in the wider confidence intervals for *Urban* in figure 2.3, although the coef-ficient is easily statistically significant. Even with these caveats, however, the analysis here indicates that the incumbency advantage—the hallmark of the localized, personalistic elections under SNTV—has receded greatly.

Before concluding this section, let me make a quick remark about the overall model fit. While there are various ways to estimate the explanatory power of statistical models, I focus here on the proportional reduction in errors, or PRE. PRE compares the proportion of incumbent "win" and "loss"—the two possible values of Win_i—that the model correctly predicts relative to a base model that simply expects incumbents to perform at modal rates. Under SNTV, this base model assumes that both LDP and JSP incum-bents always win. The same is true for LDP incumbents under MMM, but, in sharp contrast, the modal DPJ incumbent is expected to lose.

Table 2.1 lists the proportional reduction in errors for each model, as well as the pseudo-R^2, an alternative measure for estimating model fit.[3] In the models for SNTV (1 and 2), the PRE is very small, both yielding 1

---

3 The "pseudo-R^2" ranges from 0 to 1 and approximates how much of the variation in the dependent variable is accounted for by the explanatory factors. It is similar in interpretation to the R^2 commonly calculated for ordinary least squares regressions. As with the PRE estimates, the pseudo-R^2 indicates that *Last Margin* and *Party Swing* have more explanatory purchase after 1996. The model fit as estimated by the pseudo-R^2 was quite low under MMD-SNTV elections (0.06 for the LDP, 0.07 for the JSP) but much higher under MMM (0.46 for the LDP and 0.33 for the DPJ).

percent or less improvement in predictive power. By contrast, the models of MMM elections do much better. By incorporating previous margins of victory, partisan swing, and the urbanization of electoral districts, Model 3 explains whether LDP incumbents won or lost 58 percent better than the base prediction that its incumbents were always reelected. Similarly, Model 4 improves our ability to predict the fate of DPJ incumbents by more than 40 percent. One interpretation is that the influence of the omitted variables is much greater in the SNTV cases, because the successes of the LDP and JSP were affected by the presence of minor parties that are no longer serious contenders under MMM (Scheiner 2012). The broader implication, however, is that the partisan swing and past margins of victory explain a greater proportion of electoral fluctuations besetting incumbents today than in the past.[4]

One unresolved question, however, is whether bigger fluctuations in party support are likely to benefit the DPJ more than the LDP, or vice versa. To put it differently, should the LDP focus on trying to regain its rural dominance by doubling down on redistributive policies and patronage favors, or should it concentrate its policy agenda on appealing to national interests more broadly? I turn to this issue next.

Urbanization of the Median Voter in Japan

Recent election outcomes suggest that some of the goals of electoral reform have been met. Electoral cohesiveness has been strengthened, seen by the increased predictive power of partisan vote swings on incumbent reelection. Similarly, electoral volatility has become a fact of life, given that an incumbent's previous vote margin no longer insulates him or her from national vote trends. These two indicators *should* co-vary: greater cohesiveness implies that copartisans increasingly share a common fate, which in turn means that past individual performance should also be less important.

---

4 I have replicated this analysis using different dependent variables. Instead of the dichotomous *Win*, I have tried using (1) *Margin*, the vote margin in the current election between the incumbent and the first loser, and (2) *Votes*, the vote share of the incumbent in the current election. Both models were estimated with the use of an ordinary least squares (OLS) regression. One small difference is that for the model using *Votes* as the dependent variable, I replaced *Last Margin* with the more appropriate *Last Votes* as an explanatory factor. The regression results are included in appendix A. There are some notable findings. First, as in the logistic model discussed in the text, the substantive coefficient sizes of *Last Margin* and *Last Votes* drop after electoral reform. By contrast, the coefficient size of the *Partisan Swing* increases, except for the model predicting the *Last Margin* for LDP incumbents. Finally, I find that *Urban* becomes statistically insignificant at conventional levels after electoral reform, echoing the findings in the logistic regression that the LDP's dominance in rural districts is fading.

Of course, the statistical analysis in the previous section does not eluci-date *why* cohesiveness and volatility have increased, but we can postulate a number of plausible explanations. For one, the gradual reduction in com-petitive parties to two per district means that voters have an easier and more explicit choice between competing policy platforms and prime ministerial candidates. For another, voter partisanship has been decreasing significantly. This may seem counterintuitive, given that partisan vote swings are bigger now than ever before. But if we define partisanship narrowly as voters' long-term affinity to specific parties, then what we observe in Japan today is a growth in independent, nonpartisan voters, as shown earlier in figure 2.2.

Equalization of Seat Apportionment

This brings us to the next question: How much more valuable are rural than urban votes? In the past, the LDP's solid lock on rural districts made competition over urban votes the only way for opposition parties to expand their Diet presence, but high malapportionment limited the ultimate signifi-cance of urban electoral warfare. However, the growing nationalization of elections and increasing competitiveness of the DPJ in rural districts imply that the value of regional dominance is eroding.

To answer this question, we must look more carefully at one of the fun-damental effects of the 1994 electoral reform: Japan's changing electoral ge-ography. One finding from the preceding regression analysis is that under MMD-SNTV, the LDP and JSP carved out distinct geographical bases of support in rural versus urban areas. Given the agglomeration of industrial centers in coastal port cities, it is not surprising that the union-backed JSP would be more successful in urban environs with more blue-collar workers. After electoral reform, however, more DPJ candidates have become competi-tive in rural areas. This is no accident: the DPJ has strategically sought to nationalize its voter base instead of simply protecting its urban seats. Take the case of the agricultural sector, an important source of votes and dona-tions for the LDP. Under Prime Minister Junichiro Koizumi's market reform initiatives, the government promoted the liberalization of rice distribution and focused subsidies on larger agribusinesses that could take advantage of economies of scale to increase profits. This predictably upset small-scale, part-time farmers who are electorally influential and organized in rural areas. In 2009, the DPJ swooped in by promising subsidies to all farmers regardless of size, allowing it to win in rural districts that had consistently voted for the LDP in the past.

This is not to say that the LDP and DPJ are equally competitive in all districts. Since 2000, the median urbanization level of constituencies won by

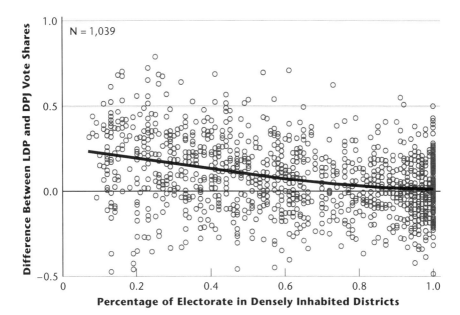

FIGURE 2.4 Partisan Support and District Geography
Source: Electoral data shared by Steven R. Reed.

LDP candidates, as measured by the percentage of voters residing in densely inhabited districts (DID), is 0.53. By contrast, the median DPJ victor hails from districts with a much higher DID value of 0.72. Figure 2.4 displays a scatter plot and quadratic regression line of relative LDP and DPJ support. The vertical axis denotes the difference between LDP and DPJ vote shares in each district in the 2000, 2003, 2005, and 2009 elections, with positive values indicating greater LDP support. The horizontal axis is the district's DID level. We can clearly see that the LDP's advantage over the DPJ is greater in rural areas, denoting the persistence of geographical divisions in electoral support.[5]

The dominance of the LDP in rural areas has been a long-term problem for its competitors. Traditionally, rural districts have enjoyed an outsized electoral influence due to high degrees of malapportionment. Because of rapid reindustrialization in the postwar period, more people moved from rural to urban regions than vice versa, leaving the former with progressively fewer voters relative to their number of seats. In effect, it was possible to win a rural seat with substantially fewer votes than to win an urban seat. This malapportionment can be ameliorated by periodically reallocating seats or by redrawing district boundaries. Indeed, the Supreme Court has interpreted

5 This relationship holds even if we draw separate scatter plots for each election.

Article 14 of the Japanese constitution—mandating political, social, and economic nondiscrimination—to mean that the gap between the number of voters per representative cannot deviate by more than 3:1 between the most and least populated districts (Ohmiya 1992). The Diet is required to reallocate seats after every quinquennial census, but in practice, the LDP routinely ignored this principle except when the Supreme Court threatened to void election results (McElwain 2008). The LDP's tactic is not surprising in light of Raymond Christensen and Paul Johnson's (1995) finding that malapportionment produced a statistically significant bump in how disproportionately LDP votes were translated into Diet seats.

Following the 1994 electoral reform, however, the preexisting 129 multimember districts were transformed into 300 single-member districts. Two important rules were built into the regulations governing constituency design. First, each prefecture was automatically given one seat, with additional seats distributed based on population size.[6] While this meant that underpopulated rural prefectures continued to be awarded more seats than technically warranted, the resulting distortion was still much less than under MMD-SNTV. Second, the independent Boundary Demarcation Commission was established in 1994. Its mandate was to apply neutral administrative criteria for district boundaries and seat allocations in order to keep malapportionment below 2:1. Every government since then has implemented the commission's recommendations, and Christensen (2002) finds no discernible partisan bias in recent seat apportionment patterns.

Figure 2.5 is a box plot displaying changes in malapportionment levels, based on each district's number of voters per representative relative to the median district. By definition, the box for each year is centered on "1," or the median constituency. Districts that are *over*apportioned seats—relatively few voters per representative—have values less than 1, while those that are *under*apportioned have values greater than 1. The horizontal box in figure 2.5 captures the 25th to 75th percentile range, the extended lines show the 5th and 95th percentiles, and the dots indicate outliers. As we can see, malapportionment expanded to 5:1 between the most and least populated districts in the 1960s and 1970s, but since electoral reform, the disparity has fallen dramatically, to around 2:1. Indeed, the last time malapportionment was so low was 1958—the first election in which the LDP competed.

The reduction in malapportionment has profound consequences for electoral outcomes in Japan. As discussed earlier, voter identification with political parties—especially with the LDP—has been significantly stronger

6 This method is similar to the distribution of legislative seats to each state in the U.S. House of Representatives.

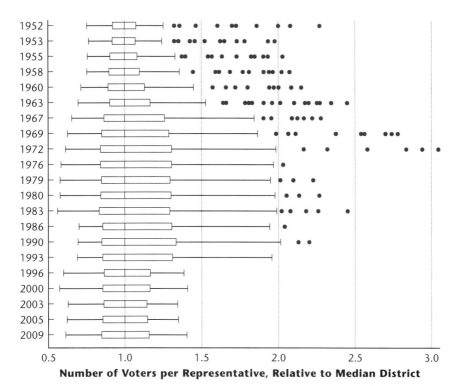

FIGURE 2.5 Malapportionment Declining after Electoral Reform
Source: District population data shared by Steven R. Reed.

in rural areas. This also made public policies that were favorable to rural districts, such as fiscal redistribution and trade protection for the construction and agricultural sectors, electorally efficacious. However, the declining value of rural votes following reapportionment, coupled with the rising percentage of independent votes (see fig. 2.2) and the greater sensitivity of election contests to partisan swings (see simulations in fig. 2.3), suggest that the LDP's strategic focus on rural districts may backfire. Indeed, given that the 2009 election produced the decisive ouster of the LDP, the geographical biases of the electoral system may no longer favor the LDP at all.

Calculating Distribution Biases

In this section, I estimate how cross-district variation in electorate size can produce a malapportionment bias. While institutional safeguards now exist to ensure population parity of at least 2:1, migration between censuses and some flexibility in the Boundary Demarcation Commission's guidelines mean that rural votes continue to count more than others. The question is whether the size of this bias, which allowed the LDP to capture more seats than its popularity warranted, has declined since the 1994 electoral reform.

We can estimate the relative salience of malapportionment biases through algebraic transformations of electoral data. Bernard Grofman, William Koetzle, and Thomas Brunell (1997) focus on two key measures: the average vote share of each party across all districts, and the population size of the electorate in each district.[7] I leave a full discussion of this methodology to Grofman et al. but review each component piece here. First, P_i is the mean vote share of Party i in all districts where i has run candidates. Second, M_i is the population-corrected vote share of a party, which is calculated by multiplying each party's district vote share by that district's electorate ratio. Mathematically, these two indicators are calculated as follows:

- $P_i = \sum_{j}^{J} (p_{ij})/S$, or the mean vote share of Party i in all Districts $j \in J$ that year.

  ○ "p_{ij}" is the vote share obtained by Party i in District j.

  ○ S is the total number of contested seats across all districts.

- $M_i = \sum_{j}^{J} (p_{ij} d_j)$, or the population-corrected vote share of Party i.

  ○ "$d^{(j)}$" is the ratio of the raw electorate—the number of eligible voters—in District j to the total raw national electorate.

Malapportionment bias is calculated as $M_i - P_i$, or the difference between Party i's population-corrected vote share and its mean district vote share. Mathematically, P_i captures the status quo by weighting each district's vote share equally. M_i estimates the counterfactual scenario of perfect apportionment by discounting the party's vote share in districts with small electorates and increasing its weight where the electorate is larger. As a result, parties like the LDP that consistently win more votes in less populated, overapportioned districts would have a smaller M_i than P_i. A negative value in the difference between M_i and P_i indicates that Party i is currently more popular in

---

7 There are a number of ways to measure these sources (and others) of partisan bias. For example, Johnston, Rossiter, and Pattie (1999) advocate an alternative process called Brookes' method, named after Richard Brookes, who estimated partisan biases in New Zealand. Substantively, both Grofman, Koetzle, and Brunell (1997) and Johnston, Rossiter, and Pattie (1999) produce similar results, and so I focus on the former in this chapter.

overapportioned districts, and so would do worse if population imbalances were corrected. By contrast, a positive value tells us that Party i would do better without malapportionment, because its current support is concentrated in districts with too many voters. If all districts are already equally apportioned—that is, the number of voters is identical—there will be no difference between M_i and P_i.

Declining Malapportionment Bias to the LDP

I have calculated each of these component parts for the MMD-SNTV (1958–93) and MMM periods (1996–2009). In this section, I use raw vote shares for each party, although I reestimate two-party vote shares between the LDP and DPJ later. Figure 2.6 compares the malapportionment biases of the LDP and the JSP/DPJ. To reiterate, each line indicates how much the national vote shares of each party would change $(M_i - P_i)$ if we corrected for cross-district variation in malapportionment. Negative values mean that the party would be worse off. Not surprisingly, we find that the LDP benefited significantly from malapportioned rural districts, generating an average vote boost of 2.4 percent (prereform) and 2.7 percent (postreform). While the JSP was not significantly affected by malapportionment during the SNTV period, the DPJ is actually quite similar to the LDP, benefiting by 3.3 percent more votes on average under MMM. This convergence in the benefits of malapportionment to the LDP and DPJ—which was also apparent in the regression results in figure 2.3—reflects the increasing nationalization of the

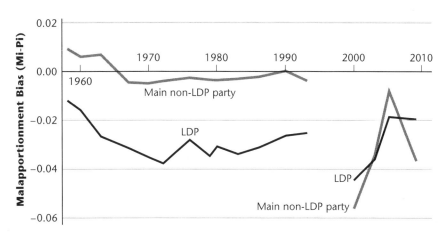

FIGURE 2.6 Malapportionment Bias in Electoral Competition, 1958–2009 Elections

Source: Author.

Note: Non-LDP refers to the JSP from 1958 to 1993 and to the DPJ from 2000 to 2009.

DPJ's support and its ongoing efforts to penetrate the traditional support bases of the LDP.

Given that the LDP and DPJ are now (mostly) in a two-party contest in almost every district, it is worthwhile to compare their relative performances directly. As alluded to earlier, the Grofman et al. methodology was designed for two-party elections. In a two-party setting, gains made by one party are inherently losses to the other, since vote shares must sum to 1. In a multiparty setting, however, different non-LDP parties could gain from some factors more than others. For example, the Kōmeitō may be harmed by malapportionment because it competes mainly in urban areas, while the Communist Party receives no benefits because it runs candidates in every district. The operationalization in figure 2.6 does not make this distinction and simply treats the LDP and the JSP/DPJ as each competing against a bloc of other parties. This makes sense if there is regional variation in party competition, as during MMD-SNTV when the LDP faced different constellations of opposition parties in every district. However, the LDP and DPJ are in direct competition in almost every single-member district today. We should thus replicate the analysis from figure 2.6 by recalibrating each party's post-MMM vote share as a two-party share.[8]

In a two-party setting, any gains or losses to the LDP are picked up by the DPJ; that is, vote shares always sum to 1. Table 2.2 lists the malapportionment bias to the LDP in the 2000, 2003, 2005, and 2009 elections. It indicates no malapportionment benefits to the LDP, with any gains or losses being less than 0.5 percent of the national vote. This reflects the striking change to electoral geography after reform. While malapportionment

TABLE 2.2

Disappearing Malapportionment Benefits to the LDP

	Malapportionment bias, two-party share[a]
2000	0.004
2003	0.000
2005	0.001
2009	0.001

Note: [a] Malapportionment bias = $M_i - P_i$. Positive values indicate that the DPJ benefits more from malapportionment bias than does the LDP.

Source: Author.

8 Instead of calculating each party's votes relative to all ballots cast, I reestimate vote shares as ratios of the LDP plus DPJ votes. In other words, the LDP's two-party vote share = (Absolute LDP Votes)/(Absolute LDP + DPJ Votes).

produced a sizable boon to the LDP during the MMD-SNTV period, most benefits vis-à-vis their main opponents were erased when MMM was instituted. We can attribute this shift to new laws now in place, especially the creation of the Boundary Demarcation Commission, that ensure periodic redistricting. In effect, the concentration of LDP supporters in rural areas no longer translates into disproportionately better aggregate performance.

Conclusion

Before discussing the larger implications of this chapter, I will briefly summarize the main empirical findings. My first result is that incumbent reelection is increasingly determined by partisan swings, not past performance or local networks. Traditionally, electoral incumbents were insulated from challengers because voters prioritized candidate characteristics at the polls. Since the switch to the MMM system in 1994, however, both electoral volatility and cohesiveness have increased, indicating that contests today are determined by party- and national-level trends in voter sentiment. Second, I show that the reapportionment of seats in 1994 reduced the value of dominating rural districts. While the LDP's parliamentary majorities used to stem from the concentration of its supporters in rural regions, those rural votes are less valuable because there are now relatively more urban seats. As a result, there are weaker benefits to the LDP of having a geographically narrow voter base.

There are two broader implications of this study to future developments in Japanese politics. First, greater electoral volatility implies a low likelihood of future single-party dominance. The number of floating voters has increased since the 1990s, and those voters are more likely to make ballot decisions based on their evaluations of competing party leaders, not ideological convictions. As Michio Umeda and I have shown (McElwain and Umeda 2011), leader popularity is significantly more volatile than party affinity, increasing the odds of large vote swings. Furthermore, the high salience of party leaders makes Diet members less tolerant of unpopular leaders who lower their individual reelection odds, resulting in higher frequencies of government turnover outside of elections. Figure 2.7 shows the average tenure (in days) of prime ministers in a broad range of developed democracies after 1990, using data from the ParlGov database (Döring and Manow 2011).[9] Japan is second on the list, trailing Italy, and it is well short of the average survival rate of most premiers.

9 Many countries' ideological cleavages and party systems changed significantly after the collapse of the Soviet Union and the declining salience of the capitalism versus communism debate in the early 1990s. As such, it can be seen as a time of electoral turmoil in many countries, not only Japan.

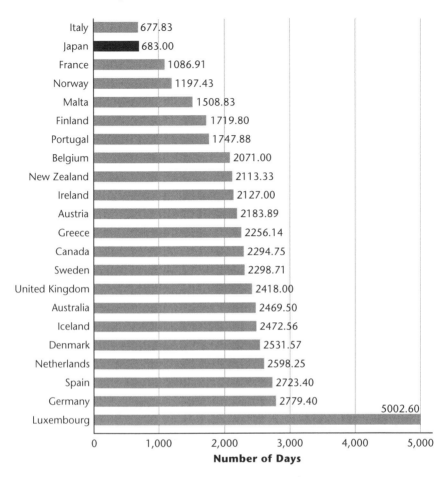

FIGURE 2.7 Average Prime Minister Longevity after 1990 (in Days)
Source: Data from the ParlGov database (Döring and Manow 2011).

Second, any party that seeks future success needs to appeal to both urban and rural regions. Indeed, the growing devaluation of rural votes suggests that Prime Minister Koizumi's attempts to sever the LDP's overreliance on its traditional base were strategically appropriate. His policy priorities, such as the privatization of public-sector companies, were more attractive to urban voters, who are more amenable to free market competition and reductions in pork barreling. However, Koizumi's initiatives were strongly opposed by many LDP incumbents, whose own electoral survival depended on meeting the demands of rural constituents. The DPJ has tried to capitalize on rural mistrust of Koizumi's agenda by promising greater wealth redistribution and trade protection for vulnerable industries. In effect, the

DPJ's victory in 2009 was predicated on its decision to become more like the LDP, while preserving its legacy of urban appeal. Looking forward, I believe it is costly for parties to rely on narrow support in specific regions, since the growth in electoral volatility signifies the lack of any safe bailiwicks.

At the same time, weaker incumbency advantage implies shorter time horizons for politicians, which in turn makes the enactment of fundamental policy reforms challenging. Koizumi's advocacy of structural reform was predicated on "pain now, gains later." This intertemporal trade-off requires political parties to stand their ground over an extended time period. The LDP could afford to do this in the past because of a reliable rural support network. However, growing volatility will tempt parties to prioritize incremental short-term payoffs, such as firing unpopular leaders quickly, instead of tackling major policy issues such as social welfare or tax system overhaul. For vote swings to restabilize, parties must become more ideologically attractive and coherent, but there are few indications that this transition is coming in the near future.

Appendix A

TABLE A.1

Alternative Models of Estimating the Partisan Swing

System: Party: DV:[a]	SNTV LDP Votes	SNTV JSP Votes	MMM LDP Votes	MMM DPJ Votes	SNTV LDP Margin	SNTV JSP Margin	MMM LDP Margin	MMM DPJ Margin
Last Votes	0.757 $(45.13)^{**}$	0.721 $(33.26)^{**}$	0.577 $(15.65)^{**}$	0.523 $(8.30)^{**}$				
Last Margin					0.552 $(18.79)^{**}$	0.411 $(10.51)^{**}$	0.423 $(10.94)^{**}$	0.316 $(4.10)^{**}$
Party Swing	0.79 $(13.21)^{**}$	0.853 $(18.13)^{**}$	0.893 $(15.70)^{**}$	0.864 $(15.11)^{**}$	0.834 $(9.63)^{**}$	0.612 $(11.41)^{**}$	0.537 $(6.73)^{**}$	0.899 $(9.77)^{**}$
Urban[b]	−0.004 $(5.05)^{**}$	−0.001 −1.14	−0.051 $(4.14)^{**}$	−0.039 −1.84	−0.003 $(3.91)^{**}$	0.000 −0.13	−0.026 −1.47	−0.046 −1.79
Constant	0.054 $(14.95)^{**}$	0.051 $(11.02)^{**}$	0.245 $(10.28)^{**}$	0.254 $(6.23)^{**}$	0.033 $(11.51)^{**}$	0.024 $(6.93)^{**}$	0.127 $(8.25)^{**}$	0.119 $(5.33)^{**}$
N	3,299	1,427	631	253	3,307	1,430	631	253
R-squared	0.54	0.53	0.55	0.57	0.29	0.18	0.3	0.36

Notes: Robust t statistics in parentheses; * significant at 5%; ** significant at 1%.

[a] Each dependent variable ranges from 0 to 1.

[b] *Urban* ranges from 1 to 4 under SNTV and 0 to 1 under MMM.

Source: Author.

References

Brookes, Ralph H. 1960. "The Analysis of Distorted Representation in Two-Party, Single-Member Elections." *Political Science* 12 (2): 158–67.

Christensen, Raymond. 1994. "Electoral Reform in Japan: How It Was Enacted and Changes It May Bring." *Asian Survey* 34 (7): 589–605.

———. 2002. "The Drawing of Electoral Boundaries in Japan." Paper presented at the annual meeting of the American Political Science Association, Boston.

Christensen, Raymond, and Paul E. Johnson. 1995. "Toward a Context-Rich Analysis of Electoral Systems: The Japanese Example." *American Journal of Political Science* 39 (3): 575–98.

Cox, Gary W., and Frances McCall Rosenbluth. 1995. "The Structural Determinants of Electoral Cohesiveness: England, Japan, and the United States." In *Structure and Policy in Japan and the United States*, edited by Peter F. Cowhey and Mathew D. McCubbins, 19–34. Cambridge: Cambridge University Press.

Curtis, Gerald L. 1971. *Election Campaigning Japanese Style*. Tokyo: Kodansha International.

———. 1999. *The Logic of Japanese Politics: Leaders, Institutions, and the Limits of Change*. Studies of the East Asian Institute. New York: Columbia University Press.

Döring, Holger, and Philip Manow. 2011. "Parliament and Government Composition Database (ParlGov): An Infrastructure for Empirical Information on Parties, Elections, and Governments in Modern Democracies." Accessed November 15, 2011. http://parlgov.org/stable/index.html.

Estévez-Abe, Margarita. 2006. "Japan's Shift Toward a Westminster System: A Structural Analysis of the 2005 Lower House Election and Its Aftermath." *Asian Survey* 46 (4): 632–51.

Grofman, Bernard, William Koetzle, and Thomas Brunell. 1997. "An Integrated Perspective on the Three Potential Sources of Partisan Bias: Malapportionment, Turnout Differences, and the Geographic Distribution of Party Vote Shares." *Electoral Studies* 16 (4): 457–70.

Horiuchi, Yusaku, and Jun Saito. 2003. "Reapportionment and Redistribution: Consequences of Electoral Reform in Japan." *American Journal of Political Science* 47 (4): 669–682.

Johnston, R. J., David Rossiter, and Charles Pattie. 1999. "Integrating and Decomposing the Sources of Partisan Bias: Brookes' Method and the Impact of Redistricting in Great Britain." *Electoral Studies* 18 (3): 367–78.

Kabashima, Ikuo, and Ryosuke Imai. 2002. "Evaluation of Party Leaders and Voting Behavior: An Analysis of the 2000 General Election." *Social Science Japan Journal* 5 (1): 85–96.

Krauss, Ellis S., and Benjamin Nyblade. 2005. "'Presidentialization' in Japan? The Prime Minister, Media, and Elections in Japan." *British Journal of Political Science* 35 (2): 357–68.

Krauss, Ellis S., and Robert J. Pekkanen. 2011. *The Rise and Fall of Japan's LDP: Political Party Organizations as Historical Institutions*. Ithaca, NY: Cornell University Press.

Maeda, Ko. 2010. "Factors Behind the Historic Defeat of Japan's Liberal Democratic Party in 2009." *Asian Survey* 50 (5): 888–907.

McElwain, Kenneth Mori. 2008. "Manipulating Electoral Rules to Manufacture Single-Party Dominance." *American Journal of Political Science* 52 (1): 32–47.

———. 2009. "How Long Are Koizumi's Coattails? Party-Leader Visits in the 2005 Election." In *Political Change in Japan: Electoral Behavior, Party Realignment, and the Koizumi Reforms*, edited by Steven R. Reed, Kenneth Mori McElwain, and Kay Shimizu. Stanford, CA: Walter H. Shorenstein Asia-Pacific Research Center.

McElwain, Kenneth Mori, and Michio Umeda. 2011. "Party Democratization and the Salience of Party Leaders." *Journal of Social Science* 62 (1): 173–93.

McKean, Margaret, and Ethan Scheiner. 2000. "Japan's New Electoral System: *La plus ça change . . . .*" *Electoral Studies* 19 (4): 447–77.

Nyblade, Benjamin, and Steven R. Reed. 2008. "Who Cheats? Who Loots? Political Competition and Corruption in Japan." *American Journal of Political Science* 52 (4): 926–41.

Ohmiya, Takeo. 1992. *Senkyo-seido to giin-teisuu no zesei* [The electoral system and correcting legislative apportionment]. 3rd ed. Tokyo: Hokuju Shuppan.

Ramseyer, J. Mark, and Frances McCall Rosenbluth. 1993. *Japan's Political Marketplace*. Cambridge, MA: Harvard University Press.

Reed, Stephen R. 2009. "Party Strategy or Candidate Strategy: How Does the LDP Run the Right Number of Candidates in Japan's Multi-Member Districts?" *Party Politics* 15 (3): 295–314.

Reed, Steven R., Ethan Scheiner, and Michael F. Thies. 2012. "The End of LDP Dominance and the Rise of Party-Oriented Politics in Japan." *Journal of Japanese Studies* 38 (2): 353–76.

Reed, Steven R., and Michael F. Thies. 2001. "The Causes of Electoral Reform in Japan." In *Mixed-Member Electoral Systems: The Best of Both Worlds?*, edited by Matthew Soberg Shugart and Martin P. Wattenberg, 152–72. New York: Oxford University Press.

Sato, Seizaburo, and Tetsuhisa Matsuzaki. 1986. *Jiminto seiken* [The LDP administration]. Tokyo: Chuo Kouron-sha.

Scheiner, Ethan. 2005. *Democracy Without Competition in Japan: Opposition Failure in a One-Party Dominant State*. Cambridge: Cambridge University Press.

———. 2012. "The Electoral System and Japan's Partial Transformation: Party System Consolidation Without Policy Realignment." *Journal of East Asian Studies* 12 (3): 351–79.

Tufte, Edward R. 1973. "The Relationship between Seats and Votes in Two-Party Systems." *American Political Science Review* 67 (2): 540–47.

3 The Electoral System and Japan's Partial Transformation

PARTY SYSTEM CONSOLIDATION WITHOUT POLICY REALIGNMENT

Ethan Scheiner

Japan's electoral system, which emphasizes first-past-the-post, single-member district rules, promoted a party system that became consolidated around the Liberal Democratic Party (LDP) and the Democratic Party of Japan (DPJ). At the same time, Japan's electoral rules created reason to expect that the two parties might not differ markedly in their policy positions, and might provide obstacles to new partisan alignments that would offer more clearly distinct policy options. Put differently, Japan's electoral rules encouraged the development of what was essentially a two-party system, but one in which party alternation in power might not produce sharp policy change. The massive unpopularity of the DPJ in 2012 led to a dramatic shift in the party system as new alternatives emerged, but the rules continued to provide significant incentives that make very likely a return to a roughly two-party system—but not necessarily greater policy differentiation between the parties.

Over 1996–2009, Japanese politics were transformed—but in a way that remained unsatisfying to a significant portion of the Japanese public that had yearned for bold policy change. Once a party system dominated by the Liberal Democratic Party (LDP) with only awkward opposition from a fragmented group of challengers, Japan came to approximate a two-party

Thanks to Steph Haggard, Ellis Krauss, Phillip Lipscy, T.J. Pempel, Steve Reed, Mike Thies, and the two anonymous reviewers for helpful comments on earlier drafts. This chapter was originally published in the *Journal of East Asian Studies*, Vol. 12, #3. Copyright © 2012 by the East Asia Institute. Used with permission by Lynne Rienner Publishers, Inc.

system where party alternation was possible in any given election. Indeed, for the first time since its formation in 1955, the LDP lost its position as the largest party in Japan's House of Representatives (HR), as the Democratic Party of Japan (DPJ) overwhelmingly won the 2009 election. Nevertheless, as highlighted in the introduction to this book (and in the specific example of transportation policy discussed by Lipscy in chapter 8), despite the transformation of the party system and three-plus years of non-LDP government, the DPJ did not institute a major shift away from the policies of the LDP.

I argue that the electoral system governing elections to the HR played a significant part in promoting the transformation of the party system, but also helped limit the impact on policy of these partisan changes. Japan's now-defunct single nontransferable vote (SNTV) system in the HR had helped keep Japan's opposition parties fragmented. But the country's post-1993 electoral system—a "mixed member majoritarian" (MMM) system, which focuses especially on first-past-the-post (FPTP), single-member district (SMD) rules—helped the opposition come together around a single party. This chapter highlights how the FPTP rules helped promote a system in which electoral competition in each district came to focus on two principal candidates, and with those two candidates usually representing the LDP and DPJ. Moreover, the considerable power held by the central government in Japan, along with shifts in policy and campaign behavior by both the LDP and DPJ, meant that the leading parties were nationalized parties (see McElwain, chapter 2 in this volume), genuinely competing throughout most of the country.

This chapter also highlights two important reasons, related to the electoral system itself, why the new rules did not quickly push the DPJ to promote major policy change. First, Japan's SMD system did in fact appear to promote party efforts to make policy appeals to the Japanese median voter (see Rosenbluth and Thies 2010) as expected by the classic work by Downs (1957), but these efforts actually made it likely that elections would be decided by "valence" issues rather than policy positions. More specifically, as I show in this chapter, LDP and DPJ candidates who competed in a given SMD were likely to converge in the policy appeals that they made to their constituents. However, this convergence actually made it difficult for voters to distinguish between the two candidates/parties on policy. As a result, just as has been the case in other countries that use FPTP, such as the UK and New Zealand, the Downsian convergence has meant that since 2005 elections in Japan have centered not on policy positions, but rather on general notions of "party image"—including voters' sense of which party is most competent or oriented toward reform (Reed, Scheiner, and Thies 2012).

Second, Japan's electoral system, especially the emphasis on plurality rules, further restricted greater policy change by creating disincentives for partisan realignments that would promote both greater policy coherence within parties and differentiation between the leading parties. Multi-district FPTP rules help permit variation in policy positions across the various politicians within any given party. Not surprising, therefore, in Japan many politicians within the two major parties have shared policy views more in line with members of the other party than with members of their own. Nevertheless, Japan's electoral rules created significant electoral risks for politicians who might want to switch parties, which, as I highlight later in this chapter, was demonstrated by the results of the 2012 election that undercut the DPJ's dominant place as the leading counterweight to the LDP. As a result, there has been much less of a move to create a new, more ideologically coherent, partisan alignment that would promote significant differences between the leading parties and, in turn, greater policy change when there is party alternation in power.

Japan's MMM Electoral System and the Effects We Might Expect from It

Classic work by Duverger (1954) and Downs (1957) gives us good reason to expect Japan's MMM electoral system to produce two-party competition focused on policy programs, and then, in turn, to promote policy change when party alternation in power occurs. To be sure, the rules are well designed to lead to two large parties. However, the system is not necessarily well set up to bring about significant policy change when new governments come into power.

Theoretical Expectations about Two-Party Politics

The electoral system that is used to elect members of Japan's House of Representatives does offer some opportunities for the promotion of a multiparty system, but the strongest elements of the system promote relatively stable two-party politics.

In 1994, Japan enacted legislation to use the MMM electoral system to conduct House of Representatives elections. First used in 1996, the system gives voters two ballots for elections to the HR: one for a candidate in a first-past-the-post, single-member district and one for a party in proportional representation (PR). In Japan, the overwhelming share of seats—300 out of the 480 total—are allocated through the SMD tier.

The PR portion of Japan's electoral system creates some opportunities for a multiparty system to emerge in Japan, but also introduces some constraints on party proliferation. PR rules tend to be "permissive"; they allow even parties that receive a small share of the vote to win seats. In this way, it is possible for even small parties such as the Kōmeitō and the Japan Communist Party (JCP) to win seats. At the same time, though, the lower the district magnitude—that is, the number of seats allocated within a given district—the less permissive an electoral system will be. Japan's 180 PR seats are divided into 11 blocs. PR blocs such as Kinki, which has 29 seats, certainly promote party proliferation through the low vote share needed for representation, but five blocs have fewer than 15 seats. The smallest, Shikoku, with only six seats, requires a substantially larger share of the vote, and therefore reduces competition to a small number of parties that will win seats.

Meanwhile, the SMD tier of Japan's system creates significant incentives for a two-party system. Perhaps the most well-known theory within political science is Duverger's Law (Duverger 1954), which holds that FPTP systems tend toward two viable parties. Over the years, the law became more precise, arguing that FPTP systems tend to be capped at two parties per district (Cox 1997). The logic of the theory is that, since only candidates who win many votes can win under FPTP rules, voters and elites who prefer small parties will strategically transfer their support to a potentially competitive option. With SMDs being winner-take-all contests, this strategic winnowing-down process should continue until there are only two candidates, Candidate #1 (the ultimate winner) and Candidate #2, upon whom all those opposed to Candidate #1 strategically pin their hopes. The lack of information about who the top contestants are makes it likely that there will be more contestants in the initial election under FPTP rules, but as a result of learning and strategic behavior over time, the system should come to focus on no more than two candidates per district (especially in socially homogeneous societies).

In theory, the simultaneous existence of a PR vote may lead more parties to compete in SMDs in Japan, but there is only weak evidence to support such a point. Scholars such as Ferrara, Herron, and Nishikawa (2005) argue that mixed systems like Japan's lead to a "contamination" effect:[1] Weak parties continue to run candidates in SMDs in an effort to drum up votes for the party in PR. However, sophisticated analysis of vote patterns in Japan by Maeda (2008) finds no support for this contamination argument.

---

1 Another type of possible contamination effect comes from the House of Councillors (HC), where the more permissive rules (high district magnitude national PR races and multimember district SNTV for each prefecture) have helped small parties remain afloat. It is conceivable that the existence of these parties in the HC has allowed some to continue to contest House of Representatives races.

Moreover, cross-national analysis by Moser and Scheiner (2012, chapter 2) and Singer (2013) demonstrates no statistically discernible difference in the number of parties contesting elections under FPTP rules in MMM systems and in "pure" FPTP systems (although it is difficult to imagine that there is not at least some degree of influence of each tier on the other in mixed-member systems).

Another feature of Japan's political system makes it likely that the district two-party competition becomes projected across the country, thus leading to two major *national* parties. In some countries, such as Canada, significant federalism allows for regionally based parties, which makes it possible for different parties to win FPTP seats around the country, leading to a larger number of parties overall. However, other contexts promote the projection of district-level two-party competition to a national two-party system. Where there is a plurality-elected national presidency, elites in different districts will have a strong incentive to coordinate in an effort to win the national presidency (Cox 1997). A similar incentive exists in countries like Japan in which government power is centralized (Chhibber and Kollman 1998, 2004).[2] In such systems, voters and elites in districts around the country have an incentive to join together with like-minded voters and elites in other districts to try to create a national majority party, which can control the central government that makes the key policymaking decisions for most of the country. In this way, each of the two principal parties in each district is likely to join forces with one of the parties in each of the other districts in the country in order to try to gain the majority of seats necessary to control the powerful central government. Under such a scenario, it is likely that the same two parties will become the two leading contenders in most districts across the country.

In short, Japan's electoral system is well designed to elect a few parties under its PR rules, but the incentives generated by the SMD portion of the system should help lead to the consolidation of the party system largely around two principal parties.

Theoretical Expectation about Policy-Based Elections

The switch to MMM was expected to promote greater competition over policy ideas between parties. The SNTV electoral system—which contained multiple seats per district and allowed candidates to win seats with a fairly

---

2 As Shimizu discusses in detail in chapter 5, since the early 2000s Japan has become somewhat more decentralized, giving its prefectures somewhat greater government fiscal authority, but overall most power remains in the hands of the central government.

small share of the vote—had forced large parties to permit significant intra-party competition between their candidates. Elections, therefore, in large part hinged on personal differences among candidates (especially within the LDP). In contrast, the PR component of MMM ought to promote more "issue"-oriented politics by creating a vote for political parties, rather than for individuals. Moreover, the first-past-the-post component of MMM usually means that candidates need a large share of the vote in order to win an SMD, and therefore gives candidates an incentive to appeal broadly within the district. The classic work by Downs (1957) leads us to expect that candidates will present centrist policy appeals designed to attract the support of the median voter in order to gain the majority of the vote needed to win in this FPTP setting.

Nevertheless, even if FPTP candidates seek to appeal to voters in a Downsian fashion, government policy need not necessarily reflect significant differences among parties. To begin with, when candidates converge on ideology, voters need to use other criteria, such as attention to "valence" issues—including the relative experience ("quality") of the candidates, images of party competence, or views of the parties as agents of "change"—to make their vote decisions (Downs 1957, 44, 136). It should not be surprising to find that valence-based voting is common in FPTP systems. In the United States, where primary elections (which determine party nominees) lead to more candidate-centered politics, voters tend to emphasize candidates' experience or quality in making their vote decision when candidates converge ideologically (Buttice and Stone 2012). And voters' perceptions of the party image, especially views of the parties' relative competence, have become the center of elections when party-issue positions converge in the more party-centered cases of the UK (Clarke et al. 2004, 2009; Green 2007; Green and Hobolt 2008) and New Zealand (Vowles 2009). As such, FPTP rules do not necessarily lead to significant differences between parties on the issues, and elections, therefore, may be about convincing voters about the relative valence qualifications of the various options. In these scenarios, with few significant policy differences between the leading parties, there is no reason to expect major policy changes to accompany party alternations in power.

Theoretical Expectations about Parties' Ideological Consistency and Partisan Realignment

In addition, FPTP does not require consistency across all members of a party, and different seat holders within a party may not hew to the same positions. If anything, the presence of multiple districts that use plurality rules allows parties to offer various signals about ideological stances, which in turn makes it harder for voters to identify parties' true positions (Aldrich, Dorabantu, and Fernandez 2009). Parties frequently put forward national policy manifestos, but they need not match the positions of the individual candidates. As a result, there can be substantial variation in the policy positions across the candidates and incumbent politicians within parties under FPTP, thus potentially hindering the parties' ability to stake out bold new policy positions.

Moreover, FPTP systems present obstacles to overcoming ideological diversity of this kind across a given party's candidates. First, FPTP makes it much more difficult to create new parties that might help realign the party system around more coherent policy positions by each party. Both the district- and national-level logic involved in Duverger's Law and its projection to the national level implies stability in the two principal parties that contest elections in specific districts and across the country. Once a two-party system is established—whether within a given FPTP district or across the country in an FPTP system where government power is heavily centralized—the party system will be in a state of equilibrium that is difficult to alter. Voters and elites have little incentive to support a third party within most districts: Within the district, drawing support away from one of the two main alternatives would be likely to lead to a spoiler effect, whereby the third-party candidate does not win enough support to take the seat, but does shift enough votes away from another candidate so that the latter loses as well. Such an outcome would be the worst option for many voters and elites who then see their least favorite candidate elected as a result. Also, even if the third-party candidate is able to win enough votes to take the district seat, that single seat is unlikely to help a third party gain control over the national government. As a result, unless the third-party candidate becomes part of a national party coalition, the district would be left with a representative who is unlikely to be a major player in national policymaking. For these reasons, once the two-party system is established, it would take extraordinary circumstances for other parties to overcome the central position held by the two leading parties.

Second, FPTP systems create strong electoral incentives for incumbents not to leave one of the two leading parties (even if to join the other). To begin with, incumbents from the majority party should be less likely to leave the party because of the risk of losing access to the advantages of power— including, potentially, control over the government budget. Moreover, switching parties can create problems for incumbent politicians, since many voters may have supported them previously because of their party affiliation, and the politicians' previous party may marshal its resources to defeat any switchers from the party in the next election. Party switching is not common in most systems, but has been especially widespread under Brazil's open-list PR system, which has promoted generally weaker partisan ties and a highly personalistic relationship between voters and politicians (Desposato 2006). Especially where party primaries are not used to select party nominees for office, FPTP systems tend to create incentives for less personalistic politics (Carey and Shugart 1995). Not surprising, then, party switching tends to be extremely uncommon in systems that use FPTP rules,[3] with the largest amount of party switching occurring in Canada (O'Brien and Shomer 2013),[4] where the heavily federal system creates weaker incentives for politicians to affiliate with parties that are strong in the national government (Scheiner 2006).

Japan's MMM rules may make party switching even more unlikely. In Japan, candidates can run both in an SMD and on a party list. In many cases, candidates lose the SMD race but then win office through PR, leaving a large number of districts represented by both an SMD incumbent and a PR incumbent. In these cases, even if incumbents wanted to leave their party for policy reasons, they would face problems in joining the other major party, since it would already have an incumbent within that district.

In sum, any given party under FPTP rules may contain politicians with wildly varying policy positions, and Japan's MMM rules create disincentives for new party creation and switching that might otherwise "correct" policy differences between politicians within the major parties. With less consistent policy positions across the politicians within each party, it becomes less likely that Japan's parties will make dramatic policy shifts away from the status quo, especially since there may even be similarities across parties in the policy positions of many of their incumbents.

MMM, Japan's Two (Plus) Party System, and Policy Convergence without Differentiation

In fact, the electoral system promoted a two (plus) party system in Japan, but the system did not promote significant policy change with the DPJ's entry into the government. As expected in the work by Downs (1957),

3 In the United States, it is striking that two of the highest-profile party switches in recent years—the cases of Joseph Lieberman and Arlen Specter—in the Senate occurred when the incumbents faced difficulty gaining their party's nomination.

4 Interestingly, O'Brien and Shomer find only weak evidence of a link between personalistic electoral rules and party switching. But they do find a strong negative correlation between legislative party unity and party switching, and research by Carey (2007, 2009) shows a strong link between personalistic electoral rules and low levels of legislative party unity.

candidates within SMDs converged on policy, and elections came to be decided by valence considerations. As a result, there was no major policy differentiation between the parties that could promote greater policy change with party alternation.

The New Two (Plus) Party System

Many Japanese had hoped that the new system would quickly bring an end to the LDP's dominance in the House of Representatives and that there would be a decline in the clientelistic politics that was common among many LDP politicians. The fact that the LDP continued to control the HR until 2009 and clientelism continued to play front and center in Japanese politics led many observers to be gravely disappointed by the reforms (Scheiner 2008; Scheiner and Tronconi 2011). Nevertheless, the new system actually changed Japanese party politics in precisely the way it should have—most notably, shaping the number of parties in the country in the ways that the electoral system literature would predict. The PR component of the system has helped keep a few small parties afloat, but the FPTP rules (combined with the fact that the central government is the primary policy mover) led to what is largely a two-party system.

PR has played an important part in supporting the survival of a number of parties in Japan. Parties like Kōmeitō, the Socialists (SDPJ), and the Communists, who had been a part of Japanese politics for years, and new ones such as Your Party (Minna no Tō) gained more seats under PR than they did under SMDs.[5] The Laakso-Taagepera index of the effective number of parties is the most commonly used measure of party fragmentation that takes into account the different shares of votes or seats won by each party.[6] In each election under the HR mixed system in Japan, the effective number of parties score (a measure weighted by either votes or seats won by parties) in PR has been at least 3.0.

Nevertheless, as highlighted most clearly by Reed (2005), the incentives created by the SMD tier of the system played perhaps the dominant role in shaping the number of parties—principally in ways expected by the electoral system literature. As figure 3.1 shows, SMDs did not lead immediately to a two-party outcome. In 1996 the average (i.e., mean for all districts) effective

5 In 2009, Kōmeitō won 21 PR seats and no SMDs. The SDPJ won 4 PR seats and 3 SMDs. The JCP won 9 PR seats and no SMDs. Your Party won 3 PR seats and 2 SMDs.

6 The effective number of parties index is calculated by squaring the proportion of the vote or seat shares of each party and then dividing 1 by the sum of all the squares:

$$N_v = 1/\Sigma (v_i)^2 \text{ or } N_s = 1/\Sigma (s_i)^2$$

number of candidates score (measured by votes) was nearly 3.0. This substantial number of parties in SMDs is not surprising, in part because it was the initial election under a new electoral system that voters and elites were still learning to navigate. Moreover, the party system was very much in flux in 1996, as the opposition was divided principally between the DPJ and the then-much-larger New Frontier Party (NFP).

A key part of the logic behind Duverger's Law and the idea of two viable candidates per district is that voters and elites will turn away from candidates in third or worse place, but Japan's first election under its new system in 1996 showed no signs of such behavior. Cox's (1997) analysis highlights "SF ratios" (second-first ratios) as an opportunity to analyze strategic behavior. In districts under FPTP rules, the *second* loser is the third-place candidate and the *first* loser is the second-place candidate. Where there is significant strategic behavior consistent with Duverger's Law, few votes will go to the third-place candidate (second loser) relative to the second-place candidate (first loser), and the SF ratio in a district will be roughly zero. Figure 3.2 presents histograms that indicate the distribution of SF ratios in SMDs across Japan in each election under the mixed system. As the figure shows, in 1996 there did not appear to be much Duvergerian strategic behavior: Very few districts had SF ratios near zero.

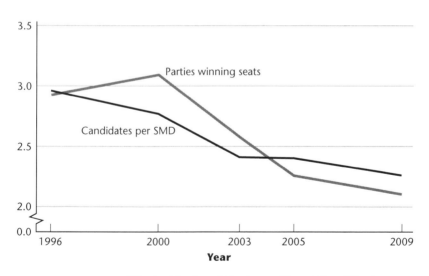

FIGURE 3.1 Effective Number of Parties per Year—Mean Effective Number of Candidates per SMD and Effective Number of Parties (Based on Each Party's Share of SMD and PR Seats)

Source: Author.

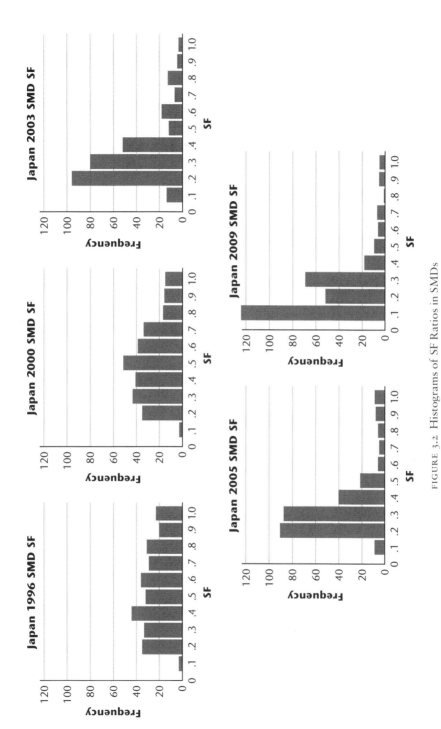

FIGURE 3.2 Histograms of SF Ratios in SMDs

Source: Author.

Note: Third-place vote divided by second-place vote.

However, once the opposition consolidated around the DPJ in 2000, Japan's party system increasingly matched the expectations of Duverger's Law. In each election, a larger number of SMDs developed very low SF ratios, thus indicating greater strategic behavior by voters and elites (see fig. 3.2). In addition, the average effective number of candidates dropped in each election (see fig. 3.1). By 2009, a majority of SMDs had quite low SF ratios, and the average effective number of candidates score for the 300 SMDs was 2.26. The 2.26 figure is lower than the average effective number of candidates in most pure FPTP systems outside the United States (Moser and Scheiner 2012, chapter 2).

Two Nationalized Parties

Moreover, the district-level two-party system became nationalized. In the first election under the mixed system, the effective number of parties winning seats of any kind across the country was nearly 3.0 (see fig. 3.1). That number even increased in 2000, as the NFP had splintered. However, from that point on, the number of parties winning seats in Japan dropped dramatically in each election. Even including PR seats won by each party, by 2009 the effective number of parties' score (measured by the parties' share of all seats) was a mere 2.1.

Accompanying (and possibly helping cause) the shift in the number of parties was a change in what drove district-level electoral success in Japan. Prior to 2005, perhaps the leading predictor of whether a candidate would win a given SMD was the political experience of the candidate: Incumbents and new candidates with substantial experience in political office were more likely to win an SMD race than less experienced candidates (Reed, Scheiner, and Thies 2012; Scheiner 2006). However, beginning in 2005, candidates' party affiliation became at least as important a predictor of SMD success (Reed, Scheiner, and Thies 2012). Probably the best predictor of an SMD victory in 2005 was if the candidate was a member of the LDP, and in 2009 it was if the candidate was a member of the DPJ.

This shift was undoubtedly due in part to moves by the leading parties to respond to the incentives created by both the FPTP system and the centralized government structure. The shift was also very much a result of LDP Prime Minister Koizumi's efforts in the 2005 election to focus politics nationally on himself and his own proposed reforms, thus increasing the nationalization of electoral politics. Whatever the reason, though, there were big vote swings across much of the country to LDP candidates in 2005 and to DPJ candidates in 2009.

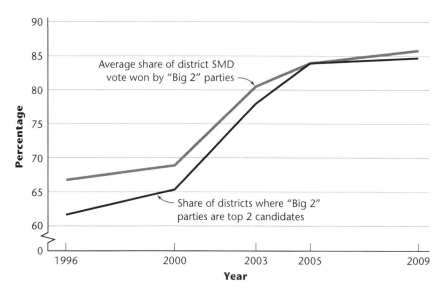

FIGURE 3.3 Dominance of the "Big 2" Parties (LDP and NFP in 1996,
LDP and DPJ in 2000–09) in SMDs
Source: Author.

In the process, the party system clearly came to focus on only two specific parties—the LDP and DPJ—and their candidates across the country's
SMDs. Figure 3.3 illustrates the proportion of all SMDs in the country in
which the top two candidates in the district were both from the "Big 2"
parties—i.e., the LDP and NFP in 1996 and the LDP and DPJ in later years.
The figure also illustrates the average share of each SMD's vote that was for
candidates from the Big 2 parties. As figure 3.3 shows, there was a marked
increase over time in the focus of the system on the Big 2 parties. In 1996,
only in 185 SMDs were the top two candidates from the Big 2 parties, and
Big 2 party candidates won on average only 67 percent of the SMD vote.
However, the concentration of SMD competition on the LDP and DPJ increased substantially over time, especially once Ichirō Ozawa's Liberal Party
merged with the DPJ in 2003. By 2009, the LDP and DPJ took first and second place in 254 out of Japan's 300 SMDs, and accounted for, on average,
86 percent of the SMD vote.[7]

Moreover, there was a good strategic reason, consistent with district-
level Duvergerian analysis, for many of the cases in which the Big 2 parties

7 In addition, of the districts that did not have the top two candidates from the Big
2 parties, only a small number had neither party in the top two: 20 districts in 1996, 17 in
2000, 5 in 2003, 2 in 2005, and 3 in 2009.

did not take both of the top two places in the SMD race: Voters and elites ought only to remove their support from a candidate who is unlikely to do well. Incumbents are especially likely to be successful, and so ought to be especially likely to retain support, even if not from one of the top two parties. In a significant share of districts in which candidates outside the LDP and DPJ were among the top two competitors, the non–Big 2 party candidate was the incumbent within the SMD. Out of all the districts in which the LDP and DPJ did not grab the top two spots, a non–Big 2 party candidate was the incumbent in 39 percent of the districts in 2000, 30 percent in 2003, 69 percent in 2005, and 35 percent in 2009.[8] Indeed, this entire discussion of the nationalization of Japan's leading parties is consistent with the findings presented in this volume by McElwain, who shows that Japan's national parties gained importance after reform and the vote in each district swings in line with the vote in other districts across the country.

Convergence—but Also Greater Emphasis on Party Image

As expected by the first analyses of the new system (see especially Reed and Thies 2001), the FPTP system does seem to have encouraged campaign appeals designed to attract the median voter on issues, and candidates do appear to have responded to the incentives from FPTP to converge on policy. However, convergence under FPTP appears to have led voters to make their vote choice on the basis of valence considerations—most notably, the *image* of the parties.

There are mixed views on whether more issue-based politics have accompanied the introduction of the new electoral system. Hirano (2006) demonstrates convincingly that the new rules led candidates to broaden their campaign appeals beyond just a small geographically based constituency, but the most common view is that this broader-based campaigning has not been more issue-oriented (see Steel 2008). However, it seems certain that the reduced intraparty competition under the new electoral system encouraged parties to put forward more coherent policy platforms, which the DPJ did in 2003, with the LDP immediately following suit. In addition, Martin (2011) argues that there has become greater party competition over issues of security and defense, and Rosenbluth and Thies (2010) argue that both the LDP and DPJ use issues to appeal to the median voter, especially in the area of political economy.

8 The particularly high number in 2005 is due to the fact that, prior to the election, Prime Minister Koizumi had pulled the LDP nomination from a number of high-profile politicians. Most of these politicians continued to run in 2005, but under a new party banner (or as independents).

Most analyses examine differences in the appeals made in party manifestos and general party statements, but FPTP affects district-level candidates most directly, and we can analyze the types of appeals that individual candidates make. Japan has an excellent source of data for an analysis of legislative candidates' electoral appeals: At the beginning of the 12-day campaign period for each HR election, all SMD candidates are allocated advertisement space to present their individual platform (*senkyo kōhō*) in a publicly funded newspaper within their districts. Along with my collaborators Jed Kawasumi and James Adams, I have coded the issues that individual FPTP candidates from the LDP and DPJ discussed in these platforms in the 2003 and 2009 electoral campaigns. We create a series of dichotomous dummy variables indicating, for each of a large number of specific policy areas, whether the candidate took a specific position.

Because we do not have data on the SNTV period, we cannot make statements about how the change in electoral rules affected campaigning, but with the data on two elections, we can suggest how campaigning changed over time under the FPTP rules and the consolidation of the party system around two parties. To begin with, we find a sharp increase from 2003 to 2009 in the proportion of candidates from both parties who took specific positions on policies. In 2003, only 69 percent of all candidates made specific issue appeals in at least one policy area, but the number jumped to 85 percent in 2009. Moreover, position-taking increased for *both* major parties, going from 82 to 90 percent of DPJ candidates and from 56 to 82 percent of LDP candidates.

Voters and parties alike became greatly concerned about the effects of the weakened economy on potentially vulnerable groups, and large numbers of candidates made specific policy proposals in these areas.[9] As figure 3.4 indicates, overall there was a substantial increase in the proportion of candidates mentioning specific policies to promote agriculture, small and medium-sized enterprises (SMEs), and the economic safety net.[10]

However, even more striking is the *convergence* of candidates on these issues over time. As figure 3.5 shows, there was a big jump between 2003 and 2005 in the number of districts in which candidates from both the LDP and DPJ mentioned specific policy positions: Candidates from both parties

9 Our coding does not indicate whether candidates took positions in support of groups in these areas, but in fact, nearly every policy proposal mentioned was in support of the groups.

10 The proportion of LDP candidates proposing specific policies to support SMEs dropped slightly, but overall, there was an increase in proposals to support them, thanks to the big increase in the number of DPJ candidates doing so.

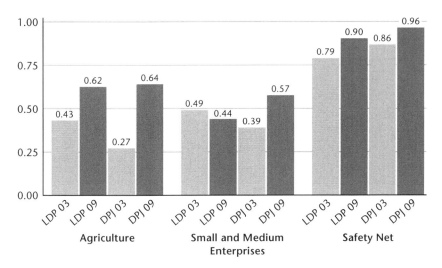

FIGURE 3.4 Proportion of Candidates in Each Party Mentioning Certain
Key Issues in Their Campaign Platforms (by Party and Year)
Source: Author.

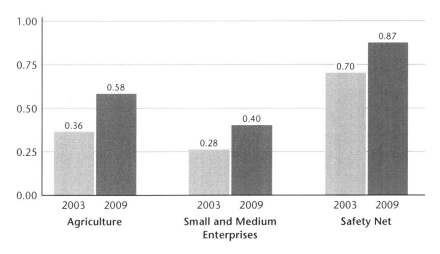

FIGURE 3.5 Proportion of Districts Mentioning a Specific Issue in
Which Both an LDP and a DPJ Candidate Discuss the Issue
Source: Author.

mentioned specific positions in the area of agriculture in 36 percent of districts in 2003 and in 58 percent of districts in 2009. On SME policy, there was a jump from 28 to 40 percent; and on safety net issues, there was a jump from 70 to 87 percent of all districts in which both candidates took specific positions. To be sure, the data do not permit us to recognize differences in the positions taken by the candidates, but the key point here is that over time under the new electoral system, candidates appeared to be more likely to state their issue positions openly, and stated positions that were at least roughly similar to those of their district opponent in a number of different policy areas.

Equally noteworthy, as candidates came to highlight issue positions and converge on them, there was a shift in what determined victory in FPTP races. During the earlier years of elections under Japan's MMM system, such as 2003, when candidates were less likely to highlight their policy positions in their campaign platforms, the most important determinant of electoral success by candidates in FPTP elections was a valence consideration related to the *candidates*—that is, how politically experienced the candidates were (Reed, Scheiner, and Thies 2012). However, once parties became nationalized—partly a result of the FPTP system—elections were no longer first and foremost about individual district candidates. Parties converged on their issue positions, as did candidates facing each other in most districts, but elections did not seem to become *about* the parties' relative policy positions. Instead, with nationalized parties and district candidates who largely shared issue positions with one another, voters' valence concerns with respect to the *parties*—in particular, a sense of which party was the most committed and competent to address reform (Rosenbluth and Thies 2010)—drove electoral outcomes in 2005 and 2009.

The 2005 election became a referendum on LDP Prime Minister Koizumi's reform agenda. In 2009, the LDP lost all credibility to handle either reform or the economy, and the DPJ successfully took up the mantle of reform. Interestingly, as highlighted by Gaunder's analysis in this volume, the LDP in 2005 and the DPJ in 2009 were able to use their support for female candidates as evidence of their reform bona fides. The result of all these changes was that, beginning in 2005, the personal qualities of individual candidates mattered far less in shaping victory in FPTP races. Instead, and much like elections in FPTP systems like the UK and New Zealand, party image became the key to candidate success: Irrespective of individual candidates' political experience, LDP candidates were more likely to win FPTP races in 2005, and DPJ candidates were more likely to win in 2009 (Reed, Scheiner, and Thies 2012).

This new emphasis on party image made party alternation in power more likely, but the lack of differences in the parties' issue positions made it less likely that party alternation in power would actually produce markedly new policies.

Intraparty Divisions and the Impediments to Party Realignments

There are divisions within the LDP and DPJ, and many observers and politicians have hoped and expected to see new party switches and party realignments that could create more ideologically coherent parties (Sato 2011). The hope has been that new parties emerging through a realignment based on shared ideology would promote significant policy differences between one another. With such realignment, significant policy change would be more likely to occur in conjunction with party alternation in power.

Nevertheless, even despite intraparty divisions within the DPJ, during the party's first three years in power, incumbents were generally reluctant to jump ship from the new ruling party. Japan's FPTP system—especially in conjunction with the dual candidacy rules used in Japan's MMM system— produces disincentives for politicians to consider leaving the two leading parties, thus creating significant obstacles to successful party realignments.

Divisions within the Parties

Scholars such as Pempel (1998) have long expected significant policy changes to emerge in Japan because of the divide that has grown within the LDP between politicians who represent the interests of urban residents and the competitive sectors of the economy, on one side, and rural residents and the weaker sectors of the economy, on the other. In addition, there was a widely held view that the DPJ was a mish-mash of largely incompatible groups, put together only for the sake of trying to win elections (Scheiner 2006, chapter 9), and it remained internally divided even after victory in 2009 (Pempel 2010). Indeed, the view of many was that "conservative" members of the DPJ actually had more in common with the LDP than with the rest of the DPJ (Scheiner 2006, chapter 9), and that politicians like Koizumi in the LDP had more in common with the DPJ than with many in the longtime ruling party. As Aldrich, Dorabantu, and Fernandez (2009) suggest, plurality rules help permit greater variation within parties, because seat holders are ultimately chosen by voters in their local constituency. In this way, divisions within the major parties are likely to remain for some time.

In fact, as the DPJ came to represent a more diverse set of districts, because of its recent success in gaining rural seats in 2007 (HC) and 2009

(HR), the new ruling party faced conflicting pressures from its seat hold-ers over its policy programs. Most notably, the DPJ's growth in rural areas emboldened the portion of the party led by Ozawa, who strongly promoted rural interests and opposed the leadership's efforts to raise the country's consumption tax rate.[11]

How the Rules Produced Disincentives to Split from the LDP and DPJ

From the time of the LDP's loss in 2009, analysts considered the possibil-ity of the longtime ruling party splitting, but in reality the Japanese context created little few incentives for a major split in the party. Even for LDP mem-bers who might have wanted to join the DPJ, there would have been few seat openings. In the 2009 election, the DPJ won 221 SMDs, and in another 43 the DPJ candidate lost the SMD but then won a PR seat. As a result, there were a mere 36 SMDs with no DPJ incumbent occupying the seat, thus cre-ating few available landing spots for anyone wanting to try to join the DPJ.

It is also unclear what sort of division within the LDP might have driven a wedge that could have split the party into major groupings. The LDP was long divided between urban and rural politicians (Scheiner 2006). However, in the 2009 election, of the 64 SMDs won by the LDP, only 10 were in urban areas. As a result, after 2009 there was no meaningful urban wing of the LDP that might necessitate separate urban and rural parties for LDP members.

To be sure, splits in the LDP did occur, but the LDP did not appear on the verge of serious fracture. Most notably, in April 2010 a few high-profile members left the LDP to form the New Sunrise Party (Tachiagare Nippon) and the New Renaissance Party (Shintō Kaikaku). Ultimately, though, a mere handful of LDP incumbents left the party to join these new alterna-tives and neither new party won more than three seats in the ensuing 2010 upper-house election. Moreover, the LDP's victory in the 2010 upper-house election even helped the party to regain its traction to a degree, and stemmed the tide of further potential defections.

There were a number of potential lines of division within the DPJ. There were large numbers of both urban and rural politicians. However, especially after leadership within the DPJ shifted from Yukio Hatoyama to Naoto Kan in 2010, the sharpest split within the party was between forces that sup-ported and forces that opposed Ozawa. This divide became particularly evident in the 2010 campaign and election for the party's presidency, which pitted Ozawa against Kan. Out of 406 Diet members casting valid votes in

---

11 The divisions between Ozawa and the leadership were not only restricted to policy. Issues related to the party's organization and leadership were at least as important as well.

the presidential election, 200 voted for Ozawa. It was expected that if Ozawa left the party—which had often been considered a possibility because of both his legal problems and his clashes with other leaders of the party—a large number of DPJ members might leave with him. Nevertheless, Japan's electoral rules created a strong incentive for most politicians, even those who supported Ozawa, to remain within the DPJ. Strategic electoral considerations appeared to play an important part in shaping HR members' willingness to support Ozawa (see Scheiner 2011). And, as I discuss in this section, electoral considerations growing out of the imperatives of Japan's FPTP and dual-candidacy rules were not favorable for most candidates to leave the DPJ in support of Ozawa.

Among the DPJ Diet members, the vote for the party presidency was by secret ballot, but a number of members made their votes public.[12] Out of the 263 DPJ HR members listed as supporting one of the two candidates or remaining undeclared, 80 voted for Kan, 74 voted for Ozawa, and 109 did not declare their support.[13] I should note, also, that it is one thing to vote for Ozawa in the DPJ presidential election, but it is quite another to actually leave the party on Ozawa's behalf when doing so meant leaving the party that controls the government. Presumably, it would take someone with very good reasons to actually leave the party that controls the reins of the national government.

Perhaps most importantly, it is unlikely that most of the Ozawa supporters would simply leave the DPJ with Ozawa without considering how it would affect their future electoral chances, and few of Ozawa's supporters faced district conditions that would give them a strong position to leave the party. Of the 74 HR members who openly supported Ozawa in the DPJ presidential election, 14 had run in an SMD in 2009, lost the SMD race, and then won in PR. These "zombie" politicians would face a very unwelcoming district environment were they to leave the DPJ. If these HR members were to leave the DPJ, it would undoubtedly be to a party that would win fewer seats of any kind, including PR seats. As a result, it would be much harder for them to gain PR seats in future elections. In addition, the district race would be even more difficult: Out of the 14 PR HR members

12 I am very grateful to Steve Reed for sharing his data on publicly stated support for Kan versus Ozawa by HR members. Much of the data on the Kan-Ozawa vote are drawn from *Yomiuri Shimbun* (September 15, 2010 and December 1, 2010).

13 Because of the secret ballot, it is difficult to know precisely the number who voted for Ozawa in the HR, but the fact that roughly three-fourths of the DPJ's total Diet membership is made up of HR members gives us a rough clue as to how many voted for each candidate in each house. Most likely, no more than roughly half of the undeclared group supported Ozawa.

who openly supported Ozawa, the districts of 13 were won in 2009 by the LDP, and the DPJ would undoubtedly run a challenger as well, thus making victory in the SMD very unlikely for any of these Ozawa-supporting zombies.[14] In short, the winner-take-all nature of the FPTP rules gives even the staunchest of Ozawa-supporting zombies little incentive to leave the DPJ. If they were to leave the party, they would be very likely to lose their seats in the next election.

The FPTP rules also gave the 60 SMD winners from the HR who openly supported Ozawa in 2010 little incentive to leave the DPJ. Nearly any politician who were to leave the DPJ would face a DPJ challenger in the SMD in the next election. Moreover, of the 60 SMD winners who openly supported Ozawa in the presidential election, many were likely to face a difficult electoral environment in the next election, especially if they left the DPJ:

- Eleven saw their LDP opponent in 2009 win a PR seat after losing the SMD race. These PR incumbents would be a powerful challenge in the next election, and they would make the LDP less interested in accepting a politician from the DPJ in that same district.
- Nine won their SMD by less than 5 percentage points in 2009. Such candidates faced great uncertainty in the next election about their chances of being reelected.
- Twenty won their SMD by less than 10 percentage points in 2009. Such candidates also faced great uncertainty about their chances of success in the next election, given the large number of "extra" votes that went to DPJ candidates in 2009 with the wave of national support for the party that year.
- Thirty-eight won their seats in a district whose rank and file supported Kan over Ozawa in the presidential race in 2010. Defectors from the DPJ were likely to face a strong challenge from the DPJ in the next election.

In short, a large share of the 60 SMD incumbents who were strong supporters of Ozawa faced a context in which the next HR election would likely be hard fought, and a very large share was likely to be strongly opposed by the DPJ rank and file in the district if they were to leave the DPJ. Ultimately, out of this 60, there were 42 who (a) in the next election would likely face a PR incumbent from the LDP or an LDP candidate who had lost to them by less than 10 percentage points in 2009, or (b) came from a district that

14 Similarly, out of the 18 zombies who did not openly declare their support for Kan or Ozawa, the SMDs of 17 were won in 2009 by LDP candidates.

supported Kan by more than 10 percentage points over Ozawa in the 2010 presidential election.[15] In other words, *of Ozawa's strong supporters, only 18 faced a relatively "safe" environment for leaving the DPJ*.[16] The winner-take-all, head-to-head competition of FPTP rules gave incentives to very few supporters of Ozawa to actually leave the DPJ.[17]

Events and the Election of 2012

The focus of this chapter is on the electoral system's role in helping to undermine greater policy innovation by the 2009–2012 DPJ government, but I would be remiss not to mention major changes in Japan's party system that occurred in 2012. In an earlier version of this chapter, written in the spring of 2012, I opined: "Japan is now well established to be a competitive two-party system, where alternation in power between the LDP and DPJ is a common practice but where party alternation in power need not necessarily introduce significant policy change" (Scheiner 2012, 374). However, on December 16 of that same year, the DPJ was crushed by the LDP in the lower-house election, and won a mere 57 (out of 480) seats. Moreover, a number of "third-force" (i.e., non-LDP and non-DPJ) parties competed on roughly equal footing with the DPJ in many SMDs. Although I included the hedge that the Japanese system was "well established" to be a competitive two-party system, my words sounded pretty foolish after December 16, when Japan no longer looked like a two-party system. Nevertheless, the incentives created by the electoral system remain, and there continues to be

15 If we count any candidate whose district voted for Kan over Ozawa, rather than just those where Kan won by more than 10 percentage points, there were 48 HR members who would face a difficult environment if they were to leave the DPJ.

16 Out of the 88 SMD winners who did not openly declare support for any candidate in the election, 17 had a PR incumbent in their district, 9 won by less than 5 percentage points, 26 won by less than 10 percentage points, and 77 were in a district in which Kan defeated Ozawa. To put it all together, out of the 88 there were 80 who (a) in the next election would likely face a PR incumbent from the LDP or an LDP candidate who had lost to them by less than 10 percentage points in 2009, or (b) came from a district that supported Kan by more than 10 percentage points over Ozawa in the 2010 presidential election.

17 In many ways, the type of candidate who was best set up to leave the DPJ was one who faced no strong LDP candidate in the SMD. Such candidates might face less of a challenge from all sides, or might be able to link up with the LDP. However, of the DPJ zombies, none ran in a district that had no LDP candidate in 2009. Of the SMD winners in the DPJ, eight did not face an LDP candidate in 2009. Of this eight, two openly supported Kan in the DPJ presidential election, two openly supported Ozawa, and four did not declare.

good reason to believe that Japan's party system will become more consolidated around a smaller number of alternatives again.

The broad reason for the 2012 shift in Japan's party system was the massive loss of popularity of the DPJ, which made it no longer the clear non-LDP alternative in a FPTP, majoritarian type of system. The logic behind Duverger depends on the assumption that voters know which two candidates are the viable two (Cox 1997; Moser and Scheiner 2012), and the DPJ's overwhelming loss of popularity put its position as the alternative to the LDP in doubt. It is beyond the scope of this chapter to explain *why* the DPJ's loss of popularity—in contrast to the loss of popularity of most other large parties in FPTP systems—led to the collapse of its clear position as one of the two leading parties. Future work will pay considerable attention to this question.

However, what is most important for the purposes of this chapter is that the events of 2012 serve to underscore the powerful incentives for consolidation provided by FPTP rules. Japanese politicians whose behavior ran counter to these incentives paid dearly in 2012.

Ozawa's Defection

Prior to summer 2012, the most significant defections from the DPJ were consistent with the logic laid out in this chapter and did not involve a major split of the party: In February 2011, 16 HR members of the DPJ left the party's parliamentary caucus in support of Ozawa (and in opposition to Kan).[18] However, strikingly, these defectors were principally first-term politicians (with strong ties to Ozawa) who were pure PR candidates in 2009. Most were so poorly ranked on the lists that it took an enormous DPJ landslide for them to win their seats in 2009. As a result, they had little chance of winning seats in future, more competitive elections. To be sure, these moves suggest that other DPJ members who were elected from poorly ranked positions on the party's PR list in 2009 might have had some reason to leave the party in the hope of gaining a better slot on, for example, the LDP's list (or even winning one of the few seats of a small new party) in the next election. However, this logic really applies only to a very small number of HR legislators from the DPJ: Of the 308 candidates who won office for the DPJ in 2009, 264 were the party's candidate in a single-member district. Given the dangers of having to run against a new DPJ candidate if they were to leave the party, the incentives were much weaker for these SMD candidates to switch out of the DPJ.

---

18 This "split" did not involve the members actually leaving the party but did reduce their likelihood of supporting DPJ policy.

Indeed, when Ozawa finally bolted from the DPJ to form a new small party in July 2012 in response to the party's efforts to raise Japan's consumption tax, relatively few politicians left with him.[19] Recall that Ozawa won the votes of 200 Diet members in the 2010 DPJ presidential election. Moreover, Ozawa's House of Representatives faction within the DPJ contained roughly 80 members.[20] Nevertheless, only roughly 40 House of Representatives members, along with a dozen in the House of Councillors, joined Ozawa in leaving the ruling party at the time.[21] Ultimately, despite the presence of a number of politicians aligned with Ozawa, it appears that the incentives growing out of Japan's electoral rules constrained many from joining Ozawa in splitting the party, thus hampering significant party and policy realignment.

DPJ Defectors and Third-Force Party Candidacies in the 2012 Election

Once Prime Minister Noda dissolved the lower house on November 16, 2012, additional politicians left the DPJ and the pace of third-force new-party formation increased. By the time of the election, there were three main third-force parties. The first was Your Party (Minna no Tō, or YP), which had formed just prior to the 2009 election and won a very small number of seats in the 2009 and 2010 elections. The second was the Japan Restoration Party (Ishin no Kai, or JRP), led by Osaka mayor Toru Hashimoto and Tokyo governor Shintaro Ishihara, with its principal base of support in Osaka (a prefecture that, outside of Tokyo, is the least dependent in Japan upon the central government). The third party was the Tomorrow Party (Mirai no Tō, or TPJ), led by Shiga Governor Yukiko Kada and Ozawa.

The election was not kind to the defectors, but the defections also hurt the DPJ. Of the 67 DPJ defectors who ran for a new party in 2012, *only one*, Ozawa, won an SMD seat. Moreover, in the 39 districts in which the DPJ ran a new candidate against an incumbent defector, no DPJ candidates won, and in only two districts did a DPJ candidate even finish second.

As discussed earlier, FPTP rules—especially when they are part of a strongly centralized political system—create significant obstacles to new

---

19 Ozawa led a group that voted against the DPJ's proposed consumption tax increase. In response, the DPJ expelled Ozawa and his followers from the vote, and Ozawa and his group resigned from the DPJ nearly simultaneously.

20 See the June 20, 2012 *Daily Yomiuri* article. http://www.yomiuri.co.jp/dy/national/T120619004682.htm.

21 See the June 3 and 5, 2012 *Daily Yomiuri* articles. http://www.yomiuri.co.jp/dy/national/T120702005371.htm, and http://www.yomiuri.co.jp/dy/national/T120704005099.htm.

parties that seek to gain strength in established party systems. Under FPTP, candidates outside the top two parties typically achieve little, except perhaps creating a spoiler effect. New parties usually have great difficulty starting up in plurality systems (see, for example, Pridham 1988). Indeed, even in 2010 in the UK, during a period of great voter unhappiness with Labour and the Conservatives, as well as tremendous policy convergence by the leading parties, the leading third party, the (British) Liberal Democratic Party, still took less than 10 percent of all seats.

Incredibly, the "third" parties played a much more significant role in Japan in 2012, but the outcome in Japan makes clear why there is little precedent for such parties to succeed. The third-force parties contested races in many districts, leading to a substantial increase in the number of parties, but also providing the LDP with many victories that a consolidated non-LDP force probably would not have permitted. The average effective number of candidates per district in 2012 shot up to 2.99. There is strong evidence that votes for the third-force party candidates came largely at the expense of votes for DPJ SMD candidates, rather than those from the LDP. The inability of the DPJ and third-force parties to coordinate was a boon to the LDP. Combined DPJ and third-force party votes would have defeated the LDP in 75 of the LDP's 237 SMD victories in 2012 (and would have taken two of Kōmeitō's nine SMD wins). Such a coordinated non-LDP force (i.e., DPJ and third-force parties) would have prevented the LDP from winning a majority, and would have reduced the total number of seats won by the LDP- Kōmeitō coalition to 248 and increased the DPJ+third force total to 215 seats.[22] Such a result would have been markedly different from the 325-139 thrashing that did occur.

Put differently, the non-LDP cohort encountered significant electoral failure in 2012 because of behavior that ran counter to the incentives created by Japan's FPTP rules. It is difficult to imagine that the principal non-LDP set of parties and candidates will continue to ignore these incentives. There is, therefore, good reason to expect a return to politics more like the consolidation seen especially between 2000 and 2009—provided there is no significant electoral reform (something that is being discussed in Japan today).

Conclusion

The heavy emphasis on the FPTP rules that govern the election of 300 out of Japan's 480 House of Representatives seats promoted a two-party

---

22 See http://themonkeycage.org/blog/2012/12/27/the-japanese-general-election-of-2012 -sometimes-lucky-is-better-than-popular/, and the analysis in Pekkanen, Reed, and Scheiner (2013).

system that became consolidated around the LDP and DPJ at both the district and national levels. At the same time, these very FPTP rules promoted policy convergence among the leading parties, which therefore led to an emphasis in Japanese elections on the image of the parties, with elections decided by which party voters deemed to be most likely to address the issue of reform competently. FPTP also permitted ideological variance across the incumbents in each major party, and FPTP created disincentives for major new-party formation or realignments that might create more ideologically cohesive parties. As a result, Japan developed a roughly two-party system, but one in which the parties did not differ markedly on the issues, and the advent of party alternation did not introduce a sharp break from previous government policies.

To be sure, it is possible to imagine other outcomes occurring in Japan's FPTP system. Following the lead of Margaret Thatcher and the Conservative Party three decades ago in the UK, one party could have sought victory by creating a sharper distinction between itself and its opposition. Nevertheless, the LDP's rural base has typically made it unlikely that it would propose a major policy initiative that could appeal widely in Japan. And it was difficult to imagine the DPJ proposing such a bold and sustained policy effort given its lack of policy coherence in areas where it differed from the LDP.

It is also possible that the recent decline of the DPJ and the rise of the third-force parties might generate a party realignment that makes bold and broadly appealing policy initiatives more likely. At the same time, the DPJ and the third-force parties each continue to maintain substantial intraparty differences of opinion on policy, and it is not at all obvious that a coordinated non-LDP force would break from the 2009–2012 experience of the DPJ and institute significant policy innovation.

References

Adams, James F., Jed Kawasumi, and Ethan Scheiner. 2010. "Running on Character or Running on Policy? An Analysis of Japanese Candidates' Campaign Platforms." Paper presented at the annual meeting of the American Political Science Association, Washington, DC, September 2–5.

Aldrich, John, Sinziana Dorabantu, and Marco Antonio Fernandez. 2009. "Perceptions of Party Positions on the Left-Right Scale." Paper presented at the annual meeting of the American Political Science Association, Toronto, Canada, September 3–6.

Buttice, Matthew K., and Walter J. Stone. 2012. "Candidates Matter: Policy and Quality Differences in 2006." *Journal of Politics* 74 (3): 870–87.

Carey, John. 2007. "Competing Principals, Political Institutions, and Party Unity in Legislative Voting." *American Journal of Political Science* 51 (1): 92–107.

———. 2009. *Legislative Voting and Accountability*. Cambridge: Cambridge University Press.

Carey, John, and Matthew S. Shugart. 1995. "Incentives to Cultivate a Personal Vote: A Rank Ordering of Electoral Formulas." *Electoral Studies* 14: 417–39.

Chhibber, Pradeep, and Ken Kollman. 1998. "Party Aggregation and the Number of Parties in India and the United States." *American Political Science Review* 92 (2): 329–42.

———. 2004. *The Formation of National Party Systems: Federalism and Party Competition in Canada, Great Britain, India, and the United States.* Princeton, NJ: Princeton University Press.

Clarke, Harold, David Sanders, Marianne C. Stewart, and Paul M. Whiteley. 2004. *Political Choice in Britain*. Oxford: Oxford University Press.

———. 2009. *Performance Politics and the British Voter*. New York: Cambridge University Press.

Cox, Gary W. 1997. *Making Votes Count: Strategic Coordination in the World's Electoral Systems.* New York: Cambridge University Press.

Daily Yomiuri. Various issues.

Desposato, Scott W. 2006. "Parties for Rent? Ambition, Ideology and Party Switching in Brazil's Chamber of Deputies." *American Journal of Political Science* 50 (1): 62–80.

Downs, Anthony. 1957. *An Economic Theory of Democracy*. New York: Harper and Row.

Duverger, Maurice. 1954. *Political Parties: Their Organization and Activity in the Modern State*. London: Methuen.

Ferrara, Federico, Erik S. Herron, and Misa Nishikawa. 2005. *Mixed Electoral Systems: Contamination and Its Consequences*. New York: Palgrave Macmillan.

Green, Jane. 2007. "When Voters and Parties Agree: Valence Issues and Party Competition." *Political Studies* 55 (3): 629–55.

Green, Jane, and Sara B. Hobolt. 2008. "Owning the Issue Agenda: Explaining Party Strategies in British General Election Campaigns." *Electoral Studies* 27 (3): 460–76.

Hirano, Shigeo. 2006. "Electoral Institutions, Hometowns, and Favored Minorities: Evidence from Japan's Electoral Reforms." *World Politics* 59 (1): 51–82.

Laakso, Markku, and Rein Taagepera. 1979. "'Effective' Number of Parties: A Measure with Application to West Europe." *Comparative Political Studies* 12 (1): 3–27.

Maeda, Ko. 2008. "Re-examining the Contamination Effect of Japan's Mixed Electoral System Using the Treatment-Effects Model." *Electoral Studies* 27: 723–31.

Martin, Sherry L. 2011. "Issue Evolution and Electoral Politics in Contemporary Japan." In *The Evolution of Japan's Party System: Politics and Policy in an Era of Institutional Change,* edited by Leonard J. Schoppa. Toronto: Toronto University Press.

Moser, Robert G., and Ethan Scheiner. 2012. *Electoral Systems and Political Context.* New York: Cambridge University Press.

O'Brien, Diana Z., and Yael Shomer. 2013. "A Cross-National Analysis of Party Switching." *Legislative Studies Quarterly* 38 (1): 111–41.

Pekkanen, Robert, Steven R. Reed, and Ethan Scheiner, eds. 2013. *Japan Decides 2012: The Japanese General Election.* New York: Palgrave Macmillan.

Pempel, T.J. 1998. *Regime Shift: Comparative Dynamics of the Japanese Political Economy.* Ithaca, NY: Cornell University Press.

———. 2010. "Between Pork and Productivity: The Collapse of the Liberal Democratic Party." *Journal of Japanese Studies* 36 (2): 227–54.

Pridham, Geoffrey. 1988. "The Social Democratic Party in Britain: Protest or New Political Tendency?" In *When Parties Fail,* edited by Kay Lawson and Peter H. Merkl. Princeton, NJ: Princeton University Press.

Reed, Steven R. 2005. "Japan: Haltingly Toward a Two-Party System." In *The Politics of Electoral Systems,* edited by Michael Gallagher and Paul Mitchell, 277–94. New York: Oxford University Press.

Reed, Steven R., Ethan Scheiner, and Michael F. Thies. 2012. "The End of LDP Dominance and the Rise of Party-Oriented Politics in Japan." *Journal of Japanese Studies* 38 (2): 353–76.

Reed, Steven R., and Michael F. Thies. 2001. "The Consequences of Electoral Reform in Japan." In *Mixed-member Electoral Systems: The Best of Both Worlds?* edited by Matthew Soberg Shugart and Martin P. Wattenberg. Oxford: Oxford University Press.

Rosenbluth, Frances, and Michael Thies. 2010. *Japan Transformed: Political Change and Economic Restructuring.* Princeton, NJ: Princeton University Press.

Sato, Akira. 2011. "Big Bang: Conservative Merger Expected from Political Supernova." *Asahi Shimbun Weekly Aera,* March 2.

Scheiner, Ethan. 2006. *Democracy Without Competition in Japan: Opposition Failure in a One-Party Dominant State.* New York: Cambridge University Press.

———. 2008. "Does Electoral System Reform Work? Electoral System Lessons from Reforms of the 1990s." *Annual Review of Political Science* 11: 161–81.

————. 2011. "Evolution of Japan's Party System—Consolidation or Realignment?" Paper presented at the conference "Political Change in Japan II: One Step Forward, One Step Back," Stanford University, February 4–5.

————. 2012. "The Electoral System and Japan's Partial Transformation: Party System Consolidation Without Policy Realignment." *Journal of East Asian Studies* 12 (3): 351–80.

Scheiner, Ethan, and Filippo Tronconi. 2011. "Unanticipated Consequences of Electoral Reform in Italy and Japan." In *A Natural Experiment on Electoral Law Reform: Evaluating the Long Run Consequences of 1990s Electoral Reform in Italy and Japan*, edited by Daniela Giannetti and Bernard Grofman, 95–112. New York: Springer.

Singer, Matthew. 2013. "Was Duverger Correct? Single-Member District Election Outcomes in Fifty-three Countries." *British Journal of Political Science* 43 (1): 201–220.

Steel, Gill. 2008. "Policy Preferences and Party Platforms: What Voters Want vs. What Voters Get." In *Democratic Reform in Japan: Assessing the Impact,* edited by Sherry L. Martin and Gill Steel. Boulder, CO: Lynne Rienner.

Vowles, Jack. 2009. "The 2008 Election: Why National Won." In *New Zealand Government and Politics,* 5th ed., edited by Raymond Miller, 365–82. Melbourne: Oxford University Press.

Yomiuri Shimbun. Various issues.

4 The Survival of "Third Parties" in Japan's Mixed-Member Electoral System

Steven R. Reed

This chapter analyzes the resources and strategies of Japan's third parties since the introduction of the mixed-member electoral system in 1994, in an effort to explain why some third parties have failed while others have survived. The chapter examines the policy profile, electoral strategy, and resource bases of small parties in order to determine what distinguishes the survivors from the failures. It finds that the key factor for third-party survival in Japan is party organization rooted within civil society, with the capacity to elect significant numbers to local assemblies. Third parties that fail primarily have little organization of their own and depend upon candidate *kōenkai*, a less efftective organizational structure under the new mixed electoral system.

In 1994, Japan adopted a new electoral system, a combination of single-member districts (SMDs) and proportional representation (PR). As predicted by Duverger's Law (Duverger 1954), the party system has moved toward a two-party system featuring competition between the Liberal Democratic Party (LDP) and the Democratic Party of Japan (DPJ).

Duverger's Law is based on two linked generalizations. First, at the district level, SMDs tend to produce bipolar competition between two candidates. This generalization is one of the most reliable in political science. Within three or four elections after adoption, most SMDs will feature bipolar competition (Reed 2001, 2007). You can make money betting on it.

Second, at the national level, through a process that Gary W. Cox (1997) calls "linkage," SMD candidates tend to associate with either the government or the opposition, leading toward bipolar competition at the national level. This second generalization is also reliable but tends to take longer to realize. Consolidation into two, and only two, parties seldom reaches completion. Parties in the national legislature may not merge and, as in the case of Italy, may actually proliferate, producing not a two-party system, but a bipolar two-coalition system (D'Alimonte 2001). Even in Britain, the classic case of a two-party system, a third party has persisted and regional parties have emerged. SMDs thus tend to reduce the choice set offered to voters to two, and only two, at both the district and national levels, but at varying speeds and to differing degrees.

As the choice set is steadily reduced to only two major parties, the voters, candidates, and smaller parties are all pressured to choose: Are you part of the government or of the opposition? At the theoretical equilibrium, every voter and candidate will have chosen one major party or the other and all small parties will have disappeared. As noted earlier, however, this theoretical equilibrium is never completely realized. Some "third parties" resist the pressure to choose and continue to run candidates under the unfavorable terms offered by single-member districts. Some of these parties fail as predicted but others survive. Those that survive represent theoretically important exceptions to Duverger's Law. In this chapter, I will analyze the resources and strategies of Japan's third parties since the introduction of the mixed-member electoral system, in an effort to explain why some third parties have failed while others have survived.

For the purpose of this analysis, I define *third party* as any party other than the LDP or DPJ that has won at least two seats in a general election. I exclude minor parties that have won no seats, or those such as the Liberal Alliance (Jiyū Rengō), New Party Nippon (Shintō Nippon), and Shintō Daichi, that serve as vehicles for a single candidate and win a maximum of one seat per election. I also exclude the New Frontier Party (NFP), because it was the second-largest party in the 1996 election and did not last long after that. Nine parties fit this definition, of which only three have persisted. The jury is still out on one, so we have three cases of third-party survival, five cases of third-party failure, and one case that has yet to either succeed or fail.

What distinguishes the survivals from the failures? I examine three hypotheses: policy profile, electoral strategy, and resource base. First, small parties must give voters some reason to refrain from voting strategically, that is, to vote for a small party instead of for one of the parties that will be running the government after the election. Parties that present a policy profile not represented by either major party should thus be better able to survive. Second, a new electoral system represents a challenge to all parties. Those parties that first find the optimal strategy for dealing with the new system should have a better chance of survival than those that fail to do so. Finally, small parties with more resources and/or resources more appropriate to the new electoral system should be better able to survive than those with fewer or less appropriate resources. I find no support for the first hypothesis, limited support for the second, but strong support for the third. The small parties that have survived under the new electoral system are those that possess a party organization rooted in civil society.

Third-Party Survival

The literature on third parties has focused primarily on their emergence and success in consolidated party systems (Hino 2012). One of the most consistent findings of these studies is that new parties arise when the established parties fail to respond to an issue of public concern (Rosenstone, Behr, and Lazarus 1996; Hirano 2008). Not only do small parties arise when major parties fail to respond to an issue, but major parties can combat the small-party challenge by responding to those issues (Meguid 2005). Though I focus here not on new-party emergence but on third-party survival, the questions are similar enough to warrant testing the hypothesis that the third parties that survive are those that represent a policy profile distinct from those of the two major parties.

The literature on electoral systems focuses on electoral strategy. To take a simple example, a party that hopes to win single-member districts would be wise to run only one candidate per district. The DPJ accomplished this goal better than the LDP, giving the DPJ an advantage over its rival. If there were an optimal strategy for third parties, those parties that approach that optimum first should have an advantage and be more likely to survive. I will examine the nomination strategies in both the SMD and PR tiers, asking whether the survivors followed different strategies from those followed by the failures.

Analyzing the two major parties, I found that the DPJ strategy was better than the LDP strategy, but the LDP continued to win more seats (Reed 2011b). The reason for this discrepancy was the LDP's advantage in resources, its initial endowment of organization, and quality candidates. I apply the same logic to third parties.

There are three ways in which a third party can win SMDs. First, a third party with a geographically concentrated vote can finish first in a few SMDs and win a seat against major-party competition. Examples include the Canadian regional parties based in Quebec and the British regional parties representing Scotland and Wales. However, no Japanese third party has the resource of a sufficiently concentrated vote to win a single SMD.

The second possibility is common in Japan but rare elsewhere: Run a candidate who has a strong enough organization to win no matter what the party label is. Under the previous SNTV electoral system featuring multimember districts (MMD), the LDP won elections by depending upon candidates to organize their own vote. These personal support organizations, known as *kōenkai*, were, to varying degrees, independent of the party (Krauss and Pekkanen 2011, chapter 2). LDP candidates could defect from the party, form a new party, and win by taking their *kōenkai* with them. Winners always had the option of returning to the LDP because the party coveted the candidate's *kōenkai* (Reed 2009). Many candidates had developed *kōenkai* under the old system that proved strong enough to win an SMD under the new system. Indeed, some candidates had enough support to win two SMDs. Kouno Youhei's *kōenkai* in the old Kanagawa 5th MMD proved strong enough to elect him in the new Kanagawa 15th SMD and to elect his son in the new Kanagawa 17th SMD. In other countries that enacted major electoral reforms in the 1990s, candidates did not possess this resource, and the resources available to parties and candidates explains many of the differences between countries that enacted similar reforms (Di Virgilio and Reed 2011).

Several third parties under the new electoral system were thus little more than collections of LDP defectors and their *kōenkai*. As I will demonstrate, such parties failed to survive under the new system. Eventually, strong candidates either join a major party or retire. In the latter case, a third party with no other resources has no way of recruiting a new candidate to replace the retiree.

A few of the old parties developed resources other than candidate *kōenkai*. The Socialists are based in the union movement. The Communist Party has a strong party organization featuring a variety of "front organizations" that form a communist subculture similar to, though smaller than, those found in Western Europe. Kōmei is based on a religious group, the Souka Gakkai, which has developed the best-organized subculture in Japan. No other group, including such LDP favorites as the medical professions, the construction industry, and agriculture, comes close to matching the vote-mobilizing capacity of this religious group (Klein and Reed, under review). These three parties also won significant numbers of seats in local assemblies, and local elections have proven effective in maintaining small parties in Europe (Kestel and Godmer 2004; Bowyer 2008, 612; Butler and King 1965, 100). An organizational base in civil society and local government has proven to be the key resource for winning PR seats under the new electoral system.

Japanese Third Parties

Only one third party survived intact from the old party system: the Japan Communist Party (JCP). The rump of the Japan Socialist Party (JSP) also survived, as the Social Democratic Party of Japan (SDP). These are the only two third parties to have run in each of the elections since 1996. One other party, Shintō Sakigake, was founded in 1993 and ran in 1996 but disbanded before the second election under the new system.

Three third parties formed from the remnants of the New Frontier Party (NFP), the failed first attempt to create a major party alternative to the LDP. Kōmei had been an important player under the old system before joining the NFP, and it re-emerged as an independent party after the failure of the NFP. The Liberal Party was a vehicle for Ozawa Ichiro after the failure of the NFP. The Liberals joined a coalition with the LDP but left before the 2000 election. The party then merged with the DPJ before the 2003 election. The Conservative Party split from the Liberals when Ozawa led the latter out of the coalition with the LDP. The Conservatives were designed as a vehicle to facilitate the re-entry of their candidates into the LDP and disappeared once that had been accomplished. The Independent Club (Mushozoku no Kai) served as an umbrella for several conservative candidates who could not get a major party nomination or who had not yet decided which party to join.

Finally, two new parties, both splinters from the LDP, fit the definition used here, the People's New Party (Kokumin Shintō, or PNP) and Your Party (Minna no Tō). The PNP is a single-issue party, focused almost exclusively on undoing Prime Minister Koizumi's postal reforms. Your Party split from the LDP in the 2009 election. It is a vehicle for its leader, Watanabe Yoshimi, but has also taken an aggressive stance on reform while criticizing both major parties.

I will first discuss the five parties that failed, and then the three parties that survived. I will then turn to the newest third party.

The Failures

The five parties that failed are Shintō Sakigake, the Conservative Party, the Independent Club, the People's New Party, and the Liberal Party.

Shintō Sakigake

Shintō Sakigake (New Party Harbinger, or hereafter Sakigake) was one of the three new parties that defeated the LDP in 1993. It was also the first group to leave the LDP to protest its failure to enact political reform, and a key member of the Hosokawa coalition government that ensued. However, along with the JSP, Sakigake refused to participate in the Kaishin parliamentary group that led to the formation of the NFP. It chose instead to participate in a coalition with the LDP, allowing the LDP to return to power. The party was successful in the 1993 election and in coalition politics thereafter, but as the 1996 election approached, most of its candidates chose to join the newly created DPJ. The party was disbanded before the 2000 election, and candidates who ran for Sakigake in 1996 either retired from politics soon thereafter or joined one of the two major parties.

Of the 35 candidates with Sakigake backgrounds who ran in an SMD in the 1996 election, 22 (63 percent) ran for the DPJ, while only 11 (31 percent) continued to run for Sakigake. Choosing the DPJ seems to have been a wise decision. A third of those running for the DPJ, including four of five incumbents, won their respective SMDs. Only 19 percent of those running for Sakigake and only two of eight incumbents were able to do the same. In 1996 Sakigake ran 17 candidates. The party nominated 13 in SMDs, the 11 who had run for the party in 1993 plus two from the Japan New Party. Eleven were nominated in PR, of whom nine were cross-listed in an SMD. The party won only two SMDs in 1996, just barely qualifying as a third party under our definition. It did not come close to winning a PR seat.

Sakigake was a party of reform, with a strong environmental policy profile. Once the party disbanded, a remnant continued as a green party, running in the PR tier of the upper house, though winning no seats. Yet the environment was not prominent on the political agenda at the time, and both major parties took relatively strong stands on the issue. Sakigake's policy stances were not sufficiently different from the major parties to draw a significant number of votes away from either of them.

Sakigake's strategy for dealing with the new electoral system can only be described as ad hoc. The party presented PR lists in only five of the 11 PR blocs. Nine of the party's SMD candidates were also nominated in the PR tier. Takemura, the party's founder, did not accept PR nominations, being assured of winning his SMD. The party nominated three candidates in SMDs in PR blocs where Sakigake did not present a PR list, and nominated two PR candidates who were not nominated in any SMD. Both were political secretaries and were presumably nominated as a stepping stone toward a political career. One candidate achieved that goal, winning a seat with an LDP nomination in the 2005 general election. It is hard to see any strategy behind this pattern of nominations.

Sakigake's only resource was a few strong candidates and their *kōenkai*, only two of whom, Takemura, the party's founder, and Sonoda Hiroyuki, proved strong enough to win their respective SMDs. Takemura ran again in 2000 as an independent before retiring, while Sonoda negotiated his way back into the LDP. All of the party's strong candidates thus chose one of the two major parties, either in 1996 or 2000, or retired from politics. Parties that depend upon candidates and their *kōenkai* tend to rapidly succumb to the pressures of Duverger's Law.

The Conservative Party

When Ozawa Ichiro led his Liberal Party out of the coalition with the LDP and Kōmei, many decided not to follow. The 26 who chose to stay in the coalition formed the Conservative Party. From the beginning, the party seemed designed to be little more than a halfway house back into the LDP. In traditional LDP fashion, those who won rejoined the LDP. Three of the losers also rejoined the LDP. The negotiations at the SMD level were often complex and involved the other options available to the local LDP party branch. A losing Conservative who happened to be the strongest candidate available was usually allowed to rejoin the party.

The Conservative Party nominated only three candidates in the PR tier in 2000 and none in 2003. In neither case did the party follow the standard practice of nominating their SMD candidates in the PR tier. Their three PR candidates were all politicians facing the end of their careers, each having lost several elections under several different banners. The Conservatives had no resources other than a group of candidates and their *kōenkai*, and like Sakigake, they soon failed.

The Independent Club

Five candidates who had run for the NFP in 1996 either could not or would not join either of the two major parties. Instead, they organized a temporary grouping under the label of the Independent Club (Mushozoku no Kai). The new electoral system is not kind to candidates without a party label, usually called independents but more accurately called unaffiliated candidates. Candidates without a party nomination often band together simply to avoid the handicaps associated with being unaffiliated. There have been several such parties, but the only one to win enough seats to qualify as a third party under the definition used here has been the Independent Club .

As a matter of convenience rather than policy, such parties are willing to nominate almost any otherwise unaffiliated candidate who wants to run. The Independent Club thus had no trouble picking up a few other candidates and even ran two candidates in the PR tier in 2000, but it won only the seats in which the candidates had strong enough *kōenkai* to win on their own. The relatively successful candidates soon joined one of the two major parties, three to the LDP and two to the DPJ. One, Nakata Hiroshi, moved on to become the mayor of Yokohama. Another, Watanabe Kōzō, joined the DPJ and became something of a TV personality, playing the role of the conscience of the party.

The People's New Party

In 2005 Prime Minister Koizumi forced his pet project, the privatization of the post office, through the lower house of the Diet against the fierce opposition of many within his own party. Blocked in the upper house by members of his own party, he dissolved the Diet and called an election. In that election he not only refused to nominate those who had voted against that bill, but he also ran "assassins" against them, candidates with LDP nominations who had signed a pledge to support the bill. Most of these postal rebels ran as independents hoping to return to the LDP if they won their SMDs. Those who won were indeed allowed to return. A few, however, refused to return and instead formed two new political parties, the People's New Party (PNP, Kokumin Shintō) and the New Party Japan (Shintō Nippon). Only the former won enough seats to qualify as a third party under the current definition, and it has not proven very successful in the electoral arena, winning only four seats in 2005 and three in 2009.

The PNP is a collection of candidates, several with strong *kōenkai*, plus the organization of retired postmasters. This organization was an important backer of the LDP before Koizumi's reforms but is now an implacable enemy. The PNP takes a clear position on postal reform, one different from either of the major parties but also of little concern to voters. Committed to overturning the Koizumi reform of the post office, the party joined the DPJ in a coalition after the 2009 election in order to achieve this goal. The PNP brought very few seats to the coalition but presumably facilitated the organizational support of the postmasters to DPJ candidates.

Technically, the PNP has yet to fail, but it is clearly in the process of doing so. A revision of postal privatization was passed, with LDP support, in April 2012, leaving the party with no clear unifying issue. Its leader, Kamei Shizuka, disagreed with the DPJ cabinet's tax policy and decided to leave the coalition in March 2012. The only member of the party to follow his lead, however, was his daughter. In the 2012 election, the party won only one seat and was forced to discuss the option of disbanding. As befits a *kōenkai*-based candidate, party members plan their individual political futures as independent political entrepreneurs.

The Liberal Party

When the NFP broke up, Ozawa formed the Liberal Party. He then joined the LDP in a coalition, but he left the coalition before the 2000 election. Only 24 of his party, a little less than half, followed him. The Liberals ran in only one general election, in 2000, merging into the DPJ before the next election, in 2003, and must thus be counted as a failure. It was absorbed into one of the major parties as predicted by Duverger's Law. Yet, the Liberals cannot be considered a typical failure.

In the 2000 election, the Liberals finished fourth in the total number of seats won, following the LDP, DPJ, and Kōmei. The party won a few more seats than the JCP and the SDP, two of the three parties that survived through the 2009 election. Finally, the party managed to win more PR (22, of whom 14 were double-listed in an SMD) than SMD (4) seats. The party's PR vote was over three times its SMD vote. What explains the relative success of the Liberals in 2000? The party did not have a distinctive policy profile, but it did have something of a distinctive image. As the party leader, Ozawa had an image as a reformer. He clearly made the best television advertisement of the 2000 campaign. Ozawa appears as a robot that repeatedly runs into walls and other barriers but breaks through and keeps on going. The ad neatly expresses both Ozawa's failures since leaving the LDP and his persistence. Nevertheless, it is hard to argue that the party was popular when those 22 candidates who ran for the NFP in 1996 and the Liberals in 2000 lost over 20,000 votes on average. By contrast, those NFP candidates who opted for the Conservatives lost fewer than 6,000 votes and those who ran for the DPJ gained almost 11,000 votes.

Nor did the Liberals have any particular organizational backing, though Ozawa is well connected with the LDP organizational base. Another hypothesis that springs to mind whenever Ozawa is involved is money, but the Liberal candidates were not particularly well funded in 2000. The Liberal candidates do seem to have committed more than their share of election law violations, but that cannot explain their relative success. The party did, however, pursue an aggressive nomination strategy not used by any other third party.

The Liberal Party fielded 61 candidates in the SMDs despite the string of failures that had preceded that election and even though the 2000 election was yet another failure for most of those candidates. Over half of the Liberal candidates in 2000 found their careers in the SMDs to be over after that election, though some continued their political careers elsewhere. The party also followed an aggressive PR nomination policy, running in every PR bloc and nominating 57 of its SMD candidates and 15 pure PR candidates, for a total of 76 candidates. One thing that Ozawa had learned from his mentor, Tanaka Kakuei, was how to find and recruit potential candidates.

Unlike the four other failures described previously, the Liberals were not simply a collection of candidates, each with a *kōenkai*. Except for Ozawa himself, the candidates with strong *kōenkai* chose to join the Conservatives in the hope of eventual re-entry into the LDP instead of following Ozawa into the Liberal Party. Only 30 of the Liberal candidates who ran in the SMDs in 2000 had any significant organization of their own in their districts, and most of those were members of a local assembly hoping to move up to the national level, not established members of the Diet. Twelve others were political secretaries. Ozawa is well known for having a large corps of secretaries to help his candidates win elections. These secretaries were presumably trying to make the transition from assistant to candidate.

The relative success of the Liberals in the 2000 election seems best explained by this aggressive nomination policy, but one may doubt whether this strategy could have been maintained over the long run. How would Ozawa have continued to attract candidates if he could not offer them a chance of victory and a chance at power? As we will see, the JCP can run candidates in most SMDs despite winning very few seats by utilizing its organizational base, but the Liberals had no such base. The Liberal strategy thus seemed better designed as preparation for joining the DPJ than for long-term survival. In 2000 the DPJ was having trouble finding SMD candidates (Scheiner 2006). The merger with the Liberals largely solved that problem in 2003.

Merger with the Liberals transformed the DPJ from irrelevance to near dominance in Ozawa's base, Iwate Prefecture (four SMDs). In the 1996 and 2000 elections, the DPJ was unable to find a candidate to run in the 2nd and 4th districts and finished fifth or sixth whenever it nominated candidates in the 1st and 3rd districts. Three of the four Liberal SMD winners in 2000 were from Iwate, and its losing candidate won a PR seat. Since the merger, the ex-Liberal DPJ candidates have won three of the four SMDs. Since Ozawa left the LDP in 1993, Iwate politics has been structured by the rivalry between Ozawa's *kōenkai* and the LDP, with Ozawa winning most of the battles. Whatever party Ozawa joined defeated the LDP in Iwate.

In addition, the DPJ got the four Liberal SMD incumbents (three, including Ozawa, from Iwate) and six other candidates in districts where the DPJ had not been able to run in 2000. In four other districts the DPJ candidate had retired or won some other election, leaving the nomination open. These vacancies were filled by ex-Liberal candidates. In four other districts the DPJ candidates lost the nominations to Liberal candidates who had not won their districts but who had finished well above the DPJ candidates. The ex-Liberal candidates thus represented a clear upgrade over the old DPJ candidates. Finally, six Liberals left their 2000 SMD to take an open nomination in another district. The DPJ thus gave up little or nothing and gained 24 candidates. The Liberals were able to negotiate a merger into the DPJ based on their performance in the 2000 election, instead of being simply absorbed by the larger party, but they did not bargain from a position of strength.

The merger certainly worked out well for Ozawa, who became one of the top three leaders of the DPJ, later winning the post of party leader. The DPJ continued to benefit from Ozawa's ability to find more and better candidates but it also suffered from Ozawa's legal problems and his unwillingness to hew the party line. Ozawa was instrumental in bringing about the DPJ victory over the LDP in 2009, but he continued to operate as an independent entrepreneur within the party, using the candidates he had recruited into the party as a weapon against the leadership. Removed from leadership positions by Prime Minister Kan and unable to support Prime Minister Noda's tax hike, Ozawa finally led over 40 DPJ incumbents out of the party to form the People's Life First Party (Kokumin Seikatsu Dai-ichi), which had been the title of the DPJ's 2009 manifesto. Ozawa's fifth party, renamed the Future of Japan Party (Nihon no Mirai no Tō), had 61 seats when the election began but only nine when the votes had been counted. Its future is in doubt.

The Survivors

The third parties that survived are the Social Democratic Party of Japan (SDP), the Japan Communist Party (JCP), Kōmei, and Your Party.

The Social Democratic Party of Japan (SDP)

The Social Democratic Party of Japan (SDP) is the successor to the Japan Socialist Party (JSP), the largest opposition party under the previous party system. In 1996 the party changed its name to the Social Democratic Party of Japan. Many JSP candidates opted to join the newly founded Democratic Party of Japan (DPJ), partly for ideological reasons but also as a practical means of winning in an SMD. A few joined other parties for various reasons, and those who refused to accept policy moderation formed the New Socialist Party (NSP). Of the 136 candidates with a JSP background that ran in the 1996 election, 67 (including four running as DPJ affiliated independents, or 49 percent) ran for the DPJ and only 28 (including five running as SDP-affiliated independents, or 20 percent) for the SDP. More ran for the leftist NSP (34, or 25 percent) than for the SDP.

Choosing to run for the NSP proved to be electorally disastrous. NSP candidates won an average of only 9,620 votes, and none won seats. Those nominated by the DPJ won an average of 43,286 votes, and one-third of them won seats. Those nominated by the SDP won an average of 41,156 votes, and over half won seats. In 1996 the choice between the DPJ and the SDP did not seem particularly relevant to a candidate's electoral fate. The DPJ had yet to establish itself as the primary alternative to the LDP. It was the smaller of two large parties challenging the LDP in that election. Yet by the 2003 general election, the DPJ had established itself as the only realistic alternative to the LDP, while the SDP was reduced to six seats, only one of which was won in an SMD.

If the Liberals were the most successful of the failures, the SDP is the least successful of the survivors. The JSP had been in steady decline since 1969, interrupted only in 1989 and 1990 by a short-lived revival. This decline is also evident in the number of Socialists represented in local assemblies. Especially since 2003, the SDP has also been losing union support, votes, and candidates to the DPJ.

In 2005, two SDP candidates decided to leave the SDP and run for the DPJ. In Kumamoto 3rd district, Yokomitsu Katsuhiko, who had won a PR seat in 2003, chose to run for the DPJ in 2005. He won a DPJ PR seat in 2005 and his SMD in 2009. It is unlikely that he could have done either by running for the SDP against a DPJ candidate and certainly would not have been a member of the party in power after the 2009 election. Similarly, in Kagoshima 3rd district, Hamada Ken'ichi left the SDP for the DPJ. He had run without competition from a DPJ candidate since 1996 but had won only once, a PR seat in 1996. Running for the DPJ, he increased his vote in 2003 but still lost. He was slated to run again in 2009 but retired for health reasons in 2006. Two defections are a serious matter for a party with only seven seats in the 2005 election, but the defection of Tsujimoto Kiyomi after the 2009 election was more damaging than the loss of a single candidate.

Tsujimoto was a rising star in the SDP and was considered a future party leader. She won her SMD, Osaka 10th, against both Kōmei and DPJ competition in the 2000 election. In the Diet she became famous for her aggressive questioning of Prime Minister Koizumi. A scandal forced her to resign from the Diet in 2002, and she did not run in 2003. However, she was back in 2005, losing to the LDP incumbent but finishing ahead of the DPJ and winning a PR seat for the SDP. In 2009 the DPJ withdrew from the district in her favor, and she defeated the LDP incumbent by a large margin. The SDP entered into a coalition with the victorious DPJ after that election. The DPJ initiated a new system in which ministers would choose their own political vice ministers and form a team of politicians to lead the ministry. Tsujimoto was sought by several ministries and played a significant role on the team that won her services. When the SDP left the coalition, Tsujimoto was upset to the point of shedding tears in front of the television cameras. In July of 2010 she left the SDP and in September joined the DPJ parliamentary group. She received an appointment on the crisis management team established after the 2011 earthquake. She was slated to run for the DPJ in the 2012 election.

As the least successful of the survivors, the SDP must have both its survival and its decline explained relative to the other two survivors. What makes the SDP different from the failures and what makes it different from the more successful third parties, the Communist and Kōmei? Let us turn first to nomination strategy.

The SDP's nomination strategy gives priority to the SMDs, much like the major parties but unlike the other survivors. In the five elections under the new electoral system, 88 percent of PR candidates also ran in SMDs. Most of these SMD candidates were listed as tied at first on the PR list, allowing their performance in the SMD to determine their electoral fate. Though a few pure PR candidates were given high list positions, most were given positions below the cross-listed candidates. These latter candidates appeared to be running not to win the current election but as a stepping stone in their political careers. One reason that the party gives priority to SMDs despite having little chance to win any of them is that the party believes that running a candidate in the SMD increases its PR vote. A consensus seems to be emerging in the literature that running a candidate in an SMD does not reliably increase a party's PR vote (Ferrara, Herron, and Nishikawa 2005; Maeda 2008), but perhaps we can forgive the SDP for simply learning from experience. In table 4.1 I have separated districts into those in which an SDP candidate exited (ran in the previous election but not in the current election), those in which an SDP candidate entered (ran in the current election but not in the previous one), and those in which there was no change between elections. In every election, the SDP did better in PR in the districts that it entered and did worse in the districts that it exited. One can thus see how the party came to the conclusion that running a candidate in the SMD increases the PR vote.

TABLE 4.1

Change in the SDP's PR Vote by Entry or Exit of an SMD Candidate

	All	2000	2003	2005	2009
SMD exit	−4,287 (n=92)	+1,702 (n=15)	−12,873 (n=21)	−1,206 (n=36)	−5,310 (n=20)
SMD same	−289 (n=942)	+5,446 (n=230)	−8,191 (n=192)	+2,619 (n=252)	−2,294 (n=267)
SMD entry	+5,392 (n=86	+12,232 (n=41)	−5.611 (n=20)	+6,071 (n=12)	+124 (n=13)

Source: Calculated from Steven R. Reed and Daniel M. Smith, The Japan SMD Data Set, March 20, 2011 version.

People also tend to learn from prominent cases, and Tsujimoto presents an extreme case of a candidate's effect on the party's PR vote. When Tsujimoto ran in Osaka 10th in 2000, the SDP PR vote almost tripled, from 12,805 to 33,899. When she did not run in 2003, the party's vote fell back to 9,747 votes, only to rise again to 27,198 votes when she again ran in 2005. In 2009, running on the SDP ticket but with the endorsement of the DPJ, the SDP lost 10,000 PR votes, a fact that may well have affected her decision to leave the party. The SDP acts as if it believes that running candidates in SMDs increases its PR vote despite the scientific evidence to the contrary. In this, the party is like basketball players who believe in the "hot hand" theory, that you should shoot more when you are "hot." Statistical analyses have repeatedly shown that players are no more likely to make a basket after making one but also that they are more likely to shoot again after making one (Matson 2012).

The SDP changed strategies after a drop in votes and seats in the 2003 election. It nominated many fewer candidates, but only six went unchallenged by the DPJ. There is little evidence that the DPJ stepped down in these six in order to gain SDP support. They appear instead to be districts in which the DPJ could not find a candidate of its own to run against a safe LDP incumbent. In 2009 the number of unchallenged SMDs rose to 16, seemingly evidence of electoral cooperation, but closer examination indicates that the situation was more complex and any agreements were negotiated at the prefectural and district levels, not the national level.

Akita is a case in point. In 2009 the DPJ endorsed the SDP candidate in the 2nd district and the two parties formed a joint campaign organization to elect the DPJ candidate in the 3rd district. A reading of the local newspapers, however, indicates that these two decisions were not part of an agreement between the two parties. First, the DPJ and SDP supported rival candidates in the 2009 gubernatorial election that immediately preceded the general election. The SDP and the Federation of Labor Unions chose to support the LDP candidate, running as an independent, while the DPJ supported the successor to the incumbent anti-LDP candidate, also running as an independent. The DPJ decision to endorse the SDP candidate in the 2nd district was influenced by the fact that the incumbent governor's son was running for the DPJ in the 1st district. The DPJ won the 1st district in 2005 but by a small margin and SDP support seemed a way to guarantee his victory. As it turned out, the DPJ landslide would have elected the DPJ candidate under any circumstances but SDP support must have seemed attractive when nominations were being made.

The SDP had a presence in the 2nd district dating from 1996, but the DPJ first fielded a candidate only in 2003. In 2009, the DPJ held "open auditions" (*kōbo*) but found no attractive candidates willing to run, though one of the rejected candidates ran under the banner of Your Party. The decision to endorse the SDP candidate was thus less a matter of cooperation than a lack of an appropriate candidate. To make matters worse, the DPJ's losing gubernatorial candidate decided to run as an independent, ignoring party discipline. In effect, the DPJ ran a candidate in the district in which the party had agreed to step down. According to exit polls, 72 percent of DPJ supporters voted for the rebel independent while only 13 percent voted for the DPJ-endorsed SDP candidate. The rebel soon returned to the DPJ fold, so the DPJ wound up winning a seat in a district that it had ceded to the SDP while the SDP gained nothing.

Another seemingly clear example of electoral cooperation is Hosaka Nobuto, a candidate with high priority for the SDP. In 2009 he left Tokyo 6th district to run in Tokyo 8th in order to get DPJ support. Tokyo 8th, however, featured the LDP candidate Ishihara Nobuteru, a rising star within the party and the governor's son. The DPJ thus ceded a hopeless SMD to the SDP. Similarly, the DPJ withdrew from Gunma 5th because the DPJ could not run a candidate in the district in which Yanba Dam was under construction. The DPJ manifesto had featured this dam as a waste of money that would not be built if the DPJ were to win the election. In Fukuoka 11th, Kumamoto 5th, and Miyazaki 3rd the DPJ candidate of 2005 had found a more favorable election by 2009. In Hyogo 8th, the DPJ nominated no candidate but supported Tanaka Yasuo of New Party Japan instead of the SDP candidate. In none of these cases did the DPJ give up anything of value. The SDP received only the districts where the DPJ had no alternative candidate.

In Osaka 10th the DPJ ceded the seat to Tsujimoto, one of the SDP's strongest candidates. The decision paid off when, as described previously, Tsujimoto left the SPD and moved toward joining the DPJ. Similarly, the DPJ ceded Ehime 2nd district to an SDP candidate who, after she lost, ran for the DPJ in the 2010 House of Councillors election. Electoral cooperation in these two cases produced a candidate gain for the DPJ and a candidate loss for the SDP. The only clear case of negotiated electoral cooperation occurred in Toyama. The DPJ was allotted the 1st district, the SDP the 2nd district, and the PNP the 3rd district. Even then, only the DPJ candidate won his SMD.

The DPJ is currently getting what it wants from the SDP without giving much in return. The SDP's union support is moving steadily toward the DPJ, and some of the SDP's best candidates are leaving to the DPJ. It is hard to see how the SDP will survive the new electoral system. The SDP joined the DPJ in coalition after the 2009 election but soon left. It can no longer expect DPJ cooperation in elections and seems doomed to further decline.

The SDP maintains the "historic mission" of its predecessor, the JSP, protecting the "peace constitution." It has not only proved to be willing to sacrifice electoral gain in order to pursue this mission, but it also has merged with the NSP in a reinforcement of that commitment. The electorally rational solution would seem to be to merge with the DPJ, but that would violate its historic mission. Neither does this mission serve as a policy stance that distinguishes the SDP from other parties because it is also represented by the Communists. The SDP won only two seats in the 2012 election. The most likely scenario for the SDP would thus seem to be a slow but inevitable decline, probably to the point of extinction.

The Communist Party

The Japan Communist Party (JCP) has never received much more than 10 percent of the vote, and its support in the polls never attained even that level. In most districts in most elections, one could find the Communist candidate simply by looking for the candidate with the fewest votes in the district. The party has never participated in a coalition at the national level. In 1993, when the LDP was defeated after 38 years of one-party rule, the new coalition government excluded only two parties: the LDP and the JCP.

At first, the JCP did well under the new electoral system, winning over 20 seats in each of the first two elections, all but two in the PR tier. After the two-party system consolidated in the 2003 election, however, the party was reduced to only nine seats, all won in the PR tier. However, the party was able to maintain those nine seats for three consecutive elections, making it the second most successful third party after Kōmei. The secret to the JCP's survival is a strong party organization that creates a significant presence in local assemblies. The party has been able to win between 4 and 5 percent of the seats in prefectural assemblies since 1971, with no sign of decline. This organizational structure allows the party to survive without winning any SMD seats.

The JCP has become a PR party despite running more candidates in SMDs than any other third party. The JCP nomination policy is unique in both tiers. For the first three elections under the new system, the party continued a tradition started in 1960 of running a candidate in every district for both houses of the Diet. The party fielded a candidate even when it had not the slightest chance of winning a seat. A few exceptions to this rule were made in 2005, and the policy was finally abandoned in 2009. Even so, the JCP nominated candidates in a little over half of the SMDs, more than any other third party.

In the PR tier, the party decides who will win seats and who will not. Although 65 percent of PR candidates are also nominated in an SMD, the party made no use of the tied ranking provision until 2009, and the exceptions made that year were lower on the list and unlikely to affect the outcome. Every candidate is ranked by the party, leaving nothing to be determined by the SMD results. Pure PR candidates may be ranked high or low, but the candidates who are awarded JCP seats are determined by the candidate's rank on the PR list and thus by the party leadership.

The JCP seems capable and willing to be a pure PR party, running in many SMDs but winning no SMD seats. The key is party organization and local government seats. The party is essentially continuing it traditional role in postwar politics, making only minor adjustments in the new electoral system. That role has been and continues to be the uncompromising and omnipresent receptacle for protest votes.

Kōmei

Kōmei is based on the Sōka Gakkai religious group. It had proven to be a successful third party under the old electoral system, but it understood the threat posed by SMDs. The party could not win a single SMD without the electoral cooperation of a major party. In 1996, a merger with the NFP seemed like it might solve Kōmei's SMD problem, but after the NFP disintegrated, the party needed another partner. In 2000, the numbers indicated that Kōmei and the LDP could solve each other's problems in the SMDs, and the parties moved toward coalition.

Electoral cooperation, however, proved difficult to implement, because the two parties had campaigned as enemies in the 1996 election. Kōmei ran in 18 SMDs, and in 11 of those districts the Kōmei candidate faced competition from an LDP candidate. Thereafter, the LDP was able to prevent its candidates from running only in those districts where Kōmei had won in 2000 (Reed and Shimizu 2009). In 2003 the LDP managed to talk one more candidate into accepting a guaranteed PR nomination in return for ceding Tokyo 12th district to Ota Akihiro, a future leader of Kōmei. The LDP made an extraordinary effort to convince LDP supporters to vote for Ota, and exit polls suggest that 56 percent of them followed their party's advice. Relatively successful cooperation was the norm thereafter until 2009. In that election, the LDP defeat brought down Kōmei as well. Kōmei won no SMDs and dropped two seats in the PR tier. That still left the party with 21 PR seats, more than any other third party and only four down from its peak in 2003. Kōmei needs major party cooperation in the SMDs but can survive in the PR tier on its own.

Kōmei nomination policy in the SMDs since 2000 has been simple: nominate candidates only in those districts negotiated with the LDP. PR nomination policy is also simple. Since 2000, with only one exception in 2003 and 2005 and no exceptions in 2009, SMD candidates were not cross-listed in PR. PR candidates did not run in SMDs because to do so would have violated agreements negotiated with the LDP. SMD candidates were expected to win their SMDs and, as in the JCP, the party decided which candidates would win PR seats. Kōmei thus won PR seats much like the JCP, but it won SMDs by cooperating with a major party, an option not available to the JCP.

Kōmei also pioneered an innovative strategic use of the mixed-member system: trading Kōmei votes to the LDP SMD candidate in return for LDP votes to Kōmei in PR. This strategy is carried out at many levels but is made manifest when an LDP candidate actively campaigns for supporters to "vote Kōmei in PR." Based on newspaper reports, I have located 14 cases of this type of campaigning. The simple analysis presented in table 4.2 lends preliminary support to the idea that the practice does indeed produce PR votes for Kōmei. In each election, Kōmei's PR vote went up more (or, in 2009, went down less) in those districts with an LDP candidate urging supporters to vote Kōmei in PR.

Until 2009, things went according to plan. Candidates who were slated to win either their SMD or a PR seat did so with impressive regularity. It is not yet clear what happened to LDP-Kōmei cooperation in 2009. Sporadic reports based on newspaper exit polls clearly indicate that LDP supporters voted for the DPJ in significant numbers and that LDP candidates lost a significant number of votes from Kōmei supporters in the SMDs. Large numbers of LDP supporters also seemed to have abandoned Kōmei candidates in the SMDs. The extreme case was Osaka 5th, where exit polls indicate that Taniguchi Takayoshi won 75 percent of LDP supporters in 2005 but only 14 percent in 2009. In other districts, LDP support dropped from about 70 percent to about half. Overall, Kōmei SMD candidates in 2009 lost an average of 16,000 votes in their respective SMDs.

Since the failure of electoral cooperation with the LDP in the 2009 election, Kōmei is rethinking its future. Kōmei might choose to become a pure

TABLE 4.2

The Effect of LDP SMD Candidates Urging Their Supporters to "Vote Kōmei in PR"

	Change in Kōmei PR Vote			
	All	2003	2005	2009
Vote Kōmei in PR	+1,897 (n=14)	+6,378 (n=4)	+2,692 (n=5)	−2,481 (n=5)
Other districts	+ 68 (n=820)	+3,224 (n=229)	+825 (n=295)	−3,138 (n=295)

Source: Calculated from Steven R. Reed and Daniel M. Smith, The Japan SMD Data Set, March 20, 2011 version.

PR party, something like the JCP. This would probably be the optimal strategy for maximizing influence over public policy. Even with no SMDs, Kōmei could win about 20 PR seats and continue to be a serious player in coalition politics. Abandoning the SMDs would free the party's hand in such negotiations, allowing it to ally with either the LDP or the DPJ. It would also allow the party to support SMD candidates from either party, giving it a voice in government no matter which major party is in power. The cost, of course, would be fewer total seats.

If, however, Kōmei decides to maximize seats, it must win SMDs and it needs the cooperation of one of the major parties to do so. The path toward cooperation with the DPJ, however, would be at least as rocky as the path toward cooperation with the LDP was leading up to the 2000 election, but the path toward cooperation with the LDP has already been paved. In addition, because of the complementarities in the distribution of their votes, cooperation with the LDP would produce more seats than would cooperation with the DPJ. The policy costs of maximizing seats would include locking itself into a coalition with the LDP even though Kōmei policy preferences are closer to those of the DPJ. A coalition with the LDP has already forced Kōmei to swallow several painful policy compromises.

Kōmei is indeed facing hard choices. This is the fate of third parties in a two-party system. Yet both of Kōmei's options are more attractive than those available to any other third party. If Kōmei chooses to become a pure PR party, it will win over twice as many seats as the other PR party, the JCP. If it chooses to ally itself with the LDP, it will be in a much stronger bargaining position vis-à-vis its major party partner than any other third party would be. The resource that gives Kōmei this flexibility is its solid organizational support.

Your Party

Your Party (Minna no Tō, literally "everyone's party") was founded before the 2009 election by Watanabe Yoshimi. It is, on the one hand, the vehicle of a single politician with a powerful kōenkai, much like Ozawa's Liberals in 2000. Watanabe dominates Tochigi Prefecture much like Ozawa dominates Iwate Prefecture, though to a lesser degree. Watanabe's kōenkai was sufficient to defeat both major parties in his own district, but the party was unable to field candidates in the four other SMDs in the prefecture. Neither was Watanabe's party able to match Ozawa's in the number of candidates fielded or the number of seats won, nominating only 14 SMD candidates and winning only five seats. Your Party has no organizational base either in civil society or in local assemblies. Based on the preceding analysis, Your Party would appear doomed to failure, but it has one resource that no other third party possesses: a distinctive policy profile.

Your Party successfully projected the image of being the party most committed to reform in the 2009 election. It took votes from both major parties wherever it nominated a candidate and where it presented a PR list, and it did so again in the 2010 House of Councillors election (Reed 2111b). It is the first Japanese third party that has been able to use a rallying cry common among third parties around the world: "A pox on both your houses!"

Watanabe also seemed to understand the need for a local base. In the 2010 unified local elections the party pursued an aggressive nomination strategy. The results of the local elections offer both hope and worries for the party's viability in the longer run. On the one hand, starting from scratch, Your Party won 41 prefectural assembly seats, the biggest gain of any party, putting it ahead of the SDP's 30 but far behind the JCP's 80 or Kōmei's 171. On the other hand, 68 percent of its seats were won in Tochigi and Kanagawa. The former is Watanabe's stronghold and the latter is home to the party's second in command, Secretary General Eda Kenji.

Though it is the most viable of the new parties, Your Party has yet to break out of dependence upon its leaders and their *kōenkai*. The 2012 election presented the party with another chance because neither of the major parties seemed capable of enacting reform. The party more than doubled its seats in the 2012 election (from eight to 18) but was overshadowed by the even newer Japan Restoration Party.

Conclusions

Duverger's Law is working in Japan. Some third parties survive as exceptions, but those exceptions depend upon the PR tier, a feature of mixed-member systems not anticipated by Duverger's Law. Most third parties have dutifully obeyed the "Law," either merging into one of the major parties or disappearing altogether. Only a few have survived through the first five elections.

I found no support for the hypothesis that a distinctive policy profile allows a third party to survive under the new electoral system. None of the survivors possesses this resource, so we can conclude that a distinctive policy profile is not a necessary condition for survival. However, Japan provides us with no cases of failures that possessed a distinctive policy profile, so we cannot conclude that policy has no effect on prospects for survival. The available data thus suggest that a distinctive policy profile, the ability to convincingly declare "a pox on both your houses," may be important for third-party emergence and original success but it is not necessary for long-term survival.

Neither do I find any optimal strategy for survival that applies to third parties across the board. Siavelis and Morgenstern argue that " . . . in certain cases party variables may trump legal/institutional ones confounding institutionalists and their theoretical propositions . . . " (2008, 19). Institutionalist predictions work well for the two major parties: They have converged on a single optimal strategy for both the SMD and PR tiers. The institutionalist prediction for third parties under SMDs, however, is extinction. In order to explain survival, we must look elsewhere and we find the answer right where Siavelis and Morgenstern predict, in party variables.

The key to survival proves to be organization. The third parties that failed had little organization of their own and depended primarily upon candidate *kōenkai*. *Kōenkai* were effective political organizations under MMD but are not the stuff from which to build a third party under the new mixed-member system. *Kōenkai* still function and can win elections for individual candidates, but *kōenkai* follow the candidate, and candidates tend to leave third parties. And, sooner or later, those candidates retire. The small parties that have survived had strong organizations and the capacity to elect significant numbers to local assemblies. Only the parties that had such organizations in 1996 had the capacity to survive thereafter in the PR tier. The initial endowment of small parties, resources developed under the old system, constrained that party's choice set in responding to the new system. This is a powerful form of path dependence; you cannot use resources that you do not possess (Di Virgilio and Reed 2011).

The choice set of a third party depends not only upon the electoral system but also on the resources available to that party. The best-known example is that a third party can win SMDs on its own power only if its vote is geographically concentrated. Third parties with geographically dispersed support do not have this option. Nor is it a simple matter to develop a geographically concentrated base in order to win SMDs. It is a matter of resources, not of strategy. Similarly, in Japan the option of depending upon the PR tier is not available to all third parties. Only those parties with a solid organizational base have a proven ability to win seats in the PR tier. Parties that depend solely on candidate *kōenkai* cannot choose the strategy of maximizing PR seats, because that maximum will be zero.

What is required to make a PR strategy viable is the support of an organization that can mobilize enough votes to affect electoral outcomes but does not depend upon winning elections for organizational survival. Such an organization is not constrained by the incentive structures created by the electoral system, because it need not maximize seats or votes. These organizations are therefore free to deviate from the logic of Duverger's Law. Many such organizations fit easily into the category of "civil society," but the key is the capacity to mobilize votes, combined with the capacity to survive without winning elections. Although a network of local assembly members may not fit easily with the concept of civil society, such networks do allow parties to survive without winning national elections. The local office rewards the activists who keep the party functioning between national elections, and those activists should also prove willing to run in a national election even when there is no hope of winning a seat.

References

Bowyer, Benjamin. 2008. "Local Context and Extreme Right Support in England: The British National Party in the 2002 and 2003 Local Elections." *Electoral Studies* 27:611–20.

Butler, David, and Anthony King. 1965. *The British General Election of 1964*. London: Macmillan.

Cox, Gary W. 1997. *Making Votes Count*. New York: Cambridge University Press.

D'Alimonte, Roberto. 2001. "Mixed Electoral Rules, Partisan Realignment, and Party System Change in Italy." In *Mixed Member Systems: The Best of Both Worlds?* edited by M. S. Shugart and M. P. Wattenberg. New York: Oxford University Press.

Di Virgilio, Aldo, and Steven R. Reed. 2011. "Nominating Candidates under New Rules in Italy and Japan: You Cannot Bargain with Resources You Do Not Have." In *A Natural Experiment on Electoral Law Reform: Evaluating the Long Run Consequences of 1990s Electoral Reform in Italy and Japan*, edited by Daniela Giannetti and Bernard Grofman. New York: Springer.

Duverger, Maurice. 1954. *Political Parties*. New York: Wiley.

Ferrara, Frederico, Erik S. Herron, and Misa Nishikawa. 2005. *Mixed Electoral Systems*. New York: Palgrave Macmillan.

Herron, Erik S., and Misa Nishikawa. 2001. "Contamination Effects and the Number of Parties in Mixed-Superposition Electoral Systems." *Electoral Studies* 20:63–86.

Hino, Airo. 2012. *New Challenger Parties in Western Europe*. London: Routledge.

Hirano, Shigeo. 2008. "Third Parties, Elections and Roll Call Votes in the Late Nineteenth-Century U.S. Congress." *Legislative Studies Quarterly* 33 (1): 131–60.

Kestel, Laurent, and Laurent Godmer. 2004. "Institutional Inclusion and Exclusion of Extreme Right Parties." In *Western Democracies and the New Extreme Right Challenge*, edited by Roger Eatwell and Cas Muddle. London: Routledge.

Klein, Axel, and Steven R. Reed. Under review. "Religious Groups in Japanese Electoral Politics." In *Komeito: Politics and Religion in Japan*, edited by George Ehrhardt, Axel Klein, and Steven R. Reed.

Krauss, Ellis, and Robert Pekkanen. 2011. *The Rise and Fall of Japan's LDP: Political Party Organizations as Historical Institutions.* Ithaca, NY: Cornell University Press.

Maeda, Ko. 2008. "Re-examining the Contamination Effect of Japan's Mixed-Member System Using the Treatment-Effects Model." *Electoral Studies* 27:723–31.

Matson, John. 2012. "The Not So Hot Hand." *Scientific American* (February): 14.

Meguid, Bonnie M. 2005. "Competition between Unequals: The Role of Mainstream Parties in Niche Party Success." *American Political Science Review* 99 (3):347–59.

Reed, Steven R. 2001. "Duverger's Law Is Working in Italy." *Comparative Political Studies* 34 (3): 312–27.

———. 2003. "並立制における小選挙区候補者の比例代表得票率への影響" [The effect of the PR tier on SMD nomination strategies in mixed-member systems] 『選挙研究』 [Electoral studies] 18: 5–11.

———. 2007. "Duverger's Law is Working in Japan" 『選挙研究』 [Electoral studies] 22: 96–106.

———. 2009. "Party Strategy or Candidate Strategy: How Does the LDP Run the Right Number of Candidates in Japan's Multi-Member Districts?" *Party Politics* 15: 295–314.

———. 2011a. "The Evolution of the LDP's Electoral Strategy: Towards a More Coherent Political Party." In *The Evolution of Japan's Party System: Politics and Policy in an Era of Institutional Change*, edited by Leonard Schoppa. Toronto: Toronto University Press.

———. 2011b. "Winning Elections in Japan's New Electoral Environment." In *Japanese Politics Today*, edited by Purnendra Jain and Takashi Inoguchi. New York: St. Martin's Press.

Reed, Steven R. and Kay Shimizu. 2009. "Avoiding a Two-Party System: The LDP versus Duverger's Law." In *Political Change in Japan: Electoral Behavior, Party Realignment, and the Koizumi Reforms*, edited by Steven R. Reed, Kenneth Mori McElwain, and Kay Shimizu. Stanford, CA: Shorenstein Asia-Pacific Research Center.

Rosenstone, Steven J., Roy L. Behr, and Edward H. Lazarus. 1996. *Third Parties in America: Citizen Response to Major Party Failure.* Princeton, NJ: Princeton University Press.

Scheiner, Ethan. 2006. *Democracy without Competition in Japan.* Cambridge: Cambridge University Press.

Siavelis, Peter M., and Scott Morgenstern. 2008. "Political Recruitment and Candidate Selection in Latin America: A Framework for Analysis." In *Pathways to Power: Political Recruitment and Candidate Selection in Latin America*, edited by Peter M. Siavelis and Scott Morgenstern. University Park: Pennsylvania State University Press.

5 Electoral Consequences of Municipal Mergers

Kay Shimizu

The dominance of Japan's Liberal Democratic Party (LDP) was long buttressed by the existence of a strong political support base in the rural areas, led by local politicians who worked on behalf of national LDP politicians seeking reelection. In recent years, municipal mergers have drastically weakened the LDP's support base by reducing the number of local politicians and redrawing electoral district boundaries. Surprisingly, the main opposition party, the Democratic Party of Japan (DPJ), could not take full advantage of the new institutional arrangements. Instead, local politicians have become more independent of both major parties. As a result, at a time of increasing numbers of floating voters, neither of Japan's two major parties has a reliable local base across the country. To succeed, both parties must pay attention to the changing needs of the increasingly independent—and very often still rural—localities.

In August 2009, in what was perhaps the most memorable lower-house election in the postwar period, Japan's ruling Liberal Democratic Party (LDP) suffered a catastrophic loss to the opposition party, the Democratic Party of Japan (DPJ). For the first time since it came to power in 1955, the LDP was no longer the ruling party, handing over the political reins to the ecstatic but inexperienced DPJ. What explains this 2009 electoral loss by the LDP and, more generally, Japan's changing political landscape?

I would like to thank the organizers and participants at the Stanford Conference on Japanese Politics for their very constructive comments. Thanks also go to Kozo Miyagawa and Mai Shintani for assistance with data and research. This chapter was originally published in the *Journal of East Asian Studies*, Vol. 12, #3. Copyright © 2012 by the East Asia Institute. Used with permission by Lynne Rienner Publishers, Inc.

Undoubtedly, the LDP suffered a large and significant electoral loss, losing 155 seats in single-member districts and 22 seats in the proportional representation seats, winning a total of only 119 seats. Meanwhile, the opposition party, the DPJ, won 195 new seats for a total of 308 seats, handing the LDP the worst electoral loss in its history. While there is no question as to the magnitude of this loss and its significance for both the LDP and Japanese politics more broadly, this event was also the culmination of a much longer and more gradual trend; the LDP had been losing votes in every election for nearly two decades. Since entering into coalition rule for the first time in 1993, the LDP's popularity had been in decline. Thus, rather than explaining the 2009 LDP defeat as a one-time event, this chapter extends the analysis back several elections in an attempt to better understand the LDP's gradual loss of its support base over time.

One significant but largely unnoticed institutional change that has altered politics dramatically over the past decade has been municipal mergers. Municipal mergers in Japan, like administrative redistricting in many democratic countries, were an institutional answer to structural changes in the political economy, including depopulation, aging, and fiscal decline. Smaller municipalities without a stable source of income had become particularly costly to maintain. Merging municipalities allowed a fiscally strapped LDP to cut expenditures by drastically reducing the number of local government units and consequently the administrative costs of maintaining local public servants, including politicians, bureaucrats, and public school teachers. Concurrently, municipal mergers also redrew the boundaries of many electoral districts. While the reduction in fiscal expenditures was most certainly the intended outcome for the LDP, the political effects of changes to electoral district boundaries were perhaps less well understood.

Typically, incumbents interested in reelection design redistricting to provide political advantages. While measures to minimize partisan advantage and incumbent protection may be in place, aside from equalizing the population of districts, the electoral expectation from redistricting is that the resulting map benefits incumbents the most.

This was not the case for Japan. By the latter half of the 1990s, Japan faced plummeting fiscal incomes (Noble 2010) and thus needed to cut expenditures, especially the local allocation tax distributed to stabilize fiscally weak localities. Therefore, in contrast to electoral redistricting resulting from a legally mandated requirement to adjust the number of elected representatives per population, redistricting in Japan occurred as a byproduct of municipal mergers primarily aimed at fiscal conservation. In particular, the effort focused on reducing the number of small, fiscally strapped municipalities in rural areas that were eating a disproportionately large share of government expenditures. The electoral consequences of Japan's municipal mergers were not a central part of the calculation when incumbent politicians put them in place. As a result, as I show in this chapter, the incumbent LDP incurred electoral losses from the very municipal mergers that it promoted.

However, the DPJ opposition has not directly benefited from these institutional changes. Rather, these mergers have contributed to the increasing independence of local politicians and Japan's still influential rural voters more generally, creating a conundrum for political parties seeking national leadership and policy change.

In the remaining sections, I examine the process of municipal mergers and their electoral consequences and what they have come to mean for politicians seeking election in Japan today. I use data from prefectural assembly elections in 2003 and 2007, the two elections straddling the years when the majority of municipal mergers took place, to examine the electoral effects of those mergers. By comparing the actual electoral results from 2007 with simulated results generated as if there had been no electoral boundary changes from municipal mergers, I show that municipal mergers hurt the LDP, especially in rural areas long considered to be LDP strongholds. In other words, the LDP's loss of its rural support base was in part an unintended consequence of its efforts to address structural problems through institutional change. But the effects of municipal mergers do not stop there. The loss of LDP support did not necessarily translate into DPJ gains; rather, local politicians have become more independent of both major parties. These findings help shed light on the weakening of patron-client ties between national and local politicians; on the decrease in district-level stability and the increase in volatility as described by McElwain in chapter 2; and on the need for candidates and parties in Japan to broaden their appeal in order to be electorally competitive.

After briefly explaining how structural changes in Japan's society and economy have led to the overall weakening of political support for the LDP, I consider alternative explanations for the LDP's loss of its rural support base and discuss how in many ways municipal mergers were the LDP's attempt to address its declining popularity. However, while municipal mergers directly tackled fiscal deficits and other macro-level problems, the overall effect alienated some of the LDP's strongest supporters. I demonstrate how this occurred by first looking at the process of municipal mergers and the various forms these mergers took. I then compare municipalities that merged with those that stayed intact to show how mergers broke apart the rural electoral districts previously under the LDP's control. Finally, I compare electoral results from after the mergers to results simulated under the assumption that no mergers took place to see how mergers affected support for the LDP. I conclude by examining the broader implications of these municipal mergers.

Structural Changes and the LDP's Gradual Decline

Both popular sentiment and structural factors contributed to the LDP's decline. In urban areas, more than a decade of economic stagnation convinced voters to abandon whatever loyalty they still had to the LDP and to vote for a new leadership. The DPJ took advantage of these trends and portrayed itself first and foremost as an alternative to the LDP. Thus, the DPJ's campaign slogan of "change" appealed to a wide spectrum of urban voters.

What was perhaps more shocking for the LDP was its loss of seats in the rural areas, traditionally considered its stronghold. Here, voters looked for alternatives to the LDP in large part as a consequence of demographic change and industrial maturity. In contrast to urban areas, rural Japan has seen an even faster pace of aging and depopulation as young people continue to move to urban areas in search of higher wages and greater conveniences. Japan's hinterlands are now well connected to urban centers via high-speed railways and multilane highways. These areas no longer desire pork in the form of transportation infrastructure or recreational facilities, long the specialty of LDP national politicians; rather, they seek greater social stability and better employment opportunities to care for their older residents and to retain younger workers.

The DPJ, while running on a strong urban support base, also sought to take advantage of weakening LDP support in Japan's rural areas. The DPJ's electoral mastermind Ichiro Ozawa appealed to rural voters by distributing direct income subsidies, playing the LDP's own game using a different weapon. However, fiscal austerity in the wake of the global economic recession limited the effectiveness of this new weapon. The electoral success of the LDP in the 2010 upper-house elections in rural single-member districts and the return of the LDP in the 2011 nationwide local government elections show that, although the LDP may have weakened, the DPJ has yet to catch on to the underlying currents of political change in Japan, especially in the rural areas.

Possible Explanations for the LDP's Loss

Several scholars have tried to explain the LDP's decline in recent years. Perhaps the most rigorously studied and often cited cause is the 1994 change in electoral rules from a multimember district system to a single-member district system. This electoral rules change has surely stimulated some changes in political behavior; for example, politicians must now rely more on their party line and leadership to carry them through electoral campaigns than on their individual ability to bring pork home from Tokyo, as argued in other chapters in this book (e.g., McElwain in chapter 2 and Scheiner in chapter 3), among others. Having operated successfully under the old system with contradictory incentives, the LDP struggled to adjust its decades-old party structure and leadership to one that was more effective under the new single-member district (SMD) system. However, institutions purported to support politicians in a multimember district (MMD) system seemingly survived the change to an SMD system, at least for the time being. For example, *kōenkai* (electoral support groups) continue to support individual candidates over parties despite predictions of their demise (Krauss and Pekkanen 2011), and candidate-centered politics remains fairly strong (Christensen 1998; McKean and Scheiner 2000; Otake 1998). The true effects of the rules change may still be observed in the future, as studies also show that *kōenkai* are not as influential as they once were (Krauss and Pekkanen 2011) and party-oriented politics appears to be taking root, though gradually (Reed, Scheiner, and Thies 2013). Electoral reform, however, was limited to the lower house and cannot adequately explain the LDP's decline in local elections.

Yet another often-cited explanation, especially in the media, is the backlash against Prime Minister Junichiro Koizumi's reforms. Although radical and popular during his time, many of the changes that Koizumi set in place have now been reversed. One now often hears that Koizumi's efforts toward structural change in Japan, both for his own party and for the broader economy, were too radical. Many have resisted the changes he set in motion, and some (including his immediate successor Prime Minister Shinzo Abe, who invited back those Diet members Koizumi had kicked out of the LDP) have reverted to the pre-Koizumi days. The current stall in the privatization of the postal system, Koizumi's pet project, is one such example.

Although legal stipulations for municipal mergers were established long before his time,[1] Koizumi himself also strongly supported municipal mergers in conjunction with broader plans for decentralization (see Hasunuma in chapter 10). Although decentralization remains incomplete, municipal mergers

---

1 Municipal mergers in Japan have a long history, beginning in the 1870s during the Meiji era, but the most recent round of mergers, the so-called Grand Mergers of the Heisei Era (*Heisei no dai gappei*), began in earnest in 1995 with the passing of the General Decentralization Law (*chihou bunken ikkatsu hou*). In the forty-first lower-house elections in 1996, all three major parties, including the LDP and the DPJ, included municipal mergers in their party manifestos.

reached their peak between 2003 and 2005 in the middle of Koizumi's popular leadership. The 3,232 municipalities in March 1999, the beginning of this wave of mergers, dwindled to 1,820 by April 2006, Koizumi's last year as prime minister. Municipal mergers helped reduce fiscal expenditures for many local governments, but this reduction came at the cost of lost jobs for many local bureaucrats and politicians. Local assembly members typically kept their positions during the months immediately after the mergers, often serving out their terms, but by the 2007 prefectural assembly elections many had lost their positions. But the unpopularity of the Koizumi reforms does not explain *why* they and the LDP became unpopular. What or where was the incongruence between Koizumi's plans, which were extremely popular during his term in office, and the reality on the ground once attempts were made to put these plans into action?

In contrast to explanations of the LDP's loss that focus on the effects of electoral rules change or the failure of Koizumi's structural reforms, the media and talking heads have focused on "the word on the street," or sentiments seemingly most often voiced by the general public: economic decline and *kakusa*, or growing economic inequalities. According to popular analysis, voters blame the long-ruling LDP for creating an increasingly competitive and thus unequal society, thereby shattering their long-held self-image of a small island country, largely middle class. Major national newspapers, including *Asahi Shinbun*, have carried several series of articles highlighting the growing economic divide between the high-income earners in Japan's urban centers and the lower-income earners or unemployed in the rural hinterlands (*Asahi Shimbun* 2009). Many of these articles and news stories are anecdotal, highlighting the hardships suffered by individuals. More systematic data on the number of citizens living in poverty remain spotty, as evidenced by the DPJ government's revelations on numerous senior citizens gone "missing," but Japan's undeniable economic decline continues to feed this viewpoint. This frustration with long-term economic decline and inequality also does not explain the renewed support for the LDP in the 2010 upper-house elections or the 2011 local elections. The LDP may be in decline, but the DPJ has not made solid gains. The LDP now holds the majority in the upper house, where rural areas remain disproportionately strongly represented, creating a major constraint for policy change. In order to explain the LDP's loss of its rural support base and the inability of the DPJ to grab and hold rural voters in its camp, I examine here what has happened to the LDP's local rural support base, especially in the small and fiscally poor towns and villages that relied on the LDP's ability to bring back pork from Tokyo.

Municipal Mergers

Municipal mergers (*shi cho son gappei,* or *Heisei no dai gappei* as this current round is called) addressed Japan's twin problems of demographic change and fiscal income decline by merging smaller towns and villages with larger towns and cities. Using prefectural assembly data from 2003 and 2007,[2] the election years straddling the period when most municipal mergers occurred, I show that the municipal mergers designed to address demographic change and fiscal income decline inadvertently led to a decline not only in the total number of local politicians, but more specifically, in the number of *LDP-aligned* local politicians. Table 5.1 shows the decline in the number of municipalities from 3,190 in April 2003 to 1,800 by October 2007, the dates closest to the 2003 and 2007 elections for which data are available.

The most recent round of municipal mergers in Japan began in 1995, when the LDP was coming out of its first experience with a partial loss of power, having been forced to join a coalition government for ten months in 1993–1994. At this time, almost two years after the banking crisis, demographic

TABLE 5.1

The Decline in the Number of Subprefectural-Level Units

Date	Cities (*shi*)	Towns (*cho/machi*)	Villages (*son/mura*)	Total
1947.08	210	1,784	8,511	10,505
1965.04	560	2,005	827	3,392
1995.04	663	1,994	577	3,234
1999.04[a]	671	1,990	568	3,229
2003.04[b]	677	1,961	552	3,190
2006.04	779	844	197	1,820
2007.10	782	823	195	1,800
2010.03	786	757	184	1,727
2012.04	767	748	184	1,699

Sources: 1947–2010: Ministry of Internal Affairs and Communications; 2012: Local Authorities Systems Development Center website.

Notes: [a] 1999.04–2010.03 marks the period of the *Heisei no dai gappei* (mergers of the Heisei era). [b] 2003.04–2007.04 marks the period straddled by the nationwide general local elections of 2003 and 2007.

2 In this analysis, data from Saitama, Tokyo, Ibaraki, and Okinawa prefectures are excluded. These four prefectures hold local elections in off years and are thus not on the same four-year cycle as the remaining 43 prefectures included in this analysis.

change and fiscal decline had become evident, especially in rural areas where the LDP had traditionally been strong. The LDP's weakened political position vis-à-vis the opposition parties made it necessary for the LDP to reduce total (national) fiscal expenditures while still protecting rural areas long supported by LDP-controlled fiscal redistributions from the central government.

On the one hand, municipal mergers were the LDP's response to popular calls for a reduction in fiscal spending, especially in sparsely populated rural areas that received disproportionately large sums of public funds on a per capita basis. By merging depopulated areas, the LDP would achieve large cuts in spending through a reduction in the number of public employees and facilities. However, the LDP knew that those areas hardest hit by depopulation and economic decline were also areas with traditionally strong LDP support. To compensate for the coming decline in fiscal redistributions from the center, the LDP provided fiscal cushions to municipalities planning to merge. The content of the Law for Exceptional Measures for Municipal Mergers (amended in 1995 and 1999) promoted mergers by providing generous fiscal incentives upfront. In addition, newly merged governments were guaranteed to have a smaller reduction in the local allocation tax (LAT), one of two types of fiscal transfers from the central to local governments slated to be cut in the overall decentralization process. By reducing overall fiscal expenditures but providing short-term protection for merging municipalities, the LDP launched a two-pronged preemptive attack on the problems just around the corner: depopulation and fiscal weakening in areas of traditional LDP support, and overall fiscal decline in the national coffers long used to compensate these very areas in exchange for their electoral support.

Where the LDP miscalculated was perhaps in the electoral effects of the process by which municipal mergers were decided. Unlike Greece, where fiscal deficits also motivated municipal mergers but where the central government used legal measures to systematically merge municipalities that fell under nationally specified rules, the Japanese government left the ultimate decision to merge up to the municipalities themselves. Specifically, residents could vote to initiate the establishment of a merger consultation commission, but the ultimate decision-making power lay in the hands of local assemblies. This lack of central-level, top-down control and regulation in the merger process, combined with citizen participation, added complexity and unpredictability to what was often already a highly contentious issue. Most importantly, it took power out of the hands of incumbent LDP national politicians and placed it in the hands of the localities.

Municipalities debated hotly over how the mergers would proceed. First, there was the question of whether or not a particular municipality would change its boundaries, either through a straightforward merger with another municipality or through a splitting of the original municipality into several smaller municipalities, each of which would decide to merge with another larger municipality or to form a new municipality among themselves, sometimes inviting smaller municipalities away from neighboring municipalities. Citizens had the power to initiate merger discussions, but the final decisions on the new municipal boundaries were left in the hands of municipal assemblies. At stake were not only the geographic boundaries that would define the new municipal divisions, but also the survival of public facilities, such as municipal offices and public schools, bureaucratic positions, and even the right to name the new municipality.

Disputes also often arose around the fiscal health of merging municipalities, especially in cases where depopulated and fiscally weak municipalities sought to merge with larger, wealthier municipalities that were unwilling to take on what they saw as additional mouths to feed. The smaller municipalities themselves were often uncertain of the fiscal benefits of forgoing their rights to generous central government subsidies in exchange for possible longer-term fiscal health.

Municipal Mergers: Political Effects

Most importantly for this study, however, was the effect of municipal mergers on electoral outcomes. By redrawing municipal boundaries, often in complex ways that crossed many former municipal boundaries, municipal mergers created new electoral districts with unforeseen electoral effects. While demographic and fiscal changes largely determined which municipalities merged, the process that determined how new municipal and electoral boundaries were drawn ultimately led to miscalculated LDP losses.

Yusaku Horiuchi and Jun Saito argue that the municipal mergers contributed to the loss of the LDP in two ways (Horiuchi and Saito 2009; Saito 2010). First, the total reduction in the number of local politicians hurt the LDP by cutting the number of publicly paid foot soldiers who had long been some of the most reliable vote-gathering forces for the LDP. This reduction included the elimination of mayors and the heads of each merged municipality. By reducing the total number of subprefectural units, and thus local politicians, the LDP, which relied more heavily on local politicians for votes than other parties, took a disproportionately heavy blow after the mergers. Second, Horiuchi and Saito argue that the reduction in the number of municipalities and foot soldiers and the increase in geographic size of each municipality also hurt the LDP by increasing the geographic area of representation for each local politician, thereby diminishing their ability to effectively monitor the voting behavior of their constituents. Thus, the remaining local politicians were not only reduced in number, but each politician was less effective in vote collection relative to the premerger times.

This chapter agrees with Saito (2010) in that municipal mergers have indeed cost the LDP many foot soldiers in rural localities where they once ruled strong, but their reduction alone does not explain the full extent of the effect of the mergers. Local politicians who are still loyal to the LDP acknowledge that LDP national politicians no longer have the allure for rural voters that they once had.[3] Nor do local politicians feel that their districts have become too large to oversee. Mergers have increased the size of *municipalities*, but the number of *electoral districts* in each prefecture has changed very little, if at all. This means that the geographic size of each electoral district remained fairly constant before and after the mergers. Local districts today are also much smaller than the pre-1994 lower-house districts.

Rather, the larger geographic size of merged municipalities has contributed to the growing independence of localities. Merged municipalities have larger total fiscal capacities and thus tend to be more fiscally independent than their premerger units. Larger municipalities can also take advantage of economies of scale, making a larger lump sum go further, even those larger municipalities that have adopted smaller fiscally strapped municipalities. Moreover, municipalities that exceed a certain size get additional benefits in the form of higher administrative status and larger fiscal distributions from Tokyo. This is especially true for the twenty ordinance-designated cities (*seireishitei toshi*), each of which exceeds 500,000 in population. In short, by directly addressing the problem of fiscal shortages, mergers have also made municipalities less indebted and less dependent on central-level politicians.

Data

To better understand the electoral effects of municipal mergers, this chapter uses subprefectural-level (*shi-ku-cho-son*, or municipal-level) data and prefectural assembly data to assess the extent to which the mergers influenced electoral outcomes for the LDP. The data come from the subprefectural-level demographic and industrial structure data in the Japanese population census (1995, 2000, and 2005), municipal boundary data from

3 Author interviews with local LDP-aligned politicians, 2008, 2009.

the Japanese Ministry of Internal Affairs and Communications, and the prefectural assembly election data from the 2003 and 2007 nationwide local elections (Japanese Ministry of Internal Affairs and Communications 1995, 2000, 2005).

This analysis uses prefectural assembly elections data from 2003 and 2007 for four reasons. First, between 1999 and 2010,[4] the total number of subprefectural units declined from 3,229 in 1999 to 1,727 in 2010, almost halving the number of subprefectural units.[5] However, the largest decline occurred between 2003 and 2006, when the total number of subprefectural units declined from 3,190 to 1,820, a decline of 43 percent (see table 5.1). Thus, this chapter analyzes the changes between the two elections straddling this period of rapid and numerous mergers. Second, prefectural assemblies allow the examination of local electoral conditions while still assessing national partisan effects. Local politicians often do not explicitly align themselves with national parties; the farther down the level of government one goes, the less significant party alignment becomes. Prefectural assembly members are one (or two if one counts prefectural governors as one level above prefectural assembly members) level below Diet representatives, and they too often receive endorsements from multiple parties—including local parties active only in their prefectures—and are not always singularly aligned with the LDP or its opposition parties. If one takes the analysis farther down to the subprefectural levels, deciphering party affiliation becomes even more difficult, thus adding too much uncertainty to the analysis.

Third, the use of prefectural assemblies as the unit of analysis allows comparison across time while keeping prefectural boundaries intact. Municipal mergers drastically changed the number of local politicians at the subprefectural level in a nonuniform manner. Where municipalities merged, some localities immediately decreased the total number of local politicians, while other localities kept the same number of local politicians for the time being. Still other localities came up with complicated ways of adjusting the total number of local politicians elected to their newly formed local assemblies. This variation in how localities adjusted the number of assembly members makes it difficult to compare changes over time in the strength of LDP allegiance at the subprefectural level. The prefectural boundaries,

4 Mergers conducted during this period are considered part of a nationwide movement called *Heisei no dai gappei*.

5 Japanese Ministry of Internal Affairs and Communications, www.soumu.go.jp/english/index.html.

however, have not been influenced by municipal mergers, thus making prefectural assemblies viable for cross-temporal analysis.

Finally, the very nature of municipal mergers means that many municipalities have moved from one electoral district to another or have been merged with other municipalities to create entirely new electoral districts at the subprefectural level. These newly formed municipalities did not exist previously, so we cannot conduct cross-temporal analyses at that level. In contrast, the number of prefectures has remained the same over this time. By conducting cross-temporal analysis to look at the changes in the number of LDP-aligned prefectural assembly members as municipalities merged, I investigate the electoral effects of municipal mergers and structural change more broadly. In the analysis, I also use electoral data from 2003 and 2007 to simulate an election in which municipal mergers do not occur in these years. If the electoral results from the simulated election show the LDP winning more seats than it actually won in 2007, such a finding would provide further evidence of the negative effects of municipal mergers on the LDP's electoral support.

Some limitations to the data exist. Municipal mergers have made it extremely challenging to create comparative data spanning multiple years. One of the main obstacles lies in matching electoral district data to municipal data. While local-level elections in some prefectures clearly indicate how municipal mergers have influenced electoral districts, other prefectures do not aggregate such data in one location. Also, municipal mergers occur in an ad hoc manner, with each locality deciding when to merge. This makes matching electoral data (including candidate background and vote count data) to municipal data challenging. The years between 2003 and 2005, when most of the municipal mergers occurred, are relatively well recorded, but the years preceding 2003 and the years after 2005 often have missing or erroneous data.

Ideally, this analysis would also be conducted for the DPJ at the local level to compare and contrast the effects of mergers on both the LDP and the DPJ. However, the DPJ is a much younger party and did not create a strong nationwide support base in the localities, especially rural areas. The number of DPJ-affiliated prefectural assembly members was much smaller—about one-third the number affiliated with the LDP. These limitations make a cross-national and cross-temporal analysis of the effects of mergers on the DPJ almost impossible. Given these constraints, I attempt to examine the effects of mergers primarily from the vantage point of the LDP, the traditionally dominant party in Japan's localities.

Analysis: Characteristics of Municipalities Involved in Mergers versus Those That Remained Intact

Municipal mergers purportedly targeted the smallest towns and villages in Japan that had a declining or aging population and that were facing fiscal decline. A descriptive analysis of all subprefectural localities that existed in 1995, the year of the national census closest to when municipal mergers began, gives a more accurate picture of local governments before the mergers.[6] For simplicity, I call these subprefectural units municipalities; the term refers to all subprefectural levels of government, including cities, wards, towns, and villages. Municipalities can be divided into two groups: those whose boundaries remained largely intact throughout the post-1995 period, and those that were involved in mergers or splits. Municipalities that absorbed a much smaller municipality also belong to the first group, the group that remained "largely" intact. Dividing all municipalities into these two groups places 1,602 municipalities in the intact group and 1,768 municipalities in the merged group.

As discussed earlier, the decision to merge or split municipalities occurred voluntarily within and among municipalities. Although demographic change and fiscal decline were often what drove these changes, there were no laws regulating or enforcing such changes based on nationally set criteria. As such, I first examine the data to see if the municipalities involved in the mergers indeed conformed to these assumptions and predictions about what type of municipalities actually ended up merging with other municipalities. Table 5.2 summarizes the findings.

Table 5.2 shows that municipalities that remained intact were, in fact, overwhelmingly larger in population (approximately six times as large) and much more densely inhabited or urban than their merged counterparts. In contrast, those municipalities that were merged were much smaller in population and much less densely inhabited. Figures 5.1 and 5.2 further illustrate the differences in population and demographic distribution. Figure 5.1 shows that the population sizes of merged municipalities were on average much smaller than those municipalities that remained intact. Figure 5.2 shows that merged municipalities had a greater percentage of older residents. These figures suggest that, although municipal mergers were voluntary and were left in the hands of local residents and assemblies, those that did merge often did so out of demographic and fiscal necessity.

6 There have been several rounds of municipal mergers in the past, including the previous round in the Showa period, from 1953 to 1961. Here, I refer to the most recent round of municipal mergers, beginning in the mid-1990s.

TABLE 5.2

Comparison between Intact Municipalities and Merged Municipalities

		Population	Population over 65 (percentage)	Densely inhabited districts (percentage)
Average	Intact	65,509	17.8	36.7
	Merged	11,666	22.6	6.1
Maximum	Intact	802,993	41.3	100.0
	Merged	453,300	47.4	100.0
Minimum	Intact	237.0	5.0	0.0
	Merged	198.0	7.5	0.0
Standard deviation	Intact	1.5	1.4	1.9
	Merged	1.6	1.0	6.6

Source: Author's own calculations with data from the Statistics Bureau of Japan.

I further investigate potential differences in these two groups of municipalities, especially for signs of greater support for the LDP. For example, the LDP has long had the strong support of Japan's farmers and those employed in the primary sector. Figure 5.3 shows that merged municipalities in fact had higher percentages of their working population employed in primary industries. In contrast, one sees from figure 5.4 (showing the construction industry, another industry with traditionally strong support for the LDP) that the difference between the two groups of municipalities in terms of the percentage of workers employed in construction is minimal. However, unlike the primary industry, the construction industry and its employees tend to be dispersed among both rural and urban areas. Thus, it appears safe to say that, by and large, municipal mergers occurred in areas where the LDP traditionally had a stronghold.

While demographic change and fiscal decline may be reasons for merging municipalities, these causes by no means determine *how* municipalities went about the actual process of merging. More specifically, while a sparsely populated and economically weak municipality A may need and want to merge with another larger and wealthier municipality B, municipality A has a number of different choices to make. First, A must decide whether to stay intact as one municipality, and then it must decide with which municipality it will merge. Both decisions depend in part on the municipality or municipalities with which A could merge. The larger,

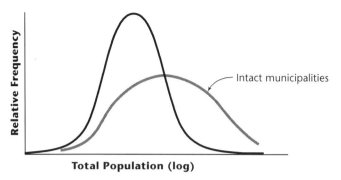

FIGURE 5.1 Distribution of the Population Size
Source: Author's own calculations with data from the Statistics Bureau of Japan.

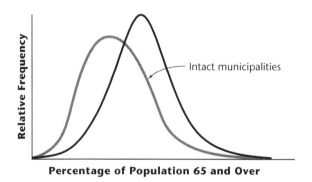

FIGURE 5.2 Distribution of the Percentage of the Population Over 65
Source: Author's own calculations with data from the Statistics Bureau of Japan.

wealthier municipality that will absorb all or part of municipality A must also come to agreement with municipality A on how the merger will take place. These negotiations, which ultimately determine the geographic—and thus demographic, economic, and political—characteristics of the newly formed municipality, all greatly impact the electoral outcome that results from the merger. Municipal mergers are not simply about the reduction in the number of subprefectural-level units and the number of local politicians, and thus the expected savings in fiscal expenditures. The exact geographic location in which the final boundaries are drawn is a result of much debate, and its implications are not always clear for all parties involved.

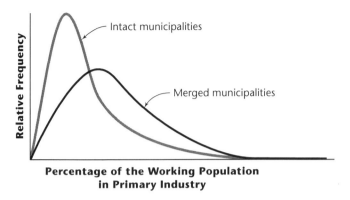

FIGURE 5.3 Percentage of the Working Population in Primary Industry
Source: Author's own calculations with data from the Statistics Bureau of Japan.

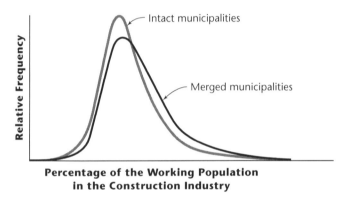

FIGURE 5.4 Percentage of the Working Population in the Construction Industry
Source: Author's own calculations with data from the Statistics Bureau of Japan.

Electoral Outcome as a Result of a Municipal Merger: The Case of Kagoshima Prefecture

To illustrate the electoral impact of municipal mergers, I begin by closely examining the case of one prefecture, Kagoshima. Of the 114 municipalities that existed in 1995, 71 municipalities underwent some kind of merger by the end of 2010, leaving Kagoshima with 43 municipalities (19 cities, 20 towns, and 4 villages). Thus, among Japan's 47 prefectures, Kagoshima is one of the more "merged" prefectures, with more than half of its municipalities merging during this time period.

In the 2003 local elections, Kagoshima's then 96 municipalities were divided into 24 electoral districts; in 2007, there were 49 municipalities divided into 23 electoral districts. However, in both elections, there was a total of 54 seats in the prefectural assembly up for election. The total number of prefectural assembly members did not change, despite the numerous municipal mergers and the slight reduction in the number of electoral districts.

Like most prefectures in Japan, Kagoshima's municipal mergers took on a variety of forms. Some municipalities split into multiple municipalities, and each of those smaller municipalities merged with a number of larger municipalities. Other municipalities remained intact and simply merged with a larger municipality. Still other municipalities merged with a number of similar-sized municipalities to make a new municipality. When new municipalities were created or when municipal mergers occurred, electoral districts were also redrawn. While most of the adjustments to electoral districts were simply made according to the new boundaries created by the municipal mergers, some new electoral districts were created as entirely new districts straddling multiple old electoral districts. Thus, while the number of electoral districts saw little change (24 to 23) between 2003 and 2007, in actuality, 11 electoral districts disappeared or were disbanded, and 10 new electoral districts were created between these two elections.

In 2003, 80 candidates, of which 43 were LDP-endorsed or -affiliated, ran for 54 assembly seats. Of them, 37 seats went to LDP-affiliated or -aligned candidates.[7] In terms of vote count, a total of 640,591 votes were cast in the electoral districts where at least one LDP candidate ran. Of those votes, 354,106 votes went to LDP candidates, giving them 55.3 percent of the total votes. A similar calculation was conducted for the 2007 elections. In this election, 82 total candidates ran for 54 seats; 45 LDP candidates ran, and they won 38 seats and 61.3 percent of the total votes. To better understand the electoral effects of these mergers, I simulated from these numbers a scenario in which municipal mergers and electoral redistricting did *not* take place. This simulation allows a comparison of the true 2007 electoral results with the simulated results that assumed no mergers or redistricting. The results are shown in table 5.3.

The actual election results from above were used to calculate the percentage change in the votes cast for the LDP and non-LDP candidates between

---

7 This analysis excludes electoral district 5, in which there were no LDP candidates. Thus, the votes from that district (15,056) are not counted in the total number of votes used to calculate the percentage of votes that went to LDP candidates. Nine other electoral districts had LDP candidates, but these candidates won seats without an actual election, because the number of candidates equaled the number of seats. In each of these nine districts, all the candidates were LDP candidates.

TABLE 5.3
Simulated Data for Kagoshima Prefecture,
Assuming 2003 Electoral Districts Remain Intact

	2003	2007	Simulation
LDP votes	354,106	398,044.2	392,901
Non-LDP votes	286,485	250,931.8	247,690
Total votes	640,591	648,976	640,591
LDP seats	37	38	40
Non-LDP seats	17	16	14
LDP vote (percentage)	55.3	61.3	
Non-LDP vote (percentage)	44.7	38.7	
Change in percentage of LDP votes		1.110	
Change in percentage of non-LDP votes		0.865	

Source: Author's own calculations.

2003 and 2007. The change in LDP votes was 1.110, and the change in non-LDP votes was 0.865. Assuming that these changes in the percentage of votes won would remain the same if municipal mergers had not occurred and electoral districts had remained exactly the same as they had been in 2003, I calculated the simulated electoral outcomes. By keeping the total number of votes the same as in the 2003 elections, but using the percentage of LDP votes won in 2007, I calculated that the LDP candidates would have won a total of 392,901 votes and the non-LDP candidates would have won 247,690 votes. I then applied these same assumptions and methods to each electoral district, assuming the same percentage change in the number of LDP and non-LDP votes to calculate how many seats could have gone to the LDP in 2007 had the municipal mergers not occurred and had the electoral districts remained unchanged. As a result, the simulation shows that the LDP could have won two more seats than what it actually won in 2007, for a total of 40 seats.

To further verify that municipal mergers cost the LDP these seats, I investigated where these additional two seats would have come from. One of these seats would have come from an electoral district with three seats in 2003 called Hioki-gun, which disbanded into four distinct electoral districts by 2007. Of the eight villages originally belonging to Hioki-gun, four villages together formed Hioki-shi, which became a new electoral district with two seats in 2007. The remaining four villages merged with other municipalities and dispersed into three other electoral districts. The other seat would have come from an electoral district with three seats in 2003, called Soh-o-gun. Soh-o-gun also originally had eight villages, which disbanded into three distinct electoral districts by 2007. Of the eight villages originally belonging to Soh-o-gun, three villages together formed Soh-o-shi, which became a new electoral district with just one seat in 2007. The remaining five villages merged with other municipalities and dispersed into two other electoral districts.

These findings suggest that municipal mergers are not simply about the reduction in the number of local politicians, especially at the subprefectural level in the towns and villages, but are just as much about electoral redistricting. Municipal mergers have forced the redrawing of electoral districts or the creation of new electoral districts, thereby breaking apart electoral districts that used to form the LDP's core rural support base. Once long-held districts are broken, it may take many years to rebuild candidate or party support. In assembly elections in Japan at the subnational level, rebuilding an electoral support base can be even more difficult because elections remain under the multimember system where multiple candidates are elected from the same electoral district. Under these conditions of intraparty competition, where the personal vote matters more than the organizational or party vote and electoral support tends to be more geographically concentrated, local politicians can easily lose a large portion of their core supporters through electoral redistricting. Another possible reason for the LDP's loss is that the newly formed municipalities are larger and more urban and are thus less likely to support the LDP.

Of course, the municipal mergers not only changed and often reduced the number of electoral districts themselves, but also greatly reduced the number of subprefectural-level local politicians, including not just the prefectural assembly members, but the mayors and assembly members of the cities, towns, and villages as well. According to Saito (2010), this reduction in the number of local politicians dealt an especially hard blow to the LDP Diet members who relied on these local politicians as crucial members of their vote-gathering organizations and *kōenkai*. While this simulation does not and cannot take into account the LDP vote loss in prefectural assembly elections resulting from the reduction in the number of local politicians, if there had been such an effect, the percentage of LDP votes would have been *negatively* impacted between 2003 and 2007. Since the simulation found an *increase* in the percentage of total LDP votes in Kagoshima between 2003 and 2007, taking this bias into account would further strengthen the argument. Had there not been a reduction in the number of local politicians from mergers, the LDP may have gained even more than the two seats that it could have gained (assuming no mergers) between 2003 and 2007.

Electoral Outcome as a Result of Municipal Mergers: National-Level Simulation

I next extend the analysis done in Kagoshima to the rest of Japan for 2003 and 2007. Four prefectures— Saitama, Ibaraki, Tokyo, and Okinawa— have been omitted from this analysis, because these prefectures hold elections on off years. The remaining 43 prefectures all hold local elections at the same time every four years. Table 5.4 illustrates the results of this analysis.

Between the years 2003 and 2007, each of the 43 prefectures had at least one merger. Together, these prefectures reduced the number of municipalities by 1,316 municipalities, from 2,926 municipalities down to 1,610 municipalities, roughly a 45 percent reduction. The most mergers occurred in Niigata (76 municipalities) and the fewest in Osaka (one municipality).

During the same period, 24 of the 43 prefectures reduced seats in their prefectural assemblies. In these prefectures, the average number of seats reduced per prefecture was 3.2 seats, or 5.9 percent. In the remaining prefectures, seat numbers either did not change or increased by just one seat, with one exception, in Shizuoka Prefecture, which increased its assembly by 11 seats. The number of municipal mergers is only very weakly correlated with the reductions in assembly size, with a correlation coefficient of just 0.30. Niigata Prefecture, which had the most mergers, reduced its assembly by nine seats, the largest reduction among the 43 prefectures, but other prefectures with many mergers, such as Hiroshima, Nagasaki, Gifu, and Okayama, did not make significantly large adjustments. This dissonance between municipal mergers and adjustments to assembly size occurs because the number of seats for prefectural assemblies is determined by each prefecture, independent of other prefectures. Until 2011, there was an upper limit on the size of the prefectural assembly, which was partially derived from population size. However, assemblies have long remained well under this legally set upper limit, making the limit largely irrelevant while signaling that mergers were not singularly responsible for declining assembly size. These two observations diminish the argument that mergers weakened the LDP by reducing the number of local politician foot soldiers, at least as it pertains to prefectural assemblies, and at least for the time being. While the general trend has been to decrease the number of assembly members, changes in the size of assemblies appear to be largely independent of the number of mergers in each prefecture.

Comparing the LDP's performance in prefectures that reduced the size of their assemblies with those that did not, the LDP lost more seats in the former. Between 2003 and 2007, the total number of LDP-aligned prefectural assembly members declined from 1,244 to 1,175, a reduction of 69 seats: it lost 87 seats in 18 of the 24 prefectures that reduced their assembly size, while gaining 24 seats in the remaining six prefectures. This suggests that the shrinking size of assemblies may be partly to blame for the weakening of LDP support in the localities. However, during this time, the number of DPJ-aligned prefectural assembly members increased from 196 to 352; the total number of LDP-aligned seats still far outweighs the number of DPJ-aligned seats at more than triple its numbers, supporting the view that the DPJ still has a long way to go in building a local support base. Seats won with no voting (where the number of candidates equaled the number of seats) also show similar trends: in 2003, the LDP won 361 seats versus just 17 for the DPJ, while in 2007 the LDP won 278 such seats versus 46 for the DPJ. The strong LDP showing in the most recent 2011 nationwide local elections also supports this view.

Next, I applied the same simulation conducted on Kagoshima Prefecture to the remaining prefectures in Japan. The results in table 5.4 show that had there been no mergers, the LDP could have won 30 more seats than what it actually won in 2007, for a total of 1,205 seats. Mergers potentially lost the LDP 93 seats in 21 prefectures and possibly gave it 63 seats in 19 prefectures. While the reduction in assembly size and mergers do not appear to be directly correlated, the shared trends toward reduction in both assembly size and the number of municipalities are a result of macro-level changes in population size, aging, and fiscal decline. Still, the reduction in LDP seats from mergers (93) appears greater, if only slightly, than the reduction in LDP seats from shrinking assembly size (87).

To summarize, the overall decline in LDP support among local rural voters is clear, but it has not necessarily translated into local support for the DPJ or any particular opposition party. Rather, local politicians and rural voters have become increasingly independent. As mentioned earlier, local party affiliations below the prefectural level are often quite nebulous and loose, with many local assembly members representing local parties that exist only within their own prefectures or receiving endorsements from multiple parties, a phenomenon called *ainori* (carpooling) or *ohru yotou* (all

TABLE 5.4

Simulated Results for Prefectural Assembly Elections, 2003 and 2007

Prefecture	LDP 2003	LDP 2007	LDP Change in seats	LDP 2007 simulated	Effect of merger on LDP	2003 Assembly Seats	2007 Assembly Seats	Change in assembly seats	Change in municipalities '03–'07
Hokkaido	47	46	-1	47	-1	110	107	-3	-32
Aomori	21	24	3	24	0	51	48	-3	-27
Iwate	14	13	-1	9	4	51	48	-3	-23
Miyagi	23	30	7	28	2	63	61	-2	-33
Akita	24	19	-5	26	-7	48	45	-3	-44
Yamagata	26	27	1	26	1	46	44	-2	-9
Fukushima	37	29	-8	30	-1	58	58	0	-30
Tochigi	25	32	7	27	5	54	50	-4	-18
Gunma	42	33	-9	40	-7	56	50	-6	-31
Chiba	59	50	-9	59	-9	97	95	-2	-24
Kanagawa	44	35	-9	42	-7	107	107	0	-4
Niigata	34	29	-5	34	-5	62	53	-9	-76
Toyama	31	28	-3	29	-1	45	40	-5	-20
Ishikawa	26	24	-2	23	1	46	47	1	-22
Fukui	15	24	9	18	6	40	40	0	-18
Yamanashi	22	15	-7	22	-7	42	38	-4	-30
Nagano	6	11	5	6	5	59	59	0	-39
Gifu	32	26	-6	32	-6	49	48	-1	-55
Shizuoka	30	35	5	25	10	63	74	11	-31
Aichi	55	57	2	55	2	106	104	-2	-25
Mie	18	18	0	18	0	51	51	0	-40

Prefecture	LDP 2003	LDP 2007	LDP Change in seats	LDP 2007 simulated	Effect of merger on LDP	2003 Assembly Seats	2007 Assembly Seats	Change in assembly seats	Change in municipalities '03–'07
Shiga	23	16	-7	20	-4	47	47	0	-24
Kyoto	25	24	-1	23	1	62	62	0	-18
Osaka	40	45	5	40	5	112	112	0	-1
Hyogo	26	25	-1	24	1	93	92	-1	-47
Nara	23	21	-2	23	-2	48	45	-3	-8
Wakayama	17	23	6	16	7	46	46	0	-20
Tottori	19	21	2	20	1	38	38	0	-20
Shimane	22	21	-1	24	-3	39	37	-2	-38
Okayama	35	27	-8	33	-6	56	55	-1	-51
Hiroshima	42	33	-9	42	-9	70	66	-4	-56
Yamaguchi	32	28	-4	33	-5	53	54	1	-34
Tokushima	16	20	4	19	1	42	41	-1	-26
Kagawa	26	29	3	27	2	45	45	0	-20
Ehime	31	29	-2	31	-2	50	47	-3	-49
Kochi	18	13	-5	16	-3	41	39	-2	-18
Fukuoka	45	40	-5	40	0	88	88	0	-30
Saga	30	27	-3	25	2	41	41	0	-26
Nagasaki	27	19	-8	24	-5	51	46	-5	-56
Kumamoto	29	24	-5	25	-1	55	49	-6	-42
Oita	23	21	-2	19	2	46	47	1	-40
Miyazaki	27	26	-1	21	5	45	45	0	-14
Kagoshima	37	38	1	40	-2	54	54	0	-47

Source: Author's own calculations.

parties in power). This trend has been growing since the early 1990s and has accelerated in recent years (Kawamura 2003). Additionally, in 2003, 661 assembly members with no party affiliation won seats (excluding assembly members specifically affiliated with parties labeled "no affiliation"); in 2007, 570 such assembly members won seats. In 2007, the number of local parties with no specific affiliation with a national party also increased.

Several factors, including mergers, have contributed to the growing independence of local politicians and to rural voters' detachment from national parties. First, mergers themselves have made many localities more independent by merging fiscally weak municipalities with larger cities and towns. Local politicians in these merged municipalities can now access larger budgets, have greater capacity to carry out larger projects, often have elevated their status within the subnational government hierarchy (obtaining city or ordinance-designated city status), and can lure bigger businesses and other sources of income. In short, their dependence on national politicians and their parties for pork and other benefits has diminished. Second, fiscal austerity has made less money available from the central government, making an affiliation with a national party and its politicians less valuable. The slow but gradual transition toward decentralization begun in the 1990s has also made local governments more independent of Tokyo and more eager to take matters into their own hands. One sign of this growing independence is the recent popularity and national prominence of prefectural governors and municipal mayors, such as former governor and now mayor Toru Hashimoto of Osaka and current mayor Takashi Kawamura of Nagoya. The increase in the number of local referenda and recalls also signals the growth of political activity in once-sleepy local governments. The aftermath of the March 11, 2011, triple disasters has also served to illustrate the growing independence of local governments that have taken matters into their own hands.

Third, not only are national politicians bringing home less pork, but they are now operating under electoral incentives that no longer necessarily match the needs of local politicians. Lower-house politicians, in particular, have turned to more programmatic and partisan policies that often do not promote the more particularistic interests of individual localities. Local politicians, in contrast, continue to campaign in small, multimember districts against copartisans. Their electoral districts are much smaller than the pre-1994 multimember districts for lower-house members. For example, Hokkaido had five multimember districts for lower-house members but still has 48 electoral districts for its prefectural assembly. Akita, a much smaller prefecture, had two multimember districts for lower-house members but still has 14 electoral districts for its prefectural assembly. Local politicians competing in these geographically limited environments cannot abandon particularistic interests for national campaign slogans. This growing divide in the electoral incentives of national and local politicians also contributes to the erosion of patron-client relationships between national and local politicians within each party and weakens partisan support among local voters.

Conclusion

Municipal mergers have weakened the LDP's local support base, particularly in the rural areas that were once its stronghold. This weakening stems in part from an institutional change—municipal mergers; whereas the number of municipalities are reduced, the number of local politicians and bureaucrats supporting the party are also reduced. But the scope of the analysis of municipal mergers and their electoral effects needs to be much broader. A closer look at municipal mergers reveals that the process of mergers, which was left primarily in the hands of localities, broke apart and remolded electoral districts along new and unexpected boundaries, costing the LDP valuable seats. Neither the LDP nor the opposition parties have been able to adjust to either of these changes—neither the reduction in the number of local foot soldiers nor the boundary changes of electoral districts—leaving all parties without a strong local support base. Furthermore, the mergers have created stronger, more independent localities whose politicians and voters are more removed from national parties. These findings shed light on why rural voters now behave much like swing voters, leaving party politics in Japan unstable.

The erosion of the LDP's rural support base and the greater independence of local politicians and rural voters have important implications for party politics at the national level. This is because rural voters still play a significant role in national elections, thanks to their still-significant overall numbers, the continued malapportionment that overweighs rural areas, and the growing and politically active senior rural population. Despite the macroforces of depopulation underlying the mergers, the actual number of people who vote in rural areas has not decreased and has the potential to continue to increase for the short-to-medium term. The key to understanding the future role of Japan's rural voters may lie in the details of their demographics. Rural voters as a whole (those who are eligible to vote) are decreasing in population due to continued urbanization and overall population decline, but the population of senior voters is increasing. In 1970, at the beginning of the LDP's rise, 7.1 percent of the population was over 65, the official definition of *senior*; in 1995, it was 14.5 percent, and in 2007, it was up to 21.5 percent. This increase is predicted to peak in about 2055 at around 43 percent of the population. The rate of growth of the senior population far exceeds the rate of decline of the total population in both rural and urban areas. In absolute numbers, in 2005, of Japan's 127.65 million population, 25.56 million were senior; in 2020, the total population will decrease to 124.11 million, but the senior population will increase to 34.56 million (Ministry of Internal Affairs and Communications). More than half of this increase in the senior population will reside in rural areas, and traditionally senior citizens have been more likely to vote than younger generations. Thus, rural voters, and particularly the senior voters, will remain crucial for winning national and local elections, but they have become more difficult for the parties to harness and keep.

In the longer term, however, as population decline and urbanization continue, constituents in merged rural areas may have a smaller political voice unless they find a way to organize around national-level issues. Today, such organization remains difficult due to blurred partisan cleavages and the remaining roots of particularistic politics. Channels of communication between localities and the center—and opportunities to cultivate the next generation of party candidates and leaders—have also been weakened. The LDP is an aging party desperately in need of younger blood, but many young candidates have lost their seats in recent rounds of elections. The same applies for the DPJ and other opposition parties that are also experiencing a shortage of viable candidates. The reduction in the number of local politicians also weakens the communications and ties between national politicians and their constituents. In the future, parties seeking electoral success in Japan must work to rebuild their support base under the new realities of this changing electoral landscape.

References

Asahi Shimbun. 2009. "Inequalities Among Local Governments in Tuition Assistance." *Asahi Shimbun*, October 26.

Christensen, Ray. 1998. "The Effects of Electoral Reforms on Campaign Practices in Japan." *Asian Survey* 38 (10): 986–1004.

Horiuchi, Yusaku, and Jun Saito. 2009. "Removing Boundaries to Lose Connections: Electoral Consequences of Local Government Reform in Japan." Paper presented at the Annual Meeting of the Midwest Political Science Association, Chicago, April 2–5.

Japanese Ministry of Internal Affairs and Communications, Statistics Bureau. 1995, 2000, 2005. "Population Census of Japan." Tokyo: Japanese Ministry of Internal Affairs and Communications.

Kawamura, Kazunori. 2003. "Chapter 10: Local Politics (*Chiho Seiji*)." In *Access Nippon (Akusesu Nippon)*, edited by Hiroshi Hirano and Masaru Kohno. Tokyo: Nihon Keizai Hyoronsha.

Krauss, Ellis S., and Robert Pekkanen. 2011. *The Rise and Fall of Japan's LDP: Political Party Organizations as Historical Institutions*. Ithaca, NY: Cornell University Press.

McKean, Margaret, and Ethan Scheiner. 2000. "Japan's New Electoral System: La plus ça change. . . ." *Electoral Studies* 19: 447–77.

Noble, Gregory W. 2010. "The Decline of Particularism in Japanese Politics." *Journal of East Asian Studies* 10 (2): 239–73.

Otake, Hideo. 1998. *How Electoral Reform Boomeranged*. Tokyo: Japan Center for International Exchange.

Reed, Steven R., Ethan Scheiner, and Michael F. Thies. 2012. "The End of LDP Dominance and the Rise of Party-Oriented Politics in Japan." *Journal of Japan Studies* 38 (2): 353–76.

Saito, Jun. 2010. "Local Government Reform and the Demise of the LDP." Paper presented at the Horiba International Conference, Tokyo, August 19–20.

The DPJ

6 Building a Party: Candidate Recruitment in the Democratic Party of Japan, 1996–2012

Daniel M. Smith, Robert J. Pekkanen, and Ellis S. Krauss

The Democratic Party of Japan (DPJ) was founded in 1996 from several disparate groups, including ex-members of the Japanese Socialist Party (JSP) and the Liberal Democratic Party (LDP). Mergers in 1998 and 2003 further expanded its ranks. As such, the DPJ began its history with incumbent candidates of diverse career and social backgrounds, and struggled to recruit quality new candidates in other districts, due in part to a lack of local politicians affiliated with the party. However, by the time it took control of government in 2009, the party had grown substantially. By 2012, 75 percent of DPJ candidates were new recruits of the party—some recruited with familiar methods from the founders' former parties, and others with a novel open recruitment process known as *kōbo*.

In this chapter, we examine how the party has evolved in character and grown over time, with an extensive data set of the recruitment methods, personal backgrounds, and electoral and legislative careers of DPJ candidates for the House of Representatives from 1996 to 2012, as well as personal interviews with DPJ politicians and party staff. We find that the DPJ has been largely successful at using innovations in candidate recruitment to diversify its candidate pool and gradually build the party from weak beginnings. However, we also find that members who started their careers in the LDP and other founding parties continue to dominate the DPJ leadership. We believe that understanding how the party has evolved up to this point may shed light on its potential paths to rebuilding itself following its devastating loss in 2012.

The 2012 election headline about the Democratic Party of Japan (DPJ) can only be its huge loss of seats and tumble from power, just three years after its historic victory over the long-ruling Liberal Democratic Party (LDP) in the 2009 election. But in the first five elections after its founding in 1996, the DPJ had made remarkable growth as a party—first, becoming the main opposition party to the LDP in 2000, and then ascending to the role of governing party in 2009. Especially in the run-up to the 2009 election, observers praised the DPJ for the new and diverse range of candidates that it presented to the electorate. Most celebrated of all were the "Ozawa girls": young, educated women who in many cases were nominated to run against targeted LDP incumbents (most of whom were older men), in a strategy that has been credited to then–secretary-general and later party-defector Ozawa Ichirō. Many of the new candidates nominated by the DPJ seemed to break the mold of the traditional image of politicians and offer an alternative type of politician to a public that was eager for change. The diversity of candidates was also in part the product of an innovative open recruitment process (*kōbo*), which the party first began to experiment with in 1999. The *kōbo* system of recruitment diverges from traditional methods of recruitment by increasing the opportunities for would-be candidates of nontraditional backgrounds to attract the attention of the party, and increasing the role of the central party organization in candidate selection. How did this novel approach to candidate selection help the DPJ grow and evolve in character over time?

Candidate selection is an important component of party organization and democratic representation (Ranney 1981; Gallagher and Marsh 1988; Norris 1997; Cross 2008; Hazan and Rahat 2010), because a party's candidates are a reflection of its priorities and values. The candidate selection process in large part determines who runs for office, which in turn constrains the options facing voters at election time. Who gets elected, and who gets appointed to important posts in the party and government after election, also shapes how voters are represented and which policies their government will pursue. Candidate selection, elections, and legislative organization are thus at the heart of party politics and democratic representation alike. In recognition of this fact, scholars are crafting a burgeoning literature on candidate selection, most notably on the efforts of U.S. congressional parties in the United States to recruit "quality" candidates, typically defined as candidates with prior local-level legislative experience (e.g., Jacobson 1983; Carson, Engstrom, and Roberts 2007). The comparative literature on candidate selection is also growing (e.g., Gallagher and Marsh 1988; Norris 1997; Rahat and Hazan 2001; Narud, Pedersen, and Valen 2002; Rahat 2007; Hazan and Rahat 2010).

However, there are still relatively few studies of candidate recruitment and selection in Japan. Moreover, almost all of these concern the erstwhile (and now once again) dominant party, the LDP, and focus particularly on how its factions and candidate support organizations (known as *kōenkai*) influence the process. Most of these studies address candidate selection only during the long period of LDP dominance, prior to Japan's major electoral reform in 1994 (e.g., Satō and Matsuzaki 1986; Shiratori 1988; Fukui 1997), though a few notable studies consider the changes in the recruitment processes and characteristics of LDP candidates since reform (Krauss and Pekkanen 2004; Asano 2006; Krauss and Pekkanen 2011; Di Virgilio and Reed 2011; Smith 2012; Tsutsumi 2012; Endo, Pekkanen, and Reed 2013; Smith 2013).

Yet, apart from more general articles on the impact of Japan's electoral reform on the success of party candidates (e.g., Maeda 2009; Reed, Scheiner, and Thies 2012), or the failure of the opposition parties to build strength in local assemblies (Scheiner 2006), there have been only a few scholarly works that examine the evolution of the DPJ's candidate recruitment and selection processes, or how they have shaped the DPJ into its current form. Most of these studies have been concerned primarily with the form and extent of factions among its representatives (e.g., Köllner 2004; Schmidt 2011) or the impact of women in the party on its gender-related policies (Gaunder 2012).

Only three studies to our knowledge directly investigate the types of candidates that the DPJ has offered the electorate. Looking at the party of origin of DPJ candidates, Miura, Lee, and Weiner (2005) find a trend toward more "conservative" candidates nominated over time from 1996 to 2003, despite the party's need to present a more progressive policy platform to draw a contrast with the LDP. However, the authors do not go beyond investigation of candidate type based on their previous party affiliations (or resemblance to the latter) to a distinct analysis of other characteristics, and their analysis precedes the important 2005, 2009, and 2012 elections. More recently, Weiner (2011, 79–92) presents a sophisticated study of the electoral strengths and weaknesses of the party over time, highlighting as a key area for research the ability or inability of the DPJ to produce quality candidates.[1] Weiner argues that the DPJ took a step backward in 2009 in its efforts to recruit quality candidates, and concludes that even its landslide victory was not enough to make it a genuine counterpart to the LDP in this respect (Weiner 2011, 83).

Lastly, Hamamoto (2011) chronicles changes over time in the background characteristics of first-time DPJ candidates and Diet members, tracking the

---

1 The quality of DPJ candidates is one of three main areas that Weiner (2011) explores. In addition, Weiner challenges the myth that the DPJ is excessively dependent upon volatile urban areas and that the DPJ is hostage to its ex-Socialist members.

three characteristics (of many included in the analysis) that were most prominent among each group in the five elections from 1996 to 2009. Hamamoto notes that local politicians have consistently been one of the largest groups of new recruits (and elected members), but their numbers amount to between only 20 and 30 percent of individuals.[2] Since 1996, the proportion of candidates and Diet members from a labor organization background has decreased rapidly, and the two other largest groups have fluctuated between Diet member secretaries, businessmen, and business employees. These are not exactly pathways to recruitment that produce high-quality alternatives to LDP incumbents or new LDP candidates with experience in local politics. In addition, 8 percent or less of new DPJ candidates have had backgrounds in the bureaucracy or mass media (TV news), backgrounds that both Scheiner (2006) and Weiner (2011) consider "quality" characteristics.

Indeed, the DPJ's failure to recruit quality candidates—especially those with previous electoral experience at the local level or in the House of Councillors—features prominently in the scholarly literature on the party (Scheiner 2006; Weiner 2011). It may not be going too far to say that the mainstream scholarly view is that the LDP dominated Japanese politics for so long, and the opposition (including the DPJ) perpetually lost, in large part because of the opposition's inability to recruit quality challengers (Scheiner 2006). Scholars fault the DPJ for this even in its landmark 2009 victory, which is viewed as the result of increased support for the DPJ as a party rather than an increase in the quality of its candidates (Weiner 2011; Reed, Scheiner, and Thies 2012). Similarly, the party's dramatic defeat in 2012 was the result of voter dissatisfaction with the DPJ government, rather than a decrease in the quality of its candidates (Reed, Scheiner, Smith, and Thies 2013; Smith 2013).

Reed, Scheiner, and Thies (2012) make a compelling argument that the nature of electoral choice in Japan is now dominated by party image and policies, such that the characteristics of individual candidates—particularly whether or not they can be considered "quality"—matters less. Nevertheless, given the DPJ's remarkable growth and ascension to power in 2009, we believe it is worthwhile to delve further into the party's organization, who its candidates and representatives are, and where they come from. This will be a crucial component in systematically determining the nature and identity of the party, how it has evolved to this point, and its possible future, particularly in the aftermath of its devastating loss to the LDP in the 2012 election.

---

2 For comparison, between 30 and 50 percent of new LDP candidates during the same period had local political experience.

In this chapter, we make our own contribution toward understanding the evolution of the DPJ, with an extensive analysis of all DPJ candidates in House of Representatives elections (including by-elections) from 1996 to 2012. Our data set includes information on candidates' personal backgrounds, electoral district characteristics, and party, parliamentary, and government positions,[3] as well as new data on the recruitment process used for each candidate. We also draw from interviews with DPJ politicians and party staff.[4] In the 17 years and six general elections since its founding, the DPJ grew and changed in character, and by 2012 approximately 75 percent of candidates who ran under the DPJ label had first entered national politics as new recruits of the party—some recruited with familiar methods from the founders' former parties, and others with the new *kōbo* recruitment process. Our first concern is what type of candidates the party has recruited, how these candidates differ from DPJ members who were first recruited by other parties, such as the Japan Socialist Party (JSP) and the LDP, and how they differ from other new DPJ candidates by the nature of the recruitment process used (i.e., *kōbo* or not). Second, we investigate how successful the party's candidates have been in winning votes and elections over time and advancing their careers in the party.

Our most important contribution in this chapter is to examine the actual candidate selection process used by the DPJ in recruiting new candidates, and how variations in this process are reflected in candidate characteristics and postselection electoral and legislative careers. Our study is the first to our knowledge to systematically investigate how the DPJ's recruitment processes have helped shape the party's organization.[5] For the DPJ, candidate recruitment is of special interest, because the party has experimented with *kōbo* since as early as 1999, a process that has furnished a sizable proportion of its nominated candidates since 2000 and that inspired the LDP to adopt a similar process in 2004 (Sekō 2006). How successful has the DPJ been at

3 Data up to 2009 come from Krauss and Pekkanen's Japan Legislative Organization Database (J-LOD), which is now part of a much larger comparative project, funded by the National Science Foundation (NSF, grants SES 0751662 and SES 0751436), involving 12 countries, some of which experienced electoral reform in the 1990s and some of which did not (co-PIs: Krauss, Pekkanen, and Matthew Søberg Shugart). The authors thank NSF, and Shugart for his support of this research and the larger project of which this is a part. The authors also thank Michael Thies for supplying the 2012 electoral data.

4 *Kōbo* and interview data collected by Smith. Smith thanks the Japan-U.S. Educational Commission (Fulbright Japan) for its financial support during field research in Tokyo from 2010 to 2011.

5 In a recent study in Japanese, Shoji (2012) describes the *kōbo* processes in the DPJ and LDP, and examines a few district case studies, but does not evaluate candidate characteristics or electoral and legislative careers.

growing as a party through this new approach to recruitment? We will look particularly at whether the introduction of *kōbo* has influenced the type of candidates that the DPJ has nominated, and whether the characteristics and postselection careers of *kōbo*-selected candidates vary significantly from candidates selected through more traditional means.

In the next section, we briefly review the background and origins of the party. We then describe the process through which new candidates have been recruited by the DPJ, focusing particularly on the use of *kōbo* in some district races. Using our data on DPJ candidates for the House of Representatives, we then explore whether new candidates recruited through the *kōbo* process differ systematically from those recruited by the DPJ's founding-party predecessors or new candidates recruited through more conventional means. Finally, we examine differences in postselection electoral and legislative careers and whether those careers have varied by the method and path to DPJ candidacy.

Background: The Origins and Development of the DPJ

In many ways, the DPJ is the product of the 1994 electoral reform from a single, nontransferable vote (SNTV) system—under which voters cast one vote in a multimember district (MMD) of magnitude M, and the top M vote-getters are elected by plurality rule—to a hybrid mixed-member majoritarian (MMM) system in which voters cast two votes: one vote to elect a candidate in one of 300 single-member districts (SMD), using plurality rule (first-past-the-post), and one vote for a (closed) party list in one of 11 regional proportional representation (PR) districts with a total of 180 (initially 200) seats. Under the SNTV system, the LDP's dominance of the party system and the ideological fragmentation of the Cold War meant that new opposition parties were relegated to narrow niche positions. The LDP's main opposition, the JSP, was for its part ideologically rigid and never earned more than a third of the seats in the Diet since the 1960s. With the Cold War over, and implementation of the new electoral system in 1996, the prospect for a larger, center-left opposition party to challenge the LDP became apparent.

Prior to the 1993 election, several new moderate parties, such as the Japan Renewal Party and New Party Sakigake, were formed from LDP members who bolted the party to support reform. After the LDP lost its majority in that election, myriad complicated discussions followed, especially among leaders from the more moderate former Socialists and these small parties. The aim of those involved was to establish a "third-force" liberal party positioned between the conservative LDP and the leftist JSP. These parties succeeded in passing electoral reform in 1994, but the coalition soon fell apart, and the

LDP came back to power via an LDP-JSP-Sakigake coalition government with JSP leader Murayama Tomiichi holding the premiership. That coalition collapsed in 1996, and former Sakigake members Hatoyama Yukio and Kan Naoto formed the DPJ. Hatoyama was a fourth-generation LDP politician before leaving the party in 1993 with several other defectors to form Sakigake with Kan, who was a former Socialist Democratic Federation member and health minister in the LDP-JSP-Sakigake coalition government of 1994–1996.[6]

In the first election under the new MMM system in October 1996, the DPJ ran 143 candidates in the SMDs and an additional 18 purely on the PR list.[7] However, the expected new wave of support did not materialize, because the party suffered from inconsistent policy stands by its leaders on the issue of coalition with the LDP, and the fact that it was financed almost entirely by Hatoyama's personal family fortune (Fukui and Fukai 1997, 26). The party won only 52 seats (17 SMD, 35 PR), the same number that it had held prior to the dissolution of the House of Representatives. Instead, the LDP again captured the plurality of the votes and seats, increasing its total from before the election. The biggest opposition winner was the moderate New Frontier Party (NFP), newly formed from many of the same parties that had been in the reform coalition of 1993–94 that passed electoral reform, and the creature of the omnipresent master party creator (and destroyer) Ozawa Ichirō. When the NFP broke up in 1998, as Ozawa disbanded the party and left to form his own Liberal Party, it left 11 opposition parties in its wake. Six of these merged with the DPJ in April, becoming the "New" DPJ (Uriu 1999, 118; Higashi 2008; Koellner 2011, 26–27). The DPJ was now composed of diverse "refugees" from prereform parties, including conservatives from the LDP, moderate conservatives and liberals from the Sakigake and the Socialist Democratic Federation, and moderate leftists from the former JSP, as well as individuals who were newly recruited after reform.

The addition of these new centrist and moderately conservative politicians from the NFP, however, changed the party's overall character. By the 2000 election, many more candidates had come from or resembled former LDP and Sakigake politicians (and those in between) than former Socialists or Democratic Socialists (Miura, Lee, and Weiner 2005, 57; Hamamoto 2011, 37). After Ozawa's Liberal Party also merged with the DPJ in 2003, the

6 For details on the complicated ins and outs of these discussions leading to the formation of the DPJ in 1996, see Tachibana (2008, in Japanese), Koellner (2011, 25–26), and Uekami and Tsutsumi (2011, 1–12, in Japanese).

7 All but two SMD candidates were dual-listed in the PR tier: 72-year-old former Socialist Mikami Ryōki in Miyagi 6th District, and 51-year-old university professor Sutō Nobuhiko in Kanagawa 7th District.

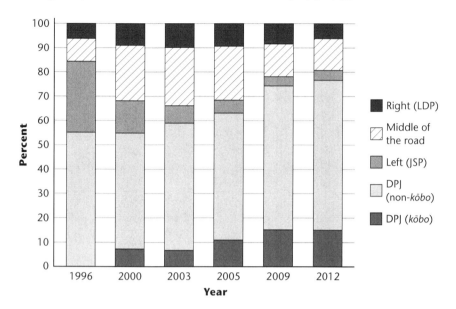

FIGURE 6.1 Party Group of Origin of All DPJ Candidates
in House of Representatives Elections, 1996–2012
Source: J-LOD.
Note: Includes by-election candidates, who are grouped with the previous general election.

imprint of the former Socialists on the party declined even further (Miura, Lee, and Weiner 2005, 56–63). Over time, the proportion of DPJ candidates who had no background in any party but the DPJ, or who came from "middle of the road" parties rather than the left (JSP) or the right (LDP and New Liberal Club) before reform, increased, while those of leftist origin declined greatly (figure 6.1 and appendix table B.1).[8]

8 Middle-of-the-road parties include the Sakigake and Sakigake-affiliated independents; the Democratic Socialist Party (DSP), which split off from the Socialists in 1959–60; Kōmeitō; the parties that split off from the LDP over the issue of reform, such as the Japan New Party, the New Frontier Party, and the Japan Renewal Party; and Ozawa's Liberals and affiliated independents. In other words, middle-of-the-road parties are all the parties that were more reformist and to the left of the LDP and New Liberal Club but also to the right of the JSP. No former Communists have joined the DPJ. Since we are primarily interested in recruitment differences, each candidate's party of origin is coded based on his or her party affiliation at the time of that candidate's first run for the House of Representatives—that is, the party that was first involved in recruiting/selecting the candidate to run for office. This coding differs from that of Weiner (2011), who groups candidates by both former party affiliation and similar background characteristics to a former party, and also differs from that of Hamamoto (2011), who uses the last party affiliation of the candidate prior to joining the DPJ.

Two major tendencies defined the DPJ between 1998 and 2005. The first was its increasing emergence as the major opposition party to the again-ruling LDP. As electoral theorists predicted, the MMM system—with over 60 percent of its seats allocated through the SMD tier—would produce a predominantly two-party system but with limited opportunities for smaller parties to continue to win seats through the PR tier. In 1996, LDP and DPJ candidates were the top two vote winners in just 35 of the 300 SMDs; but by 2003, the two parties finished in the top two positions in 234 SMDs, and in 2009, 254.[9]

The second tendency was the party's continuing struggle to form a cohesive party ideology from the diverse views of its representatives. It combined European-style social welfare liberalism with support for a market economy and maintaining a strong U.S.-Japan alliance with a more strictly constitutional (Article 9) view of foreign policy. Offering itself as an alternative to the LDP on both of these fronts, it often resorted to either avoidance of confronting internal party differences or settling for the lowest common denominator (Koellner 2011, 27). All of this was reinforced by the complicated party origins and policy loyalties of its members (Miura, Lee, and Weiner 2005). This ideological balancing act was complicated even further when Ozawa's Liberal Party merged with the DPJ. The merger brought with it new representatives but also a greater conservative coloration to the party, and the strategic brilliance, but inexorable threat to harmony, of Ozawa himself.

Nevertheless, the DPJ had come a long way, and managed to outpoll the LDP for the first time in the party vote in the PR tier in the 2003 election, helped by the party's introduction of a "manifesto" of policy promises. The popularity of the DPJ's manifesto forced the LDP to defensively introduce one as well (Tsutsumi and Uekami 2011). Indeed, as the LDP seemed to founder, there were hopes of the DPJ finally taking power. This was not to be, however, as the DPJ suffered a crushing defeat in the 2005 election, in large part because of Prime Minister Koizumi Junichirō's postal privatization agenda and the subsequent internal party theater with rebel LDP politicians, which stole the thunder of the DPJ's reform message.[10]

---

9 In the 2012 election, due to the split of the DPJ and subsequent rise of "third-force" parties, only 165 SMDs featured the LDP and DPJ in the top two positions.

10 The DPJ voted against Koizumi's postal privatization bills not because it differed substantially with the policy but because it differed on the "details." This stance both confused the voters' image of the DPJ as a reform party and enabled Koizumi to cast himself as the reformer against the rebels in his own party. If the DPJ had voted for his bills, they would have passed and the LDP's great 2005 election victory may not have occurred.

In the next four years, however, under the leadership primarily of Ozawa and Hatoyama, and using a strategy of attracting new and fresh-faced candidates and adopting policy positions that challenged the LDP where it was weak, the DPJ rebuilt itself—both in the urban districts that had been the party's base until 2005, and even in the LDP's formerly impregnable strongholds in rural Japan. In this feat, the DPJ was greatly aided by the LDP itself, which had adopted policies that were unpopular in rural Japan, including Koizumi's structural reforms and agricultural reforms that alienated small farmers. The LDP prime ministers who followed Koizumi (Abe Shinzō, Fukuda Yasuo, and Asō Tarō) also showed themselves incapable of producing popular and effective leadership, and each lost popularity quickly and resigned within a year of taking office (see Krauss and Pekkanen 2011, 226–59).

The DPJ's first victory came in 2007, when it captured control of the House of Councillors. Then, in the 2009 general election, the party sealed the deal with a huge majority win in the House of Representatives, capturing 308 seats and increasing its representation by 195 seats, the first true electoral defeat for the LDP since it was founded in 1955. Of the DPJ's new representatives (many of them female), over a hundred were known as "Ozawa's children," because they were personally groomed and trained (and often financed) for the election by Secretary General Ozawa. With so many of its representatives new to the Diet, and with other veterans never having been in government, many observers were uncertain about the preparedness of the DPJ to lead. The continued rivalry and policy divergence of its experienced leaders further dampened its three-year term in power.

Prime Minister Hatoyama struggled with public support and eventually resigned after a year in office, damaged especially by an ill-advised and ineptly managed attempt to renegotiate a difficult agreement with the United States on the relocation of the Futenma airbase from southern to northern Okinawa. His successor, Kan, made contradictory statements during the 2010 House of Councillors election campaign about raising the consumption tax to help contain Japan's massive public debt, and the party lost its majority in that chamber.[11] Kan held on as prime minister but then faced both a land purchase scandal involving Ozawa (who, no longer secretary general, was indicted but eventually acquitted of criminal charges), and the March 11, 2011, triple disaster of the 9.0 earthquake, the massive tsunami, and the Fukushima nuclear reactor meltdown. He finally stepped down in

11 The DPJ actually won the House of Councillors election in terms of votes cast, but the structure of that chamber's electoral system advantaged the LDP in single-member rural constituencies, which helped the LDP to win more seats.

September 2011 and was succeeded by the former finance minister, Noda Yoshihiko, who was viewed as a stable conciliator who could help mend internal party fracturing between pro-Ozawa and anti-Ozawa groups.

In July 2012, Ozawa and 48 of his supporters defected from the DPJ in opposition to the Noda government's plan to increase the consumption tax, and formed the People's Life First Party, which later merged with other parties to become the Tomorrow Party of Japan. This fracturing of the DPJ increased doubts about the party's future, and its support rate declined steadily in the months preceding the House of Representatives election in December 2012 (Pekkanen and Reed, 2013). In that historic election, the LDP won big (294 seats), and the DPJ was decimated, winning just 57 seats—a mere five more than it began with in 1996 (Reed, Scheiner, Smith, and Thies, 2013).

Despite the massive defeat it suffered in the 2012 election, there is no indication that the DPJ will disband, and having first become the chief opposition party and then unseating the long-dominant LDP in just 11 years, the party is still worthy of closer study. Further, it remains the only viable center-left opposition party in the current party system. In the next section, we turn our attention to an examination of the recruitment procedures through which it grew and evolved as a party.

The Recruitment of New Candidates

Perhaps the best way to gauge the evolution of the DPJ as a party is to examine the types of candidates that it has offered to the electorate. The candidate selection process is an important first step in determining who will become the elected representatives of the people. After all, most elections weed out at most a few hundred candidates, while candidate selection reduces the pool in many countries from tens or even hundreds of millions of eligible candidates to a few hundred or at most a few thousand who make it onto the ballot for national office. As mentioned previously, candidate recruitment has already been pointed out as a key failing of opposition parties in their long failure to break the dominance of the LDP (Scheiner 2006). From a party perspective, choosing the best candidates is a matter of vital interest.

There is a vast literature arguing that the electoral system powerfully influences the types of candidates who are selected by parties—particularly when it comes to the representation of women and minorities (e.g., Duverger 1955; Rule and Zimmerman 1994)—because parties respond to the incentives structured by how votes are translated into seats, and will want to maximize both. However, the candidate selection method itself can also matter greatly (Gallagher and Marsh 1988; Norris 1997; Hazan and Rahat 2010). For instance, Hazan and Rahat (2010) identify four dimensions— *candidacy* (who is eligible?), the *selectorate* (who decides?), *decentralization* (where is the decision made, centrally or locally?), and the *appointment or voting system* (is it majoritarian or proportional?)—that can theoretically alter the nature and outcome of the candidate recruitment process. The first dimension, candidacy, can vary from more inclusive (any citizen can seek the nomination) to more exclusive (parties restrict candidacy to party members or impose additional requirements) in nature. The second dimension, the selectorate, can also be more inclusive (e.g., open primaries) or more exclusive (e.g., party elite or a single leader decides the nomination).

These differences in the recruitment process can ultimately have an effect on the types of candidates who are selected. For example, we might expect a candidate chosen in a local district by local actors to exhibit more ties to that locality (such as birthplace in the district or prior experience in local politics) than a candidate chosen by the national party organization, because party leaders at the national level may have broader goals in mind (for example, better gender representation or the recruitment of policy experts) that trump local concerns.

In the case of the DPJ, we have a wonderful opportunity to study a party that used two different candidate selection methods at the same time over the course of a few elections. As we describe later, the DPJ used a more traditional, decentralized, and exclusive method for recruiting many candidates but also deliberately introduced an entirely new method of recruitment in some districts: the *kōbo* open recruitment system, whereby interested would-be candidates apply directly to the national party to be considered for a party nomination. The *kōbo* system increases the inclusiveness of the candidacy pool, while at the same time placing greater centralized control in the hands of national party actors for shaping the recruitment process. We take advantage of this innovation to see how *kōbo*-recruited candidates compare, in terms of background characteristics and electoral success, to candidates that the DPJ recruited using other methods, including incumbent candidates who joined the DPJ from other parties.

Recruitment patterns under the old SNTV system were remarkably stable. Candidate nomination decisions in the LDP played out predominantly at the local level, with the national headquarters approving only the local decisions and settling disputes. The choice of candidate was also heavily influenced by factions and the personal support networks (*kōenkai*) of exiting Diet members, who could pass the resources of their *kōenkai* organization to a successor. For this reason, LDP nominations often favored the son or other relative of the outgoing Diet member, or his personal secretary. LDP candidates were also frequently recruited from the national bureaucracy, or from local and prefectural assemblies (Shiratori 1988; Fukui 1997).

In the JSP, the party's main support organization, the General Council of Trade Unions of Japan (*Sōhyō*), had a strong influence in candidate recruitment, but prefectural party branches also played a role in proposing candidates to the national headquarters for approval. For these reasons, more than half of all candidates from the JSP were active in *Sōhyō* prior to running for office, while another third were members of local or prefectural assemblies (Shiratori 1988; Fukui 1997).

The middle-of-the-road parties used a variety of methods for recruiting new candidates. For example, the Democratic Socialist Party (DSP) was supported mostly by the Japanese Confederation of Labor (*Dōmei*), which represents unions that are less militant and more business-oriented than those represented in *Sōhyō*.[12] DSP candidates were also chosen locally and thus were drawn mostly from among local politicians and *Dōmei* trade union leaders. In contrast, new recruits to many of the other middle-of-the-road parties, most of which were splinters from the LDP, were chosen in various ways, often from among younger local politicians, former secretaries, bureaucrats, and graduates of the Matsushita Institute of Government and Management who were attracted by the new party leaders and the prospects for political change. Some parties, like the Japan New Party (JNP), also experimented with *kōbo*.

The DPJ initially had a weak organizational base in local prefectures and among local assembly members (Scheiner 2006; Uekami and Tsutsumi 2011, 12–13) and was able to field candidates in only 143 SMDs in 1996. So the party needed to seek innovative new ways to attract candidates to stand under its label in subsequent elections. One important way that it did so was through the *kōbo* system. In 1999, the DPJ began to employ *kōbo* to recruit candidates, with personnel from the national party headquarters heavily involved in determining the nomination. The adoption of *kōbo* was driven primarily by the need for more quality candidates capable of competing with the LDP in SMDs, as well as the desire to recruit more female candidates. In fact, a special round of *kōbo* held in August 1999 was limited to recruiting women. The *kōbo* system has only been used to supply SMD

12 The DSP is best considered as a middle-of-the-road party, and not in the leftist grouping. At the time of its creation, this was the consensus view of the party and the key to its positioning in the party system. Moreover, although the DSP drew much of its support from *Dōmei*, *Dōmei* was itself moderate rather than leftist, and the DSP was more moderate than the JSP on both domestic and foreign-policy issues.

candidates where the prefectural party organization (*kenren*) could not find a suitable candidate on its own, or where the national party headquarters did not approve the local choice.[13] The *kenren* are also primarily responsible for supplying the candidates for the party list (PR tier) who are not dual-listed in SMD contests. Some *kōbo* candidates have been nominated to run in prefectural districts for the House of Councillors as well.

The DPJ's *kōbo* process consists of four main steps. First, interested and eligible[14] applicants submit a two-page form to the party with their personal qualifications, preferred electoral districts, a recent photograph, and a short essay describing their feelings about a chosen theme, their interest in becoming a candidate for the DPJ, and how they would appeal to voters.[15] Second, after an initial screening of applications by party staff in the Election Strategy Committee at party headquarters, successful applicants are further screened in an interview with DPJ Diet members and are ranked.[16] Third, candidates who pass this stage are registered as "approved" (*gōkaku*) candidates and enter into negotiations with party leaders about where to run, given their personal preferences, strengths (such as local ties), and the districts where the DPJ is in need of a candidate.[17] Since 1999, the party has screened over 5,000 individuals through the *kōbo* process, and over 600 have been approved as candidates (table 6.1).

In the final step to nomination, approved candidates must meet with local party organization officials in the district for final approval to make sure that the candidates chosen by the national headquarters "match" well with the local organization and members. This step ensures that local party supporters will cooperate and mobilize for the nominated candidate. Sometimes the local organization is presented with several candidates from which to choose a suitable match. If the proposed candidate is not acceptable to the local organization (which sometimes happens), the national headquarters proposes

13 Interview by Smith with a senior staff member of the DPJ, June 15, 2011, Tokyo. In a few cases, party leaders such as Ozawa Ichirō recruited celebrity candidates or academics and other policy experts without using the *kōbo* or *kenren* systems, but these cases were not identifiable, so they are coded here simply as non-*kōbo*.

14 Candidates are required to have held Japanese citizenship for at least 25 years.

15 In the latest post-2009 round of *kōbo* (2009), primarily for the 2010 House of Councillors election, the theme was "Politics after the change in government: what I want to tackle."

16 In the past, interview committees consisted of approximately three Diet members and three party staff members.

17 One exception is the February 2005 *kōbo* before the 2005 House of Representatives election, when applications were collected only for the specific districts where a candidate was still needed after the previous *kōbo* in 2004.

TABLE 6.1

Number of Applicants and Approved Candidates
in DPJ Kōbo Contests, 1999–2009

Kōbo Round	Number of Applicants	Number Approved	Percent Approved
March 1999	564	94	16.7%
August 1999 (women only)	56	37	66.1%
April 2002	416	46	11.1%
February 2004	713	81	11.4%
February 2005*	231	—	—
May 2006	1314	164	12.5%
November 2009	1982	208	10.5%

Source: DPJ Election Strategy Committee.

Notes: *The number of approved candidates in 2005 is not available since that round of *kōbo* was for specific SMD races. Similarly, the number of applicants and approved candidates is not available for the three district-level *kōbo* contests held in 2012.

an additional candidate (or candidates) from the list of approved candidates until a consensus is reached.

Since its adoption, a total of 79 candidates recruited through the *kōbo* system have been nominated in SMD races in the House of Representatives.[18] The proportion of new candidates chosen through the *kōbo* system increased over time and by 2009 constituted two out of every five new SMD candidates. In total, since the party was reformed in 1998 as the "New DPJ," nearly a fifth of its new candidates have been selected through *kōbo*. However, given the large number of DPJ incumbents after 2009 and the hasty recruitment of new candidates following party defections, *kōbo*-recruited candidates only ran in a handful of districts in the 2012 election (Smith 2013). Table 6.2 shows summary statistics on the number and percentages of new *kōbo* versus non-*kōbo* candidates recruited by the DPJ to run in SMD elections from 1996 to 2012 and the electoral results for each type. It is interesting to note that *kōbo* candidates have a higher overall success rate than non-*kōbo* candidates, a topic we will revisit later in this chapter when we analyze postselection careers. There is an informal party rule that any candidate who loses his or her SMD race three times consecutively (without being elected through the PR list) is not renominated. However, most candidates are replaced or opt not to

18 Recruitment data obtained from the DPJ's Election Strategy Committee at party headquarters in Tokyo in June 2011. Data include by-election candidates, who are grouped with the previous general election. Details are listed in appendix table C.1.

TABLE 6.2

Recruitment Method and Electoral Success of New DPJ Candidates in SMDs, 1996–2012

	Method	1996	2000	2003	2005	2009	2012	Total
Number of candidates	*Kōbo*	—	18	9	20	29	3	79
	Non-*kōbo*	81	89	71	35	43	41	360
Percentage of candidates	*Kōbo*	—	17%	11%	36%	40%	7%	18%
	Non-*kōbo*	100%	83%	89%	64%	60%	93%	82%
Number elected in SMD (on PR list)	*Kōbo*	—	3 (1)	1 (3)	0 (1)	22 (6)	0 (0)	26 (11)
	Non-*kōbo*	5 (7)	14 (5)	12 (15)	3 (6)	19 (20)	1 (0)	54 (53)
Percentage elected (SMD or PR list)	*Kōbo*	—	22%	44%	5%	97%	0%	47%
	Non-*kōbo*	15%	21%	35%	22%	91%	2%	30%

Source: J-LOD and DPJ Election Strategy Committee for 1996–2009; 2012 *kōbo* data based on newspaper references.

Notes: By-election candidates are grouped with the previous general election. SMD losers who were elected via the PR list during the term due to a resignation or death are counted as list winners.

run again before that time. Weiner (2011) emphasizes that not running repeat losers as candidates is one of the ways the DPJ has improved as a party. The party has also instituted an age limit of 65 years for new candidates.

Given the more inclusive pool for candidates and the more centralized selectorate in the *kōbo* system, do the background characteristics of new candidates recruited by *kōbo* differ in any substantial ways from new candidates recruited by more traditional means? Do both types of new DPJ candidates differ from those of the DPJ's founder parties? We have two general hypotheses:

- Candidates recruited by the DPJ will come from backgrounds different from those of candidates who were originally recruited by other parties, especially the JSP, and who later joined the DPJ. Specifically, we expect the following in relation to its founder parties:
  - Fewer new DPJ candidates will come from the more traditional sources of candidates such as labor unions, agricultural associations, and the bureaucracy.
  - Newly recruited DPJ candidates will have proportionally fewer quality candidates.
- New DPJ candidates selected through *kōbo* will also differ from new candidates selected through more traditional means, especially in terms of quality. Specifically, given the original purpose of introducing *kōbo* (to recruit more women and to find candidates where

quality local politicians could not be found) and the national scope of the process, we expect the following:

- *Kōbo* candidates will include more women.
- *Kōbo* candidates will include fewer quality candidates.
- *Kōbo* candidates will include fewer individuals with a local background—namely, having been born in the prefecture where they are running.

As for what attributes define a "quality" candidate, there is a disagreement in the literature. For example, the narrow definition most often used in the U.S. politics literature (e.g., Jacobson 1990) is that a quality candidate is merely one with prior experience in local elective office. However, Scheiner (2006, 136–7) uses a wider definition that also includes "legacy candidates" from political dynasties, former national bureaucrats, and former TV news reporters. Weiner (2011) uses this definition as well but includes incumbents in his analysis, who would also count as quality.

There are advantages and disadvantages to both of these definitions. The broader definition assumes somewhat validly that, in the Japanese context, hereditary politicians, bureaucrats, and TV news reporters have an advantage over other candidates who lack these backgrounds and therefore should be included. Such an inclusion, however, complicates any comparative analysis with the stricter definitions used in other countries and arguably may stretch the definition to include too many candidates (where does the objective measure of quality end?). We prefer the narrower definition of *quality* as experience in local politics or in the House of Councillors. However, we will also show results for a broader definition along the lines of that used by Scheiner (2006) and Weiner (2011) to see if there are any noticeable differences in outcomes.[19]

Patterns in DPJ Candidate Characteristics

We are first interested in whether, and how, first-time candidates recruited by the DPJ differ systematically from candidates for the DPJ who were originally recruited by one of the DPJ's founder parties. While the JSP historically relied heavily on labor unions for its supply of candidates, the LDP and its splinter groups more frequently recruited candidates from the bureaucracy and interest groups related to agricultural interests, such

19 We include all "legacy" (*nisei*) candidates who are related to a current or former Diet member in our broad coding of "quality," not simply "hereditary" (*seshū*) candidates who directly succeed their relatives in candidacy. Similarly, we also include other celebrities, such as movie and TV actors and famous athletes, along with TV news reporters, since the name recognition of such candidates is likely to be as valuable.

as *Nōkyō*. To what degree has the DPJ shifted from such patterns when recruiting its own new candidates? Second, how have these new candidates differed from each other, depending on their method of recruitment: a nationalized *kōbo* versus a more conventional process?

A total of 725 individuals have stood for election at least once as a DPJ candidate since the party's founding in 1996—514 (71 percent) of these candidates were first nominated to a national election by the DPJ. Table 6.3 shows the percentage of these individuals who exhibit each of several common background characteristics. The individuals are grouped by party of origin in order to illustrate differences between the backgrounds of candidates that the DPJ has recruited and those of candidates who joined the party after being recruited by other parties.[20] In contrast, table 6.4 illustrates the change over time in the percentage of newly recruited DPJ candidates who exhibit each trait, separated by the type or arena of recruitment: SMD candidates recruited through the *kōbo* system, SMD candidates selected without the use of *kōbo*, and candidates who were only nominated to the PR list (without dual-listing).[21]

There are clear differences between the DPJ candidates of different party origins and new DPJ recruits. Most notably, as Scheiner (2006) and Weiner (2011) have pointed out, the DPJ has had difficulty in recruiting quality candidates. The comparative data in table 6.3 show that by the stricter definition of quality, newly recruited DPJ candidates are overall less likely to be of high quality than those originally recruited by the more established parties that formed the DPJ. In addition, fewer quality candidates are recruited through *kōbo* than through more traditional means. As table 6.4 shows, it is not until 2009 that those candidates recruited via the *kōbo* system include a substantial percentage of quality candidates. However, using a broader definition of *quality* that includes other background characteristics that might be perceived by Japanese voters to give the candidate an advantage—former bureaucrats, media personalities, legacy candidates—there are somewhat less dramatic differences between *kōbo* and non-*kōbo* candidates over time (table 6.4).

---

20   Some candidates who were first nominated by the DPJ may have been previously involved in the party organization or local politics of one of the other parties. We cannot trace all such prior involvements, so we instead use the party affiliation of the individual at the time that she or he first stood for election to the House of Representatives. A few DPJ-affiliated independents are grouped with the DPJ.

21   It is possible that some candidates who were ultimately nominated as pure PR candidates on the party list were originally unsuccessful *kōbo* applicants for an SMD contest, but in general the list is composed of candidates nominated by the prefectural organizations (*kenren*).

TABLE 6.3

Comparison of DPJ Candidate Backgrounds by Party Group of Origin

Characteristic	DPJ	Left (JSP)	Middle-of-the-Road	Right (LDP)	Total
Quality (elective experience)	29%	29%	35%	43%	31%
Quality (broad definition)	43%	46%	55%	80%	47%
Female	19%	8%	4%	4%	15%
Local (born in prefecture)	68%	78%	66%	76%	69%
Bureaucracy	8%	0%	13%	18%	9%
Labor Union	5%	54%	10%	0%	9%
Agriculture	3%	2%	1%	4%	2%
Total N	513	59	104	49	725

Source: J-LOD for 1996–2009; 2012 electoral data courtesy of Michael Thies.

Notes: Data represent percentages of all *individual* DPJ candidates since 1996 (no duplicates; includes by-election candidates) with each background characteristic, grouped by the party that initially recruited them to run for a House of Representatives election. Party groupings are detailed in appendix table B.1. Each individual can have more than one background characteristic, so percentages do not add up to 100%. The broad definition of *Quality* includes the narrow definition of individuals with prior elective experience (at the local level or House of Councillors) plus former national bureaucrats, celebrities such as TV media personalities and professional sports athletes, and relatives of current or former Diet members. Some candidates are missing exact data for place of birth, so *Local* is based on 694 of the 725 individuals. *Bureaucracy* includes only national-level bureaucratic positions. *Labor union* includes any prior position within a labor union organization. *Agriculture* includes any ties to the agricultural cooperatives, *Nōkyō*, including prior occupation as a farmer.

In the first election in 1996, the DPJ drew on labor unions for 12 percent of its SMD candidates and for 27 percent of its pure PR candidates. However, the unions quickly declined as an arena for recruiting new candidates for the House of Representatives.[22] Instead, the DPJ has begun to attract more candidates with local-level elective experience and ex-bureaucrats. Many of these candidates initially sought nomination as LDP candidates but turned to the DPJ after being rejected or passed over by the LDP, in many cases for a legacy candidate (Sekō 2006). Bureaucrats' support for the LDP also began to waver by the 2000s following frustration with administrative and structural reform, and the emerging prospect of a non-LDP government (Muramatsu 2010, 83). Despite the DPJ's often public rhetoric

22 According to a DPJ party staff member (interviewed in June 2011 in Tokyo), labor union candidates are infrequent applicants to the *kōbo* process as well but are still present on the House of Councillors party list, where the organized vote of unions can still make a difference.

TABLE 6.4

Percentage of New DPJ Candidates with Each Characteristic, by Year and Type/Arena of Recruitment

Characteristic	Recruitment	1996	2000	2003	2005	2009	2012	Total
Quality (elective experience)	SMD (kōbo)	—	0	0	0	31.03	0	11.39
	SMD (non-kōbo)	28.4	26.97	22.54	45.71	30.23	43.9	30.56
	Pure PR	45.45	0	33.33	40	38.64	—	38.24
Quality (broad definition)	SMD (kōbo)	—	11.11	11.11	25	55.17	33.33	31.65
	SMD (non-kōbo)	39.51	40.45	40.85	68.57	53.49	46.34	45.28
	Pure PR	45.45	50	33.33	40	40.91	—	41.18
Female	SMD (kōbo)	—	27.78	0	0	13.79	66.67	13.92
	SMD (non-kōbo)	18.52	20.22	12.68	14.29	27.91	21.95	18.89
	Pure PR	27.27	50	33.33	0	27.27	—	26.47
Local (born in prefecture)	SMD (kōbo)	—	56.25	55.56	60	65.52	33.33	59.74
	SMD (non-kōbo)	69.57	62.03	61.43	80	74.42	68.29	67.66
	Pure PR	57.14	0	83.33	60	88.64	—	80.95
Bureaucracy	SMD (kōbo)	—	11.11	11.11	10	17.24	0	12.66
	SMD (non-kōbo)	3.7	7.87	14.08	20	9.3	0	8.61
	Pure PR	0	0	0	0	2.27	—	1.47
Labor Union	SMD (kōbo)	—	5.56	0	0	3.45	0	2.53
	SMD (non-kōbo)	12.35	0	7.04	0	2.33	0	4.44
	Pure PR	27.27	0	16.67	0	4.55	—	8.82
Agriculture	SMD (kōbo)	—	0	0	5	3.45	0	2.53
	SMD (non-kōbo)	1.23	3.37	1.41	2.86	4.65	0	2.22
	Pure PR	0	0	16.67	0	6.82	—	5.88
Total N	SMD (kōbo)	—	18	9	20	29	3	79
	SMD (non-kōbo)	81	89	71	35	43	41	360
	Pure PR	11	2	6	5	44	0	68
	All types	92	109	86	60	116	44	507

Source: J-LOD for 1996–2009; 2012 electoral data courtesy of Michael Thies.

Notes: Data represent percentages of all first-time DPJ candidates in House of Representatives elections since 1996 (no duplicates) with each background characteristic. By-elections are included, grouped with the previous general election. Each individual can have more than one background characteristic. The broad definition of *Quality* includes the narrow definition of individuals with prior elective experience (at the local level or House of Councillors) plus former national bureaucrats, celebrities such as TV media personalities and professional sports athletes, and relatives of current or former Diet members. Some candidates are missing exact data for place of birth, so *Local* is based on 477 of the 507 individuals. *Bureaucracy* includes only national-level bureaucratic positions. *Labor Union* includes any prior position within a labor union organization. *Agriculture* includes any ties to the agricultural cooperatives, *Nōkyō*, including prior occupation as a farmer.

criticizing the bureaucracy, disaffected or ambitious bureaucrats began to seek the party nomination, often through the *kōbo* process.[23] A smaller trend is visible in the increase over time in candidates with an agricultural background, particularly on the PR list. This may have been part of the DPJ's strategy to cut into the LDP's rural stronghold, particularly in 2009. However, new candidates with a background in the bureaucracy, unions, or agriculture were completely absent in 2012, when the DPJ scrambled to find candidates and relied mainly on Diet member secretaries and local politicians for its new recruits (Smith 2013).

There is a striking contrast between newly recruited DPJ candidates and candidates from different party group origins in terms of gender (table 6.3). Female candidates are much more common among DPJ recruits, though this is no doubt partly a result of the electoral reform and a concomitant increase in female candidates generally since 1996, rather than distinct differences in party priorities per se. Surprisingly, however, apart from the 2000 election when one of the preceding *kōbo* contests focused specifically on female recruitment, women have less often been nominated as a result of the *kōbo* selection process. Even though one of the stated reasons for introducing the *kōbo* system was to close the gender gap in the DPJ, both among its candidates and also among voters (Kawamoto 2008, 266), for the 2003 and 2005 elections, the system did not produce any new female candidates at all (table 6.4).

Interestingly, DPJ and middle-of-the-road party recruits are less likely to run in the prefectures of their birth, a difference that may be the result of the localized recruitment practices of the JSP and the LDP. The gap between new SMD candidates selected through *kōbo* and non-*kōbo* methods in terms of having local ties (being born in the prefecture containing the SMD) also underscores the relationship between local selection and nominating candidates with local ties. On average, *kōbo* candidates are roughly 12 percent less likely to be "locals" than non-*kōbo* candidates.

Postrecruitment Careers of New DPJ Candidates

How have various DPJ candidates fared electorally and in advancing to key leadership posts in the party? Weiner (2011) provides compelling arguments against the (mis)perception that the DPJ is dominated by ex-Socialists. He demonstrates how retiring or losing ex-Socialist DPJ Diet members have

23 Interview by Smith with former bureaucrat and first-time DPJ representative Oizumi Hiroko, June 15, 2011, Tokyo. Ms. Oizumi ran and lost as a non-*kōbo* recruit for the DPJ in Yamaguchi 1st District in the 2003 election and again in the House of Councillors 2004 election, but later contested the party's *kōbo* to win nomination in Ibaragi 6th District in 2009. She lost her seat in 2012.

been replaced over time by candidates with no ties to the former JSP. Through this replacement process, the number of ex-Socialists has gradually diminished to just 10 percent of the House of Representatives delegation (Weiner 2011, 92). Weiner's definition of "ex-Socialist" includes individuals with public sector union backgrounds who never ran under the JSP label. In contrast, Hamamoto (2011) tracks party backgrounds based on the last party affiliation that each candidate held before joining the DPJ. By this measure, Hamamoto records an even lower figure for ex-JSP members—just below 4 percent of members after the 2009 election. Our measurement of party group of origin, which is based on the first party of recruitment, is more similar to that of Hamamoto. Figure 6.2 shows graphically how the percentage of elected DPJ members who were initially candidates of another party has diminished over time. We expect these trends to continue in the future, though 2012 witnessed a huge drop in the percentage of elected DPJ members who were recruited to the party after its formation in 1996.

So, Weiner (2011) is correct not only to point out that few current DPJ members have ties to the former JSP (and fewer will in the future), but also in his larger point that the DPJ should not be considered in any way "hostage" to the party's ex-Socialist members. However, there is another part to

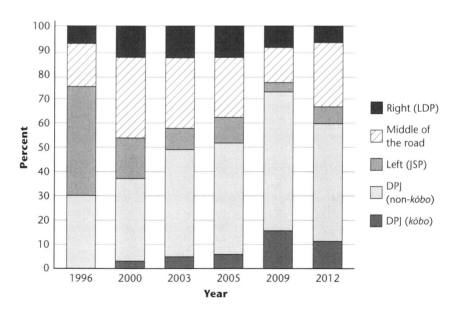

FIGURE 6.2 Party Group of Origin of DPJ Members
of the House of Representatives, 1996–2012
Source: J-LOD.
Note: Includes Diet members elected midterm through by-elections and resignations.

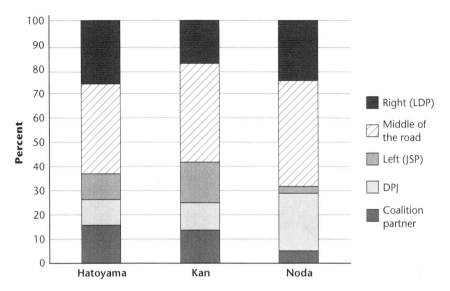

FIGURE 6.3 Cabinet Composition by Party Group Origin: Ministers
Appointed to Hatoyama, Kan, and Noda Cabinets

Source: J-LOD.

Note: Two non-partisan "technical" ministers, and former LDP Diet member Yosano Kaoru
(appointed to the Kan cabinet) are grouped with "Coalition partner."

the picture. DPJ candidates who were originally recruited after the party's
founding have had *at most* six elections of experience, and so most are still
backbenchers in the party. Even though the ex-Socialist members may be
shrinking in number (along with members from other non-DPJ origins),
they are disproportionately senior in the party. Therefore, when we examine
the composition of the top party leadership, particularly the post-2009 DPJ-
led cabinets (figure 6.3), we see a different picture.

When it comes to the cabinet, members who were first recruited into
national office by the DPJ are underrepresented. Only 11 percent of the
ministers in the Hatoyama (2009–2010) and Kan (2010–2011) cabinets were
originally recruited by the DPJ. The Noda (2011–2012) cabinet featured a
higher percentage of DPJ-origin ministers, at 24 percent. However, not one
of the cabinet ministers of DPJ origin was selected through the *kōbo* process.
Roughly 40 percent of each DPJ cabinet has been composed of members
originally recruited by the middle-of-the-road parties, such as the Democratic Socialist Party, JNP, and Socialist Democratic Federation.

Meanwhile, although ex-Socialists have declined rapidly as part of the
overall DPJ delegation in the House of Representatives, they have been well
represented in the cabinet. Although they made up less than 4 percent of DPJ
Diet members after the 2009 election, roughly 10 percent of appointments

to the Hatoyama cabinet went to ex-Socialists, as well as nearly 17 percent of appointments to the Kan cabinet. They made up only 3 percent of Noda's appointees, which was more on a par with their overall percentage in the Diet. This may have also reflected ideological differences between Kan, who got his start in the more liberal Socialist Democratic Federation, versus Noda, who got his start as a JNP nominee.

To what extent have newly nominated DPJ candidates selected through different methods been successful at getting votes? Between 1996 and 2003, DPJ-recruited candidates represented 50 to 60 percent of all candidates, but only 30 to 50 percent of all DPJ winners (figs. 6.1 and 6.2). As previously noted, several scholars have attributed this to the lack of quality candidates among the DPJ's new recruits (Scheiner 2006; Weiner 2011; Reed, Scheiner, and Thies 2012). We know that by the 2005 and 2009 elections, candidate characteristics (such as quality) mattered less, and party label mattered more. But we are also interested in examining whether the introduction of *kōbo* has been a successful strategy for finding electorally viable candidates. Have candidates selected through *kōbo* been able to compete in district races, despite their often lacking many of the characteristics traditionally viewed as making a high-quality candidate? Or do non-*kōbo* candidates from more traditional backgrounds account for the gradual increase in success of DPJ candidates, especially prior to 2009?

Table 6.2 shows the election results for new SMD candidates nominated by the DPJ in elections from 1996 to 2012. Under the new MMM system, SMD candidates who are dual-listed can either win their SMD contest outright or be elected on the party list in the PR tier (as a so-called zombie), if the proportion of their SMD vote relative to the winner in their district (*sekihairitsu* in Japanese, or "best-loser ratio") is high enough to secure a place among the party's reranked list candidates. Apart from the 2005 and 2012 elections, *kōbo* candidates have been more successful at being elected overall than new non-*kōbo* candidates. The electoral success of *kōbo* candidates is further surprising considering that one of the initial purposes of the system was to recruit quality candidates in the districts where the local party organizations could not find a suitable candidate, and often where candidates would face an incumbent challenger. Moreover, non-*kōbo* candidates tend to be stronger than *kōbo* candidates in terms of quality and local ties to the district.

Yet the values in table 6.2 cannot tell us how much the success of *kōbo* candidates is the result of their personal characteristics (or excitement brought about by the more "democratic" candidate selection process) versus the characteristics of the districts in which they were nominated. To better address this concern, we must control for variation in both candidate quality and district "winnability." Table 6.5 shows the results of an ordinary least squares (OLS) regression analysis on the percentage of the winning candidate's vote earned by first-time DPJ candidates in SMD races. As previously mentioned, this calculation is referred to as the *sekihairitsu* and measures how close a candidate came to winning the race. A value of 100 percent for *sekihairitsu* represents a winning candidate, whereas any lower value represents the percentage of the winning candidate's vote earned by a losing candidate.

We use *sekihairitsu* rather than the simple measure of winning or losing, or raw percentage of the vote, because it gives us a better sense of how competitive a candidate was, relative to the other candidates in the same district, especially since so many new DPJ candidates had to compete against LDP incumbents. Due to the practice of dual-listing and reranking the PR list in accordance with an SMD candidate's performance in the district contest, a higher *sekihairitsu* is also important even to candidates who ultimately lose the election, since it may secure them a seat through the party's PR list. We estimate the effect of *kōbo* selection, the quality of the candidate (using both the narrow and broad definitions), the amount of money the candidate spent in the race (as a percentage of the legally allowed amount), gender, age, and district characteristics of whether an incumbent from another party (usually the LDP) was running, the effective number of candidates in the race, population density, and the DPJ's normal party support in the SMD (based on its support in House of Councillors PR elections within the SMD boundaries),[24] to test whether first-time candidates selected through *kōbo* systematically performed differently from non-*kōbo* candidates, even when running in similar electoral contexts and with similar career backgrounds. We exclude the 2012 election from this analysis because we lack detailed data on campaign expenditures and district-level characteristics at the time of this writing. In addition, only three new candidates to our knowledge were selected through *kōbo* (hastily applied at the local level) in 2012, which makes it a less suitable year for testing the differences between *kōbo* and non-*kōbo* candidates.

The regression analysis results indicate no significant difference between the *sekihairitsu* values of *kōbo* and non-*kōbo* candidates when controlling for quality (both narrowly and broadly defined) and the characteristics of the district. In fact, until 2009, one of the most important factors contributing to a new DPJ candidate's increased *sekihairitsu* was the party's popularity in the district. In general, each additional percentage point of support for the DPJ in a district is associated with roughly 3 additional percentage

TABLE 6.5

OLS Regression Coefficients of Percentage of Winning Candidates'
Vote Earned by New DPJ Candidates in SMDs, 1996–2009

	1996	2000	2003	2005	2009
Kōbo *recruit*		3.907	5.398	−3.776	5.686
		(5.475)	(6.120)	(6.292)	(4.030)
Quality (elective office)	−5.519	−3.217	−8.167	2.542	−0.206
	(8.507)	(6.909)	(6.319)	(8.494)	(5.028)
Quality (broad definition)	11.51	14.15**	9.308*	7.387	2.462
	(7.922)	(5.821)	(4.784)	(6.752)	(4.926)
Expenditures/limit	0.493***	0.0554	0.234	0.342	0.263
	(0.155)	(0.134)	(0.146)	(0.225)	(0.224)
Female	4.832	5.880*	7.573	−2.496	−1.864
	(6.769)	(3.293)	(5.236)	(5.735)	(6.893)
Age	−9.443	3.498	−6.495	6.088	−1.339
	(5.707)	(4.778)	(5.983)	(11.15)	(4.585)
Open seat	−0.201	−0.569**	−0.211	−0.398	0.159
	(0.260)	(0.217)	(0.210)	(0.382)	(0.252)
Effective number of candidates	10.30*	6.394	8.706	19.55	−0.269
	(5.642)	(7.304)	(5.325)	(23.23)	(9.753)
Population density	0.219	0.306***	0.501***	0.0911	0.168**
	(0.139)	(0.0811)	(0.0758)	(0.101)	(0.0714)
Party HC PR normal vote	3.726***	3.932***	2.711***	2.437**	0.452
	(1.222)	(0.933)	(0.804)	(1.049)	(0.776)
Constant	−57.59**	−19.94	−24.10	23.58	61.04**
	(24.76)	(18.56)	(22.11)	(26.79)	(26.31)
Observations	77	101	77	52	71
R-squared	0.446	0.494	0.592	0.332	0.175

Notes: OLS regression with *Sekihairitsu* as the dependent variable. *Expenditures/limit* is the percentage of the total allowed amount of election expenditures that the candidate claimed. *Open seat* is coded 1 only when no incumbents (SMD or list) were running in the district. *Effective number of candidates* is the Laakso Taagepera Index (Laakso Taagepera 1979). *Population density* is the percentage of residents in the SMD who live in census-defined densely inhabited districts. *Party HC PR normal vote* is the best estimate of the normal percentage of voter support for the party in the SMD, constructed using the party's actual vote shares within the boundaries of the SMD in House of Councillors national PR elections. This measure is courtesy of Steven R. Reed. By-elections are excluded, so the number of observations is slightly lower than the number of new candidates in table 6.2. Standard errors in parentheses. *** $p < 0.01$, ** $p < 0.05$, * $p < 0.1$.

points in a new candidate's *sekihairitsu*. Given these results, we cannot say that the introduction of *kōbo* as a method of candidate recruitment has itself compensated for the party's comparative disadvantage in terms of quality candidates, but we can say that it has not produced candidates who are in any significant way "weaker" than candidates recruited through more conventional means. It may even have helped the party's popularity overall if it helped project an image of innovation or fresh faces.

Discussion

In this chapter, we have explored the evolution of the DPJ's membership since the party's founding, and the differences in background characteristics and electoral success of new candidates recruited to the party through different methods. Our findings indicate an interesting but variegated pattern to DPJ recruitment of new candidates. First, confirming the previous analyses by Miura, Lee, and Weiner (2005), Weiner (2011), and Hamamoto (2011), we find that the ideological and partisan background of DPJ candidates has indeed changed over time. Former Socialists have especially declined, and a vast majority of today's DPJ candidates have no prior experience in other parties. Interestingly, however, we find that in terms of cabinet appointments during the DPJ's period in government from 2009 to 2012, the "pure DPJ" Diet members were underrepresented, relative to their percentage in the overall House of Representatives, while former Socialists (at least until Noda) and former LDP and middle-of-the-road party members were more dominant.

There are some possible implications of this for the manner in which the party governed. With a more diverse cabinet in terms of partisan (and ideological) backgrounds, it may have been more difficult to reach consensus in the cabinet than in the party as a whole. All of the party's leaders, and most of the cabinet ministers, got their start in other parties. Considering that the DPJ tried strongly to centralize policymaking in the cabinet and create a Westminster-style system, this may imply that it centralized decisions in a more diverse and contentious body. After the 2012 loss, perhaps we can anticipate a more cohesive party—though such a prediction is premature at this point. Under Kan and Noda, the DPJ did not show particularly centralized leadership in the policymaking process, and there are signs that it may be moving back structurally toward resembling the former LDP process (Pempel 2012). A more decentralized policymaking process within the DPJ, or the retirement of its senior leaders (such as Hatoyama in 2012) and replacement by more centrist members might at least produce greater consensus within the party. The departure of Ozawa and his followers in 2012 (all but six of whom lost in the election) certainly may help to produce greater consensus, too. Much depends on how the DPJ can rebuild itself after its devastating 2012 electoral loss.

Our most important findings concern the practice and consequences of the DPJ's innovative *kōbo* method of recruitment. This open style of recruitment was supposed to diversify the candidates the party supported, especially by attracting more female candidates, and compensate for the party's difficulty in recruiting "quality" candidates. Our analysis here reveals a diverse and somewhat surprising picture. The *kōbo* process has not dramatically helped the DPJ close the gender gap, although the DPJ nominates more female candidates than most other major parties. Also, until the 2009 election, *kōbo* candidates have been of lower quality, by all definitions, than non-*kōbo* candidates.

However, we find that *kōbo*-recruited candidates have actually been *more* successful over all at being elected than non-*kōbo* candidates, in part because of their revival rates in the PR tier through the dual-listing provision, rather than as a result of being superior in terms of winning the SMDs outright. But we find no statistical difference between *kōbo* and non-*kōbo* candidates' electoral competitiveness when controlling for candidate quality and party support in the district. In short, *kōbo* cannot be considered a better recruitment method when other options (candidates) are available. But it *has* helped expand and diversify the pool of candidates, and candidates recruited through *kōbo* have not fared any worse electorally than non-*kōbo* candidates. In this sense, *kōbo* was a successful way for the party to cope with the difficulty of growing its candidate pool and building its membership from such a varied and weak organizational base.

Another possible explanation for our null findings in terms of differences in the electoral success of *kōbo* and non-*kōbo* candidates is that candidate characteristics and methods of recruitment do not matter as much under the more party-centered MMM electoral system as they did in the past under the SNTV system. As Reed, Scheiner, and Thies (2012) show, voter choice in recent elections has been shaped more dominantly by party labels and platforms than by the characteristics of individual candidates, at least in terms of quality. With the rise of many more floating voters and the increasing influence of party and party leader image as a determinant of the vote, it may be that party image and popularity now wash out any impact of candidate background or candidate recruitment method.

On the other hand, it is unclear how much the diversity of new *kōbo* candidates and the media hype surrounding fresh faces such as the "Ozawa girls" contributed to the party image in a way that mattered more for electoral success than simply whether or not they had prior elective experience. It is at least a hypothesis worth investigating further in the future.

Appendix B

TABLE B.1

Party of Origin of All DPJ Candidates in House of Representatives Elections, 1996–2012

Party Name	Grouping	1996 N	1996 %	2000 N	2000 %	2003 N	2003 %	2005 N	2005 %	2009 N	2009 %	2012 N	2012 %	Total N	Total %
Democratic Party of Japan	DPJ	92	55.09	147	54.44	164	58.16	189	61.76	241	72.81	199	74.53	1,032	63.59
DPJ Independent	DPJ			1	0.37	2	0.71	4	1.31	4	1.21	5	1.87	16	0.99
Japan Socialist Party	Left	45	26.95	32	11.85	18	6.38	13	4.25	11	3.32	9	3.37	128	7.89
JSP Independent	Left	4	2.4	4	1.48	2	0.71	3	0.98	2	0.6	2	0.75	17	1.05
Democratic Socialist Party	Middle	2	1.2	12	4.44	11	3.9	11	3.59	6	1.81	4	1.5	46	2.83
DSP Independent	Middle			1	0.37	1	0.35	1	0.33	1	0.3	1	0.37	5	0.31
Socialist Democratic Federation	Middle	1	0.6	1	0.37	1	0.35	1	0.33	1	0.3	1	0.37	6	0.37
Kōmeitō	Middle					2	0.71	1	0.33	1	0.3			4	0.25
New Frontier Party	Middle			23	8.52	19	6.74	19	6.21	11	3.32	12	4.49	84	5.18
Sakigake	Middle	1	0.6	4	1.48	4	1.42	4	1.31	1	0.3	1	0.37	15	0.92
Sakigake Independent	Middle					1	0.35	1	0.33	1	0.3	1	0.37	4	0.25
Japan New Party	Middle	9	5.39	14	5.19	14	4.96	14	4.58	9	2.72	7	2.62	67	4.13
Japan Renewal Party	Middle	1	0.6	4	1.48	4	1.42	2	0.65	3	0.91	1	0.37	15	0.92
Liberal Party	Middle					7	2.48	8	2.61	5	1.51	2	0.75	22	1.36
Liberal Alliance	Middle					1	0.35	1	0.33	1	0.3			3	0.18
Independent	Middle	2	1.2	3	1.11	3	1.06	5	1.63	4	1.21	4	1.5	21	1.29
People's New Party	Middle									1	0.3	1	0.37	2	0.12
Liberal Democratic Party	Right	5	2.99	11	4.07	13	4.61	13	4.25	12	3.63	5	1.87	59	3.64
LDP Independent	Right	5	2.99	12	4.44	15	5.32	16	5.23	16	4.83	12	4.49	76	4.68
New Liberal Club	Right			1	0.37									1	0.06
Total		167	100	270	100	282	100	306	100	331	100	267	100	1,623	100

Sources: J-LOD for 1996–2009; 2012 electoral data courtesy of Michael Thies.

Notes: By-election candidates are included, grouped with the previous general election. Party of recruitment is based on the party at the time of the first observation in our data set, which goes back as far as the 1980 general election.

Appendix C

TABLE C.1

SMD Contests with a Kōbo-*Recruited*
New DPJ Candidate, 2000–12

Prefecture	District (Year)
Aichi	9 (2003); 10 (2005)
Aomori	1 (2012)
Chiba	10 (2000); 1 (2003); 2, 9, 11 (2009); 3 (2012)
Fukuoka	2 (2005)*; 11 (2005); 8, 9 (2009)
Fukushima	1 (2009)
Gifu	4 (2005); 4 (2012)
Gunma	2 (2000); 4 (2003); 5 (2005); 1 (2009)
Hiroshima	1 (2005); 3 (2005)
Hyogo	4 (2003); 7 (2005); 2 (2009)
Ibaragi	1 (2000); 2, 6 (2005)
Ishikawa	2, 3 (2009)
Kagoshima	3 (2000)
Kanagawa	16 (2000); 2, 3, 13, 17 (2009)
Kumamoto	5 (2003); 2 (2009)
Miyagi	4 (2005)
Miyazaki	2 (2000); 3 (2005)
Nagano	1 (2000); 5 (2005)
Niigata	2 (2005)
Okayama	5 (2000); 2, 4 (2003); 5 (2005); 1, 3 (2009)
Osaka	1, 18, 19 (2000); 16 (2003)
Saitama	2, 6 (2000); 8, 13, (2009)
Shizuoka	2 (2000); 3 (2005); 3, 7, 8 (2009)
Tochigi	1 (2000); 3 (2005); 1 (2009)
Tokushima	2 (2000)
Tokyo	4, 10, 13, 14, 16, 23 (2009)
Tottori	1 (2005)
Toyama	1 (2000)
Yamagata	4 (2002)*
Yamaguchi	1, 3 (2005)

Source: DPJ Election Strategy Committee (2012 data based on newspaper references).

Note: * denotes by-elections.

References

Asano, Masahiko. 2006. *Shimin Shakai ni okeru Seido Kaikaku: Senkyo Seido to Kōhosha Rikurūto* [System reform at the level of civil society: Electoral reform and candidate recruitment]. Tokyo: Keio University Press.

Carson, Jamie L., Erik J. Engstrom, and Jason M. Roberts. 2007. "Candidate Quality, the Personal Vote, and the Incumbency Advantage in Congress." *American Political Science Review* 101 (2): 289–301.

Cross, William. 2008. "Democratic Norms and Candidate Selection." *Party Politics* 14 (2): 596–619.

Di Virgilio, Aldo, and Steven R. Reed. 2011. "Nominating Candidates under New Rules in Italy and Japan: You Cannot Bargain with Resources You Do Not Have." In *A Natural Experiment on Electoral Law Reform: Evaluating the Long Run Consequences of 1990s Electoral Reform in Italy and Japan*, edited by Daniela Giannetti and Bernard Grofman. Studies in Public Choice, vol. 24, 59–73. New York: Springer.

Duverger, Maurice. 1955. *The Political Role of Women*. Paris: UNESCO.

Endo, Masahisa, Robert Pekkanen, and Steven R. Reed. 2013. "The LDP's Path Back to Power." In *Japan Decides 2012: The Japanese General Election*, edited by Robert Pekkanen, Steven R. Reed, and Ethan Scheiner. New York: Palgrave.

Fukui, Haruhiro. 1997. "Japan." In *Passages to Power: Legislative Recruitment in Advanced Democracies*, edited by Pippa Norris, 98–113. Cambridge: Cambridge University Press.

Fukui, Haruhiro, and Shigeko N. Fukai. 1997. "Japan in 1996: Between Hope and Uncertainty." *Asian Survey* 37 (1): 20–28.

Gallagher, Michael, and Michael Marsh, eds. 1988. *Candidate Selection in Comparative Perspective: The Secret Garden of Politics*. London: Sage Publications.

Gaunder, Alisa. 2012. "The DPJ and Women: The Limited Impact of the 2009 Alternation of Power on Policy and Governance." *Journal of East Asian Studies* 12 (3): 441–66.

Hamamoto, Shinsuke. 2011. "Minshutō ni okeru Yakushoku Haibun no Seidoka" [DPJ personnel system change]. In *Minshutō no Soshiki to Seisaku* [DPJ organization and policies], edited by Takayoshi Uekami and Tsutsumi Hidenori, 29–70. Tokyo: Tōyōkeizai Shinpansha.

Hazan, Reuven Y., and Gideon Rahat. 2010. *Democracy Within Parties: Candidate Selection Methods and Their Political Consequences*. New York: Oxford University Press.

Higashi, Yasuhiro. 2008. "Minshutō no Hata Age" [Raising the flag of the DPJ]. In *Minshutō Jūnen-shi* [DPJ ten-year history], edited by Tamiyoshi Tachibana, 43–80. Tokyo: Daiichi Shorin.

Jacobson, Gary C. 1983. *The Politics of Congressional Elections*. Boston: Little, Brown.

———. 1990. *The Origins of Divided Government: Competition in the U.S. House Elections, 1946–88*. Boulder, CO: Westview Press.

Kawamoto, Suguru. 2008. "*Chihō Nettowāku Katsudō*" [Local network movements]. In *Minshutō Jūnen-shi* [DPJ ten-year history], edited by Tamiyoshi Tachibana, 248–68. Tokyo: Daiichi Shorin.

Koellner, Patrick. 2011. "The Democratic Party of Japan: Development, Organization, and Programmatic Profile." In *The Routledge Handbook of Japanese Politics*, edited by Alisa Gaunder, 24–35. New York: Routledge.

Köllner, Patrick. 2004. "Factionalism in Japanese Political Parties Revisited or How Do Factions in the LDP and DPJ Differ?" *Japan Forum* 16 (1): 87–109.

Krauss, Ellis S., and Robert J. Pekkanen. 2004. "Explaining Party Adaptation to Electoral Reform: The Discreet Charm of the LDP?" *Journal of Japanese Studies* 30 (1): 1–34.

———. 2011. *The Rise and Fall of Japan's LDP: Political Party Organizations as Historical Institutions*. Ithaca, NY: Cornell University Press.

Laakso, Markku, and Rein Taagepera. 1979. "Effective Number of Parties: A Measure with Application to West Europe." *Comparative Political Studies* 12 (1): 3–27.

Maeda, Ko. 2009. "Has the Electoral-System Reform Made Japanese Elections Party-Centered?" In *Political Change in Japan: Electoral Behavior, Party Realignment, and the Koizumi Reforms*, edited by Steven R. Reed, Kenneth Mori McElwain, and Kay Shimizu, 47–66. Stanford, CA: Shorenstein APARC.

Miura, Mari, Kap Yun Lee, and Robert Weiner. 2005. "Who are the DPJ? Policy Positioning and Recruitment Strategy." *Asian Perspective* 29 (1): 49–77.

Muramatsu, Michio. 2010. *Seiken Sukuramu-gata Rīdāshippu no Hōkai* [The collapse of scrum-like politico-bureaucratic leadership]. Tokyo: Tōyōkeizai Shinpansha.

Narud, Hanne Marthe, Mogens N. Pedersen, and Henry Valen, eds. 2002. *Party Sovereignty and Citizen Control: Selecting Candidates for Parliamentary Elections in Denmark, Finland, Iceland and Norway*. Odense, DK: University Press of Southern Denmark.

Norris, Pippa, ed. 1997. *Passages to Power: Legislative Recruitment in Advanced Democracies*. New York: Cambridge University Press.

Pekkanen, Robert, and Steven R. Reed. 2013. "Japanese Politics Between the 2009 and 2012 Elections." In *Japan Decides 2012: The Japanese General Election*, edited by Robert Pekkanen, Steven R. Reed, and Ethan Scheiner, 8–19. New York: Palgrave Macmillan.

Pempel, T. J. 2012. "Is the Democratic Party of Japan Just a Reincarnation of the LDP?" http://www.nippon.com.

Rahat, Gideon. 2007. "Candidate Selection: The Choice Before the Choice." *Journal of Democracy* 18 (1): 157–70.

Rahat, Gideon, and Reuven Y. Hazan. 2001. "Candidate Selection Methods: An Analytical Framework." *Party Politics* 7 (3): 297–322.

Ranney, Austin. 1981. "Candidate Selection." In *Democracy at the Polls: A Comparative Study of Competitive National Elections*, edited by David Butler, Howard R. Penniman, and Austin Ranney, 75–106. Washington, DC: American Enterprise Institute for Public Policy Research.

Reed, Steven R., Ethan Scheiner, Daniel M. Smith, and Michael F. Thies. 2013. "The Japanese General Election of 2012: The LDP Wins Big by Default." In *Japan Decides 2012: The Japanese General Election*, edited by Robert Pekkanen, Steven R. Reed, and Ethan Scheiner. New York: Palgrave Macmillan.

Reed, Steven R., Ethan Scheiner, and Michael F. Thies. 2012. "The End of LDP Dominance and the Rise of Party-Oriented Politics in Japan." *Journal of Japanese Studies* 38 (2): 353–76.

Rule, Wilma, and Joseph F. Zimmerman, eds. 1994. *Electoral Systems in Comparative Perspective: Their Impact on Women and Minorities*. Westport, CT: Greenwood Press.

Satō, Seizaburō, and Tetsuhisa Matsuzaki. 1986. *Jiminto Seiken* [LDP rule]. Tokyo: Chūō Kōronsha.

Scheiner, Ethan. 2006. *Democracy without Competition in Japan: Opposition Failure in a One-Party Dominant State*. New York: Cambridge University Press.

Schmidt, Carmen. 2011. "DPJ Factions: Benefits or Threats?" *Hitotsubashi Journal of Social Studies* 43 (1): 1–21.

Sekō, Hiroshige. 2006. *Jimintō Kaizō Purojekuto 650 Nichi* [LDP reform project: 650 days]. Tokyo: Shinchōsa.

Shiratori, Rei. 1988. "Japan: Localism, Factionalism, Personalism." In *Candidate Selection in Comparative Perspective: The Secret Garden of Politics*, edited by Michael Gallagher and Michael Marsh, 169–89. London: Sage.

Shoji, Kaori. 2012. "Nihon no Nidai Seitō to Seitō Kōhosha Kōbo Seido: Jimintō Miyagi Kenren no Keiken ga Shimesu Seido no Evolution" [Japan's two-party system and open recruitment: Evidence of system evolution in the experience of the LDP party branch in Miyagi Prefecture]. *Gakushuin Daigaku Hōgakukai Zasshi* 48 (1): 307–41.

Smith, Daniel Markham. 2012. "Succeeding in Politics: Dynasties in Democracies." Ph.D. dissertation. University of California, San Diego.

———. 2013. "Candidate Recruitment for the 2012 Election: New Parties, New Methods, . . . Same Old Pool of Candidates?" In *Japan Decides 2012: The Japanese General Election,* edited by Robert Pekkanen, Steven R. Reed, and Ethan Scheiner, 101–22. New York: Palgrave Macmillan.

Tachibana, Tamiyoshi, ed. 2008. *Minshutō jūnen-shi* [DPJ ten-year history]. Tokyo: Daiichi Shorin.

Tsutsumi, Hidenori. 2012. "Kōhosha Sentei Katei no Kaihō to Seitō Soshiki" [Opening up the candidate selection process and party organization]. *Senkyo Kenkyū* 28 (1): 5–20.

Tsutsumi, Hidenori, and Takayasohi Uekami. 2011. "Minshutō no Seisaku: Keizokusei to Henka" [DPJ policy: Continuity and change]. In *Minshutō no Soshiki to Seisaku* [DPJ organization and policies], edited by Takayoshi Uekami and Tsutsumi Hidenori, 225–53. Tokyo: Tōyōkeizai Shinpansha.

Uekami, Takayoshi, and Hidenori Tsutsumi. 2011. "Minshutō no Keisei Katei, Soshiki to Seisaku" [DPJ formation process, organization, and policies]. In *Minshutō no Soshiki to Seisaku* [DPJ organization and policies], edited by Takayoshi Uekami and Tsutsumi Hidenori, 1–28. Tokyo: Tōyōkeizai Shinpansha.

Uriu, Robert. 1999. "Japan in 1998: Nowhere to Go but Up?" *Asian Survey* 39 (1): 114–24.

Weiner, Robert. 2011. "The Evolution of the DPJ: Two Steps Forward, One Step Back." In *The Evolution of Japan's Party System: Politics and Policy in an Era of Institutional Change,* edited by Leonard J. Schoppa, 63–98. Toronto: University of Toronto Press.

7 The Development of DPJ Partisanship from a Fraction to a Majority (and Back Again?)

Yukio Maeda

Previous research on aggregate partisanship focuses primarily on stable party systems, and provides few clues to understanding the process that a new political party follows to develop support among the electorate. Thus, it is worthwhile to analyze how DPJ partisanship has grown since the party was first formed in 1996.

In this chapter, I empirically examine the growth of DPJ partisanship using a time-series statistical analysis of Jiji monthly opinion polls from the party's founding to December 2011. I also examine the quantity of news reports about the DPJ in the mass media, which changes as a function of the electoral fortunes of the party over the years. I show that an increase in DPJ partisanship is a consequence of electoral victory, rather than a prerequisite of it, and that a government party has an advantage over opposition parties in attracting the attention of the mass media, and consequently, the support from the electorate.

New political parties rarely succeed in gaining the support of a majority of respondents in opinion polls. Established political parties control a large share of the electorate, so new parties face an uphill struggle in convincing independents and supporters of other parties to support them. In their classic article, Seymour Martin Lipset and Stein Rokkan (1967) argue that the

This chapter was originally prepared for presentation at the 2012 annual conference of the Association for Asian Studies, Toronto. I am grateful for constructive criticism from the panelists, audience members, and an anonymous reviewer. I also thank Daniel Smith for his suggestion to add "and Back Again?" to the title of this chapter. Margaret Gibbons kindly provided a few rounds of proofreading and advice. This research is supported by Grants-in-Aid for Scientific Research (B) No. 11002710, "The DPJ Government and Party Organization."

party systems in Europe had been frozen since suffrage was extended to the mass population. While new political parties have entered the field in most Western democracies since then, most of them either have disappeared or remain minority parties, as Lipset and Rokkan may have anticipated. Indeed, in advanced industrial democracies it is not common for a new party to win over a majority of the public within its first several years of activity.

This pattern also held true in Japan until very recently. The Liberal Democratic Party (LDP) never allowed another party to surpass its support rate in opinion polls until the twenty-first century. During the reign of the LDP and LDP-led coalition governments (1955–2009), many new parties entered the arena of electoral competition but faded away sooner or later, except Kōmeitō.[1] However, just 10 years after its founding, the Democratic Party of Japan (DPJ) was supported by a majority of the public in opinion polls. Its remarkable success makes the DPJ a striking case worth serious examination.

The primary hypothesis in this paper is that the amount of media coverage of political parties influences aggregate partisan support in opinion polls. It is likely that the temporal increase in political information during electoral campaigns produces a short-term surge in party support in opinion polls. Similarly, a high support rate for a political party may be buttressed by the mass media's constant supply of information about the party. As most people acquire political information only through the mass media, it is crucial to examine the impact of media coverage on the electorate's support for political parties.

Previous Research

In order to place the exceptional rise of Japan's DPJ in the context of public opinion research, it is necessary to review the existing studies briefly. The academic study of aggregate partisanship has advanced greatly during the last quarter century. Scholars demonstrated how partisan balance in the results of opinion polls changes over time, and described what influences its movements. Statistical techniques employed for analysis have increased in sophistication during the same period (MacKuen, Erikson, and Stimson 1989; Box-Steffensmeier and Smith 1996; Erikson, MacKuen, and Stimson 2002; Green, Palmquist, and Schickler 2004).

However, previous research on aggregate partisanship focuses primarily on stable two-party systems, namely the United States and the United

---

1 The Japan Communist Party is older than the LDP. Founded in 1922, it operated underground until Japan's defeat in 1945.

Kingdom, and provides few clues to understanding the process that a new political party follows to develop support among the electorate. These studies show how the economy, the approval ratings of incumbent presidents or prime ministers, political scandals, and international crises influence the distribution of mass partisanship (Norpoth 1987b, 1987a; Erikson, MacKuen, and Stimson 2002; Green, Palmquist, and Schickler 2004; Lebo and Norpoth 2011). Furthermore, many of these studies analyze the relative balance between two major parties rather than focus on a party itself.

In states with stable two-party systems, it makes sense to focus on shifts in the balance or ratio of support between partisan groups. However, when a party system is in transition, examining how support for a new party develops over time is a better approach than focusing on shifts in partisan balance. By examining public support for a new party, one can better understand the dynamics of partisanship for a minority party and how it can develop into a majority. Thus, a time-series analysis of mass support for the DPJ will contribute not only to our understanding of historic political change in Japan, but also to the theoretical discussion on how aggregate partisanship for a new party evolves over time.

No study has systematically examined the evolution of support for the DPJ, which is not surprising considering that the party has existed for only 15 years. Several studies examine LDP partisanship in opinion polls over a long period of time, and they provide a baseline for assessing DPJ support. As is often the case with time-series analysis of polling data (Norpoth 1987b; MacKuen, Erikson, and Stimson 1989; Norpoth, Lewis-Beck, and Lafay 1991; Anderson 1995), all of the LDP partisanship studies point out the importance of economic conditions. Inoguchi (1983) finds that personal income levels and consumer prices influence LDP support. Nishizawa (2001) shows that economic conditions, mediated through subjective economic evaluations, affect support for the LDP. Nakamura (2006) also demonstrates that household income affects both LDP support and cabinet approval.

However, we cannot assume that these findings on the impact of the economy on partisan support can be directly applied to the DPJ while in opposition. Though bad economic conditions may weaken support for a ruling party, an economic downturn is highly unlikely to influence support for an opposition party in the same way. Voter evaluations of the economy are asymmetrical, which means that voters might punish a government for a recession but fail to reward it for good economic growth (Norpoth 1987b). In a similar way, voters might punish a government for a recession without rewarding the opposition for it. Thus, while the economy must be taken into account as a potential explanatory variable, I expect that economic trends have limited influence on the popular support for an opposition party such as the DPJ.

Another element affecting public opinion is political events such as wars and scandals (Mueller 1970; Kernell 1978; Norpoth 1987b, 1987a). Fortunately, Japan has been only tangentially involved in military conflict since 1945 and, while there has been no shortage of scandals, the existing studies using Japan's polling data have not addressed the topic of scandals in depth.

Elections themselves are important political events that influence the dynamics of mass partisanship over time. Polling specialists in academia and journalism point out that partisan support increases just before and after an election as independents are drawn toward one party or another (Sakaiya 2006). Though the number of partisan voters increases briefly, many voters return to being independent as time passes. According to the conventional explanation, the number of partisan voters (for whichever party) increases when people are confronted with an opportunity to cast their ballots. At the same time, the various news media disseminate information about political parties in order to aid people in choosing among competing alternatives. The flow of information plays an important role in shaping partisanship in opinion polls because partisanship is not deeply rooted in the hearts and minds of most Japanese people. Partisanship in Japan is referred to as *party support*, a term that reflects the lack of a strong affective component in evaluating political parties. Party support is far more cognitive than party identification, which in the U.S. context signifies affective psychological attachment to a party. If people acquire enduring partisan attitudes through socialization at home and in their local community (Campbell et al. 1960), a change in the news supply may not affect partisan attitudes in the electorate. However, as the DPJ has a history of just over 15 years, it is unlikely that people have acquired stable affective partisan attitudes toward it.[2] Lacking enduring partisanship, people constantly update their evaluations of the DPJ as they are exposed to new information. Furthermore, evaluations may erode if little news is supplied over a certain length of time. By "erosion" I do not mean more negative evaluations, but rather, a lack of evaluations. Thus, when a party receives little news coverage, I expect that its rate of popular support will decline.

This expectation leads to a prediction that the level of support for the DPJ changes as the supply of news on the DPJ from the mass media changes. Simply stated, the more extensive the supply of news on the DPJ, the higher its support in opinion polls will become. The idea that popular support for

2 For the distinction between affective and cognitive partisanship, see Miyake (1991).

opposition parties and the amount of news coverage are interrelated is actually not new. If one browses through a pile of old Japanese newspapers, one can find this idea spelled out many times, but in an ad hoc fashion. It has never been systematically tested and is worth serious examination.

Data and Measurement

The data set analyzed for this chapter is constructed from the Jiji Press monthly polls, which are employed in almost all studies of Japanese public opinion (Inoguchi 1981; Ikeda 1992; Miyake, Nishizawa, and Kouno 2001; Maeda 2005). Jiji has been conducting its monthly poll using the same format since June 1960.[3] This chapter analyzes survey data in the period after September 1996, when the DPJ was officially established.[4] The number of respondents is slightly over 1,300 for each survey. Jiji pollsters always conduct four days of fieldwork in the first half of each month; the schedule is fixed and does not change due to political events. The measure of support for the DPJ is simply the number of people who name it in response to the question "Which political party do you support?," divided by the total number of respondents.[5] Those who choose "Don't know" are included in the denominator.[6]

To gauge the supply of news on the DPJ in the mass media, I employ the Yomidasu database of articles published in *Yomiuri Shimbun*, which has a circulation of roughly 10 million for its morning edition, the highest in Japan. Though both *Asahi Shimbun* and *Mainichi Shimbun* provide similar databases, Yomidasu was chosen in part for a practical reason: Its interface is better suited for converting search results into a spreadsheet format than those provided by the other newspapers. It is also important to use a news source other than Jiji Press for measuring media coverage, because Jiji's reporting on the DPJ may be affected by the results of its polls, before or

3 There was one major change in a follow-up question to the initial question on partisan support. It does not affect the analysis in this chapter, because it occurred in 1994, before the formation of the DPJ.

4 Technically speaking, the current DPJ was established in 1998 through the merger of the old DPJ and a few other minor parties. For this chapter, I do not distinguish between the two periods.

5 Jiji interviewers neither read nor show a list of political parties to respondents in the monthly polls. Due to this lack of prompting, Jiji opinion polls regularly report higher percentages of independents than surveys conducted by other news agencies.

6 In the literature of American political science, *macropartisanship* is defined as Democratic identifier divided by the total number of those who support either of the two major parties. Not only those who responded "Don't know" but also independents are excluded from the definition.

after they are published. (See appendix D for the procedure used to calculate the amount of news flow using the Yomidasu database.) The amount of news on the DPJ is simply the number of news items on the DPJ reported in *Yomiuri Shimbun* for each month.

Descriptive Analysis

Figure 7.1 shows the simple time-series plot of support for the DPJ and the LDP in the Jiji monthly polls from October 1996 through December 2011. DPJ support seems to have grown in a few discrete steps, not with a smooth linear trend. Though several spikes appear, the average level of DPJ support seems to have jumped up a few times. Figure 7.2 has such "imagined" steps overlaid on DPJ support. It seems that DPJ support did not grow gradually but went up in stages, as if climbing up a stairway step by step. And after moving one step up, it plateaued until it had to go up (or down) another step.

What caused such steplike changes in the support for the DPJ? For the observer of Japanese politics, it is clear that DPJ support in opinion polls jumped up when the DPJ gained a significant share of seats in the Diet in national elections. The first step appears in November 2003, when the mainstream mass media announced the beginning of a full-fledged two-party system in Japan (Yomiuri Shimbun Tokyo Honsha Yoronchosabu 2004). After the DPJ and the Liberal Party merged immediately before the 2003

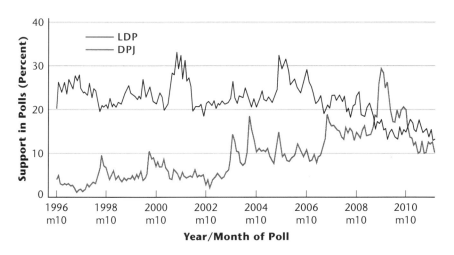

FIGURE 7.1 Party Support Rate, Oct. 1996–Dec. 2011
Source: Jiji monthly poll.

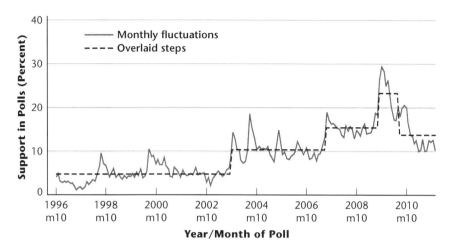

FIGURE 7.2 Trends in DPJ Support, Oct. 1996–Dec. 2011: Steps Overlaid

Source: Jiji monthly poll.

lower-house election, the DPJ won 177 seats—the largest number of seats won by an opposition party in postwar Japan. The second step appears in July 2007, when the DPJ recorded a large victory and gained a majority in the upper house. The third step appears in September 2009, at the time that the DPJ finally won the government.

However, the DPJ enjoyed high levels of support only briefly. The DPJ's setback in the 2010 upper-house election seems to have pushed down support for the DPJ systematically. As the drop in support became apparent about 10 months after the change of government, the trend is less clear and depends on a subjective judgment as to whether there was another downward step after the 2010 upper-house election, or if support for the DPJ had been gradually declining after September 2009 due to the many missteps and failures of the DPJ government. The difference between steplike shifts in support before the change of the government and the more linear downward trend afterward warrants separate treatment for these two periods in subsequent analyses.

Going back to the period when the DPJ was in opposition, the major hypothesis in this chapter is that the amount of media reporting on political parties influences aggregate party support in opinion polls. This hypothesis may apply only to parties in opposition for a simple reason: The mass media always report what the government does because it is their professional obligation to monitor the government and disseminate political news to the public. The mass media report both good and bad aspects of government

activities constantly. The seemingly different movements of DPJ support before and after the change of government in September 2009 make intuitive
sense, because mass media report on the government and opposition parties
differently.

It may seem obvious that the mass media report the activities of opposition parties only when they are newsworthy. A little less obvious is that
when different parties commit factually equivalent blunders (bribery, gaffes,
public in-fighting, and so on), the ruling party's missteps receive more coverage. Also, opposition parties can generally control damage more quickly
than ruling parties, for which the stakes are higher. If a series of negative
news stories damages its reputation, an opposition party usually takes swift
remedial action, mostly through removing from leadership posts those who
are involved in a scandal. Unlike governing parties, those in opposition are
not forced to respond to criticism in the Diet, and once remedial actions
have been taken, the media's attention shifts elsewhere.

Parties receive some positive press coverage as well, but it is difficult to
sustain positive news coverage, because that requires a party to constantly
take newsworthy and popular action. Except for short bursts of negative
or positive news coverage during a brief time period, most news reports on
the opposition are neither favorable nor unfavorable toward them. Reporters
mostly relate parties' electoral and legislative activities. Still, neutral press
coverage is very important for opposition parties, because they lack their
own machinery to carry out large-scale public relations. People are not likely
to support a political party without knowing what it is actually doing. Thus,
news coverage is a prerequisite of support for opposition parties.

The time-series graph of support for the DPJ and the number of news
reports in *Yomiuri* on the DPJ are displayed in figure 7.3. Visual inspection
is dependent on subjective judgment and prone to misinterpretation, but
support for the DPJ in opinion polls and the number of news reports on the
DPJ exhibit similar trajectories after the 2003 lower-house election.[7] The
influence of press coverage on public support for the DPJ will be systematically analyzed in the next section.

Jiji poll respondents' evaluation of the national economy is used as a
control variable in the analysis. While the Jiji poll also asks respondents
about their households' economic condition, I use their assessment of

---

7 Actually, the two lines also seem to move in tandem before the 2003 election, but
the number of news reports did not move up as much as the support for the DPJ in polls.
The graph of the news items lacks the upward step in the fall of 2003, which is apparent
in the support for the DPJ.

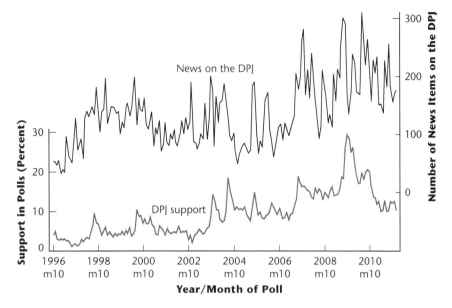

FIGURE 7.3 Media Coverage and DPJ Support, Oct. 1996–Dec. 2011
Sources: Jiji monthly polls and Yomiuri database.

the state of the national economy because people are less likely to blame the government for their personal financial situations than for the overall economy (Kinder and Kiewiet 1979).[8]

Data Analysis

Before proceeding to examine multivariate relationships, checking the time-series property of DPJ support is in order. Because the popularity of the DPJ is observed over time in monthly polls, it is necessary to understand its own dynamics over time before proceeding to a more elaborate analysis (McCleary and Hay 1980; Vandaele 1983; Bisgaard and Kulahci 2011). Following previous studies on support for the LDP, such as Nishizawa (2001), I employ the Box-Jenkins ARIMA (autoregressive integrated moving average) approach here.

8 The survey question asks, "Do you think that current economic conditions are the same as last month, worse than last month, or better than last month?" Respondents are given five choices, ranging from very positive to very negative, with the middle being neutral. I use the sum of the two negative answers as an economic evaluation score rather than the sum of the two positive answers, simply because negative evaluations provide more variability than positive evaluations.

In ARIMA modeling, simply stated, time-series variables are expressed as a combination of autoregressive and moving average processes. A simple case of the first-order autoregressive and the first-order moving average process, which is denoted as ARIMA (1,0,1), can be expressed as follows:

$$Y_t = \varphi Y_{t-1} + \epsilon_t + \theta \epsilon_{t-1} + c$$

As shown in the preceding equation, the value of Y at time t is expressed as a function of its value at time $t-1$, the weighted average of disturbances (ϵ) in time t and $t-1$, and a constant (c). Both φ and θ are parameters to be estimated. When Y does not hover around its mean value over time, usually a first difference is used for the sake of statistical analysis.

In constructing a regression model with time-series variables, it is necessary to take a few steps to identify the relationships between independent and dependent variables. First, an appropriate ARIMA structure is identified for the independent variable to construct a "filter" that removes time dependency from the original time series. This procedure is called prewhitening in the terminology of the Box-Jenkins method (Vandaele 1983; Norpoth 1986). Then the same prewhitening filter is also applied to the dependent variable to uncover the relationships between the independent and dependent variables.[9]

To initially identify time-series characteristics of DPJ support and news reports on the DPJ, I use only the first 85 monthly observations, from October 1996 to October 2003; using the entire series could obscure the nature of a time series due to large changes in the mean level present in the time series (McCleary and Hay 1980; McDowall et al. 1980).[10] For evaluating broader economic conditions, I use the entire period. After several rounds of data exploration and estimation, I chose ARIMA(1,0,0) for DPJ support, ARIMA(1,0,1) for news reports on the DPJ, and ARIMA(0,1,0) for evaluation of the overall economy or economic conditions. I provide technical information in the appendix for interested readers.

To show how media reports and DPJ support are related to each other, estimates of cross-correlation between prewhitened news reports and filtered DPJ partisanship are graphically presented in figure 7.4. Intuitively speaking, this is a kind of Pearson's product-moment correlation between two variables over time. The height of the bars represents the size of correlations

9 For a detailed instruction in the context of a specific software program such as Stata, see McDowell (2002).

10 When a large break is not taken into account, it can inflate autocorrelation and lead to an erroneous conclusion.

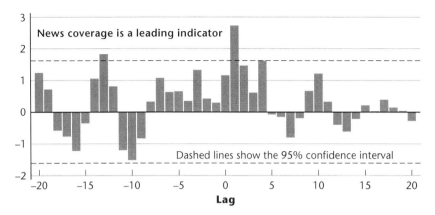

FIGURE 7.4 Cross-Correlation between Amount of News Coverage and DPJ Support
Sources: Jiji monthly polls and Yomiuri database.

between the prewhitened leading variable (news reports on the DPJ) and the filtered response variable (support for the DPJ).

In this case, statistically significant correlations appear at lags 1, 4, and -13. The lags at 1 and 4 indicate that when the number of news reports on the DPJ increases, the support rate for the DPJ follows with one- to four-month delays. However, it is unclear as to why cross-correlation is significant at lag -13. The implication is that the amount of press coverage on the DPJ increases 13 months after DPJ support increases in opinion polls, which does not make sense substantively. However, as the odds of a correlation being significant by coincidence are 1 out of 20 at the significance level of 0.95, I leave this result as it is for now. The most important finding here is that DPJ support responds to an increase in news reports on the DPJ with delays of one to four months, which is theoretically expected.

The same procedure is applied to the relationship between the evaluation of economic conditions and DPJ support. Cross-correlation between prewhitened economic conditions and the filtered DPJ support is also graphically presented below in figure 7.5. It is clear that these two variables are unrelated after taking account of temporal dynamics.

Having roughly identified the interrelationship between variables through a piece-by-piece procedure, we then combine these elements into a single regression format. In order to model a step-by-step pattern of rising and falling support for the DPJ, dummy variables are constructed for national elections. For example, for the 2003 lower-house election, the dummy variable is 0 through October 2003 but 1 from November 2003. It is constructed as a permanent change (. . . 0 0 0 0 1 1 1 1 . . .) rather than a pulse.

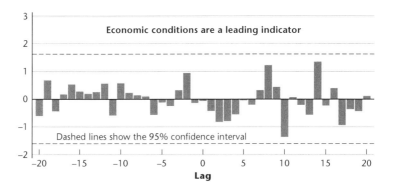

FIGURE 7.5 Cross-Correlation between National
Economic Conditions and DPJ Support
Source: Jiji monthly poll.

The 2007 upper-house election is coded as a permanent change. However, for elections that did not produce a lasting increase but only a short-term boost—namely, the upper-house elections of 1998 and 2004—the dummy variable is coded as a pulse (. . . o o o o I o o o o . . .). Because the dynamics of party support may have been altered after the change of government, I analyze support for the DPJ as an opposition party and support for the DPJ as a governing party separately. Estimates from the time-series regression model are shown in table 7.1.

The first column shows the estimates when the impact of national elections is taken into account. Both the 2003 lower-house and the 2007 upper-house elections elevated the support rate for the DPJ by roughly 6 percentage points. By winning these two elections, the DPJ gained roughly 12 percentage points in mass political support, a significant political change. However, the 1998 upper-house and the 2000 lower-house elections, which are modeled as pulses, registered 3 percentage-point temporary boosts. The 2004 upper-house election recorded close to a 6 percentage-point temporary increase. The model is adequately specified as the Ljung-Box Q (chi-square) test of residual autocorrelation failed to reject the null hypothesis of no serial correlation for 12 and 24 lags, respectively.

The second column displays the main findings in this chapter. After taking account of "shocks" produced by national elections, we find that the amount of news reporting on the DPJ still influences its support in the subsequent few months. If the number of news items increases by 50, DPJ support rises by 0.5 percentage points in the next month, but the effects linger on through the fourth month. After the 2007 upper-house election, the number

TABLE 7.1

Time-Series Regression on DPJ Support Rates (October 1996–August 2009)

	(1)	(2)	(3)	(4)
1998 Upper-House Election (pulse)	3.154*	3.105	3.123	3.218
	(1.338)	(1.787)	(1.984)	(2.227)
2000 General Election (pulse)	3.670**	3.540**	3.558**	3.448**
	(0.601)	(0.653)	(0.672)	(0.666)
2004 Upper-House Election (pulse)	5.739**	5.538**	5.492**	5.757**
	(0.433)	(0.425)	(0.428)	(0.450)
2003 General Election (step)	5.659**	5.305**	5.332**	5.358**
	(0.705)	(0.671)	(0.670)	(0.669)
2007 Upper-House Election (step)	5.668**	3.956**	3.797**	3.945**
	(0.832)	(0.614)	(0.685)	(0.616)
News Reports on DPJ at month t		0.005	0.005	0.005*
		(0.002)	(0.002)	(0.002)
News Reports on DPJ at month t-1		0.009**	0.009**	0.009**
		(0.003)	(0.003)	(0.003)
News Reports on DPJ at month t-2		0.004	0.004	0.004
		(0.003)	(0.003)	(0.003)
News Reports on DPJ at month t-3		0.004	0.003	0.004
		(0.003)	(0.003)	(0.003)
News Reports on DPJ at month t-4		0.009**	0.008*	0.009**
		(0.003)	(0.003)	(0.003)
Cabinet Approval			−0.017	0.008
Level in the 3rd column, first difference in the 4th column			(0.018)	(0.013)
Evaluation of the National Economy			−0.006	0.029
Level in the 3rd column, first difference in the 4th column			(0.019)	(0.023)
AR(1) of DPJ support	0.727**	0.686**	0.683**	0.691**
	(0.061)	(0.065)	(0.066)	(0.065)
Constant	4.504**	1.239	1.980	1.158
	(0.571)	(1.242)	(1.414)	(0.078)
Observations	155	151	151	151

Notes: Standard errors in parentheses; ** significant at 0.01; * significant at 0.05 in two-sided test.

Ljung-Box Q-test for residual autocorrelation				
Q(12)	16.14	16.06	15.81	14.58
Q(24)	34.28	34.66	35.44	34.06

Source: Jiji monthly poll.

of articles on the DPJ in *Yomiuri* rose sharply to roughly 200 per month and DPJ support rose as well. Increased press coverage makes a substantial difference in the support rate for the DPJ in monthly opinion polls. A high support rate partly depends on the flow of political information through the mass media.

The third and fourth columns demonstrate that the impact arising from the media is not an artifact of omitting cabinet approval under LDP governments or evaluations of national economic conditions. In the third column, cabinet approval and evaluations of the economy in their original scales are added to the regression equation but produce practically no effect at all on the DPJ's support rate while in the opposition. The impacts of national elections and news coverage remain intact as well. In the fourth column, the first differences of cabinet approval and economic evaluations are tested in place of their original scales, but this also makes little difference.

These results clearly show that cabinet approval and economic conditions do not influence DPJ support directly. The relationship between cabinet approval and support for opposition parties may need some elaboration, because this link has received scant academic attention in the past. People make judgments on political parties based on what they know, which is why the amount of news coverage makes a difference for opposition parties. Information delivered through the mass media enables individuals to assess political parties, and yet the link between attitudes toward a cabinet and attitudes toward an opposition party is tenuous. News reports on cabinets certainly have an impact on support for the governing party, because people easily recognize the relationship between a cabinet and the governing party. However, reporters rarely frame a story negatively for a cabinet and positively for the opposition in a single article. Thus, it is not surprising that cabinet approval had no influence on DPJ support when the party was in opposition. The same logic applies to the influence of the economy on support for the DPJ. Because the DPJ did not have any policy means to control the economy, we do not expect to find a link between economic conditions and support for the DPJ within the aggregated opinion polls.

However, this disconnect implies that opposition parties are unable to take advantage of dismal cabinet approval rates or unfavorable economic conditions that beleaguer the governing party. A malfunctioning cabinet may diminish support for the governing party, but voters' images of opposition parties will not necessarily improve. Similarly, recessions are most likely to hurt the government, but their impact is asymmetrical and does not enhance support for the opposition. Thus, it is only through an increase of press coverage that an opposition party can extend its popular support base, because only the mass media can deliver the news on its legislative and electoral activities to the electorate. As demonstrated by the Japan Socialist Party in 1989, an opposition party may benefit from protest votes cast in a backlash against a ruling party, but it will not hold on to those voters if it fades from public view.

Having demonstrated the model of DPJ partisanship during its opposition period, I now turn to popular support for the DPJ as a governing party, albeit in brief. The question is whether the rate of DPJ support is connected to shifts in cabinet approval ratings and evaluations of national economic conditions after the DPJ took control of the government. Figure 7.6 shows cabinet approval levels and support for the DPJ from September 2009 through December 2011.[11] Though cabinet approval ratings are much more volatile than support for the DPJ, there is a similarity in the trajectories of the two time series. It is also apparent that support for the DPJ declined after it lost the majority in the upper house, although the decline became apparent in the Jiji polls three months after the election. This delayed response can be attributed to the fact that the Diet was in session for only eight days after the July 2010 upper-house election and did not reopen until October. So the decline of DPJ partisanship started when it was confronted by an opposition with a larger share of seats in the Diet.

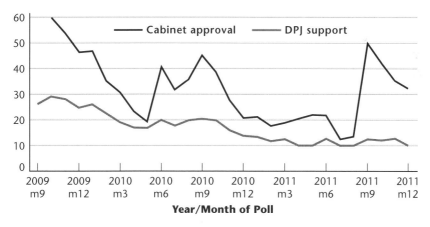

FIGURE 7.6 Approval for the DPJ Cabinet and Support for the DPJ
Source: Jiji monthly poll.

11 Cabinet approval for September 2009 is omitted, because Yukio Hatoyama had not yet become prime minister. During the interview period for September 2009, the Aso cabinet (LDP) was serving as caretaker.

The same time-series regression model for the DPJ in opposition is applied to the support for the DPJ as a governing party. Only the amount of news reporting on the DPJ with a one-month lag is included in the estimation, due to the limited time period. The 2010 upper-house election is included as a step variable. Otherwise, the model is essentially the same as the one in table 7.1. Table 7.2 shows the results.

Because the time series is very short, this result should not be taken too seriously.[12] However, the amount of news reporting on the DPJ in the previous month is no longer statistically significant. On the other hand, cabinet approval now exercises influence on DPJ support. When cabinet approval falls 30 percentage points, from 60 to 30, it leads to a 3.0 percentage-point

TABLE 7.2

Time-Series Regression on DPJ Support Rates
(September 2009–December 2011)

2010 Upper-House Election (Step)	−1.043
	(7.551)
News Reports on DPJ at month t-1	0.001
	(0.007)
Cabinet Approval (Original Level)	0.134**
	(0.028)
△Evaluation of Economic Conditions (the first difference)	−0.013
	(0.036)
AR(1) of DPJ support	0.967**
	(0.081)
Constant	13.630*
	(5.696)
Observations	27

Notes: Standard errors in parentheses; ** significant at 0.01; * significant at 0.05 in two-sided test.

Ljung-Box Q-test for residual autocorrelation		
	Q(12)	11.84
	Q(24)	20.60

Source: Jiji monthly poll.

12 An autocorrelation coefficient closest to 1 implies that differencing may be required for DPJ support. However, because this time series is too short for serious time-series analysis, I simply replicate the model for DPJ support as an opposition party.

decline in DPJ support. While it does not sound like a massive shift, the average DPJ support during the Kan cabinet was 14.6 percent. Thus, on average, dissatisfaction with the cabinet made 20 percent of supporters abandon the DPJ. Considering the influence of media polling in Japanese politics these days, cabinet approval ratings have a nontrivial impact.

Discussion

This paper has demonstrated that support for the DPJ developed through two crucial victories in national elections and has been sustained by a constant supply of information regarding the DPJ through news reports in the mass media. Though I exclusively analyzed the impact of newspaper reporting levels, that does not mean that television and Internet sources are unimportant. Rather, a newspaper (specifically, *Yomiuri*) has been selected simply because it provides the most practical measure of the amount of information disseminated. While the amount of reporting on the DPJ is hard to compare across the various types of mass communication, it is likely that the other major newspapers and TV news programs follow a pattern similar to that of *Yomiuri*, because they rely on similar sources (Freeman 2000). The flow of information on political parties through the mass media significantly shapes the distribution of partisanship in the electorate. More specifically, when the DPJ was in opposition, the increase in news reports on the DPJ led to increased support for the DPJ in opinion polls.

This explanation is not limited to the case of the DPJ in opposition but should be applicable to other political parties in similar situations. LDP partisanship declined after it lost the 2009 lower-house election, largely due to its loss of prominence in the mass media. Because people are no longer as exposed to news about the LDP as they were when it was in government, they are less aware of what the LDP is doing at a particular moment. This diminished awareness makes them less likely to name the LDP as their party of choice during survey interviews.

The mass media in Japan try to be neutral and fair to different political parties (Kabashima, Takeshita, and Serikawa 2010, 172–73), but neutrality does not translate into equal space or time for each party. The governing party is a focus of news reports, and a sizable majority of news items is allocated to the government (Ishikawa 1990). Thus, there is a governing-party premium in news reporting, which in turn contributes to a bonus in support rates for the governing party in opinion polls (Maeda 2011). It is no wonder that LDP support declined after, not before, its defeat in the 2009 lower-house election.

The same story can be applied to the rise and fall of other political parties. For example, support for the Social Democratic Party of Japan (SDPJ)—the fast-shrinking successor of the Japan Socialist Party—is very low, hovering around 1 percent in various opinion polls. However, it jumped up to 3 or 4 percentage points when it broke up the coalition with the DPJ due to disagreement over the American military bases in Okinawa Prefecture. However, the SDPJ enjoyed higher support only briefly. In Kyodo News opinion polls, the SDPJ had the support of 4.5 percent of respondents immediately after it left the coalition at the end of May 2010 but support went back to less than 1 percent by the end of August as its news coverage shrank. Thus, two to four months are long enough for people to lose links between widely reported political events and their choice of political parties in interviews. These lags of four months are not very different from the estimates obtained in this chapter. It is very difficult for an opposition party to maintain media coverage through its own efforts. The case of the DPJ in opposition was unusual in one respect: It gained recognition as a serious contender for power against the LDP after the 2003 election and held a majority in the upper house after the 2007 election, which led to an unusual amount of media coverage as an opposition party. The extensive media coverage was necessary to sustain a high support rate in opinion polls.

After it took over the government, DPJ support was strongly linked to cabinet approval, as expected, while LDP support was decoupled from cabinet approval. I suspect that the LDP support rate became a function of the amount of news coverage that it received, as once was the case for the DPJ. The situation is exactly reversed for the two parties. People tend not to choose a party in opinion interviews unless they know what a particular party stands for or what it is actually doing on the national political scene. For the parties in opposition, the amount of news devoted to them is crucial in cultivating support among the electorate. This chapter demonstrated the role of mass media in shaping public support for opposition parties. Without understanding the dynamics between the mass media and public opinion, one cannot understand how parties in opposition gain followers in the electorate.

Appendix D

Procedure for extracting news on the DPJ from the database; Time-Series Diagnoses

Keyword: 民主党（*Minshutō*, Democratic Party of Japan)[13]

Sources: Newspapers distributed in the Tokyo area (both morning and evening editions)

News items under the following classifications: "Politics," "First page," "Second page," "Third page," "First page in evening," "Second page in evening," "Third page in evening"

13 The term 民主党 is also used to refer to the U.S. Democratic Party. To eliminate these references, all the news items under the classification "international" are removed. Some news on the U.S. Democratic Party still remains after this filter, but I do not think it distorts the measurement in a systematic way.

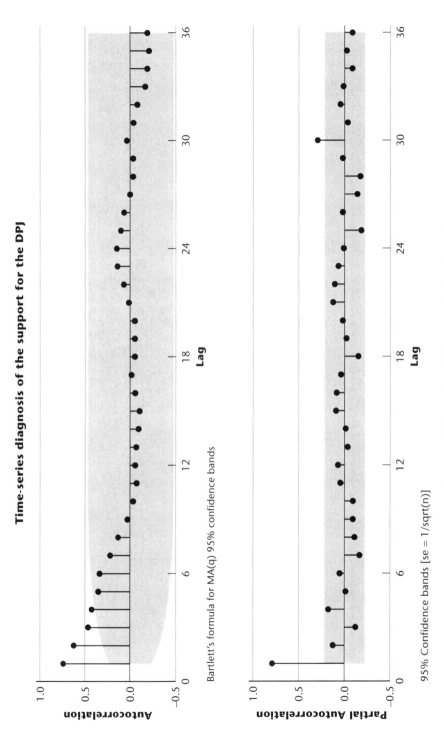

FIGURE D.1 Autocorrelation and Partial Autocorrelation of DPJ Support

TABLE D.1

Estimates of the DPJ Support Rate (1996.10–2003.10)

	ARIMA(1,0,0)	ARIMA(0,1,0)	ARIMA(0,0,1)	ARIMA(1,1,0)	ARIMA(1,0,1)	ARIMA(0,1,1)	ARIMA(1,1,1)	ARIMA(2,0,0)
constant	4.782	0.055	4.657	0.048	4.796	0.047	0.034	4.799
	(0.743)	(0.153)	(0.300)	(0.138)	(0.830)	(0.127)	(0.023)	(0.851)
AR(1)	0.776			−0.215	0.819		0.754	0.692
	(0.091)			(0.127)	(0.107)		(0.093)	(0.154)
AR(2)								0.108
								(0.151)
MA(1)			0.521		−0.108	−0.228	−1.000	
			(0.112)		(0.175)	(0.112)	(1180.099)	
sigma	1.226	1.294	1.519	1.264	1.221	1.264	1.211	1.219
	(0.069)	(0.075)	(0.100)	(0.074)	(0.077)	(0.074)	(714.618)	(0.076)
N	84	84	84	84	84	84	84	84
ll	−136.78	−140.83	−154.48	−138.91	−136.43	−138.91	−136.55	−136.32
aic	279.56	285.66	314.96	283.81	280.86	283.82	281.11	280.64
bic	286.85	290.52	322.25	291.10	290.58	291.12	290.83	290.37
Q(6)	10.17	14.74	65.24	8.60	8.17	8.88	9.68	7.37
Q(12)	13.10	17.84	68.67	12.87	11.68	13.38	12.92	10.78
Q(24)	21.36	25.61	75.54	24.13	21.77	24.64	20.80	20.58

Shaded cells indicate the null hypothesis of white noise is rejected at the 0.05 level.

Dickey-Fuller test for unit root for DPJ in different periods:

1996.10–2003.10 (85 months)   Z(t) = −2.978 p-value is 0.0370
2003.11–2007.08 (46 months)   Z(t) = −3.608 p-value is 0.0056
2007.09–2009.08 (25 months)   Z(t) = −3.265 p-value is 0.0165

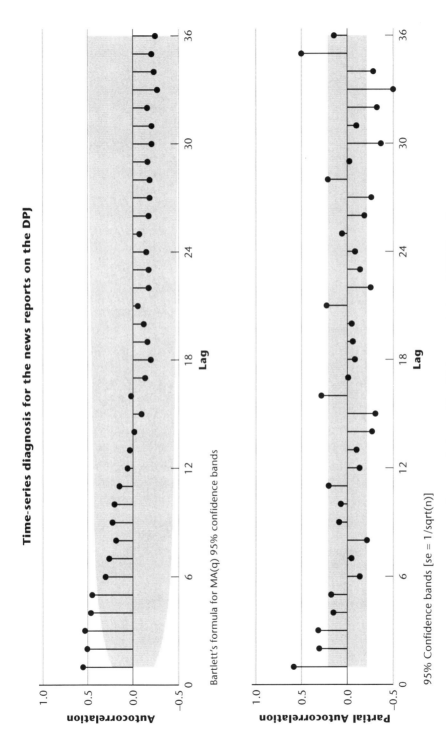

FIGURE D.2 Autocorrelation and Partial Autocorrelation of DPJ News Reports

TABLE D.2

Estimates of DPJ News Reports (1996.10–2003.10)

	ARIMA(1,0,0)	ARIMA(0,1,0)	ARIMA(0,0,1)	ARIMA(1,1,0)	ARIMA(1,0,1)	ARIMA(0,1,1)	ARIMA(1,1,1)	ARIMA(2,0,0)
constant	113.977	1.75	113.778	1.422	109.027	1.076	1.086	113.468
	(8.024)	(3.959)	(5.345)	(2.548)	(19.178)	(1.160)	(1.204)	(11.223)
AR(1)	0.57			−0.448	0.944		−0.071	0.406
	(0.087)			(0.100)	(0.058)		(0.180)	(0.107)
AR(2)								0.296
								(0.122)
MA(1)			0.425		−0.625	−0.674	−0.641	
			(0.112)		(0.137)	(0.092)	(0.149)	
sigma	31.938	35.409	34.156	31.868	29.385	29.319	29.279	30.633
	(2.597)	(2.439)	(2.997)	(2.170)	(2.165)	(2.225)	(2.228)	(2.370)
N	84	84	84	84	84	84	84	84
ll	−410.35	−418.82	−415.89	−410.07	−403.62	−403.26	−403.16	−406.93
aic	826.71	841.63	837.78	826.15	815.23	812.53	814.33	821.87
bic	834.00	846.50	845.07	833.44	824.95	819.82	824.05	831.59
Q(6)	10.89	20.04	35.49	13.71	4.72	4.32	4.21	8.24
Q(12)	15.22	26.17	45.33	17.55	7.70	8.59	8.79	10.33
Q(24)	32.53	53.81	64.05	43.89	23.43	25.52	26.13	28.57

Shaded cells indicate the null hypothesis of white noise is rejected at the 0.05 level.

Dickey-Fuller test for unit root for the news reports on the DPJ in different periods:

1996.10 − 2003.10 (85 months) $Z(t) = -4.583$ p-value is 0.0001
2003.11 − 2007.08 (46 months) $Z(t) = -3.549$ p-value is 0.0068
2007.09 − 2009.08 (25 months) $Z(t) = -2.352$ p-value is 0.1558

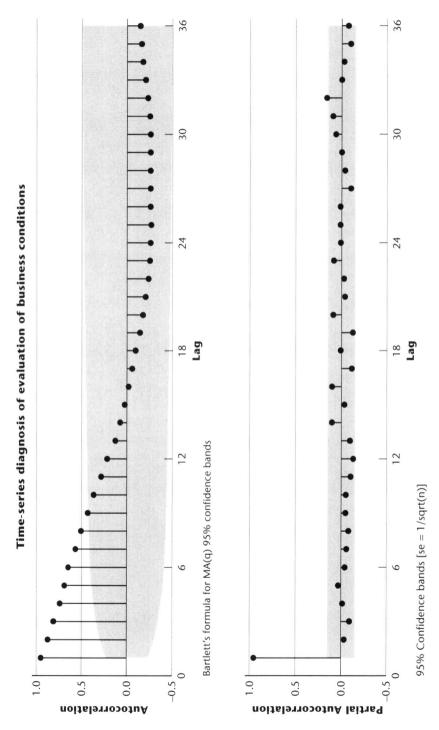

FIGURE D.3 Autocorrelation of Negative Evaluation of Business

TABLE D.3

Estimates of the Evaluation of Business Conditions (1996.10–2011.12)

	ARIMA(1,0,0)	ARIMA(0,1,0)	ARIMA(0,0,1)	ARIMA(1,1,0)	ARIMA(1,0,1)	ARIMA(0,1,1)	ARIMA(1,1,1)	ARIMA(2,0,0)
constant	36.402	0.114	37.522	0.114	36.447	0.114	0.112	36.459
t	(6.705)	(0.413)	(1.404)	(0.434)	(6.638)	(0.434)	(0.411)	(6.599)
AR(1)	0.941			0.006	0.937		−0.996	0.978
	(0.027)			(0.062)	(0.030)		(0.058)	(0.064)
AR(2)								(0.040)
								(0.063)
MA(1)			0.783		0.035	0.005	0.985	
			(0.051)		(0.069)	(0.062)	(0.101)	
sigma	5.225	5.296	9.743	5.297	5.222	5.296	5.262	5.221
	(0.211)	(0.214)	(0.614)	(0.218)	(0.218)	(0.218)	(0.250)	(0.219)
N	182	182	182	182	182	182	182	182
ll	−560.26	−561.65	−673.05	−561.64	−560.15	−561.64	−560.67	−560.12
aic	1126.53	1127.29	1352.10	1129.28	1128.29	1129.28	1129.35	1128.24
bic	1136.14	1133.70	1361.71	1138.90	1141.11	1138.90	1142.16	1141.06
Q(6)	1.58	1.36	435.22	1.35	1.31	1.35	1.72	1.27
Q(12)	3.65	2.76	561.34	2.74	3.36	2.74	3.74	3.33
Q(24)	17.43	16.02	607.38	15.98	16.88	15.98	16.40	16.76

Shaded cells indicate the null hypothesis of white noise is rejected at the 0.05 level.

Dickey-Fuller test for unit root for evaluation of business conditions:
1996.10–2011.12 (183 months)   Z(t) = −2.429   p-value is 0.1338

References

Anderson, Christopher. 1995. *Blaming the Government: Citizens and the Economy in Five European Democracies*. New York: M.E. Sharpe.

Bisgaard, Søren, and Murat Kulahci. 2011. *Time Series Analysis and Forecasting by Example*. Hoboken, NJ: Wiley.

Box-Steffensmeier, Janet M., and Renée M. Smith. 1996. "The Dynamics of Aggregate Partisanship." *American Political Science Review* 90 (3): 567–80.

Campbell, Angus, Philip E. Converse, Warren E. Miller, and Donald E. Stokes. 1960. *The American Voter*. New York: Wiley.

Erikson, Robert S., Michael MacKuen, and James A. Stimson. 2002. *The Macro Polity*. Cambridge: Cambridge University Press.

Freeman, Laurie Anne. 2000. *Closing the Shop: Information Cartels and Japan's Mass Media*. Princeton, NJ: Princeton University Press.

Green, Donald, Bradley Palmquist, and Eric Schickler. 2004. *Partisan Hearts and Minds*. New Haven, CT: Yale University Press.

Ikeda, Kenichi. 1992. "Naikaku Shijiritsu No Hensen" [Changes in cabinet approval]. In *Nihon No Seitou to Naikaku: 1981–91*, edited by Jiji Tsushin and Chuo Chosa. Tokyo: Jiji Tsushin.

Inoguchi, Takashi. 1981. "Naikaku Shijiritsu No Hensen (Bunseki)" [Changes in party support (analysis)]. In *Sengo Nihon No Seito to Naikaku*, edited by Jiji Tsushin. Tokyo: Jiji Tsushin.

———. 1983. *Gendai Nihon Seiji Keizai No Kouzu: Seifu to Shijo* [Contemporary Japanese political economy: Government and market]. Tokyo: Toyo Keizai.

Ishikawa, Masumi. 1990. "Media—*Kenryoku He No Eikyouryoku to Kenryoku Kara No Eikyoryoku*" [Media's impact—"to the powers that be" to "from the powers that be"]. *Leviathan* (7): 30–48.

Kabashima, Ikuo, Toshio Takeshita, and Yoichi Serikawa. 2010. *Media to Seiji, Kaiteiban* [Media and politics, revised edition]. Tokyo: Yuhikaku.

Kernell, Samuel. 1978. "Explaining Presidential Popularity: How Ad Hoc Theorizing, Misplaced Emphasis, and Insufficient Care in Measuring One's Variables Refuted Common Sense and Led Conventional Wisdom Down the Path of Anomalies." *American Political Science Review* 72 (2): 506–22.

Kinder, Donald R., and D. Roderick Kiewiet. 1979. "Economic Discontent and Political Behavior: The Role of Personal Grievances and Collective Economic Judgments in Congressional Voting." *American Journal of Political Science* 23 (3): 495–527.

Lebo, Matthew, and Helmut Norpoth. 2011. "Yes, Prime Minister: The Key to Forecasting British Elections." *Electoral Studies* 30 (2): 258–63.

Lipset, Seymour Martin, and Stein Rokkan. 1967. "Cleavage Structures, Party Systems, and Voter Alignments: An Introduction." In *Party Systems and Voter Alignments*, edited by Seymour Martin Lipset and Stein Rokkan, 1–64. New York: Free Press.

MacKuen, Michael B., Robert S. Erikson, and James A. Stimson. 1989. "Macropartisanship." *American Political Science Review* 83 (4): 1125–1142.

Maeda, Yukio. 2005. "Jiji Tsushin Sha Yoron Chosa Ni Miru Naikaku Shijiritsu No Suii 1989–2004" [Changes in cabinet approval in Jiji monthly opinion polls]. *Chuo Chosa Hou* (569): 1–9.

———. 2011. "Minsyutou Shijiritsu No Seicho to Antei" [The developmennt of DPJ support]. In *Minsyuto No Soshiki to Seisaku: Ketto Kara Seikenkotai Made*, edited by Takayoshi Uekami and Hidenori Tsusumi. Tokyo: Toyo Keizai.

McCleary, Richard, and Richard Hay. 1980. *Applied Time Series Analysis for the Social Sciences*. Beverly Hills, CA: Sage Publications.

McDowall, David, Richard McCleary, Errol Meidinger, and Richard A. Hay Jr. 1980. *Interrupted Time Series Analysis*. Thousand Oaks, CA: Sage Publications.

McDowell, A. 2002. "From the Help Desk: Transfer Functions." *Stata Journal* 2 (1): 71–85.

Miyake, Ichiro. 1991. "Type of Partisanship, Partisan Attitudes, and Voting Choices." In *The Japanese Voter*, edited by Scott C. Flanagan, Shinsaku Kohei, Ichiro Miyake, Bradley M. Richardson, and Joji Watanuki, 226–264. New Haven, CT: Yale University Press.

Miyake, Ichiro, Yoshitaka Nishizawa, and Masaru Kouno. 2001. *55 Nen-Taiseika No Seiji to Keizai* [Politics and economics under the party system of 1955]. Tokyo: Bokutaku.

Mueller, John E. 1970. "Presidential Popularity from Truman to Johnson." *American Political Science Review* 64 (1): 18–34.

Nakamura, Estuhiro. 2006. "Tahenryou Choki Kioku Moderu Wo Mochiita Seitoshiji to Naikakushiji No Kankeisei No Bunnseki" [Analyzing the dynamic relationship between the cabinet support rate and the LDP support rate using the multivariate long memory model]. *Senkyogakkai Kiyou* (6): 107–26.

Nishizawa, Yoshitaka. 2001. "Jiminto Shiji to Keizai Gyoseki Hyoka" [The support for the LDP and economic evaluation]. In *55 Nen-Taiseika No Seiji to Keizai* [Politics and economics under the party system of 1955], edited by Ichiro Miyake, Yoshitaka Nishizawa, and Masaru Kohno, 121–38. Tokyo: Bokutaku.

Norpoth, Helmut. 1986. "Transfer Function Analysis." In *New Tools for Social Scientists: Advances and Applications in Research Methods*, edited by William Dale Berry and Michael S. Lewis-Beck, 241–273. Beverly Hills, CA: Sage Publications.

———. 1987a. "The Falklands War and Government Popularity in Britain: Rally without Consequence or Surge without Decline?" *Electoral Studies* 6 (1): 3–16.

———. 1987b. "Guns and Butter and Government Popularity in Britain." *American Political Science Review* 81 (3): 949–59.

Norpoth, Helmut, Michael S. Lewis-Beck, and Jean-Dominique Lafay. 1991. *Economics and Politics: The Calculus of Support*. Ann Arbor: University of Michigan Press.

Sakaiya, Shiro. 2006. *Seijiteki Joho to Senkyo Katei* [Political information and electoral process]. Tokyo: Bokutaku.

Vandaele, Walter. 1983. *Applied Time Series and Box-Jenkins Models*. New York: Academic Press.

Yomiuri Shimbun Tokyo Honsha Yoronchosabu. 2004. *Nidaiseitou Jidai No Akebono: Heisei No Seiji to Sennkyo* [The beginning of the era of the two-party system]. Tokyo: Bokutaku.

Domestic Policy

8 A Casualty of Political Transformation?

THE POLITICS OF ENERGY EFFICIENCY IN THE
JAPANESE TRANSPORTATION SECTOR

Phillip Y. Lipscy

The Democratic Party of Japan (DPJ) came to power in 2009 promising significant transportation-sector reform, but it has struggled to implement its
proposals. I argue that the DPJ's initiatives faltered due to the legacy of *efficiency clientelism*. Historically, Japanese transportation policy combined two
imperatives: (1) to encourage efficiency by raising the cost of energy-inefficient
transportation, and (2) to redistribute benefits to supporters of the incumbent
Liberal Democratic Party (LDP). Because of the legacy of efficiency clientelism,
DPJ campaign pledges—designed to appeal broadly to the general public by
reducing transportation costs—ran up against the prospect of sharp declines in
revenue and energy efficiency. Efficiency clientelism was well suited to political
realities in Japan prior to the 1990s, but recent developments have undercut
its viability. This raises profound questions about the sustainability of Japan's
energy-efficiency achievements.

I would like to thank Steph Haggard, Ethan Scheiner, participants at the conference
"Political Change in Japan" at Stanford University in February 2011, and two anonymous reviewers for excellent feedback. I also thank Yasuhiro Daisho, Akihiko Hoshi,
Takashi Naono, and Lee Schipper, as well as members of the following organizations
who were exceedingly generous with their time and resources: METI, MLIT, IEEJ, JARI,
and NTSEL. The broader project of which this chapter is a part has benefited greatly
from the support and generosity of Sakurako and William Fisher, the Japan Foundation
Center for Global Partnership, the FSI Takahashi Fund, the Japan Fund at Stanford
University, Shorenstein APARC, and the UPS Endowment Fund. Excellent research as-
sistance was provided at various stages by Siddharth Bellur, Rosalind Boone, Kimberly
Cheng, Lily Guo, Colleen Jiang, Jun Jiang, Erica Kang, Jared Poelman, Zheng Wu, and
Cathy Zhu. This chapter was originally published in the *Journal of East Asian Studies*,
Vol. 12, #3. Copyright © 2012 by the East Asia Institute. Used with permission by Lynne
Rienner Publishers, Inc.

Since the early 2000s, the Democratic Party of Japan (DPJ) has placed heavy emphasis on transportation-sector reform. In its first campaign manifesto, published in preparation for the 2003 lower-house election, the DPJ proposed to eliminate highway tolls, abolish government funds earmarked for road construction, and drastically reduce taxes related to automobile ownership (Democratic Party of Japan 2003). The 169th Diet session held in 2008 became known as Gasoline Kokkai (gasoline Diet), because the DPJ maneuvered aggressively for a reduction of the gasoline tax.[1] The DPJ came to power in 2009 campaigning on a platform that heavily emphasized transportation-sector reform. For example, in the 2009 DPJ manifesto, measures related to transportation constituted 23 percent of projected costs associated with policy proposals through FY 2013, and were second only to the child allowance, which accounted for 49 percent.[2]

In light of the DPJ's enthusiasm for transportation reform as a minority party, it is striking how little change occurred once the party came to power. The gasoline tax, the subject of a heated showdown with the LDP in 2008, was retained in all but name and was replaced with a CO_2 tax that left gasoline prices virtually unchanged. Plans to eliminate highway tolls were scaled back dramatically, with selective reductions occurring in 2010 on an experimental basis, followed by cancellation of the program in 2011 in order to raise revenue for reconstruction following the Tohoku earthquake.[3] Plans to eliminate various taxes associated with automobile ownership were reconsidered, with the automobile acquisition tax retained at status quo levels and the weight tax reduced modestly.[4]

What accounts for this puzzling pattern of DPJ policymaking in the transportation sector? Popular and media accounts have mostly focused on factors such as lack of leadership and the shortcomings of key individuals such as Hatoyama Yukio, Maehara Seiji, and Ozawa Ichiro.[5] Such factors undoubtedly played a role in muddling the decision-making process of the

---

1 The DPJ was able to force a temporary expiration of the *zantei ze* (temporary tax) in April 2008 due to its control of the upper house and parliamentary rules that forbade the lower house from overturning upper-house decisions for 60 days.

2 Calculated from the table on pp. 6–7 of *Democratic Party of Japan* (2009).

3 An exception was made for the Tohoku region through March 2012 and for those displaced by the nuclear accident in Fukushima through September 2012.

4 Although the precise rate depends on automobile class and type, the reduction was about 20 percent for a typical compact vehicle. For more detail, see "Heisei 22 nendo zeisei kaikaku ni tomonau jidosha juryo zei no henko ni tsuite," www.mlit.go.jp/common/000111305.pdf.

5 For example, see Yamazaki (2010); Mulgan (2010); and "Flip-Flop on Highway Tolls," *Asahi Shimbun*, April 24, 2010.

DPJ once in office. However, in this chapter, I analyze the DPJ's transportation policies from a broader perspective, focusing on political changes over the past two decades (Lipscy and Scheiner 2012) and historical patterns of Japanese transportation policymaking.

More specifically, I argue that Japanese efficiency policies in the post–oil shocks period often followed a predictable pattern, which I call *efficiency clientelism*. Efficiency clientelism coupled the achievement of energy-efficiency goals—an important national prerogative for Japan after the 1970s oil shocks—with the political survival of the Liberal Democratic Party (LDP). Policies were implemented that were consistent with two outcomes: (1) imposing diffuse costs on the general population in the direction of encouraging greater energy conservation or energy efficiency, and (2) redistributing the revenues or economic rents attributable to higher costs in order to benefit narrow, organized supporters of ruling politicians.

Efficiency clientelism was effective precisely because of the symbiosis between energy-efficiency goals and Japan's postwar political arrangements—an electoral system that encouraged particularism over broad, public appeal (Rosenbluth 1989; Sakakibara 1991; Ramseyer and Rosenbluth 1993; McCubbins and Rosenbluth 1995; Scheiner 2005), LDP one-party dominance, and an elite bureaucracy with considerable autonomy and agenda-setting power (Johnson 1982; Okimoto 1990). However, these elements of postwar Japanese politics have weakened over the past two decades. Electoral reform in 1994 shifted the incentives of politicians from narrow targeting of interest groups toward broad, public appeal (Cox, Rosenbluth, and Thies 1999; Hirano 2006; Rosenbluth et al. 2009; McElwain 2012; Scheiner 2012). This has made it increasingly difficult to justify policies that generously benefited narrow groups such as rural residents and infrastructure-related industries at the expense of the general transportation user. The bureaucracy, which has played an important role in designing and implementing energy-efficiency measures, has been severely delegitimized by repeated scandals (Pharr 2000; Ozeki 2009), and administrative reforms have gradually shifted power in favor of politicians. Finally, the DPJ emerged as a serious, credible competitor of the LDP and took over the reins of power in 2009 (McElwain 2012). In effect, important underpinnings of Japanese energy efficiency in the transportation sector have been undermined by political changes over the past two decades.

Ironically, the elements that made efficiency clientelism effective prior to political transformation also became a liability as the DPJ gained power. As a minority party, the DPJ targeted its message to Japan's new electoral realities by adopting policy positions designed to appeal broadly to the general public. In the transportation sector, this meant attacking traditional mechanisms that raised costs and delivered benefits to core LDP supporters. However, once in power, the DPJ was confounded by the "efficiency" dimension of efficiency clientelism; dismantling status quo policy arrangements in the transportation sector would lead to a sharp deterioration in energy efficiency. This dilemma put the DPJ in an awkward position. On the one hand, the DPJ appealed to the environmentalist sensibilities of its urban support base by advocating steep reductions in CO_2 emissions. On the other hand, policy measures such as the elimination of highway tolls and gasoline taxes would lead to greater transportation activity and fossil fuel consumption, increasing pollution and emissions.[6] This conundrum forced the DPJ to scale back and ultimately abandon its core policy objectives in the transportation sector.

DPJ transportation policymaking was constrained by two additional factors attributable to the evolution of Japanese politics over the past two decades (Lipscy and Scheiner 2012). First, in recent years, the policy positions of the LDP and DPJ have moved toward convergence, motivated by an electoral system that emphasizes the preferences of the median voter (Scheiner 2012; McElwain 2012). By the time the DPJ came to power, LDP reformists had partially implemented several of the DPJ's transportation initiatives, eliminating some low-hanging fruit and limiting the scope for DPJ reform once in office. Particularly important was the 2008 decision by LDP prime minister Fukuda Takeo to transfer transportation revenues from the Road Improvement Special Account to the general account budget. This severed the explicit connection between transportation taxes and redistribution to traditional LDP supporters; any reduction in transportation taxes under a DPJ government would directly impact general revenues. Consequently, the DPJ's transportation reform initiatives encountered strong intraparty resistance from budget hawks and the Ministry of Finance.

Second, each major party in Japan remains internally divided, due to disincentives against switching parties (Scheiner 2012), and organized, particularly local, interest groups continue to exert important influence over national-level policymaking vis-à-vis both parties (Shimizu 2012). As I discuss in this chapter, the DPJ's plans for highway tolls came under heavy intraparty contestation during the implementation process, not only from budget hawks, but also from politicians closely tied to labor unions of alternative transportation industries. These groups feared the adverse effects of cost advantages gained by automobile transportation. The DPJ's highway toll plan was modified repeatedly to accommodate such interests.

---

6 Kamioka (2010) provides an extensive technical treatment of this issue.

I proceed in my discussion as follows. In the next section, I present an overview of Japan's energy-efficiency policies and place them in historical and cross-national context. In particular, I illustrate that Japan's energy profile in the transportation sector stands out from that of its international peers. I then characterize the historical pattern of policymaking in Japan vis-à-vis transportation energy efficiency, which I call efficiency clientelism. A set of case studies follows, illustrating how efficiency clientelism promoted energy efficiency in Japan's transportation sector. I then discuss the DPJ's transportation policies in light of this historical context and political changes over the past two decades. I conclude with a discussion of the implications of this study for the future of energy-efficiency policymaking in Japan.

Japanese Energy Efficiency in Comparative Perspective

Since the oil shocks of the 1970s, Japan has been a global leader in energy efficiency. Japan's economy is extremely energy efficient based on a variety of measures such as energy intensity and CO_2 intensity, and Japanese energy-efficient technologies are among the most advanced in the world (Barrett and Therivel 1991; Barrett 2005). Cooperation on energy efficiency has also been a major Japanese foreign-policy objective. Japan has leveraged its strong record on energy efficiency by, among other things, taking an active role in facilitating international agreement on the Kyoto Protocol restricting CO2 emissions and promoting energy efficiency as a major component of its foreign aid program (Tanabe 1999; Seki 2002; Hamanaka 2006; Oki 2007; Ministry of the Environment 2007).

However, to date, the politics of Japanese energy efficiency has been an underexplored topic. Most existing accounts of Japanese policymaking in this area have focused on either energy security issues (Eguchi 1980; Samuels 1983; Nemetz, Vertinsky, and Vertinsky 1985; Kim and Shin 1986; Bobrow and Kudrle 1987; Samuels 1987; Hein 1990) or broader environmental policy (Simcock 1974; McKean 1981; Reed 1981; Iijima 1984; Reich 1984; Broadbent 1998; Tsuru 2000; Funabashi 2006; Miyauchi 2006; Nakazawa 2006; Terao and Otsuka 2007). Those analyses that do deal explicitly with energy efficiency tend to be descriptive in nature and focus on technical and engineering aspects of the issue rather than on political and policymaking processes (Nagata 1993; Kasahara et al. 2005; Ministry of Economy, Trade, and Industry (Japan) 2007; Wicaksono 2008; International Energy Agency, various years; Kiang and Schipper 1996).

Because energy efficiency is a multifaceted issue spanning multiple sectors, it is affected by a range of factors. It is worth emphasizing at the outset that I am not claiming that the theoretical account that follows is the only mechanism that has contributed to energy efficiency in Japan, or that it is even the most important one. Many factors account for Japan's relative efficiency, and several important policy initiatives fall outside the scope of this analysis. For example, Japan's stringent fuel economy standards owe a great deal to the interests of domestic automobile firms, which specialize in fuel-efficient automobiles and are therefore relatively supportive of strong regulatory standards compared to automobile firms in other countries. Close, frequent, and informal consultation between bureaucrats and private-sector actors allows for realistic regulatory measures that may be more difficult to implement in legalistic societies such as the United States (Lipscy 2009).

In addition, some factors unrelated to politics are also important contributors to Japanese energy efficiency (Kiang and Schipper 1996). For example, Japan's geography plays a role in making energy conservation measures feasible; with densely populated urban centers in relatively close proximity to each other, Japan is much more suited to high-speed rail transportation than more sprawling countries such as the United States or Canada.[7] Japan's climate is also relatively temperate, which implies less energy used for heating and cooling than in Russia or Singapore. Some observers also point to Japanese culture, which has purported advantages such as being more frugal, collectivist, or in tune with nature.[8]

In this chapter, I focus on energy efficiency in the transportation sector for several reasons. First, transportation reform has been a key policy platform of the DPJ and, more broadly, a major source of contention in Japanese politics in recent years. Second, because of the complex, multifaceted nature of energy efficiency, limiting the analysis to a single sector makes it more feasible to gather in-depth information from relevant databases and policymakers. Third, Japan clearly stands out in transportation-sector energy efficiency in several respects. The Japanese government often promotes the fact that Japan has maintained the most stringent fuel economy standards and consequently has the most fuel-efficient automobile fleet of any developed economy. However, Japan is somewhat weaker in actual, realized automobile energy efficiency, due to greater traffic congestion compared to other countries (Lipscy and Schipper 2013).

7 It is worth noting, however, that the degree of urban concentration is itself endogenous to policy choices over long time horizons. It is more feasible to live in suburban areas requiring long automobile commutes in the United States in part because automobile transportation is less costly than in Japan.

8 For example, Alexander Jacboy, "Japan's Culture Offers Hope for the Environment," *Japan Times*, April 28, 2007.

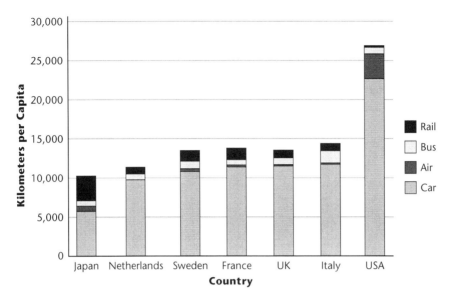

FIGURE 8.1 Passenger Kilometers per Capita by Travel Mode, 2007
Source: Various national sources.

Where Japan truly stands out is in aggregate distances traveled and transportation mode share (see figure 8.1).[9] Compared to other developed countries, a far greater percentage of Japanese transportation is accounted for by rail, which is generally the most energy-efficient mode of transportation currently available.[10] On a per-capita basis, automobiles account for a much lower share of passenger kilometers in Japan, even compared to countries with similar geographic and demographic characteristics. In addition, Japanese citizens travel shorter distances compared to their international peers. As figure 8.1 shows, on a per-capita, annualized basis, Japanese travel about 25 percent less than the French and 62 percent less than Americans.

There are good reasons to suspect that these transportation outcomes are at least partially a consequence of government policies. As illustrated in tables 8.1 and 8.2, highway tolls and taxation of automobiles in Japan have been maintained at extremely high levels compared to other countries. Travel is generally expensive in Japan regardless of mode share, and among

9 Although I have opted for simplicity here for the purpose of illustration, Japan stands out even after controlling for potentially confounding factors such as land area, population density, urbanization, climate, and level of development. A more detailed analysis is available in Lipscy (2011) and Lipscy and Schipper (2013).

10 In some cases, rail may be inferior to other modes if ridership is consistently low, as is sometimes the case in rural areas.

TABLE 8.1

Highway Tolls, 2002

	Japan	France	Italy	United States	United Kingdom	Germany
Toll highways (as a percentage of total)	100	74.8	86.2	8.9	0	0
Average toll (US$/km)	$0.21	$0.07	$0.05	n/a	n/a	n/a[a]

Source: Japan Public Highway Corporation.

Note: [a] Germany started imposing a toll only on trucks, equivalent to $0.12/km, in 2005.

TABLE 8.2

Automobile Taxation, 2002

	Japan	United Kingdom	France	Germany	United States
Tax per automobile (US$)	$5,800	$4,700	$3,750	$3,300	$1,500

Source: Japan Automobile Manufacturers Association.

Note: Assumes ownership for nine years, with the following vehicle characteristics: 1800 cc, 1100 kg, purchase price of 1.8 million yen.

modes, automobile travel is particularly costly in comparison to other developed economies. Naturally, this imposes both an income effect (less total travel) and a substitution effect (opting for nonautomobile travel) on the Japanese traveler. In sum, although factors such as geography and culture may make Japan particularly suited to energy conservation, government policies also stack the decks in favor of short travel distances and away from automobile transportation. The following section lays out my theoretical perspective on how Japanese political arrangements have facilitated this transportation profile.

Efficiency Clientelism in Japan

One important element of Japanese energy-efficiency policy that emerged after the 1970s oil shocks was what I call efficiency clientelism. In this section, I describe efficiency clientelism and how it contributed to the maintenance of overall energy efficiency in Japan. To be effective and sustainable, any policy measure promoting energy efficiency must be compatible with the political realities of the country in which it is implemented. Under efficiency clientelism, a policy measure has two principal effects: (1) it imposes diffuse costs on the general population in the direction of encouraging greater energy conservation or energy efficiency, and (2) it redistributes the revenues or economic rents attributable to higher costs to benefit narrow, organized supporters of the ruling politicians.

The first element of efficiency clientelism stems from Japan's experience in the 1970s oil shocks, which highlighted the country's dependence on foreign energy sources and consequent economic vulnerability. Japan's response was shaped by its political institutions, characterized by close cooperation between an elite bureaucracy, politicians, and private-sector actors (Johnson 1982; Samuels 1987; Okimoto 1990). Energy efficiency emerged as a centerpiece of Japan's response.[11] In recent years, an additional motivation has been provided by environmental concerns and Japan's international treaty obligations concerning CO_2 emissions reductions.

In the transportation sector, the Ministry of Land, Infrastructure, Transport, and Tourism (MLIT) has been primarily responsible for developing efficiency policies in coordination with the Ministry of Economy, Trade, and Industry (METI) and the Ministry of the Environment (MOE).[12] Since the 1970s, these bureaucracies have acted as important advocates for energy efficiency within the Japanese government, and bureaucrats have steered policy outcomes toward efficiency through their influence over specific regulatory design and enforcement.[13] Although the bureaucracy has advocated efficiency measures in part because of broader public policy considerations, there were also direct benefits for the bureaucrats themselves. Efficiency policy was frequently designed to facilitate *amakudari*—employment destinations for retired bureaucrats—by benefiting private firms and quasi-public institutions in closely related fields.[14]

Japan stands out cross-nationally in the emphasis placed on energy efficiency by the public bureaucracy as well as the historically influential role that bureaucrats have played in policy design and implementation. One indicator that underscores this point is the amount of public-sector resources devoted to energy efficiency. Figure 8.2 plots information from the Energy Charter Secretariat, which collects data on national energy-efficiency

---

11 Although Japan also pursued other strategies, such as source diversification and a buildup of nuclear energy, these are not directly relevant to transportation policy. For an early overview, see Samuels (1987, chapter 6).

12 Prior to administrative reorganization, the equivalent actors were the Ministry of Transport, the Ministry of Construction, the Ministry of International Trade and Industry, and the Environmental Agency.

13 Personal interview, MLIT official, June 10, 2011.

14 Inose (2008) provides a particularly incisive critique of these practices in the transportation sector.

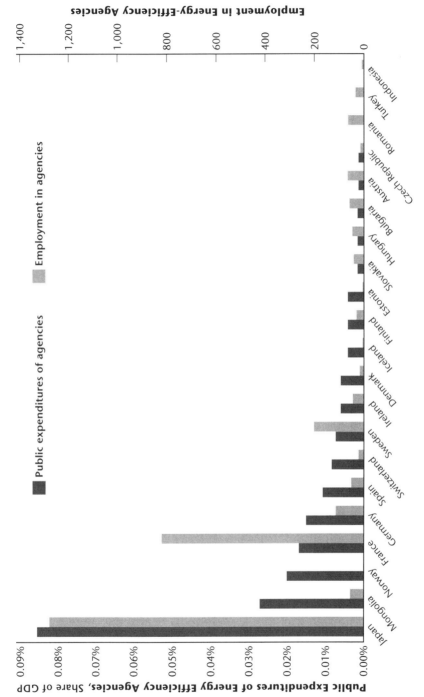

FIGURE 8.2 Energy Efficiency Spending and Employment by Government Agencies, 2005

Source: Energy Charter Secretariat.

agencies.[15] As the figure shows, Japan is virtually sui generis in terms of both spending per GDP and number of public employees devoted to energy efficiency–related activities. The only country that is somewhat comparable is France, which employs slightly more employees per capita than Japan but devotes considerably fewer public resources.

The second element of efficiency clientelism is largely consistent with clientelist models of Japanese politics (Curtis 1971; Scheiner 2005; Kitschelt 2000; Fukui and Fukai 1996; Woodall 1996; Richardson 1997). By its nature, transportation policy is wide ranging in its effects and is politicized. Virtually all citizens in developed countries utilize some form of motorized transportation in their daily lives. The provision and maintenance of transportation infrastructure requires considerable fiscal outlays and a large labor force, making it a common mechanism through which governments channel resources to preferred constituencies. For this reason, in Japan, as is customary elsewhere, politicians have played an important role in directing the allocation of transportation budgets to benefit their political supporters. This is exemplified by Tanaka Kakuei's *Nihon Retto Kaizo Keikaku* (Japan reforming plan), which emphasized the construction of road and rail infrastructure to promote the economic development of rural areas and also formed the basis for much of Japan's redistributive politics toward the end of the twentieth century (Tanaka 1972).

Japan's electoral system and fiscal centralization long favored policies designed to benefit particularistic interest groups at the expense of the general public (Rosenbluth 1989; Sakakibara 1991; Ramseyer and Rosenbluth 1993; McCubbins and Rosenbluth 1995; Scheiner 2005). These electoral incentives allowed governments under the LDP to impose high, diffuse costs on transportation use by the general public but nonetheless retain office by securing support from narrow, organized groups. As I illustrate in the next section, Japanese transportation policies frequently established a direct link between high costs for the general user, which encouraged energy conservation, and redistribution in favor of LDP constituents. Special accounts were established to channel revenues from transportation taxes toward favored groups such as rural residents and the construction industry. Onerous highway tolls on heavily utilized urban routes subsidized road construction and maintenance in rural areas. Exceptions to high costs, such as those for

15 There are some problems with this type of data, such as inherent ambiguity about what tasks certain agencies perform and which of their employees are devoted to energy efficiency, although the charter has attempted to account for this in their data collection. Japan's high numbers are primarily driven by METI and the New Energy and Industrial Technology Development Organization (NEDO).

lightweight vehicles, were designed to favor small-business owners and rural residents.

Efficiency clientelism as practiced in Japan developed incrementally over time as the incentives of politicians, constituencies, and bureaucrats lined up in favor of policies serving the dual objectives of energy efficiency and clientelistic redistribution. One illustrative example is the shinkansen bullet train network. The shinkansen predates energy-efficiency concerns, with the first route between Tokyo and Osaka completed in 1964. However, the expansion of the network came to be justified and defended on redistributive and efficiency grounds. The classic expression of the redistributive dimension was the expedited construction in 1982 of the Jōetsu Shinkansen, which connects Tokyo to Niigata, the home prefecture of Tanaka Kakuei. LDP politicians saw the shinkansen as a mechanism to revitalize rural economies, from which they drew a disproportionate share of their political support. However, expansion of the shinkansen network has also been promoted by the bureaucracy as a means to enhance energy efficiency and, in more recent years, reduction in CO_2 emissions, by shifting passenger volumes from less energy-efficient air and automobile travel.[16]

In sum, Japan's political institutions led to a pattern of policymaking that encouraged energy efficiency by diffusely raising the cost of inefficient transportation, while also redistributing resources to organized supporters of the LDP. In the following section, I examine several specific policy areas that illustrate how efficiency clientelism facilitated energy conservation in Japan.

Efficiency Clientelism in Practice

In this section, I illustrate how efficiency clientelism operated in practice by examining three policy areas: gasoline and automobile taxes, highway tolls, and subsidies for lightweight automobiles. Each of these policy areas illustrates a distinct mechanism through which efficiency clientelism operated: (1) taxation of energy inefficient automobile transportation, with revenues explicitly earmarked for activities that benefited LDP supporters; (2) the administration of expensive highway tolls through the creation of quasi-government monopolies, which redistributed toll revenues from urban to rural routes; and (3) subsidization of energy-efficient automobiles in a manner that disproportionately benefited rural residents. While the specific mechanisms varied, each of these policy measures met the dual objectives of efficiency clientelism: encouraging energy efficiency by the general transportation user while delivering asymmetrical benefits to core constituents of the LDP.

16 Personal interview, MLIT officials, September 22, 2010.

Gasoline and Automobile Taxes

Japan briefly experimented with a gasoline tax in the pre–World War II period, but the first continuous taxation policy was established in 1949 in the *Kihatsu Yuzeiho* (gasoline tax law).[17] In 1974, in the aftermath of the 1973 oil shock, the tax was increased on a *zantei* (temporary) basis to raise revenues and encourage the conservation of gasoline (Ministry of Land, Infrastructure, Transport, and Tourism 2002). Aside from the gasoline tax, Japan has imposed a variety of hefty, direct taxes on automobile ownership. All purchases of automobiles are subject to a vehicle acquisition tax of 3 percent. In addition, the *jidosha juryo zei*, or automobile weight tax, is assessed every three years. The weight tax was established in 1971 and was raised sharply during the oil shocks. Although the precise calculation of the tax is complex, a standard compact car is generally assessed 45,000 yen (US$600) every three years, with heavier (generally less energy-efficient) vehicles taxed at higher rates.

The revenues from these automobile-related taxes were specifically earmarked for clientelistic purposes.[18] All revenues from the temporary gasoline tax were designated to the Road Improvement Special Account, which benefited the construction industry and rural residents disproportionately by supporting expansion and maintenance of the road network. Similarly, three-fourths of the revenues from the automobile weight tax were assigned to the Road Improvement Special Account, and one-fourth was designated directly to local governments in rural areas (*shichoson*) (Ministry of Land, Infrastructure, Transport, and Tourism 2002).

These taxes proved durable because they served the dual purposes of energy conservation and redistribution of resources to rural residents and the construction industry. After the oil shocks, raising the cost of gasoline and automobile ownership was seen as an effective means to encourage energy conservation (Furukawa 2007). In more recent years, the taxes have been defended by environmentally oriented politicians and members of the bureaucracy on the grounds that they will help Japan reduce CO_2 emissions and meet its commitments under the Kyoto Protocol.[19] The taxes also directly benefited key constituencies of the LDP, particularly the construction industry and rural residents, who benefited from expansion and maintenance of the road network.

Gasoline and automobile taxes, however, impose diffuse costs on the Japanese public, directly through higher prices of operating automobiles and indirectly through higher costs associated with the production and distribution

17 The full text is available at http://law.e-gov.go.jp/htmldata/S32/S32HO055.html.
18 Inose (2008) provides a detailed overview and critique.
19 Personal interview, MLIT official, June 10, 2011.

of goods. The gasoline tax is deeply unpopular; for example, in a *Toyo Keizai* 2010 poll, although 59 percent of respondents recognized the need for future tax increases and 46 percent supported an increase in the consumption tax (generally considered the third rail of Japanese politics), only 17 percent supported an increase in gasoline taxes.[20]

Highway Tolls

Toll roads have existed in Japan since at least 1871, when the Meiji government promulgated Dajo Kanfukoku No. 648, allowing for the collection of duties on private roads for the purposes of construction and maintenance (Furukawa 2009). However, highway tolls are a much more recent development: Japan had no highways until the construction of the Meishin Expressway, which connected Nagoya and Osaka, in 1963. In 1956, the Japanese government invited World Bank economist Ralph J. Watkins to chair a commission on road improvement. Watkins lamented, "The roads of Japan are incredibly bad. No other industrial nation has so completely neglected its highway system."[21] He recommended the establishment of highway tolls as an economical means to realize the rapid development of Japan's road infrastructure (Hagen et al. 1956).

Acting on these recommendations, the Japanese Diet passed national highway legislation in 1956, which established the Japan Highway Public Corporation (JHPC), a quasi-public "special corporation" to construct and administer Japan's toll roads. Construction on the Meishin Expressway was initiated in 1958 (Japan Automobile Manufacturers Association 2006). The JHPC was created for two primary reasons: (1) to coordinate road construction and maintenance, which would otherwise be administered separately by the Ministry of Construction and prefectural and local governments; and (2) to supplement public funds with private financing, which the JHPC could raise directly (Furukawa 2009). The JHPC, along with three regional special corporations,[22] effectively monopolized Japan's highways and set toll levels in close consultation with the Ministry of Transport and the Ministry of Construction.

20 "Zozei wa fukahi to kangaeru hito wa roku wari jaku" [Nearly 60 percent see increases in taxes inevitable], *Toyo Keizai*, May 31, 2011.

21 For example, see the discussion in Road Bureau of the Ministry of Land, Infrastructure,Transport, and Tourism (2010).

22 They were the Metropolitan Expressway Public Corporation (administration of highways in Tokyo and the immediate vicinity), Hanshin Expressway Company (administration of highways in Osaka and the immediate vicinity), and Honshu-Shikoku Bridge Expressway Company (administration of bridges between Honshu and Shikoku).

During the initial phase of development in the 1960s, highway tolls were established on a road-by-road basis, with the general presumption that tolls would be reduced or eliminated as construction costs were recouped. For example, initial plans called for the elimination of tolls on the Meishin Expressway by 1988, when loans from the World Bank would be fully repaid (Furukawa 2009; Sato 2010). However, in 1972, as part of Tanaka Kakuei's Nihon Retto Kaizo Keikaku, revenues from highway tolls were pooled to support the development of highway infrastructure in rural areas (Sugimoto 2004). This effectively served to redistribute the revenues from profitable routes within and among urban centers such as Tokyo, Osaka, and Nagoya, to uneconomical routes in rural areas, which doubly benefited from improved infrastructure and the associated construction and maintenance employment. As a consequence, tolls remained high on the heavily utilized Tomei and Meishin routes connecting Japan's metropolitan areas, even after the relevant loans were paid back in full.

Figure 8.3 provides one illustration of how Japanese highway tolls acted as a redistributive mechanism. The x axis of the graph is the average population density of the prefectures where the terminal interchanges are located for each highway.[23] For example, the Tomei Expressway, which connects Tokyo and Nagoya, is plotted with a population density that is the average of Tokyo and Aichi in the graph.[24] The y axis is highway profitability by route, measured in hundreds of million yen as of 2001 and inclusive of operating costs and interest payments associated with construction loans.[25] As the graph indicates, unprofitable highway routes in Japan are concentrated in rural areas with low population density—for example, the Akita Expressway, which connects two sparsely populated regions in Iwate and Akita prefectures. In comparison, major urban routes such as the Tomei and Meishin deliver the bulk of profits to the highway system, even though loans associated with initial construction have been repaid.

This pricing structure facilitates energy efficiency in Japan's transportation sector by suppressing intercity automobile transport and shifting passengers to more energy-efficient rail.[26] Consider, for example, travel between

23 Data are from Sugimoto (2004).

24 This is an imperfect measure, because it does not capture variation in population density en route. However, most Japanese highways are short in distance and terminate at major or local population centers, so the measure should perform reasonably well as a proxy in most cases.

25 The Japan Expressway Holding and Debt Repayment Agency, established in 2005, no longer reports profitability figures by route inclusive of costs associated with highway construction.

26 See the extensive analysis in Yai (2009) and Kamioka (2010).

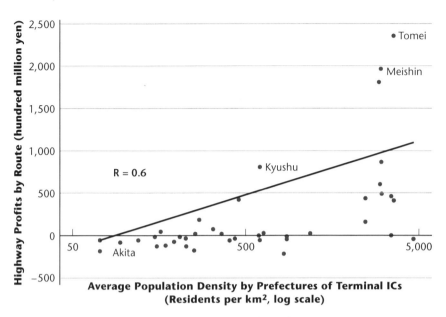

FIGURE 8.3 Profitability of Highways and Population Density, 2001
Sources: Sugimoto (2004) and Statistics Bureau, Ministry of Internal Affairs and Communications.

Tokyo and Osaka versus travel between San Francisco and Los Angeles in California.[27] In Japan, driving is made highly unattractive by highway tolls: the cost of tolls and gasoline alone come to about $200, and the trip takes around six hours, assuming no traffic.[28] In comparison, the shinkansen bullet train costs about $170 with a total trip length of 2.5 hours. Flying has become competitive in recent years, with prices ranging from $145 to $275, depending on the carrier, but given the time required to reach airports and to board planes, the shinkansen is generally faster for most business travelers within a 500-mile travel distance.[29] In comparison, in the United States, rail travel is impractical: a trip between San Francisco and Los Angeles takes 11 hours and costs $53. Driving is faster and cheaper, taking about six hours and costing about

27 Distance and travel time information is obtained from Google Maps. Pricing information is obtained from relevant carriers and average local gasoline prices from the Energy Information Administration and the Oil Information Center. All data are as of June 2011. The distance between San Francisco and Los Angeles is somewhat greater, about 380 miles, compared to about 320 miles between Tokyo and Osaka, but this does not bear significantly on the results.

28 A trip based on travel between Kasumigaseki and Minatomachi during a regular business day. Tolls are 13,500 yen, and the cost of gasoline amounts to about 4,000 yen as of summer 2011. I use an exchange rate of 80 yen to the dollar throughout.

29 Personal interview, MLIT official, September 2010.

$30–$50 for gasoline. Flying is more expensive but much faster—about $100 to $250 and roughly three hours, even accounting for time spent at airports.

Lightweight Automobiles

One unique element of Japanese policy in the transportation sector has been the promotion of *keijidosha*, or kei-cars. Kei-cars are defined by restrictions on engine displacement and car size and are subject to a variety of incentives such as lower taxes and insurance costs and relaxed registration requirements. For example, in 2010, compared to a regular compact vehicle, a kei-car purchased for personal use was subject to reductions in taxes as follows: 2 percent reduction in the automobile acquisition tax, $530 reduction in the automobile weight tax, and $270 reduction in the yearly automobile tax.[30] Government support for kei-cars was initially implemented in Japan after World War II as a means to advance motorization.[31] However, government support continued and expanded even after Japan became one of the largest automobile markets in the world.

Kei-cars, because they tend to be lighter and smaller, are generally more energy efficient than regular automobiles. In 2006, regular automobiles in Japan emitted about 0.19 kg CO_2 per passenger kilometer, compared to about 0.15 kg CO_2 for the average kei-car (Lipscy and Schipper 2013). For this reason, MLIT officials have advocated public support for kei-cars as a means to facilitate automobile fuel efficiency and reduce CO_2 emissions.[32] This government support has contributed to the expanding share of kei-cars in Japan's automobile fleet despite economic development, which generally pushes consumers toward more expensive, larger automobiles; the proportion of kei-cars in Japan's fleet has increased from about 10 percent in the 1970s to above 25 percent by 2007 (Lipscy and Schipper 2013).

Subsidization of kei-cars has also been politically attractive because it serves a key constituency of the LDP—residents of rural areas. Government subsidies for kei-cars are particularly generous in rural areas of Japan, where the absence of practical public transit means that many households own two vehicles. According to surveys, kei-cars are particularly popular in rural areas as a second vehicle, which housewives use for errands and chores (Ozeki 2009). In addition to the benefits mentioned, kei-car owners in rural areas receive a 20 percent discount on highway tolls and a waiver on the mandatory registration of a parking space associated with the vehicle.

30 Dollar figures computed at 80 yen per dollar. The automobile weight tax is assessed every three years.

31 For an overview, see Ozeki (2009).

32 Personal interview, MLIT officials, September 22, 2010.

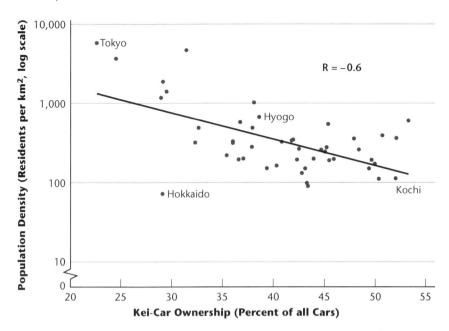

FIGURE 8.4 Kei-Car Ownership and Population Density, Japan's 47 Prefectures
Sources: MLIT; Statistics Bureau, Ministry of Internal Affairs and Communications.

As figure 8.4 illustrates, kei-car ownership in Japan is inversely related to population density. Ownership is highest in rural prefectures such as Kochi, Nagasaki, Shimane, and Okinawa, where kei-cars account for over 50 percent of automobiles. In comparison, in Tokyo, which has the lowest share, kei-cars account for only 23 percent of automobiles (Miyazaki, Hikaru, and Akaba 2009). Hence, a major justification for maintaining subsidies for kei-cars is to assist the economic well-being of rural areas by facilitating the availability of cheap cars.[33]

Kei-car subsidies provide a clear illustration of how efficiency clientelism has functioned in Japan. The subsidies long predate concerns about energy efficiency and CO_2 emissions. However, the policy was sustained and reinvigorated well after the initial goal of motorization was accomplished, as officials recognized the utility of promoting automobile fuel efficiency in rural areas, where public transportation is relatively underdeveloped. The policy proved durable as the benefits accrued disproportionately to rural residents—a crucial, overrepresented constituency of the LDP under Japan's prior electoral system.

33 Personal interview, MLIT officials, September 22, 2010.

Efficiency Clientelism and the DPJ

Across the policies associated with efficiency clientelism, an important consideration was compatibility with the core constituencies of the LDP—for example, rural residents, the transportation industry, and the construction industry. Japan's energy-efficiency measures in the transportation sector were designed to redistribute resources from the general public to this narrow support base of the incumbent party. Over the past two decades, several changes to the Japanese political system have undermined the sustainability of these redistributive arrangements and upended Japan's transportation policymaking.

First, electoral reform in 1994 replaced the old multimember district, single nontransferable vote (MMD-SNTV) system with a mixed system placing greater emphasis on plurality voting in single-member districts. This reform has shifted the electoral strategy of politicians away from narrow appeal to particularistic interest groups—the construction industry, for example—toward broader appeal to the median voter (Rosenbluth and Thies 2010; Scheiner 2012). Second, as the status of bureaucrats has declined with adverse economic performance and a series of scandals (Pharr 2000; Ozeki 2009), initiatives have been implemented to shift power away from the bureaucracy to politicians. This shift has diminished the influence of the bureaucracy, which has been an important advocate for efficiency measures. Finally, the DPJ emerged as a serious competitor to the LDP and took over control of the government in 2009.[34]

These changes have affected basic elements of Japan's transportation policy. In an electoral system that incentivizes politicians to seek broad support from the electorate, high, diffuse costs associated with transportation have increasingly come under attack. Public opinion polls have generally found dissatisfaction with high prices. According to a *Kyodo* poll, 72 percent of the general public opposed the gasoline tax in 2007.[35] A poll by the Cabinet Office in 2005 also found significant opposition to highway tolls, with 30 percent saying current levels were satisfactory or tolerable, compared to 52 percent who supported lower tolls.[36] Similarly, a survey by the Japan Automobile Manufacturers Association (JAMA) found that 57 percent of survey respondents supported elimination or reduction of the automobile weight tax.[37]

---

34 Cross-national studies have found that increases in party competition tend to be associated with declines in clientelistic policies. For example, see Kitschelt and Wilkinson (2007).

35 "Naikaku shijiritsu 41 percent," *Kyodo Tsushin Yoron Chosa*, January 12, 2008.

36 Cabinet Office (Japan), "Doro ni kansuru yoron chosa," July 2005.

37 "Jidosha no zeikin ni tsuite," Japan Automobile Manufacturers Association Report No. 91, 2001.

Japan's old MMD-SNTV electoral system allowed politicians to largely sidestep such diffuse opposition from the general public. For example, the temporary gasoline tax rate was raised repeatedly in 1976, 1979, and 1993. As a result of these tax hikes, the gasoline tax in Japan rose roughly 90 percent between 1974 and 1993. In comparison, the tax rate has never been raised since electoral reform in 1994. This is in contrast to Europe, where governments have continued to raise gasoline taxes as a means to facilitate reductions in CO_2 emissions.[38] This stagnation since 1993 has lowered Japan's relative gasoline tax rate from about 80 percent of the Organisation for Economic Co-operation and Development (OECD) average rate in 1980 to about 60 to 70 percent in recent years.[39]

As a minority party, the DPJ sought popular appeal by attacking the high cost of transportation, portraying existing arrangements as wasteful giveaways to special-interest groups. The DPJ took up the banner of transportation reform most clearly in 2003, when it adopted a set of proposals formulated by Yamazaki Yasuo, a former partner at Goldman Sachs who had run unsuccessfully for governor of Tokushima Prefecture in 2002. Yamazaki argued that elimination of highway tolls would stimulate economic activity by reducing transportation costs, while the costs could be covered by eliminating waste and converting Japan Public Highway Corporation bonds into Japanese government bonds, which carried a lower interest rate (Yamazaki 2003). Yamazaki was named MLIT minister in the DPJ's shadow cabinet, and the party adopted his ideas in its first campaign manifesto, prepared for the 2003 lower-house election.[40]

From that point on, transportation reform remained a central element of the DPJ's policy platform. In 2008, the DPJ manufactured a political showdown with the LDP over extension of the temporary gasoline tax. Having replaced the LDP as the largest party in the upper-house election of 2007, the DPJ refused to approve the extension. Under Japan's parliamentary rules, the LDP could utilize its two-thirds lower-house majority to overrule the DPJ, but it had to wait until 60 days after the upper house had rejected the relevant legislation. The DPJ held up the legislation and forced a brief repeal of the temporary gasoline tax in April during the 60-day waiting period.[41]

---

38 For example, Germany implemented a gasoline tax hike of 10 cents per year between 1999 and 2003 as part of its Ecological Tax Reform (ETR).

39 Calculated based on prices for regular unleaded gasoline (US$/liter in purchasing power parity, or PPP). Data from the International Energy Agency.

40 See, for example, Iwami (2008, 90); Yamazaki (2008).

41 See, for example, Linda Seig, "Japan Parliament Set to Clash over Gasoline Tax," Reuters, January 28, 2008; Sachiko Sakamaki, "Fukuda Renews Japan Gas Tax, Facing Down Opposition," Bloomberg, April 30, 2008.

The DPJ took maximum advantage of the political theater surrounding gasoline. Yamaoka Kenji, chair of the Diet Affairs Committee, referred to the ongoing Diet session as the Gasoline Kokkai (gasoline Diet) and remarked that he would force the LDP into a Gasoline Kaisan (gasoline dissolution of Parliament). The DPJ formed a Gasoline Nesagetai (gasoline price cut unit), composed of 52 lower-house members and led by Kawauchi Hiroshi. The unit spread out across the country to publicize the issue and picketed the Diet building in an attempt to thwart gasoline-related legislation.[42]

Importantly, the LDP was subject to similar electoral incentives during this period (Scheiner 2012; Lipscy and Scheiner 2012; McElwain 2012). Both parties faced strong incentives to adopt populist policies with broad appeal to the general public, and given the unpopularity of status quo transportation policies, it was natural that electorally minded reformists in each party seized upon the issue. In the LDP, Prime Minister Koizumi Junichiro made reform of the transportation sector a key element of his *seiiki naki kozo kaikaku* (reform without sanctuaries). Koizumi boosted his popular appeal by portraying traditionalists within his own party as *teikoseiryoku* (the forces of resistance), and he succeeded in privatizing Japan's major highway corporations in 2004. In 2008, LDP prime minister Fukuda Takeo co-opted a DPJ policy proposal to shift revenues associated with the Road Improvement Special Account to the general account budget (Furukawa 2008). This effectively severed the connection between highway tolls and gasoline taxes on the one hand and road construction and maintenance on the other, putting an end to the redistributive element associated with these policies. LDP prime minister Aso Taro similarly implemented a reduction of highway tolls in March 2009, although it was limited to weekends and holidays on nonurban routes.

Elimination of highway tolls and gasoline taxes remained popular, and they were retained as central components of the DPJ's 2009 campaign manifesto.[43] However, by the time the DPJ came to power, reforms by the LDP had obviated the relationship between transport taxes and tolls on the one hand and redistribution to particularistic interest groups on the other. In effect, transportation taxes were stripped of their explicitly clientelistic character by 2009. What remained was the environmental and fiscal impact of dramatically cutting government taxation on automobile transportation.

Once in power, the DPJ was confounded by the "efficiency" dimension of efficiency clientelism. The DPJ, with its urban support base, sees itself

42 "Minshuto 'gasoline nesagetai' hossoku," *Sankei Shimbun*, January 15, 2008.
43 Democratic Party of Japan, "The Democratic Party of Japan's Platform for Government," 2009.

as more of a green party, compared to the LDP.[44] One of Prime Minister Hatoyama's signature announcements upon entering office was a 25 percent CO_2 emissions-reduction target, which was considerably more aggressive than any previously proposed by the LDP. However, the DPJ's campaign pledges related to transportation clearly ran counter to these environmentalist goals. In general, reduction of highway tolls and gasoline taxes encourage automobile travel versus more energy-efficient modes of transportation, primarily air and rail.[45] Thus, simulations indicate that elimination of highway tolls would raise Japanese CO_2 emissions immediately by about 4 million tons per year (Yai 2009). Similarly, expiration of the temporary gasoline tax is projected to raise CO_2 emissions by about 8 million tons immediately and 24 million tons per year by 2015, as consumers adjust their purchasing decisions and behavior in response to the price shift (Ministry of the Environment 2008). In combination, these policy changes would increase Japan's transportation sector CO_2 emissions by more than 10 percent per year.

These environmental externalities posed a major roadblock to the DPJ's transportation reform proposals. Along with environmentally oriented party members, the Social Democratic Party, the DPJ's coalition partner, vocally objected to the elimination of highway tolls on the grounds that they would run counter to emissions-reduction goals.[46] Furthermore, major intra-urban and interurban highway routes, including the Meishin and Tomei, were removed from proposed reductions due to the potential for an adverse environmental impact. MLIT minister Maehara Seiji explained that these urban routes were left out because they "are likely to become congested, with adverse effects for CO_2 emissions."[47] However, recall that these are the most utilized routes that should have become toll-free earliest as the World Bank loans were repaid. Perversely, environmental concerns transformed the DPJ's highway toll-reduction plans into an updated version of Tanaka

44 Personal interview, DPJ party official, June 6, 2011.

45 In some instances, where local roads are congested due to expensive highway tolls, this effect could be mitigated or even reversed. Prior to the Tohoku earthquake of March 11, 2011, MLIT was conducting pilot studies to examine the net effect of local highway toll elimination on realized emissions. These studies were called off as the political climate changed after the earthquake and elimination of tolls became highly unlikely. Personal interview, MLIT officials, June 10, 2011.

46 For example, see Social Democratic Party (Japan), "Kosoku doro no muryoka/1000 yen ni tsuite," August 16, 2009, www5.sdp.or.jp/policy/policy/other/090816.htm; "Fukushima toshu, minshu no kosoku muryoka to kodomo teate ni iron," *Yomiuri Shimbun*, August 27, 2009.

47 See "Kosoku muryoka de Tomei, Meishin wa jogai," *Kyodo Tsushin*, November 25, 2009; "Kosoku muryoka, Tomei Meishin Honshu-Shikoku Renrakusen wa Jogai," *Asahi Shimbun*, November 20, 2009.

Kakuei's Nihon Retto Kaizo Keikaku—high tolls on heavily utilized, urban routes, coupled with toll-free rural routes. Unsurprisingly, popular support for the DPJ's highway toll policy plummeted.[48]

The fact that revenues from transportation taxes were now earmarked for the general budget also engendered objections from the Ministry of Finance and budget hawks within the DPJ. One of the signature initiatives of the new DPJ government was the *jigyo shiwake*, a process by which *individual* government programs were screened and streamlined. MLIT's proposed budget for the elimination of highway tolls and gasoline taxes became candidates for rationalization under the *jigyo shiwake*. Finance Minister Fujii Hirohisa and Senior Vice Minister of Finance Noda Yoshihiko argued that the cuts should be scaled back dramatically.[49] The budget allocation for highway tolls was ultimately reduced to about one-sixth of the original proposal (Yamazaki 2010).

Internal divisions also impeded the implementation of DPJ transportation initiatives. Constraints attributable to first-past-the-post electoral rules, the nearly co-equal status of the upper house, and newfound political leverage exerted by local politicians have left both the DPJ and LDP internally divided between reformers and traditionalists in recent years (Scheiner 2012; Shimizu 2012). These divisions led to speculation during the initial stages of Koizumi's term of office that he might split the LDP to join ranks with reformist elements in the DPJ. For example, Kan Naoto of the DPJ noted in 2001, "If Koizumi submits his reform proposal to the Diet, and it is something we can sympathize with, the DPJ will support it. Even if the DPJ and part of the LDP support the proposal, it will likely be rejected in the Diet. At that point, the Prime Minister must decide whether he gives up or takes his case to the people."[50] However, Koizumi ultimately pursued reform within the LDP, campaigning against traditionalist politicians in his own party (Reed, McElwain, and Shimizu 2009).

Just as Koizumi encountered resistance to transportation reform within his own ranks, the DPJ faced significant internal divisions between politicians hoping to please the broad electorate and those catering to local

48 For example, in a *Yomiuri* poll conducted in April 2010, only 23 percent of respondents approved of the DPJ's handling of the highway toll reduction plan. Other DPJ policies included in the survey received more favorable support: free high schools (54 percent), agricultural policy reform (50 percent), child allowance (43 percent). "Hatoyama naikaku shijiritsu kyuraku 33 percent," *Yomiuri Shimbun*, April 5, 2010.

49 "Kosoku muryoka, shinkansen ga koho: sasshin kaigi no jigyo shiwake," *Kyodo Tsushin*, October 29, 2009; "Kosoku muryoka 'soan wa matomatte iru' Maehara Kokko Daijin," *Response*, December 4, 2009.

50 My own translation of excerpt in Inose (2008, 27).

interests. Particularly fierce resistance was encountered from politicians with close ties to labor unions associated with Japan Railways,[51] ferry operators,[52] and bus operators.[53] These groups feared that highway toll reductions and automobile-related tax reductions would lead to a shift away from their businesses in favor of private automobile transportation. The DPJ repeatedly modified its proposals to accommodate these groups— for example, by increasing the tolls on the bridges connecting Honshu to Shikoku to accommodate ferry operators (Yamazaki 2010).

The DPJ's transportation policy gradually moved toward de facto maintenance of the status quo with minor adjustments. The automobile acquisition tax remained unchanged. The automobile weight tax, which was slated for elimination, was instead reduced modestly.[54] The gasoline tax was replaced by a new CO_2 tax, implemented beginning in 2011 over a three-year period. The revenues from the tax were directed to support the development of green technologies such as renewable energy. However, this was a largely symbolic gesture, since revenues generated from the gasoline tax had already been transferred to the general account budget. The tax effectively replicated the preexisting gasoline tax in all but name. According to forecasts, gasoline prices are projected to rise by about 0.76 yen per liter (about 3 cents per gallon), and the expected reduction in CO_2 emissions associated with the tax is only about 1 percent cumulatively by 2020.[55]

The March 11, 2011, Tohoku earthquake, which devastated northeast Japan and led to a nuclear crisis at the Fukushima Dai-Ichi plant, put a decisive end to the DPJ's plans to eliminate highway tolls. Plans for toll reductions had already been scaled back dramatically by early 2011. After the earthquake, the DPJ chose to "freeze" plans to eliminate highway tolls in order to raise revenues for reconstruction. However, senior MLIT vice-minister Ikeguchi noted, "The government cannot quite say that it is abandoning [the toll elimination policy], so it wrote 'freeze,' but in reality, it is

51 "'Kosoku muryoka' JR shien no Minshuto giin wa itabasami," *Asahi Shimbun*, September 14, 2009.

52 "'Kosoku muryoka ni danko hantai' kansai ferry 7 sha ga uttae," *Kyodo Tsushin*, October 29, 2009.

53 "Bus kyokai ga kosoku muryoka ni hantai: Kokkosho ni kinkyu yobousho," *Kyodo Tsushin*, October 19, 2009.

54 Although the precise rate depends on automobile class and type, the reduction was about 20 percent for a typical compact vehicle. For more detail, see "Heisei 22 nendo zeisei kaikaku ni tomonau jidosha juryo zei no henko ni tsuite," www.mlit.go.jp/common/000111305.pdf.

55 "Zeisei taiko wo kakugi kettei," *Yomiuri Shimbun*, December 17, 2010; "11 nendo zeisei kaisei," *Mainichi Shimbun*, December 17, 2010.

a foregone matter."[56] Toll roads remained free only for the disaster-affected Tohoku region through March 2012 and for those displaced by the nuclear accident at Fukushima through September 2012.

Conclusion: The Future of Energy Efficiency in Japan

Japan's economy stands out for being remarkably energy efficient. In this chapter, I have argued that one important pillar of Japanese energy-efficiency policy has been destabilized by political developments over the past two decades. Under what I call efficiency clientelism, policies served a dual role: to promote energy efficiency while also delivering economic benefits to key constituencies of the LDP. Political changes since the 1990s have diminished the feasibility of such arrangements. In particular, electoral reform, which incentivizes broad public appeal, has made it more difficult to sustain policies that encourage energy efficiency by imposing diffuse costs on the general public. The DPJ pursued an electoral strategy that sought popular support by attacking policies associated with efficiency clientelism, such as high highway tolls and gasoline taxes. However, this put the DPJ in a conundrum once in power; its policy initiatives in the transportation sector ran directly counter to its ambitious environmentalist objectives.

Political change over the past 20 years leaves Japanese transportation energy-efficiency policy in a state of uncertainty and flux. Although policies that facilitated efficiency in the past remain under challenge, no credible alternative mechanisms have emerged. Unlike previous policies under efficiency clientelism, there is no clear political constituency in Japan for new measures such as a CO_2 tax. Surveys indicate that popular support for the CO_2 tax has ranged between about 25 percent and 40 percent in recent years.[57] Officials indicate that the only enthusiastic supporter of the CO_2 tax is the Ministry of Finance, which favors the measure from a revenue standpoint.[58] Although unions associated with alternative transportation industries played an important role in reducing the scope of highway toll reductions under DPJ rule, there are also compelling interest groups on the other side of the issue—for example, the automobile industry and affiliated unions. Green energy producers are hardly a formidable political constituency on par with rural residents and the construction industry in the heyday of LDP rule.

56 For example, "Kosoku muryoka, fukkatsu konnan," *Jiji Press*, August 8, 2011 (my translation of Japanese original).

57 Japan Cabinet Office, "Chikyu ondanka taisaku ni kansuru yoron chosa," various years.

58 Personal interview, MLIT official, June 10, 2011.

Will Japan be able to remain a global leader in energy efficiency despite these shifts? Besides these political challenges, Japan faces the more practical difficulty of diminishing returns. Because Japan has already achieved relatively high levels of energy efficiency, incremental improvement is expensive and sometimes impractical. For example, one initiative that MLIT has been working on is to shift commercial freight from trucks to rails.[59] However, as a practical matter, further improvements have proved challenging. Japan has already achieved high utilization on existing rail tracks, which means there is very little spare capacity open for commercial use. This is a particularly difficult problem once freight trains arrive in major metropolitan areas such as Tokyo and Osaka. In urban areas, there is no idle capacity during peak hours in the morning and evening, so commercial trains must stop. Between Tokyo and Osaka, trains must also pass through several urban areas, and moving through these areas without delay is difficult. Because land is scarce in Japan and population densities in urban areas are high, further expansion of the capacity of the rail network will take an excruciatingly long time. A major shift from truck to rail freight in Japan is highly unlikely precisely because Japan already relies so heavily on rail transportation.

However, there are some trends in Japan that will likely have a beneficial long-term impact on energy efficiency and CO_2 emissions. Japan's demographic profile—an increasingly older and smaller population—is often cited as a negative factor for its economy and international standing. However, Japan's demographics are helpful when considering energy use and CO_2 emissions. A shrinking population will require less energy over time. Senior citizens tend to drive less than the young. The continuing movement of people into densely populated urban areas, such as Tokyo, means greater use of more energy-efficient public transportation. In addition, *kuruma banare* (moving away from cars) among young Japanese is frequently reported by the media, and government surveys indicate that ownership of automobiles by Japanese below the age of 40 has declined sharply in recent years.[60] There are therefore some important factors, largely orthogonal to efficiency policy, that are moving Japan toward greater energy efficiency and lower emissions.

It is also important to emphasize again that efficiency clientelism is not the only policy model that has contributed to Japanese energy efficiency. Japanese fuel economy standards are the most stringent in the world and

59 Personal interview, MLIT officials, June 11, 2009.
60 Ministry of Internal Affairs and Communications, "Zenkoku shohi jittai chosa," 2010.

will likely remain so for the foreseeable future. Also of note are policy innovations such as the "top-runner" program. This program, introduced under the Energy Conservation Law in 1998, has been applied to a range of areas, including fuel economy standards. The program is designed to automate improvements in efficiency over time by setting target improvements based on the current highest-efficiency product in each sector. It is the first program of its kind and is widely recognized as an important innovation in energy-efficiency policymaking. It is an open question whether the bureaucracy will continue to retain the initiative and autonomy necessary to maintain the effectiveness of programs such as top-runner, but to date, the program appears to enjoy widespread support.

Japanese policymakers may also be able to compensate for losses in transport energy efficiency by pursuing greater efficiency in other sectors. In transportation, the crucial choices that affect total energy consumption—how far to travel, whether to fly or to ride the train, what kind of automobile to purchase—are decentralized, individual-level decisions. For this reason, it is difficult to facilitate efficiency without imposing higher costs on energy use by the general public. Maintaining such diffuse, high costs has become less feasible under Japan's current electoral system. By contrast, in the industrial sector, energy efficiency is typically achieved by targeting a relatively small set of energy-intensive producers. Power generation lies somewhere in between; utilities are concentrated, but overall electricity consumption is determined by the autonomous decisions of individuals. Hence, the prognosis for Japanese energy efficiency in sectors aside from transportation may be more encouraging in comparison.

An obvious extension of this chapter would be to consider the relationship between electoral arrangements and energy efficiency in a wider set of countries. Elsewhere, I have examined two other episodes of electoral reform in the OECD—in Italy and in New Zealand—and found changes in energy efficiency consistent with the Japanese experience outlined here. Cross-national evidence also points to higher energy prices and greater transportation energy efficiency in nonmajoritarian electoral systems, where it is more feasible to design political arrangements imposing diffuse costs on the general population (Lipscy 2011).[61] However, this remains a largely unexplored topic, and much research remains to be done.

61 There is also a related literature on the cross-national variation between general price levels and electoral systems, but it does not consider energy policy or the potential environmental externalities of energy price differentials (Rogowski and Kayser 2002; Chang et al. 2010).

References

Barrett, Brendan. 2005. *Ecological Modernization and Japan*. London: Routledge.

Barrett, Brendan F. D., and Riki Therivel. 1991. *Environmental Policy and Impact Assessment in Japan*. London: Routledge.

Bobrow, Davis, and Robert Kudrle. 1987. "How Middle Powers Can Manage Resource Weakness: Japan and Energy." *World Politics* 39 (4): 536–65.

Broadbent, Jeffrey. 1998. *Environmental Politics in Japan: Networks of Power and Protest*. Cambridge: Cambridge University Press.

Chang, Eric, Mark Kayser, Drew Linzer, and Ronald Rogowski. 2010. *Electoral Systems and the Balance of Consumer-Producer Power*. New York: Cambridge University Press.

Cox, Gary, Frances McCall Rosenbluth, and Michael Thies. 1999. "Electoral Reform and the Fate of Factions: The Case of Japan's LDP." *British Journal of Political Science* 29 (1): 33–56.

Curtis, Gerald. 1971. *Election Campaigning Japanese Style*. New York: Columbia University Press.

Democratic Party of Japan. 2003. *DPJ Manifesto for 2003 General Election*. Tokyo: DPJ.

———. 2009. *DPJ Manifesto for 2009 General Election*. Tokyo: DPJ.

Eguchi, Yujiro. 1980. "Japanese Energy Policy." *International Affairs* 56 (2): 263–79.

Fukui, Haruhiro, and Shigeko N. Fukai. 1996. "Pork Barrel Politics, Networks, and Local Economic Development in Contemporary Japan." *Asian Survey* 36 (4): 268–86.

Funabashi, Harutoshi. 2006. "Minamata Disease and Environmental Governance." *International Journal of Japanese Sociology* 15 (1): 7–25.

Furukawa, Kotaro. 2007. "Jidosha kanren zeisei no genjo to kadai" [Current situation and issues related to automobile-related taxation]. *Reference* (August): 5–99.

———. 2008. "Doro tokutei zaigen no ippan zaigen ka" [Transfer of the road improvement special account to the general account budget]. *National Diet Library Issue Brief*, No. 619.

———. 2009. "Kosoku doro no tsuko ryokin seido: Rekishi to genjo" [Regulations concerning highway tolls: History and present situation]. *Reference* (October): 99–118.

Hagen, E., F. W. Herring, G. E. McLaughlin, W. Owen, H. M. Sapir, and R. J. Watkins. 1956. *Report on Kobe-Nagoya Expressway Survey*. Tokyo: Ministry of Construction.

Hamanaka, Hironori. 2006. *Kyoto giteisho wo meguru kokusai kosho: COP3 ikou no kosho keii*. Tokyo: Keio Gijuku Daigaku Shuppankai.

Hein, Laura. 1990. *Fueling Growth: The Energy Revolution and Economic Policy in Postwar Japan*. Cambridge, MA: Harvard University Press.

Hirano, Shigeo. 2006. "Electoral Systems, Hometowns, and Favored Minorities: Evidence from Japan's Electoral Reforms." *World Politics* 59 (1): 51–82.

Iijima, Nobuko. 1984. *Kankyo mondai to higaisha undo* [The pollution problem and the victims' movements]. Tokyo: Gakubunsha.

Inose, Naoki. 2008. *Doro no kecchaku*. Tokyo: Bunshu Bunko.

International Energy Agency. Various years. "Energy Policies of IEA Countries: Japan." Paris: IEA.

Iwami, Takao. 2008. *Minshuto 10 nen shi*. Tokyo: Dai Ichi Shorin.

Japan Automobile Manufacturers Association (JAMA). 2006. *Japan's Auto Industry*. Tokyo: JAMA.

Johnson, Chalmers A. 1982. *MITI and the Japanese Miracle: The Growth of Industrial Policy, 1925–1975*. Stanford, CA: Stanford University Press.

Kamioka, Naomi. 2010. *Kosoku muryoka ga nihon wo kowasu*. Tokyo: Commons.

Kasahara, Satoru, Sergey Paltsev, John Reilly, Henry Jacoby, and A. Denny Ellerman. 2005. "Climate Change Taxes and Energy Efficiency in Japan." In *MIT Joint Program on the Science and Policy of Global Change Report No. 121*. Cambridge, MA: Massachusetts Institute of Technology.

Kiang, Nancy, and Lee Schipper. 1996. "Energy Trends in the Japanese Transportation Sector." *Transport Policy* 3 (1): 21–35.

Kim, Dalchoong, and Euisoon Shin. 1986. *Energy Policies in Korea and Japan: Comparison and Search for Cooperation*. Seoul: Yonsei University Press.

Kitschelt, Herbert. 2000. "Linkages Between Citizens and Politicians in Democratic Polities." *Comparative Political Studies* 33 (6–7): 845–79.

Kitschelt, Herbert, and Steven I. Wilkinson. 2007. "A Research Agenda for the Study of Citizen-Politician Linkages and Democratic Accountability." In *Patrons or Policies? Patterns of Democratic Accountability and Political Competition*, edited by H. Kitschelt and S. I. Wilkinson. New York: Cambridge University Press.

Lipscy, Phillip Y. 2009. "The Political Economy of Energy Efficiency in Japan." Paper presented at the annual meeting of the American Political Science Association, Toronto, September 3–6.

———. 2011. "Efficiency Clientelism." Paper presented at the Princeton Conference on Environmental Politics, Princeton, NJ, December 2–3.

Lipscy, Phillip Y., and Ethan Scheiner. 2012. "Japan Under the DPJ: The Paradox of Political Change Without Policy Change." *Journal of East Asian Studies* 12 (3): 311–22.

Lipscy, Phillip Y., and Lee Schipper. 2013. "Energy Efficiency in the Japanese Transport Sector." *Energy Policy* 56: 248–58.

McCubbins, Mathew, and Frances McCall Rosenbluth. 1995. "Party Provision for Personal Politics: Dividing the Vote in Japan." In *Structure and Policy in Japan and the United States*, edited by P. F. Cowhey and M. McCubbins. Cambridge: Cambridge University Press.

McElwain, Kenneth Mori. 2012. "The Nationalization of Japanese Elections." *Journal of East Asian Studies* 12 (3): 323–50.

McKean, Margaret. 1981. *Environmental Politics in Japan*. Berkeley: University of California Press.

Ministry of Economy, Trade, and Industry (METI). 2007. "Comparison of Energy Efficiency Across Countries." Tokyo: METI.

Ministry of the Environment (MOE). 2007. "Nihonkoku seifu to chuka jinmin kyowakoku tono kankyo energy bunya ni okeru kyoryoku suishin ni kan-suru communique." Press release, Tokyo. MOE.

———. 2008. "Kankyozei wo meguru saikin no jokyo ni tsuite" [Recent situation concerning the environmental tax]. In *Chuo kankyo shingikai sogo seisaku/chikyu kankyo godo bukai*. Tokyo: MOE.

Ministry of Land, Infrastructure, Transport, and Tourism (MLIT). 2002. "Doro seibi taikei no arikata" [Considering the system of road maintenance]. In *Report of the Council for Decentralization Reform*. Tokyo: MLIT.

Miyauchi, Taisuke. 2006. "Pursuing the Sociological Study of Environmental Governance in Japan: An Introduction to the Special Issue." *International Journal of Japanese Sociology* 15 (1): 2–6.

Miyazaki, Takuro, Sugiura Hikaru, and Jun Akaba. 2009. "Keijidosha no user to shijo kankyo." *JAMAGAZINE*, February.

Mulgan, Aurelia George. 2010. "Ozawa Taking His Toll on Japan's DPJ Government." *East Asia Forum*, May 5.

Nagata, Yutaka. 1993. "Comparative Analysis of Energy Intensity Between the U.S. and Japan." EMF SR 5. Stanford, CA: Energy Modeling Forum, Stanford University.

Nakazawa, Hideo. 2006. "Between the Global Environmental Regime and Local Sustainability: A Local Review on the Inclusion, Failure and Reinventing Process of the Environmental Governance." *International Journal of Japanese Sociology* 15 (1): 69–85.

Nemetz, P. N., I. Vertinsky, and P. Vertinsky. 1985. "Japan's Energy Strategy at the Crossroads." *Pacific Affairs* 57 (4): 553–76.

Oki, Hiroshi. 2007. *Kireina chikyu wa nihon kara: Kankyo gaiko to kokusai kaigi*. Tokyo: Hara Shobo.

Okimoto, Daniel I. 1990. *Between MITI and the Market: Japanese Industrial Policy for High Technology*. Stanford, CA: Stanford University Press.

Ozeki, Kazuo. 2009. "Keijidosha no rekishi wo furikaeru." *JAMAGAZINE*, February.

Pharr, Susan J. 2000. "Officials' Misconduct and Public Distrust: Japan and the Trilateral Democracies." *In Disaffected Democracies: What's Troubling the Trilateral Countries?* edited by S. J. Pharr and R. D. Putnam. Princeton, NJ: Princeton University Press.

Ramseyer, Mark, and Frances McCall Rosenbluth. 1993. *Japan's Political Marketplace.* Cambridge, MA: Harvard University Press.

Reed, Steven R. 1981. "Environmental Politics: Some Reflections Based on the Japanese Case." *Comparative Politics* 13 (3): 253–70.

Reed, Steven R., Kenneth Mori McElwain, and Kay Shimizu. 2009. *Political Change in Japan: Electoral Behavior, Party Realignment, and the Koizumi Reforms.* Stanford, CA: Shorenstein APARC.

Reich, Michael R. 1984. "Mobilizing for Environmental Policy in Italy and Japan." *Comparative Politics* 16 (4): 379–402.

Richardson, Bradley. 1997. *Japanese Democracy: Power, Coordination, and Performance.* New Haven, CT: Yale University Press.

Road Bureau of the Ministry of Land, Infrastructure,Transport, and Tourism. 2010. *Michi no rekishi* [History of Japanese roads]. Tokyo: MLIT.

Rogowski, Ronald, and Mark Andreas Kayser. 2002. "Majoritarian Electoral Systems and Consumer Power: Price-Level Evidence from the OECD Countries." *American Journal of Political Science* 46 (3): 526–39.

Rosenbluth, Frances McCall. 1989. *Financial Politics in Contemporary Japan.* Ithaca, NY: Cornell University Press.

Rosenbluth, Frances McCall, Mathew McCubbins, Jun Saito, and Kyohei Yamada. 2009. "Median Districts and District Medians: Electoral Adaptation to Majoritarian Politics in Post-1994 Japan." Paper presented at the annual meeting of the American Political Science Association, Toronto.

Rosenbluth, Frances McCall, and Michael F. Thies. 2010. *Japan Transformed: Political Change and Economic Restructuring.* Princeton, NJ: Princeton University Press.

Sakakibara, Eisuke. 1991. "The Japanese Politico-Economic System and the Public Sector." In *Parallel Politics: Economic Policymaking in the United States and Japan*, edited by S. Kernell. Washington, DC: Brookings Institution Press.

Samuels, Richard J. 1983. *State Enterprise, State Strength, and Energy Policy in Transwar Japan.* Cambridge, MA: International Energy Studies Program. Massachusetts Institute of Technology.

———. 1987. *The Business of the Japanese State: Energy Markets in Comparative and Historical Perspective.* Ithaca, NY: Cornell University Press.

Sato, Masahiko. 2010. *Nihon kokumin no tame no kosoku doro muryoka* [Elimination of highway tolls for the Japanese people]. Tokyo: Meiji Daigaku.

Scheiner, Ethan. 2005. *Democracy Without Competition in Japan: Opposition Failure in a One-Party Dominant State.* Cambridge: Cambridge University Press.

———. 2012. "The Electoral System and Japan's Partial Transformation: Party System Consolidation Without Policy Realignment?" *Journal of East Asian Studies* 12 (3): 351–79.

Seki, Soichiro. 2002. "Kyoto giteisho no hijun to waga kuni no torikumi." *Nihon boueki kai geppo* 582. Japan Foreign Trade Council.

Shimizu, Kay. 2012. "Electoral Consequences of Municipal Mergers." *Journal of East Asian Studies* 12 (3): 381–408.

Simcock, Bradford Lincoln. 1974. *Environmental Politics in Japan.* Cambridge, MA: Harvard University Press.

Sugimoto, Yuzo. 2004. "Kosoku doro no seisaku cost to zaiseito yushi seido kaikaku" [The policy cost of highways and reform of FILP]. *Kaikei Kensa Kenkyu* 29: 99–114.

Tanabe, Toshiaki. 1999. *Chikyu ondanka to kankyo gaiko: Kyoto kaigi no kobo to sonogo no tenkai.* Tokyo: Jijitsushinsha.

Tanaka, Kakuei. 1972. *Nihon retto kaizo ron.* Tokyo: Nikkan Kogyo Shinbun Sha.

Terao, Tadayoshi, and Kenji Otsuka, eds. 2007. *Development of Environmental Policy in Japan and Asian Countries.* New York: Palgrave Macmillan.

Tsuru, Shigeto. 2000. *The Political Economy of the Environment: The Case of Japan.* Vancouver: University of British Columbia Press.

Wicaksono, Agung. 2008. *Energy Efficiency in Japan.* Singapore: Institute of Southeast Asian Studies.

Woodall, Brian. 1996. *Japan Under Construction: Corruption, Politics, and Public Works.* Berkeley: University of California Press.

Yai, Tetsuo. 2009. "Kosoku doro ryokin hikiage ni yoru kankyo men heno eikyo" [The effect of highway toll reduction on the environment]. In *Prime Minister's Office Task Force on Global Warming and Climate Change Meeting Number 5, Appendix 2.* Tokyo.

Yamazaki, Yasuyo. 2003. "Kosoku doro wa tada ni dekiru." *Chuo Koron,* September.

———. 2008. *Doro mondai wo toku.* Tokyo: Diamond.

———. 2010. "Kosoku doro muryoka wo kobande iru no wa dare ka" [Who is rejecting elimination of highway tolls?]. *Japan Business Press,* April.

9 Information and Communications Technology (ICT) Policy in a Post-LDP Japan

CAUGHT BETWEEN DISTRIBUTIVE POLITICS
AND STRATEGIC POLICY AGAIN?

Kenji E. Kushida

Japan's ICT policy, which straddled the two logics of Japan's political economy—strategic/developmental, and clientelistic/distributive—continued to be pulled in both directions after the DPJ came to power. The DPJ's campaign promises had suggested it would curtail the distributive elements of politics while focusing on bold reforms. In ICT, bold reforms were initially promulgated, but they contained a surprising degree of seemingly distributive regional infrastructure projects. Moreover, policy volatility was high, as the bold reform proposal itself was retracted as personnel were reshuffled in an internal DPJ political upheaval. This chapter shows how politicians leading the policymaking process over bureaucrats (the DPJ's mantra) can pave the way for bold reform initiatives, but that the very nature of having political leadership responsible for policy can lead to greater policy volatility and politicized policy.

Japan's information and communications technology (ICT) policies provide a useful vantage for analyzing policymaking under the Democratic Party of Japan (DPJ). Until the mid-1990s Japan's ICT sector straddled both sides of the two very different political logics operating in Japan's political economy—the *strategic* or *developmental*, and the *distributive* or

Earlier drafts of this chapter were prepared for a conference held by the Japan Studies Program at the Stanford University Walter H. Shorenstein Asia-Pacific Research Center in February 2011, and a panel at the Association for Asian Studies (AAS) annual meeting in Toronto, Canada, in March 2012. The author thanks the organizers of the Stanford conference, the discussant Ethan Scheiner, and the participants for insightful comments. The author also thanks Eiji Kawabata for organizing the AAS panel, the Japan Foundation Center for Global Partnership for funding the panel, and Marie Anchordoguy, panel participants, an anonymous reviewer, and Trevor Incerti for valuable feedback.

clientelistic. On the one hand, the ICT sector was historically considered a strategic industry, receiving favorable industrial policy treatment, led by government official, to build the technological capabilities of Japanese firms while protecting them from imports. On the other hand, ICT was often used by politicians for electoral advantage, with regional deployments of costly infrastructure. Political involvement during critical junctures in the industry's restructuring often hindered reforms to strategically enhance the sector's international competitiveness.

Upon coming to power in 2009, one of the DPJ's core policy claims was to make a clean break from the LDP's distributive, pork-barrel–oriented politics. Japan's ICT policy area is an excellent test bed for assessing the degree to which this was carried out. If the DPJ indeed jettisoned LDP-style distributive politics, we would expect less focus on costly regional infrastructure deployments and more on strategic policy aimed at enhancing industrial competitiveness. The DPJ's dramatic break from the LDP's traditional regional-oriented distributive policies in areas such as transportation raised expectations for the same in ICT. This chapter therefore asks two simple questions: What was the nature of Japan's ICT policies under the DPJ? And, were these policies less regionally distributive compared to Japan's ICT policies under the LDP?

The answers to these questions are quite revealing. This chapter finds that, contrary to expectations based on the party's own promises and its track record in other notable policy areas, Japan's ICT policy under the DPJ took a surprisingly distributive and politicized turn after initial plans for broad, strategic reforms. This was caused by a fundamental structural tension within the DPJ that focused the party on distributive politics, combined with severe political infighting within the party that led to high levels of policy volatility.

There are several implications of having political power alternation in Japan that can be drawn from these findings. First, new patterns of interest group politics became possible, as firms that were previously policy outsiders could become policy insiders. Second, it became clear that although increasing political leadership vis-à-vis bureaucratic management did enable bold new reforms to be articulated, the very fact of having politicians at the helm of policy opened the possibility of intraparty political infighting, ultimately resulting in greater levels of policy volatility.

The implication for Japan's ICT policy revealed by this study is that the bureaucratic organization of the ministries responsible for ICT policy could dilute political attention away from ICT. This increased the difficulty of promulgating effective strategic policy.

In this chapter I first establish the significance of examining Japan's ICT sector, and review how the politics driving Japan's ICT policies mirrored

Japan's "dual structure" political economy. I conclude this section by providing a basis for the expectation that the DPJ's policies would weaken the distributive aspect of Japan's ICT policies. The next section examines the surprising distributive content of the DPJ's ICT policies, which uncovers the new interest group dynamics driving the policy trajectory. The next section analyzes the reversal of DPJ's initial vision for bold reform due to political struggles within the DPJ. The chapter concludes with some implications for how these cases help us understand what to expect from political dynamics in a post-LDP Japan.

Japan's ICT Sector: Between Strategic and Distributive

The economic significance of ICT sectors in any advanced country cannot be understated. As a set of sectors, ICT usually encompasses computer hardware, software, networks, telecommunications equipment and services, and, more recently, digital content industries. ICT has been a crucial driver of economic growth in advanced industrial countries since the 1980s. U.S. economic growth in the 1990s was driven in large part by the computer and semiconductor industries. Firms such as Microsoft, Intel, and Cisco grew to join America's largest companies, ushering in an era of American global dominance in ICT.

In Japan, ICT is the largest economic sector, accounting for approximately 10 percent of Japan's nominal gross domestic product (GDP) in 2008, at 96.5 trillion yen. During the country's five years of sustained (albeit slow) growth from 2002 to 2007, ICT contributed approximately 34 percent of the country's GDP growth (MIC 2010c, 26). Moreover, Japan's ICT sector has been one of the few dynamic and exciting growth sectors after the bubble burst in 1990. Despite its overall stagnant economic growth in the 1990s and its banking crisis in 1997, Japan's mobile telecommunications sector experienced rapid and profitable growth. In the late 1990s and early 2000s, new entrants and startup firms spearheaded broadband services markets and online services.

Beyond its size, growth, and dynamism, ICT has driven some of the most important transformations in economic activity around the world (Jorgenson and Wessner 2007; Zysman et al. 2013). It has enabled new services, new business models, and a transformation of existing activities. It played a critical role in transforming the services portion of the economy, once thought immune to significant productivity gains, into a driver of productivity increases and economic growth (Baumol 1967). In this chapter we are primarily concerned with telecommunications-related parts of the industry, which are more heavily influenced by government policy than computers and semiconductors.

ICT as a Set of Policy Issues

ICT sectors in virtually all countries have been shaped heavily by government policies. Crucially, the domestic architecture of ICT markets in particular countries has influenced their international competitiveness, which has in turn shaped global markets.

Since telecommunications originated as national or government-owned monopolies of national network infrastructure in most countries, the wave of privatization and liberalization that swept the telecommunications sectors of the advanced industrial countries from the 1970s through 1990s decisively shaped their domestic ICT industries. For example, in the United States, a Department of Justice antitrust suit filed in the mid-1970s led to a 1982 settlement resulting in AT&T splitting itself apart. In the United Kingdom, the government decided to privatize British Telecom in 1982, and it was put into effect in 1984. In Japan, Nippon Telegraph and Telephone (NTT) was thrown into a prolonged political battle over privatization and liberalization from the late 1970s, with privatization beginning in 1985. Monopoly communications operators were often among the largest companies in their respective countries, and the diversity of political processes driving liberalization and privatization led to a variety of ICT industry structures and market dynamics.

These industry structures and market dynamics, in turn, have influenced the relative global competitiveness of ICT sectors. For example, a consistent policy stance by the FCC since the 1980s enabled the Internet to develop as an open platform, in which third-party content providers could innovate and experiment without interference from the network carriers (Bar et al. 2000). Firms such as Yahoo, and later Google, used the U.S. online environment with early lead users to develop strong global presences. In South Korea, key policy issues such as a ban on cellular handset subsidies helped focus manufacturers on global handset markets (Kushida 2008). In Japan, however, the choice of a proprietary digital cellular standard played a major role in isolating the domestic industry from global markets—to the detriment of Japanese firms (Kushida 2011; Funk 2002). Thus, while some forms of government policy can yield positive market outcomes, if done badly, they can be detrimental to the domestic industry's global competitiveness.

Japan's Historical ICT Politics: Between the Distributive and Strategic

Japan's ICT sector has long been pulled in two separate directions by the contrasting political logics of Japan's postwar "dual economy." On the one hand, the internationally competitive, export-oriented sectors that drove Japan's rapid postwar growth followed the logic of *strategic* or *developmental* politics and policies. Politicians ceded control to elite bureaucrats who employed a variety of policy tools to channel resources to strategic sectors, actively facilitating technology transfers from abroad, and engaging in infant industry protection (with a credible threat of removing that protection to promote competitiveness in export markets). The Ministry of Finance (MOF), Bank of Japan, and Ministry of International Trade and Industry (MITI) were the main policy actors and were given considerable autonomy (Johnson 1986a; Woodall 1996).

On the other hand, domestic-oriented sectors such as agriculture, construction, and regional finance were part of Japan's *clientelistic* or *distributive* political logic. Politicians were heavily involved in protecting these sectors from international competition in exchange for votes and financial contributions (Woodall 1996). The sectors became inefficient and were not globally competitive, but this was relatively unnoticed during Japan's rapid economic growth through the 1980s. After the bubble burst in 1990, however, their inefficiencies were revealed as an acute problem, slowing economic recovery and growth (Katz 1998).

The financial system was the linchpin of this dual economy. On the strategic side, the bank-centered financial system in place until the late 1980s took consumer deposits and allocated capital to bureaucratically chosen strategic areas. On the distributive side, the postal savings system offered greater reach and slightly higher interest rates than banks, channeling consumer savings into the Fiscal Investment and Loan Program (FILP). FILP was essentially a "second budget" for politicians, who could allocate funds to pork-barrel projects for their districts to stay in power.[1]

Japan's ICT sector straddled these two logics. In its inception in the late 1800s, communications was a strategic industry deemed critical for industrialization and development. After initially importing equipment and expertise to establish a communications network, the government assisted in the creation of Japan's industrial giants such as NEC, Hitachi, and Fujitsu to raise the level of domestic technological capabilities. The government aided these firms' efforts to obtain foreign technology, actively pushing them to develop their own communications equipment. The government's focus on ICT as a strategic sector continued in the postwar era, with NTT receiving large procurement budgets approved by the National Diet. NTT procurement and joint research and development (R&D) with manufacturers subsidized the latter's R&D operations in other areas, such as semiconductors and consumer electronics (Fransman 1995; Anchordoguy 2001).

---

1 For more on the ties binding the two parts of Japan's dual economy, see Vogel (1999).

From around the 1980s, after Japan's rapid growth era of the 1950s through the 1970s considerably enriched the country, and the LDP's model of distributive, pork-barrel politics became firmly entrenched—largely thanks to Prime Minister Tanaka Kakuei—Japan's communications sector was increasingly influenced by the distributive political logic. As shown in more detail later, politicians jumped at opportunities to facilitate costly infrastructure developments in their local regions. One outcome was vast amounts of capital spent on networks that were quickly rendered obsolete. More seriously, in the debates over how to privatize and break apart NTT, political interventions enabled NTT to retain its structural integrity, considerable R&D resources, and special mechanisms to raise funding. These factors enabled NTT to dominate the domestic market and lead equipment manufacturers along its preferred technological trajectory—which ended up being disastrous for the latter's global market competitiveness (Kushida 2011).

The communications sector received a large amount of political attention, partly due to the configuration of government organizations overseeing the sector; the Ministry of Posts and Telecommunication (MPT) regulated both telecommunications and the postal savings system under the same roof. The postal savings system, which funded FILP, was a powerful political draw for specialist LDP politicians (known as *zoku*, or "tribes"). These powerful, regional distribution-oriented politicians became involved in shaping Japan's ICT regulation at critical junctures such as the privatization of NTT.

Expectations of a Departure from Clientelism in ICT Policy

There were several credible reasons to expect the DPJ to depart from the LDP's longstanding patterns of ICT policies. At the broadest level, beyond ICT, the period of 1993–94, when the LDP was out of power, was a time when several important reforms were undertaken, since the coalition government in power was free from the LDP's traditional vested interests. Most critically, it was not dependent on local votes, enabling the government to push through the electoral rule changes that decreased the LDP's ability to leverage its size and clientelistic ties to local voters.[2] Other reforms included the Administrative Procedure Law, which weakened bureaucracies' discretionary authority to engage in informal administrative guidance and interpret and implement broadly written laws with ministerial ordinances.

---

2 The effects of this electoral rule shift comprise a major thrust of scholarship in Japanese politics. Most scholars agree that it created incentives toward more popular, rather than narrower, regional issues. See, for example, other chapters in this volume and Ikuo Kabashima and Gill Steel (2011).

With the DPJ coming to power, it was reasonable to expect that they would be free from the traditional regional concerns of the LDP, as well as from ties to NTT that had led to the distributive and nonstrategic aspects of policy in the sector.

Second, even before the DPJ came to power, Japan's ICT policy itself had been increasingly focused on enhancing competitiveness, both in the domestic market and globally, since the late 1990s. As Japan fell behind in international indicators of ICT competitiveness such as Internet diffusion, and later, as its mobile communications became increasingly isolated from global markets, the government engaged in a "policy regime shift" (Kushida and Oh 2007; Kushida 2006). A series of deregulations enabled new entrants and new business models, while a wave of new regulations increased regulatory strength over NTT, facilitating competitors to use its infrastructure and enabling the rapid growth of broadband markets. Explicit government policies began aiming to reshape the mobile industry to make the dynamics of competition within Japan closer to that of other advanced industrialized countries (Kushida 2011).

A comparison with other early dramatic policy shifts by the DPJ, particularly in transportation infrastructure policy—a notoriously distributive policy area—added to the expectation that ICT policy would depart from historical patterns as well. An active reformist DPJ minister, Maehara Seiji, became the DPJ's first minister of the Ministry of Land, Infrastructure, Transport, and Tourism (MLIT). Free from the LDP's traditional vested-interest support groups, he quickly revised the longstanding division of labor between Tokyo's airports that had been detrimental to Japan's efforts to raise the global competitiveness of Tokyo (Shirahaze and Morita 2010). The LDP had long maintained a division of labor between Tokyo's two international airports. Narita International Airport, 35 kilometers away in Chiba Prefecture, handled most international flights, with Haneda Airport, far closer to the city center, limited to domestic flights with the exception of select chartered international flights. The LDP's bargain with Chiba Prefecture to allow Narita Airport to be built in the first place—and which had been the focal point of major demonstrations opposed to its construction in the 1970s—had led to failures of previous attempts to revive Haneda as Tokyo's international gateway (*Nikkei Weekly* 2000; *Nikkei Weekly* 2009).

In another dramatic shift, the DPJ promised to abolish the high road tolls for Japan's expressways. This was a deliberate attempt to distance itself from the LDP, which had promised in the late 1960s to lower highway tolls, but instead reneged and took the proceeds to finance local projects for its constituents. The LDP had, in essence, exchanged toll revenue—funding infrastructure projects aimed at localities, and providing jobs and infrastructure—for votes.[3]

Thus, conditions seemed ripe for change in ICT policy as well. The LDP was out of power, breaking longstanding political ties between NTT and *zoku* politicians. The DPJ's first minister of the Ministry of Internal Affairs and Communications (MIC), Haraguchi Kazuhiro, was also a young active reformer. Very soon after taking office, Haraguchi articulated several bold proposals for reorganizing NTT and reshaping the sector to make it more competitive.

Japan's ICT Policy under the DPJ: Back to the Distributive?

The DPJ's initial ICT vision, however, to the surprise of many, contained a strong focus that appeared classically distributive. The distributive component was shaped primarily by two forces: the DPJ's internal politics, and a new set of interest group politics that happened to align with the traditional distributive agenda.

In the DPJ's internal politics, MIC minister Haraguchi was solidly in the camp of Ozawa Ichiro, the party president. Ozawa was a classic LDP pork-barrel distributive-style politician in the Tanaka Kakuei faction. Ozawa had split from the LDP in the mid-1990s and was responsible for orchestrating the DPJ's successful 2009 campaign. He effectively mobilized rural votes for the DPJ by promising cash subsidies to key interest groups such as agriculture—a reversion to traditional LDP-style distributive politics.

The new set of interest group politics was that Haraguchi aligned himself with Softbank's entrepreneurial president, Son Masayoshi. Son was traditionally an ICT policy "outsider" who had complained loudly in the past for being excluded from closed-door meetings between carriers, bureaucrats, and occasionally politicians who had decided key policy matters in the sector (Kushida 2012). Softbank's policy agenda happened to align with historical regional distributive ICT policies, with a strong interest in government-sponsored, nationwide fiber-optic infrastructure deployment in order to offer extremely fast broadband services.

Haraguchi's Broadband Ambitions: The "Haraguchi Vision" and "Path of Light"?

The DPJ's first ICT plan appeared in a document presented by MIC minister Haraguchi in December 2009, entitled the "Haraguchi Vision." A major

---

3 The DPJ eventually reneged on this promise as well. See chapter 8 in this volume by Phillip Y. Lipscy.

portion of this document was a "Vision for an ICT Restoration." The wording deliberately included *Ishin* (Restoration), from the Meiji Restoration, when Japan was transformed from a feudal political, economic, and social structure to a modern industrial country, led by young, ambitious reformers.

The Vision for an ICT Restoration contained specific targets. For example, it called to double Japan's overall ICT investments by 2020 to return Japan to a 3 percent growth rate; to implement digital textbooks in all elementary and middle schools by 2015; to install electronic government systems to enable 24-hour-365-days-a-year service; to create electronic health records; and to facilitate greater productivity in agriculture through IT. Most dramatically, Haraguchi proposed that 100 percent of Japan be covered by high-speed broadband by 2020 (Haraguchi 2009).

In March 2010, Haraguchi shortened the broadband target date to 2015. He put together a working group consisting of a number of professors and experts drawn from research institutes and management consulting companies to formulate specific measures to implement a "Path of Light" plan.

The Path of Light Plan: What Is at the End of the Light?   In May 2010, this working group published "The Basic Direction to Realize the 'Path of Light' Plan." This was an extraordinarily ambitious plan on several fronts. First was the extremely fast data transmission speed, stipulating 100 Mbps or greater to all households. This is faster than most broadband services available in the world in urban areas, let alone remote rural areas (typical U.S. residential broadband is approximately 1.5 to 15 Mbps). Second, it went to great lengths to specify 100 percent household coverage, no matter how remote or costly. Third, it had no hesitation in offering government subsidies to realize this goal (MIC 2010a).

The highly ambitious nature of this policy is evident when compared to its U.S. and EU counterparts. The high-speed broadband plan announced in the United States by the FCC in 2009 aimed to provide 100 million households with 100 Mbps (50 Mbps uplink) broadband by 2020. Nationwide broadband coverage aimed for 4 Mbps, but with no specific target date. The proposed funding mechanism entailed establishing a "Connect America Fund," but as of 2011, concrete plans were still under negotiations and subject to interest group lobbying. In the EU, the Europe 2020 strategy articulated in 2010 stipulated that all EU citizens would get broadband access by 2013, with speeds of 30 Mbps or greater by 2020. By 2020, 50 percent or more of the broadband speeds were to be 100 Mbps or greater.[4]

4 European Commission, "Europe 2020." http://ec.europa.eu/europe2020/index_en.htm.

Haraguchi's Path of Light plan was extraordinary also because Japan was already among the world's most broadband-connected countries. By 2009, approximately 90 percent of Japan's households had access to at least 100 Mbps broadband through fiber-optic cables. Strong demand by the remaining 10 percent was unlikely, since of this 90 percent of households with FTTH (fiber-to-the-home) access, only approximately 30 percent actually subscribed to FTTH services (Ida 2011). The last 10 percent, however, was the most expensive to install, including mountainous areas, islands, and other areas difficult to access.

Moreover, Japan, more than elsewhere, had already discovered that promoting the usage of high-speed broadband was far more difficult than facilitating its build-out.[5] By 2002, Japan had the fastest and lowest-priced broadband worldwide, partly due to government policies that facilitated competition on the one hand, and subsidies for building core network infrastructure on the other (Kushida 2006). Yet, the widespread availability of high-speed broadband did not necessarily advantage Japanese firms in global markets, as firms such as Google (including YouTube), Apple's iPhone and App Store platform, and various cloud computing services made deep inroads. In particular, the government discovered that facilitating the usage of broadband in areas such as health care and education was much more difficult than initially anticipated (Kushida and Zysman 2009).

Japan's Historical Distributive ICT Policies

The Path of Light plan, stemming from the Haraguchi Vision, resonated strongly with the distribution portions of Japan's historical ICT policy. Let us review some of those plans in detail.

Let There Be Fiber: NTT and MPT's Historical Fiber-Optic Ambitions.   From at least the late 1970s, NTT espoused a long-range plan of migrating the entire nation's telephony network infrastructure to fiber-optic networks. As a first step, NTT began investing massive amounts of capital into a nationwide deployment of Integrated Services Digital Network (ISDN) infrastructure, widely touted worldwide as the next-generation network. NTT, with the full support of MPT, raced ahead to develop and deploy ISDN,

---

5 An MIC official stationed in a regional area described the challenge of his job: going around sparsely populated and overwhelmingly senior areas of Japan trying to convince residents that broadband would introduce new conveniences to their lives. He was forced to be ambiguous on the details, however, since few such households had or used PCs, and applications such as remote health monitoring had yet to be widely commercialized (interview with MIC official, October 1, 2009).

becoming the first to introduce it, and covering 90 percent of the population by the early 1990s (Fransman 2006). By 2000, Japan had far greater ISDN diffusion than most other countries in the world (OECD 2005).

A distinctive feature of NTT's ISDN deployment was the degree of regional deployment, and the cost associated with highly advanced (but mostly unused) ISDN public telephones. In 1990, NTT introduced ISDN public telephones sporting digital and analog data ports. These were deployed not only in urban areas, but in many rural areas as well—although in an era predating mainstream Internet diffusion, there were few users and even fewer devices that could take advantage of them. Whereas the proportion of these ISDN public telephones was a small fraction of the 800,000 deployed nationally, their per-unit and development costs were undoubtedly the world's highest. By the early 2000s, NTT had invested an estimated 9 billion USD into ISDN networks and related switching technology, known as ATM (Asynchronous Transfer Mode) (Cole 2006).

NTT's focus on nationwide fiber-optic deployment was so strong that it intentionally delayed Japan's adoption of a cheaper and far faster broadband technology, DSL (digital subscriber line). The sudden global popularity of the Internet around the world caught NTT by surprise. The Internet is based on a set of protocols, TCP/IP, that follow a technological paradigm that is fundamentally different from ATM. DSL essentially rendered ISDN obsolete by sending data at far higher speeds over conventional copper wires. In the late 1990s, even as DSL and broadband were spreading rapidly around the world, NTT showed little interest and even suppressed early feasibility tests (Tojo 2010). NTT's longstanding plan was to follow a migration path from ISDN to FTTH, deploying a proprietary (non-Internet) service and custom terminals. FTTH as simply a high-speed Internet connection for PCs was not part of its vision.

In the 1990s, MPT actively supported NTT's competitors to construct fiber-optic backbone networks. It facilitated low-interest loans through the Development Bank of Japan and used a semipublic organization (the Telecommunications Advancement Organization) to subsidize interest payments. By 1999, over 75 billion yen worth of loans had been allocated (Kushida 2011).

ICT-Flavored Pork: "Teletopias" and "New Media Communities."   The LDP's history of shaping ICT strategies toward its distributive goals is most clearly illustrated by its involvement in a series of regional development plans in the mid-1980s.

The plans originated as bureaucratic turf wars between MITI and MPT. Both sought to extend their jurisdiction over value-added IT networks; MITI was in charge of computers and MPT oversaw networks. As the two technologies converged, each wanted to claim the new territory as its own. In 1983, MITI proposed a plan for 11 "New Media Communities" to receive heavy investments in the latest communications networks and new, experimental services. MPT, not to be outdone, immediately proposed to create several "Teletopias"—essentially the same concept. Major capital investments were planned for these strategies; NTT published investment estimates of anywhere between 20 to 100 trillion yen for its next-generation networks.

LDP politicians jumped en masse at the opportunity to bring (and take credit for) major investments to their districts. They immediately and enthusiastically supported both ministries' plans. In the fall of 1983, LDP members created the "Diet Members' League for the New Media," led by Kanemaru Shin and Sato Moriyoshi, both key figures in the LDP's Tanaka faction. An astonishing 220 LDP members joined the new group upon its creation. MITI's plan, tellingly, included Tanaka's local district, Nagaoka (Johnson 1989, 225).

Other parts of Japan's clientelistic political economy—construction and transportation—also entered the political fray. The Ministry of Construction (MOC), supported by construction-*zoku* politicians, submitted bills to the Diet in 1984 that included large budgets to construct regional ICT infrastructure. The Ministry of Transportation (MOT), supported by the transportation-*zoku*, quickly followed, proposing fiber-optic cables along government-owned railway lines. In the end, a 1986 cabinet proposal combined the plans of all the ministries, offering tax credits and support from the Development Bank of Japan (DBJ). As Chalmers Johnson summed it up, the resulting bill was "an omnibus pork barrel bill that [gave] something to everybody" (Johnson 1989, 227).

The Politics Driving the "Path of Light": New Insiders

The drivers of the Path of Light plan were far different from previous NTT- and MPT-led plans or the heavily LDP-pushed regional distribution plans. First of all, NTT vociferously opposed the plan, especially when the deadline was shortened to 2015. Second, the bureaucracies were minimally involved, and other Diet members were not particularly active on the issue. Instead, Softbank, long a policy outsider, gained major influence in shaping Japan's ICT policy.

Softbank, founded in the 1980s by ethnic Korean-Japanese entrepreneur Son Masayoshi, was a rapidly growing IT services company. Since the late 1990s, it had expanded to offer broadband, mobile, and fixed-line telecommunications services, but it had always been an outsider in the policy process. In fact, Son had gone to extreme lengths to obtain wireless spectrum, taking out ads in national newspapers and even waging a lawsuit against MIC. He charged that major decisions always occurred behind closed doors between incumbent carriers, the ministry, and LDP politicians.[6]

The DPJ's ascent to power provided Softbank with an unprecedented opportunity to access policy. One of Son's staff in the president's office was a former DPJ member who facilitated direct meetings between Son and Minister Haraguchi (Ida 2011, 201–202). Softbank concentrated its lobbying efforts on Haraguchi and was the first to use the term "Path of Light" in its proposal. This proposal advocated not only 100 percent FTTH access, but also the entire replacement of NTT's existing telephone network with an IP (Internet Protocol)–based fiber-optic network.

Softbank's interest in getting the government to pay for nationwide broadband and an IP-based fiber network was simple. Its vision was to provide a broad portfolio of online services through a large variety of subsidiaries and affiliates offering content firms. To this end, it had launched a price war in DSL in the early 2000s, demonstrating that it was willing to incur several years of losses to facilitate greater broadband penetration. It also purchased nationwide cellular infrastructure and was Japan's exclusive provider for the Apple iPhone. Softbank had entered the FTTH business, but withdrew within a few years after finding it infeasible to compete against NTT.

NTT strongly criticized Softbank's plan as unrealistic, leading to a widely publicized debate. Softbank took out full-page advertisements in major newspapers, comparing its own calculations with those of the status quo; it contended that, under its plan, prevailing telephone rates could remain unchanged while FTTH broadband prices could be lowered approximately 15 dollars. NTT was put in the awkward position of opposing a plan it had long advocated, since it was also being threatened with a potential breakup, as discussed later. It contended that the core network could be converted to IP by 2025 and that household fiber-copper installation should occur only when consumers signed up for FTTH. While many considered Softbank's proposal self-serving, others, such as Kyoto University economics Professor Ida Takanori (who turned down approaches from both Softbank and NTT), pointed out that Softbank did raise some legitimate points. Conventional telephone switches are vastly more expensive to operate and maintain vis-à-vis IP equipment, and conversion to an all-IP network would be more efficient if done in blocs rather than piecemeal by household (Ida 2011).

6 For details, see Kushida (2012).

Softbank's lobbying clearly influenced Haraguchi's plans. His March 2010 "Haraguchi Vision 2.0," announced three months after the original, incorporated much of Softbank's vocabulary, including the label "Path of Light." Softbank had also brought to the table the issue of breaking apart NTT. As the task force of experts began calling in various firms to testify, the basic plan they worked from closely resembled Softbank's proposal (Interview notes, 2011).

What does Softbank's role in Haraguchi's Path of Light strategy signify? First, even though the policy initially seemed traditionally distributive, it was not simply a repeat of historical clientelism. Instead, the alignment of actors and their positions were a departure from historical patterns. It was neither NTT nor MIC driven, there were no bureaucratic turf wars at stake, and the familiar pattern of ministries and NTT lobbying their respective *zoku* politicians did not occur. Instead, a former outsider provided input to a reform-minded minister, who went ahead with relatively little consultation with the ministry. Despite the minister calling for a long-term goal that NTT had long supported, NTT was opposed, but not due to a MIC-NTT conflict. The fault line of conflict was between NTT and Softbank, with the latter prepared to battle NTT more aggressively than any other firm.

The DPJ's Attempt at Restructuring the Sector: Abandoning the Strategic

Arguably the most important policy measures to enhance the international competitiveness of Japan's ICT sector included breaking up NTT and consolidating the government's ICT policymaking functions. Many of Japanese firms' woes in global markets can be traced to NTT's sheer size, its procurement practices, R&D resources, and intention to lead manufacturers. With rare exceptions, its innovation model was closed and focused on the domestic market. At the same time, regulatory fragmentation has led to policy duplication and has frustrated Japan's attempts to take advantage of its highly developed mobile and broadband environment.

The DPJ initially floated the idea of breaking up NTT and reorganizing the regulatory structure. Part of Minister Haraguchi's Path of Light strategy called for an examination of the issue of breaking apart NTT, entailing the creation of an independent company that would exclusively manage the FTTH networks and lease out capacity to all other carriers, including NTT. This was not a trivial matter, since intense debates had raged several times since the early 1980s. Here, too, the debates followed a political logic that departed from historical patterns. Then, partway through the debates, an upheaval within the DPJ led to its hasty abandonment of these issues.

Without strong political will, the powerful interest groups quickly pressured the DPJ to drop the issue.

To understand NTT's power is to understand its scale. NTT had long been Japan's largest company, dwarfing all others in the sector. In 1994, even after the Japanese asset bubble had burst, NTT had the largest market value of any company in the world, at $129 billion, with the second largest being the Shell Group, at $92 billion (Fransman 1995). In 1998, just before NTT was restructured into a holding company, its operating revenue was $91 billion. This compares with $62 billion for former monopoly AT&T, $37 billion for Deutsche Telecom, and $29 billion for France Telecom and Telecom Italia, all former government-owned monopolies like NTT.

Competition policy in Japan therefore always revolved around the rules over NTT, such as interconnection and access rates, and the scope of its business; any new area that it entered put competitors at jeopardy through its sheer size and ownership of nationwide infrastructure.

A History of Conflict over Breaking Up NTT: MPT's Attacks

A history of conflict between NTT and MPT grew out of their organizational origins, as products of complex political battles and compromises.

From the establishment of the communications sector until after World War II, Japan's communications networks and services were operated directly by the Ministry of Communications. The ministry was broken apart by the Allied Occupation forces, as it had been central to wartime censorship and propaganda. NTT became a fully government-owned public corporation, enjoying a monopoly in domestic communications until 1985.

MPT became the primary supervisor of NTT, but in practice, having grown out of the Ministry of Postal Affairs, it lacked expertise and political clout. NTT received its budget from the National Diet after approval from the MOF, and the prime minister appointed NTT's president and vice president.[7]

A complex political struggle beginning in the late 1970s and culminating in 1985 led to the partial privatization of NTT, new competitors in the sector, and a vast expansion of MPT's regulatory powers. An intense political and bureaucratic struggle involved MPT, MITI, MOF, LDP *zoku* politicians, NTT, NTT's "family" of equipment suppliers, NTT's labor union, the opposition Socialist Party, and big business in the form of the Japan Federation

---

7 NTT frequently gave testimony directly to the Diet, circumventing MPT, and the approximately 30 staff members of the telecommunications office in MPT were all dispatched from NTT. When NTT applied for licenses, therefore, the officials within MPT inspecting the applications were none other than NTT employees (Vogel 1996).

of Economic Organizations (Keidanren).[8] NTT, though privatized, avoided a breakup. MPT became a full-fledged "policy bureaucracy," gaining new regulatory powers that enabled it to conduct R&D and shape the sector through licenses and administrative guidance.

From 1985 onward, political battles occurred roughly every five years, with MPT pushing to split apart NTT, while NTT and its labor union fought back. MPT could draw upon the political clout of the Special Postmasters' Association *(Zentoku)*, due to its position of overseeing postal affairs. "Special postmasters" were local notables in rural areas appointed to provide postal services from their homes, and they could deliver votes. Yusei-*zoku* LDP politicians therefore often sided with MPT. NTT itself was Japan's largest corporation in terms of number of employees, with an array of local construction subcontractors and firms that could deliver both votes and financing—the basis for their influence with NTT-*zoku*. NTT's labor union (the Japan Telecommunications Workers' Union, or JTWU), a longtime supporter of the opposition Socialist Party, opposed splitting apart NTT. Its influence on policy was in mobilizing the Socialist Party to reach a compromise with the LDP. The complex settlement led to a postponement of the breakup issue for five years.

In 1990, MPT again pushed to break apart NTT, while NTT and JTWU opposed. This time MITI and MOF aligned against MPT for their own reasons—MITI to prevent MPT from gaining more clout, and MOF to prevent a decline in NTT's share value, of which the government held the largest portion and which had declined markedly. The Japan Socialist Party's victory in the 1989 upper-house elections put JTWU's demands on the table.[9] This united opposition threatened to overwhelm MPT's position, but MPT succeeded in mobilizing Yusei-*zoku* politicians.

A compromise postponed the discussion until 1995 while enhancing the operational independence of NTT's divisions, such as long distance and local, forcing it to disclose unit-based financial reports. The compromise spun off NTT's wireless services division, then small and considered relatively insignificant, but which later grew to become NTT's primary revenue driver.[10]

---

8 For details on the complex battle, see Johnson (1989) and Vogel (1996).

9 In addition, equipment manufacturers followed NTT for fear of losing their R&D procurement budgets, and Keidanren, divided between pro-breakup and anti-breakup camps, depending on their relationship to NTT, called for more time to deliberate (Kawabata 2006).

10 The decision to give NTT's wireless R&D labs to the new company, against the concerns of some MPT officials, proved to be a major factor in isolating Japan's cellular market, as it later developed at an explosive rate (Kushida 2011).

In 1995, the debate reopened, once again pitting MPT against NTT, NTT's competitors, and Japan's major industrial firms, which pushed for a breakup, against NTT, the JTWU, the Socialist Party, and equipment firms, which opposed. The LDP at the time was in a coalition with the Socialist Party, and the latter took JTWU's position of staunchly opposing any weakening of NTT. With a lower-house election looming, Prime Minister Hashimoto postponed the issue for a year. In March 2006, the issue was reopened but was unsuccessful in mobilizing enough LDP support to push through a strong compromise, leading to another one-year postponement. Hashimoto's new government after October 1996 was a coalition without the Socialist Party, severely weakening JTWU's influence. As a result, the ruling coalition was willing to seek a compromise on restructuring NTT, paving the way for a deal brokered by Hashimoto and political leaders and allowing NTT to restructure itself into a holding company. This agreement was reached behind closed doors, astonishing even the participants in MPT's deliberation council, who learned about the agreement in the newspapers.[11] NTT became a holding company, with two massive regional carriers (NTT East and West), the mobile subsidiary (NTT DoCoMo), long distance (NTT Communications), and general IT solutions (NTT Data).

In 2000, MPT called for reforms that would force NTT Group companies into greater competition with one another and weaken their financial and personnel ties. NTT, unsurprisingly, opposed these ideas and began lobbying its *zoku* politicians, even mobilizing some of its managers to participate in pre-election campaigns for the LDP in the summer upper-house elections. Before the legislative revision proposals were presented to LDP members in March 2001, however, MPT was reorganized into MIC.

This organizational change of the ICT regulator altered the political resources available to it, shifting the balance of power in political debates. When MPT's telecommunications functions were combined with the Ministry of Home Affairs and the Management and Coordination Agency to form MIC, postal affairs regulation moved to the Postal Affairs Agency. As a result, MIC officials in charge of telecommunications policy could no longer draw on broader Yusei-*zoku* as effectively, leaving only a few LDP members knowledgeable about ICT policy on their side. NTT-*zoku*, however, remained, strengthening NTT.[12]

As a result, MIC's attacks on NTT in early 2001 were ineffective, and instead, its own regulatory jurisdiction came under attack. The LDP threatened

11 Interview with the former chair of the MPT deliberation council, March 14, 2002.
12 Interviews with MIC officials, the former chair of the MPT deliberation council, telecommunications journalists, September 5–6, 2011.

MIC that if the latter pursued a breakup of NTT too vigorously, the LDP would detach a new organization, the Telecommunications Carriers Dispute Resolution Commission, from the MIC. This would create an independent regulator, weakening MIC's power to shape the market and pursue its agenda of strengthening regulations over NTT to prevent it from dominating the market. MIC ended up dropping its plans to promote competition among NTT regional firms and to raise the possibility of an NTT breakup in another two years. In the final bill submitted to the Diet in April and passed in June 2001, MIC did obtain some policy concessions, particularly in strengthening competitors' access to NTT's networks to offer broadband services, but the reorganization of NTT was off the table.

This brings us to the DPJ's initial talk of breaking up NTT.

The DPJ's Politics of Breaking Apart NTT

When Minister Haraguchi raised the issue of breaking apart NTT again in 2010, neither the political alignments nor the political dynamics followed historical patterns.

Softbank, as part of its lobbying for the Path of Light plan, first floated the idea of breaking apart NTT, but in a new way. Softbank's idea was to follow the example of Australia and Singapore to create a firm dedicated to building and operating a network infrastructure—in this case, fiber—and leasing it out to carriers who provided the actual services. The initial Haraguchi Vision of December 2009 did not advocate a breakup of NTT, but the following April, an NTT breakup was on the agenda for Haraguchi's "Task Force for ICT Policy in a Global Era."

The industry conflict became clear during the early Path of Light strategy hearings, when major ICT service firms were invited to state their positions. Those who stood to benefit from a weakened NTT, as well as access to low-cost nationwide fiber infrastructure, supported a breakup. These included NTT's major competitors KDDI, Softbank, and eAccess, along with an industry association, the Telecommunications Services Association (of which the major NTT companies were not members).[13]

Firms opposing the NTT breakup included NTT itself and two other carriers whose own fiber deployments were their competitive advantage. K Opticom, a Western Japan–based power company subsidiary, had been particularly aggressive in spreading FTTH to the Kansai area with low prices, and J-Com was Japan's largest cable operator expanding rapidly into broadband services.

13 The proceedings of the task force, as well as documents such as the membership list, are available on the MIC home page. http://www.soumu.go.jp/menu_news/s-news/01tsushin01_01000017.html.

Observers wryly noted that although NTT had long depicted its nation-wide fiber plans as serving the national interest, this debate revealed that NTT was interested only in deploying fiber if it could do so on its own terms. A curious contention by NTT's president during the proceedings to oppose 100 percent coverage, that an easy-to-use terminal device for FTTH was required for the network to be useful to most users, harked back to its plan from the early 1990s before widespread Internet diffusion.

The initial momentum spearheaded by Haraguchi, however, did not play out through *zoku*-style political maneuvers with each side mobilizing their own political supporters. Instead, a political upheaval within the DPJ during its first year in power brought the reform inertia to a screeching halt.

The DPJ's Reversal: The Specter of Ozawa in ICT Politics

The DPJ's first prime minister, Hatoyama Yukio, resigned on June 2, 2010, marking a major structural shift of power within the DPJ. ICT reforms became collateral damage.

Although Hatoyama was the party president and therefore prime minister, Party Secretary Ozawa Ichiro wielded much of the power and influence. Over the course of the 1990s, Ozawa's various political maneuvers arguably did more to shape Japanese politics in the 1990s than any other politician. When Ozawa left the LDP in 1993, he split the party, bringing an end to its continuous rule since 1955. As part of the coalition government that replaced the LDP, his alienation of the Socialist Party led to the unlikely coalition of longtime opponents, bringing the LDP back into power in coalition with the Socialist Party. A decade later, after he merged his party with others to create the DPJ, he became the party president of the DPJ. Yet, embroiled in a campaign-financing scandal, he was forced to step down as party president even as he engineered the DPJ's 2009 electoral victory that brought it to power.

Once the DPJ took power, Ozawa's position as party secretary created a contradiction between the DPJ's platform and its operational reality. The platform was to consolidate power in a strong prime minister and the cabinet, as Ozawa had advocated in his book, *Blueprint for a New Japan* (1994). However, having resigned as party president, Ozawa did not have a government post when the DPJ was elected, creating an uncomfortable tension in the leadership structure and undermining the DPJ's credibility with the public. Moreover, Ozawa's political-funding scandals plagued the DPJ from the start, and Hatoyama became embroiled in a funding scandal of his own. As the DPJ broke promise after promise—to cut expenditures by approximately $32 billion, to end highway toll and gasoline taxes, and to move a U.S. military base away from Futenma in Okinawa—Hatoyama's approval ratings plummeted. As the July 2010 upper-house election loomed, Hatoyama and Ozawa lost support within the DPJ, leading to their resignations.

The problem for ICT policy was that reformist minister Haraguchi was an Ozawa supporter. He won his first term in the House of Representatives in 1996 as a member of Ozawa's New Frontier Party. When Hatoyama's successor, Kan Naoto, reshuffled his cabinet in September 2010, Haraguchi was removed as MIC minister and assigned to the House of Representatives General Affairs Committee.

A comprehensive reversal of Haraguchi's policy initiatives ensued. Funding for major items in his Haraguchi Vision was slashed from the budget, including funding for items that he had revived the previous year as minister. The Path of Light plan itself was given a *B* ranking in the DPJ's budget evaluation. A comparison with METI's ICT-related policies, which were not driven by an active reformist DPJ minister and were therefore relatively conservative, is telling. While 83 percent of METI's ICT-related policies were given an *A* ranking, only 8 percent of MIC's ICT-related policies received *A's*, and 19 percent received *D's*.

Haraguchi's successor, Katayama Yoshihiro, was originally a Ministry of Home Affairs official. In 1998, on the eve of the ministry's absorption into MIC, he left to become governor of Tottori Prefecture. With little experience or interest in ICT policy, he focused his energies on other areas of the ministry. Without strong leadership or political support, MIC was weakened against NTT's labor union, a core DPJ supporter, and NTT itself, both of which opposed splitting apart NTT.[14]

The final recommendation of the task force presented in November 2010 was considerably less ambitious than its initial and midterm stance toward NTT. It sketched three scenarios: (1) spinning off NTT's fiber operations to an independent company; (2) making it into a subsidiary under the NTT Holding Company; and (3) strengthening internal controls to maintain some independence of the infrastructure operations. The task force recommended the third, which kept NTT intact (MIC 2010b). In a more dramatic reversal, it jettisoned both the goal to attain 100 percent broadband coverage and a timeline, let alone the 2015 target. NTT, on its part, with an informal understanding that this was a concession to silence the breakup debate, agreed to lower its FTTH access rates to competitors (Okui 2011).

The point about Minister Katayama not concentrating his energies on MIC's telecommunications policy leads us to the issue of reforming Japan's

14 Interview with MIC official, September 5, 2011.

ICT regulatory structure, since the fact that MIC's jurisdiction extends to areas unrelated to ICT is an artifact of Japan's politics shaping its government organization.

Restructuring Japan's ICT Regulator(s)

Restructuring Japan's ICT regulator has been a long-term issue for Japan's capacity to enact strategic ICT policy. After the DPJ came to power, Haraguchi initially raised the idea of combining and specializing Japan's fragmented ICT regulatory structure, but his removal from MIC halted this plan.

In contrast to countries such as South Korea, which created a Ministry of Information and Communications in the early 1990s,[15] Japan's ICT regulation was decentralized, hindering its ability to promulgate and implement coherent strategies. METI's jurisdiction included high-tech industries, MIC covered information and communications, and the Ministry of Education, Culture, Sports, Science, and Technology (MEXT) was responsible for driving advanced science and technologies and strengthening industry-academia ties. In 2001, the government had established the IT Strategy Headquarters in the cabinet office, which promulgated a series of strategies that helped facilitate Japan's broadband markets.

The government's inability to effectively coordinate with a coherent set of policies became pronounced as various technological areas converged. As e-commerce and electronic payment systems became a commercial reality in the late 1990s, METI and MIC set up parallel divisions. Firms complained that they were confused about which ministry's jurisdiction they fell under, and ended up having to expend energy to coordinate with both. In 2003, MIC promulgated the "Ubiquitous Japan (u-Japan)" strategy, calling for the adoption of Japan's high-speed broadband services in areas such as health care, agriculture, transportation, education, and government. However, each of these areas fell under a different ministerial jurisdiction, such as the Ministry of Health, Labor, and Welfare (MHLW), and MLIT, and MEXT. MHLW, in particular, was not only cautious about implementing medical IT systems for safety reasons, but it was also subject to its own political pressures from the powerful doctors' association, the Japan Medical Association. Only the area of e-government—installing IT systems for government services— benefited from the ministerial structure, since MIC housed the former Ministry of Home Affairs.[16]

---

15 For details, see Kushida and Oh (2007).
16 Interview with MIC official, September 5, 2011.

In his early days in office, Haraguchi called for the creation of a unified Ministry of Information, Communications, and Culture to oversee Japan's ICT policy capabilities. However, enhancing bureaucratic power flew in the face of the DPJ's platform to weaken the bureaucracies. Haraguchi instead pressed for greater specialization as a first step, including in his Haraguchi Vision 2.0 the proposal to spin a piece of MIC specializing in broadcasting rights, with a plan to grow it into a digital content management agency. However, when Haraguchi was removed from MIC, this idea was removed from the final task force report under his successor. Thus, the status quo remained.

Conclusion and Implications

This chapter has addressed the question of how Japan's ICT policies and politics shifted under the DPJ. It began with the longstanding observation that Japan's ICT policies were pulled in two directions—the distributive and the strategic—mirroring the logics of Japan's "dual" political economy. The expectation was that, under the DPJ, running on a platform of departing from the LDP's clientelistic model of politics, Japan's ICT policies would have a far weaker distributive influence.

An initial examination, however, revealed a surprisingly strong focus on distributive goals. Further analysis showed that the politics behind the distributive plan actually stemmed from new interest group politics, which departed considerably from previous LDP distributive plans. On the strategic side, this chapter found that an internal DPJ upheaval halted early strategic visions for the sector to enhance its international competitiveness, by breaking apart NTT and consolidating regulatory functions.

On balance, after two years of DPJ rule, Japan's ICT policies are remarkable in their level of continuity from the LDP era. However, in the interim, new political dynamics began to drive policy, but the DPJ's internal politics reverted the industry and regulatory structure to the status quo. With a weaker distributive policy pull, however, there is less risk of massive infrastructure projects that end up as obsolete investments. However, the political volatility has demonstrated that the strategic capacity is not likely to be strengthened either.

There are several observations from this longitudinal study of multiple issues in a single sector. While this is one sector, it is a critical one in and of itself, and others, such as power and other highly regulated services, share several broadly similar features, such as large, regulated firms and traditionally strong distributive components. First, we see the curious reality of marked policy continuity driven by a new set of politics. An alternation of power can lead to outsiders becoming insiders, but the outsiders may end up, for different reasons, advocating a similar policy trajectory as before.

Second, stronger political leadership, with a greater policy orientation, can lead to greater volatility in the policy trajectory. Internal party politics can shift policy trajectories when key political leaders are replaced. Therefore, if parties rotate in power and the political leadership is strengthened even further, we can expect greater volatility, which can decrease the government's strategic capacity.

Third, the most powerful of interest groups can remain quite powerful—a point relevant for the March 2011 nuclear disaster involving the Tokyo Electric Power Company, the largest corporate customer for major Japanese firms. In ICT, NTT is still powerful, despite the reconfiguration of its direct political support base for the incumbent party—the labor union being a longtime supporter of the DPJ rather than NTT's management networks with the LDP. In issues where labor and management's interests are aligned, such as a breakup, strong political will must be sustained to drive change.

Finally, the configuration of bureaucracies can matter a great deal in how political changes affect policy. If MIC were not housing several very different types of functions, with personnel operating largely along old ministerial silos, it would have been unlikely that a ministerial replacement would shift the policy momentum so drastically.

For the future of ICT in Japan, there was much disappointment after Haraguchi left, except for NTT and its supporters. The fragmentation of regulatory capabilities makes strategic policy difficult, and a strong NTT makes reforms difficult. Change will continue to be strongly shaped by NTT, and the best that regulators can do is to support new entrants and technologies to force it to adjust and adapt.

Overall, we can expect that without strong political leadership, radical reform will be difficult, resulting in a continuing pattern of moving a number of steps forward, followed by a few steps of reversal. Yet, the irony of MIC's experience is that when it had stronger political leadership, the backlash was stronger as well.

References

Anchordoguy, Marie. 2001. "Nippon Telegraph and Telephone Company (NTT) and the Building of a Telecommunications Industry in Japan." *Business History Review*, no. 75 (Autumn): 507–41.

Bar, François, Stephen Cohen, Peter Cowhey, Brad DeLong, Michael Kleeman, and John Zysman. 2000. "Access and Innovation Policy for the Third-Generation Internet." *Telecommunications Policy* 24 (6–7): 489–518.

Baumol, William J. 1967. "Macroeconomics of Unbalanced Growth: The Anatomy of Urban Crisis." *American Economic Review* 57 (3): 415–26.

Cole, Robert E. 2006. "Telecommunications Markets in World Markets: Understanding Japan's Decline." In *How Revolutionary Was the Digital Revolution? National Responses, Market Transitions, and Global Technology*, edited by John Zysman and Abraham Newman, 101–124. Stanford, CA: Stanford University Press.

Fransman, Martin. 1995. *Japan's Computer and Communications Industry: The Evolution of Industrial Giants and Global Competitiveness*. New York: Oxford University Press.

———. 2006. "Introduction." In *Global Broadband Battles: Why the U.S. and Europe Lag While Asia Leads*, edited by Martin Fransman. Stanford, CA: Stanford University Press.

Funk, Jeffrey. 2002. *Global Competition between and within Standards: The Case of Mobile Phones*. New York: Palgrave Macmillan.

Haraguchi, Kazuhiro. 2009. "Haraguchi Vision." MIC. http://www.soumu.go .jp/main_content /000048728.pdf.

Horikoshi, Ko. 2010. "'Hikari No Michi' Jitsugen Ni Muke NTT to Kyougou Ga Tairitsu" [NTT and competitors face off in road toward "Path of Light"]. Nikkei ITPro. http://itpro.nikkeibp.co.jp/article/NEWS/20100421/ 347305/?ST=network.

Ida, Takanori. 2006. "Broadband, the Information Society, and National Systems." In *Global Broadband Battles: Why the U.S. and Europe Lag While Asia Leads*, edited by Martin Fransman, 65–86. Stanford, CA: Stanford University Press.

———. 2011. *Jisedai Intaanetto No Keizaigaku* [The economics of the next-generation Internet]. Tokyo: Iwanami Shinsho.

Johnson, Chalmers A. 1986a. *MITI and the Japanese Miracle: The Growth of Industrial Policy, 1925–1975*. 1st Tuttle ed. Tokyo: Charles E. Tuttle.

———. 1986b. "Tanaka Kakuei, Structural Corruption, and the Advent of Machine Politics in Japan." *Journal of Japanese Studies* 12 (1): 1–28.

———. 1989. "MITI, MPT, and the Telecom Wars: How Japan Makes Policy in High Technology." In *Politics and Productivity: The Real Story of How Japan Works*, edited by Chalmers Johnson, Laura Tyson, and John Zysman. New York: Harper Business.

Jorgenson, Dale Weldeau, and Charles W. Wessner, eds. 2007. *Enhancing Productivity Growth in the Information Age*. Washington, DC: National Academies Press.

Kabashima, Ikuo, and Gill Steel. 2011. *Changing Politics in Japan*. Ithaca, NY: Cornell University Press.

Katz, Richard. 1998. *Japan: The System That Soured: The Rise and Fall of the Japanese Economic Miracle*. Armonk, NY: M.E. Sharpe.

Kawabata, Eiji. 2004. "Dual Governance: The Contemporary Politics of Posts and Telecommunications in Japan." *Social Science Japan Journal* 7 (1): 21–39.

———. 2006. *Contemporary Government Reform in Japan: The Dual State in Flux*. New York: Palgrave Macmillan.

Kushida, Kenji E. 2006. "Japan's Telecommunications Regime Shift: Understanding Japan's Potential Resurgence." In *How Revolutionary Was the Digital Revolution? National Responses, Market Transitions, and Global Technology in the Digital Era*, edited by Abraham Newman and John Zysman, 125–47. Stanford, CA: Stanford University Press.

———. 2008. "Wireless Bound and Unbound: The Politics Shaping Cellular Markets in Japan and South Korea." *Journal of Information Technology and Politics* 5 (2): 231–54.

———. 2011. "Leading without Followers: How Politics and Market Dynamics Trapped Innovations in Japan's Domestic 'Galapagos' Telecommunications Sector." *Journal of Industry, Competition and Trade* 11 (3): 279–307.

———. 2012. "Entrepreneurship in Japan's ICT Sector: Opportunities and Protection from Japan's Telecommunications Regulatory Regime Shift." *Social Science Japan Journal* 15 (1): 3–30.

Kushida, Kenji E., and Seung-Young Oh. 2006. "The Political Economies of Broadband Development in South Korea and Japan." Stanford Japan Center Discussion Paper DP-2006-002-E.

———. 2007. "The Political Economies of Broadband in South Korea and Japan." *Asian Survey* 47 (3): 481–504.

Kushida, Kenji E., and John Zysman. 2009. "The Services Transformation and Network Policy: The New Logic of Value Creation." *Review of Policy Research* 26 (1–2): 173–94.

MIC (Ministry of Internal Affairs and Communications). 2010a. "'Hikari No Michi' Kousou Jitsugen Ni Mukete—Kihonteki Houkousei" [Basic direction to realize the "Path of Light" plan]. MIC. http://www.soumu.go.jp/main_content/000066358.pdf.

———. 2010b. "'Hikari No Michi' Kousou Jitsugen Ni Mukete Torimatome an" [Toward realizing the "Path of Light" plan]. http://www.soumu.go.jp/main_content/000092955.pdf.

———. 2010c. "Information and Communications in Japan: 2010 White Paper." Tokyo:MIC.

Nikkei Weekly. 2000. "Tokyo Airport Bids for Global Flights: Ministry Considers Increasing International Air Traffic at Haneda, but Chiba Protests Competition." May 1, 4.

———. 2009. "Minister's Comments on Airports Spark Hubbub." October 19.

OECD. 2005. "Source OECD Telecommunications Database, Vol. 2005."

Okui, Noriaki. 2011. "'Genba Yose' to 'Haraguchi Hazushi'" [Moving toward Genba, removing Haraguchi]. *Nikkei ITpro*. http://itpro.nikkeibp.co.jp/article/COLUMN/20110112/356002/?k2.

———. 2011. "Soumusho vs. Keisanshou" [MIC versus METI]. *Nikkei ITpro*. http://itpro.nikkeibp.co.jp/article/COLUMN/20110112/356008/.

Oonishi, Katsuaki, ed. 2000. *Joho Tsushin: Nihon No Biggu Ban Indasutorii* [Information communications: Japan's Big Bang industry]. Tokyo: Otsuki Shoten.

Ozawa, Ichiro. 1993. *Nihon Kaizou Keikaku* [Japan transformation plan]. Tokyo: Kodansha.

Ozawa, Ichiro, Louisa Rubinfien, and Eric Gower. 1994. *Blueprint for a New Japan: The Rethinking of a Nation*. 1st ed. Tokyo; New York: Kodansha International.

Shirahaze, Shoichi, and Masataka Morita. 2010. "Government Shifts Course in Aviation Policy." *The Daily Yomiuri*, May 28, 7.

Suda, Yuko. 2005. *Tsushin Gurobaru-Ka No Seijigaku: "Gaiatsu" to Nihon No Denki Tsushin Seisaku* [The politics of globalization in telecommunications: "External pressure" on Japanese policies]. Shohan ed. Tokyo: Yushindo Kobunsha.

Tojo, Iwao. 2010. *Tokyo Metallic Monogatari* [The Tokyo metallic story]. Tokyo: JCast. http://www.j-cast.co.jp/2010/09/j-cast_books.html.

Vogel, Steven K. 1996. *Freer Markets, More Rules: Regulatory Reform in Advanced Industrial Countries*. Ithaca, NY: Cornell University Press.

———. 1999. "Can Japan Disengage: Winners and Losers in Japan's Political Economy, and the Ties That Bind Them." *Social Science Japan* 2 (1): 3–21.

———. 2006. *Japan Remodeled: How Government and Industry Are Reforming Japanese Capitalism*. Ithaca, NY: Cornell University Press.

Woodall, Brian. 1996. *Japan under Construction: Corruption, Politics, and Public Works*. Berkeley: University of California Press.

Zysman, John, Stuart Feldman, Kenji E. Kushida, Jonathan Murray, and Niels Christian Nielsen. 2013. "Services with Everything: The ICT-Enabled Digital Transformation of Services." In *The Third Globalization? Can Wealthy Nations Stay Rich in the Twenty-First Century?*, edited by Dan Breznitz and John Zysman, 99–129. New York: Oxford University Press.

Zysman, John, Stuart Feldman, Jonathan Murray, Niels Christian Nielsen, and Kenji E. Kushida. 2011. "The New Challenge to Economic Governance: The Digital Transformation of Services." In *Innovations in Public Governance*, edited by Ari-Veikko Anttiroiko, S. J. Bailey, and Pekka Valkama. Amsterdam: IOS Press.

10 Decentralization and the Democratic Party of Japan

Linda Hasunuma

The LDP-Kōmeitō coalition accelerated decentralization reforms and transformed the geographical, political, and financial structure of Japan's local governments. Because these reforms were blamed for deepening regional inequalities, the DPJ was able to capitalize on this issue and won majorities in both houses by pledging to restore "people's livelihoods." Once in power, however, the DPJ faced incentives to restore resources to rural areas because rural voters were still pivotal in the upper house and had switched their support from the LDP to the DPJ. Electoral incentives forced the DPJ not only to put the brakes on decentralization, but also to reverse some of those policies in order to provide a cushion to groups that had been made worse off by the previous government's reforms of local governments. The party that had once championed decentralization while in opposition was restoring resources to rural areas—much like the old LDP.

The authors in this edited volume explore how politics and policies changed with the historic transfer of power to the Democratic Party of Japan (DPJ), and these discussions focus on the political dynamics and policies at the national level. The goal of this chapter, however, is to place the focus on local governments to see what impact the change in power to the DPJ had

I thank Stephan Haggard, Ethan Scheiner, Phillip Lipscy, and two anonymous reviewers of an earlier draft of this chapter, for their extremely helpful comments and suggestions. All errors are my own.

on politics at that level, especially with respect to the wave of decentralization reforms that began in 1999. Did decentralization and these changes to local governments continue under the DPJ?

While in opposition to the LDP-Kōmeitō coalition, the DPJ was a strong advocate of decentralization, but once in power, it faced incentives to slow down these reforms because these policies, including the municipal mergers, were thought to be responsible for deepening regional and income inequalities. Rural voters had switched their support to the DPJ in the 2007 upper-house election over this issue of inequality. Faced with the competing incentives of a lower house that represents urban interests and an upper house that still overrepresents rural interests, the DPJ abandoned decentralization and expanded social welfare spending to maintain its core and new bases of support in both houses. Its single greatest legacy at the local level thus far is that it restored and expanded allocations to rural areas that the previous governments had cut, thereby behaving much like the old LDP. The party that once championed decentralization had to slow down and even reverse some decentralization policies because of the electoral incentives it faced in each chamber.

What Changed? Decentralization under the DPJ

The DPJ could not impose greater burdens on local governments because it had won both houses of the Diet on its campaign promise to address the growing social inequalities generated by the previous LDP-Kōmeitō governments. In its 2009 manifesto, the party pledged to improve the quality of life or people's livelihoods, and to reduce wasteful spending, especially in public works. The 2009 manifesto highlighted decentralization as one of the party's five key principles in its vision for political change. The party wanted to reform Japan "from centralized government to regional sovereignty" and argued that "local affairs will be decided at the local levels." The DPJ wanted to make the central-local relationship more equal and abolish the way subsidies were distributed. Until 2007 and 2009, the DPJ had greater success with urban and suburban voters, so the party's platform emphasized measures to change the existing political structure and redistribute more resources to them. The party's policy document, "Index 2009," had a vision for decentralization that was even bolder than that of the former governments and prioritized the replacement of Japan's 47 prefectures into about a dozen regional governments (*doshusei*) (Yokomichi 2011).

The DPJ platform favored shifting resources from specific rural interests to broader social policies, yet once the party won the upper house, spending for rural areas, especially through the Fiscal Investment and Loan Program (FILP), increased.[1] Budget plans from the Ministry of Finance and the Ministry of Internal Affairs and Communications show decreases in public works and transportation grants in the FILP during the DPJ years as promised, but social welfare spending also increased, deepening Japan's growing debt problem. This is evident in table 10.1, which shows the decline in the FILP from 2001–2007 during the LDP-Kōmeitō years, and then an increase in 2009–2010 when the DPJ was in power.

Table 10.2 shows the decreasing revenues and the increases in overall expenditures and social welfare spending, especially in the 2010 budget.

The DPJ provided income support to farmers, fishermen, workers, and small and medium-sized enterprises to promote regional/local economic development. Its home-page news section included slogans like, "Politics equals people's lives" and "Restoring people's lives." On the National Policy Unit's website, one of the budget plans was called a "Fiscal 2010 Budget: A Lifesaving Budget." Despite the DPJ's commitment to decentralization, greater regional autonomy, and reforms to improve the overall economic condition of the country, the party's pledges to address inequalities and unemployment required greater expenditures at the national and local levels. The *kakusa*, or inequality, issue gave the DPJ the window of opportunity it needed to win the upper house in 2007 and the lower house in 2009.

The DPJ deepened the deficit problem because of the incentives that it faced to cultivate and maintain support from its core and new constituencies in both houses. Furthermore, the DPJ immediately dismantled the Council on Economic and Fiscal Policy (CEFP), which the LDP had institutionalized to push through politically controversial reforms to local

---

1 The FILP was critical to the LDP's strategy of supporting its electoral base in rural areas. Until 2001, all postal savings deposits, pensions, and life insurance deposits went directly to the FILP. The FILP reforms and the decreases show the decreasing value of pork and public works–oriented local fiscal policies under the new electoral incentives in the lower house, because these were evidence of cuts to the LDP rural bases. The annual percentage of change in the FILP allocations to local governments from 2003 to 2007 (these years reflect the Trinity Reform years) decreased by over 10 percent in every year except 2004, because that is when it was first implemented. "How Does the Fiscal Investment and Loan Program Work?" http://www.mof.go.jp/zaito/zaito2001e/e04.htm. See Park (2011) for more analysis of the politics behind the FILP.

TABLE 10.1

Reductions in the Fiscal Investment and Loan Program (FILP), 2002–2011 (in billion yen)

Amount	2002	2003	2004	2005	2006	2007	2008	2009	2010	2011
Local governments	16,523.9	18,484.5	17,484.3	15,536.6	13,946.6	12,510.8	12,477.6	14,184.4	15897.6	13,734
Annual percent change		11.9	5.4	11.1	10.2	10.3	0.3	13.7	12.1	13.6
Japan finance corp. for municipal enterprises	1,900.0	1,780.0	1,614.0	1533.0	1,406.0	1350.0	210.0	0	0	0
Small and medium-sized enterprise units	—	—	—	—	—	—	0	1400.3	2515.1	2,340

Sources: Data are based on the individual plans for the years (2003–2011) from the Japanese government's Ministry of Finance's *Fiscal Investment and Loan Program (FILP) Budgets*.

TABLE 10.2
Expenditures, LDP-Kōmeitō vs. DPJ Years

Fiscal year	General expenditures	Tax revenues	Local allocation tax grants	Social security	National debt servicing	Government bonds
2005	82,182.90	44,007.00	16,088.90	583.8	873.60	526,927.90
2006	76,686.00	45,878.00	14,558.40	193.1	319.40	531,701.50
2007	82,908.80	53,467.00	14,931.60	567.0	2,237.20	541,458.40
2008	83,061.30	53,554.00	15,613.60	641.5	835.60	545,935.60
2009	88,548.00	46,103.00	16,573.30	3052.0	80.50	593,971.70
2010	92,299.20	37,396.00	17,477.70	2434.2	405.30	642,345.90
2011	92,411.60	40,927.00	16,748.50	1439.3	900.00	667,627.80

Sources: Data from the Ministry of Finance website, "Japan's Fiscal Condition," December 24, 2010, http://www.mof.go.jp/english/budget/budget/index.html, and the fiscal year 2011 budget, http://www.mof.go.jp/english/budget/statistics/201006/index.html.

finances.[2] The CEFP had legislative agenda-setting power and the support of the prime minister. The different policymaking structure in the DPJ's National Policy Unit and Government Revitalization Unit, and the weaker party leadership of the DPJ created more opportunities for local interests to make greater demands on the center than during the Koizumi and subsequent LDP-Kōmeitō coalition years. Over time, however, since the DPJ has been in government, the National Policy Unit has become more or less defunct. The DPJ government has had a relatively weak executive that has not been able to coordinate policy effectively to manage Japan's economy and other urgent policy challenges related to the disasters of March 2011.

In 2010, the DPJ was committed to a "strong economy, strong public finances, and a strong social security [system]" based on its Fiscal Management

2 "The Council on Economic and Fiscal Policy is a consultative organ placed within the cabinet office. Its purpose is to facilitate full exercise of the prime minister's leadership while sufficiently reflecting the opinions of private-sector experts in economic and fiscal policy formation. The Council is headed by the prime minister, and includes the chief cabinet secretary, the minister of state for economic and fiscal policy, other relevant ministers (minister for internal affairs and communications; minister of finance; minister of economy, trade, and industry), the head of the relevant institution (governor of the Bank of Japan), and four private-sector experts" (http://www.keizai-shimon.go.jp/english/about/index.html#roles). See Wataru Kitamura (2006) for his explanation of how the CEFP helped the prime minister advance decentralization reforms. Also see Estevez-Abe (2008, 273–75) for her analysis of *shingikai* (legislative advisory councils) versus the CEFP and Gene Park (2011).

Strategy statements (National Policy Unit 2010). To achieve this new trinity of goals to strengthen Japan's economy and social safety net, the party had to implement significant structural reforms, limit spending at the local and national levels, and raise tax revenues. The budget plans demonstrated the party's concern over growing unemployment and the dual challenge of trying to promote practices to reform the economy and promote efficiency and competitiveness, while addressing the social impact of Japan's demographic crisis and years of economic stagnation. These plans addressed key challenges to the Japanese government but were ambitious in scope for a party with no previous experience in government.

The DPJ also tried to direct the flow of central resources to its local political bases and fulfill some of its 2009 manifesto pledges by increasing multiple areas of welfare spending on behalf of women, seniors, children, and workers. Whichever party is in power in the future will face the challenges of trying to win support for short-term electoral gain versus imposing difficult cuts for long-term economic stability. The incentives posed by the lower and upper houses make it hard to cut local spending because parties will need to continue to appeal to rural interests, which are overrepresented in the upper-house districts. The outcome of the change in government to the DPJ was increased spending at a time when the tax revenue base had decreased.[3] Because the DPJ won on a platform of social protections, it put the brakes on decentralization and, in many areas, reversed the cuts imposed under Koizumi by allocating special budgets to address those shortfalls.

Central-Local Relations Before the DPJ

To understand and appreciate the institutional constraints that the DPJ faced, it is necessary to provide historical context and background on how and why decentralization reforms were even implemented in the last decade. The effects of these reforms created conditions that permitted the DPJ to expand its voter base and win national elections, so it is helpful to see what exactly changed and why. Before decentralization, Japan's system of local governments was very centralized and financial resources were allocated by the national government. Because the LDP dominated the national legislature from 1955 to 1993, the LDP's interests defined the nature of central-local relations. (Steiner 1965; Reed 1986; Pempel 1998; Muramatsu 1997; Scheiner 2006). The LDP maintained its legislative majorities by redistributing income from richer, urban areas to its core supporters in economically

---

3 Decentralization was initially a DPJ issue, but was co-opted by Koizumi during the years that the LDP faced greater electoral challenges from the DPJ (Hasunuma 2010).

weaker, rural areas. This system served a political purpose in that it equalized emerging income inequalities between rural and urban regions when Japan was rapidly transforming its economy after the Second World War. This gave the new postwar government the political stability that it needed to meet its economic recovery goals (De Wit 2002, 1997). The centralized local finance system was the key mechanism for redistributing wealth to the LDP's electoral base in rural areas, and locked in these privileges for decades.[4]

This system rewarded faithful LDP supporters in local governments of rural and economically underdeveloped regions by providing a steady stream of public works and subsidies for consistent voter turnout in elections. LDP governments continued to support these rural local governments because of the electoral incentives it faced under the single nontransferable vote (SNTV). (See table 10.3 for a comparison of the political system under the former and current electoral rules in the lower house.) Under SNTV, though the LDP did not win majorities with rural votes alone, it could consistently win enough votes from many rural constituencies in both chambers, and it had a reliable base in rural areas. Therefore, policies disproportionately reflected this electoral and rural bias.

The upper-house districts overlap the prefectures and their populations; this system was designed in 1947 and reflected the demographic distribution of that time. The dramatic urban population growth and rural population decline over time was not corrected for in the upper-house districts (Hayes 2009). Rural interests are still overrepresented in the upper house, so Japanese trade policies and subsidies privilege the farming and fishing interests. The Japanese government has consistently protected agricultural interests, which is why the economy remains closed to imports of agricultural goods, and this is a continued source of conflict in trade negotiations. This is also why the price of agricultural food items is high for Japan's consumers. Rural and agricultural interests continue to wield power over policies because even though the lower-house electoral system was reformed and malapportionment was addressed at the time of the reform, the upper house was not reapportioned to reflect Japan's more urban population. Organized farming and fishing interests are still powerful because of the upper-house districts, and this is evident in Japan's subsidies for rural areas and in its trade policies. There are institutional incentives to protect rural interests, and like the LDP before it, the DPJ also had to respond to these powerful interests and incentives after winning a majority in the upper house in 2007.

4 See Scheiner (2006) for a discussion of how the centralized local finance system privileged the LDP.

TABLE 10.3

MMD-SNTV vs. SMD + PR and Local Governance

Electoral rule	1947–1993	1994–present	
	MMD-SNTV	SMD	Closed-list PR
No. of districts	~129	11 regions	
No. of seats	~511	300	180
Average district size	4	1	16.4
Intraparty competition	Always	No	No
Malapportionment	Yes	Much less	
Campaigns	Expensive, candidate-centered	Policy-oriented, manifestos, and party-based	
Pivotal voters	Organized interests	Floating, independent, and urban voters	
Party organization	Decentralized, dominated by factions	Centralized under the prime minister and cabinet	
Policymaking process	Bottom-up, decentralized, bureaucratic influence	Top-down, centralized, prime minister and cabinet influence	
Policy outputs	Targeted goods, pork	Public goods, universal benefits, less pork	
Local government	Centralized	Decentralizing	
	Prefectures key to centralized control (law gave PM authority to hire and fire governors)	Law allowing PM to hire and fire governors abolished	
		More special status, designated, and core cities take on prefectural duties	
	Equalize regional inequalities to provide social welfare to rural areas (jobs, income)	Greater inequalities, and laws passed to assure greater fiscal accountability and transparency	
	Complex formula for redistribution (many variables subject to political influence)	Simpler formula for redistribution (based on population and area)	
	3,200 municipalities	1,700 municipalities	

Source: Table adapted from Rosenbluth and Thies (2010).

Previous attempts to reform the rural-oriented local finance system were derailed by LDP politicians who were dependent upon rural voters, and by local government officials and bureaucrats with interests in maintaining the status quo. Local finance was thought to be the "third rail" of Japanese politics because, under the old incentives, cutting off these constituencies would mean certain defeat in elections (De Wit 1997). In fact, when the LDP, under Koizumi's leadership, advanced fiscal decentralization reforms and began to cut off support to rural areas, it lost the upper house to the DPJ in 2007. Matters pertaining to local finance, which helped break the bond between the LDP and rural voters, played a crucial role in creating the political conditions and opportunities that the DPJ needed to finally bring about a change in power at the national level.

Coalition Governments and Decentralization

Changes made to local finance undertaken during the Koizumi administration played a significant role in helping the DPJ come to power. The centralized system of local finance had been an effective political tool for the LDP for nearly 40 years, delivering the party consistent majorities in national elections (Scheiner 2006). However, coalition governments (including those led by the LDP) that were formed in the middle and late 1990s passed laws to change this system. For the first time in 40 years, decentralization reforms to local governments were passed in 1995, 1999, and again in the early 2000s.[5] (See table 10.4.)

The local finance system had to be reformed because it contributed to much of the political and economic stagnation in Japan. To rein in wasteful spending and reduce the deficit, Japan had to make changes to its central-local relations and reevaluate the way that resources were allocated to localities; this also reflected the growing importance of urban and floating voters, and the demographic realities of the country. Japan had become a mostly urban country, but the political and local finance system did not reflect these changes until the electoral reform and formation of coalition governments.

These early coalitions placed decentralization on the legislative agenda in the mid-1990s (Otake 2000; Nakano 2010; Hasunuma 2010). Decentralization introduced competition, accountability, and transparency to local finances, and eliminated numerous local governments and recipients of national resources through municipal mergers. One of the most important changes to local finance undertaken by the LDP-led coalition came in the

---

5 These reforms were undertaken at times of crises, such as the "lost decade" and after an electoral reform ended 38 years of government by the LDP.

TABLE 10.4

Recent Changes in Japan's Central-Local Relations

Year	PM (and parties in government)	Changes
1989	Kaifu (LDP)	Outline on the promotion of reforms to central-local relations (his political and administrative reform bill failed in 1990)
1991	Kaifu Miyazawa (LDP)	The PM can no longer remove elected local officials (June 1994) Introduction of Core City System via amendment to the Local Autonomy Law
1995	Murayama (LDP+JSP+NPH)	Decentralization Promotion Law passed by the Diet
1996	Hashimoto (LDP+JSP+NPH) (11/96, LDP)	July 1997, 2nd Advisory Report of the Decentralization Committee
1999	Obuchi (LDP+Kōmeitō+LP)	Omnibus Decentralization Law of 1999 Agency-delegated function abolished Central government Dispute Resolution Council established Abolition of the approval system for bond offerings System for local government input on the calculation of the local allocation tax Abolition of the approval system for nonstatutory general taxes from the Local Tax Law Municipal Mergers Law

2002	Koizumi (LDP+Kōmeitō+CP until 2003)	Establishment of Zones for Structural Reform implemented in 2003 Local governments allowed to issue bonds Fiscal decentralization, Trinity Reforms 2003 More fiscal decentralization and a proposal to change the local grant allocation system; over 5 trillion yen in taxation authority to be transferred to the regions from the central government
2007	Abe (LDP+Kōmeitō) Fukuda (LDP+Kōmeitō)	*Dōshūsei* proposals debated (to eliminate 47 prefectures and establish 10–14 regional governments) 10% of the fiscal decentralization was implemented Local bond issues discussed, but very little action, press, or progress
2008	Aso (LDP+Kōmeitō)	*Dōshūsei* bill proposed
2009–2011	DPJ	FILP Improvement Loans increase Regional Revitalization Plans with a focus on strengthening agriculture, forestry, and fisheries Administrative Bureau (need to follow up on the agencies developed during the last LDP years to monitor local accounting) Greater investment in small and medium-sized enterprises and social welfare

Sources: Organisation for Economic Co-operation and Development, *OECD Economic Survey of Japan 2006*; Toshiyuki Masujima, *Administrative Reform in Japan: Trends in the Latter Half of the Twentieth Century and Future Directions in the Twenty-first Century* (Institute of Administrative Management, 2006); Council of Local Authorities for International Relations (CLAIR), "Municipal Mergers in Japan," CLAIR Fact Sheet (2009); Hiroshi Ikawa, *Recent Local Financial System Reform (Trinity Reform)*. [Tokyo]: CLAIR, 2007; *Annual Report on the Japanese Economy and Public Finance 2006, 2006*, Cabinet Office, Government of Japan; *Annual Report on the Japanese Economy and Public Finance 2007, 2007*, Cabinet Office, Government of Japan; *Plans for the Years (2003–2011)* from the Japanese government's Ministry of Finance's Fiscal Investment and Loan Program (FILP) Budgets; *Japan's Government and Administration at a Glance*, 2006. (Institute of Administrative Management); and various issues of the *Nikkei Shimbun*.

Notes: JSP: Japanese Socialist Party
    NPH: Shintō Sakigake, or New Party Harbinger
    LP: Liberal Party
    CP: Communist Party

form of the 1999 Omnibus Decentralization Law, which promoted the voluntary amalgamations of municipalities by March 2006 (Shirai 2004). The municipal mergers transformed the physical organization of local governments by dramatically reducing the total number of rural municipalities. The decentralization reforms continued in successive LDP-led coalition governments. According to the Council on Economic and Fiscal Policy (the CEFP) Basic Policies set forth in 2003, the plan was to reduce the number of recipients of the local allocation tax (LAT) (MOFA 2003). The municipal mergers were part of this effort, because this would reduce the total number of LAT recipients. The country went from having 3,200 to 1,700 municipalities in a few short years.[6]

Reduced Support for Local Governments: Koizumi's Reforms

The pace of decentralization accelerated under Koizumi's leadership. In 2001, when the LDP was in coalition with the Conservative Party and the New Kōmeitō, the CEFP in the Cabinet Office proposed decentralization laws (Kitamura 2006; Park 2011). Stating that there would be "no sacred cows" with the reform vision he had planned for the country, Koizumi proposed to reform the three pillars of the local finance system: local subsidies, tax revenue sources, and the distributive system (Schoppa 2001). These proposals constituted the basis of the Trinity Reforms, proposed for 2004 through 2006, which proposed cuts to local governments in three important ways. These included reducing the amount of support transferred to local governments from the national government, shifting the burden of local revenue collection from the national government to local governments, and cutting public subsidies to rural areas. These reforms marked, for the first time in decades, a severe cut in support from Tokyo to rural areas, and contributed to the growth of financial inequalities among regions.[7] The Trinity Reforms abolished grants of national treasury subsidies and obligatory shares by 4.7 trillion yen between fiscal year 2004 and 2006. From the 2003 fiscal year budget, the total for reforms to the national treasury subsidy amounted to

6 A law was passed in 2005 to accelerate the consolidation of municipal mergers by the end of March 2006.

7 Taro Aso, who later became the LDP's third prime minister after Koizumi (from 2008 through 2009), stated that the number of groups that did not receive money from the central government would increase in 2003 because the calculation would be based on population. Aso stated, "If we think about villages and cities, those groups are about 4.3 percent of the total. By 2004, if we calculate by population, groups that will no longer receive payments will go up to 17.3 percent" (based on my translations of CEFP minutes from 2003).

5.2 trillion yen. This is in excess of 40 percent of the national treasury subsidies and obligatory shares at the time of fiscal year 2003 (Ikawa 2008).

The consequences of Koizumi's reforms on local financing were severe. The tax revenue reductions that were transferred from the central governments to the local governments totaled about 3 trillion yen out of 82 trillion yen. The local allocation tax decreased significantly from 23.9 trillion yen in the 2003 fiscal year budget, at the start of the Trinity Reforms, to 18.8 trillion yen in the 2006 fiscal year budget, a reduction of 5.1 trillion yen (21.3 percent) (Ikawa 2008). Overall, by 2006, there was a reduction of 6.1 trillion yen from the total 89.3 trillion yen for local financing since fiscal year 2001.

The Trinity Reforms altered the manner in which the local allocation tax, or subsidies to local governments, was calculated; this greatly reduced the number of recipients and the amounts distributed. From 2001 through 2006, the percentage of areas not receiving local transfers went up from 11.5 percent to 18.4 percent (MIC 2007). The total reduction in the LAT and extraordinary financial bonds was 12 percent that same year ("On the Three-in-One Reforms" 2005). The amount of 1.3 trillion yen for local public nursery schools, child protection, home care insurance administration, and retirement homes was discontinued or scaled down. The 2004 budget also had local government sources implement programs on their own rather than from subsidies. As a temporary measure, income taxes and personal residential taxes were used as a source of revenue and allocation. This change made the allocation of tax resources more proportionate to the population.

By establishing a closer connection between population and the allocation of tax resources, Koizumi's reforms benefited urban over rural areas. According to the Ministry of Internal Affairs and Communications White Paper from 2007, the following categories of investment expenses were estimated by the new formula (by population and area) for the prefectural level: social welfare (by population), senior citizen health and welfare expenses (by population over 65), agriculture administration (by agricultural land area), and forestry administration expenses (forest area). For municipalities, education and social welfare allocations were determined by population, and agricultural administration was based on the number of farming households (which was declining) (*Japan Statistical Yearbook* 2007). The number of workers in forestry, fisheries, and mining determined other industrial and economic expenses for municipalities. Larger and more populous governments would receive more resources now, and the distributions would be more proportionate to population and needs. The previous system did not use such objective criteria so that it could build in opportunities to provide resources to pro-LDP rural governments, which had smaller populations and weaker tax bases, for political purposes. Rural areas were hit hard by these changes to local governments and finances. They had much higher rates of unemployment and depended solely on agriculture for income, so they were more dependent on the old style of subsidies. Knowing full well about the consequences that these reforms would have on rural areas, the LDP continued to cut local support even after Koizumi's resignation in 2006 (Ministry of Internal Affairs and Communications 2009, 26–29).

The Trinity Reforms generated considerable opposition from a wide array of interests. The National Governors Association, along with other local officials and academics, were greatly concerned about cuts to education and children's allowances (Kayama 2003). In the Diet, meanwhile, there was extended debate over the question of how these cuts would affect financially weak governments that depended on LAT transfers. Indeed, much of the criticism directed against the Trinity Reforms came from within the LDP itself, with many LDP members opposing reforms that could undermine the provision of minimum services to poorer areas. The Trinity Reforms marked a turning point for the LDP, signaling the advent of a new era in which the LDP's now-vanishing rural base could no longer be counted on. The urban-rural and social protection versus neoliberal values cleavages broke the bond between the LDP and the rural base. Rural voters felt abandoned and the DPJ moved right in, replicating similar policies to the LDP before Koizumi.

The DPJ used this issue of the "pain" and inequality caused by "neoliberal reforms" to win elections in the upper and lower houses. It then increased budget allocations to soften the blow of these reforms and to improve the "quality of life" for Japan's people, especially weaker members of society and workers. Its vision and plans promised to strengthen local governments by providing additional loans and by supporting those working in agriculture, forestry, and fisheries. In addition to increasing support to rural workers, the DPJ allocated more resources for social welfare policies to address the concerns that urban voters had about housing, senior care, child care, education, and employment.

Internal and External Constraints on the DPJ

The DPJ's local government policies reflected the party's own policy-making structure at the time. The DPJ's National Policy Unit consisted of 30 members and lacked the same kind of party cohesion and executive leadership that existed under Koizumi; this could be why it became ineffective over time. Already, the larger size of the policymaking body meant greater delays, conflicts, and demands on the overall budget priorities for the country. The political current changed and the DPJ capitalized on that change, but it required targeting benefits to groups once beholden to the LDP to sustain its electoral support, especially in the upper house. Despite the DPJ's commitment to decentralization in its previous manifestos, the party focused more on the consequences of these reforms for the people of Japan, and on revitalizing the economies of these regions through increases to small and medium-sized enterprises (see table 10.1).

Local Finances Under the DPJ

The electoral reform and correction of the malapportionment problem allowed for greater representation of Japan's middle class and urban and consumer interests in the lower house (Rosenbluth and Thies 2010). The incentives generated by SMDs drove campaigns, policies, and resource distribution in a new direction (see table 10.3, about the old and new electoral systems). There is growing evidence that the municipal mergers changed the electoral fortunes of the LDP (Horiuchi and Saito 2009; Yamada, Horiuchi, and Saito 2009; and Shimizu in chapter 5 of this book). Preliminary evidence from budget data shows a decrease during the previous LDP administrations, especially near the end of the Koizumi years. The DPJ prioritized social welfare issues broadly and targeted them to specific constituencies in key upper-house prefectures. We can observe increases in the levels of local spending and the FILP again.

Electoral Constraints

The party faces two distinct electoral environments and, in some sense, competing incentives: to support rural interests in the upper house, because of the overrepresentation of rural interests in the upper-house districts; and to respond to the incentives of the new mixed-member majoritarian (MMM) system where urban and floating voters want an end to the old LDP style of politics that privileged rural interests at the expense of cities, and that prefer more broad, universal benefits in the areas of education, employment, medical services, and support for seniors. The language and priorities of the budget plans from 2008 to 2011 prioritized social safety net measures for Japan's people. In response to the recession, DPJ budgets prioritized employment insurance, assistance in job searches and job creation in local areas, and tax breaks for small and medium-sized businesses to reduce layoffs. Many jobs were eliminated not only by the recession, but also by the municipal mergers; nearly 1,500 local governments disappeared. Shimizu, in chapter 5, analyzes how the mergers resulted in a greater number of independent local governments and continued to break the bonds between the LDP and rural localities.

Outcomes and Effects of the DPJ Government

After coming to power, the DPJ made a point of funneling support back to local and regional governments. Mulgan shows the DPJ's influence in spending. Of the 593 roads that were to be built based on the 2010 budget, "more than half (321) are roads that DPJ prefectural federations and governors requested. Of these, *190 have had their works expenses increased*" from the time the draft 2010 budget was settled. Mulgan refers to these increases as "political additions" (2010). Again, political interests directed the flow of central resources; only this time, the resources went to prefectures of electoral interest to the DPJ. This is not surprising, but it set the country back and reversed several years of improvements in reducing public works spending at the local levels (Noble 2010). Undoubtedly, some of these are rural governments critical for winning upper-house votes.

The DPJ has used its prefectural chapters to publicize the amount of budget allocations designated for public works to local governments. With the next upper-house election in mind, the DPJ funneled public works subsidies to local governments. More money was sent to prefectures where the party was weak, while DPJ strongholds had to "settle for less." Key election battlegrounds received the biggest "political additions," especially Tottori, where LDP defector Kotaro Tamura was standing for the DPJ in what is a traditional LDP base. Money deliberately went to prefectural constituencies that the DPJ hoped to win (Mulgan 2010).

In this sense, the DPJ was acting very much like the old SNTV-LDP, at least in upper-house campaigns. The dynamics at the lower level seemed to be a little different as the DPJ tried to pursue income support benefits that targeted a broader spectrum of voters than, say, the public works subsidies doled out to prefectures in the upper house. In any case, the party was compelled to court specific and broad interests simultaneously, and the economic plans from the Cabinet Office and FILP plans document these increases (see tables 10.1 and 10.2). Spending in social welfare expanded during the DPJ years.[8]

The Council on the New Economic Measures issued a report in 2008 that laid out the priorities to increase support for child care and medical services, raise wages for employment, and reduce insurance premiums and gas and electric utilities costs. It also proposed to provide a safety net for nonregular workers and those in small and medium-sized businesses. The theme was to "ease anxiety." In 2009, the economic plans highlighted innovations

---

8 This is problematic in that greater spending in social welfare may be due to increasing expenditures for social security and the increasing number of recipients for such benefits over time. However, the DPJ allocated resources to education and unemployment.

in business, and employment opportunities for seniors, youth, and women. Again, in the 2009 Economic Emergency Measures report, job-related improvements were suggested, especially to help with job searches and child care to support women's employment.

The economic plans after the DPJ came to power included measures to support "people's daily lives"; FILP improvement loans to "revitalize" local governments as evident in the increasing allocations to small and medium-sized enterprises; and a vision of strengthening agriculture, forestry, and fisheries. The 2010 plan also more than doubled the amount that went to Okinawa—a major political sore spot for the DPJ government with respect to the military base issue. In 2009 the Okinawa Development Finance Corporation (one of the many FILP agencies) received 200 billion yen; in 2010 it received 500 billion yen. There were also increases in the Expressway and Debt Repayment Agency, from 470 to 670 billion yen from 2009 to 2010. The evidence is in the budget plans. The DPJ funneled more money through the local finance system to areas that would benefit them politically. The change in power at the national level clearly generated changes in spending at the local level.

These upper-house political incentives seem to have reversed some of the gains made by the CEFP and Koizumi in trying to reform the old local finance system. Not surprisingly, money to localities was used for political gain in national elections, which explains why the budget deficit problem deepened after the DPJ came to power. It was trying to buy off supporters in the upper house and then was pursuing policies that appeal to urban voters and that required greater expenditures in social welfare as well, especially in the areas of aging, education, and income support. Whichever party is in power at the national level determines how much money is spent at the local levels, and under the DPJ, local spending increased significantly for the first time in several years, especially for social welfare, and that may be its biggest legacy for local governance.

In the most recent draft 2011 budget, there was a 690 billion yen decrease in the amount of tax allocations to local governments, and this was the first cut in five years, but the reality is that these amounts were to be supplemented by a 1 trillion yen special account fund, which resulted in an increase of central government grants to local governments for the fourth consecutive year. The central government grants helped poorer localities with revenue shortfalls. Such increases under the DPJ government led to greater conflicts between the Ministry of Internal Affairs and Communications, which requested these increases, and the Finance Ministry, which found these requests excessive.

The DPJ did not control the budget process in a way that imposed and maintained reductions in local expenditures, but created opportunities to allocate more resources for political purposes. This reflects the decentralized nature of the party and the fact that there seems to have been less party discipline and unity under a powerful executive; this made it harder to impose cuts or measures to improve fiscal discipline. The projections for the next 10 years are alarming, and it is obvious that this level of spending at the national and local levels cannot be sustained. The government knows what it needs to do: make painful cuts and raise taxes, but there is no political will to do so. The short-term political costs to the DPJ in imposing fiscal discipline may make the country's fiscal situation worse in the long term, and the lack of policy and internal unity and the lack of effective leadership hurt the party in the 2010 upper-house elections.

The DPJ's decentralization reforms were largely unsuccessful. It seems that there is a desire among voters for the government to take more action in addressing the major fiscal policy challenges of the day. Perhaps this is just stating the obvious, but the DPJ—and any government at the national level—faces a great challenge in having to make significant cuts or raise taxes to improve the country's long-term fiscal health, while providing some kind of cushion to the people of Japan who will bear the brunt of these cuts in the short term.

Conclusions

Regardless of which party is in power at the national level, that government will have to learn how to achieve this delicate balance, and manage its short-term political interests versus the long-term well-being of the Japanese economy. The DPJ did not do enough to address the fiscal crisis, because it prioritized building and maintaining its new political bases of support by funneling resources to them. This may have worked in the short run but was not sustainable in the long run. With respect to local finances and the country's fiscal health, the DPJ took Japan off course and deepened the country's fiscal crisis. The politics of compassion, easing anxiety, and improving the quality of life may cost the country much more in the long run. This is why the 2011 FILP plans showed a significant decrease in FILP budget requests from 2010 through 2011 and the party selected a new finance minister in 2011. There was growing media and public scrutiny about the DPJ's inability to manage the national economy.

The tragic events of March 2011 only increased these fiscal and political challenges for the DPJ. The DPJ selected Yoshihiko Noda, a finance minister, as its new prime minister to restore faith in the party's leadership and the management of the country's finances. The DPJ came to power on the promise of change. However, the previous reforms to local governments, and the competing electoral incentives of the two chambers, limited how much the DPJ could actually do. These conditions also created incentives for this new party in power to spend more on social welfare to carry out its mandate and build a new base of electoral support.

Without strong executive leadership, party unity, and a policymaking apparatus to promote timely and necessary reforms to the economy, the DPJ had a more ad hoc and undisciplined approach to local finances. Furthermore, the party's commitment to social welfare came at a time of declining tax revenues, deepening the country's deficit crisis. It seems that this failure to address serious fiscal and economic issues undermined the DPJ's legitimacy and popularity because it lost its majority in the last 2010 upper-house election. Nevertheless, regardless of which party wins a majority in the lower house, the parties face electoral and institutional constraints in each chamber. Urban and independent voters are pivotal in lower-house elections, and rural voters will remain pivotal in upper-house elections. This volume shows us that while much has changed in Japan's political system, some institutional features, interests, and incentives remain the same. With change, there is also familiar continuity, which slows the pace and breadth of the changes that are possible in Japanese politics.

Furthermore, few studies in comparative and Japanese politics connect the electoral and party system changes at the national level to the changes in local governance. However, changes to local governance can influence national politics and the electoral fortunes of parties, as demonstrated in this and the other chapters in this volume. The Democratic Party of Japan's victories in the 2007 upper-house and 2009 lower-house elections provide evidence that changes to local finances did indeed change national politics because rural voters felt abandoned by the LDP and switched their support to the DPJ. This context is important because the DPJ had an opportunity to court the LDP's abandoned interests in the rural areas and capitalize on a platform of protecting society from the perceived and actual inequalities generated by the Koizumi administration. In essence, despite all these changes to the party system and the promises of change made by the DPJ, rural voters became pivotal swing voters in the upper-house election of 2007, and still influence lower-house elections. Though Koizumi's reforms may have sacrificed rural local governments at the altar of reform, the existing upper-house institutions continue to guarantee the influence of rural areas on national policies for years to come.

The DPJ restored spending to localities and expanded social welfare spending overall; not just to senior citizens, but in areas like education and job training and especially employment. The DPJ's expansion of the budget meant that the government would need to triple the consumption tax to 15 percent to gain some control over its growing debt (*Nikkei* 2011). The catastrophic damage caused by the Tohoku earthquake and tsunami of March 2011 posed the greatest challenge yet as the government had to fund reconstruction efforts in an era of declining revenues and expanding budgets. This tragedy also gave the DPJ an opportunity to further consolidate localities, create more efficient local entities, and rebuild local governments to better handle the country's demographic and financial realities. Whichever party wins the lower house in the next election will have unprecedented challenges in managing the increasing demographic and fiscal pressures that Japan faces today.

References

Anderson, Gregory E. 2004. "Lionheart or Paper Tiger? A First-Term Koizumi Retrospective." *Asian Perspective* 28 (1): 149–82.

Annual Report on the Japanese Economy and Public Finance 2006. 2006. Cabinet Office, Government of Japan. Tokyo.

Aoki, Ichiro. 2008. "Decentralization and Intergovernmental Finance in Japan." PRI Discussion Paper Series (No. 08A-04). Policy Research Institute, Ministry of Finance, June.

Bawn, Kathleen, and Michael F. Thies. 2003. "A Comparative Theory of Electoral Incentives: Representing the Unorganized under PR, Plurality, and Mixed-Member Electoral Systems." *Journal of Theoretical Politics* 15 (1): 5–32.

CLAIR (Council of Local Authorities for International Relations). 2004. "Local Government in Japan." http://www.clair.or.jp.

———. 2006. *The Trinity Reform.* CLAIR Fact Sheet, no. 10. Tokyo.

———. 2009. *Municipal Mergers in Japan.* CLAIR Fact Sheet, no. 9. Tokyo.

Democratic Party of Japan website. 2011. "Hatoyama Expresses DPJ Resolve to Make Correction of Inequalities Theme of Forthcoming Diet Session." http://www.dpj.or.jp/english/news/070124/01.html

DeWit, Andrew. 1997. "Trench Warfare on the Tax Fields: Bureaucratic Turf and Japan's Centralized Tax State." Unpublished dissertation, University of British Columbia.

———. 2002. "Dry Rot: The Corruption of General Subsidies in Japan." *Journal of the Asia Pacific Economy* 7 (3): 355–78.

"Distribution of Laspeyres Indices of All Local Public Entities" and "Municipalities with Higher Laspeyres Indices (As of April 1, 2003)." 2006. In *Japan's Government and Administration at a Glance 2006*, 51. Tokyo: Institute of Administrative Management, Government of Japan.

Estevez-Abe, Margarita. 2008. *Welfare and Capitalism in Postwar Japan*. New York: Cambridge University Press.

Fukui, Haruhiro. 1970. *Party in Power: The Japanese Liberal-Democrats and Policy Making*. Berkeley: University of California Press.

Hasunuma, Linda. 2010. "Restructuring Government: Party System Change and Decentralization in Japan." Unpublished PhD dissertation, University of California, Los Angeles.

Hayes, Louis D. 2009. *Introduction to Japanese Politics*. New York: M.E. Sharpe.

Horiuchi, Yusaku, and Jun Saito. 2003. "Reapportionment and Redistribution: Consequences of Electoral Reform in Japan." *American Journal of Political Science* 47 (4): 669–82.

———. 2009. "Removing Boundaries to Lose Connections: Political Consequences of Local Reform in Japan." Unpublished manuscript.

Ikawa, Hiroshi. 2007. "Recent Local Financial System Reform (Trinity Reform)." Up-to-date Documents on Local Autonomy in Japan, no. 2. Tokyo: CLAIR.

———. 2008. "15 Years of Decentralization Reform in Japan." Up-to-date Documents on Local Autonomy in Japan, no. 4. Tokyo: CLAIR.

Ito, Hirofumi. 2002. "Fundamental Issues in the Local Allocation Tax System." *Local Government Review in Japan* (30). Japan Center for Local Autonomy.

Japan Statistical Yearbook. 2007. Statistics Bureau. Ministry of Internal Affairs and Communications. Statistical Research and Training Institute.

Japan's Government and Administration at a Glance, 2006. 2006. Institute of Administrative Management, Tokyo.

Joumard, Isabelle, and Tadashi Yokoyama. 2005. "Getting the Most Out of Public Sector Decentralization in Japan." Economics Department Working Paper, No. 416. January 27, ECO/WKP 3, Organisation for Economic Co-operation and Development.

Kayama, Michihiro. 2003. "The Three-in-One Reforms and the Local Allocation Tax." *Local Government Review in Japan*, no. 31, 1–15. Tokyo: Japan Center for Local Autonomy.

Kitamura, Wataru. 2006. "The Foundations of the 'Trinity' of Local Government Finance Reform." In "Beyond the 'Lost Decade': The Lessons of Economic Crisis and the Koizumi Reforms." *Social Science Japan* no. 34 (March).

Krauss, Ellis, and Robert Pekkanen. 2004. "Explaining the Party Adaptation to Electoral Reform: The Discreet Charm of the LDP." *Journal of Japan Studies* 30 (1) (Winter): 1–34.

Lin, Chao-chi. 2009. "How Koizumi Won." In *Political Change in Japan: Electoral Behavior, Party Realignment, and the Koizumi Reforms*, edited by Steven Reed, Kenneth Mori McElwain, and Kay Shimizu, 109–31. Stanford, CA: Shorenstein Asia-Pacific Research Center.

Local Autonomy in Japan: Past, Present, and Future. 2006. Tokyo: Ministry of Internal Affairs and Communications.

MOFA. 2003. "Basic Policies for Economic and Fiscal Management and Structural Reform 2003." Tokyo: Ministry of Foreign Affairs. http://www.mofa .go.jp/policy/economy/japan/reform0306.html.

Ministry of Internal Affairs and Communications. 2007. *FY 2005 Settlement. White Paper on Local Public Finance*. Tokyo: Financial Management Division, Local Public Finance Bureau, Ministry of Internal Affairs and Communications. http://www.soumu.go.jp/iken/zaisei/19data/2007e_c_visual.pdf.

———. 2009. *FY 2007 Settlement: White Paper on Local Public Finance, 2009. Illustrated*. Tokyo: Financial Management Division, Local Public Finance Bureau, Ministry of Internal Affairs and Communications. http://www .chihousai.or.jp/english/07/pdf/WhitePaperonLocalPublicFinance2009.pdf.

Morita, Akira. n.d. "Government Reform in Japan." http://innovation.pa.go .kr/include/file_down.php?id=2074.

Mulgan, Aurelia George. 2010. "Japan: Is the DPJ Taking a Leaf Out of the LDP's Book?" East Asia Forum: Economics, Politics, and Public Policy in East Asia. http://www.eastasiaforum.org/2010/02/24/japan-is-the-dpj -taking-a-leaf-out-of-the-ldps-book/.

Muramatsu, Michio. 1997. *Local Power in the Japanese State*. Berkeley: University of California Press.

Nakano, Koichi. 2010. *Party Politics and Decentralization in Japan and France*. Nissan Institute/Routledge Japanese Studies. New York: Routledge.

Nakano, Minoru. 2002. *New Japanese Political Economy and Political Reform: Political Revolution from Above*. Florence: European Press Academic Publishing.

National Policy Unit website. 2010. http://www.npu.go.jp/en/policy/policy01/ index.html#g.

Nikkei. 2011. "Japan Sees Bleaker Long-Term Finances Without Tax Hike." January 21.

Noble, Gregory W. 2010. "The Decline of Particularism in Japanese Politics." *Journal of East Asian Studies* 10 (2) (May-August): 239–73.

Nonaka, Naoto. 2000. "Characteristics of the Decision-Making Structure of Coalitions." In *Power Shuffles and Policy Processes: Coalition Government in Japan in the 1990s*. Tokyo: Japan Center for International Exchange.

OECD (Organisation for Economic Co-operation and Development). 2006. *Economic Survey of Japan, 2006*. July.

"On the Three-in-One Reforms in the 'Basic Policies on Economic and Fiscal Management and Structural Reform 2004.'" 2005. 2–16, 45–50. Japan Center for Local Autonomy, The Nippon Foundation.

Otake, Hideo, ed. 2000. *Power Shuffles and Policy Processes: Coalition Government in Japan in the 1990s*. Tokyo: Japan Center for International Exchange.

Park, Gene. 2011. *Spending Without Taxation: FILP and the Politics of Public Finance*. Stanford, CA: Stanford University Press.

Pempel, T. J. 1998. *Regime Shift: Comparative Dynamics of the Japanese Political Economy*. Ithaca, NY: Cornell University Press.

Reed, Steven R. 1986. *Japanese Prefectures and Policymaking*. Pittsburgh, PA: University of Pittsburgh Press.

Reed, Steven R., and Michael F. Thies. 2001. "The Causes of Electoral Reform in Japan." In *Mixed-Member Electoral Systems: The Best of Both Worlds?*, edited by Matthew Soberg Shugart and Martin P. Wattenberg, 152–72. New York: Oxford University Press.

———. 2001. "The Consequences of Electoral Reform in Japan." In *Mixed-Member Electoral Systems: The Best of Both Worlds?*, edited by Matthew Soberg Shugart and Martin P. Wattenberg, 380–403. New York: Oxford University Press.

Rosenbluth, Frances McCall, and Michael F. Thies. 2010. *Japan Transformed: Political Change and Economic Restructuring*. Princeton, NJ: Princeton University Press.

Sakakibara, Eisuke. 2003. *Structural Reform in Japan: Breaking the Iron Triangle*. Washington, DC: The Brookings Institution.

Samuels, Richard J. 2007. *Tokyo's Grand Strategy and the Future of East Asia: Securing Japan*. Ithaca, NY: Cornell University Press.

Scheiner, Ethan. 2006. *Democracy Without Competition in Japan: Opposition Failure in a One-Party Dominant State*. New York: Cambridge University Press.

Schoppa, Leonard J. 2001. "Locating the LDP and Koizumi in Policy Space: A Party System Ripe for Realignment." *Social Science Japan* 22 (December): 9–15.

Schwartz, Frank. 2001. *Advice and Consent: The Politics of Consultation in Japan*. New York: Cambridge University Press.

Shimizu, Kay. 2008. "Survey on Wages of Local Government Employees." *Japan Statistical Yearbook*. Data downloaded as an Excel file (1985–2007).

Shirai, Sayuri. 2004. "The Role of the Local Allocation Tax and Reform Agenda in Japan—Implications for Developing Countries." Policy and Governance Working Paper Series, April, no. 32.

Steiner, Kurt. 1965. *Local Government in Japan*. Stanford, CA: Stanford University Press.

Tanaka, Hiraki. 2008. "Evaluation in Local Governments in Japan." Local Government Paper Series, no. 14. Council of Local Authorities for International Relations.

Tiebout, Charles. 1956. "A Pure Theory of Local Expenditures." *Journal of Political Economy* 64 (October): 416–24.

Treisman, Daniel. 2007. *The Architecture of Government: Rethinking Political Decentralization*. New York: Cambridge University Press.

Yamada, Kyohei, Yusaku Horiuchi, and Jun Saito. 2009. "Electoral Incentives and Municipal Government Consolidation in Japan." American Political Science Association. Toronto Meeting Paper. Available at SSRN: http://ssrn.com/abstract=1449022.

Yokomichi, Kiyotaka. 2011. "Movement in Decentralization in Japan After the First Decentralization Reform." *Up-to-Date Documents on Local Autonomy in Japan*, no. 8. CLAIR; Institute for Comparative Studies in Local Governance (COSLOG); and the National Graduate Institute for Policy Studies (GRIPS).

11 The DPJ and Women

THE LIMITED IMPACT OF THE 2009 ALTERNATION
OF POWER ON POLICY AND GOVERNANCE

Alisa Gaunder

The Democratic Party of Japan (DPJ) saw 40 of its 46 female candidates elected in the 2009 lower-house election; 26 were first-time candidates. Recently, both the Liberal Democratic Party (LDP) and the DPJ have supported more women as "change" candidates in response to changing electoral incentives that favor broad appeals. The DPJ's victory, however, has not had a large impact on women in terms of governance or policy. An exploration of child allowance, day care provision, and dual surname legislation under the DPJ reveals that low seniority and the lack of a critical mass have prevented DPJ women from overcoming significant veto points. The electoral incentives of the emerging two-party system have resulted in a larger number of women in office, but the volatility of the system has sustained a weak voice for women in policymaking.

Both the 2005 and 2009 lower-house elections in Japan broke records for female representation. Specifically, the number of women elected increased from 34 in 2003 to 43 in 2005, with women increasing their representation from 7.1 percent to 9.4 percent of the 480 seats. The majority of this increase came from the success of women in the Liberal Democratic Party (LDP). Twenty-six women were elected in the LDP; 16 were first-time candidates. In this election, Prime Minister Junichiro Koizumi strategically nominated a significant number of conservative women to run against the postal rebels he had kicked out of the party. In 2009, the total number of women

This chapter was originally published in the *Journal of East Asian Studies*, Vol. 12, #3. Copyright © 2012 by the East Asia Institute. Used with permission by Lynne Rienner Publishers, Inc.

in the lower house increased further to 54, constituting 11.3 percent of the total seats. Significantly, however, a large number of women elected under Koizumi did not retain their seats. Instead, this increase is largely related to the support of women candidates by the Democratic Party of Japan (DPJ). The DPJ saw 40 of its 46 female candidates elected; 26 were new candidates. The success of these women was part of the DPJ's landside victory over the LDP, marking what many see as the beginning of true party alternation in Japanese politics.

In this chapter, I explore the implications of party alternation for women in politics in Japan. Overall, the DPJ's ascendance to power has not had a large impact on women in terms of either governance or policy, at least in the short term. This outcome is related to the more strategic, as opposed to institutionalized, support of women in elections and the relative lack of seniority of female legislators in general. The electoral incentives of the emerging two-party system have resulted in a larger number of women in office, but the volatility of the system has sustained a weak voice for women in policymaking.

The increasing trend in female representation at least partially reflects the changes in the electoral environment over the past decade and a half. As Kenneth McElwain (2012) points out, elections have become nationalized in recent years. In addition, the two-party system has stabilized. Moreover, Ethan Scheiner (2012) illustrates how party competition has increasingly centered on valence issues. The LDP's and the DPJ's support of women in recent elections backs this assertion. In the midst of economic stagnation and high voter disillusionment, female candidates cast as "change" candidates can potentially tap into a larger portion of the electorate.

The new electoral environment also has increased the potential for larger partisan swings, as seen in 2005 and 2009. Much of the success of LDP women in 2005 and DPJ women in 2009 is related to the fact that LDP candidates tended to win in 2005 and DPJ candidates tended to win in 2009, irrespective of gender. Partisan affiliation was the greatest predictor of success for newcomers in single-member districts (SMDs) in 2005 and 2009 (Reed, Scheiner, and Thies 2012).

While party popularity partially explains why women have done well, it is not the only reason. Party leaders must select women to begin with and place them in competitive districts or high on the proportional representation (PR) list. The LDP significantly increased its number of women candidates in 2005, as did the DPJ in 2009. Prior to these elections, each party supported a relatively stable number of women, especially in SMDs.

Both parties have increased their number of female candidates in times of high party popularity, not because of a commitment to gender issues, but because of a strategic desire to attract votes in the new electoral environment. Indeed, the SMD portion of the combined electoral system provides incentives for parties to reach out to the median voter through broad appeals, such as promoting women as symbols of reform. The trend toward large electoral swings, however, has hampered the ability of women to affect policy by reducing their ability to gain seniority. As we shall see, this factor largely explains the DPJ's limited success on women's issues. Moreover, many of the women's policies pursued by the DPJ have not differed significantly from those supported by the LDP. Such policy convergence also reflects each party's desire to attract the median voter, a point highlighted by Lipscy and Scheiner (2012).

I begin my exploration of the impact of the alternation of power on women in politics by investigating the DPJ's internal party policies for female candidates. I then review the electoral performance of female DPJ candidates from 1996 to 2010. I suggest in these early sections that while the DPJ has slightly more favorable nomination and recruitment practices, the DPJ's support of women has not been significantly different from the LDP's since 2005. In recent elections, both parties have used women candidates to bolster their reform credentials and appeal to urban, floating voters. Next, I explore the impact of women within the DPJ on governance since the alternation of power in 2009, arguing that the DPJ has followed a pattern similar to the LDP's in its limited involvement of women in the policymaking process. In the final section, I discuss the DPJ's progress on three policies that affect women—child allowance, day care provision, and dual surname legislation. While the DPJ successfully passed child allowance legislation, it has been forced to scale it back significantly since the 2011 earthquake disaster. Meanwhile, little progress has been made on either day care or dual surname legislation. I posit that the limited success is related to the low seniority of the still small, though increasing, number of women in the DPJ and the Diet who have been unable to overcome significant opposition from the LDP on child allowances, from bureaucratic ministries regarding day care provision, and from the People's New Party on dual surnames.

The DPJ's Internal Party Policies and Women

The DPJ's nomination and recruitment practices are slightly more favorable to women candidates, at least in comparison to its main competitor, the

LDP. Unlike the now defunct Japan New Party, the DPJ did not incorporate quotas for women candidates as part of its party platform. However, the DPJ's open recruitment program, its Water and Seeds program to support women financially and its upper-house election policy that encourages the nomination of female candidates have all contributed to the promotion of a growing number of female candidates. These female candidates had varying levels of success in the 2005 and 2009 lower-house elections and in the 2007 and 2010 upper-house elections, the main elections analyzed in this chapter.

The open recruitment program provides women with a path to nomination outside the old boys' network at the local level. The DPJ's Committee for Gender Equality oversees the recruitment of women for party nomination. It considers female applicants to the open recruitment program, along with female candidates recommended through other channels. Those selected from the open recruitment program are assigned to districts where the local party branch does not have a recommended candidate.[1] The open recruitment program is open to both men and women.

The DPJ was the first party to implement an open recruitment program, which began in 1999. The LDP introduced a similar program shortly thereafter. Neither party draws a substantial number of candidates through open recruitment, but it has opened the door to some successful political novices. The DPJ has received 50 to 1,300 applications for candidacy through this program for various elections between 1999 and 2007, and women have constituted anywhere between 10 and 17 percent of the applicants deemed suitable for consideration by the party.[2] In the DPJ, women recruited from this program have often been nominated in districts where they had no chance of winning. Nevertheless, some women have pulled out surprise victories.[3] Significantly, not one of the new DPJ women elected in 2009 was selected through this program (Iwamoto 2010). Instead, party leader Ichiro Ozawa hand-picked most of these candidates. The continued reliance on party "patrons" reflects the limited success of this institutional innovation for women.

The DPJ's Water and Seeds program specifically targets female candidates. The DPJ established this program in 1999 to provide monetary support

1 DPJ Election Campaign Committee staff member, personal interview, March 19, 2009.

2 Ibid.

3 For example, Hiroko Mizushima defeated LDP incumbent Hajime Funada, a third-generation politician with a developed personal support group, in Tochigi Prefecture in 2000.

for female candidates running at both the national and local levels. The DPJ party literature explains the rationale for the program in the following way:

> Water is transparent, but it is a necessity for a seed. We, the DPJ, think that we would be such water and help women to get over the various hurdles in their daily lives and help them to take part in politics when they face an important decision point. . . . A seed first absorbs a small amount of water, and then, it receives the sun and rainwater fully and grows bigger by itself. (DPJ 2007; my translation)

As of 2007, the DPJ boasted that this program had supported 172 candidates for local and national office (DPJ 2007). The LDP does not have a comparable program of financial assistance for female candidates.

The money provided by the Water and Seeds program provides only a "start." The current level of support is based on the level of office that the candidate is seeking (see table 11.1). Overall, the Water and Seeds program covers only one-half to one-third of the deposit that a candidate must pay to enter a local or prefectural race. For example, it costs 600,000 yen to enter a prefectural election, and candidates are given only 300,000 yen (Oki 2010).

Finally, since 2005, the DPJ has had an official party-level policy regarding the support of female candidates in upper-house elections. According to this policy, in upper-house districts with three seats the party would support two candidates, and the second of the two candidates would be a woman.[4] The then–DPJ president Ozawa promoted this policy in the 2007 upper-house election, and it remained party policy in the 2010 upper-house election. In contrast, the LDP has no comparable nomination policies for women.

In 2007, Ozawa also implemented a policy of selecting female candidates for certain constituencies where they would provide an effective contrast to

TABLE 11.1

Financial Support Provided by Water and Seeds Program

National Assembly	2 million yen
Prefectural Assembly	300,000 yen
Government Ordinance City Assembly	200,000 yen
Municipality (city/ward/village) Assembly	100,000 yen

Source: DPJ (2007).

4 DPJ Election Campaign Committee staff member, personal interview, March 19, 2009.

older, old-style conservative LDP politicians.[5] Ozawa continued this strategy in selected single-member districts in the 2009 lower-house election. This informal policy mimicked Koizumi's nomination strategy in the 2005 lower-house election.

Overall, open recruitment, the Water and Seeds program, and the upper-house nomination policy address key obstacles that female candidates face when running for office. The Water and Seeds program and the upper-house nomination policy explicitly tackle female monetary support and nomination, putting the DPJ ahead of most other parties in Japan in terms of supporting women. These policies, however, are limited when compared to internal party quotas used by parties in other countries (Krook 2009). As we shall see, the electoral trends for women in the DPJ reflect the limited scope of these institutional supports.

Electoral Performance of Female DPJ Candidates

Female representation has gradually increased in Japan in the postwar period. Female representation in the lower house was 1.4 percent in 1986, 7.3 percent in 2000, 9.4 percent in 2005, and 11.3 percent in 2009 (Cabinet Office 2005, 46; Inter-Parliamentary Union 2011). The increases in recent years are at least partially related to electoral reform in 1994. The old multimember district system with a single nontransferable vote did not favor female candidacy, especially given the bottom-up nomination process that was dominated by old boys' networks. Incumbents with established personal support networks (*kōenkai*) proved very difficult to unseat (Darcy and Nixon 1996, 14). The current system, which combines 300 SMD seats with 180 PR seats, is more accommodating to women candidates.

Most scholars agree that closed-list PR systems are more advantageous for women seeking office (Rule 1987, 1994; Matland 2002; Norris 2004). Parties are more likely to nominate women to PR lists, and voters who might be reluctant to support women in a single-member district are less likely to avoid parties that have both women and men on the party list (Norris 2004). PR systems also are more amenable to "positive action strategies" to promote female representation, such as quotas and reserved seats (Norris 2004, 191).

In mixed SMD/PR systems, women also perform better in the PR tier (Moser and Scheiner 2012). Japan has supported this trend in most instances since electoral reform. The PR portion, however, is quite small in Japan, and

5 DPJ Election Campaign Committee staff member, personal communication, October 24, 2007.

no "positive action strategies" have been tied to PR at the national or party level. Women have done less well in the SMD portion, as predicted by the comparative literature. SMDs favor incumbents, increasing the barriers of entry for all candidates, but especially women who lack the seniority and resources to build the support mechanisms necessary to win a plurality of the vote (Carroll 1994; Darcy, Welch, and Clark 1994).

Japan's combined system has resulted in large electoral shifts in both SMD and PR in recent years. These shifts have increased the total number of women elected but have prevented women from gaining seniority. When large parties like the LDP and DPJ gain a large portion of the PR vote, women who are often "bottom-of-the-list" PR candidates are favored.[6] For example, in 2009, 12 of the DPJ women elected were at the bottom of the PR list (Iwamoto 2010). These politicians will struggle to gain reelection, given the diminished popularity of the DPJ since gaining control of the government.

While electoral system rules are important, party ideology also matters.[7] Parties of the left are more likely to support and elect women (Norris 1985; Rule 1987). In fact, small parties of the left in PR systems have often pressured larger parties to support women after making women a large portion of their party lists (Matland and Studlar 1996). Contagion from the left, however, has not occurred in Japan, and the DPJ's centrist position has made it less receptive to women than more progressive parties.

The DPJ's support of female candidates followed a fairly stable pattern from 1996 to 2005. After the 2005 lower-house election, however, the party adjusted its strategy and adopted the upper-house policy discussed earlier. In 2009, the DPJ adopted Koizumi's strategy of supporting women as change candidates. Overall, the 2007 and 2010 upper-house and the 2005 and 2009 lower-house elections suggest that party strategy largely explains the number of women nominated, while party popularity influences the overall success (or failure) of female candidates.

6 See Matland (1993) for a discussion of the importance of the number of parties in the PR system.

7 Moser and Scheiner (2012) also point out that electoral rules are not completely determinative, noting that countries that do not see women as leaders have lower female representation regardless of electoral rules in place. According to the World Values Survey in 2005, 43.9 percent of the Japanese population surveyed agreed that "men make better political leaders than women do." This places Japan with several other Eastern European countries and far from industrial democracies such as Germany, where the percentage of people who agree with this statement rests under 20 percent (Moser and Scheiner 2012).

TABLE 11.2

Total Number of Women Elected to the
Lower House by Party Since Electoral Reform

Party/Election	1996	2000	2003	2005	2009
LDP	4	8	9	26	8
DPJ	3	6	15	7	40
Kōmeitō	...	3	4	4	3
Socialists	3	10	3	4	2
JCP	4	4	2	2	1

Source: Author compilation.

Lower-House Elections (1996–2003)

During the period 1996–2003, the DPJ ran more female candidates than the LDP. While the DPJ tended to nominate more women candidates, these candidates had a much lower success rate from 1996 to 2003 when compared to LDP female candidates (Gaunder 2009, 246). This fact suggests that while the LDP was less likely to nominate female candidates, it tended to nominate women in districts where they were competitive. In contrast, the DPJ often nominated women as sacrificial lambs in districts where the DPJ as a whole was much less competitive. The success rates for DPJ women candidates were lower than the success rates for DPJ male candidates throughout this period (Gaunder 2009). As shown in table 11.2, the total number of women elected in the LDP and DPJ is quite similar during this period, with the DPJ electing more women than the LDP in 2003 only.

Women in the 2005 and 2009 Lower-House Elections

In 2005, a record 43 women successfully won office in the lower-house election. This increase was primarily due to LDP prime minister Koizumi's electoral strategy. Koizumi placed high-profile "assassins" as the official LDP candidates in the districts of postal rebels who had voted against postal privatization in the lower house and later had been kicked out of the party. Ten of the assassins were women. Six of the 10 female assassins won in SMDs outright; the others were saved by PR. In addition, Koizumi placed women at the top of seven of the 11 PR bloc lists, and every woman who ran in an SMD was given a high placement on the PR list. As a result, all 26 women who ran either won in the SMD or were saved by the PR list. Koizumi supported these women to highlight his reformist credentials. In contrast, the DPJ saw only seven women elected to the lower house, down from a total of 15 in 2003. This result is consistent with the DPJ's overall inability to compete against Koizumi's LDP in the 2005 election.

Koizumi's female "children," however, did not fare well in the 2009 lower-house election, due to the general unpopularity of the LDP and Koizumi's departure from politics.[8] Only eight LDP women won seats: two in SMDs and six in PR. Moreover, only four of the 10 Koizumi female assassins recaptured seats. Overall, three-fourths of the new LDP women lost their seats, with only four of the 16 first-term women returning.

In contrast, DPJ women did quite well in 2009, thanks to Ozawa's adaptation of the 2005 Koizumi strategy combined with increasing DPJ popularity. Specifically, Ozawa and the DPJ chose several female candidates to run against senior LDP male politicians in SMD contests in 2009. In addition, the DPJ gave these women high PR rankings to "save" them if they lost the SMD contest. For example, Eriko Fukuda, a 28-year-old woman who sued the government over the hepatitis C scandal, beat former defense minister Fumio Kyuma. Ai Aoki, a former TV personality and member of the upper house, defeated the head of the New Kōmeitō, the LDP's coalition partner. As mentioned earlier, the DPJ saw 40 of its 46 female candidates elected, 26 of whom were new candidates. While these women did well, much of their success was related to the overall partisan shift to the DPJ.[9]

DPJ Women in the 2007 and 2010 Upper-House Elections

The DPJ began its successful strategy of supporting women against old-style LDP opponents in the 2007 upper-house election. In this election, 26 women were elected to the upper house, with most of the new women coming from the DPJ. Following its new upper-house election policy (detailed earlier), the DPJ saw 14 women elected—11 of whom were new. Three were elected from PR and eight from constituencies.

The DPJ nominated more women candidates in the 2010 upper-house election, but these women were less successful than in 2007. Both male and female candidates saw a drop in their success rates in 2010, suggesting that at least part of the explanation rests with the party's overall popularity. Also, in

8 Koizumi's "children" refers to first-term LDP candidates elected in 2005 under Koizumi's leadership.

9 Maeda's investigation of four of the so-called Ozawa's girls, who received a large amount of media coverage in 2009, suggests that these women did not do proportionately better than other DPJ candidates; their vote share gain did not differ dramatically from the vote share gain of other DPJ candidates (Maeda 2010, 899–900).

2010, Ozawa decided to run two candidates in both two-seat and three-seat constituencies. The commitment to two candidates in two-seat constituencies was new. Perhaps this made sense when the DPJ's popularity was at its height, but by the time the upper-house election occurred, the DPJ's popular support had plummeted.[10] Nevertheless, in 2010, Ozawa extended his strategy of supporting women and nominated a woman as the second candidate in six of the 12 two-seat constituencies; however, only one woman won. DPJ women ran in all five of the three-seat constituencies, and one woman won. Overall, 20 women ran in the constituencies and only four won; seven ran in PR and only two won. The flaw in Ozawa's strategy was that the DPJ simply did not have enough popular support to elect two candidates, especially in two-seat constituencies. Moreover, after Ozawa was implicated in a political funding scandal, his position in the party was marginalized, and he was no longer able to financially support the candidates he had initially selected (Ogai 2010).

The DPJ, like the LDP, has chosen to support women as symbols of change since 2005. This electoral strategy has emerged as elections have become more nationalized and parties have greater incentives to appeal to broader audiences. Female candidates in both the LDP and DPJ have struggled to maintain their seats in subsequent elections, due to both declining party popularity and weaker party support following the departure of Koizumi and the marginalization of Ozawa. Such electoral volatility is likely to continue and further inhibit a sustained presence of women in the Diet. As will become apparent in the sections to follow, the junior status of a large number of women in the Diet has limited their ability to capture significant leadership positions or influence policy.

Implications for Governance

As noted earlier, female representation in the lower house of the Japanese Diet has increased in recent years. Nevertheless, it remains well below the average of 19.5 percent for lower-house female representation in the 188 countries surveyed (Inter-Parliamentary Union 2011). One important question that emerges in response to the gradual increase of female representation, however, is the extent to which the increase of women in politics has affected governance and policy. The investigation of the DPJ since 2009

10 According to an *Asahi Shimbun* poll on May 31, 2010, support for the Hatoyama cabinet had fallen to 17 percent. Support for the Kan cabinet, which replaced the Hatoyama cabinet prior to the upper-house election, was 60 percent in a June 9, 2010, *Asahi Shimbun* poll (Mansfield Asian Opinion Poll Database, at www.mansfieldfdn.org). Kan's support for the consumption tax during the election campaign, however, partially negated this boost.

illustrates that women politicians and women's issues remain marginalized; this is due in part to the volatility of the new nationalized party system, which has prevented women politicians from gaining seniority and instead has simply promoted them as symbols of change.

Women have had a limited impact in governance since the inauguration of the DPJ government in 2009. In fact, the DPJ's inclusion of women in governance has not significantly departed from norms under the LDP. Since Prime Minister Kaifu appointed two women to his cabinet in 1989 to counter the popularity of the Socialist Party's successful female candidates in the 1989 upper-house election, the inclusion of women on the cabinet has been relatively standard in Japanese politics. The LDP, however, usually appointed women to oversee less powerful ministries that had some relation to traditional gender roles, such as education, health and welfare, and gender equality. Koizumi broke from tradition and appointed a record five women to his cabinet in 2001, even appointing Makiko Tanaka to the more powerful cabinet position of foreign minister. After Koizumi's departure, the appointment of women returned to lower levels.

The DPJ has followed this formula for women on the cabinet. The Hatoyama, Kan, and Noda cabinets have contained one or two women. With the exception of Renho, the second-term upper-house member who has served as the state minister in charge of government revitalization on the Kan and Noda cabinets, most female ministers have been appointed to ministries that oversee issues of concern to women—consumer affairs, birthrate, gender equality, and the like. Overall, the limited pool of women in any given party helps women get selected for cabinet positions, but for the most part, women in both the LDP and the DPJ have been relegated to cabinet positions that deal with "soft" issues, often related to gender concerns.

The new female members of the DPJ elected in 2009 also have been marginalized by the DPJ. Concerned that the influx of freshman members could tarnish the party's image as a competent governing party, Ozawa allegedly implemented a gag order on all new DPJ representatives, forbidding them from making public statements on policy (Ogai 2010).[11] This "gag order" fit with the DPJ's desire to move the Japanese system closer to a Westminster parliamentary system, where backbenchers play a minimal role, instead remaining subordinate to the cabinet. This party policy limited the voice of first-term DPJ women.

11 According to *Asahi Shimbun*'s weekly magazine, *AERA*, the DPJ faxed the new legislators a memo immediately after the election, asking them "to carefully respond to information from the mass media due to the cases that also occurred with Koizumi's 'children'" (*AERA*, September 21, 2009, 21).

Connections to Ozawa also limited the overall impact of the influx of women on governance. Ozawa's "girls," as they were referred to in the media, were relatively young and inexperienced and lacked a strong commitment to gender issues. These characteristics have made them good followers but have not resulted in innovative policy leadership, something that is rare for most junior politicians in Japan, male or female.

Implications for Policy

The policy implications of the change in government for women have been minimal, certainly falling short of expectations. Women's groups, as well as other activist organizations, put great hope in the DPJ's campaign pledge to "put people's lives first" (DPJ 2009a). The DPJ's 2009 manifesto also suggested that it would make issues of gender equality and discrimination a priority. Specifically, the 2009 manifesto asserts, "We will realize equal treatment such that people doing the same work at the same workplace can receive the same wage, and we will promote work life balance" (DPJ 2009a). Similar pledges appeared in the 2010 manifesto released prior to the 2010 upper-house election. These pledges, however, have not resulted in concrete policy proposals. In particular, the DPJ has failed to address the weaknesses in the revised Equal Employment Opportunity Law (EEOL), such as its failure to adequately regulate practices that continue to promote significant wage and promotion differentials between men and women.[12] It also has not seen the EEOL as the vehicle to address many of the work/family balance issues that dual-income families face. Instead, it has chosen to address the work/family balance issue by proposing the merger of day care centers and kindergartens.

Since coming to office, the DPJ has had more success with welfare-type provisions that appeal to the median voter than with policies of particular interest to more progressive women. The DPJ oversaw the initial passage of child allowance legislation in 2010, but it failed to enact its plan to unify day

12 The LDP implemented the Equal Employment Opportunity Law (EEOL) in 1986. This law encouraged companies to promote antidiscrimination against women in hiring, job assignments, and promotions and prohibited such discrimination in dismissals and training. It also sought to protect women from overtime or extra shifts. Revisions in 1997 strengthened the antidiscrimination provisions from voluntary to mandatory and added limited sanctions for noncompliance. It also framed antidiscrimination in terms of affirmative action. Revisions in 2006 extended the antidiscrimination provisions to both women and men. Overall, the EEOL and subsequent revisions have struggled to balance antidiscrimination provisions with protection (see Schoppa 2006, 174–79).

care centers and kindergarten care. Dual-surname legislation appears to be a dead issue.

While the DPJ responded to electoral incentives to appeal to urban, floating voters with its support of women's issues, it was unable to fulfill its campaign promises, due to the weak voice that women politicians have in the party. Electoral volatility has meant that few women have gained seniority in either the LDP or the DPJ. Moreover, absent a critical mass, women in the DPJ have been unable to pursue a coherent policy platform; instead, policies have been hampered by key veto points in the system, many of which also stymied the LDP while it was in office. Ironically, while the nationalized party system provides incentives for parties to pursue policies that appeal to the median voter, such as women's issues, it also contributes to party fragmentation and politician turnover, which prevent reform.

Child Allowances

One of the DPJ's initial accomplishments was the passage of the child allowance provisions in March 2010. Child allowances, a pivotal piece of the 2009 manifesto, were highlighted throughout the 2009 lower-house election campaign. The public showed initial enthusiasm for this policy. One poll immediately following the election indicated that 60 percent of the public thought that the child allowance policy should be implemented.[13] Another poll revealed that the public ranked policies that addressed the declining birthrate and child care in third place, trailing only social security and the economy/employment.[14]

The DPJ was committed to fulfilling its promise on child allowances. In the extraordinary session of the Diet after the election, the DPJ focused on its budget with an eye to cutting "wasteful" government spending in order to finance more expansive child allowances (along with abolishing senior high school fees and highway tolls—other key costly provisions in its manifesto).

The law that passed the Diet in March 2010 aimed toward the goals for child allowances in the 2009 manifesto. In that manifesto, the DPJ promised to increase the monthly child allowance to 26,000 yen per child without any parental income restrictions. Given the financial burden, the DPJ decided to gradually introduce the allowance. In 2010, families received 13,000 yen per child monthly for every child of junior high school age or younger. The total

13 *Asahi Shimbun* poll, released September 18, 2009. Cited in Mansfield Asian Opinion Poll Database (P09-23). www.mansfieldfdn.org/backup/polls/2009/poll-09-23.htm.

14 *Nikkei Shimbun* poll, conducted September 16–17, 2009. Cited in Mansfield Asian Opinion Poll Database (P09-24). www.mansfieldfdn.org/backup/polls/2009/poll-09-24.htm.

cost of the partially implemented program in 2010 was estimated to be 2.25 trillion yen (Matsutani 2010).

The gradual introduction of the allowances opened the opportunity for backpedaling. In December 2010, the DPJ announced that it would be unable to fulfill its promise to raise the allowance to 26,000 yen by fiscal year 2011. Instead, the party pledged to increase the amount for parents with children three years old and under by 7,000 yen to 20,000 yen. This plan became imperiled following the March 2011 disaster. The DPJ withdrew the bill to increase the allowance to 20,000 yen on March 30, 2011, in response to sharp criticism from the opposition that government funds needed to be directed toward reconstruction (Takahara 2011b). The DPJ did convince the opposition parties to extend funding for the original child allowance bill for six months as a "stopgap measure."[15] In the end, the DPJ agreed to essentially repeal the new child allowance legislation in order to gain LDP and Kōmeitō support of the issuance of bonds to cover the current deficit. In this agreement, the DPJ pledged to reinstate income restrictions for household eligibility to participate in the child allowance program.[16] The abolition of income restrictions had been a major way that the DPJ legislation had differed from the LDP child allowance policy.[17]

Child allowances represent a broad appeal to the median voter. In its 2009 manifesto, the DPJ stated, "We will increase the disposable income of households and encourage consumption by supporting policies such as a child allowance, free high school education, abolition of highway tolls and abolition of provisional tax rates" (DPJ 2009a, 17). For the longer term, the DPJ argued that child allowances would provide greater incentives for having children. Indeed, couples often cite the expense of child-rearing as the main prohibitive factor for having more children.[18] Critics, however, note that a child allowance will not necessarily encourage women to have more children (Boling 2007, 133). From the perspective of work-oriented women,

15 "Diet OKs Monthly Child Allowances," *Japan Times*, April 1, 2011.

16 According to this agreement, households earning approximately 9.6 million yen or more were no longer eligible to receive the child allowance beginning in fiscal year 2012 ("DPJ Bends on Child Allowances," *Japan Times*, August 5, 2011).

17 The DPJ reached an agreement with the LDP and Komeito in March 2012. The agreement calls for 15,000 yen monthly for each child under three years old and 10,000 yen monthly for the first two children between three years old and middle school. The income restriction was reinstated as part of the compromise ("'Child Benefit' to Likely Pass Diet by End of March," *Daily Yomiuri Online*, March 16, 2012).

18 According to a 2005 survey conducted by the National Institute of Population and Social Security Research, two-thirds of married couples who were surveyed pointed to child-rearing expenses as the largest constraint against having children (Kato 2009).

the policy does nothing to address the structural features that make it difficult for working women to have children, such as the inflexibility in the labor market, unpaid maternity leave, and the insufficient number of day care centers. In this way, as Leonard Schoppa points out, the policy "does little to challenge male breadwinner social structures and norms" (Schoppa 2011, 202).

Regardless of the motivation behind the legislation, though, the allowances proved unsustainable financially following the March 2011 disaster. Even before the disaster, the DPJ started to question the efficacy and financial sustainability of the very generous allowance initially passed. Thus, as Phillip Lipscy's exploration of transportation in chapter 8 of this book also reveals, fiscal constraints have limited the DPJ's ability to fulfill its policy goals (Lipscy 2012).

Day Care

Prior to the March 2011 disaster, eliminating waiting lists for day care centers joined child allowances and seven other reform areas to receive funding priority in the 2011 fiscal budget (DPJ 2010). Proponents see the creation of more day care centers as the crucial element for both fertility and employment/pension issues. The DPJ hoped to respond to this demand for more child care by merging day care centers and kindergartens over a ten-year period beginning in 2013.

In Japan, day care centers serve children from infancy to five years old and are seen as a support for working parents. Kindergartens are available to, but not mandatory for, children ages three to five. Kindergartens focus on educating young children, not caring for children of working parents. While day care centers are oversubscribed, kindergartens are not at capacity, due in part to the declining birthrate. In 2009, kindergarten and day care centers enrolled 84.4 percent of three- and four-year-old children. This rate of enrollment is quite high in comparison to the 71.2 percent average for member countries of the Organisation for Economic Co-operation and Development (OECD). In contrast to other OECD countries, though, parents incur a much larger percentage of the cost for preschool education. In Japan, households bear 38.3 percent of the cost of preprimary education, the highest percentage among 24 OECD peer countries (MEXT 2009). The cost varies from public to private facilities. For example, in the Tokyo area, public day care tuition is based on parent income and ward and ranges from 0 to about 60,000 yen a month for infant care and from 0 to about 30,000 yen a month for children three and older (Tartan 2007).

The merger of day care centers and kindergartens would capitalize on the fact that kindergartens are under capacity, while day care centers suffer from excess demand. Specifically, due to the declining birthrate, kindergartens were only at 69 percent capacity in May 2009. In April 2010, the number of children on waiting lists for government day care centers stood at 26,275 (Takahara 2010). Many speculate that the potential demand is even larger than the official waiting lists, as many housewives who might be enticed to join the workforce have simply written off this option, given the insufficient supply of day care facilities (Tartan 2008).[19] The DPJ promoted the integrated facilities (referred to as *kodomo-en*) to provide care for children of working mothers from birth. Children of nonworking mothers would be accepted from age three. The LDP attempted to implement a similar consolidation in 2006 with its creation of *nintei kodomo-en* (authorized children's facilities). Over 500 *nintei kodomo-en* exist, but these facilities currently face several bureaucratic and organizational obstacles (Takahara 2010).

While the DPJ's plan sounds like an effective way to redistribute government resources, its proposal for mandated mergers faced some daunting obstacles. The largest obstacle, one that has plagued the LDP's *nintei kodomo-en,* is the fact that kindergartens and day care centers are currently overseen by different bureaucratic ministries. The Ministry of Education, Culture, Sports, Science, and Technology (MEXT) administers kindergartens, while the Ministry of Health, Labor, and Welfare (MHLW) oversees day care centers. The desire of each ministry to maintain control of its bureaucratic turf complicates attempts at consolidation. The tensions between these two ministries ultimately stymied the LDP's efforts to move in the direction of consolidation (as politicians with strong connections to the ministries lobbied against integration), and these tensions have plagued the joint facilities currently in operation, mainly by increasing the amount of red tape involved (Takahara 2010). Kindergarten administrators also stand in opposition to integration, because such consolidation could result in longer hours of operation and changes in type of education provided (Takahara 2010).

In reaction to these constraints, the DPJ backed away from mandated mergers in January 2011. Instead, the DPJ decided to promote subsidies for day care centers and kindergartens that chose to merge voluntarily (Takahara 2011a). The provision of subsidies is clearly a reaction to the

19 Tartan (2008) cites a study in 2005 in the *Asian Economic Journal* that estimated that the number of women who wanted to work but wrote off the option due to insufficient day care facilities roughly equaled the number of children between ages one and three currently enrolled in day care.

resistance from the bureaucracy and kindergarten personnel and represents significant concessions on the part of the DPJ.

Dual Surname

For a certain subset of mainly young, female, progressive supporters, the DPJ's inaction on the dual-surname issue has been a significant disappointment, especially given the party's apparent commitment to this issue while in the opposition. The dual-surname legislation seeks to amend the Japanese Civil Code, which states that couples must register under a single family name once married. The law does not stipulate which name must be used, but in practice most couples take the husband's family name. The wife's name tends to be adopted only when the family lacks a male heir. Feminist scholars along with activist organizations have long pointed to current stipulations in the Civil Code as undermining equal citizenship for women (Shin 2008; Mikanagi 2011). Instead, the law is seen as promoting traditional patriarchal notions of family that no longer reflect reality for many dual-income couples. Even the United Nations has stepped into the debate, with the Convention on the Elimination of Discrimination Against Women (CEDAW) calling on Japan to allow for dual surnames to better support gender equality (Brasor 2009).

The expectation for action on the dual-surname issue stems from the DPJ's long support of this issue while in the opposition. In fact, the DPJ has submitted legislation to amend the Civil Code in support of dual surnames every year since 1998, most recently in April 2009, just prior to its landslide lower-house victory in August 2009 (DPJ 2009b).

Significantly, however, support for the dual-surname policy was left out of the DPJ's 2009 manifesto. This omission suggests that the DPJ did not believe that this issue would attract a large number of floating, independent voters. As the prospects for governing increased, the party began to shy away from the issue, which resonated more with progressive women. As its time in government progressed, internal party divisions over the issue became more apparent. Ultimately, however, the inclusion of the People's New Party (PNP) in the governing coalition thwarted progress on this initiative.

The inclusion of two key supporters of the dual-surname policy in Hatoyama's cabinet initially boded well for the introduction of dual-surname legislation, despite the omission of the policy from the DPJ's 2009 manifesto. Hatoyama appointed senior DPJ member Keiko Chiba as justice minister, and Social Democratic Party president (and coalition partner) Mizuho Fukushima as minister of gender equality. Both Chiba and Fukushima had been vocal supporters of the dual-surname policy. They even coauthored a book in 1993 titled *Fufubessei* [Separate surname]. Chiba highlighted the dual-surname issue upon her inauguration as justice minister, promising to introduce legislation to the regular session of the Diet in 2010. Hatoyama also publicly endorsed the legislation, stating, "I'm in favor of the law change in principle and it is not premature [to introduce a new name system] because it has been debated for a long time" (Munakata and Ichinose 2010). Public opinion also has been shifting in favor of the issue over time (Mikanagi 2011, 135). For example, a poll taken immediately after Chiba's inauguration found 48 percent in favor of dual surnames and 41 percent against.[20]

In the end, however, the legislation stalled. Divisions within the DPJ along with strong opposition from the PNP prevented the cabinet from reaching an agreement (Munakata and Ichinose 2010). Shizuka Kamei, the leader of the PNP and former LDP member, expressed traditional conservative party objections to the bill, stating, "I don't think it's good [for married couples] to use different surnames when family bonds are weakening" (Munakata and Ichinose 2010). Conservatives see the dual-surname issue as attacking the traditional foundation of the Japanese family. These types of objections stalled the legislation when initially introduced by the Ministry of Justice under the LDP in 1996.

In 2011, activists turned their attention to the courts. Five people filed suit in Tokyo District Court on February 14, 2011, claiming that the provision in the Civil Code that stipulates that couples must have a single surname violates the constitution's equality provisions (*Japan Times* 2011). Court action could pressure the DPJ in the future.

Toward an Explanation of Limited Policy Success

As we have seen, the nationalized party system has provided incentives to both the LDP and the DPJ to support more female candidates in order to appeal to the broader public and to illustrate each party's commitment to the valence issue of change. The volatility of the emerging two-party system, however, has meant that women have struggled to retain their seats across elections. As a result, the majority of women in the DPJ lack seniority, which in turn limits their influence on policy.

20 *Asahi Shimbun* poll, released October 14, 2009. Cited in Mansfield Asian Opinion Poll Database (09-26). www.mansfieldfdn.org/backup/polls/2009/poll-09-26.htm.

Women in the Diet in general and in the DPJ in particular fall short of constituting a critical mass. Proponents of critical mass suggest that legislative bodies need to be composed of somewhere between 20 and 35 percent women before female legislators can affect the political culture and legislative priorities of these lawmaking bodies. The key question addressed has been how long it will take for women to move from being tokens to being influential participants (Kanter 1977, 966). Many political scientists have approached this puzzle by attempting to determine whether the presence of a significant percentage of women in a legislative body results in a substantive change in policy priorities (Mansbridge 1999; Norris and Lovenduski 1989; Phillips 1995; Thomas 1994). The results from this body of work are varied, with much depending on the country under investigation (Grey 2002; Lovenduski and Norris 2003; Swers 1998).

Significantly, a study of the passage of parental leave and child care policies in 20 OECD countries, including Japan, found that the number of women in parliament increased the likelihood of policy passage. This finding suggests that a threshold might be less important than a simple increase in numbers (Lambert 2008). In light of this, one would expect more activity on women's issues under the DPJ, given the recent increase in the number of female politicians. Several women's issues have been considered by the DPJ, but little progress has been made, due primarily to the fact that these mainly junior women have been excluded from the policymaking process.

Not only is the DPJ composed of mostly junior women, but it also does not have a clear policy stance on women's issues. The variety of women's policies that the DPJ has considered since taking office illustrates fragmentation within the party. The DPJ policies do not affect women in similar ways. Child allowances, day care provision, and dual surnames are connected only in the broadest sense, that they are all policies that affect women; however, women in various positions are affected differently. Child allowances primarily target housewives and provide incentives for women to stay at home and have more children. Japan's declining birthrate is a motivating factor behind this legislation. In contrast, the provision of day care is of most concern to women who want to remain in the workforce after childbirth. With limited spaces in child care, women are often faced with the choice of either working outside the home or rearing children (Schoppa 2006). Increasing day care provision could potentially address this dilemma and provide incentives for women to have children and stay in the workforce. In contrast, the dual-surname issue has less to do with fertility or the political economy and more to do with concerns over equality, citizenship, and democracy.[21] As with day care provision, the main supporters of the dual-surname legislation are professional women. The support of policies with conflicting incentives is not limited to women's issues. Lipscy, in chapter 8, exposes a similar phenomenon in transportation policy where the popular appeals of abolishing gasoline taxes and highway tolls conflict with the DPJ's goals to reduce CO_2 emissions.

Given the relatively small number of mainly junior women in the DPJ and the absence of a unifying policy stance, it should not be surprising that veto points, which also influenced the LDP, stymied progress on most women's policies. Child allowances passed partially because of the speed of action when a "policy window" was open (Kingdon 1984). The election of the DPJ was interpreted as a strong call for this legislation, and the DPJ acted quickly to pass it. In the end, fiscal constraints forced the DPJ to succumb to pressure from the opposition and retract this policy. The competing bureaucratic ministries backed by kindergarten employees acted as key veto points against the merger of day care centers and kindergartens. Similarly, the dual-surname legislation eventually failed due to strong opposition from the DPJ's coalition partner, a major veto point, despite initial support from (female) Justice Minister Chiba and Prime Minister Hatoyama. In both cases, the supporters of the policies are weaker and less organized than those opposed to the policies.[22] The absence of a clear base of support for these policies within the DPJ has hindered progress on women's issues.

Conclusion

For women in politics, the inauguration of the DPJ government represents a baby step forward but not a significant change from the LDP (or at least from the LDP under Koizumi). While the DPJ's Water and Seeds and open recruitment programs helped women overcome some constraints to running for office, these programs were insufficient to guarantee continued support of women, especially once they have been elected. The DPJ's upper-house policy to run a woman in three-seat constituencies was a step in the right direction but not nearly as sweeping as a party quota for both the lower and upper houses. Without a sustained commitment to nominate a significant number of women across elections, the number of women will

21 Some have noted that day care provision along with maternity leave and parental leave also are related to citizenship, as the ability to fully participate in the economy speaks to issues of equality (Lambert 2007, 3).

22 See Lambert (2008) for a discussion of the impact of veto points on maternal employment policies.

remain small. The women elected in 2005 and 2009 reflect the popularity of the LDP (in 2005) and the DPJ (in 2009) as well as the public's desire for change. These attitudes can shift. The less the valence issues of change and reform resonate with the public, the less likely women will be tapped by their parties without more comprehensive institutional supports.

Meanwhile, women for the most part remain in marginal cabinet positions and sit outside the important decision-making circles within parties. The DPJ is no exception. While the DPJ successfully supported a large number of women in the 2007 upper-house and 2009 lower-house elections, these women lacked the seniority and experience necessary to significantly influence the policy agenda at that point. Their chances of reelection also were lower because of their reliance on Ozawa's financial support, especially given Ozawa's marginal position in the DPJ. Indeed, when facing reelection, Ozawa's "girls" likely found themselves in a similar position to Koizumi's female "children."

For the female legislators in the DPJ who would have liked to pursue issues such as day care and dual surnames, obstacles still existed. First, a large number of women in both the LDP and DPJ have very junior status. While the importance of strict seniority has diminished since electoral reform, junior women do not have a large voice in the policymaking process. And even senior women, such as Kciko Chiba, have struggled against the more conservative voices within the DPJ. Moreover, significant veto points remain regardless of the party in power.

This study, like other chapters in this volume, also illustrates how the nationalized party system has created pressure for policy convergence. As Lipscy and Scheiner highlight, this convergence is related to the incentives to focus on the median voter (2012). The fact that the DPJ has made more progress on issues related to women as mothers than to women as workers suggests that the differences between the LDP and DPJ are not that large. Moreover, the main difference in the DPJ's child allowance policy rested with its commitment to eliminate income restrictions for household eligibility. When faced with budgetary constraints, the DPJ ended up repealing this reform. The DPJ's day care proposal also was not significantly different from what the LDP had attempted to enact. Both parties ended up succumbing to bureaucratic resistance.

The DPJ is a moderate party, not a progressive one like the Japan Socialist Party (JSP) during the period of LDP dominance. Indeed, much evidence exists that since its formation the DPJ has moved from a center-left party to a party firmly in the center ideologically (Kabashima and Steel 2006; Koellner 2011; Miura, Lee, and Weiner 2005). While its centrist position has enhanced its electoral performance, it has not allowed it to champion issues of concern to more progressive women, especially after those women have gained office. Unlike the JSP in the 1980s, the DPJ has not pushed for gender equality issues (Johnson 1992). Indeed, the women elected as DPJ politicians were unable to find a common voice. In the end, more women in significant leadership positions are necessary to accomplish reform, a particularly difficult task given the volatility of national elections.

Electoral reform opened the door to greater female representation. The PR portion of the combined system lowers the barriers to female nomination. Moreover, the nationalized campaigns characteristic of the emerging two-party system provide incentives to parties to support women, in order to indicate change and reform. The new electoral system, however, also has produced more volatile elections. The resultant partisan shifts have meant that several female politicians have not been reelected. In addition, the DPJ felt pressure to move to the middle to attract more votes. The DPJ's abandonment of the dual-surname issue is representative of this shift. Its child allowance and day care policies also differ only slightly from the LDP's. The election of more women across elections cannot completely reverse these larger electoral trends. Still, the sustained support of women in both the LDP and DPJ is required for ensuring the type of presence necessary to more substantially influence governance and policy in the future.

References

Boling, Patricia. 2007. "Policies to Support Working Mothers and Children in Japan." In *The Political Economy of Japan's Low Fertility*, edited by Frances McCall Rosenbluth, 131–54. Stanford, CA: Stanford University Press.

Brasor, Philip. 2009. "The Forgotten DPJ Promise on Women's Rights." *Japan Times*. September 20. http://search.japantimes.co.jp/cgi-bin/fd20090920pb.html.

Cabinet Office. 2005. *Heisei 17 danjo kyodo sanka jisho* [Cabinet white paper for planning gender cooperation]. http://www.gender.go.jp/whitepaper/h17/danjyo_hp/danjyo/pdf/DKH17H01.pdf.

Carroll, Susan J. 1994. *Women as Candidates in American Politics*. 2nd ed. Bloomington: Indiana University Press.

Darcy, Robert, and David L. Nixon. 1996. "Women in the 1946 and 1993 Japanese House of Representative Elections: The Role of the Election System." *Journal of Northeast Asian Studies* 15 (Spring): 3–19.

Darcy, Robert, Susan Welch, and Janet Clark. 1994. *Women, Elections, and Representation*, 2nd ed. Lincoln: University of Nebraska Press.

DPJ (Democratic Party of Japan). 2007. *Minshuto WS kikin "Water and Seed/ Tane to Mizu* [DPJ WS Fund "Water and Seed"]. http://www.dpj.or.jp / danjo/candidates.

———. 2009a. "2009 Change of Government: The DPJ's Platform for Government." http://www.dpj.or.jp/english/manifesto/manifesto2009.pdf.

———. 2009b. "Sentakuteki fufubessei seido no donyue mimpo no ichibu kaiseian o sangiin ni teishutsu" [The introduction of an elective system of separate conjugal surnames: Presentation to the House of Councillors of a bill on a partial revision of the Civil Code]. April 24. http://www.dpj.or.jp/ news/?num=15817.

———. 2010. "DPJ Policy Research Committee Submits Party Budget Proposal to the Government." December 6. http://www.dpj.or.jp/english/ news/?num=19485.

Gaunder, Alisa. 2009. "Women Running for National Office in Japan: Are Koizumi's Female 'Children' a Short-Term Anomaly or a Lasting Phenomenon?" In *Political Change in Japan: Electoral Behavior, Party Realignment, and the Koizumi Reforms*, edited by Steven R. Reed, Kenneth Mori McElwain, and Kay Shimizu, 239–59. Stanford, CA: Shorenstein Asia-Pacific Research Center.

Grey, Sandra. 2002. "Does Size Matter? Critical Mass and New Zealand's Women MPs." *Parliamentary Affairs* 55 (January): 19–29.

Inter-Parliamentary Union. 2011. "Women in National Parliaments." http:// www.ipu.org/wmn-e/classif.htm.

Iwamoto, Misako. 2010. "Who Are 'Ozawa's Girls'? Political Recruitment of DPJ." Paper presented at the Japanese-American Women's Symposium (JAWS), August 28–September 4, 2010, Washington, DC.

Japan Times. 2011. "Women Sue to Keep Surnames in Marriage." *Japan Times Online.* February 16. http://www.japantimes.co.jp/news/2011/02/16/ national/women-sue-to-keep-surnames-in-marriage/.

Johnson, Linda. 1992. "The Feminist Politics of Takako Doi and the Social Democratic Party of Japan." *Women's Studies International Forum* 15 (3): 385–95.

Kabashima, Ikuo, and Gill Steel. 2006. "How the LDP Survives." *Japan Echo* (June): 7–15.

Kanter, Rosabeth Moss. 1977. "Some Effects of Proportions on Group Life: Skewed Sex Ratios and Responses to Token Women." *American Journal of Sociology* 82 (March): 965–90.

Kato, Mariko. 2009. "Parties Wave Flag for Child-Rearing." *Japan Times.* August 13. http://search.japantimes.co.jp/cgi-bin /nn20090813f1.html.

Kingdon, John. 1984. *Agendas, Alternatives and Public Policies.* Boston: Little, Brown.

Koellner, Patrick. 2011. "The Democratic Party of Japan: Development, Organization and Programmatic Profile." In *The Routledge Handbook of Japanese Politics*, edited by Alisa Gaunder, 24–35. London: Routledge.

Krook, Mona Lena. 2009. *Quotas for Women in Politics: Gender and Candidate Selection Reform Worldwide*. Oxford: Oxford University Press.

Lambert, Priscilla. 2007. "The Political Economy of Postwar Family Policy in Japan: Economic Imperatives and Electoral Incentives." *Journal of Japanese Studies* 33 (Winter): 1–28.

———. 2008. "The Comparative Political Economy of Parental Leave and Child Care: Evidence from Twenty OECD Countries." *Social Politics: International Studies in Gender, State and Society* 3 (Fall): 315–44.

Lipscy, Phillip Y. 2012. "A Casualty of Political Transformation? The Politics of Energy Efficiency in the Japanese Transportation Sector." *Journal of East Asian Studies* 12 (3): 409–39.

Lipscy, Phillip Y., and Ethan Scheiner. 2012. "Japan Under the DPJ: The Paradox of Political Change Without Policy Change." *Journal of East Asian Studies* 12 (3): 311–22.

Lovenduski, Joni, and Pippa Norris. 2003. "Westminster Women: The Politics of Presence." *Political Studies* 51 (March): 84–102.

Maeda, Ko. 2010. "Factors Behind the Historic Defeat of Japan's Liberal Democratic Party in 2009." *Asian Survey* 50 (5): 888–907.

Mansbridge, Jane. 1999. "Should Blacks Represent Blacks and Women Represent Women? A Contingent 'Yes.'" *Journal of Politics* 61 (August): 628–57.

Matland, Richard E. 1993. "Institutional Variables Affecting Female Representation in National Legislatures: The Case of Norway." *Journal of Politics* 55 (3): 737–55.

———. 2002. "Enhancing Women's Political Participation: Legislative Recruitment and Electoral Systems." In *Women in Parliament: Beyond Numbers*, edited by Julie Ballington and Azza Karam, 93–111. Stockholm: International IDEA.

Matland, Richard E., and Donley T. Studlar. 1996. "The Contagion of Women Candidates in Single-Member District and Proportional Representation Electoral Systems: Canada and Norway." *Journal of Politics* 58 (3): 707–33.

Matsutani, Minoru. 2010. "Ins, Outs of New Child Allowance." *Japan Times*. April 1. http://search.japantimes.co.jp/cgi-bin /nn20100401f1.html.

McElwain, Kenneth Mori. 2012. "The Nationalization of Japanese Elections." *Journal of East Asian Studies* 12 (3): 323–50.

MEXT. 2009. "White Paper on Education, Culture, Sports, Science and Technology." http://www.mext.go.jp/b_menu/hakusho/html/hpab200901/ 1305844.htm.

Mikanagi, Yumiko. 2011. "The Japanese Conception of Citizenship." In *The Routledge Handbook of Japanese Politics*, edited by Alisa Gaunder, 130–39. London: Routledge.

Miura, Mari, Kap Yu Lee, and Robert Weiner. 2005. "Who Are the DPJ? Policy Positioning and Recruitment Strategy." *Asian Perspective* 29 (1): 49–77.

Moser, Robert G., and Ethan Scheiner. 2012. *Electoral Systems and Political Context*. New York: Cambridge University Press.

Munakata, Michiko, and Masato Ichinose. 2010. "DPJ Wavers on Maiden Names Law." *Japan Times*. April 10. http://search.japantimes.co.jp/cgi-bin/nn20100410f1.html.

Norris, Pippa. 1985. "The Gender Gap: America and Britain." *Parliamentary Affairs* 38 (2): 192–201.

———. 2004. *Electoral Engineering: Voting Rules and Political Behavior*. Cambridge: Cambridge University Press.

Norris, Pippa, and Joni Lovenduski. 1989. "Women Candidates for Parliament: Transforming the Agenda." *British Journal of Political Science* 19 (January): 106–115.

Ogai, Tokuko. 2010. "Women's Advancement in the Election 2010 for the House of Councillors and Election Strategies of Mr. Ozawa, Democratic Party of Japan." Paper presented at the Japanese-American Women's Symposium (JAWS), Washington, DC, August 28–September 4.

Oki, Naoko. 2010. "Candidate Recruitment Strategy of the Democratic Party of Japan in Local Election." Paper presented at the Japanese-American Women's Symposium (JAWS), Washington, DC, August 28–September 4.

Phillips, Anne. 1995. *The Politics of Presence*. Oxford: Oxford University Press.

Reed, Steven R., Ethan Scheiner, and Michael F. Thies. 2012. "The End of LDP Dominance and the Rise of Party-Oriented Politics in Japan." *Journal of Japanese Studies* 38 (2): 353–76.

Rule, Wilma. 1987. "Electoral Systems, Contextual Factors, and Women's Opportunity for Election to Parliament in Twenty-Three Democracies." *Western Political Quarterly* 40 (3): 477–98.

———. 1994. "Parliaments Of, By, and For the People: Except for Women?" In *Electoral Systems in Comparative Perspective: Their Impact on Women and Minorities*, edited by Wilma Rule and J. Zimmerman, 15–30. Westport, CT: Greenwood Press.

Scheiner, Ethan. 2012. "The Electoral System and Japan's Partial Transformation: Party System Consolidation Without Policy Realignment." *Journal of East Asian Studies* 12 (3): 351–79.

Schoppa, Leonard. 2006. *Race for the Exits: The Unraveling of Japan's System of Social Protection*. Ithaca, NY: Cornell University Press.

———. 2011. "Policies for an Aging/Low Fertility Society." In *The Routledge Handbook of Japanese Politics*, edited by Alisa Gaunder, 201–11. London: Routledge.

Shin, Ki-young. 2008. "'The Personal Is the Political': Women's Surname Change in Japan." *Journal of Korean Law* 8 (1): 161–79.

Swers, Michelle L. 1998. "Are Women More Likely to Vote for Women's Issue Bills Than Their Male Colleagues?" *Legislative Studies Quarterly* 23 (August): 435–48.

Takahara, Kanako. 2010. "Kindergartens, Day Care Centers May Merge." *Japan Times*. November 17. http://search.japantimes.co.jp/cgi-bin/nn20101117i1.html.

———. 2011a. "Preschool, Day Care Integration Plan Eases." *Japan Times*. January 25. http://search.japantimes.co.jp/cgi-bin/nn20110125a5.html.

———. 2011b. "DPJ Withdraws Child Allowance Bill as Opposition Digs Its Heels In." *Japan Times*. March 31. http://search.japantimes.co.jp/cgi-bin/nn20110331a5.html.

Tartan, Suzannah. 2007. "Taking Time for Younger Children." *Japan Times*. December 18. http://search.japantimes.co.jp/cgi-bin/fs20071218a1.html.

———. 2008. "Making Day Care Fit Real Needs." *Japan Times*. January 22. http://search.japantimes.co.jp/cgi-bin/fs20080122a1.html.

Thomas, Sue. 1994. *How Women Legislate*. Oxford: Oxford University Press.

Foreign Policy

12 The Democratic Party of Japan's New (but Failing) Grand Security Strategy

FROM "RELUCTANT REALISM" TO "RESENTFUL REALISM"?

Christopher W. Hughes

This chapter challenges the dominant negative critiques of the foreign policy of the Democratic Party of Japan (DPJ). The DPJ possesses a coherent grand strategy vision, capable of securing Japan's national interests in an age of multipolarity and centered on a less dependent and more proactive role in the U.S.-Japan alliance, strengthened Sino-Japanese ties, and enhanced East Asian regionalism. However, the DPJ has failed to implement its policy, due to domestic and international structural pressures. Consequently, the DPJ is defaulting back into a strategy in the style of the Liberal Democratic Party (LDP). Japanese and U.S. policymakers should recognize the risks of a strategy characterized not by "reluctant realism" but by a more destabilizing "resentful realism."

The Democratic Party of Japan (DPJ) assumed office in September 2009 pledging fundamental change from the previous Liberal Democratic Party (LDP) regime, not only in domestic policy but, just as crucially, in foreign policy. The DPJ has already encountered significant resistance and setbacks in domestic policy, not least in its unsure response to the "3/11"

The original outline of this essay was inspired by time that I spent as the Edwin O. Reischauer Visiting Professor of Japanese Studies at the Department of Government, Harvard University. I made subsequent presentations in 2009–10 at Harvard, George Washington University, University of Southern California, and the University of Washington. For the invitations to speak, incisive comments on the outline, and overall help with the project, I would like to thank Susan Pharr, Dick Samuels, Llewellyn Hughes, Mike Mochizuki, Saadia Pekkanen, Robert Pekkanen, Kenneth Pyle, Ellis Krauss, Saori Katada, Kōda Yōji, and Amy Catalinac. Any errors of interpretation or fact are my own. This chapter was originally published in the *Journal of Japanese Studies*, Vol. 38, #1. Copyright © 2012 by the Society for Japanese Studies. Used with permission.

disasters, but it is arguably in its foreign and security policy that it has provoked the most sustained criticism and counterpressures. The DPJ has found itself embroiled in fierce controversy over its impact on the future trajectory of Japan's international orientation vis-à-vis the United States and East Asia. The degree of controversy over foreign policy has been so great as to threaten to spill back and overwhelm the domestic agenda. This phenomenon has been demonstrated by the DPJ's contribution to the downfall of the first DPJ prime minister, Hatoyama Yukio, in June 2010 over the imbroglio on the relocation of the U.S. Marines' Air Station Futenma, and then the precipitous decline in public support for his immediate successor, Prime Minister Kan Naoto, following tensions with China and Russia over territorial issues in late 2010. Meanwhile, Noda Yoshihiko, Kan's successor since September 2011, has clearly taken heed of the implications for domestic stability and thus far has moved cautiously in the foreign-policy field.

The DPJ has triggered debate on the future course of Japan's foreign and security policy on a number of levels, with most analyses marked by an extraordinary degree of fear and loathing of DPJ policy in Japan itself, as well as in the United States and other partner countries. The Japanese and international media have been at the forefront of efforts to ladle criticism upon the DPJ for its foreign and security policy, naturally supported by opposition policymakers in Japan, and those prepared to defend the DPJ have been few and far between.[1]

Consequently, the debate on DPJ foreign policy has been dominated by two sets of highly negative discourses, which at times have come close to caricaturing the administration as a collection of fools and knaves.[2] The first set has characterized DPJ leaders as essentially foolish due to their naïve and wrongheaded foreign-policy prescriptions, which fail to recognize the realities and challenges to Japan of the current international system, and most especially Japan's limited ability to influence U.S. security strategy and to promote compensatory new forms of cooperation in East Asia. In a similar vein, the DPJ has been criticized as simply confused in its foreign policy, really possessing no coherent or consistent international strategy, as demonstrated by the disarray of Hatoyama and eventually the party over the Futenma issue. Meanwhile, the second set of discourses has characterized the DPJ as knavelike in seeking to renegotiate the international pledges made to the United States under the preceding LDP administration, and

---

1 For one view defending the DPJ that has found its way into the mainstream, see Packard (2010).

2 For U.S. officials allegedly viewing Hatoyama as "hapless" and "loopy," see Kamen (2010).

perhaps concomitantly, having elements of its leadership holding a hidden agenda to dismantle the U.S.-Japan alliance.

These discourses conclude not only that the DPJ has thus far botched its immediate management of foreign and security policy, but that it has also initiated, whether deliberately or inadvertently, a process of longer-term shift, and drift, in Japan's strategy. The DPJ is now thought to be diverting Japan from the trajectory laid down by the LDP—a trajectory that in recent years, and especially under the premiership of Koizumi Jun'ichirō, has generally been viewed as setting a benchmark to be emulated of close U.S.-Japan alliance ties and concomitant Japanese international proactivity. In turn, the conclusion of these discourses is that any DPJ deviation from this trajectory is by definition a fundamentally negative development for U.S.-Japan ties, and by logical extension, anything detrimental to the bilateral relationship as the foundation of Japanese foreign and security policy must be detrimental to Japan's overall international position (Green 2011). The final conclusion appears to be that the DPJ needs, then, to be nudged back onto the correct pathway for international policy and that inevitably it is the duty of the United States, as the prime international partner, in "tough love" fashion, to cajole, or if necessary coerce, Japan back onto the straight and narrow. Secretary of Defense Robert Gates attempted to do something akin to this when he visited Japan in October 2009 and expressed opposition to the DPJ's stance on Futenma (Green 2009a).

In the midst of this maelstrom over the DPJ's foreign policy, more sober and nonpartisan academic analyses have been in short supply.[3] This chapter is an attempt to deliver a more detailed, nuanced, and objective analysis of DPJ foreign policy. It grounds its analysis on deeper and more wide-ranging empirical evidence than presented to date on the DPJ's international outlook, and contextualizes the administration's moves thus far within the larger sweep of Japanese international policy so as to divine just how much the party has deviated or is likely to deviate from the LDP's postwar trajectory. The chapter further considers the overall possible implications for Japan's grand strategy.

The chapter argues that, contrary to much of the near-universal condemnation of the DPJ, the party does in fact possess a grand strategy, or at least a *vision* of a grand strategy, worthy of serious consideration and potentially capable of promoting Japan's national interests and role as a key international actor. This grand strategy certainly differs in many respects from that of the LDP, but it is explicit in its framing, with no hidden

---

3 For sound academic analysis of the DPJ before it took power, see Easley et al. (2010).

agendas. In addition, it indeed has been openly articulated by the DPJ's top leadership for a number of years, including the last five party presidents prior to Noda—Okada Katsuya, Maehara Seiji, Ozawa Ichirō, Hatoyama, and Kan—and those other party members most actively engaged in foreign policy and security issues. Those critics who feel that the DPJ has ambushed the United States with its agenda simply appear to have been overly fixated on the LDP while failing to read the Japanese tea leaves and to prepare for the possibility of domestic and international policy transition.

Moreover, the DPJ's grand strategy is remarkably coherent in that, despite inevitable internal factionalism, most of the key elements have been shared by the party's top leadership, thus making its policy in many ways as feasible as that of the LDP ever was. Furthermore, the DPJ vision appears sophisticated and realistic, shorn of much ideological sentiment (in contrast to recent LDP administrations dabbling with emotive historical revisionism and value-oriented diplomacy) and instead attempting to carefully rethink and calibrate Japan's international ambitions and capabilities against its external challenges.[4] The DPJ's vision, if examined in depth, I argue, is also not necessarily problematic for U.S. strategy and in many ways may be more complementary and beneficial than that of the LDP.

Hence, the DPJ can be argued to possess a relatively plausible and viable foreign policy, one certainly no less credible in inception than those of previous LDP administrations. In this sense, the advent of the DPJ certainly does contain the potential to shift Japan in new strategic directions. However, the more prosaic part of the DPJ foreign- and security-policy story is that, even though the party might envision a grander reorientation for Japan internationally, it has struggled and will likely continue to struggle to implement such a strategy, due to a combination of domestic policymaking and international structural pressures. The final outcome is that, bedeviled by these difficulties—many of its own making—the DPJ risks defaulting back to the easier international strategy practiced by the LDP.

Yet, there is here an interesting sting in the tail. Even as the DPJ might acquiesce or be coerced into returning to a path of so-called reluctant realism, its fundamentally different vision and recognition of the perils of this LDP-style strategy vision will lead it to kick, probably forlornly, in frustration at the extinguishing of its hopes for greater international autonomy (Green 2009b). The result will be more a sense of resentful realism and a storing up of further tensions between Japan and the United States.

4 For the definitive account of contending LDP foreign-policy strands, see Samuels (2007).

DPJ Grand Strategy Vision: Finally Facing Up to the Realities of Multipolarity

The DPJ—unsurprisingly, and in little contrast to the LDP—has argued consistently in its manifestos and elsewhere for the last decade that it seeks a position for Japan as a proactive and responsible international power (*Minshutō* 2005a, 2009, 2010). Nevertheless, the DPJ's policy prescription, even if similar to that of the LDP in terms of overall ambitions, diverges more strongly in terms of the administration's analysis of the international environment and the subsequent measures taken to strengthen Japan's position. The DPJ not only was less reticent than the LDP in critiquing U.S. unilateralism under the George W. Bush administration but also was more explicit in indicating that the travails of the United States in Afghanistan and Iraq are manifestations of a deeper and long-term malaise in U.S. power. The DPJ leadership talks more openly about U.S. relative hegemonic decline and the already apparent limits to its ability to manage single-handedly the international system (Ozawa 2007; Nagashima 2009). Similarly, DPJ policymakers are more willing to acknowledge as inevitable the rise of China to great power status, or even hegemonic status, and are not even shy about discussing Japan's own recent relative economic and political decline vis-à-vis the United States and China. There is also a strong acceptance of the "rise of the rest," in the shape of India, a resurgent Russia, a stronger South Korea, and further afield, Brazil and a more integrated European Union (EU) (Hatoyama 2000; Hashimoto 2005; Maehara 2011; Kan 2011a). In short, the DPJ leadership, although not often using the terminology openly, perceives the potential passing of U.S. unipolarity and a concomitant shift in the balance of power toward multipolarity (Hatoyama 2009; Okada 2010).

The DPJ's recognition of multipolarity is seen to pose immediate regional challenges for Japan. DPJ leaders readily admit that Japanese and U.S. interests now and in the future may not always coincide and hence that Japan cannot as in the past unhesitatingly entrust its security to the United States (Hashimoto 2005, 122–23; Sutō et al. 2002, 38). Moreover, the DPJ has sensed that, as the international ground shifts under Japan's feet, it faces the risk of becoming trapped between a rising China and a United States desperate to maintain international primacy. For Japan this entails the risk of becoming embroiled in a Sino-U.S. conflict or, just as worrisomely, being marginalized in a Sino-U.S. regional condominium, as in talk of G2 governance (Hatoyama 2002; Hatoyama 2010; *Asahi Shimbun* 2010a).

LDP administrations were certainly not blind to U.S. relative hegemonic decline and the shift toward multipolarity, as shown by the diplomatic and security demarches to India and Russia under Koizumi and his successors (Hughes 2009). However, for the DPJ the analysis of Japan's necessary response to the changing international system is significantly different. Whereas the LDP toward the end of its period in government became increasingly fixated on the backward-looking (and somewhat contradictory) agendas of ending the postwar era (*sengo dakkyaku*) and of tackling U.S. hegemonic decline while maintaining the status quo by merely investing deeper in the bilateral alliance, the DPJ has shown a more forward-looking posture. The DPJ has arguably leapfrogged ahead of the LDP in attempting to move beyond debates on ending the postwar period. It is instead beginning a rather belated process of contemplating how to extricate Japan from the more recent legacies of the Cold War era and how to address the issues presented by the emerging realities of a new international system (Hoshi 2009).

The DPJ thus advocates that the key for Japan in meeting its international challenges and responsibilities is not, in LDP fashion, to replicate past patterns of foreign-policy behavior but to begin to break out of these constraints. Just as the DPJ has called for a revolution in domestic policy in terms of escaping reliance on the bureaucracy, so it has called for something akin to a revolution in international policy by breaking Japan's past dependence on the increasingly rickety crutch of U.S. hegemony. DPJ leaders argue that Japan throughout and since the Cold War period has been to varying degrees dependent (*izon*) or overdependent (*kajo na izon*) upon or blindly devoted (*tsuizui*) to or even clinging (*bettari*) to the United States (Hatoyama 2001). The result has been that even though the U.S.-Japan bilateral relationship has enabled Japan to develop certain types of international responsibilities, usually in line with U.S. priorities, at other times Japan's easy reliance on the United States (*Amerika makase Nihon no gaikō*) has meant that it has been able to shirk or defer commitments to the United States if these are viewed as particularly risky, as well as to obviate the need to develop a wider set of cooperative foreign and security relations with other powers (Sutō et al. 2002, 36).

In turn, Japan's ability to always fall back on the cushion of the U.S.-Japan relationship has allowed it to develop a form of "closed," "warped" (*kussetsu*), or "U.S.-dependent" (*taibei izon*) nationalism, whereby its policymakers have fiddled with issues of historical revisionism, safe in the knowledge that they are insulated from the full consequences and wrath of East Asian neighboring countries by U.S. security guarantees (Hatoyama 2002). The DPJ further argues that the LDP's comfortable dependence on the United States enabled Japan to pass up opportunities for enhanced East Asian cooperation. Japan instead pursued policies akin to "blocking regionalism"—deliberately overproliferating regional cooperation frameworks as a means to dilute and check China's concentration of power in any one regional forum, rather than a genuine attempt to build durable and effective frameworks to lessen Japan's dependence on the United States.

Japan's perilous overdependence on the United States and the international situation, as seen by the DPJ, carries clear implications for its future international strategy. Japan must redress its dependence on the U.S.-Japan bilateral relationship, not by weakening or abandoning the alliance but by moving to develop a broader set of complementary and counterbalancing international ties and by exploiting the opportunities of emerging multipolarity. Japan must maneuver to strengthen bilateral relations with a rising China and, for some DPJ leaders, try to reestablish a more symmetrical triangular balance of power (*seisankakukeiron*) among itself, the United States, and China (Hatoyama 2009c).[5] In many ways, the DPJ is advocating just a recentering of Japanese diplomacy to establish more equidistance between the United States and China, so as to maximize its potential intermediary role, a tradition of diplomacy upheld by the LDP until the perceived disastrous stewardship of Koizumi.

In similar fashion, the DPJ champions renewed efforts in East Asian regionalism. In contradistinction to the LDP, though, the DPJ leadership shares a stronger "cognitive" rather than "tactical" attachment to regionalism, viewing the growth of regional frameworks not simply as a means to hinder the rise of China while the real efforts of Japanese diplomacy are devoted to the U.S.-Japan alliance. Instead, the DPJ views regional frameworks as a viable international strategy in their own right, as already demonstrated in other regions such as Europe, well suited to bringing effective governance to an increasingly multipolar international order. Hence, for the DPJ, the concept of the East Asian Community—strongly shared by nearly every leading member of the DPJ at least until recent tensions with China and the advent of Noda—even if never viewed as usurping the U.S.-Japan alliance in the set of Japanese international priorities, is seen as more than a diversionary tactic. In addition, it offers Japan a useful alternative to increasingly exclusive dependence on the United States and an opportunity to build an "open" form of nationalism conducive to improved ties with regional neighbors.

The DPJ's assessments of the changing international structure are given coherence, above all, by a shared belief in the restoration of a more autonomous (*jishu-teki*) and independent (*jiritsu-teki*) Japanese diplomatic posture.

---

5 Other notable DPJ advocates of this thesis are Ozawa, Yamaoka Kenji, and Koshiishi Azuma.

The DPJ contends that the only effective path for Japan to increase its international contribution and, in fact, become a more reliable or "normal" ally and partner is not for Japan to shield behind the United States, as under the LDP, but instead to step out from the shadow of the United States and to undertake greater international responsibilities in a more self-reliant fashion.

U.S.-Japan Alliance: Seeking Balanced Autonomy

DPJ interest in rearticulating the U.S.-Japan relationship has been interpreted as predicated on anti-Americanism, a view fueled by an abridged translation of Hatoyama's article originally intended for the September 2009 edition of the Japanese journal *Voice* but appeared in the *New York Times* in August 2009 and in which he criticized U.S.-inspired globalization and free-market fundamentalism (Hatoyama 2009b).[6] Setting aside the fact that Hatoyama's critique of globalization is not unique to the DPJ, to the LDP, or to domestic opinion in the United States itself and other countries, the DPJ's willingness to reexamine ties with the United States should not be viewed as a simplistic reaction against U.S. domination or as an expression of hope for the winding down of the relationship. On the contrary, the DPJ leadership, by raising questions about the future of the U.S.-Japan relationship, sees itself engaged in a constructive attempt to resolve deep-rooted and long-avoided issues in the relationship and to thereby better sustain and strengthen the alliance for the longer term.

Indeed, it is ironic that the DPJ in openly pondering the means to rationalize and sustain the alliance has attracted near-universal criticism, whereas its LDP predecessor has received universal praise in its management of the bilateral relationship. This is despite the fact that the LDP, more often than not in its half-century in power, and even under Koizumi, resorted to expediency, buck passing, and minimalist security commitments in managing the alliance (as seen in the dispatch of the Japan Self-Defense Forces [JSDF] to support the United States in the "war on terror"), and to boot, demonstrated toward its end increasing signs of erratic neo-nationalism—all traits that do not argue for the long-term structural strength of the alliance (Hughes and Krauss 2007). The open and relatively thoughtful efforts by Hatoyama and other DPJ leaders to rearticulate the basis of the U.S.-Japan alliance contrast sharply with the mantra-like, yet still opaque, justifications

6 For the full Japanese version of Hatoyama's September 2009 article in *Voice* and an accompanying full official English translation, see Hatoyama (2009c) and "My Political Philosophy," http://www.hatoyama.gr.jp/profile/fraternitye.html. For the analysis that drew attention to Hatoyama's comments and possible implications for U.S.-Japan relations, see Landler and Fackler (2009).

for the necessity of the alliance purveyed by Koizumi and many other LDP leaders.

The DPJ's agenda for reforging the U.S.-Japan alliance is largely transparent and certainly does involve scaling back bilateral commitments in certain areas. The DPJ, in light of what it views as the willful stretching of alliance cooperation to encompass the JSDF dispatch to support ill-advised U.S.-led coalition operations in the "war on terror," has made it clear that it intends future U.S.-Japan alliance military cooperation to be predicated upon tighter functional and geographical interpretations of the constitution and the security treaty (Hashimoto 2005). The DPJ leadership is fond of advocating a "close and equal U.S.-Japan relationship" (*kinmitsu de taitō Nichibei kankei*) or "equal alliance" (*taitō na Nichibei dōmei*). This alliance vision eschews the LDP's simple expedient followership of the United States in out-of-area military operations and instead focuses on a more forthcoming Japanese military role alongside the United States in East Asia itself. This focus addresses the purport of Articles 5 and 6 of the bilateral security treaty and completes much of the 1990s agenda of alliance strengthening for regional contingencies that the LDP in the end hedged away from. Hence, the DPJ administration in the wake of the 2010 clash with China over the Senkaku Islands was relatively comfortable in opening discussions with the United States over the possibility of remodeling the "common strategic objectives" of the alliance first laid down in 2006, and even possibly the U.S.-Japan Defense Guidelines, in order to respond more effectively to China's rising military presence (*Japan Times Online* 2010c; *Asahi Shimbun* 2011).

Alliance Adjustments and New Support

The DPJ, in order to fulfill its vision, has a specific program of modifications to alliance cooperation, with which it has experienced varying degrees of success. After internal debate and hesitance in regard to the U.S. reaction, the DPJ, in line with its consistent manifesto pledges and opposition over the last decade to the deployment of the Maritime Self-Defense Force (MSDF) in the Indian Ocean to provide refueling in support of the U.S.-led coalition in Afghanistan, allowed the Replenishment Support Special Measures Law to lapse in January 2010 and terminated the MSDF mission. The DPJ instead instituted a $5 billion package over five years for civilian support for Afghan reconstruction in the areas of police training, employment of former combatants, and development of agriculture and energy. The DPJ has argued that this type of large-scale civilian contribution was more suited to Japan's own national capabilities and to the immediate needs of the coalition on the ground than a continued or new JSDF mission with a highly

circumscribed military mandate and requiring the investment of great domestic political energy simply to pass the National Diet legislation required
for dispatch. The United States, for its part, despite viewing the MSDF mission as an important symbol of U.S.-Japan alliance solidarity and Japanese
military support for the struggle in Afghanistan, accepted that cessation of
the JSDF mission was largely inevitable and relatively insignificant in terms
of the overall military effort surrounding Afghanistan.

If the DPJ's ending of the MSDF Indian Ocean mission proved rela-
tively straightforward for alliance management, then far greater travails
have awaited attempts to review U.S.-Japan base agreements in Okinawa.
The DPJ's interest in renegotiating elements of the May 2006 U.S.-Japan
Defense Policy Review Initiative (DPRI) and Roadmap for Realignment
Implementation relating to the planned relocation of the U.S. Marine Corps
(USMC) Air Station Futenma from Ginowan City to Camp Schwab and
Cape Henoko near Nago City has been construed as an act of Japanese
duplicity. This is partly because the United States had been engaged in three
sets of protracted negotiations for close to 13 years over the potential new
site for Futenma, and because the previous LDP administration had already
concluded in February 2009 an agreement on joint funding of the relocation
of approximately 8,000 III Marine Expeditionary Unit personnel and 9,000
of their dependents to Guam. This movement has been seen as the precondition for shifting other USMC assets in Okinawa, including Futenma.
The LDP, moreover, had gone so far as to interpret the Guam International
Agreement as essentially a treaty, gaining National Diet approval in May
2009 (MOFA 2009d). Furthermore, the DPJ's potential renegotiation of the
Futenma agreement has been interpreted as part of a longer-term conspir-
acy to unravel the entire U.S. base infrastructure in Japan, a desire allegedly traceable back to Hatoyama's advocacy since the late 1990s of moving
toward a regional security environment that would allow the creation of a
U.S.-Japan security pact without the need for the stationing of U.S. forces
(*chūryū naki anpo*) (Hatoyama 1998).

Once again, leaving aside the fact that the United States for its part
would find it hard to regard the Guam International Agreement as a binding
treaty, given that this necessitates Congressional approval, and the fact that
Japan as a sovereign and democratic state with a change of domestic administration is entitled to renegotiate international agreements, the DPJ's actions in seeking to review the Futenma relocation should not be interpreted
as underhanded or as part of a hidden agenda (McCormack 2009). The DPJ
has asserted in various iterations of its *Okinawa bijon* (Okinawa vision)
since 2002 that it seeks a major reduction in the disproportionate burden

on Okinawa Prefecture of hosting 75 percent of U.S. bases in terms of land area. The DPJ indicated first in 2005 and then again in 2008 that it preferred the relocation of Futenma outside Okinawa, or even outside Japan itself, in line with changes in the international security environment (*Minshutō* 2002; *Minshutō* 2005b; *Minshutō* 2008).

In addition, although it is true that certain members of the DPJ top leadership question the degree of necessity and actual operational functions for the defense of Japan and the surrounding region of the USMC presence— Ozawa Ichirō, most notably in talks with then–Secretary of State Hillary Clinton in February 2009, commented that the presence of the U.S. 7th Fleet alone might be sufficient for the alliance—they do not view revisiting the Futenma agreement as a means to weaken the alliance. Indeed, Hatoyama and Okada had long stated publicly that the DPJ had abandoned the policy of a U.S.-Japan security pact without bases (*Asahi Shimbun* 2009b). Instead, the DPJ perceived itself as engaged in an effort to strengthen the long-term durability and fundamental basis of the U.S.-Japan alliance by seeking to remove once and for all the nagging thorn of Futenma in the side of the bilateral relationship. In this sense, the DPJ shares the LDP's sensibility in being seen to lessen the burden on Okinawa but has diverged in its belief that the current U.S.-Japan plans for a new facility at Henoko serve more in reality to consolidate and intensify in apparent perpetuity the U.S. presence in the prefecture. The DPJ considers these agreements not only inequitable but also politically unsustainable in Okinawa and in the rest of Japan and thus ultimately counterproductive to alliance solidity.

What is true, though, is that the DPJ leadership once in government lacked the discipline and skill to handle the volatile Futenma issue. Hatoyama failed in the first months of the DPJ administration to contain his own and key cabinet ministers' open musings about the possibility of revisiting the Futenma agreements and alternative sites for relocation in other parts of Okinawa or mainland Japan or outside Japan. Hatoyama poorly coordinated policy with his Social Democratic Party of Japan (SDPJ) and People's New Party coalition partners and further agitated local political opinion in Okinawa at the National Diet representative, gubernatorial, prefectural assembly, mayoral, and municipal assembly levels. In turn, the DPJ's one-sided ruminations understandably began to ring alarm bells about Japanese intentions in the Barack Obama administration, with the United States then compounding these problems with its seemingly poor communication with the new DPJ administration by means of press agents, divisions between the State and Defense departments over the best means to respond, and then Secretary of Defense Robert Gates's robust stance during his visit to Japan in October 2009—all precipitating the mini-crisis in U.S.-Japan relations (USDOD 2009).

Insufficient space prevents this chapter from cataloguing the litany of mistakes made by the Japanese and U.S. sides in trying then to dig the alliance out of this crisis, but those mistakes culminated in Hatoyama's resignation in June 2010. The DPJ has arguably, though, proved neither more nor less wise than the LDP in managing the Futenma issue, essentially repeating the same mistakes over the past 14 years of publicly pledging to relocate the base without first deciding where the new site should be or consulting sufficiently with the local populations of alternative sites and resorting to stimulus packages to buy local support (Sotooka 2010).

Moreover, the DPJ has progressively acquiesced in following the LDP plans for relocation. Hatoyama upon resigning in June made it clear that he had come to accept the deterrent arguments associated with the USMC presence in Okinawa (although in February 2011 he claimed that his legitimization of the base agreement using the importance of the USMC was a simple political "expedient" [hōben] that he had never believed in). Even Ozawa, a known critic of the plans for landfill relocation at Cape Henoko, in his DPJ presidential leadership debates with Kan in September 2010, accepted the need to respect the existing bilateral agreements (*Japan Times* 2010a). Kan, for his part, seemed to have largely bought the relocation arguments, although he was clearly attempting to delay implementation, given the mounting domestic political obstacles.

If the Futenma debacle has proved to be a crucial stress point for U.S.-Japan relations, it should not be viewed as fully illustrative of the condition of the alliance or the DPJ's wider plans for bilateral cooperation. For instance, in regard to the DPRI and realignments outside Okinawa, the DPJ has not sought to interfere with, but to actually support, the process. The DPJ has continued to push Iwakuni City to accept the relocation of the U.S. carrier wing from Atsugi, a crucial piece of the DPRI puzzle; and meanwhile other U.S. realignments continue unimpeded at U.S. Air Force Yokota and Camp Zama. (Interestingly, however, it is the United States that apparently has backed out of DPRI agreements relating to the Japanese mainland by scaling down plans for the relocation from Washington State of the U.S. Army's I Corps command structure and accompanying capabilities for rapid deployment in the defense of Japan and other contingencies, choosing instead only to relocate command capabilities [*Asahi Shimbun* 2010d; *Tokyo Shimbun* 2009].)

The DPJ was also thought likely to have pressed the United States on host nation support (HNS) and the Status of Forces Agreement (SOFA).

The DPJ promised in its election campaign to review Japan's high commitment, compared to other U.S. allies, of up to 75 percent of the costs of U.S. military facilities (Calder 2007, 192–94). The DPJ did attempt to pare away at the HNS budget, with the Ministry of Defense (MOD) budget request for 2011 including a modest reduction of 1 percent (*Asahi Shimbun* 2010e; MOD 2010). The DPJ's stance in this regard, though, was little divergent from the LDP, which itself engineered a total reduction of 25 percent in the HNS budget between 2001 and 2009 (Nishihara and Tsuchiyama 2010, 125; Bōei Nenkan Kankōkai 2004, 373; Bōei Nenkan Kankōkai 2010, 354). However, in the end, the DPJ, while not acceding to U.S. requests for an actual increase in HNS, was wary of alienating its ally in the midst of the security scares in late 2010 and agreed to maintain the same level of HNS at ¥188 billion annually for 2011–15 (*Asahi Shimbun* 2010g).

Similarly, the DPJ has maintained a long-term interest in revising the SOFA—again mentioned in its manifestos and the *Okinawa bijon* as part of creating a more equal alliance—but since taking power has restrained its immediate ambitions (*Minshutō* 2008, 4; *Japan Times Online* 2009a). The DPJ has advocated a clause in the SOFA to obligate the United States to hand over at the request of the Japanese authorities military personnel who are unindicted suspects of any crime, rather than the current practice of the United States agreeing only to look favorably upon Japanese requests in extreme criminal cases such as murder and rape. The DPJ has further argued for a clause obligating the United States to accept Japanese environmental inspections and to restore any damage to the environment on its bases. The DPJ's SOFA plans in some ways might privilege Japan over other allies in the area of criminal indictments, while bringing it more in line on environmental measures (*Yomiuri Shimbun* 2010b). The first area of proposed revision is clearly difficult for the United States but might be resolved with changes to Japanese procedures for the detention and questioning of criminal suspects; the United States has indicated that it is relatively open-minded about the need to incorporate environmental clauses (*Asahi Shimbun* 2010f).

Nuclear (Non) Issues?

The DPJ's stance on nuclear issues has been regarded as problematic for the U.S.-Japan alliance, but in fact the evidence thus far is that the DPJ is just as, if not more, in tune with current U.S. nuclear strategy as the LDP. The DPJ after assuming power launched investigations into U.S.-Japan secret pacts (*mitsuyaku*), forged by the Ministry of Foreign Affairs (MOFA) under

LDP administrations in the 1960s and 1970s and involving the transit of nonstrategic nuclear forces (NSNF), or tactical nuclear weapons, through Japanese territory in contravention of the third of the Three Nonnuclear Principles. MOFA in the investigations attempted to defend its stance with the line that the United States and Japan simply had divergent understandings of whether the introduction of nuclear weapons was covered by bilateral prior consultation under the security treaty, whereas an expert panel concluded that MOFA had maintained tacit agreements with the United States to allow the transit of nuclear weapons and thus a secret pact in the "general" sense, even if not in the narrower sense of a formal written agreement.[7]

The DPJ extracted its pound of political flesh from the LDP and MOFA over the secret pacts but most interestingly has not used the investigations to push for fundamental change in nuclear policy. Hatoyama responded to the investigations by simply restating Japan's commitment to the nonnuclear principles. Foreign Minister Okada indicated that Japan had no intention to codify the principles into law, a type of policy often proposed by the SDPJ. Then Prime Minister Kan did indicate that Japan might want to consider codification of the principles but made no substantive initiatives in that direction (*Asahi Shimbun* 2010h). Hence, the DPJ has shifted little from the ambiguities of the LDP line: Japan retains its nonnuclear stance, somewhat strengthened by the new transparency it has shown on alliance misdemeanors in the past but retaining the flexibility to breach these principles if necessary.

Most crucially, the DPJ has not allowed the investigations to impact U.S. nuclear strategy and extended deterrence in the Asia-Pacific region. It was feared that for the DPJ the logical outcome of the investigations might be to pressure the United States by insisting on full prior consultation on the movement of NSNF, even to the point of insisting that the United States abandon its "neither confirm nor deny" policy for the deployment of nuclear weapons (*Japan Times Online* 2009b; Cossa and Glosserman 2009). DPJ policymakers, however, seem to have had little intention to provoke the United States. Okada even stated in the National Diet after the release of the secret pact reports that Japan might still consider the introduction of U.S. NSNF in a major contingency; and the Prime Minister's Council on Security and Defense Capabilities in the New Era Advisory reported in mid-2010 that it might not be wise to use the nonnuclear principles to constrain U.S. nuclear strategy (*Japan Times Online* 2010b; *Arata na Jidai no Anzen*

---

7 For the full *mitsuyaku* reports, see "Iwayuru 'Mitsuyaku' mondai ni kansuru chōsa kekka," March 2010. http://www.mofa.go.jp/mofaj/gaiko/mitsuyaku/kekka.html.

Hoshō to Bōeiryoku Kondankai 2010, 13).[8] In part, the DPJ's relaxed stance on "neither confirm nor deny" reflects the fact that the United States since 1992 has withdrawn all NSNF from its naval vessels and aircraft in the Asia-Pacific region, and the United States has informed Japan that it will retire by approximately 2014 its submarine-based Tomahawk Land Attack Missile / Nuclear (TLAM/N). But its stance somewhat reflects a pragmatic flexibility by the DPJ to work around U.S. nuclear strategy.

Other aspects of the DPJ's nuclear stance initially deemed obstructive to U.S. strategy have proved to be in broad conformity. The DPJ has advocated attempts to persuade the United States to adopt a no-first-use nuclear posture, and the International Commission on Nuclear Nonproliferation and Disarmament initiated by Japan and Australia in 2009 recommended that all nuclear-weapon states should accept this stance, seeking to reduce the salience of nuclear weapons to support U.S. initiatives for a "nuclear free world" (ICNND 2009). However, Japan and Australia at the 2010 Nonproliferation Treaty Review Conference jointly proposed merely that nuclear-weapon states should provide stronger negative security assurances not to use nuclear weapons against nonnuclear states, in compliance with the treaty, a measure fully in line with U.S. proposals in the 2010 Nuclear Posture Review (MOFA 2010).

Furthermore, the DPJ has been far more cooperative toward U.S. disarmament initiatives than the LDP. MOFA officials were reported in the May 2009 Congressional Commission on the Strategic Posture of the United States to have opposed plans for any scaling back of the uses of nuclear weapons for deterrent purposes and to have requested the United States retain NSNF, including TLAM/Ns and low-yield nuclear weapons and B-52 aircraft in Guam (Congressional Commission 2009). In contrast, Okada as foreign minister made it clear that the Japanese government, while denying that MOFA under previous LDP administrations had expressed an opinion on the appropriate level of the nuclear inventory, no longer opposed the withdrawal of nonstrategic nuclear forces, thus in effect freeing up a key plank of U.S. disarmament initiatives (MOFA 2009c). In addition, and perhaps most crucially, the DPJ has assisted nonproliferation strategy simply by abandoning the type of LDP saber-rattling talk about Japan acquiring its own nuclear deterrent.

Meanwhile, if nuclear issues under the DPJ have proved no real barrier to U.S.-Japan alliance ties, it is apparent that bilateral cooperation has

---

8 Hatoyama prior to the 2009 elections had taken a similar stance, later retracted to avoid offending the SDPJ, that the third nonnuclear principle might be breached in times of emergency. See *Asahi Shimbun* (2010c).

continued quietly to roll forward in other vital areas unaffected by the spat over Okinawa. The DPJ has remained committed to U.S.-Japan ballistic missile defense cooperation, perhaps the key driver over the last decade of bilateral integration of military doctrines and capabilities. Moreover, the United States and Japan moved ahead with an agreement in March 2010 for a bilateral information security consultation framework as part of earlier efforts started under the LDP to expand exchanges of military information, arguably a key facet of a more "normalized" relationship for the United States with any of its allies (*Naikaku Kanbō* 2010).

East Asian Regionalism: Antidote to Unipolarity and Multipolarity?

The DPJ has often liked to portray its strong vision of East Asian regionalism within Japan's grand strategy as a total break from the LDP's policy. DPJ accusations hold that the LDP under Koizumi and his successors first disrupted East Asian relations with issues of historical revisionism and then largely neglected the region to the exclusive pursuit instead of U.S.-Japan ties. However, the DPJ is in part caricaturing LDP policy because its own East Asia strategy certainly draws continuities in concepts and mechanisms proposed for regional integration. Most notably, the East Asian Community (EAC) concept trumpeted by Hatoyama first originated in Koizumi's regional diplomacy, and other key regional cooperation mechanisms the DPJ administration has committed to, such as the economic partnership agreements and comprehensive economic partnership agreements for trade liberalization and economic harmonization, were first promoted under LDP governments (Koizumi 2002).

Nevertheless, the DPJ can justifiably argue that its vision of regional policy has differed significantly from that of the LDP in regard to its determination to fully develop these concepts and mechanisms and to position East Asian regionalism as a stronger and more viable component in its own right within overall grand strategy. Hence, the DPJ argues that the LDP maintained an overly simplistic East Asia policy predicated on the assumption that as long as U.S.-Japan relations were healthy, then positive Japan–East Asia relations would follow. The DPJ disputes this axiomatic logic, given that under Koizumi U.S.-Japan relations were allegedly at their strongest but Japan found itself at serious loggerheads with China and South Korea over issues of history, and that the LDP's perceived concentration on U.S.-Japan relations was seen to erode Japan's leadership capacity in East Asia. The DPJ further argues that LDP administrations, while maintaining a nominal commitment to East Asian regionalism through the sponsoring of new frameworks such as the East Asian Summit (EAS) and the Japan-China-South Korea Trilateral Cooperation, were in reality seeking to proliferate regional forums and thereby prevent China from concentrating its rising power in any one framework. Consequently, for the LDP the game in East Asian diplomacy was to frustrate rather than foster effective regional frameworks.

The DPJ, by contrast, argues that it is fully committed to East Asian regionalism as a core component of Japan's grand strategy and is prepared to concentrate Japanese efforts in the EAC as the prime vehicle for achieving effective regional institutionalization. In advocating the EAC, however, the DPJ clearly has no intention of ceding regional leadership to China. Instead, the DPJ's strategy is to enmesh China (*Chūgoku o koritsu sasezu, Ajia no naka ni makikomi*) within a more effective macroregional framework in order to provide the necessary collective leverage among East Asian states to actively engage against any shift toward Chinese unipolarity while also avoiding attempts to pursue a containment policy (Hashimoto 2005).

The DPJ's East Asia policy has attracted considerable skepticism. U.S. policymakers took umbrage at DPJ concepts of the EAC that appeared to exclude the United States entirely and to relegate its role in an emergent region to providing security guarantees. For others, the EAC has simply been regarded as lacking practical substance and as reliant on vague ideas such as Hatoyama's *yūai* (fraternity). It is arguable, though, that criticisms by the United States and others of the EAC have been based on misreading DPJ intentions. It is clear that the EAC concepts held by Hatoyama and the DPJ have been predicated on credible and sophisticated principles as tested in East Asia and other regional contexts.

In the first instance, the EAC concept draws upon traditions of "open regionalism" in the Asia-Pacific that are designed to foster integration not by instigating a regional bloc but by lowering barriers to external interaction with other regions and the global political economy (Hatoyama 2009d). While the DPJ has advocated the EAC as the core regional format for integration, this does not preclude continued cooperation with other formats such as APEC and certainly does not raise barriers to deeper cooperation with the United States (Maehara 2005).

Second, the DPJ's concept of the EAC is founded upon a long tradition of functionalism in regional cooperation. Hatoyama in articulating the EAC concept after the November 2009 Singapore APEC Summit emphasized that further integration should spring from gradual "multilayered functional cooperation" in the areas of economic development, the environment, and protecting human life, including combating infectious diseases, responding to natural disasters, and enhancing maritime security (Hatoyama 2009a). In addition, Hatoyama's functionalist approach to EAC was underpinned by a set of common values that extend beyond just the heavily vilified *yūai*. The DPJ and Hatoyama have advocated the general values of openness, transparency, and inclusiveness, alongside functionality (MOFA 2009b, 5; Hatoyama 2010). These lack the specificity of earlier and more ideologically charged values for regional cooperation as proposed by LDP administrations, which included the so-called universally recognized values of democracy and human rights, the rule of law, and a market economy. However, the DPJ would argue that the types of values outlined by Hatoyama are attuned to the realities of East Asia's political economy and thus represent a more pragmatic way forward in regional cooperation but at the same time are open enough for the engagement in EAC of the United States and other regional frameworks. Indeed, the DPJ's less ideologically driven approach to East Asian regionalism and near total lack of interest in issues of revisiting the colonial past, demonstrated by the party hierarchy's discipline in refraining from visiting Yasukuni Shrine, contrast strongly with the LDP's fixation on issues of nationalism and historical revisionism and provide a much firmer basis for Japan to exercise leadership in regional cooperation.

If the DPJ's regionalist vision is correctly interpreted, it is not necessarily injurious to U.S. engagement and interests in East Asia. In fact, it might be supposed that an integrated and functioning region, more open and stable economically, and attempting to moderate Sino-Japanese rivalries over history and resources through effective multilateral cooperation, would be beneficial to U.S. interests. Moreover, even if the DPJ's regionalist vision is not inherently threatening to U.S. interests, it is apparent that, in similar fashion to other DPJ foreign-policy initiatives, its level of implementation has not matched its level of ambition. Hatoyama set the cat among the pigeons with his comment at the Trilateral Summit in early October 2009 that, while the U.S.-Japan alliance was important, Japan in the past had been "too dependent on the United States" (*Beikoku ni izon shisugi ita*) and needed to create a more Asia-focused policy (*Asahi Shimbun* 2009c). Nevertheless, out of consideration for U.S. concerns, Hatoyama at the Japan-ASEAN Summit later in the month took the unusual step in a bilateral context of commenting on third-country relations, stressing that the U.S.-Japan alliance remained the central axis of Japanese diplomacy and that U.S. engagement was crucial to the EAC (*Yomiuri Shimbun* 2009b).

Indeed, the DPJ government since Hatoyama's resignation, although continuing to promote the EAC vision, has increasingly slipped in its commitment for active realization. Kan's government became preoccupied with

Japan's hosting of APEC in 2010 and responding to renewed U.S. leadership initiatives in Asia-Pacific regionalism through the Trans-Pacific Partnership Agreement. At the same time, U.S. accession to the East Asian Summit in 2010, alongside the revitalization of the Trans-Pacific Partnership concept, raises the question of how far the EAC can progress as the core format for regional integration; and China's continuing preference for the ASEAN Plus Three framework over the EAC throws doubts upon whether it is possible for Japan to shift the region away from the previous pattern of proliferating and competing formats for cooperation. The DPJ's vision of the EAC—while potentially sound in conception as a means to enhance Japanese autonomy, manage the rise of China multilaterally, and maintain U.S. engagement—as yet looks difficult to implement.

Sino-Japanese Frustrations

Similarly, the DPJ's stewardship of key bilateral relationships in East Asia offers a story of opportunities to pursue new directions in foreign policy, but these have been frustrated in implementation by external pressures and lack of DPJ policy competence, with the result that Japan has shifted little from the inherently problematic positions of the LDP regime. The DPJ was regarded as particularly intent on shifting Sino-Japanese relations onto a more cooperative track. LDP leaders, following the debacles of the Koizumi era, had in fact moved to stabilize bilateral relations through creating a "mutually beneficial partnership based on common strategic interests" (*senryaku-teki gokei kankei*).[9] Nevertheless, the DPJ charged that the LDP had failed to tackle the underlying structural problems in the relationship, such as historical revisionism, resource competition, and Japan's ready dependence on the United States in managing security tensions, with resulting dilemmas of alliance entrapment and abandonment. The DPJ instead depicted itself as the true party of engagement with China and claimed that it would seek to manage ties through deepened bilateral cooperation, a more symmetric U.S.-Japan-China strategic triangle, and most especially the advancement of the EAC.

The DPJ's critics feared in the early stages of the administration that its enthusiasm for Sino-Japanese relations, combined with the desire to establish greater autonomy vis-à-vis the United States, would lead to Japanese bandwagoning with rising Chinese power. Then DPJ Secretary General Ozawa Ichirō's courting of and by China's top leadership was especially cited as evidence of this behavior. Ozawa led a delegation of 45 DPJ National Diet

---

9 For a fuller description of this concept, see MOFA (2008).

members and 390 other general participants to China in December 2007, and then led the largest delegation ever of 143 DPJ Diet members and 496 general participants to China in December 2009. Similarly, Hatoyama was identified by China as the leader of a potentially pro-China administration, and Hatoyama reciprocated with his determination to remove issues of history from the bilateral agenda and with statements in favor of placing China and East Asia more at the center of Japan's foreign policy.

The DPJ has undoubtedly sought to prioritize improved relations with China, but it has not sought to bandwagon with China, nor has it consequently adopted a soft line in defense of Japanese national interests. On the contrary, the DPJ for much of the first year of its administration adopted a highly pragmatic and hardheaded stance, far less influenced by ideology than certain previous LDP administrations, and at times as tough, if not tougher, than the LDP. The DPJ has continued to pressure China over transparency in its military expenditures and buildup. Ozawa, during his supposed bandwagoning visit to Beijing in December 2009, remarked to Minister of National Defense Liang Guanglie that China's military modernization generated a "China threat thesis in Japan, which deepens thinking about Japan's military strengthening," thereby offering an oblique caution for China to moderate its military behavior (*Asahi Shimbun* 2009a). In a similar fashion, Hatoyama at the opening session in February 2010 of the Prime Minister's Council on Security and Defense Capabilities in the New Era stated that it was necessary for the panel to consider, "without taboos," "views regarding Japan's response to military modernization by surrounding countries," again shooting an oblique reference to the potential threat from China (*Yomiuri Shimbun* 2010a).

The DPJ has demonstrated similar resolve toward China over territorial disputes and maritime security. Okada as foreign minister warned his counterpart in January 2010 that any Chinese violation of bilateral agreements over the joint development of gas fields in the East China Sea would oblige Japan to "take necessary action," implying Japanese exploration of its own part of the disputed area (*Asahi Shimbun* 2010b). Since February 2009 the DPJ has considered submitting National Diet legislation that would obligate the government to maintain the low-tide lines of the farthest-flung Japanese islands, directly in opposition to Chinese claims that atolls such as Okinotori-shima cannot be classified as islands and thereby acquire surrounding exclusive economic zones (*Japan Times Online* 2010d). Likewise, the revised 2010 National Defense Program Guidelines (NDPG) clearly identify the need to shift JSDF assets southward to garrison outlying islands in Okinawa Prefecture against Chinese incursions.

Despite the intent to improve relations through proactive but tough-minded engagement, the DPJ has found that its China policy risks replicating the record of failure of LDP administrations. The DPJ's failures can be ascribed to a lack of basic policy competence but also to the simple fact that China's rise is exerting near-relentless strategic pressures on Japan, with the result that the DPJ administration has slipped very much back into the default policy positions of the LDP. The vulnerability of the DPJ's policy in the face of Chinese pressure was graphically demonstrated with the bilateral dispute in late 2010 over the Japan Coast Guard's arrest of a Chinese trawler captain in the vicinity of the Senkaku Islands in September. Japan's subsequent release of the captain—most probably at the political behest of the DPJ's then–Chief Cabinet Secretary Sengoku Yoshito in response to Chinese "retaliatory measures," including intensification of an embargo on vital rare earth exports—generated an image of Japanese weakness. This impression of "weak-kneed" diplomacy was then reinforced by Japan's perceived scramble to restore dialogue with China, resulting only in Chinese cold-shouldering at the Asia-Europe Meeting (with an "accidental" meeting between Kan and Wen Jiabao having to be engineered as a "corridor summit" in a conference center in Brussels) and then at East Asian and APEC summits in October and November. The DPJ's mishandling of the arrest and then the leaking by the Coast Guard of a video of the trawler incident compounded the image of a lack of diplomatic competency and backbone in dealing with China, especially in the eyes of the Japanese public.

The critique of the DPJ's handling of the incident is probably overblown, given that China damaged its own diplomatic standing in the region through its assertiveness. Moreover, Japan was able to extract in September and again in October speedy and the highest-level-yet guarantees from Clinton and Gates that Article 5 of the bilateral security treaty did cover the Senkaku Islands. Nevertheless, the ready willingness of Kan and the DPJ administration to fall back on reliance upon the United States in dealing with China signifies a failure to carve out new strategic options and autonomy, and a concomitant falling back to LDP foreign-policy positions.

Multipolarity Opportunities Lost

Japanese policy toward North Korea under the DPJ reveals similar continuity with LDP administrations and thus a lack of ability to break out of past cycles of diplomacy, with resultant questions for pursuing autonomy and national interests. The DPJ's accession to power triggered apparent North Korean hopes for a softening in Japan's stance on the abductions and nuclear issues, given that previous LDP administrations (with the possible exception of Fukuda Yasuo) had been perceived as hard line and that the DPJ entered into coalition with the traditionally proengagement SDPJ. Hatoyama even spoke in December 2009 of his willingness to, in Koizumi fashion, visit North Korea if it might produce momentum on the abductions issue.

Nevertheless, despite the LDP's accusations during the September 2009 election that the DPJ would be soft on North Korea, the opposite has again proved to be the case. The DPJ government in October 2009 abolished the LDP's Abductions Task Force, establishing instead the Headquarters for the Abduction Issue, directed on a day-to-day basis by the minister of state for abductions with an increase of personnel from 30 to 40. The DPJ initiated the visit of the North Korean defector Hwang Jang Yop to Japan in April 2010 to discuss the abductions issue, and former North Korean agent Kim Hyon Hui paid a high-profile visit for the same reason in June. The DPJ as a party overall has shown a similar level of interest in pressuring North Korea on the abductions—most notably, the cross-party Diet Members' League on Abductions was reported to have increased its membership post–September 2009, indicating that declining LDP numbers were compensated for by increased DPJ participation (*Yomiuri Shimbun* 2009a). The DPJ has hotly debated whether to exert leverage on the North Korean community in Japan by excluding North Korean high schools in Japan from a national tuition waiver program because of the failure of their textbooks to acknowledge Japanese positions on the abductions issue.

The DPJ administration in respect of the nuclear and other North Korean–related security issues has maintained, in close coordination with the United States and South Korea, a similarly hard line to the LDP. The DPJ in May 2010, in the wake of North Korea's suspected sinking of the South Korean navy's corvette *Cheonan* the previous March, passed legislation to enable Japanese inspections of North Korean ships suspected of carrying weapons. This legislation was originally slated by the LDP in 2009, although the DPJ's bill devolved inspections to the Japan Coast Guard to the exclusion of the MSDF. The DPJ extended existing sanctions on banning the acceptance of North Korean exports and began to further tighten financial remittances from Japan to North Korea. Kan immediately pledged Japan's diplomatic support to South Korea and the United States following North Korea's bombardment of Yeonpyeong Island in November 2010. Kan in December 2010 even raised the extraordinary idea of investigating revisions of the JSDF Law in order to enable the JSDF to dispatch troops to North Korea to extract the abductees in the event of a Korean Peninsula emergency (*Asahi Shimbun* 2010i).

The efficacy of DPJ North Korea policy remains as equally open to question as the policy under the LDP. Even though Hatoyama and Kan after assuming office engaged in the immediate ritual of meeting Japanese abductee families, their true devotion to the cause compared to the zeal of their LDP predecessors has been doubted. This is not least because the new Headquarters for the Abduction Issue has been slow to devise fresh policies to pressure the North and has dropped the LDP's attempts since 2006 to oblige North Korea to hand over the persons responsible for carrying out the abductions.[10] In mishandling the abductions issue, though, the DPJ is not unique, given the LDP's previous catalog of failures and fitful attention. Moreover, the DPJ demonstrates continuity with the LDP not only in its hard-line position on the abductions but also in its failure to stake out a more autonomous position on Korean Peninsula diplomacy. The DPJ has defaulted, as did the LDP, to making the abductions issue a precondition for improving ties with the North and has found little diplomatic room, because of the ongoing nuclear issue and the *Cheonan* and Yeonpyeong incidents, to depart from the common front with the United States and South Korea on security issues. The DPJ's reliance on the LDP position puts Japan's immediate security and diplomatic interests in a situation of deadlock with North Korea. However, the DPJ is likely to find its diplomatic policy toward North Korea as hidebound as that of the LDP if Japan returns to negotiations with the North and its national policy autonomy remains constrained by the focus on the abductions issue and reliance on the United States for diplomatic leverage in these negotiations.

If China and North Korea policy under the DPJ looks similar to that of the LDP in execution, then this story carries over into other strategic relationships. Japanese policy toward Russia in the latter stages of the LDP had begun to show greater strategic responsiveness to the changing international structure. The Japan-Russia Action Plan of 2003 sought to reverse the previous pattern of predicating improved ties upon the reversion of the Northern Territories and was designed instead to deepen political, economic, and security ties that would later create the necessary bilateral consensus and conditions for a resolution of the territorial issue. Japanese policymakers focused on joint projects for energy development, the promotion of trade and investment, and defense exchanges, all with a look toward employing

10 For the change in Japan's position from 2006 to 2010, see Rachi Mondai Taisaku Honbu, "Rachi mondai ni okeru kongo no taio hōshin." October 16, 2006. http://www .rachi .go.jp/jp/shisei/old.housin.html, and Rachi Mondai Taisaku Honbu, "Rachi mondai no kaiketsu ni mukete." November 29, 2010. http://www.rachi.go.jp/jp/shisei/taisaku/ images/ dai4kai_shiji.pdf.

Russia as a strategic partner to counter China's rise and to influence events on the Korean Peninsula.

Nevertheless, despite steady progress in this long-term strategic agenda, LDP administrations found it increasingly hard to avoid the short-term distractions of the Northern Territories issue. Prime Minister Asō Tarō by the time of the May 2009 Japan-Russia summit was already stating that Russian movement on the Northern Territories was necessary before relations could be moved to a "higher level," thus hinting that a resolution to the territorial issue was once again becoming a precondition for improved ties and undercutting the strategic logic of the bilateral action plan (MOFA 2009a). The advent of the DPJ was thought to presage a possible breakthrough in Japan-Russia ties, given Prime Minister Hatoyama's close personal interest in Russia and the efforts of his grandfather, Hatoyama Ichirō, to normalize diplomatic relations in 1956. However, Hatoyama rapidly defaulted to a strategy similar to the LDP's—demanding the same formula that Russia should return all four islands and linking Japan's maintenance of economic cooperation with Russia to progress on the territorial issue. Japan-Russia relations then dipped dramatically with President Dmitry Medvedev's visit to Kunashiri in the Northern Territories in November 2010, with Kan adhering to a hard line by describing it as an "outrage difficult to forgive" (*yurushinikui bōkyo*) (Kan 2011b).

Japan's attempt to revitalize relations with Russia should have been part of a DPJ strategy to exploit the potentialities of a multipolar world and enhance strategic autonomy. The DPJ, however, has been unable to utilize these opportunities, and relations with other key partners exhibit a mixed record. The DPJ has been able to follow up on some of the successes of the LDP in improving strategic ties with a rising India, even though much of the initial impetus under the LDP was linked more to strengthening trilateral ties with the United States. During his visit to India in December 2009, Hatoyama affirmed the Japan-India Strategic and Global Partnership and concluded an action plan to advance the bilateral Joint Declaration on Security Cooperation. Japan subsequently concluded a comprehensive economic partnership agreement in October 2010.

However, the extent to which the DPJ can exploit Japan-India relations to pursue greater autonomy remains dubious due to India's notoriously autonomous tradition in foreign policy and to the unlikelihood that it would allow itself to be easily utilized for Japan's strategic ends, especially vis-à-vis China. Finally, Japan under the DPJ might have thought to energize relations with the EU as another potential extraregional pole, sharing a similar attachment to multilateralism, moderation in the use of military power, and the addressing of issues such as development and climate change. The DPJ government, though, has shown only limited interest in the EU, and the April 2010 Japan-EU summit designed to reinvigorate the bilateral action plan created only limited momentum for more substantial cooperation, with the slow initiation of negotiations for an economic partnership agreement and more binding agreements on political and security cooperation.

DPJ Defense Policy: Unchanged Trajectory

The LDP in the September 2009 election campaign and since then has attempted to make great play out of the accusation that the DPJ is essentially weak on defense policy, not least because of its past association with the SDPJ, and is thus unable to protect Japan from the provocations of North Korea and other neighbors. Nevertheless, the DPJ's track record demonstrates that, while it has intended to take a slightly different tack on how to channel Japan's military power, it is no less interested in defense matters and indeed, faced with the same structural pressures, has largely conformed to the trajectory of LDP defense policy.

The DPJ, in line with the more multilateralist vision of Hatoyama, Ozawa, and Okada, had pledged to enhance Japan's cooperation in security affairs with the UN, even including where necessary the use of military force to restore international peace and security under Article 42 of the UN Charter (*Minshutō* 2009). The DPJ administration has explored since October 2009 the possibility of revising the five principles for JSDF participation in UN peacekeeping operations (PKO) to enable dispatch of its forces in a wider range of scenarios. However, despite the recommendations of the Prime Minister's Council on Security and Defense Capabilities in the New Era Advisory in September 2010 and the revised NDPG of December 2010, the DPJ has yet to introduce revisions (Arata na Jidai no Anzen Hoshō to Bōeiryoku Mondankai 2010; Bōeishō 2010, 5). Instead, the DPJ administration has followed the LDP in shying away from JSDF participation in hazardous UN PKO and has opted for continued low-risk UN PKO and disaster relief in Haiti, Pakistan, East Timor, and South Sudan.

The DPJ has thus failed as yet to launch Japan on the more radical multilateral and collective security path of the type advocated by Ozawa. Instead, the DPJ has devoted most defense policymaking energy to pushing ahead with the strengthening of Japan's existing military capabilities and external military relationships. The DPJ's procurement plans in the defense budget of 2009 appeared largely indistinguishable from previous LDP administrations, with the same emphasis on qualitative upgrading and the potential for regional and global power projection.[11] The NDPG was, if anything, stronger than past LDP-guided versions, confirming that the JSDF would abandon the basic force defense concept of the 1970s and switch instead to a posture predicated on a "dynamic defense force" seeking to counterbalance specific threats and capabilities.

Similarly, the DPJ has forged ahead with the external military partnerships first developed by the LDP. The DPJ government, despite withdrawing the MSDF from the Indian Ocean, has maintained MSDF dispatch on antipiracy missions in the Gulf of Aden and has assented to the building of Japan's first overseas base in Djibouti. Japan signed an Acquisition and Cross-Servicing Agreement with Australia in 2010, its first such agreement to provide logistical support for noncombat missions to a partner other than the United States. The JSDF has continued also to explore links with South Korea, the other key U.S. military partner in the region, with its military personnel observing U.S.-Japan exercises in the Sea of Japan in July 2010 and MSDF personnel observing U.S.-South Korean exercises in December.

In addition, the DPJ, although not interested in the short term in challenging the antimilitaristic prohibitions of Article 9 or the ban on collective self-defense, has exhibited pragmatism in challenging other military taboos. The DPJ in 2010 went further than any previous LDP administration in seeking to officially overturn the arms export ban in favor of a system of licensed exports in order to preserve Japan's indigenous defense production base, although eventually it failed in this objective due to its need for SDPJ support in National Diet budget negotiations.

Conclusion: Toward "Resentful Realism"?

The DPJ's domestic difficulties in implementing its agenda are legion. The intent in this chapter has not been to provide a systematic catalog and analysis of those difficulties, but they have obviously included inter alia: coordination problems among top leadership on the instrumentalization of policies, seen most clearly in Hatoyama's inability to control Futenma relocation; the difficulties of agreeing on a common front on U.S. bases with the SDPJ and the People's New Party coalition partners; questions over the extent of Ozawa's influence on foreign policy and his involvement in policy energy–sapping domestic scandals; a possible DPJ focus on being seen to rectify the past misdemeanors of the policymaking process to the extent that

---

11   For instance, the MSDF is to procure a new DDH-22 helicopter carrier, which at 20,000 tons is one-third larger than the previous DDH Hyuga-class and the largest-ever MSDF vessel; and the MSDF's submarine fleet is to be increased by more than one-third, to its largest-ever number of 22 vessels.

it has led to posturing vis-à-vis key bureaucratic actors such as the MOFA and MOD and vis-à-vis the United States to the detriment of consistent and informed policy implementation; a simple lack of DPJ experience in how to govern and overall concentration on domestic policy priorities; and finally, a failure to communicate and expand on guiding concepts of foreign policy, such as Hatoyama's *yūai*, that are often seen to lack applicability.

Even more importantly, though, the DPJ in its attempts to implement a new grand strategy has found itself quickly constrained by, in ways not so different from the LDP, international structural pressures; and it is these pressures that are likely to prove the greatest obstacles to any new Japanese international orientation. The DPJ, most obviously, has already run into a near brick wall of U.S. resistance to certain aspects of its attempts to rearticulate the basis of the bilateral alliance. In a similar fashion, China, while indicating an early preference for cooperation with the DPJ over the increasingly testy past relations with the LDP, has already demonstrated its continuing ability to impede the new administration's longer-term plans for maintaining Japan's influence in East Asian regionalism projects and to encroach upon core national territorial interests. Likewise, North Korea, even if it cannot necessarily exert over the longer term the same degree of international structural pressures as China, has demonstrated its capacity to spook DPJ policymakers over security as it did their LDP predecessors and to consequently push Japan further into, even if uncomfortably, the arms of the U.S. security relationship.

Thus, the first overall conclusion of this chapter is that the DPJ, in encountering such early and stiff resistance, has shown and will increasingly show a propensity to edge away from attempts at implementing a more daring grand strategy. The DPJ leadership is already acquiescing in nondecisions and satisficing in regard to the toughest foreign and security-policy choices, and has curtailed many of its grander ambitions in order to avoid costly international and domestic controversies. Indeed, the DPJ, despite its instincts to the contrary, is already defaulting and is likely, in the medium term, to default to a grand strategy not that dissimilar in essence from that of the LDP, as any other options to diverge from this trajectory simply prove too difficult to implement. The result is that the DPJ is effecting for Japan an international profile just as dependent, or as overdependent, on the U.S.-Japan relationship as under the LDP. Conversely, Japan's options for a more balanced set of international relations through enhancing East Asian regionalism are likely to remain just as underdeveloped as during the LDP regime. In this sense, the DPJ, despite offering brief glimpses for Japan of enhancing its international stance, may simply oversee the final closing off of its grand strategy options and its final entrapment in the U.S.-dominated bilateral alliance.

Noda's accession to the premiership appears so far only to confirm this trend of reverting to LDP-type policies. As an attempt to restore party unity, his leadership lineup includes figures close to Ozawa and regarded as more pro-China, such as DPJ Secretary General Koshiishi Azuma, but it is clear that for now the party internal balance of power has shifted in favor of a more traditional pro-U.S. stance largely indistinguishable from that of the LDP. Although Noda's earlier pronouncements in August 2011 that Japanese Class A war criminals were not legally convicted by the Allies have undertones of LDP revisionism, his pragmatism is such that he is unlikely to antagonize Japan's neighbors on issues of history. Instead, Noda has indicated that he intends to focus energy on strengthening U.S.-Japan relations, including abiding by the existing Futenma agreements and advancing an Asia-Pacific vision of regionalism (Noda 2011). Noda's stance is likely to receive strong support from his fellow Matsushita Seikeijuku graduates, the new foreign minister, Genba Kōichirō, and the new chair of the Policy Research Committee, Maehara Seiji.

Nevertheless, there is still likely to be a sting in the tail in the story of the DPJ's grand strategy. The first conclusion should not be taken to argue that the DPJ's foreign policy will completely relapse into business as usual in foreign policy or into a mode of "reluctant realism" whereby Japan acquiesces in structural pressures, docilely accepts the ineluctability of reliance on the U.S.-Japan alliance, and pushes its international interests centered on the strategic logic of the past decade (Green 2001, 4–9). Instead, the DPJ, due to the fact that it can at the very minimum perceive perils and opportunities of multipolarity and strategic alternatives, is likely to be tempted in the medium to longer term back into revising ambitions and initiatives for increased autonomy. However, as noted earlier, even when it has learned from its miscalculations in policy implementation, the DPJ is unlikely to have the resourcefulness to be able to significantly depart from Japan's past and current trajectory due to the near crushing weight of international structural pressures and its own domestic policy shortcomings. This resultant tension between the DPJ's strategic ideals and the realistic limits of its capacity to implement them is likely to generate friction with the United States and other international partners over the longer term.

Hence, U.S.-Japan relations in early 2011, as a side-product of the "3/11" disasters and the joint JSDF and U.S. military Operation Tomodachi relief efforts, may have been strengthened in terms of military-to-military cooperation and Japanese perceptions of the importance of the U.S. military presence, and even in terms of the USMC bases in Okinawa. Nonetheless, there is a risk that this cooperation in the short term has done little more than paper over many of the major cracks in the bilateral relationship. Operation Tomodachi clearly will not create grounds for a resolution of the Futenma relocation issue where it most counts—on the ground in Okinawa itself. The U.S. and DPJ administrations remain seemingly blindly committed to the existing Henoko relocation plans in the face of likely intractable local political opposition and will continue to postpone a genuine resolution of the Futenma issue.

More importantly, even though the Futenma issue can probably be prevented from contaminating the overall relationship, it is emblematic of the need for Japan and the United States to confront larger strategic questions in their alliance. The DPJ's forced and uneasy acceptance of dependence on the United States as part of a trend of "reluctant realism" may only accentuate existing concerns over entrapment and abandonment, and may destabilize the alliance. The DPJ's current regression to a grand strategy nearly indistinguishable in execution from that of the flawed LDP policy and reliant on the United States has merely delayed addressing the long-term challenges of a rising China, Korean Peninsula instability, developments in East Asian regionalism, and a multipolarizing international system. Moreover, Japan's dependence on the United States is likely to be unsustainable in any case, as U.S. power progressively wanes in the Asia-Pacific region, thus only enhancing Japan's desperation that it has been constrained from fully articulating a complementary or alternative grand strategy. All of these factors may compound Japanese frustrations and feed more unpredictable strategic behavior—on a far larger scale than the final Futenma fiasco—as it rails against the perceived domination of the United States and being squeezed by a rising China.

The outcome, then, may not be a Japan that accepts the pathway of "reluctant realism" in train with the United States as under Koizumi, nor may it be a Japan that reverts to a path of either remodeled antimilitarism or internationalism in the form of "cautious liberalism" as under Koizumi's predecessors (Berger 2004, 137). Instead, the DPJ's failed grand strategy and subsequent steady erosion of its international standing may lead to a more assertive but also insecure, obdurate, and cantankerous Japan. In the medium term, therefore, the need may be to think of "resentful realism" as characterizing Japanese foreign-policy behavior, with a forcible outlook, borne of the insecurity of a trapped and declining power with few international options, and random frustrations expressed toward both Japan's ally and its regional neighbors. In this instance of Japan acting as a potential source of instability in the region, the United States may want to take a fresh look at the rationality of the DPJ's original vision of grand strategy and its applicability to resolving challenges for Japan's international situation. Rather than constraining Japanese autonomy, the United States may allow it to develop in service of the bilateral partnership and thus put the alliance and Japanese foreign policy on a truly and mutually sustainable track.

References

Arata na Jidai no Anzen Hoshō to Bōeiryoku Mondankai. 2010. *Arata na Jidai no Anzen Hoshō to Bōeiryoku Kondankai, Arata na jidai ni okeru Nihon no anzen hoshō to bōeiryoku shōrai kōsō heiwa sōzō kokka o mezashite.* August 13. http://www.kantei.go.jp/jp/singi/shin-ampobouei2010/houkokusyo.pdf.

Asahi Shimbun. 2009a. "'Chūgoku, zehi senshū bōei de' Ozawa kanjichō ga kokubō ni yōsei." December 11. http://www.asahi.com/politics/update/1211/TKY200912110439.html.

———. 2009b. "Jōji chūryū naki Anpo wa 'fūin' Hatoyama Shushō." December 16. http://www.asahi.com/politics/update/1216/TKY200912160427.html.

———. 2009c. "'Kitachōsen, tainichi kaizen nozomu' On shushō setsumei Nitchūkan shunō kaigi." October 14. http://www.asahi.com/politics/update/1010/TKY200910100165_01.html.

———. 2010a. "Exclusive Interview: Ozawa Declares 'War,' Calls Party Election His 'Final Battle.'" September 7. http://www.asahi.com/english/TKY201009060235.html.

———. 2010b. "Gasuden Kaihatsu 'shinten mirarenu' Okada-shi, gōi jisshi unagasu." January 17. http://asahi.com/politics/update/0117/TKY201001170172.html.

———. 2010c. "Hatoyama daihyō, hikaku sangensoku no minaoshi niten santen tōnai ni konwaku mo." August 11, 3.

———. 2010d. "Kansaiki iten 'Yotei-dōri' Bōeishō, Iwakuni shichō ni rikai motomeru." February 20. http://www.asahi.com/politics/update/0220/TKY201002200266.html.

———. 2010e. "Omiyari yosan 'Bei ni iwareru sujiai nai' Bōeishō hanpatsu." October 1. http://www.asahi.com/politics/update/1001/TKY201010010174.html.

———. 2010f. "Omoiyari yosan no taisakuhi, Bei ga gimuka yōkyū Nihon wa kyohi." October 22. http://www.asahi.com/politics/update/1022/TKY01010220198.html.

———. 2010g. "Omoiyari yosan, 5 nenkan wa genjō iji Nichibei ga gōi." December 14. http://www.asahi.com/politics/update/1213/TKY201012130410.html.

———. 2010h. "Shushō, hikaku sangensoku hōseika ni shinchō shisei 'keii fukume kentō.'" September 23. http://www.asahi.com/politics/update/0809/TKY 201008090 287.html.

———. 2010i. "Yūji nara Jieitai de rachi higaisha kyūshutsu? shushō hatsugen ni tōwaku no koe." December 10. http://www.asahi.com/politics/update/1211/TKY201012110206.html.

———. 2011. "Anpo kyōryoku kyōgi shinten de itchi Beikoku bōchōkan, Maehara gaishō to kaidan." January 13. http://www.asahi.com/politics/update/0113/TKY201101130238.html.

Berger, Thomas U. 2004. "Japan's International Relations: The Political and Security Dimensions." In *The International Relations of Northeast Asia*, edited by Samuel S. Kim. Lanham, MD: Rowman and Littlefield.

Bōei Nenkan Kankōkai, ed. 2004. *Bōei nenkan 2004*. Tokyo: Bōei Media Sentā.

———. 2010. *Bōei nenkan 2010*. Tokyo: Bōei Media Sentā.

Bōeishō. 2010. "Heisei 23 nendo ikō ni kakawaru bōei keikaku no taikō ni tsuite." December 17. http://www.kantei.go.jp/jp/kakugikettei/2010/1217bo ueitaikou.pdf.

Calder, Kent E. 2007. *Embattled Garrisons: Comparative Base Politics and American Globalism*. Princeton, NJ: Princeton University Press.

Congressional Commission on the Strategic Posture of the United States. 2009. *America's Strategic Posture: The Final Report of the Congressional Commission on the Strategic Posture of the United States*. Washington DC: United States Institute of Peace Press. http://www.usip.org/files/America's_Strategic_Posture_Auth_Ed.pdf.

Cossa, Ralph, and Brad Glosserman. 2009. "Question for Tokyo: Remember ANZUS?" *PacNet Newsletter* 71 (November 3). http://csis.org/publication/pacnet-71-remember-anzus.

Easley, Leif-Eric, Tetsuo Kotani, and Aki Mori. 2010. "Electing a New Japanese Security Policy? Examining Foreign Policy Visions within the Democratic Party of Japan." *Asia Policy* 9: 45–66.

Green, Michael J. 2001. *Japan's Reluctant Realism: Foreign Policy Challenges in an Era of Uncertain Power*. New York: Palgrave.

———. 2009a. "Tokyo Smackdown." *Foreign Policy*. October 23. http://shadow.foreignpolicy.com/posts/2009/10/23/tokyo_smackdown.

———. 2009b. "U.S.-Japan Ties under the DPJ: Reluctant Realism Redux." *CSIS Commentary*. August 7. http://csis.org/publication/reluctant-realism -redux-us-japan-ties-under-dpj.

———. 2011. "The Democratic Party of Japan and the Future of the U.S.-Japan Alliance." *Journal of Japanese Studies* 37 (1): 91–116.

Hashimoto, Gorō. 2005. "Okada Katsuya, Minshutō daihyō: gaikō bijon o kataru." *Chūō kōron* (July): 120.

Hatoyama, Yukio. 1998. "Dai 38 ki Hitotsubashi Fōramu 21: Nikkan kankei kako kara mirai." May 26. http://www.hatoyama.gr.jp/speech/0t01.html.

———. 2000. "Kongo ichinen 'tsuyoi Nihon keizai' e no taimu rimitto." *Voice,* January. http://www.hatoyama.gr.jp/masscomm/001226_05.html.

———. 2001. "Ushinawareta 20 nen o soshi seyo." *Nihon no ronten 2001.* http://www.hatoyama.gr.jp/masscomm/001226_04.html.

———. 2002. "Seijika ni okeru aikoku to wa." *Nihon no ronten.* http://www.hatoyama.gr.jp/masscomm/011109.html.

———. 2009a. "Japan's Commitment to Asia: Toward the Revitalization of the East Asian Community." Speech, November 15. http://www.kantei.go.jp/foreign/hatoyama/statement/200911/15singapore_e.html.

———. 2009b. "A New Path for Japan." *New York Times.* August 26. http://www.nytimes.com/2009/08/27/opinion/27iht-edhatoyama.html?page wanted=all.

———. 2009c. "Sofu Ichirō ni mananda 'yūai' to iu tatakai hatashirushi." August 30. http://www.hatoyama.gr.jp/profile/fraternity.html.

———. 2009d. "Speech at the Sixty-Fourth Session of the General Assembly of the United Nations." September 24. http://www.kantei.go.jp/foreign/hatoyama/statement/200909/ehat_0924c_e.html.

———. 2010. "Dai 16 kai Kokusai Kōryūkai Kaigi 'Ajia no mirai' Hatoyama naikaku sōri daijin supiichi." May 20. http://www.kantei.go.jp/jp/hatoyama/statement/201005/20speech.html.

Hoshi, Hiroshi. 2009. "Hatoyama, Okada gaikō okure-base 'datsu reisen' no muzukashisa." *Asahi Shimbun.* October 24, 15.

Hughes, Christopher W. 2009. "Japan's Response to China's Rise: Regional Engagement, Global Containment, Dangers of Collision." *International Affairs* 85 (4): 837–56.

Hughes, Christopher W., and Ellis S. Krauss. 2007. "Japan's New Security Agenda." *Survival* 49 (2): 157–76.

ICNND (International Commission on Nuclear Non-Proliferation and Disarmament). 2009. *Eliminating Nuclear Threats: A Practical Agenda for Global Policymakers,* 172–73. http://icnnd.org/Reference/reports/ent/pdf/ICNND_Report-EliminatingNuclearThreats.pdf.

Japan Times Online. 2009a. "DPJ Eyes SOFA Environment Tack." August 27. http://search.japantimes.co.jp/cgi-bin/nn20090827a2.html.

———. 2009b. "Gates Leery on Probe." October 22. http://www.japantimes.co.jp/news/2009/10/22/national/guam-move-depends-on-futenma-gates/.

———. 2010a. "Futenma Plan OK: Ozawa." September 3. http://search
.japantimes.co.jp/cgi-bin/nn20100903a1.html.

———. 2010b. "In-Country Nukes a Crisis Option: Okada." March 18. http://
search.japantimes.co.jp/cgi-bin/nn20100318a3.html.

———. 2010c. "Japan, U.S. to Launch Talks to Bolster Defense." November
18. http://search.japantimes.co.jp/cgi-bin/nn20101118a4.html.

———. 2010d. "Protection of Remote Islets Eyed." February 4. http:// search
.japantimes.co.jp/print/nn20100204a6.html.

Kamen, Al. 2010. "At the Summit, There Are Leaders and There Are Leaders."
Washington Post. April 14, 17.

Kan, Naoto. 2002. "Kyūkoku-teki jiritsu gaikō shian." *Gendai*, September,
234.

Kan, Naoto. 2011a. "Gaikō ni kansuru enzetsu: 'rekishi busuirei ni tatsu
Nihon gaikō.'" Speech in Tokyo, January 20. http://www.kantei.go.jp/jp/
kan/statement/201101/20speech.html.

Kan, Naoto. 2011b. "Heisei 23 nen hoppō ryōdo henkan yōkyū zenkoku taikai
naikaku sōri daijin aisatsu." February 7. http://www.kantei.go.jp/jp/kan/
statement/201102/07aisatu.html.

Koizumi, Junichiro. 2002. "Japan and ASEAN in East Asia: A Sincere and
Open Partnership." Speech delivered January 14. http://www.mofa.go.jp/
region/ asia-paci/pmv0201/speech.html.

Landler, Mark, and Martin Fackler. 2009. "With Shift in Japan, U.S. Sees a
Stranger as Partner." *New York Times*. September 2, 8.

Maehara, Seiji. 2005. "Agenda for Strengthening Japan-U.S. Alliance: Achieving World Peace and Happiness through Prosperity." Keynote speech at
American Enterprise Institute, October 25. http://www.dpj.or.jp/english/
news/051029/04.html.

———. 2011. "Opening a New Horizon in the Asia Pacific." Speech at the
Center for Strategic and International Studies, January 6. http://www
.mofa.go.jp/region/n-america/ us/juk_1101/speech1101.html.

McCormack, Gavan. 2009. "The Battle of Okinawa 2009: Obama vs.
Hatoyama." *Asia-Pacific Journal*, November 16. http://www.japanfocus.
org/-Gavan-McCormack/3250.

Minshutō. 2002. "Okinawa bijon." August 26. http://www.dpj.or.jp/news/
?num=10686.

———. 2005a. *Minshutō seisaku Index 2005*. http://archive.dpj.or.jp/policy/
manifesto/images/Manifesto_2005.pdf

———. 2005b. "Minshutō Okinawa bijon kaitei." August 3, 3–4. http://www
.dpj.or.jp/news/files/BOX_KOA0022.pdf.

———. 2008. "*Minshutō Okinawa bijon.*" July 8, 4–5. http://www.dpj.or.jp/
news/files/okinawa(2).pdf.

————. 2009. *Minshutō seisakushū Index 2009.* http://archive.dpj.or.jp/policy/manifesto/seisaku2009/img/INDEX2009.pdf

————. 2010. *Minshutō seiken seisaku 2010.* http://archive.dpj.or.jp/special/manifesto2010/data/manifesto2010.pdf

MOD (Ministry of Defense). 2010. *Waga kuni no bōei to yosan: Heisei 23 nendo gaisan yosan no gaiyō.* http://www.mod.go.jp/j/yosan/2011/yosan.pdf.

MOFA (Ministry of Foreign Affairs). 2008. "Joint Statement between the Government of Japan and the Government of the People's Republic of China on Comprehensive Promotion of a 'Mutually Beneficial Relationship Based on Common Strategic Interests.'" May 7. http://www.mofa.go.jp/region/asia-paci/china/joint0805.html.

————. 2009a. "Asō sōri to Pūchin Roshia shushō to no kaidan." May 12. http://www.mofa.go.jp/mofaj/area/russia/visit/0905_sk.html.

————.2009b. "Chairman's Statement of the Fourth East Asia Summit." Cha-am Hua Hin, Thailand, October 25. http://www.mofa.go.jp/region/asia-paci/eas/state0910.pdf.

————. 2009c. "Kurinton Beikokumuchōkan oyobi Geitsu Beikokubōchōkan ni taisuru rettā." December 24. http://www.mofa.go.jp/mofaj/press/kaiken/gaisho/g_1001.html#4-C.

————. 2009d. "Nakasone gaimu daijin danwa: zai-Okinawa kaiheitai no Guamu iten ni kakawaru no teiketsu no kokkai no shōnin ni tsuite." May 13. http://www.mofa.go.jp/mofaj/press/danwa/21/dnk_0513.html.

————. 2010. *New Package of Practical Nuclear Disarmament and Non-Proliferation Measures for the 2010 Review Conference of the Parties to the Treaty on the Non-Proliferation of Nuclear Weapons.* Working paper submitted by Australia and Japan. March 24. http://www.mofa.go.jp/policy/un/disarmament/npt/review2010-4/pdfs/workingpaper1005_01.pdf.

Nagashima, Akihisa. 2009. "Hatoyama seiken no gaikō anzen hoshō seisaku." In *Hyōryūsuru Nichibei dōmei: Minshutō seikenka ni okeru Nichibei kankei*, edited by Morimoto Satoshi, 23–24. Tokyo: Kairyūsha.

Naikaku Kanbō. 2010. "Jōhō to jōhō hozen." May. http://www.mod.go.jp/j/approach/agenda/meeting/seisakukaigi/pdf/14/3–2.pdf.

Nishihara, Masashi, and Jitsuo Tsuchiyama. 2010. *Nichibei dōmei saikō: shitte okitai 100 no ronten.* Tokyo: Aki Shobō.

Noda, Yoshihiko. 2011. "Waga seiken kōsō." *Bungei shunjū*, September, 94–103.

Okada, Katsuya. 2010. "Okada gaimu daijin no Nihon gaikoku tokuha'in kyōkai ni okeru kōen gaiyō." August 25. http://www.mofa.go.jp/mofaj/press/enzetsu/22/eokd_0825.html.

Ozawa, Ichirō. 2007. "Kōkai shokan, ima koso kokusai anzen hoshō no gensoku kakuritsu o: Kawabata Takiyotaka-shi e no tegami." *Sekai* 771 (November). http://www.ozawa-ichiro .jp/massmedia/contents/appear/2007/ar20071023094628.html.

Packard, George. 2010. "The United States–Japan Security Treaty at 50." *Foreign Affairs* 89 (2): 92–103.

Samuels, Richard J. 2007. *Securing Japan: Tokyo's Grand Strategy and the Future of East Asia*. Ithaca, NY: Cornell University Press.

Sotooka, Hidetoshi. 2010. "Kenshō Futenma isetsu o meguru 13 nenkan." *Sekai 801,* February, 177–94.

Sutō, Nobuhiko, Seiji Maehara, Yukio Ubukata, and Kazuya Shinba. 2002. "Gaikōnaki Nihon kara dakkyaku, senryaku, rinen no kōchiku o." *Minshu* 2.

Tokyo Shimbun. 2009. "Kyanpu Zama iten chūshi, daiichi gundan, Bei tsugō de 'saihen' henkō." December 9. http://www.tokyo-np.co.jp/article/politics/news/CK2009120902000101.html.

USDOD (U.S. Department of Defense). 2009. "Joint Press Conference with Japanese Defense Minister Toshimi Kitazawa and Secretary of Defense Robert Gates." USDOD, October 21. http://www.defense.gov/transcripts/transcript.aspx?transcriptid=4501.

Yomiuri Shimbun. 2009a. "Rachi giren renmei ga taikita kyokō shisei o kakunin, seiken kōtaigo no hatsukaigō." November 17. http://www.yomiuri.co.jp/politics/news/20091117-OYT1T00972.htm.

———. 2009b. "Shushō, Bei e no hairyō de 'Nichibei dōmei ga kijiku' to kyōchō." October 24. http://www.yomiuri.co.jp/politics/news/20091024-OYT1T01104.htm.

———. 2010a. "Chūgoku, Kita no kyōi taisho, shinbōei taikō e giron kaishi." February 20. http://www.yomiuri.co.jp/politics/news/20100218-OYT1T01247.htm.

———. 2010b. "Kiso kara wakaru Nichibei chii kyōtei." October 1, 11.

13 The New Asianism: Japanese Foreign Policy under the Democratic Party of Japan

Daniel Sneider

This article examines the foreign policy views of the Democratic Party of Japan (DPJ), from the party's founding through the end of its time in power. In 2009 the DPJ came to power in Japan, ending a half-century of conservative rule, with the hope of reshaping the post–Cold War order by rebalancing Japanese policy with a greater emphasis on Asia, inspired by a "new Asianism." Instead, the party's first year in office was marked by foreign-policy tensions—first with the United States over bases in Okinawa, followed by clashes with China in the Senkaku Islands. The DPJ moved painfully along the learning curve from opposition politics to the realities of governance. The DPJ foreign policy also evolved under the twin pressures of a more assertive China and American pressure, amplified by the Japanese bureaucracy, media, and opposition. On both sides of the Pacific, policymakers believe there was a return to the postwar consensus, particularly regarding the U.S.-Japan security relationship and particularly evident by the time of the third DPJ administration. But it would be wrong to conclude that DPJ policies, shaped during the party's formative years by key leaders who remain largely in place, were simply thrown aside. The new Asianism, which should not be understood as a "pro-China" shift but rather as an effort to manage the rise of China, remains a core identity of the DPJ.

The Democratic Party of Japan (DPJ) came to power in August 2009 with a dramatic mandate for domestic reform. Japanese voters embraced political change in the hope that a fresh force could restructure Japan's economy to face the dual challenges of an aging society and intensifying global competition.

Instead, the DPJ's first year in office was dominated by foreign and security-policy issues. Almost from its first days in office, in September 2009, the DPJ government became embroiled in an intractable dispute with the United States over American bases on Okinawa. Prime Minister Yukio Hatoyama's failure to manage that issue contributed significantly to his resignation in early June 2010. His successor, Naoto Kan, found himself under fire only a few months later for his handling of a clash with China following the arrest of a Chinese fishing-boat captain in September in the disputed territory of the Senkaku Islands in the East China Sea.

Over the course of the year, the DPJ swung from one foreign-policy message to another. In its early months in office, the Hatoyama cabinet raised doubts about the ongoing value and purpose of the U.S.-Japan security alliance, and expressed the desire to "rebalance" foreign policy with a greater emphasis on Asia. In the spring of 2010, faced with growing concerns about an increasingly assertive China, the government seemed to embrace the deterrent value of the security alliance. By the fall, stunned by the Senkaku clash and renewed tensions on the Korean peninsula, the Kan cabinet had almost entirely dropped talk of shifting Japan's foreign-policy focus to Asia.

The impact of China's more aggressive pursuit of its interests in the region became even more evident when Prime Minister Yoshihiko Noda formed the third DPJ administration in September 2011. Kan had been forced to step down as a result of the crisis following the March 11, 2011, massive earthquake and tsunami that struck northeastern Japan, and the resulting accident at the Fukushima nuclear power station. Prime Minister Noda took over with the express intention of restoring the centrality of the U.S.-Japan security alliance in Japanese foreign policy, without entirely abandoning the DPJ's broad desire to improve its relations with its Asian neighbors.

The turmoil surrounding foreign policy during the first year of DPJ rule was shaped in significant part by the combination of an uncertainty of purpose and the painful movement of the party along the learning curve from opposition politics to the realities of governance. Both Japanese and foreign observers have tended to emphasize these two factors in explaining the foreign-policy problems of the first year of DPJ rule. In that view, there was a movement to restore the postwar consensus on foreign policy, particularly regarding the U.S.-Japan security relationship (Green and Szechenyi 2010).

The restoration of harmony, if not civility, in the alliance after a year of turmoil was certainly palpable, particularly in the public statements of Japanese and American officials. Both desired to avoid open conflict, and to close ranks in response to ongoing security problems in the region. The Noda administration, in the view of critics within the DPJ itself, had in many respects brought Japanese foreign policy back to the positions of the conservative Liberal Democratic Party–led governments that preceded—and succeeded—its coming to power. But it would be wrong to conclude that DPJ policy views, shaped during its formative years by key leaders who remain largely in place, were simply replaced by a reversion to the stance of previous conservative governments in Japan.

Undoubtedly, driven in large part by the actions of the Chinese government and to some extent by events on the Korean peninsula and elsewhere in the region, the DPJ went through a return to greater realism, whether reluctantly, as some have suggested, or even resentfully. Still, the DPJ represented a significant development in the evolution of postwar Japanese foreign and security-policy thought—an attempt, however limited, to shift the paradigm away from the doctrine of total dependence and subordination to American strategic policy. That debate remains alive in Japan and therefore it is crucial to understand in more depth the foreign policy of the DPJ, from its early days through its governance, both at the level of its core leadership along with the party's parliamentary delegation, and among the expert and policy circles that advise the DPJ.[1]

We will begin with an examination of the origins and early days of the formation of the DPJ in 1995–96, and the views of the party's founders on key foreign and security-policy issues. We will explore the broad embrace of "New Asianism" by the DPJ, and its roots in and continuity with earlier debates on Japan's strategic orientation. We will then examine how the DPJ dealt with the two key issues in Japanese foreign policy—how to respond to the emergence of China as a great power and the conduct of U.S.-Japan relations, particularly since coming to power. We will conclude with some brief thoughts on what lies ahead.

Origins and Early Days of the DPJ

The DPJ emerged out of the political turmoil in the late 1980s and early 1990s that led to the formation of the short-lived coalition government led

---

1 The author conducted interviews with leading DPJ figures, including then–party president Ichiro Ozawa, in March 2009, on their foreign-policy views, finding a remarkable degree of cohesion and anticipating all the issues that subsequently emerged in the U.S.-Japan relationship. These findings were presented in a lecture at the Woodrow Wilson International Center on July 21, 2009, and in articles, including "A Japan That Can Say Maybe: The DPJ's Foreign Policy" and an accompanying interview with Ozawa (Sneider 2009b). The author conducted further interviews in September 2010 (as well as in 2011) with key figures in the DPJ, both inside and outside the Diet, including former Prime Minister Yukio Hatoyama.

by Morihiro Hosokawa in 1993. According to one of its founders, the process to form the DPJ began in February 1995, after the disappointing fall of the Hosokawa cabinet and the return of the Liberal Democratic Party (LDP) to power in a coalition with the Socialist Party.[2]

Discussions began between Hatoyama, who had broken away from the LDP to form the New Party Sakigake in 1993, and Takahiro Yokomichi, who was finishing his third term as the Socialist governor of Hokkaido. Hatoyama represented a strand of liberal conservatism, whereas Yokomichi was widely seen as the leader of a more moderate, pragmatic wing of the Socialists. The two men opposed the idea, circulating in the Japanese media, that a two-party system should be formed out of old and new conservatives. Instead, they favored a party structure that offered a clear choice between conservative and liberal views.

The two men formed a core group that also included Banri Kaieda, elected to the Diet as a member of Hosokawa's Japan New Party; Yoshito Sengoku, a Socialist Diet member; Hajime Takano, a progressive journalist and commentator; and Naoto Kan, who had been a member of Hatoyama's party. The group met regularly and secretly, late at night in a large suite at the Prince Hotel Akasaka, near the Diet building. Kan, who had joined the cabinet in a coalition with the LDP, did not participate at first but was kept informed. Others joined, including Hatoyama's brother, Kunio (who remains an LDP member even now).

Those deliberations took place within a specific strategic context. With the end of the Cold War, the Japanese left had come to accept the legitimacy and necessity of the U.S.-Japan security treaty. At the same time, some conservatives questioned the need to maintain Cold War levels of U.S. global force deployments, not only in Japan but also in Europe. In Japan, that discussion took on a sense of urgency after several American servicemen brutally raped a Japanese preteen in Okinawa in 1995.

"We were very shocked by that incident and we felt we had to begin to gradually reduce the presence of U.S. forces," Takano recounted. "The old Socialists were for 'No *Anpo*' (the U.S.-Japan security treaty), but the DPJ was for gradually reducing unnecessary U.S. bases, one by one."

Yokomichi, with the support of both Hatoyamas, went further. He set a goal of maintaining an alliance without permanent stationing of American forces in Japan, where Japanese forces would be responsible for self-defense

2 The account of the early period of the formation of the DPJ was provided to the author by Hajime Takano, one of the participants, in an extended interview conducted on September 2, 2010 and supplemented by email interviews.

and U.S. forces would use bases and storage facilities in emergencies such as a conflict on the Korean peninsula. Despite the Taiwan Straits crisis of 1995–96, the DPJ founders optimistically hoped that the region was headed toward resolving the legacy of the Cold War, both in Korea and with China.

The DPJ founders expressed unease with the dependence that has been at the core of the U.S.-Japan alliance since its inception. They sought to restore more autonomy in Japanese foreign policy.

"The notion that Japan's defense depends on the fact of other countries having bases here, the idea that as a nation we have to depend on some other nation in order for ourselves to survive, means that fundamentally we are not independent," Hatoyama said after leaving power in mid-2010.[3]

Those sentiments are hardly new to Japanese politics. Even in the early years of postwar Japan, the desire to reestablish Japanese independence was expressed on both the left and the conservative right. The doctrine forged by Shigeru Yoshida became the postwar consensus: Japan would rely on an American security guarantee, paid for with American access to strategic bases in Japan, in order to forge its own economic revival. As some scholars have pointed out, however, that consensus did not resolve the debate over how to construct a foreign policy beyond reflexive dependence on the United States.

"The alliance has made Japan a military satellite, some would even say a client state, of the United States and has been a main theme of public debate in Japan for more than 50 years," observed Professor Kenneth B. Pyle, a prominent American expert on Japanese security policy (Pyle 2010).

Viewed in that historical context, the DPJ represents a combination of both left and right advocates of greater self-reliance. While the role of the ex-Socialists has been recognized, the more significant drivers of this outlook in the party were those who came out of conservative politics. Hatoyama draws inspiration from his grandfather, Ichiro Hatoyama, a prewar and postwar conservative leader who served briefly as prime minister in the mid-1950s. The elder Hatoyama criticized Yoshida and during his premiership sought to break ranks with the United States by seeking normalization of relations with the People's Republic of China and by signing a peace treaty with the Soviet Union. The United States actively opposed those efforts, though Hatoyama did normalize relations with the Soviet Union in 1956.

This desire to restructure the security alliance was paired with the belief that Japan should focus its attention on Asia, broadly defined but

---

3 Interview with the author, September 12, 2010.

emphasizing China and Korea. In the summer of 1996, the group drafted a manifesto for the DPJ. Regarding foreign policy, the statement said:

> We must turn away from our excessive dependence on the United States, and while deepening Japan-U.S. relations and bringing them to a new dimension, we must give greater weight to our relationships with the countries of the Asia Pacific. Resting firmly on the foundation of our Constitution's peace principles, and a historical consciousness based on facts, we will take our place as a member of Northeast Asia and gain the trust of others. (DPJ 1996)

This broad statement of principle was articulated in more detail in an article in the influential monthly *Bungei Shunjū* in November of the same year. Titled "Minshuto: Watashi no Seiken Hasso" (The Democratic Party: My concept of government), it was attributed to Yukio Hatoyama, but it reflected the views of the core group (Takano drafted the section on foreign and security policy).

In the article, Hatoyama called for reaching the eventual goal of a "new *Anpo* without a permanent U.S. military presence" (Hatoyama 1996). Japan, the article argued, should take the lead in creating a post–Cold War environment in Northeast Asia that would allow the gradual shrinkage of American bases on Okinawa and the Japanese mainland. This would have to include a long-term solution to the divided Korean peninsula, it suggested, pointing optimistically to moves by the United States and South Korea to hold four-party talks with China and North Korea that could lead to replacing the 1953 armistice with a permanent peace treaty. Citing the example of the Association of Southeast Asian Nations (ASEAN) ministerial conference and the ASEAN Regional Forum on Security (ARF), the DPJ leaders called for creating a Northeast Asian regional security group along the lines of what later emerged as the Six-Party Talks on North Korea (Hatoyama 1996, 127).

In this environment, Japan could move to restructure the U.S.-Japan security alliance, including forming a free-trade agreement with the aim of "deepening it as a partnership of equals," Hatoyama wrote. At the same time, he was careful to add that if efforts to peacefully resolve problems on the Korean peninsula or elsewhere in the region were to fall short, Japan should be prepared to fulfill its obligations under the security treaty to provide bases and matériel support to U.S. forces.

Beyond the broad issue of the American forces, the DPJ strongly supported the need to reduce the concentration of U.S. bases on Okinawa, a preponderance largely intact since the Ryukyus reverted to Japanese administration in 1972. From its early days, the DPJ opposed the agreement reached by the LDP in 1996 to reduce the base presence in the more populated southern part of the island of Okinawa, while moving the Marine Air Station at Futenma to a new facility on Okinawa itself. Consistent with its later behavior in office, however, the DPJ offered no concrete solution to this thorny base relocation problem.

DJP and Japanese Security

The post–Cold War security environment encouraged many Japanese to envision an expanded global security role, largely in tandem with the United States. Beginning with the debate at the time of the first Gulf War over the dispatch of Japanese forces to support the United Nations coalition against Iraq, Japan moved incrementally to remove some of the longstanding post-war barriers to the use of Japanese armed forces beyond the constitution-ally circumscribed mission of self-defense. The LDP increasingly asserted the need to realize its longstanding of revising the American-authored con-stitution to allow Japanese armed forces to carry out missions beyond its borders.

The DPJ has not by any means been cohesive in its own views on these issues. Some in its leadership, including Hatoyama, supported constitutional revision in the past. But the DPJ clearly differed from the LDP on security policy in showing much less enthusiasm for globalizing Japan's security role in support of U.S. needs and allowing a more extended understanding of Japan's right to collective self-defense. In its early documents, and since, the party opposed broadening the interpretation of the Japanese Constitution to allow the Self-Defense Forces (SDF) to participate in multinational combat operations outside of Japanese territorial defense (Hatoyama 1996, 127).[4] The party did, however, support the use of the SDF as international peace-keepers, provided that it took place under United Nations authorization.

The DPJ's "Basic Policies on Security," published in June 1999, offered a detailed discussion of these policy areas, animated by the stated desire to establish "more autonomous security policies for Japan while fully recog-nizing the importance of Japan-U.S. relations in the area of security."[5] The document supported the role of the American military presence as "impor-tant to regional peace and security" while reiterating the aim to consolidate

4 Hatoyama wrote "We will of course hold fast to the current Japan-U.S. Mutual Security Treaty, but we cannot agree to the steady expansion of the interpretation of 'collective security authority' that is being discussed by some, and thereby to have the SDF engage in operations outside our territory, which would be to return to the Cold War era."

5 Available in translation at http://www.dpj.or.jp/english/policy/security.html.

and scale down the presence in Okinawa, "including the transfer of facilities within Japan and abroad" to ease the burden of concentration on the island. It also called for changes in the Japan-U.S. Status of Forces Agreement (SOFA) to allow for greater authority for Japanese law enforcement to investigate and prosecute crimes by American troops.

In certain respects, the DPJ's security policy endorsed the expansion of Japan's military capacities. It called for the urgent development of indigenous surveillance satellites and preparation for cyber-warfare. It cautiously supported moves to build up missile defense, in cooperation with the United States, and called for greater flexibility and preparation to respond to threats from terrorism. On the issue of Japan's inefficient system of arms procurement and development, the DPJ argued that budgets should take into account real threats rather than the traditional balance of allocation to each service. But the DPJ policy also stopped short of endorsing lifting the ban on arms exports, although some DPJ officials, including the defense minister, openly called for such change since taking power.

The security-policy outlook outlined at the founding of the party remained almost unchanged through the 2009 election that brought it to power, as expressed in party election manifestos and other documents.[6] On the specific question of the U.S. base presence, calls to reorganize and reduce the U.S. base burden on Okinawa can be found in all the election manifestos in 2003, 2007, and 2009, and in the platforms of the DPJ and allied candidates for the Diet who swept the Okinawa constituencies in 2007 and 2009 (Sneider 2009a).

The DPJ maintained these policies despite the broadening of its ranks from the late 1990s to include more conservative elements. In 1998 a group of younger and more conservative politicians joined the party, including defense specialist Seiji Maehara, later the foreign minister and considered the leading advocate of "realist" views in the party. Maehara briefly served as the party president in 2005–2006, during which time he articulated a more cautious version of the DPJ's foreign and security policy. In speeches during a visit to Washington, Maehara carefully expressed concerns about China's military buildup and sought to reassure American policymakers that the DPJ supported the security alliance and would not pursue a version of an East Asian community that excluded an American role. At the same time, he warned about a "gap in perceptions between our two nations," referring to American efforts to define a broader security role for its forces based in

6 The party documents dating back to 1999 are available in English translation on the DPJ's website at http://www.dpj.or.jp/english/policy/index.html.

Japan and for the Japanese military. Maehara pointed to the DPJ's opposition to the Iraq war, though not to a role in aiding Iraqi reconstruction, and warned that in the future, "it is quite conceivable that, despite our status as a close ally of the United States, Japan will refuse U.S. requests for cooperation if those involve international contributions that do not receive the understanding of the Japanese people" (Maehara 2005a, 2005b).

The merger of Ichiro Ozawa's small but influential Liberal Party with the DPJ in 2003 did not challenge the dominant viewpoint on foreign and security policy. Ozawa had a reputation as a conservative nationalist, even as an advocate of Japanese military buildup. While Ozawa has called for Japan to take greater responsibility for its own defense, he also has consistently opposed the expansion of Japan's global security role beyond UN-sanctioned peacekeeping and peace enforcement operations (Ozawa, Rubinfien, and Gower 1994). As an LDP leader, Ozawa had advocated support for the Gulf War in 1991 based on the formation of a UN-sanctioned international coalition. After failing in a earlier attempt, Ozawa was instrumental in pushing through the 1992 law authorizing Japanese forces to participate in peacekeeping operations (PKO) and advocated a law that would permit Japanese peacekeepers to use force under less restrictive rules of engagement.

This stance was visible when the DPJ—albeit with some dissenters from among the ex-Socialists—backed the post-9/11 decision to dispatch Japanese naval forces in a noncombat, logistical role in support of Afghanistan operations in 2002. But the DPJ broke ranks with the LDP and the Koizumi administration over their decision to support the invasion of Iraq and to lend symbolic support for that war by dispatching a small unit of SDF peacekeepers in a noncombat role in southern Iraq. For that reason, the DPJ opposed the extension of the Indian Ocean mission, arguing that Japan was now actually operating in support of the Iraq war.

At the point that Ozawa joined the DPJ, he had intimate conversations on such security issues with the leadership, particularly with Yokomichi, who became his close ally in inner party struggles.[7] They were in agreement on the need to respect the existing constitutional limits on deployment of Japanese forces overseas, though Ozawa interpreted more broadly what could be sanctioned by the UN, including the dispatch of Japanese peacekeepers to Afghanistan.

Ozawa took over the party leadership from Maehara in 2006. Under his leadership, the party won a significant electoral victory in the upper-house elections in 2007, setting the stage for the 2009 victory in the lower house of

7 Takano, interview with the author, September 2, 2010.

the Diet. The manifesto issued for the 2007 election summarized the goals of building "proactive foreign relations" as follows:

- A strong and equal U.S.-Japan relationship based on mutual trust will be built as the foundation of Japan's foreign relations.
- Japan will immediately end the dispatch of Self-Defense Forces to Iraq.
- To build world peace initiated by the United Nations, Japan will actively participate in UN peacekeeping operations and play a leading role in the reform of the UN.
- Japan will make the utmost effort to develop relations of mutual trust with China, South Korea, and other Asian nations.

On the issue of American bases in Japan, the Ozawa-sponsored manifesto called for a reexamination of the "role of the U.S. military in the security of the Asia-Pacific region and the significance of U.S. military bases in Japan," with the aim of reducing the burden of American bases in Okinawa.

Ozawa stirred controversy in February 2009 when he told reporters that Japan could manage its defense with the support of the U.S. 7th Fleet, implying that all other American forces in Japan were not necessary. In an interview with the author on March 3, when he was still serving as party president, Ozawa clarified his belief that Japanese ground forces should be able to take on responsibility for self-defense but that American naval and air forces in Japan that had a regional security role as well should remain. Ozawa clearly embraced the broad vision laid out by the DPJ founders in 1996, including the eventual reduction, if not elimination, of the U.S. Marine bases on Okinawa (Sneider 2009b).

The possible reduction of the U.S. military presence in Japan, and specifically the relocation of the Marines, is hardly unique to the DPJ or to Japanese themselves. Many American security specialists have raised this idea, particularly after the end of the Cold War.

But the DPJ never fully elaborated a vision of Japan's security, particularly how continued reliance on the United States and its nuclear umbrella would continue to fit into its desire for greater independence. The DPJ talk of taking on a greater responsibility for self-defense did not extend to a serious discussion of the need to expand defense spending beyond the de facto barrier of roughly 1 percent of GNP. More significantly, the DPJ did not address the trade-off that is at the core of the security treaty: the American obligation to come to the defense of Japan if it is attacked (Article 5) and Japan's provision of bases for U.S. forces (Article 6) "for the purpose of contributing to the security of Japan and the maintenance of international peace and security in the Far East." That failure, as we discuss below, emerged into full view after the DPJ took power and tried to implement its electoral pledge to revise the base relocation agreement in Okinawa.

The New Asianism

Along with its security views, the DPJ distinguished itself in consistently asserting the need for Japan to focus on Asia. While that view was not unique to the DPJ—as we discuss later—the prominence of this idea set the DPJ apart from its conservative LDP predecessors. In that sense, the DPJ represented a "New Asianism" in Japanese foreign policy, new in the sense that while it draws on a past intellectual debate about Japan's position between East and West, it takes place in a different global and security environment, one built on the rubble of Japan's wartime disaster and postwar dependency on the United States (Sneider and Katz 2009).

The DPJ's outlook has its roots in a Japanese debate about identity, one camp of which can be broadly labeled as Asianism, a belief that Japan's identity and strategic interests are rooted in Asia. Similar to the debate among Russian intellectuals between Slavophiles and Westernizers, other Japanese have argued that Japan, as an offshore maritime nation ready to adapt Western technology and ideas, should ally with the Western powers. Faced with the threat of Western imperialism, and noting disdainfully the failure of China and Korea to reform themselves to meet that threat, Meiji intellectual leader Yukichi Fukuzawa famously argued in his 1885 essay "Good-bye Asia" that "we do not have time to wait for the enlightenment of our neighbors so that we can work together toward the development of Asia. It is better for us to leave the ranks of Asian nations and cast our lot with civilized nations of the West" (Fukuzawa 1885).

The Asianists in Japan were themselves divided. The "Greater Asianism" camp advocated imperial advance on to the Asian mainland, clothed in the rhetoric of Japan as a "liberator" and protector of Asia from Western colonialism. Their victory over pro-Western liberals led to the tragedy of war in Asia. But there was also a small camp of anti-imperial Asianists in Japan, led by the prewar journalist Tanzan Ishibashi, an advocate of "small Nipponism," who opposed territorial expansion into Asia while expressing sympathy for the Asian nationalism of Sun Yat-sen and others. Those debates continued among conservatives in the postwar period. The anti-imperial Asianist school was represented in the 1950s by Ishibashi, who briefly served as prime minister in the late 1950s, and to a lesser extent by Ichiro

Hatoyama (grandfather of the DPJ leader), who as prime minister normalized relations with the Soviet Union and sought to establish diplomatic relations with the People's Republic of China, against the wishes of the United States (Wakamiya 1999).[8]

The DPJ founders' core combines the descendants of that conservative tradition with pragmatic elements of the Japanese left, united in renouncing Japan's colonial and imperial past in Asia and in believing that Japan is best served by taking on a leadership role in Asia. In practical terms, that has meant a focus on China and Korea in Northeast Asia, where the legacy of Japan's wartime past has been a principal obstacle to improved relations.

The DPJ's readiness to address Japan's history in Asia marks the most profound line of difference from the LDP, whose ranks include many outright defenders of Japan's wartime expansion into Asia, among them former Prime Minister Shinzo Abe. The DPJ harbors none of that wartime revisionism. On specific issues, the DPJ led the rebuke of former Air Force Chief of Staff Toshio Tamogami for publishing an essay defending Japan's wartime aggression, including the attack on the United States. After former Prime Minister Junichiro Koizumi's controversial visits to the Shinto Yasukuni shrine to Japan's war dead, the DPJ called for easing tensions with China and Korea by creating a secular national cemetery and removing the names of Japanese war criminals from the list of enshrined souls at Yasukuni.

"Within the LDP, especially Abe, there is a strong anticommunist ideology that leads to an anti-China position," DPJ leader Sengoku explained in an interview with me conducted in the spring of 2009 before the party took power. "Especially, they didn't really consider what happened in the Sino-Japanese war and the occupation of Korea. Abe didn't want to apologize to those countries. This is why relations with China, North Korea, and South Korea haven't improved. The DPJ members have a totally different perception of history. We look at the future, learning from past experience. That is why the DPJ is different from the LDP."[9]

Prime Minister Noda was a notable individual exception to that DPJ stance on wartime history issues. The son of a former Japanese officer in the Ground Self-Defense Forces, Noda held personal views on issues of wartime history that were much closer to those of the conservative nationalists of the LDP. Earlier in his career, Noda had expressed the view that the

---

8 Yoshibumi Wakamiya (1999) is by far the most comprehensive and insightful account of Japanese conservative thinking on Asia, written by the respected editor of *Asahi Shimbun*.

9 Yoshito Sengoku, interview with the author, March 5, 2009.

Class A Japanese war criminals convicted by the Allies in the Tokyo War Crimes Tribunal should not be considered criminals under Japanese law, and hence their enshrinement in Yasukuni was acceptable. He repeated this in the month before he took office. He also echoed Japanese conservatives in arguing that there was no clear proof that Korean women were coerced by the Imperial Army into performing sexual services for Japanese troops during the war.

The most controversial manifestation of the New Asianism is the DPJ's advocacy of East Asian regional integration, including the creation of an East Asian Community (EAC) that would emulate Europe. Hatoyama has been the DPJ leader most strongly associated with this idea, though his own thinking on this issue has been far from clear. In his writings and speeches, including after becoming the prime minister, he embraced a long-term vision to emulate the role of the EU in bringing peace and stability to East Asia, and he admired a philosophy of *yūai* (fraternity) that is attributed to an Austrian-Japanese writer admired by his grandfather. As discussed later in this chapter, Hatoyama's discussion of this idea after coming to power sparked significant alarm in American circles, which saw it as an attempt to steer Japan toward a China-centric regional system, excluding the United States.

Hatoyama's waffling and sometimes contradictory statements about whether the EAC would include the United States only fed that perception. He continues to deny that intent, portraying the EAC as an attempt to reproduce the European experience in Asia, over the long term.

> When you look at the countries of the East, of course the countries have a very different political structure, the economic level is quite different, the history is quite different, so it is difficult to build this kind of community. In the future, we will have to be working not only to build economic prosperity but also to create conditions in which we do not, and cannot, and must not go to war with each other. That's the idea toward which we are working. Given that ideal, we have to think as broadly as possible, to include America, and even Russia. . . . We have to proceed step by step. And while we are doing so, we don't need to talk in exclusive terms about who is a member [of the EAC].[10]

More practically, Hatoyama and other DPJ policymakers see the need to utilize multiple structures to promote regional integration, including the pan-Pacific Asia-Pacific Economic Cooperation (APEC) conference and the East Asia Summit, which the United States and Russia have recently joined. Rather than any single structure, DPJ policymakers call for creating

---

10 Yukio Hatoyama, interview with the author, September 16, 2010.

multiple regional organizations and coordination mechanisms, depending on the issue at hand.[11] Some see the China–Japan–South Korea triangular dialogue—the so-called *Nichukan* dialogue—as a potential core of a new regional community, as opposed to placing ASEAN at the center.

Maehara, who is the most alliance-centric among the DPJ leadership, differs and argues that regional integration should continue to be focused on economic policy through the ASEAN Plus 3 mechanism for at least the immediate period ahead. That should not be a "closed circle of coordination" but should be open to the United States, India, and other countries, he said.[12] While the United States is the most important partner for Japan, Maehara also supported the emergence of multiple structures for coordination, including a U.S.-China-Japan triangle, the Japan–U.S.–South Korea coordination, particularly in security, and the emergent Japan-China-Korea dialogue mechanism. Efforts to build all three triangular cooperation mechanisms were stepped up during the DPJ's rule.

Former Chief Cabinet Secretary Sengoku, in an interview conducted shortly before the party came to power, discussed the need for new multilateral structures to begin to supplant reliance on the bilateral security relationship:

> My personal, and the DPJ's, perception of Japan-U.S. policy is that the U.S. presence is through the hub and spoke [system]. Always the United States is at the center—the United States and China, the United States and Japan, the United States and Korea, the United States and Singapore. Always the United States is at the center. That is the approach the United States has taken to Asian nations.
>
> Post-Iraq, post–financial crisis, post–Cold War, and post–Bretton Woods, the biggest Japanese interest is how to survive; how to keep good relations with the United States and Europe, and keep our presence in Asia. What we want for the United States is to get together—the United States, China, Japan and Korea—to build a system of cogovernance, *"Ni-chu-bei-kan."* For example, in the field of energy, the environment and natural resources, Japan, China, United States and Korea could set up joint business schemes. How about Russia? Russia can join this.[13]

This vision reflects the reality of growing economic interdependence among the economies of Northeast Asia, including a dramatic increase in

---

11 See, for example, the writings of former senior Foreign Ministry official Hitoshi Tanaka in a series of policy briefs, "East Asia Insights," available at http://www.jcie.or.jp/insights/. Tanaka served as an adviser to Hatoyama and is considered among the DPJ's policy advisers.

12 Seiji Maehara, interview with the author, March 3, 2009.

13 Sengoku, interview with the author, 2009.

intraregional trade since the mid-1980s. On a corporate level, the economies of Northeast Asia increasingly operate as a single production chain, as Ren Ho, a prominent DPJ member of the upper house, a member of the Kan cabinet, and one of Japan's most popular politicians, points out:

> What Taiwan, mainland China, Korea, and Japan share is the strength of their technology, the strength in making things. That is a different model from the service industry priority of the United States. The basis of national policy on economic growth is different. It is something we share among these countries . . . Each of us have our own strengths in technology and we can each take our place in that regard. We need economic and trade cooperation—that is fundamental to the EAC.[14]

It would be simplistic to characterize the DPJ's focus on improving relations with Asia as an issue that sharply divides it from the LDP. The big-business community in Japan, which has traditionally backed the LDP, is a major force for easing tensions in the region and maintaining good relations with China, Korea, and others in Asia. Indeed, the parties overlap significantly on this issue.

Japan has a longstanding interest in East Asian regional integration, going back at least to the late 1970s, when Japanese and Australian academics first promoted this concept. During the boom days of Japan's economy, Japanese talked confidently about the formation of a "yen zone" in Asia, a Japanese-led economic area modeled on the European Community. While Japanese confidence has dimmed amid its own economic stagnation and China's rise, these ideas remain deeply entrenched.

In the last decade, LDP leaders from Prime Minister Junichiro Koizumi to Taro Aso have promoted this goal. Koizumi, for example, in a 2002 address in Singapore, envisioned a community formed by the 10 ASEAN members, together with Japan, China, South Korea, Australia, and New Zealand—what later became the East Asia Summit (EAS) with the addition of India (Koizumi 2002). Former Prime Minister Yasuo Fukuda inaugurated the triangular summit with China and South Korea in 2008, an outgrowth of the Plus Three meetings that took place on the sidelines of the ASEAN summit meetings.

The DPJ advocacy of East Asian regionalism thus does not sharply depart from previous Japanese policy. American concerns about forms of regionalism that might exclude the United States are also not new. The American decision to back the APEC conference in the late 1980s was prompted in part by the fear that Japan and others were moving to create a regional structure

14 Ren Ho, interview with the author, September 16, 2010.

that did not include the United States. Those concerns resurfaced with proposals by former Malaysian Prime Minister Mahathir to form an EAC that excluded the United States. In a 2005 speech in Washington, then–DPJ president Maehara felt compelled to reassure Americans that while the party supported creating an EAC, "the United States should be a significant player in this framework" (Maehara 2005b).

American policy toward the Japanese initiatives has been, and remains, reactive. The United States has opposed efforts toward regional integration that appear to exclude it, but has been relatively passive about regional integration. Ironically, Hatoyama's advocacy may have encouraged the Obama administration to decide to join the EAS, which at first had not included the United States. The move to join the EAS was accompanied, however, by the elevation of a somewhat minor trade grouping, the Trans-Pacific Partnership (TPP), into a U.S.-led vehicle for regional integration and for setting more rigorous standards than those agreed to by China, ASEAN, and others in the free-trade agreements reached within the region.

The post-Hatoyama DPJ administrations embraced the TPP both as a means of assuaging American concerns about the EAC and as a response to Chinese assertiveness. Prime Minister Kan announced the Japanese intention to join the TPP in the fall of 2010, a position also supported by his successor, Prime Minister Noda. But the DPJ was unable to fully join the ongoing multilateral negotiations on the pact, in part due to opposition from within its own ranks as well as from powerful interests such as agriculture and the insurance industry.

The China Question

Behind the discussion of improving relations with Asia and promoting East Asian regional integration lies a more complex debate in Japan, and within the DPJ, about how to respond to China's rise. The DPJ's policies have been frequently characterized by American observers and by conservative Japanese critics as an effort to align Japan with a powerful China, at the expense of the alliance with a fading American superpower. In conversations with DPJ leaders, Diet members, and others, however, there is no visible enthusiasm for trading American dominance for Chinese hegemony.

Rather, the DPJ seeks to manage China's rise through a combination of engagement and assertion of Japan's own leadership role in Asia. During the Bush years, Japanese policymakers increasingly feared that they would cede Asian leadership to the Chinese by overemphasizing the bilateral security relationship with the United States. While the United States was focused on the Middle East and Southwest Asia after 9/11, China moved with diplomatic skill to assert itself in the region, improving ties with South Korea and Southeast Asia, forming free-trade agreements, and reaping the benefits of its own emergent role as the driver of economic growth in East Asia.

Sino-Japanese relations had sharply deteriorated since 2002, triggered in part by Koizumi's visits to Yasukuni and by Japan's growing global security role and push to join the UN Security Council as a permanent member. This culminated in anti-Japanese riots in 2005, apparently sanctioned, at least initially, by the Chinese government. Japanese leaders worried that Sino-Japanese rivalry could lead to serious conflict, including clashes over oil and gas rights in the East China Sea. Those prospects alarmed the business community, with its deep investments in China. American officials also worried that these tensions might threaten regional stability.[15]

Japanese policymakers debated these issues, increasingly criticizing the LDP policy of coping with China and North Korea by drawing even closer to the United States, symbolized by the dispatch of troops to Iraq and the Indian Ocean. Given economic interdependence and overlapping strategic interests, neither Japan nor the United States could realistically manage China through some Cold War–style containment strategy.

If anything, Japanese policymakers increasingly worried that the United States would abandon them in favor of China, a fear that grew in the last two years of the Bush administration. Japan did not want to be consigned to a role of an anchor in an American hedging strategy toward China only to be left in the lurch. Japanese policymakers and politicians darkly predict a reprise of the "Nixon shock," when Kissinger made a surprise visit to Beijing, just as the United States was warning Tokyo against normalizing its relations with China.

"You may be shifting also toward China," DPJ parliament upper-house leader Hajime Ishii, a former senior LDP politician, said in an interview in September 2010. "That is natural. China is getting bigger and strong. Considering its future prospects and potential power, China may definitely be a more important country than Japan."[16]

Strategic unease about the changing balance of power is shared by policymakers in both the LDP and the DPJ. Given that long-term trend, Japanese policymakers increasingly see the need to hedge themselves, both against

15 Deputy Secretary of State Robert Zoellick, for example, endorsed efforts by American scholars to help mediate the disputes over wartime history issues.

16 Hajime Ishii, interview with the author, September 15, 2010.

American abandonment and the rise of China. The Japanese "hedge" is to maintain the security alliance with the United States while seeking to draw China into a regional and global economic and security structure.

That strategic outlook was manifested in the decision to repair relations with China after the anti-Japan demonstrations of 2005. It resulted in the surprising decision by conservative stalwart Shinzo Abe to travel to South Korea and China on the first overseas trip of his administration in 2006. Further steps followed. This action was combined with efforts to build closer ties, including security ties, with nations around China's periphery, from India and Vietnam to Australia, Russia, and most of all, South Korea.

The DPJ policy has followed on those LDP efforts. During the first year, the Hatoyama and Kan administrations actively courted India, Vietnam, and others in East Asia. This included both military and security ties such as military-to-military contacts, joint exercises, and policy coordination—not least with South Korea. In fact, the clearest implementation of the DPJ's efforts has been with Korea, including Kan's issuance of a new statement of apology at the time of the 100th anniversary of Japan's annexation of Korea, the return of seized Korean artifacts, and other gestures intended to cement closer cooperation.

In statement issued on August 10, 2010, Kan said:

> This year marks a significant juncture for the Japan–Republic of Korea relationship. In August precisely one hundred years ago, the Japan-Korea Annexation Treaty was concluded, making the beginning of the colonial rule of thirty six years. As demonstrated by strong resistance such as the *Samil* independence movement, the Korean people of that time was deprived of their country and culture, and their ethnic pride was deeply scarred by the colonial rule which was imposed against their will under the political and military circumstances.
>
> I would like to face history with sincerity. I would like to have courage to squarely confront the facts of history and humility to accept them, as well as to be honest to reflect upon the errors of our own. Those who render pain tend to forget it while those who suffered cannot forget it easily. To the tremendous damage and sufferings that this colonial rule caused, I express here once again my feelings of deep remorse and my heartfelt apology. (Kan 2010)

In public, Japanese officials avoid any hint of an effort to counter Chinese influence. But privately, some DPJ leaders speak frankly about their interest in strengthening ties with countries around China that share a fear of Chinese domination and aggressiveness. As Hatoyama put it in an interview with the author:

> From Vietnam's point of view, China is a real threat. Japan and Russia can cooperate to assist Vietnam's development, in order to constrain China or to reduce the sense of threat that Vietnam feels. Likewise, Japan and Korea can cooperate for the overall development of Siberia. Siberia is a place where China has been penetrating considerably and Russia has been alarmed and regards this as a threat. So Japan and Korea can cooperate economically to bring calm to that area.[17]

The fostering of relations with South Korea by the DPJ was in part a response to Chinese assertiveness in the aftermath of the sinking of the South Korean corvette by the North Koreans in March 2010, according to then–chief cabinet secretary Sengoku. The Chinese opposition to U.S. naval deployments in the Yellow Sea in the aftermath of that attack, and their de facto defense of their allies in the North, alarmed many in both Washington and Tokyo. In a talk delivered two years later, Sengoku described the decision of the newly formed Kan cabinet to respond to those events: "The cabinet's view was that it should promote a foreign and security-policy strategy based primarily on strengthening both the Japan-U.S. alliance and the cooperation between Japan and South Korea," he told a joint forum with Koreans (Sengoku 2012).

Contrary to some expectations, the DPJ has never shown a significant interest in pursuing engagement with North Korea, although it has favored a diplomatic approach to solving the nuclear issue. Though it has downplayed the issue of Japanese abductees promoted by the right wing of the LDP, the DPJ did not vigorously pursue a resumption of bilateral dialogue with Pyongyang. Ironically, perhaps the greatest interest in normalizing relations with North Korea comes from the LDP—not only Koizumi but from others in that party who had maintained a channel to Pyongyang. The DPJ ties are much closer to South Korea, and DPJ leaders see a closer relationship with Seoul as central to a new security structure in Northeast Asia.

The DPJ leadership also sees Russia as an important player in the region and as a balancing force to China. Key players in the DPJ advocate resolving Japan's territorial dispute with Russia in the Kurile Islands, paving the way to finally signing a peace treaty to formally conclude World War II and opening the door to much deeper economic ties. These leaders include

---

17 Hatoyama, interview with the author, September 16, 2010.

not only Hatoyama but also Muneo Suzuki, a controversial but influential former LDP leader who allied with the DPJ and chaired the foreign affairs committee of the lower house of the Diet until he was forced to resign late in 2010 due to his conviction on corruption charges. Both men, along with upper-house leader Yokomichi, not coincidentally, hail from Hokkaido, where relations with Russia are the primary foreign-policy issue. The Russian government, however, rebuffed serious discussion of a new deal on the islands, though there were some hints in that direction toward the end of the Noda administration.

In Suzuki's view, Japan must build good relations with China and Russia, along with its existing alliance with the United States, to create a basis for its long-term survival. "It is with the China-U.S.-Russia triangle that Japan can achieve its stability," Suzuki argues.[18]

Publicly, the DPJ holds a more benign view of China as a "threat" than is readily found in the Japanese right, particularly in the pages of conservative media in Japan. And before coming to power, DPJ leaders seemed to have an almost naïve belief that without the burden of defending Japan's wartime history, they would be better able to deal with bilateral problems. "There are issues between Japan and China that need to be resolved through frank discussion: the historical issue and the territorial issue," Ozawa told me in 2009. "Until we sit down and honestly discuss these issues, we can't resolve them."

Those hopes were dashed in September 2010 by the Chinese response to the fishing boat incident in the Senkakus. Early in the crisis, in conversations with a number of DPJ Diet members and others close to the party leadership, there was an expectation that the matter would be settled quickly and without further deterioration in relations. DPJ leaders and foreign-policy advisers were frankly stunned by Chinese escalatory behavior, and then further by the criticism within Japan, poured on by the media, that the leadership had capitulated to Chinese pressure, particularly the threat of economic retaliation, in releasing the boat captain. For many of them, it reinforced the ongoing value of the alliance with the United States.

"Problems that arise between Japan and the United States can, in the end, be resolved within the framework of the alliance," wrote *Asahi* editor Yoichi Funabashi (2010), considered an important voice in DPJ foreign-policy circles. "The alliance is the ballast. However, that cannot be said of the Japan-China relationship.... I feel the hubris of an emerging superpower out of China now."

---

18 Muneo Suzuki, personal interview with the author, 2009.

The perception of China as a potential threat to Japan has, of course, grown over the past decade. The 2004 National Defense Program Guideline (NDPG) was the first to identify China as a security issue for Japan:

> China, which has a major impact on regional security, continues to modernize its nuclear forces and missile capabilities as well as its naval and air forces. China is also expanding its area of operation at sea. We will have to remain attentive to its future actions. (Cabinet Office of Japan 2004)

The 2010 NDPG, prepared under the DPJ, slightly heightens that language and refers to China's military buildup as a "matter of concern for the regional and global community." It proposes a further shift of Japan's defense efforts away from the Cold War structure of repelling a potential Soviet invasion and toward a more flexible defense capability, including devoting more resources toward the defense of southwestern Japan, the area of territorial tensions with China (Cabinet Office of Japan 2010).

Despite these growing apprehensions and disappointment with China, the Kan administration carefully tried to dampen talk of an escalating clash with its powerful neighbor, and made strenuous efforts to restore official dialogue. As Kan laid out in his Diet policy speech in October 2010, Japan remained committed to the goal of deepening "our mutually beneficial relationship based on common strategic interests, from a broad perspective, including peace and prosperity in the Asia-Pacific region and increasing cooperation in the economic field."

At the same time, some observers have pointed to Foreign Minister Maehara, who oversaw the Coast Guard before moving to the Foreign Ministry, as forwarding a new anti-China policy. His hand was seen behind the decision to arrest the boat captain, a move that asserted the application of Japanese domestic law to the territory, triggering the harsh Chinese response. Some point to Maehara's expressed views of China as a "threat" during his brief presidency of the DPJ in 2005. But even at that point, when Sino-Japanese tensions were at a previous high, he rejected a hard containment approach to China.

> In some quarters, there is a tendency to view China as a potential enemy, as people see her strengthening her military power. However, I do not regard China as a potential enemy. In fact, I believe that we must not turn China into an enemy. Of course, we must not leave ourselves unprotected in the face of China's increasing military power, and to this end we need to firmly maintain the Japan-U.S. alliance. However, regarding China as an enemy and creating an environment that instigates a military buildup would not be to the advantage of anyone in this region. (Maehara 2005a)

The key role in shaping Japanese policy during the confrontation with Beijing was not played by Maehara, but by then Chief Cabinet Secretary Sengoku, who emerged as the most powerful figure in the Kan administration. Sengoku dispatched DPJ politicians, such as former deputy party head Goshi Hosono, to Beijing in the midst of the crisis, reportedly without the involvement of the Foreign Ministry, to find a way to ease tensions. In the midst of the crisis, Sengoku pointedly warned against rising Chinese nationalism and the echoing voices in Japan.

"What is more important than anything is that government officials in charge should be careful not to arouse narrow-minded, extreme nationalism in Japan, China, and other countries," Sengoku told reporters (*Kyodo News* September 21, 2010). Striking a conciliatory tone, he stressed the importance of good ties between Asia's two biggest economies for regional growth. "We want to use all possible channels not to escalate the issue and to solve it for the sake of development in East Asia and the Asia-Pacific region."

Speaking later, Sengoku defended the government's handling of the conflict against Japanese critics who sought a sterner response:

> The largest lesson is that each country or each tribe is becoming introverted, and tends to rush to protectionism in the economic domain, and in the political realm, or society, nationalism tends to flare up easily, even with a small spark. Under such circumstances, I think what our government did in handling troubles related to the Senkaku incident is not wrong at all in the medium to long term. (Sengoku 2010)

Despite this admonition, attitudes toward China within the DPJ hardened, mirroring the society as a whole.[19] Noda expressed this far more skeptical attitude toward China even before he took office. In a lengthy exposition of his "vision for government" written in the summer of 2011, while serving as finance minister, Noda acknowledged the role of China as Japan's largest trading partner, a massive market for Japanese goods, and a catalyst for the Asian economies. However, he wrote, China's military buildup and lack of transparency are a source of concern. "China's high-handed foreign posture backed by its military capabilities and recently put on display in the South China Sea and elsewhere is stoking fears that China will disrupt the order within the region" (Noda 2011a).

19 A Foreign Ministry–sponsored annual survey of feelings toward China (and South Korea) conducted in late September and early October 2012 showed that those with "friendly feelings" accounted for only 18 percent, the lowest since the survey began asking that question in 1978.

In his opening policy speech to the Diet, Noda notably dropped the goal of forming a new East Asian regional structure. In an article published in September, Noda made this clear and linked it to a tougher security stance toward China, though he was careful not to specifically mention the country: "I think there is no need to advocate a grand vision like the East Asian Community at this time. The priority now is to undertake another simulation of the posture Japan will adopt if there occurs another major incident relating to national territory or territorial seas. Unfortunately, the DPJ administration has not made sufficient efforts in this respect. While we definitely have no intention to create trouble, we need to be assertive when warranted and take action when required" (Noda 2011b).

During his premiership, Japanese relations with China and with South Korea notably deteriorated. In the case of China, tensions over the territorial dispute in the Senkakus flared up again following Noda's decision to nationalize several of the privately owned islets. Noda's government portrayed this as a step to ease conflict by preempting a bid from the nationalist governor of Tokyo to buy the islands and put facilities on them. The Chinese government clearly objected to the move before it took place in late summer of 2012, but Noda went ahead as planned, triggering an orchestrated wave of anti-Japanese demonstrations in China and terse diplomatic exchanges. With South Korea, an effort to deal anew with the comfort women issue between South Korean President Lee and Noda fell apart at a summit meeting in December 2011, leading Lee to make a provocative visit to Korean-held islands that are claimed by Japan and postpone the signing of a bilateral agreement to share security intelligence.

Despite these problems, Noda and the DPJ remained broadly committed to the goal of closer ties in the region, including in South and Southeast Asia. Even while tensions were rising with China and South Korea, negotiations moved ahead on the formation of a trilateral Free Trade Area and other Asian-centered regional trade structures parallel to the U.S.-led TPP. As a broad policy framework, the New Asianism remained an animating idea for the DPJ. But Chinese actions have clearly dampened Japanese expectations about the prospects of China joining in creating a more benign regional security system.

U.S.-Japan Relations under the DPJ

The core issue for the DPJ, as for previous Japanese governments, remains how to manage the alliance with the United States. The DPJ's inability to successfully do this has been, as discussed earlier, a major factor in the party's political decline during its first year in office (though not by any means the *only* source of its political woes).

In significant part, the tensions that arose in U.S.-Japan relations grew out of an unprecedented political transition in Japan and the unprepared-ness of both governments for the difficulties associated with that transition.

American policymakers, including those in government, initially tended to view this shift in power within the framework of more familiar transitions in the United States or other Western democracies. They sought early assurances of continuity of policy and dismissed signals of policy differences as the normal products of discontinuities that would soon be smoothed over.

Few understood the emergence of competitive politics as a newly significant factor in forming policy. As party loyalty weakens among Japanese voters, incumbency no longer guarantees reelection. Political leaders must respond to the shifting winds of public opinion. Even regarding U.S.-Japan relations, the DPJ was focused more on consolidating its electoral victory, driven by memories of the early 1990s, when an anti-LDP coalition government failed to consolidate its hold on power and opened the door to a resurgence of the LDP.

American policymakers only slowly recognized the more profound nature of the change in Japan and its implications, including the loss of traditional channels of communication based in Japan's bureaucracy. For more than a half-century of conservative LDP rule, Japanese foreign policy was effectively managed by a small coterie of professional bureaucrats working closely with the ruling party, big business, and a mass media elite. Public opinion, even protest, could impact decision-making, but problems, particularly in alliance management, were resolved behind closed doors by small numbers of consistent key players.

The August 2009 parliamentary election brought that era to an end. The LDP's grasp on power had begun to slip in the early 1990s, but it managed to retain control. This election dealt a heavy blow to the LDP's electoral machine and brought to power an opposition party largely peopled by politicians with little or no previous experience of governance.

The DPJ came to power determined to change not only the policies of the LDP but also the manner in which Japan had been governed. The party's central goal was to dismantle the collusive relationship between politicians and the government bureaucracy in all realms of public policy. Very quickly the management of foreign policy was taken out of the hands of the mandarins of the foreign and defense ministries.

As has become evident, the management of foreign and security policy in Japan is now highly subject to the needs of domestic politics and sensitive to the pressures of public opinion—ironically making Japan more like the United States. The bungled management of the Okinawa bases by the Hatoyama cabinet, particularly as portrayed in a hostile Japanese mass media, turned the issue into a domestic political disaster, driving opinion ratings of the government sharply downward.

American policymakers seemed largely unprepared for the tensions that quickly dominated the relationship. Prior to its taking power, few American experts and policymakers paid attention to the DPJ. They relied on the stability of LDP rule and on long-established relationships with Japanese policymakers committed to the postwar alliance consensus. Following the DPJ victory in the 2007 upper-house elections, some American officials woke up to the need to open lines of communication, in part sparked by the party's decision to vigorously oppose the extension of the Japanese naval deployment in the Indian Ocean. As it became more possible that the DPJ could gain power in 2009, a sense of alarm began to grow in Washington, perhaps prompting Secretary of State Hillary Clinton's February 2009 visit to Japan to more formally lock in Japanese agreement on the plan to relocate the Marine Air Station at Futenma to a new base on Okinawa, along with Japanese financial support for the transfer of some of the Marines to Guam.

The origins and thinking of the core DPJ founders had not been a subject of significant study, with a few exceptions.[20] Most American officials and experts tended to argue that the party was so divided internally between its left and right wings that it was incapable of a coherent outlook. Those experts confidently predicted that when faced with the realities of governance, the party would cast off its more radical views, including its views on the Okinawa bases and security ties with the United States.

The party's manifestos and other declarations "reflected the politics of a badly divided party with poor prospects for winning power," wrote former Bush administration national security adviser and Japan expert Michael Green just weeks before the 2009 elections. He argued that the conservative forces in the party, those who came out of the ranks of the LDP, would eventually move the party back to the center/right consensus. "The longer term trend in Japanese foreign and security policy, 'reluctant realism,' will not alter much," Green predicted (Green 2009).

Immediately following the Japanese election, some Obama administration officials urged patience on base and other problems, stressing the difficulties of transitioning to governance. But more impatient and negative views,

20 One notable exception to this was Leif-Eric Easley, Tetsuo Kotani, and Aki Mori (2010).

fueled by irritation at the chaos of decision-making within the Hatoyama cabinet, came to dominate American thinking. These were amplified by both Japanese and American media. The alarmist view of Hatoyama and the DPJ gained credence from a somewhat selective reading of Hatoyama's 1996 *Bungei Shunjū* essay and the publication of an election campaign essay in *Voice,* "My Political Philosophy," that included not only a reiteration of his foreign-policy views but also a post–financial crisis critique of American "market fundamentalism."[21]

Those mixed signals may have contributed to Hatoyama's apparent misreading of the Obama administration's willingness to renegotiate base issues on Okinawa. In the DPJ's early days in power, key advisers to the prime minister believed that the DPJ and the Obama administration shared a common view on a larger global policy framework, including advocacy of nuclear disarmament, climate change and alternative energy development, and the importance of multilateral institutions. This broader agenda, they thought, would supersede relatively minor issues such as base relocation.

Hatoyama was also apparently oblivious to the unease festering among American policymakers over his vague but provocative vision of Japan's role in Asia. This became clear within days of the new government taking office. In a speech to the UN General Assembly in September, Hatoyama outlined a vague vision for the creation of an East Asian Community, modeled on the European Union. American officials, speaking anonymously, expressed concern that the EAC would exclude the United States from the region in a form of pan-Asianism.

Those concerns deepened when Hatoyama attended the second triangular summit of the leaders of China, Japan, and South Korea, held in Beijing in October 2009. "Until now, there has been a tendency for Japan to depend too much on the United States," the Prime Minister told reporters during that visit. "While we will still consider the alliance with the United States as being important, we also want to create policy that places more emphasis on Asia" (*Asahi Shimbun* 2009).

Those familiar with Hatoyama and the DPJ's outlook were not surprised by those remarks, but the setting, with Chinese leader Hu Jintao looking on, and the content of the remarks angered American policymakers. They continue to be cited as evidence of a "pro-Chinese" attitude on the

---

21 Those perceptions were influenced by the appearance in early September of an English-language excerpt of the *Voice* essay that tended to focus on the most sensational aspects of the article. See "A New Path for Japan." http://www.nytimes .com/2009/08/27/opinion/27ihtedhatoyama.html?_r=1&scp=1&sq=Hatoyama+Opinion&st=nyt. The full essay, available at www.hatoyama.gr.jp/masscomm/090810_e.doc, was unfortunately not as widely read.

part of Hatoyama and other key DPJ leaders, such as former party secretary general Ozawa. When Ozawa led a large DPJ party delegation to China in December 2009, American commentators and officials speaking on background to the media characterized the visit as further evidence of a "pro-China" swing.

Conservative Japanese media fed this perception, encouraged quietly by disgruntled Japanese bureaucrats, and it reflected back into the American media. "Key policy people in the Obama administration, no doubt encouraged by LDP politicians and their friends in Washington, assumed the worst about Hatoyama, seeing him as vaguely anti-American and too enamored with China and an ill-defined East Asian community," noted respected American political scientist Gerald Curtis (2011). When the Hatoyama cabinet refused to back off from electoral commitments to renegotiate the Futenma relocation agreement, driven mostly by domestic political considerations, American officials and policy experts put it together as composite proof of a desire to rebalance its relations and actively break away from the security alliance. Secretary of Defense Robert Gates visited Tokyo in October 2009 to deliver a somewhat blunt warning to Tokyo not to abandon the base deal, shocking DPJ leaders who had expected a softer approach from a sympathetic Democratic administration in Washington.

American officials were privately encouraged to take a tough stance toward the DPJ, including their early efforts to find an alternative solution to the Futenma issue, by Japanese foreign and defense bureaucrats, themselves closely allied to the LDP. In a meeting with visiting Assistant Secretary of State Kurt Campbell on September 18, 2009, only days after the DPJ had taken office, senior Foreign Ministry official Akitaka Saiki was openly dismissive of the DPJ and Hatoyama's desire to build a more "equal" bilateral relationship. Relations are fine, Saiki told his American counterpart, but the DPJ is "an inexperienced ruling party" that is eager to "show it had Japan's powerful bureaucrats under control and was in charge of a new and bold foreign policy that challenged the U.S.," according to a secret American cable report on the meeting published by Wikileaks. "Saiki called this way of thinking 'stupid' and said 'they will learn'" (Roos 2009a).

In mid-October, American officials met with senior DPJ politicians and others in the defense and foreign ministries in an attempt to discuss a solution to the Okinawa base problems. DPJ leaders engaged in this issue probed the Americans for room to search for a new solution that would meet both American and Okinawa needs. But according to one cable, defense bureaucrats met privately after such meetings with their American counterparts to reveal the inner discussions of their DPJ supervisors and to counsel the Americans not to demonstrate flexibility (Roos 2009b).

The DPJ indeed "learned" some powerful lessons about the obstacles to trying to shift Japanese foreign policy away, even slightly, from the well-established moorings of the established order. The course of events over the next year, the first of the DPJ's rule, seemed almost deliberately crafted to justify predictions that the new government would founder but eventually return to the safe harbors of postwar Japanese foreign policy. After months of trying to find a solution to the Futenma base relocation that would satisfy both Okinawa public opinion and the Obama administration, in late May 2010, Hatoyama capitulated largely to American demands to maintain the existing agreement to build a new base at Henoko. Particularly after the sinking of the South Korean navy corvette *Cheonan* in March, the Hatoyama cabinet embraced the notion that the presence of the U.S. Marines on Okinawa was essential to regional security. American officials told the Japanese in public and private that they had not sufficiently understood the deterrent role of American forces in Japan, and on Okinawa in particular, against the threat of a rising China, as well as potential crisis on the Korean peninsula.[22]

The notion that the DPJ returned to pragmatism gained credence when Kan replaced Hatoyama in June 2010, a change triggered by both the campaign fundraising scandals surrounding Ozawa and by Hatoyama's failure to effectively manage the base dispute with the United States (Sneider 2010). The new DPJ government took pains to quickly signal its desire to close the gap with the United States. Foreign Minister Okada pointedly supported Secretary of State Clinton when she clashed with Chinese officials over territorial claims in the South China Sea at the ASEAN regional security meeting in Hanoi in late July. Kan also embraced the goal of Japanese participation in the TPP, a multilateral trade group that is led by the United States and that is trans-Pacific rather than trans-Asian in nature.

The perception that the DPJ had ditched its focus on Asia was solidified by what some have labeled the "Senkaku Shock." The confrontation with an aggressive China shattered hopes of forging a new relationship with China and reimposed focus on the U.S.-Japan security alliance, some analysts argued (Green and Szechenyi 2010). The appointment of Maehara as foreign minister was interpreted as yet another sign of the triumph of realist voices within the DPJ (Klingner and Cheng 2010).

The Noda administration that came into office in September 2011 was hailed by American officials as a return to more "normal" management of

---

22 See, for example, the speech delivered by U.S. Ambassador to Japan John Roos at Waseda University on January 29, 2010. http://tokyo.usembassy.gov/e/p/tp-20100129-71 .html.

alliance relations. The display of cooperation in the aftermath of the March 11, 2011, earthquake—the Operation Tomodachi dispatch of American forces to provide crucial relief assistance—seemed to signal the end of the irritations of the earlier DPJ governance. Other steps in the realm of security cooperation, from missile defense cooperation to a more visible Japanese role in Southeast Asia to counter Chinese influence, added to that impression.

To some degree, this upbeat view of the state of the alliance relationship also reflected a growing realization among American policymakers that Japan still had considerable value to the United States in the face of a more assertive and less compliant Chinese challenger. That realization prompted a belated acknowledgment of the scale of the problems of transition in Japan and of the ongoing strategic value of the alliance, as expressed graciously by Assistant Secretary of State Kurt Campbell to reporters in Tokyo in early October 2010, just ahead of the President's visit:

> This is the first fundamental transition of political power that's taken place in Japan in generations, and we experience political transitions in the United States every four or eight years. They are very difficult in themselves, so one can only imagine what such a fundamental reorientation of political power in a country like Japan might mean....
>
> I think we fully recognize that there would be some inevitable challenges associated with the new government, and I believe that we have managed those as effectively as possible. I think there has been a clear desire on both sides in recent months to step up our diplomatic engagement. I think there probably also has been a learning process on both sides of the Pacific. That learning process is not confined just to Tokyo; it is also clearly involving the United States as well.
>
> I think when we have faced difficult challenges—which we have in the course of the last year—it is a reminder to the United States how badly we need a good relationship with Japan. It is very hard to operate effectively—diplomatically, politically or strategically—in Asia without a strong relationship with Japan, and it is critical for this generation of American policymakers to in no way take Japan for granted. (Campbell 2010)

The rise of tensions between Tokyo and Seoul during the Noda administration, however, reminded American officials of the downside of a shift toward more conservative views in Japan. The prospect of open conflict over territory and wartime history issues between the United States' two main Northeast Asian allies caused considerable consternation among American policymakers. Even the rise of tensions with China was not without its problems, as some in Washington worried about Japan triggering tensions that could lead to a wider and unwanted conflict. These concerns remain very much in play.

Certainly there has been a learning curve in Tokyo—and as Campbell suggests, in Washington as well. The lack of understanding of the DPJ in Washington, and the DPJ leadership's own naïve and incoherent policy process, fueled a sense of crisis in the alliance. But it would be mistaken to assume that the core beliefs of the DPJ and the profound shift in Japanese policy that they imply have simply faded from the scene.

Rather, the evidence suggests that the DPJ has learned a different lesson, one learned by previous Japanese administrations: Politicians pay a high political price for the *perception* of an open break with the United States. As Japanese governments learned during the years of trade disputes, it is often more effective to say "yes, but" than to say no when dealing with Washington. Unfortunately, as was the case in the management of trade issues, that approach only postpones resolution and has become increasingly threadbare from overuse. The base problems on Okinawa remain no closer to being implemented than at the start of DPJ rule. The DPJ leadership tried to at least *appear* to be attempting to implement the deal—as the LDP did for some 13 years. But as it regained office in December 2012, the LDP inherited a situation basically unchanged from when it left.

The DPJ administrations were careful not to elaborate their thinking on deeper issues of the alliance and the broad security situation; they were wary of being assailed by a largely hostile Japanese media eager to find lines of conflict between Tokyo and Washington. But amidst growing political turmoil, the DPJ leaders were far more preoccupied with political survival and economic recovery in the face of growing uncertainty about Japan's future. And whether it was Okinawa or participation in the TPP, there remained significant opposition from within the DPJ to the more pragmatic path favored by Washington.

In an interview with me after leaving office, Hatoyama, who remained a powerful if discredited figure in the party, offered his own reflections on the alliance difficulties that arose during his short time in office:

> I agree there probably are a variety of misunderstandings. When the DPJ was first being established, the Cold War East-West division had already ended. If you think of the division as between conservatives and progressives, the conservatives had won—that is to say, the West had won (the CW). We believed the LDP style of bureaucratic-led politics really could not give the people the kind of policies that they wanted. Although we come from this different beginning, it doesn't mean on every fundamental issue, our foreign policy is different from the LDP.
>
> My main point in international relations is that while we regard the Japan-U.S. alliance as the keystone and foundation of Japanese international relations, at the same time, we need to work on how we can have a cordial

interchange with Asia, particularly China, how we can be a member of Asia. Up until now, we have been stressing the West. Now the question is how can we become more respected in Asia. For that, we have to deal with issues of the past.

The Japan-U.S. alliance is very important. I absolutely recognize and acknowledge that today. But in terms of looking toward the future, for America to have its military based in Japan in this way, for the defense of Japan, if you look at the entire world, this is a very peculiar or particular kind of set of conditions. Even if we are looking ahead 50 or 100 years, the time has to come when, fundamentally, the defense of this country will be taken on by the Japanese ourselves. So the question is what do we need to do now in order to be looking toward that end.

We recognize the need today for Article 5 and Article 6 (of the U.S.-Japan Security Treaty). America defends us when we need it and therefore the American military can have the bases in Japan. When we think of, for example, today's situation [in] North Korea and the military situation in Asia in general, the U.S.-Japan alliance is absolutely necessary. So we are not like the Communists who say that it is not necessary. We don't think it should be discarded.

I think it is important that we recognize the value of the existence of Japan as a base for America in the wars in wages for peace, for example in Afghanistan and Iraq and likewise, that because there is that American presence here, it acts as a constraint on other Asian nations, that makes Asia more stable and constrains other nations from behaving aggressively towards us. We believe this. . . . We need, however, to speak on a *honne* (true feelings) basis with each other about the way in which American bases are used and how Japan can cooperate with the United States within the limits of our Constitution. We need to be furthering these discussions.

Taking Up the Challenge

Despite the failure of its first experience with power, the DPJ brought to the surface an underlying and ongoing debate within Japan, and between the United States and Japan, about the future of the alliance and the security system in Northeast Asia. Rather than seeing the DPJ's New Asianism only as a threat, it would be more fruitful for Washington to see the New Asianism as an opportunity to shape a new post–Cold War order in Northeast Asia, in concert with Japan and also with the other principal U.S. ally in the region, South Korea.

The foreign-policy views of the DPJ and those of the Obama administration share elements that remain to be explored. First, both capitals seek to promote trilateral cooperation—between Japan, China, and the United States, and between Japan, South Korea, and the United States. These forms of multilateralism build upon the bilateral security alliances and are compatible with exploring broader regional integration, including the EAS and APEC. The United States should welcome a Japan that is interested, even if the interest is somewhat ineffectual, in challenging China for leadership of future regional structures.

Moreover, as the United States moves to rebalance its global posture after a decade of emphasis on the Middle East and Southwest Asia and is under the pressure of long-term budget constraints, it must expand multilateral security arrangements that can fit into the American global architecture. The DPJ's approach to Asia, which clearly includes growing ties with countries such as India, Vietnam, and Australia, could contribute to creating a security structure in Asia that can cope with the rise of Chinese power.

Chinese assertiveness and apparent ambition for regional domination certainly reminded Japan, South Korea, and the United States that the Cold War alliance system retains a strategic value. But China cannot be neatly slotted, along with North Korea, into the role played by the Soviet Union in that Cold War system. Certainly most Japanese (and Korean) policymakers do not accept that equivalency—even more so within the DPJ. There may not be sufficient clarity about what may emerge to replace that system, but the need for this discussion is more urgent than ever.

Unfortunately, the mechanism and basis for dialogue is weaker than ever in the U.S.-Japan alliance relationship.[23] The relationships built up over decades of LDP rule need to be revitalized for a new era in Japanese political life—and that is true regardless of where political change leads in Japan or in the United States. Unless Japanese and American policymakers do a better job of understanding each other, the chances that the tensions of the DPJ era of rule will be repeated, and perhaps deepened, are greater than ever.

---

23 The need for this is discussed in an excellent report from the Japan Center for International Exchange, "Reinvigorating U.S.-Japan Policy Dialogue and Study," published in December 2010. http://www.jcie.or.jp/books/abstracts/R/reinvigorating-dialogue.html.

References

Asahi Shimbun. 2009. "Japan, China Agree on Food Safety Talks." October 12.

Cabinet Office of Japan. 2004. *National Defense Program Guideline, FY 2005.* December. http://www.kantei.go.jp/foreign/policy/2004/1210taikou_e.html.

————. 2010. *National Defense Program Guideline, FY 2011.* December. http://www.kantei.go.jp/foreign/kakugikettei/2010 /summary _ndpg_e.pdf.

Campbell, Kurt. 2010. "Media Roundtable at the U.S. Embassy in Tokyo." U.S. Department of State. http://www.state.gov/p/eap/rls/rm/2010/10/149051.htm.

Curtis, Gerald. 2011. "Future Directions in U.S.-Japan Relations." Background paper in *New Shimoda Conference—Revitalizing Japan-U.S. Strategic Partnership for a Changing World.* February.

DPJ (Democratic Party of Japan). 1996. *Statement of Principle.* September. http://www.smn.co.jp/takano/who.text5.html.

Easley, Leif-Eric, Tetsuo Kotani, and Aki Mori. 2010. "Electing a New Japanese Security Policy? Examining Foreign Policy Visions within the Democratic Party of Japan." *Asia Policy* 9 (1): 45–66.

Fukuzawa, Yukichi. 1885. "Good-bye Asia" ("Datsu-A Ron"). http://personal .ashland.edu/jmoser1/japan/fukuzawa2.htm.

Funabashi, Yoichi. 2010. "Japan-China Relations Stand at Ground Zero," *Asahi Shimbun,* October 9.

Green, Michael J. 2009. "U.S.-Japan Ties Under the DPJ: Reluctant Realism Redux." *Oriental Economist.* http://csis.org/publication/reluctant-realism -redux-us-japan-ties-under-dpj.

Green, Michael, and Nicholas Szechenyi. 2010. "Green Shoots in the U.S.-Japan Alliance." *Japan Chair Platform,* November 9. Center for Strategic and International Studies. http://csis.org/publication/japan-chair-platform -green-shoots-us-japan-alliance.

Hatoyama, Yukio. 1996. "Minshuto: Watashi no Seiken Hasso" [The Democratic Party: My concept of government]. *Bungei Shunjū.* (November): 125–27.

Kan, Naoto. 2010. "Statement by Prime Minister Naoto Kan." Tokyo, August 10. http://www.kantei.go.jp/foreign/kan/statement/201008/10danwa_e .html.

Klingner, Bruce, and Dean Cheng. 2010. "Do Not Expect Much from Japan During Obama Visit." Heritage Foundation Web Memo No. 3055, November 9.

Koizumi, Junichiro. 2002. "Japan and ASEAN in East Asia—A Sincere and Open Partnership." Speech in Singapore, January 14.

Maehara, Seiji. 2005a. "Agenda for Strengthening Japan-US Alliance: Achieving World Peace and Happiness through Prosperity." Speech at AEI Conference, Washington DC, October 25. http://www.dpj.or.jp/english/news/051029/04.html.

———. 2005b. "The National Image and Foreign Policy Vision Aimed For by the DPJ." Translation of speech at CSIS, Washington DC, December 8.

Noda, Yoshihiko. 2011a. "My Political Philosophy: Let Us Take Pride in Being Born Japanese." *Voice* (October): 44–53.

———. 2011b. "My Vision for Government—Toward 'Moderate' Politics; Rebuilding Japan by Eliminating Clever Schemes and Using the 'Power of the Sun.'" *Bungei Shunjū* (September).

Ozawa, Ichirō, Louisa Rubinfien, and Eric Gower. 1994. *Blueprint for a New Japan: The Rethinking of a Nation*. Tokyo: Kodansha International.

Pyle, Kenneth B. 2010. "Troubled Alliance." *Asia Policy* 10 (1): 3–9.

Roos, John. 2009a. "'Stupid' P.M., Dead Abductees." *New York Times*. September 21. http://www.nytimes.com/interactive/2010/11/28/world/20101128-cables-viewer.html#report/japan-09TOKYO2197.

———. 2009b. "Warnings of Chinese Power." *New York Times*. October 10. http://www.nytimes.com/interactive/2010/11/28/world/20101128-cables-viewer.html#report/japan-09TOKYO2378.

Sengoku, Yoshito. 2010. Interview. *Wall Street Journal*. December 14. http://blogs.wsj.com/japanrealtime/2010/12/15/video-interview-with-japans-chief-cabinet-secretary.

———. 2012. "Forward-Looking Strategic Cooperation between Japan and South Korea." *Asia-Pacific Review* 19 (2): 1–5.

Sneider, Daniel. 2009a. "Déjà Vu on Okinawa." *Oriental Economist* (November).

———. 2009b. "Ozawa in His Own Words," *Oriental Economist* (June).

———. 2010. "Did Washington Bring Down the Japanese Prime Minister?" *Slate*, June 3. http://www.slate.com/id/2255924/.

Sneider, Daniel, and Richard Katz. 2009. "The New Asianism." *Foreign Policy*. October 13.

Wakamiya, Yoshibumi. 1999. "The Postwar Conservative View of Asia." *Tokyo: LTCB International Library Foundation.*

Disaster Response

14 The DPJ's Political Response to the Fukushima Nuclear Disaster

Kenji E. Kushida

This chapter explores the DPJ's response to the Fukushima nuclear disaster, triggered by the March 11, 2011 earthquake and tsunami. The DPJ's responses, which can be divided into initial chaotic maneuvers during the crisis, and unexpected medium-term volatility in nuclear and energy policy, were both shocking and deeply disappointing to much of the general public. The DPJ's handling of the nuclear crisis and its aftermath, much criticized in the press, contributed to rapidly declining public opinion polls, a general sense of DPJ incompetence, and its ultimate ousting from power. This chapter closely examines the disaster as it unfolded and the medium-term political dynamics following the disaster. It contends that the DPJ's immediate chaotic response was largely due to organizational, structural, and emergency preparation failings that the DPJ inherited from the LDP, which had presided over the development of Japan's energy industry and governance structure. Prime Minister Kan's highly criticized interventions in the nuclear reactor rescue efforts were largely a function of his leadership style and background, but did not significantly hinder the initial nuclear plant recovery efforts. The DPJ's medium-term policy volatility was driven by severe internal political strife—a result of structural contradictions within the DPJ when it came to power. At the same time, the LDP was becoming an increasingly effective opposition party, leading to extensive politicization of Japan's energy policy and disaster recovery.

On March 11, 2011, Japan's Tohoku region was hit with the triple disaster of the magnitude 9.0 earthquake, the massive tsunami that it triggered, and the nuclear reactor meltdowns at the Fukushima Dai-Ichi nuclear power plant.

The DPJ's response to the Fukushima nuclear disaster in particular was both shocking and deeply disappointing to most observers. First, the initial response was chaotic. Information given to the public was fragmented, and coordination between the prime minister's cabinet, the relevant government organizations, and the Tokyo Electric Power Company (TEPCO) operating the Fukushima Dai-Ichi plant seemed highly problematic. Prime Minister Kan Naoto seemed to play an active role but was later intensely criticized by much of the media, leaving a large portion of the general public in confusion. Why was the government's and the DPJ's initial response so chaotic?

Then, after the immediate crisis at Fukushima was stabilized, the DPJ's stance toward existing nuclear reactors, longer-term energy policy, and Tohoku recovery was volatile, controversial, and alienating for a broad range of voters. Prime Minister Kan requested that all nuclear power plants stop operations, and vowed to put Japan on a course of no nuclear energy. Six months later, he was ousted from power, exchanging his resignation for passage of a Tohoku reconstruction budget. His successor, Noda Yoshihiko, presided over the restarting of a nuclear reactor. Also during his tenure, the reorganization of Japan's nuclear governance structure was delayed, and Japan's long-term energy policy became highly ambiguous. To the public, it seemed as though political infighting had trumped considerations for the nation's welfare. Less than two years after the disaster, the DPJ was voted out of office in a landslide. Why did the DPJ's medium-term response to the acute Fukushima nuclear disaster entail such policy volatility and ambiguity?

This chapter addresses these puzzles of the DPJ's immediate chaotic policy response and medium-term policy volatility and confusion. It does so by closely examining the Fukushima disaster as it developed, tracing the DPJ's subsequent policy maneuverings and considering the structural and organizational challenges facing the DPJ.

This chapter contends that the government's *chaotic initial response* to the Fukushima nuclear disaster stemmed from a combination of the government's inadequate contingency planning and problematic organizational structures inherited by the DPJ, and Kan's own leadership style and negative predisposition toward industry and government bureaucracies shaped by his previous experiences. Specifically, Japan's nuclear governance structure was disastrously inadequate for dealing with emergencies that entailed widespread earthquake and tsunami damage occurring simultaneously with nuclear emergencies. Kan, previously having achieved fame by uncovering a major scandal involving bureaucracy-industry collusion in covering up HIV-tainted blood used on patients, was not disposed to act sympathetically toward government officials or TEPCO. His abrasive and individualistic leadership style fueled dissent from various quarters, exacerbating the appearance of extreme coordination failures within the DPJ.

This chapter contends that the *medium-term* policy volatility and ambiguity in the year and a half following the Fukushima nuclear disaster stemmed from structural and organizational tensions within the DPJ itself, and opportunistic politicking by the opposition LDP in the context of a "twisted Diet." The DPJ's mantra of empowering political leadership opened the door to greater policy volatility when the success of the political leadership to set the agenda was combined with internal power struggles within the party that frequently replaced the political leadership. This dynamic was magnified when severe infighting within the DPJ began in the immediate aftermath of the disaster. The "twisted Diet," in which the DPJ controlled a majority in the lower house but not in the upper house, gave leverage to the opposition LDP when it decided to use the DPJ's March 11 disaster responses as ammunition to attack the DPJ.

The Fukushima Nuclear Accident: An Overview

The magnitude 9.0 earthquake that struck off the northeastern coast of Japan on March 11, 2011, was the fourth largest in modern recorded history. It was followed shortly thereafter by a massive tsunami, as high as 30 meters in some places, devastating 500 kilometers of Japan's northeastern coast. Damage from the earthquake and tsunami precipitated the world's second-worst nuclear accident, at the Fukushima Dai-Ichi nuclear power station, owned and operated by the Tokyo Electric Power Company.

The Fukushima Dai-Ichi plant included six nuclear reactors, three of which were in operation, with the rest undergoing routine maintenance on March 11. The active reactors shut down successfully as soon as the earthquake hit, but all external power lines were severed. The plant was not designed for a prolonged loss of power, but it had several backup power sources to operate cooling pumps. When the tsunami hit the plant, it reached a height of over 12 meters—well exceeding the maximum safety design of 5.7 meters, and obliterating the 10-meter-high seawall. The tsunami destroyed most of the cooling system, largely consisting of pumps responsible for pumping seawater into the reactor building to cool the fuel rods. Critically, it also irreparably damaged the diesel electricity generators for the emergency backup cooling pumps.

The need for massive quantities of water for nuclear reactors cannot be exaggerated. Although the emergency shutdowns of Fukushima Dai-Ichi reactors 1, 2, and 3 were successful, considerable amounts of water were necessary to diffuse the heat retained by the fuel rods. Combined, the three reactors required approximately 70 tons of water *per hour* for 10 days to avoid a catastrophe (Saito 2011). Restarting the pumps, or at a minimum, the emergency cooling systems as a short-term solution, was critical.

Without sufficient power or cooling capacity, the three reactors experienced fuel core meltdowns over the next three days. Hydrogen explosions blew off three of the reactor buildings' roofs and walls. While there were no deaths from direct radiation exposure, the accident emitted at least 168 times the amount of radioactive cesium 137 compared to the Hiroshima atomic bomb of 1945. Mandatory evacuation zones of a radius of 10 km were imposed on March 11 and were expanded to 20 km the following day, affecting over 80,000 residents. The disaster was eventually declared level 7 on the International Nuclear Event Score (INES)—the maximum. Chernobyl was the only other level 7 nuclear accident, although it released approximately six times the amount of radioactive material vis-à-vis Fukushima since it was an explosion of the core reactor during active operation. In Fukushima, seawater pumped into the reactors and used-fuel storage pools created more than 100,000 tons of contaminated water, about a tenth of which was released into the ocean by mid-2011 (IIC 2012).

The DPJ's Chaotic Response

As the Fukushima nuclear disaster unfolded rapidly, the government's immediate response was chaotic. Some specific elements included a delay in declaring a nuclear emergency and ordering evacuation; initial press conferences that conveyed a sense of chaos and lack of information; Kan's controversial role in personally intervening in nuclear disaster mitigation efforts, argued to have delayed responses to the hydrogen explosions; and a fiasco involving a lack of publicizing government-owned radiation diffusion prediction maps.

Delay in Declaring a Nuclear Emergency and Ordering Evacuation

First, Prime Minister Kan Naoto's administration was criticized for the delay in informing the nation that a nuclear emergency was developing and in ordering an evacuation. As it later became clear, Fukushima Dai-Ichi plant manager Yoshida sent a fax to TEPCO headquarters and to the Nuclear and Industrial Safety Agency (NISA, located within METI) at 3:00 P.M. officially declaring that a nuclear emergency was likely to occur. This was the first time ever that such a notice was sent.[1] At 4:30 P.M., he sent another message, upgrading it to "emergency in progress," a status that automatically triggers an evacuation order.[2] This was also unprecedented. Yoshida noted that they were unable to cool the reactors and could not monitor the water levels of

---

[1] This was in accordance with Article 10 of the Nuclear Emergency Preparedness Act (Act on Special Measures Concerning Nuclear Emergency Preparedness) passed in 1999 following a nuclear criticality accident at a nuclear fabrication plant in Tokaimura, operated by JCO Co., Ltd.

[2] This is known as an Article 15 event, as stipulated in the Nuclear Emergency Preparedness Act.

reactors 1 and 2. The implications were serious, since the reactor fuel cores needed to be immersed in water; if the hot cores evaporated all the water, the cores would be exposed, and the fuel core rods would overheat and be damaged—the phenomenon commonly known as a meltdown.

However, almost two hours after receiving these declarations, at 4:54 P.M. Prime Minister Kan issued a two-minute statement in the pressroom of the prime minister's residence. He did not acknowledge that an unprecedented report of "nuclear emergency in progress" had been issued by the Fukushima Dai-Ichi plant. Instead, he said that the nuclear reactors had successfully shut down and that no radiation leakage had been observed. He took no questions. The statement was not false but was widely criticized later as downplaying the severity of the developing accident.

It took until 7:03 P.M. for Kan to declare a nuclear emergency to the nation—the first time such a declaration had been made. Statutorily, this should have triggered an evacuation order. However, the prime minister's office did not issue an evacuation order at that time. At 7:45 p.m., Chief Cabinet Secretary Edano Yukio advised the public not to panic and flee, but to stay indoors and wait (Kurokawa 2012b).

At 8:50 P.M., about four and a half hours after the "nuclear emergency in progress" was declared, the Fukushima prefectural government took matters into its own hands. It announced a 2 km evacuation radius around the Fukushima Dai-Ichi plant.

Half an hour later, at 9:23 P.M., the Kan government finally announced a 3 km evacuation radius. For people between 3 and 10 km, he ordered them to stay indoors. This was three hours after Kan had declared an emergency (Oshika 2012).

It was later determined that by around 5:00 P.M., four hours earlier, reactor 1's core was already exposed, and by 5:50 P.M., the radiation monitor began showing increased radiation levels. (See figure 14.1 for a timeline.)

Government Officials Explaining the Situation

The government's early press conferences as the nuclear disaster unfolded did little to allay the fear felt by the public upon hearing that a nuclear emergency was underway. Although the entire government seemed to have immediately changed clothes into neat, matching work uniforms on top of their suits, many of the initial officials and government representatives issuing press conferences were clearly not specialists. One of the first representatives of NISA to appear in front of the cameras, for example, used the word "meltdown" and was immediately replaced. Many of the officials were unable to respond to journalists' questions, and the public was given

FIGURE 14.1

Simplified Timeline of Events in the Fukushima Nuclear Accident

March 11	
2:46 P.M.	Magnitude 9.0 earthquake occurs. All power lines are severed to Fukushima Dai-Ichi plant. Emergency shutdown of reactors occurs. Backup power starts.
3:00 P.M.	Plant manager Yoshida declares "nuclear emergency likely to occur."
3:37 P.M.	12 m tsunami strikes plants. All backup power is lost.
4:30 P.M.	Yoshida declares "nuclear emergency in progress."
4:54 P.M.	Kan's press statement: Reactors have shut down successfully.
5:00 P.M.	Reactor 1 core exposed (estimated). Meltdown begins (estimated).
5:50 P.M.	Increased radiation levels detected.
7:03 P.M.	Nuclear emergency declared by cabinet.
7:45 P.M.	Cabinet advises public in vicinity to stay indoors.
8:50 P.M.	Fukushima government announces 2 km evacuation radius.
9:23 P.M.	Cabinet announces 3 km evacuation radius.
March 12	
7:10 A.M.	Prime Minister Kan visits Fukushima Dai-Ichi plant.
3:36 P.M.	Hydrogen explosion occurs at reactor 1.
6:25 P.M.	Cabinet expands evacuation radius to 20 km.

Source: Author.

the strong impression that the government was in over its head with no one aware of exactly what was happening. And worse yet, some of the NISA officials were clearly not nuclear specialists.

Prime Minister Kan's Visit to Fukushima Dai-Ichi

On the morning of March 12, as the nuclear disaster unfolded, Prime Minister Kan personally paid a visit to the Fukushima Dai-Ichi plant from about 7:10 A.M. to 8:00 A.M. News reports at the time were somewhat confusing: the nation was reeling from the tsunami disaster, and information about the developing nuclear catastrophe was unclear. On the one hand, some saw Kan's personal involvement as a sign that the government was responsive and that perhaps the nuclear disaster was not too serious if the country's prime minister was willing to pay a personal visit.

However, soon after the hydrogen explosions occurred and finger-pointing began, Kan's detractors began to accuse him of precipitating, or at least accelerating, the disaster by side-tracking recovery efforts on the ground. This image of Kan as an unnecessarily meddling figure persisted in media reports and a number of books.[3]

Delayed Response to the Hydrogen Explosion

At 3:36 P.M. on March 12, the hydrogen explosion blew off the roof of reactor 1. As television news coverage throughout the nation rebroadcast a long-range shot of the explosion captured by the local Fukushima television station, the government was unable to provide useful information for at least an hour. Television reporters and hastily gathered nuclear experts with varying degrees of knowledge serving as commentators were visibly (or audibly) shaken. It was not immediately obvious to most observers that it was a hydrogen explosion. To the general public, the video clearly depicted what seemed to be a worst-case scenario—a massive explosion at a nuclear reactor. Fears of radiation were foremost on people's minds, and on the government-funded public broadcaster, NHK, news station announcers immediately advised viewers to stay indoors.

The government's official press conferences took some time to acknowledge the explosion. Edano went on camera to say that a large shock sound had been reported, and they were confirming details—even as footage of the actual explosion was running frequently on all channels. He refused to acknowledge that a meltdown had occurred, despite a meltdown being almost certainly the only way that such a hydrogen explosion could occur. The government clearly conveyed the sense that they either were not on top of the details or were withholding information.

Only at 6:25 P.M., three hours after the explosion, did Kan order the evacuation radius to be expanded to 20 kilometers.

Evacuation Hazard Map Fiasco

After the two other hydrogen explosions, on March 14 and 15, the government expanded the evacuation radius to 30 kilometers. These evacuation radii were concentric circles around the Fukushima Dai-Ichi plant. However, given the wind conditions and topological features, the radioactive material did not fall in concentric circles. As it became clear soon afterward, the

---

3 For example, see *Yomiuri Shimbun* (2011a).

fallout exceeded the evacuation radius in the northwestern and southwestern directions, with very little dispersion directly west. This led to some evacuees fleeing from areas with almost no fallout, directly into areas with relatively heavy fallout.

A media firestorm was ignited later when it became clear that the government actually possessed a radiation diffusion prediction system whose predictions closely matched the actual fallout recorded later. Known as SPEEDI (System for Prediction of Environmental Emergency), the system was under the jurisdiction of the Ministry of Education, Culture, Sports, Science, and Technology (MEXT). It turned out that between March 11 and March 16, 45 simulations were conducted, clearly revealing the concentric evacuation circles to be inadequate. However, the government did not make these simulations public at the time.

Moreover, six months after the disaster, it emerged that U.S. aircraft equipped with radiation sensors had conducted numerous high-altitude fly-overs of the area and had collected and sent accurate information about the radiation spread to the Japanese government (*Yomiuri Shimbun* 2012; *Nihon Keizai Shimbun* 2012a). However, this information was not made public, nor was it used in the evacuation.

Explaining the Chaotic Response

Why was the government's initial response so chaotic, and how much was the DPJ, the Kan administration, or Kan himself to blame? The DPJ, after all, was much criticized for having difficulty with policy coordination after coming to power, and Kan came under fire for his personal involvement with detailed rescue efforts.

A close examination of the nuclear crisis as it unfolded reveals that the DPJ leadership was operating under conditions of extreme information uncertainty and communication difficulties, exacerbated by preexisting governmental organization and contingency-planning shortcomings. It is not obvious that the DPJ leadership itself was much to blame; the LDP or any other party in power would have faced the same problems. The accusation that the prime minister's excessive meddling in the rescue effort seriously hindered recovery seems greatly exaggerated. His actions also need to be put into the context of his personality, background, and previous experiences. While it is unlikely that his predecessors or successors would have become as personally involved in the rescue effort, there were aspects that aided the rescue efforts to solve information difficulties. Given the timeline of the accident as it developed there is no evidence that had Kan not intervened, the disaster would have been averted.

Physical Communication Problems: On the Ground at Fukushima Dai-Ichi

As the nuclear crisis unfolded rapidly, timely and accurate information about the details were almost impossible to convey to the public for the very simple reason that extensive damage at the Fukushima Dai-Ichi plant itself led to severe information and communication problems within the plant.

The earthquake severely damaged the operations centers, as ceiling panels came unhinged and file cabinets and furniture were strewn about the place. As backup power came on immediately after the quake, operators were able to confirm that the reactors themselves had succeeded in shutting down. However, as soon as the tsunami hit and knocked out virtually all the backup power generators, electrical switchboards, and most batteries, not only did the operations center go dark, but the control panel lights turned off as well. Critically, the nearby cellular communications tower was also damaged in the earthquake, rendering cell phones useless.

As the earthquake had damaged the operations centers at each reactor, the plant manager, Yoshida Masao, and his core team rushed to stage recovery operations at the seismically reinforced emergency operations center. Damage was relatively light at this center, which had been completed *just eight months* before the earthquake, without which there would have been no viable staging ground for the rescue operations at the plant.

After the tsunami, with massive damage on the ground and no electricity, moving between buildings, particularly after nightfall, with open manholes and other debris, created hazardous conditions. Therefore, Yoshida and his team had very little information to work with. Small crews staked out at the operations center at each reactor building, with only one telephone line connecting them to the emergency operations center. With no control panel indicators, they eventually used batteries to plug into each one to take readings. However, some indicators had been damaged and did not produce accurate readings. This misled Yoshida into initially prioritizing reactor 2, although reactor 1 turned out to be in much worse shape.[4]

To grasp the situation on the ground, Yoshida had to repeatedly send staff with flashlights into the reactor buildings to assess the situation and take readings. After 11 P.M. on March 11, as radiation levels began rising

---

4 For example, it turned out that the emergency cooling system in reactor 1, which converts steam into water, had started automatically. However, 11 minutes later, an operator had manually stopped *it because it was cooling the reactor faster than the guidelines* set by NISA. Yoshida, unaware that the system had been stopped, was given unreliable instrument readings and assumed that it was operating. He therefore prioritized cooling reactor 2 rather than reactor 1, though in reality reactor 1 was in far worse condition (Hatamura 2012).

rapidly in reactor 1, staff were not allowed into the building itself, further hindering information-gathering efforts.

Virtually the only link to the outside world from the Fukushima Dai-Ichi plant was a video conference system and a spotty satellite telephone link to TEPCO headquarters. The government did not have a direct communications link to the plant, and the plant manager had great difficulty in obtaining information about the condition of the reactors.

Information and Communication Problems at the Prime Minister's Office

Information and communication problems at the prime minister's office itself plagued the emergency operations, rendering Kan's official advisers even less useful than their structural position.

In the immediate aftermath of the earthquake and tsunami, the Emergency Operations Center became the headquarters of the prime minister's activities. The room was located in the basement of the prime minister's residence and was designed as a secure headquarters in the event of a national emergency. However, there was a critical problem with this room: It did not receive cellular signals. It received the designated emergency faxes and telephone calls, but both the prime minister and many key staff members needed cellular services to get information as they moved around. In particular, Kan, who strongly suspected that most established and well-known nuclear experts were captured by the electric power companies and could not be relied upon as objective advisers, began contacting the friends and acquaintances he trusted from college and other informal interpersonal networks. For this, he needed cellular reception.

By the following day, Kan had moved his operations headquarters to his own office on the fifth floor of the building. However, here too there were physical communication problems. While the room received cellular signals, all the official emergency faxes and phone lines were still routed to the basement operations headquarters. Faxes in particular needed to be hand-delivered by aides running up and down from the fifth floor to the basement as they worked literally day and night after the disaster hit. More than one source investigating the government's disaster response noted that the radiation diffusion prediction map from SPEEDI arrived by fax to the basement headquarters but never made it up to the fifth floor (Oshika 2012). Kan claimed to have never heard of the system itself. While the entire truth is unclear, the need to run time-sensitive data up six floors from a fax machine to the prime minister's operations headquarters certainly contributed to the information chaos within the top political leadership.

Organizationally, it was clear that one problem involved the location of the SPEEDI terminals. SPEEDI had terminals in NISA (within METI), the

Nuclear Safety Commission (NSC), MEXT, and the Fukushima prefectural government (and other local governments with nuclear reactors), but none in the prime minister's office. Yet it was the prime minister's office that ultimately issued the evacuation orders.

The U.S. military's radiation diffusion prediction reportedly arrived as an email attachment to a NISA official. There were no protocols or procedures on how to handle this information. It is not obvious that it was willfully suppressed, and may very likely have been the victim of the information chaos during the immediate disaster response.

Communication problems in the prime minister's office also hindered the ability of the advisers stipulated by Japan's formal nuclear governance structure to be effective. The formal structure is shown in figure 14.2. The NSC and the Japan Atomic Energy Commission (JAEC) are within the cabinet, advising the prime minister. Of these two, the NSC is responsible during nuclear disasters. (The JAEC advises on broader policy issues and strategies.) NISA was located within METI, with direct oversight of the electric power

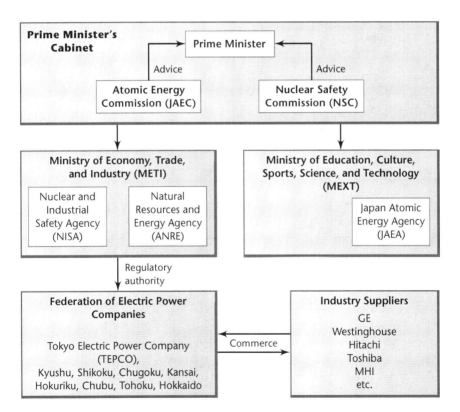

FIGURE 14.2 Organizational Chart of Japan's Nuclear Governance, March 2011

Source: Author.

companies. The Japan Atomic Energy Agency (JAEA) focuses on technical research and is under the jurisdiction of MEXT. Industry suppliers construct the actual nuclear facilities, as contracted by the electric power companies.

During the emergency, Kan quickly found that the NSC and NISA were not useful in providing live information or expertise. They were supposed to advise him from the Nuclear Emergency Agency (NEA), the establishment of which was triggered by declaration of a nuclear incident as faxed by Yoshida. However, the location where the NEA was set up, with close proximity and easy access to the prime minister's basement Emergency Operations Headquarters in mind, was in a small mezzanine along the staircase leading down to the basement. However, the space turned out to have only two phone lines, no fax (until one was installed two days later), and no cellular reception (Kimura 2012; Kurokawa 2012a). NSC, NISA, and TEPCO representatives could not get updates directly from their own organizations to advise Kan.

When NSC chairman Madarame arrived at the space, he found to his amazement that no diagrams of the Fukushima Dai-Ichi plant were available. NISA, rather than the NSC, possessed the diagrams, and for whatever reason, the diagrams were not as yet in the emergency headquarters. Given the various types of reactors and configurations in Japan's 54 nuclear power plants, Madarame, in advising the prime minister, had only his memory of the Fukushima Dai-Ichi plant and the television to go by (Kimura 2012).

To emphasize the point, *the nation's nuclear emergency center headquarters was an ad hoc office with minimal communications infrastructure, set up in the mezzanine of a staircase.* This was not simply an issue of DPJ response, but a deeper government contingency-planning issue.

The Organizational Weakness of the Prime Minister's Advisory Organizations

NISA had an organizational weakness in advising the prime minister. Because NISA was located within METI, NISA officials were not nuclear specialists, but rather METI bureaucrats who rotated through the agency every few years. They therefore tended to be economics or law majors from the University of Tokyo. In the opening hours of the crisis, NISA's top executive, Director-general Terasaka Nobuaki, was at Kan's side, informing him that the electricity had failed and that cooling was impossible at the Fukushima Dai-Ichi plant. Kan reportedly asked Terasaka if he was a nuclear specialist, to which Terasaka replied that he was a University of Tokyo economics major. Before becoming NISA's director-general in 2009, he had been director-general for METI's commerce and distribution policy. Kan repeatedly dismissed the NISA advisers who had been dispatched to him, questioning their background and forcefully pointing out that they had little operational knowledge of the nuclear power plants, let alone live information from the site of the disaster. He pointed out that they were actually relying on second-hand reports from TEPCO.

To advise the prime minister, Terasaka ended up making an emergency joint appointment for an official with a nuclear engineering background who had been assigned to the Natural Resources and Energy Agency (ANRE), also within METI. In short, NISA had to procure somebody from outside its organization to find an official with a suitable technical background to satisfy the prime minister (Kimura 2012).

In sum, there were severe structural problems with physical communications, information flows, and organizational expertise that would have created problems for any political leadership, whether DPJ or not, contributing to the DPJ government's chaotic response. From here we trace events as they occurred chronologically.

Delayed Evacuation Order: Procedural and Information Difficulties

Prime Minister Kan's delay in issuing the evacuation order was the result of several factors, only one of which was his personal judgment and the DPJ's incompetence per se. There were deeper problems with how the procedures were designed in law, and a critical lack of expertise in the government bureaucracy responsible for overseeing nuclear catastrophes: NISA.

The following occurred during the two-and-a-half-hour gap between the 4:30 P.M. fax by plant manager Yoshida declaring a nuclear "emergency in progress," which should have automatically triggered an evacuation order, and the 7:03 P.M. nuclear emergency declared by Kan.

At 4:54 P.M., Prime Minister Kan Naoto issued his aforementioned two-minute statement that the nuclear reactors had stopped with no observed radiation leakage, without acknowledging the "nuclear emergency in progress" report.

At about 5:45, the minister of METI, Kaieda Banri, arrived at the prime minister's office to join Kan and his two close aides, Terada Manabu, age 34, and Hosono Goshi, age 39, both DPJ members. Kaieda wanted Kan to immediately declare an emergency. However, although Kan listened to Kaieda's report and urgings, he left in less than 30 minutes (around 6:15 P.M.) to attend a meeting between the DPJ and the opposition, LDP, to seek cooperation in the earthquake and tsunami disaster recovery.

One must remember that, at the same time as the unfolding nuclear disaster, the government had to cope with the worst natural disaster to hit Japan since the 1923 Great Kanto Earthquake. It was the biggest challenge for the Self-Defense Forces in its history, and Prime Minister Kan was the commander-in-chief. Only after Kan returned from this meeting with the opposition parties did he proceed to finalize the emergency declaration (Hatamura 2012).[5]

There was a procedural problem, stemming from insufficient disaster preparation, that contributed to the delay in the prime minister's office declaring an evacuation. The immediate problem was that the prime minister's office lacked the know-how of exactly how to order and proceed with an evacuation order. At the prime minister's office, secretaries and aides were busy reading the relevant laws. However, this does not automatically suggest DPJ incompetence. It is not obvious that the LDP would have had such evacuation procedural know-how, since the elite bureaucracy would have been the natural repository for such procedural knowledge to support the political leadership. However, in this case, NISA staff also lacked operational knowledge to declare an evacuation.

A very serious information deficiency for advising the prime minister stemmed from the legal structure governing the situation. The relevant law was the Special Law for Emergency Preparedness for Nuclear Disasters, which had been formulated after a 1999 nuclear accident at the Tokaimura uranium reprocessing plant in Ibaraki Prefecture. The catastrophic shortcoming of this law was that *the law did not take into account the possibility that a nuclear disaster could occur simultaneously with an earthquake/tsunami disaster* that could disrupt communications and infrastructure.

The law called for a gathering of the NSC, which was to establish an emergency technical advisory group to advise the prime minister. The problem was that this advisory group could not physically gather or communicate with one other, since telecommunications networks in the Tokyo area were largely shut down; its infrastructure had been damaged while being overwhelmed with traffic. The NSC comprised about 40 members, but with communication networks offline, roads in gridlock, and all public transportation frozen, there was no way to gather the members or effectively advise the prime minister (Oshika 2012).

When Kan did finally declare a nuclear emergency, this should have triggered an evacuation order. However, Kan's staff was unable to effectively orchestrate evacuation procedures because they could not gain information about conditions on the ground, such as which roads were usable and the scope of the damage in the tsunami-ravaged areas. This was not simply a lack of experience or resourcefulness on the part of Kan's staff or the DPJ.

---

5 Kaieda later testified to a Diet investigation commission that it took time to get Kan's understanding and agreement to declare the emergency (Kurokawa 2012b).

The locus of information flows on the ground, as designed by the legal framework, should have been an off-site emergency operations center near the Fukushima Dai-Ichi plant. (The law actually stipulated the establishment of 22 off-site emergency operations centers.) The problem was that the transportation and communications paralysis, combined with the power outage, made this impossible. When a vice minister of METI, a DPJ politician, arrived by helicopter from Tokyo (after enlisting the Self-Defense Forces to get him out of the massive traffic jam within Tokyo) around midnight on March 11, the Fukushima off-site center building was still dark and unusable. Yet this was designed to be the information clearinghouse that managed information flows between the plant, the government, TEPCO, and the local municipalities—including orchestrating evacuations.

It was in this context of lacking information about the plant and local conditions that at 7:45 P.M., Chief Cabinet Secretary Edano Yukio advised the public not to panic and flee, but to stay indoors and wait, followed by the Fukushima prefectural government taking matters into its own hands and declaring an evacuation radius of 2 km at 8:50 P.M.

TEPCO's Leadership Vacuum

As the crisis unfolded, TEPCO was actually experiencing a leadership vacuum at the top. Its chairman, the real power wielder, and president were both unable to return to headquarters until the morning of March 12, more than 20 hours after the earthquake and tsunami.

The prime minister's office was unaware of their absence, fueling Kan's distrust and fear that TEPCO was grossly incompetent. Throughout the critical first day of the crisis, Kan and the government's top leadership were left dealing with TEPCO executives lower down the chain of command, and wondering why the top management was not immediately going public or giving them additional information or assurances for cooperation.

The difficulty incurred by TEPCO's chairman, Katsumata Tsunehisa, and president, Shimizu Masataka, are worth describing in detail to illustrate the lack of preparation by TEPCO and prearranged government-business coordination for the type of earthquake-triggered disaster that hit Fukushima.[6]

At the time of the disaster, Chairman Katsumata was in China on a tour with Japanese press and labor leaders. He had no way to return to TEPCO headquarters until the following morning. The Chinese government offered free use of an airplane, but the Tokyo airports of Narita and Haneda were closed. Kansai airport, near Osaka, was not an option either, since

---

6 This section draws extensively from Oshika (2012, 12–16).

domestic rail travel and freeways were all shut down due to the earthquake. Katsumata returned to Tokyo on a chartered flight the following morning. In the meantime, most communications lines were down within Japan, and it is not clear that Katsumata was able to communicate effectively with headquarters.

President Shimizu's attempts to return to headquarters would have been comical if the situation had not been so serious. On March 11 he was in Nara on a short vacation following meetings in Shikoku. His whereabouts were seemingly unknown to many of his staff. With rail and road transportation to Tokyo closed, Shimizu traveled to Nagoya, attempting to use a TEPCO-affiliated company's helicopter to fly to Tokyo. However, by the time he reached the heliport, it was discovered that the company had neither the equipment nor the permits to fly at night. Shimizu and his staff were then able to contact the government for use of a Self-Defense Forces (SDF) aircraft to fly Shimizu to Tokyo. The large C-130 transport aircraft, with Shimizu as the sole passenger, took off toward Tokyo at 11:30 P.M., eight hours after the disaster. Yet, due to a combination of questionable judgment by the minister of defense and information failures within the SDF, the plane made a U-turn at 11:45 P.M. and returned to its base in Aichi Prefecture.

What had transpired was the following. Upon hearing that Shimizu would be transported by means of C-130, the defense minister had ordered that all SDF resources should focus on rescue and recovery from the earthquake/tsunami disaster. The SDF at the time was fully consumed with the disaster, which far exceeded anything it had ever dealt with. Somewhere in the chain of command, the information that the aircraft was already airborne was lost, and the minister's order was interpreted as a command for the plane to turn back.

Shimizu had to wait until the next morning to take the helicopter, which landed him at the Tokyo heliport. From there he was stuck in the post-disaster traffic jam that gridlocked Tokyo on March 12. It took him two hours to reach TEPCO headquarters, finally arriving at about 10:00 A.M.—almost 20 hours after the disaster. By then, the Fukushima reactors were deep into the crisis—already melted down—and the first hydrogen explosion was about to occur. The prime minister's office and TEPCO had been working through the night, and Kan's mounting frustration and mistrust of TEPCO precipitated actions that were later used as fodder for attacking him, as we will see.

Kan's Personal Involvement in the Recovery Effort

As Prime Minister Kan worked through the night, he became personally involved in sending battery trucks to the Fukushima Dai-Ichi reactor. His involvement in the minute details of these operations later raised criticism that he was excessively meddling and had probably worsened the crisis.

Even before issuing the evacuation order, in the late afternoon of March 11, Kan directly dispatched power trucks carrying large batteries to the Fukushima Dai-Ichi plant. Kan was unusual as a prime minister for having an engineering background; an applied physics degree from the Tokyo Institute of Technology gave him a basic grasp of nuclear plant design and operations. He understood the critical need to supply water to the reactors and to procure electricity for the pumps.

At about 6:00 P.M., the Fukushima Prefecture Emergency Headquarters announced that TEPCO had sent eight of its power trucks, the SDF Fukushima base had sent one, and TEPCO had asked the Tohoku Electric Power Company to send any available power trucks. However, since all highways and roads surrounding the Tokyo metropolitan area were gridlocked, with many roads in the Fukushima area impassable due to earthquake damage, their progress was slow. Kan ended up spending time personally making phone calls to dispatch SDF power trucks. A whiteboard was carried into his office, with constantly updated information mapping the trucks' progress and route availability (IIC 2012).

With land routes uncertain and slow, Kan explored other options. Attempting to arrange an airlift of the power trucks, at one point Kan phoned the SDF, inquiring about the power trucks' weights and measurements. Finding the weight prohibitive for SDF helicopters, Kan also inquired of the U.S. military—but the trucks were simply too heavy. All told, 40 to 69 power trucks were dispatched by Kan's political leadership (IIC 2012; Oshika 2012).

After 9:00 P.M., one of the power trucks finally reached the Fukushima Offsite Center, 5 km from the reactor, though the building itself was not operational yet. More arrived over the next few hours. However, to everyone's dismay, they turned out to be unusable; the voltage was incorrect, and the plug sockets were incompatible. Kan was furious at TEPCO, and plant manager Yoshida's attempts on the ground to use converters within the reactor 2 building were unsuccessful, since extensive debris and damage within the plant prevented the truck from getting close. A 200-meter-long cable was needed, far longer than the cable equipped by the truck. It took some time to locate a cable within the plant, since much of the knowledge of such details was held by contract workers rather than by TEPCO staff. Then, even when someone remembered seeing a cable in a storage facility, the door lock did not easily open. As these reports flowed into the prime minister's office ("Truck arrived." "Doesn't fit!" "Needs longer cable." "Don't have cable." "Identified cable location." "Can't open door."), Kan's mistrust of TEPCO's competence and its sense of responsibility increased (Oshika 2012; IIC 2012).

Once the cable was located, transporting and connecting it was a challenge because it weighed more than one ton and most equipment was unusable. A four-ton truck with a crane was mobilized to haul the cable out of storage, and about 40 men began pulling it to where it was needed. Phones did not work, the area was pitch dark, debris was scattered, strong aftershocks kept occurring, and with manhole lids often missing, this was highly treacherous—and, critically, time-consuming—work.

At 11:50 P.M., with the power truck yet to be connected, plant manager Yoshida faxed another report to NISA: Radiation levels within the reactor building were rising.

Reactor 1 was clearly undergoing a meltdown, and it became clear that the instrument panel that Yoshida relied on was inaccurate, because it read that water levels were sufficient. Water levels were clearly insufficient, and the exposed fuel core had damaged the containment vessel, leading to radiation leakage (Oshika 2012).

All the while, the political leadership was unaware that TEPCO executives were not in command at headquarters, with Katsumata stuck in China and Shimizu's SDF transport plane just having turned back to Aichi Prefecture. Although there are no reports of Kan directly demanding that TEPCO leadership contact him, he and his aides were clearly frustrated at the lack of information from TEPCO. Kaieda later testified that they knew that the "messaging game" of indirect communications was ineffective.

Deeply mistrustful of not only TEPCO but also of government bureaucrats and nuclear researchers possibly tainted by TEPCO, Kan had already begun assembling a private group of friends for advice about the nuclear plant.

Kan's Background and Mistrust of Government-Business Ties

Kan's mistrust of TEPCO was not irrational; his background gave him strong misgivings about longstanding government-business ties. He had begun his career as a grass-roots activist and had gained widespread popularity while serving as minister of health and welfare in 1994 under the brief tenure of the non-LDP coalition government.

As minister, Kan exposed a major scandal enabled by government-business collusion. A private company had been providing untreated, HIV-tainted blood to hospitals, leading to a number of HIV infections, prominently among hemophiliacs and pregnant women. This company had been hiring retired bureaucrats from the ministry over the years, and the ministry had ignored an internal study-group recommendation advocating an immediate halt to the practice of providing untreated blood. It was government-business collusion at its worst, and the energy industry was also famous for providing post-retirement posts for bureaucrats and keeping academics on its payroll.

Kan's mistrust of TEPCO was only magnified by the leadership vacuum and its inability to provide him with satisfactory answers. His engineering background and basic understanding of nuclear reactors made it even more frustrating when neither his government advisers from NISA nor TEPCO personnel could answer his initial questions about the reactor design and the status of various parameters. These factors precipitated his much-criticized personal visit to the Fukushima Dai-Ichi plant.

Kan's Visit to Fukushima Dai-Ichi Plant, the Venting Issue, and Kan's Mistrust of TEPCO

When Kan decided to visit the Fukushima Dai-Ichi plant himself on the morning of March 12, his aides advised him against this visit from the perspective that political repercussions would be severe. Kan's decision, however, was rational given the circumstances and his doubts about TEPCO's willingness to undertake the next step of disaster aversion—a process known as venting.

Failing to restore power to the emergency cooling pumps by means of battery trucks, for which Kan blamed TEPCO's incompetence, the next option was to release the pressure inside the reaction chamber from the overheating fuel core. Unless pressure was reduced, the containment vessel itself could break or even explode in a Chernobyl-like fashion.

Most newer reactors are designed to enable venting without releasing radioactive material directly into the atmosphere, but the Fukushima Dai-Ichi reactor 1, whose pressure was rapidly rising, did not have this design.[7] Venting would release significant amounts of radioactive material into the atmosphere, thought far less than an explosion of the reaction chamber. It was therefore not a decision to be taken lightly.

Around 11:50 P.M. on March 11, plant manager Yoshida discovered that the internal pressure in the containment vessel of reactor 1 had reached 600 kilopascals (kPa), well exceeding its maximum design of 427 kPa. This was when Yoshida decided to vent the reactor.

---

7 The air vents in the reactors did not have air filters to reduce the amount of radioactive material released. These filters were installed in U.S. and European nuclear plants after the 1979 partial nuclear meltdown accident at Three Mile Island in the United States.

The venting procedure itself, however, was not easy in the damaged nuclear facility. There were two types of vents in these reactors: motor-operated valves and compressed air–operated valves. Without electricity, neither worked. Therefore, they would have to be opened manually. Yet, nobody in the operations headquarters knew the exact design or location of the manual open hatches. Moreover, this was knowledge held by contractors rather than TEPCO staff, who rarely went into the reactor buildings, and most of the contractors had left. Yoshida had to send staff with flashlights into the destroyed operations rooms in search of design schematics showing whether the vents could even be opened manually (Oshika 2012).

At the prime minister's residence, in the underground emergency operations center, Kan, Kaieda, Edano, Fukuyama, Hosono, the head of NISA, and a senior official of TEPCO debated the venting procedure. The politicians other than Kan lacked knowledge about venting, so they discussed questions such as the potential amount of radiation released and the degree of evacuation needed. By 1:00 A.M. on March 12, they decided that venting was necessary. They asked Yoshida to commence with the venting procedure after the government would announce its action at 3:00 A.M. At 3:12 A.M., Edano announced to the press that venting would occur shortly.

The political leadership expected imminent news of venting, but it never came. As Kan waited, his mistrust and suspicion of TEPCO grew. He suspected that TEPCO was unwilling to sustain the reputational damage it would incur by releasing radioactive material into the atmosphere. Yet, because not venting would produce a worse catastrophe, his concern was that TEPCO was incapable of making the difficult choices necessary at this time of crisis. After all, neither the chairman nor the president had contacted him personally. He did not know that they were not at the headquarters and would not return until the following afternoon. Sometime during the long night, Kan began saying that he would visit the Fukushima Dai-Ichi plant himself that morning.

A TEPCO executive was stationed at the prime minister's residence, former TEPCO Vice President Takekuro Ichiro. The prime minister's staff had assumed that Takekuro was in touch with the Fukushima plant directly and would be able to update them on the status of operating the venting procedure. At some point during the night, the staff was shocked to learn that Takekuro was not directly in touch with the stricken plant. Instead, he was simply relaying messages by way of TEPCO headquarters—something that the prime minister's staff was already doing. As the political leadership's frustration mounted, Takekuro could not provide clear answers to their inquiry as to why the venting had not occurred by 5:00 A.M.

The situation worsened before 6:00 A.M., when new, worrying reports came from the Fukushima Dai-Ni plant, 8 km south of the Dai-Ichi plant. At 5:44 A.M., the prime minister decided to widen the evacuation radius from 3 km to 10 km. The report from Fukushima Dai-Ni was that temperatures in three of its four reactors were rising; the tsunami had compromised its capacity to remove excess heat. It looked as though both Fukushima plants were headed for catastrophe. Receiving this news, Kan issued a second nuclear emergency decree, ordering that everyone within a 3 km radius of both plants evacuate, and that people stay indoors in the radius between 3 km and 10 km.

By this time, Kan's frustration with TEPCO for not having proceeded with the venting had reached its peak. At 6:00 A.M. on March 12, he officially decided to visit the Fukushima Dai-Ichi plant himself, leaving the prime minister's residence by helicopter at 6:30 A.M.

In the meantime, Kan had instructed METI Minister Kaieda to issue an unprecedented formal order to TEPCO to commence venting. Kaieda did so at 6:55 A.M. Kan clearly no longer trusted TEPCO to act voluntarily, assuming that it was deliberately delaying the venting procedures. It is not clear that the prime minister's office understood how difficult operations were on the ground at the plant.

Kan visited the emergency operations building at the Fukushima Dai-Ichi plant for just under an hour, meeting Yoshida and seeing the exhausted ground-level workers throughout the building. Kan was reassured by Yoshida's competence and strong leadership; this was the first time that Kan was satisfied with the answers he was given (Kan 2012). All his previous advisers from the government and TEPCO were unsure of the situation and status, largely due to communications problems. Yoshida promised that he would gain control of the situation even if it meant assembling squadrons of workers prepared to die in the attempt. During the helicopter ride, Kan was accompanied by Madarame Haruki, the chairman of Japan's NSC. Kan directly inquired whether a hydrogen explosion might occur from the reactor's zirconium case melting and reacting with water. This was a technical question requiring knowledge beyond that of most people. Madarame's answer was no; there was no oxygen, so there would be no explosion. In fact, Kan's question was highly prescient, since the zirconium reacting with water did indeed produce the hydrogen that triggered the explosion, fueled by oxygen within the reactor building. Madarame later insisted that he had stipulated that there would be no explosion of the reactor chamber itself—a far worse disaster than the building roofs (Kadota 2012).

Kan left the Fukushima plant just after 8:00 A.M. At the plant at 9:04 A.M., two-person teams began heading to the reactor building to manually open the vent. In the absence of mobile communications, the second group had to wait for the first group to return in order to get information. The first group successfully opened one of the venting valves. The second team, however, had to reach a valve located in a different area with less protection against radiation. Their analog radiation monitor soon exceeded the maximum reading as the indicator hand swung beyond the readings. Fearing immediate irradiation, they were forced to turn back before reaching the vent (Kadota 2012).[8] Yoshida deemed it too unsafe to send a third group into the reactor building.

Yoshida then attempted to connect a compressor to one of the vents that could be opened with compressed air. He sent staff to procure such a device from one of the contractors' offices. They succeeded in finding one but discovered that they could not find an adapter to connect the compressor. At 12:30 P.M., they used a truck with a crane to carry out the compressor and found something that could function as a converter.

At 2:00 P.M. they were finally able to vent reactor 1—almost 14 hours after Yoshida's decision, and 8 hours after Kan's legal order. The reactor pressure, designed for a maximum of 427 kPa, had risen to over 840 kPa at one point (Oshika 2012).

By then, the fuel core of reactor 1 had already melted through. An hour and a half later, at 3:36 P.M. on March 12, a hydrogen explosion blew off its roof and upper walls.

In the finger-pointing that occurred afterward, with TEPCO and a significant portion of the media accusing Kan of delaying recovery efforts at the plant with his personal visit, it is notable that the important facts have tended to receive scant attention. Kan ordered the venting hours before deciding to visit the plant, and the delay of two hours or so he might have caused would not have saved the reactor, given the timeline of events; the venting itself took place six hours after his departure, and the fuel meltdowns had already occurred.

---

8 One of them received a dose of approximately 106 millisieverts (mSv), far exceeding the yearly limit of 1 mSv deemed safe (the others received 89 and 95 mSv). The most exposed worker reported a headache and high body heat, suggesting that he had been irradiated, or *hibaku*—a Japanese term loaded with connotations of the Hiroshima and Nagasaki atomic bomb victims. There was no doctor within the operations center, so he was rushed to the local hospital. However, the hospital had already been evacuated, so no doctors were available there either (Oshika 2012).

The Hydrogen Explosions: Chaos from the Ground Upward

The government's delay in acknowledging the hydrogen explosion was largely due to organizational and physical problems with information flows from the plant upward rather than pure incompetence or willful information suppression by the DPJ. When the shockwave from the explosions hit, neither the emergency operations center at the Fukushima Dai-Ichi plant nor the rector buildings' operations centers knew immediately what had transpired. Many of the instruments did not work, and the operations centers themselves were windowless rooms, while the rest of the plant was thrown into chaos. TEPCO headquarters therefore did not have accurate information to relay to the prime minister's office. The prime minister, and more crucially his Nuclear Security Committee chair, Madarame, learned of the explosion from television reports.

Kan and Madarame were in the emergency headquarters together when an aide rushed in and changed the channel of the television in the room, which had just begun showing a long-range shot of the explosion. Madarame reportedly held his head in his hands, while Kan shouted something along the lines of "You told me there would be no explosion!" (Oshika 2012; *Asahi Shimbun* Special Reporting Group 2012). Put simply, NSC (and NISA) first learned about the explosion on television and were unsure until later what had exploded. They had no real-time information advantages over the media and general public, and although they immediately suspected a hydrogen explosion, they had no way of knowing whether the containment vessel itself had been breached until further readings came in from TEPCO.

On the ground, the explosion of the reactor 1 building created chaos and slowed the recovery effort. The blast damaged the emergency operations center building, blowing out the venting system responsible for filtering out the radioactive material. Until that point, they had taken great care to limit radioactive contamination in the building, with workers changing outfits for every trip outside. Now the building was completely exposed. Debris fell all over the plant, and staff rushed to confirm what had happened, assess the damage, and figure out how to continue cooling operations. Only two workers were injured, but the blast severely disrupted operations on the adjacent reactor 2. Falling debris damaged the 200-meter cable connecting the power truck to reactor 2, along with a fire truck that had been preparing to inject sea water. Workers had been close to powering up a system that would insert a boric acid solution at high pressure to cool the reactor, but fear of high radiation kept workers away; by this time, the core fuel had melted considerably. Five months later, TEPCO revealed that radiation levels near an exhaust duct between reactors 1 and 2 at this time read 10 Sieverts (Sv, or 10,000 mSv) an hour, enough to kill a person in forty minutes (Oshika 2012).

Seawater Injections: Fodder for the Campaign to Bring Down Kan

The next step in dealing with the crisis—injecting seawater—became the focal point of significant controversy later on. A barrage of media reports, which ultimately proved false and possibly were planted by TEPCO itself, accused Kan of severely accelerating the crisis, and contributed to a major public approval ratings hit for Kan.

As soon as the Fukushima Dai-Ichi plant lost all power, one of the first thoughts of plant manager Yoshida was to inject seawater directly into the reactor with fire trucks. Since the reactors were not designed for this, it entailed several risks, such as corrosion of the pipes, and what would happen to the salt left over inside the reactor after the water evaporated. In the late afternoon and early evening on March 11, Yoshida sent several crews into the reactor buildings to manually open the four or five valves that would enable direct injections of water into the reactors. It was a process that would ordinarily have been accomplished with the push of a button, but without power, staff had to traverse the inside of dark, hot reactor buildings and open them manually. The creation of this direct line to inject water from the outside was an absolutely necessary condition for the water injections that eventually prevented catastrophic explosions of the reactor vessels themselves. Timing was critical, since Yoshida sent the men before elevated radiation made it impossible to enter the reactor buildings by 11 P.M. Seawater injections were still a last resort, however, because it would mean contaminating a large quantity of seawater, and the pressure within the reactor chambers had to be lowered for fire trucks to be able to inject water (Kadota 2012).

Preparations for seawater injections were underway in parallel with the venting process, and after the hydrogen explosion of the reactor 1 building, it was clear that seawater injection was virtually the only possible way to prevent the reactors from spiraling out of control. During the late afternoon of March 12, after recovering from the hydrogen explosion, Yoshida began seawater injections.

The prime minister's office did not know this and, around 6:00 P.M. at the prime minister's office, Kan strongly advocated commencing seawater injections into the reactors. As Kan prepared to give an order to TEPCO to commence seawater injections around 7:00 P.M., Takekuro, the TEPCO executive in the prime minister's office, thought that it would look bad if TEPCO was found injecting seawater before the prime minister's office had issued the order. He therefore advised TEPCO to command Yoshida to halt the seawater injection until further notice, going so far as to get patched through to call Yoshida himself.

Yoshida, whose own life and those of the plant employees, along with anybody affected nearby who would be affected by catastrophic reaction vessel explosions, were on the line, acknowledged but disobeyed the order, continuing to pump seawater into the reactors. When Kaieda ordered TEPCO to pump seawater at 8:05 P.M., the political leadership did not know that seawater injection had already begun hours before, and TEPCO leadership was unaware that it had not stopped.

In the blame game that occurred later in May, much of the popular press was misled to believe that Kan had ordered a halt of seawater injections on his own accord, and TEPCO had obediently carried out the order, substantially worsening the disaster. *Yomiuri Shimbun*, the daily newspaper with the largest circulation in Japan, even ran the story as a headline (*Yomiuri Shimbun* 2011b). The dominant narrative in most of the media through the early summer was that Kan's irrational interference in a crucial disaster recovery effort had severely set back the recovery efforts, even precipitating the subsequent explosions. His approval rates dropped precipitously.

A full two months later, however, plant manager Yoshida spoke up and revealed that he had disobeyed TEPCO orders to stop seawater injections. (Yoshida himself had been working at the plant almost nonstop in the interim, returning home for two nights only more than a month after the disaster.[9]) Only then did the story come out that it was TEPCO's Takekuro rather than Kan who had ordered the halt in the first place. Yet, Kan's approval rates did not recover, and politicians within and outside the DPJ were calling for his resignation. Notably, the editor of *Aera*, a news magazine featuring investigative journalism, points to the source of the *Yomiuri's* false accusation as the email newsletter of the LDP's former and subsequent Prime Minister Abe Shinzo, who was likely to have been prodded by TEPCO or sympathizers (Oshika 2012). Indeed, the final paragraph of the newspaper article in question carried a quote from Abe denouncing the move and calling for Kan's resignation—an odd choice for an article that did not involve the opposition LDP in any other way than a critique of the move.

In the meantime, the crisis at Fukushima Dai-Ichi continued. For water from fire trucks to be injected, pressure within the reactor had to be released

---

9 Eight months later, Yoshida was diagnosed with esophageal cancer—not directly a result of radiation—and then suffered a stroke in July 2012.

through a safety release valve, but there was insufficient battery power to open the valve. Yoshida collected his employees' commuter car batteries to get enough power, opening the valve just past 9:00 A.M. on March 14. Foam from fire tanks was injected until the decision was made to switch back to seawater because the tanks were becoming depleted. However, at about 10:30 A.M., just as the switch was about to occur, a strong aftershock hit, causing a delay of over an hour.

Reactor 3, which was later thought to have reached temperatures exceeding 2000 degrees Celsius, had already begun to melt down at about 8:00 A.M. Earlier in the morning, at 6:50 A.M., as pressure within the reactor chamber had begun to rise, all outdoor workers were given evacuation orders. At 11:01 A.M., the reactor 3 building exploded—a much stronger explosion than that of reactor 1. A black plume like a mushroom cloud rose high into the sky. Approximately 11 people were injured, and the operations center was thrown into panic.

Efforts to sustain temperatures in reactor 2 were halted as fire trucks and hoses were destroyed. Vents had been opened approximately 25 percent, but the lack of instrumentation made it difficult to ascertain whether they remained open. It soon became clear that they had slammed shut. All workers were evacuated to the emergency operations center for some time. At this point, the battery for reactor 2's cooling system ran out, just after 1:00 P.M. Another process of gathering car batteries to open the safety valve to lower the pressure and connect fire engines was completed by about 7:20 P.M. It was then discovered that the fire trucks had run out of fuel, with no supplies on hand.

Kan, who had received this latest update about insufficient fuel, was furious, ordering helicopters to send in fuel and blaming TEPCO headquarters' incompetence for failing to provide sufficient logistical support (*Asahi Shimbun* Special Reporting Group 2012, 262–263; Oshika 2012, 120–121).

It was later estimated that reactor 2 had undergone a meltdown about 6.5 hours after the cooling system had stopped. By 10:50 P.M., Yoshida determined that the internal pressure had risen to 540 kilopascals (kPa), exceeding the 427 kPa maximum.

TEPCO's Abandonment Request Controversy and the Establishment of Joint Headquarters

After the hydrogen explosion in reactor 3, TEPCO executives began asking the political leadership whether they could abandon the Fukushima Dai-Ichi plant and regroup at the Dai-Ni plant, 8 km to the south. TEPCO President Shimizu telephoned Kaieda and then Edano numerous times, though the latter did not pick up. In events that became the focal point of intense scrutiny in subsequent investigations, TEPCO executives and Shimizu later insisted that they were not seeking permission to fully abandon the Dai-Ichi plant. They contended that they had said "retreat," implying that key personnel would stay behind to continue seawater injection operations. Kaieda and Edano dispute this view, contending that nothing was ever said about core personnel remaining. They argued that if it was simply a strategic "retreat" leaving necessary personnel, Shimizu would not have had to call each of them, and after making no headway, attempt to reach the prime minister (Kurokawa 2012b).

Kan was awakened at about 3:00 A.M. on March 15, with Kaieda, Edano, Fukuyama, Hosono, and Terada in the prime minister's office on the fifth floor. Kan was informed that TEPCO was considering abandoning the Dai-Ichi plant. Kan forcefully asserted that this could not happen. He summoned TEPCO President Shimizu at about 4:00 A.M., and Shimizu arrived at about 4:20 A.M. (IIC 2012; *Asahi Shimbun* Special Reporting Group 2012).

Kan was concerned not only about reactor 2, which was close to exploding, but also with the pools of used fuel stored in the reactor buildings of reactors 4, 5, and 6, shut down for maintenance at the time of the disaster.

The fuel rods of reactor 4 had been taken out of the reactor and placed in storage pools. The fuel rods still required cooling—at least several tons of water per hour to avoid additional nuclear catastrophe. The storage pools of these fuel rods, numbering in the thousands, were at the top of the reactor buildings.

Although the explosion that rocked the Dai-Ichi plant at 6:00 A.M. on March 15 was not from the "live" reactor 2, but actually from the building of the stopped reactor 4, in some ways, this was worse. The used fuel pool had 1,535 fuel assemblies (of which 204 were actually unused), each with a dozen fuel rods. Because the pumps had stopped, the temperature of the pool had risen from 40 degrees Celsius to 84 degrees. *Unlike the nuclear reactor cores, which were inside multiple layers of containment vessels, the storage pools were unprotected.* Once the hydrogen explosion blew off the roof and much of the walls, the pool itself was exposed directly to the outside. This could speed up the evaporation of water in the pools, which could then lead to various terrifying scenarios; if a meltdown began, the fuel rods could burn through the bottom of the containment pools, falling all over inside the reactor building. Radiation would be so strong that cleanup and cooling activities would be highly problematic, and a vast area would need to be evacuated, jeopardizing operations at the Fukushima Dai-Ni plant as well. Without sufficient protection from radiation in the operations centers, let alone near the reactor buildings, on-the-ground efforts to pump water into the reactors in both Fukushima plants would have been critically hindered; therefore, the possibility of uncontrolled reactions was a real possibility.

With the roof and walls severely damaged from the hydrogen explosion, a strong aftershock could potentially bring the entire water pool, with its fuel rods, tumbling down into the reactor building. This was not a far-fetched scenario by any means. On March 12, a day after the 9.0 earthquake and three days before reactor 4's roof and walls blew off, a magnitude 6.6 aftershock, centered in northern Niigata, occurred—a major earthquake when compared to almost any quake other than the March 11 quake. Moreover, the heavy lids of the containment vessel and the equipment that was used to move it were all stored in the upper parts of the reactor building 4, making it further vulnerable to structural collapse.

The U.S. government was highly concerned about the vulnerability of these used fuel pools. It feared that the bottom of the pool in reactor 4 had already given out, with exposed nuclear rods falling around the building. The U.S. embassy recommended evacuation of U.S. citizens living within a 50 mile (80.5 km) range, and Japan's stock market plunged as soon as news of the explosion at reactor 4 was announced.

Indeed, internal worst-case-scenario simulations within the prime minister's office suggested the possibility of an evacuation radius of 250 to 300 km. This included the entire Tokyo metropolitan area (IIC 2012). In interviews and Diet testimonies months later, Kan stated that his concern was that Japan as a country might not survive the accident if Tokyo had to be evacuated.

While receiving TEPCO President Shimizu, who replied meekly in the negative to the prime minister demanding whether they intended to abandon the Dai-Ichi plant—a response that puzzled those in attendance, since it seemed to undermine the purpose of his request to see the prime minister—led Kan to decide that the information confusion between the government and TEPCO needed to be rectified immediately. He took the unprecedented step of ordering the establishment of a joint government-TEPCO headquarters within TEPCO. He told Shimizu to get a desk ready for Hosono within half an hour, and that he, Kan, would visit TEPCO headquarters within the hour.

Kan rode into TEPCO headquarters at 5:35 A.M., announcing to the 300 or so employees working around the clock that TEPCO would not be allowed to abandon the Dai-Ichi plant. He told them that they, TEPCO, were responsible, and if they fled, there was no way the company would survive. This visit increased antagonism between TEPCO and the political leadership.

However, Kan's establishment of joint headquarters was later considered a critical positive turning point in managing the disaster (IIC 2012).

At TEPCO headquarters, Kan saw for the first time that there were video feeds from the Dai-Ichi plant emergency headquarters. Once Hosono and some of his staff were established in TEPCO's headquarters, they were able to communicate far more effectively with the prime minister's office, rather than waiting for TEPCO to relay information from the ground operations.

During Kan's visit, just after 6:30 A.M., a large explosion sound emanated from reactor 2. It later became apparent that hydrogen gas from reactor 2 had leaked into reactor 4 through a shared (and likely damaged) venting pipe. There it accumulated in the reactor 4 building, and when it ignited, the explosion blew off the roof and much of the walls. The sound of the explosion traveled back through the pipes and reverberated through the reactor 2 building. Yoshida sought permission to leave 70 critical operations staff for water injections and to take the rest of the approximately 650 staff to Fukushima Dai-Ichi plant to stage operations from there. Kan observed and interacted with the TEPCO chair and president during the exchange, because many of plant manager Yoshida's staff had been evacuated to the Dai-Ni plant. All the while, Kan continued to forcefully demand that some TEPCO staff remain at the Dai-Ichi plant to continue water injections. He was at TEPCO headquarters for approximately three hours, until 8:45 A.M. (*Asahi Shimbun* Special Reporting Group 2012; Oshika 2012).

At 11:00 A.M., Kan expanded the evacuation radius to 30 km.

Emergency Mobilization to Cool Used Fuel Pools

A positive turning point in the disaster came on March 17, almost six days after the earthquake and tsunami hit. The previous day, a SDF helicopter with TEPCO employees on board confirmed visually and through photographs that reactor 4's used fuel pool contained water and that the fuel rods were not exposed. On the morning of March 17, another SDF helicopter, reinforced with tungsten on its lower side to mitigate radiation, flew over the reactor and dumped a large bucket of water onto reactor 3, which was issuing white steam. Although the amount of water was miniscule compared to what was necessary even in the short-to-medium term—and disheartening television broadcasts seemed to show that some of the first buckets missed almost entirely—it was the first indication that the government was finally able to take some tangible measures to manage the disaster.

More importantly, on the evening of March 17, a number of SDF fire trucks equipped with aircraft catastrophe–grade fire extinguishers were collected from SDF land and air forces. At 7:35 P.M., they began dousing reactor 3 with water, taking turns for five dousings. The following day, they moved in even closer, hitting reactor 3 and expanding to cover reactor 4 from March 20. Coordination between SDF, the Fire and Disaster Management Agency, and the National Policy Agency was necessary for these actions, and the government succeeded in bringing them together (IIC 2012).

On March 20, power from the electricity grid to the Fukushima Dai-Ichi plant was finally restored. However, to the shock and dismay of all involved, the cooling systems did not restart. Monitoring instruments were unstable, and the motor to pump water to the used fuel pools did not work (Oshika 2012).

Luckily, further reinforcements for the manual hosing of the reactors and storage pools were on the way. A large concrete pump truck called *Kirin* (giraffe) was deployed on March 22. In an incredible (but in this case, positive) coincidence, it was passing through the Yokohama port enroute to Vietnam, from Germany; all parties agreed to divert it to Fukushima. Two other large concrete pumps, with cameras on top, also arrived from other parts of Japan, pumping water into the 30-meter-high fuel pools. On March 23, a pump truck with an arm reaching 63 meters high arrived from China, as a gift to TEPCO. Just after that, the world's tallest pump truck with an arm reaching 70 meters arrived from the United States. These measures were used until March 24, when the cooling pumps became operational (IIC 2012). On April 11, the government announced a 20 km radius for emergency and planned evacuation areas.

Let us now turn to the DPJ's medium-term reversals after the Fukushima Dai-Ichi reactor was stabilized.

The DPJ's Medium-Term Reversals

Soon after the Fukushima nuclear plants stabilized, Kan dramatically reversed the country's energy policy, calling for an end to nuclear power for Japan's electricity generation. Then he requested that Chubu Electric Company's Hamaoka nuclear plant, located in an area of particular seismic risk, shut down. This led to a surge in his approval ratings and a voluntary shutdown of all other nuclear plants in Japan over the next year.

However, Kan's successor, Noda Yoshihiko, almost immediately called for a new direction in Japan's energy policy, sketching several scenarios in an attempt to gain acceptance for a plan that relied on nuclear power at predisaster levels. He called for the restarting of a nuclear power plant in an area facing a potential shortage of electricity during the summer peak months. This sparked demonstrations around the country, mostly peaceful, including weekly marches in front of the prime minister's residence in the winter and spring of 2012.

Kan's New Energy Policy

In a dramatic press statement on May 6, Kan announced that as prime minister, through METI Minister Kaieda, he had requested that Chubu Electric Company shut down all reactors at its Hamaoka nuclear power plant.[10] He cited a MEXT earthquake research report released shortly before, which estimated an 87 percent probability of a magnitude 6 or greater earthquake within 30 years. Kan contended that until sufficient tsunami protection measures such as a seawall were built, it was his assessment that all reactors should be shut down.

Kan had no legal authority to command the plant to be shut down. When the media asked whether this was a request or an order, Kan replied that the legal framework did not specify the exact legal form of this request or order, and that it was up to each power company to make decisions about their plant operations. Chubu had been planning to restart reactor 3—halted for maintenance—by July to meet peak demand, but when put on the spot by the prime minister in the public spotlight, Chubu decided to halt the plant.

The Hamaoka nuclear power plant was particularly controversial, with an earthquake risk assessment of an order of magnitude greater than any other. On METI's list of earthquake probability of magnitude 6 or higher within the next 30 years, Hamaoka's 87 percent was at the top, followed by Onagawa, at 8.3 percent. All others were between 0 and 2 percent.

Kaieda had visited the plant the day before Kan's announcement and noted that the sand dunes in front of it would probably not halt a tsunami. The decision to request stopping the plant was reached in a meeting with Kaieda, Fukuyama, Hosono, Edano, Sengoku, and several METI officials, amounting to over 20 people, and announced that very day to prevent leaks to the press (Oshika 2012, 244–255).

Kan's request was quite popular. According to an *Asahi Shimbun* poll conducted immediately afterward, 62 percent approved his decision, and a *Yomiuri Shimbun* poll showed 68 percent approval. The approval rating of Kan's cabinet rose from 21 percent to 26 percent, according to the *Asahi* poll.

A few days later, in a press conference on May 10, Kan called for the need to rethink Japan's entire energy policy. In the question-and-answer session with reporters, he called for a complete overhaul of the Basic Energy Plan, the latest revisions of which had been approved by the DPJ shortly after Kan

---

10 This section draws heavily from Oshika (2012, 243–255).

took office, in June 2010. The plan had focused on reducing Japan's greenhouse gas emissions, calling for an increase in the proportion of nuclear energy from 26 percent to 52 percent by 2030. The plan called for the construction of over 14 new nuclear power plants (METI 2010).

Kan declared that Japan would reduce its projected dependence on nuclear energy from 52 percent to zero by 2030. He proposed that a bold, new sustainable energy initiative could compensate for the loss of nuclear power. In the meantime, he advocated that all reactors should remain shut down until Japan adopted an entirely new system of safety testing akin to European "stress tests." During the course of the following year, all plants were shut down, mostly under the label of "maintenance." Japan seemed to be on a course of abandoning nuclear power.

Noda's Nuclear Reversals

The DPJ's reversal was abrupt. Almost the day after Noda stepped into the prime minister's office, he began calling for a restart of the nuclear power plants (*Nihon Keizai Shimbun* 2011). He argued that it was economically essential to restart the reactors and that reducing nuclear power reliance was a possible long-term goal rather than an immediate imperative.

In January 2012, Kansai Electric Power Company's (KEPCO) Ōi nuclear power plant passed NISA's stress tests that simulated a "beyond design basis" earthquake, tsunami, and loss of offsite power events similar to the events at Fukushima in March. Two weeks later, a team of 10 International Atomic Energy Agency inspectors confirmed NISA's assessment but called for additional safety measures to mitigate serious incidents (*Daily Yomiuri* 2012a). In March, the NSC approved of the stress tests as well. In April 2012, the Noda cabinet gave its approval to restart the first nuclear plant since all were taken offline following the disaster. On July 1, KEPCO's Ōi Nuclear Power Plant's reactor 3 was restarted, followed shortly by reactor 4. While they remained the only plants operating by May 2013, the others were awaiting further safety assessments.

The Noda administration projected the sense that it was in a great rush to restart nuclear power plants. The choice of the Ōi plant as the first to restart was controversial. First, it had continued to operate after the March 11 earthquake, but a few days after it had requested approval from NISA to remain online, pressure suddenly spiked in an accumulator tank needed for emergency cooling of the reactor cores. It was then taken offline for maintenance in early July 2011. Second, experts soon pointed out that the Ōi plant was built on top of a fault line that bisected the plant and that this fault line was possibly active. Third, the plant had only a single access road that went through a tunnel, leading to questions about what would happen if the tunnel collapsed in a major earthquake—an earthquake that exceeded the tunnel's design parameters just as the March 11 earthquake had exceeded all design parameters in Fukushima. Ōi did not strike the general public as the safest plant to restart first.

The most controversial aspect was that Ōi's safety for its restart was approved by NISA, which was by then a lame-duck organization about to be decommissioned to make way for the new Nuclear Regulation Authority (NRA). In fact, the NRA's first action after its inauguration was to state that no additional reactors would be restarted until summer 2013, after the NRA completed drafting a new set of safety standards (*Daily Yomiuri* 2012b). It is possible that Ōi may not have met the NRA's more stringent criteria for restarting, and it is very clear that had the restart waited until the fall, when the NRA was established, it would not be restarted for another year at minimum.

The sense that the DPJ was rushing to restart nuclear plants while disregarding critical safety lessons learned in the Fukushima accident provoked a civil society backlash of a magnitude not seen since the U.S.-Japan Security Treaty renewal demonstrations of the 1960s. Between 100,000 and 200,000 people gathered in Yoyogi Park to protest the decision, and about 200 people blocked the road to the Ōi plant as the date for its restart approached (*Economist* 2012). Weekly peaceful demonstrations occurred in front of the prime minister's residence in the winter of 2012, initially numbering in the hundreds but growing to over 100,000 participants after Ōi was restarted.

Public opinion was divided. A *Nikkei* poll in June 2012 reported that 52.2 percent of the populace supported Noda's decision to restart Ōi, while 30 percent wanted to keep all reactors offline permanently (*Nihon Keizai Shimbun* 2012b). *Asahi* reported that 58 percent of the public preferred to abolish nuclear power within a decade rather than by 2030 (*Asahi Shimbun* 2012).

In September 2012, the cabinet adopted the position to gradually reduce nuclear energy by the year 2030. It pledged that the 40-year maximum age of plants would be strictly enforced, that no new reactors would be built, and that only plants approved by the NSC could restart.

As the December 2012 election drew near, the Noda administration's message about a nuclear phase-out became remarkably unclear. The adoption of a "no nuclear by 2030" policy divided the party and was not enshrined as official party policy until only weeks before the 2012 election in the form of a new "Innovative Strategy for Energy and the Environment." The strategy did not support new reactors but did approve recommencing the construction already underway of new reactors at Ōma and Shimane. Since nuclear reactors typically last over 40 years, this suggested an abandonment of the idea of a complete phase-out by 2030. In the electoral campaigns, the issue of immediate restarting was taken off the table entirely by the DPJ and opposition parties; their policy differences dealt only with the longer-term strategies. Voters therefore were not given a party-based policy option of nuclear abandonment. What shaped these DPJ reversals?

Politics Shaping the DPJ's Medium-Term Energy Policy Reversals

Internal political dynamics within the DPJ, as well as partisan politics between the DPJ and opposition LDP, contributed to the DPJ's medium-term reversals in its nuclear policy. These internal political dynamics stem from the political configuration of the DPJ itself—in particular, the role of Ozawa Ichiro as a polarizing figure who divided the party and drove policy fluctuations in his wake.

DPJ, the Dual-Headed Monster[11]

As has been shown in the introduction and other chapters in this volume, the DPJ suffered from a major structural problem when it came to power. Ozawa Ichiro, the stronger political force in the party, had long held a vision of the prime minister and cabinet actually running the country. To this end, he had moved to strengthen the cabinet. However, this vision was difficult to execute when he was ousted as party leader (and therefore potential prime minister) due to campaign-financing scandals. The DPJ was therefore a dual-headed monster in which the strongest figure, Ozawa, was in the party but not the government, while the prime minister, Hatoyama Yukio, was not the most powerful figure in the party.

As shown in the other Kushida chapter in this volume, this power structure created policy volatility when Ozawa and Hatoyama fell from power within the party and were replaced by Kan as prime minister and party leader. Ozawa-sympathizer politicians were removed from power, with many of the reform proposals shelved. Ozawa did not leave the party at this juncture, however, and mounted a campaign to remove Kan from power to stage a comeback. Ozawa, nicknamed the "destroyer," had strongly shaped the trajectory of Japanese politics since the early 1990s: when he defected from the LDP with his followers in 1993, the LDP lost power for the first time since 1955; when he drove key ruling coalition partners away the following year, the LDP came back to power; as his Liberal party became successful,

---

11 The author thanks Steven K. Vogel for this phrase and formulation. See Kushida (2011).

he merged it into the DPJ, becoming one of the key top leaders of the party. Ozawa actively maneuvering to unseat Kan from within his party was highly destabilizing.

Kan was in a vulnerable position from before the disaster. The DPJ lost its majority in the upper-house election in 2010, and Kan was blamed for suddenly proclaiming the need to raise the unpopular consumption tax. He was gaining a reputation for acting before thinking, and his administration's public approval ratings began to decline even before the earthquake. On the eve of the earthquake disaster, Kan was also about to face some questions about campaign finances (Oshika 2012). Prior to the earthquake, Kan's approval rating stood at 20 percent, and the DPJ was expected to suffer a series of defeats in the upcoming local elections, possibly resulting in Kan's early resignation. Put simply, both a large portion of the DPJ, as well as the opposition LDP that had gained strength in the upper house, were ready to attack Kan when the crisis hit.

Disappointingly for the general public, rather than using the crisis as an opportunity to put aside differences and work together to address the recovery, both the DPJ and LDP took the crisis as fodder to attack the Kan administration.

In addition to the attacks in the media, as we saw earlier in this chapter, Ozawa went so far as to mobilize a vote of nonconfidence by allying with the opposition LDP. In late May, while Kan was in France at an OECD meeting announcing a new energy policy to radically reduce nuclear energy and dramatically increase renewables, Ozawa's group within the DPJ joined forces with some opposition members calling for a vote of nonconfidence. On June 1, Ozawa gathered 70 DPJ members loyal to him to announce the vote of nonconfidence. Hatoyama publicly announced his support of Ozawa's move, and since the minimum number of members necessary for a decisive party vote was 81, the numbers were significant. After a meeting between Kan and Hatoyama the following day, Kan announced that he would resign after completing the tasks currently underway.

Kan's Maneuvers during Summer 2011

Kan's promise to resign appeased the dissenters, and the no-confidence motion lost handily. Immediately after the motion failed, however, Kan announced that his original comment did not imply that he would be resigning soon, and he refused to announce a specific date.

The opposition and Ozawa faction of the DPJ were furious, leading Kan to make an offer. In exchange for stepping down, he would get support, both from within the DPJ and from the LDP, to pass three pieces of legislation that had been stonewalled: a 2 million yen supplementary budget for Tohoku reconstruction, the authorization of a new bond issuance to finance reconstruction, and increased government investment in renewable energy (*Nikkei Weekly* 2011). By late August, all three pieces of legislation had passed, and Kan announced his resignation. To an embattled Kan, this was a policy success. To the general public, however, it was deeply disappointing that the Tohoku reconstruction supplemental budget was used for politicking, creating delays that would not have otherwise occurred.

When Noda came into office, he had a very different policy priority. He publicly announced that he would stake his political career on doubling the consumption tax—rather than the divisive nuclear policy issues or Tohoku reconstruction. His calls to restart a nuclear plant if necessary seemed designed to help quell the fears of big business, which would face major price increases if Japan had to continue relying on imported liquid natural gas (LNG) for much of its power generation to replace nuclear power. Noda's calm, pragmatic stance was also likely to have been designed as a counterpoint to the attributes that the media and general public seemed to punish Kan for—his seemingly impulsive and extreme policymaking style.

Conclusion

There are many lessons to be learned from the Fukushima nuclear catastrophe. Some of the most important lessons concern nuclear power safety and regulatory oversight in a world where China and much of the developing world is about to embark on major nuclear power plant building. Issues such as seawall and plant heights, compared to historical tsunami and storm surge data, for example, have become valuable avenues of inquiry (Lipscy, Kushida, and Incerti 2013).

Numerous studies have attempted to uncover why the disaster occurred and whether it could have been avoided (IAEA 2011; Kurokawa 2012b; Hatamura 2012; IIC 2012; Ohmae 2012; Saito 2011; Acton and Hibbs 2012). If distilled to its essence, the proximate causation can be traced to design flaws of the plant itself. When external power was lost—a possibility for any nuclear power plant—the on-site backup power sources needed to have minimal risk of failure. The height of the seawall, height of the plant, and underground location of the backup power generators almost guaranteed a catastrophic inability to cool the reactor. Supporting this point, the Onagawa nuclear power plant, 116 kilometers to the north, was hit by a tsunami of the same height but because it was built on high enough ground it escaped tsunami damage. Some nuclear reactors, notably in Switzerland, have gas turbines on-site to provide emergency backup power in the event of complete external power loss.

The deeper policy question is why the Fukushima Dai-Ichi plant was allowed to continue operations without significant upgrades, such as repositioning backup generators on higher ground, as in the case of newer nuclear power plants in Japan, or raising seawalls. Explanations ranging from regulatory capture to a closed "nuclear village" of experts relying on one another to propagate a "myth of nuclear safety" have been raised (IIC 2012). Aoki and Rothwell point to the organizational structure of Japan's nuclear governance, which worked well under normal conditions but was not well suited to cope with large unexpected emergencies (Aoki and Rothwell 2013).

Our inquiry in this chapter has focused on the role of the DPJ. Why was the DPJ's initial response so chaotic, and how much was it responsible for worsening the disaster? A detailed examination of the events as they unfolded reveals that it was a combination of the government's inadequate contingency planning and problematic organizational structures that made the crisis response extremely difficult for any ruling party. Kan's own personal leadership style, his engineering background, and previous experience with government-business collusion contributed to a particularly abrasive relationship between the government and TEPCO. Yet, as the detailed narrative also shows, it is not clear that Kan significantly contributed to worsening the nuclear accident itself. Arguably the biggest government failure was the evacuation that did not take into account the data from SPEEDI or the U.S. military. However, there is a strong case to be made that this failure was a systemic problem deeper than the DPJ's policy execution, since the evacuation itself had never been planned at an operational procedural level.

The DPJ's medium-term policy reversals in its energy plan were driven largely by the party's internal politics. Severe intraparty fighting, combined with a mantra of political leadership exerting influence over the bureaucracy, created a greater likelihood of policy volatility. In particular, the maneuvers of Ozawa Ichiro, whose loss of power led to Kan's ascension, moved aggressively to undermine Kan's leadership. While ultimately unsuccessful in grabbing power for himself and eventually leaving, Ozawa damaged Kan's reputation to the point that Kan's successor, Noda, saw political gain in abandoning Kan's stance on several issues. In particular, he immediately jettisoned Kan's opposition to nuclear power in favor of a more moderate road that was widely perceived as more pragmatic—both to business interests and a large silent proportion of the population that was not actively pro–nuclear power but saw the pragmatic need to prevent electricity prices from spiking drastically for the sake of the economy.

An accident of the magnitude of the Fukushima Dai-Ichi nuclear disaster rarely hits advanced industrial democracies in peacetime. The effects of such a disaster may have been expected to jolt the general voting public into galvanizing the political leadership to understand swift and deep reforms. The surprise and disappointment in Japan and for Japanese was how quickly the issue became fodder for political attacks and maneuvering within the ruling party, and for the opposition parties. The introduction and other chapters in this volume provide electoral structural explanations for the policy paralysis under the DPJ, as well as other policy areas that exhibited policy volatility according to the shifting power configurations of actors within the country. The new Nuclear Regulatory Commission was finally formed in the fall of 2012, well behind schedule. The early indications of stricter governance are encouraging, but this disaster serves as a cautionary tale of when political structural factors and politicking can lead to a paralysis just when everybody hopes for swift and decisive change, with political actors setting aside their differences to quickly craft solutions and reforms.

References

Acton, James M., and Mark Hibbs. 2012. "Why Fukushima Was Preventable." Washington, DC: Carnegie Endowment for International Peace.

Aoki, Masahiko, and Geoffrey Rothwell. 2013. "A Comparative Institutional Analysis of the Fukushima Nuclear Disaster: Lessons and Policy Implications." *Energy Policy* 53: 240–247.

Asahi Shimbun. 2012. "Survey: Scrap Nuclear Power Soon, More Than Half of Japanese People Say." August 25.

Asahi Shimbun Special Reporting Group, ed. 2012. *Purometeusu no wana: akasarenakatta fukushima genpatsu jiko no shinjitsu* [The trap of Prometheus: The truth about the Fukushima disaster]. Tokyo: Gakken.

Daily Yomiuri. 2012a. "IAEA OK's Stress Test Review Process." February 1.

———. 2012b. "NRA Chief: 'No Plant Restarts Before Summer.'" September 26.

Economist. 2012. "Japan's Anti-Nuclear Protests: The Heat Rises." July 21.

Hatamura, Yotaro, ed. 2012. "Final Report: Investigation Committee on the Accident at Fukushima Nuclear Power Stations of Tokyo Electric Power Company." Tokyo: ICANPS. http://icanps.go.jp.

IAEA (International Atomic Energy Agency). 2011. "The IAEA International Fact-Finding Expert Mission of the Fukushima Daiichi NPP Accident Following the Great East Japan Earthquake and Tsunami." In *IAEA Mission Report*. IAEA.

IIC (Independent Investigation Commission on the Fukushima Dai-Ichi Nuclear Accident). 2012. *Fukushima Genpatsu jiko dokuritsu kenshou iinkai chosa/kenshou houkokusho* [Fukushima nuclear accident independent investigation commission research and evaluation report]. Tokyo: IIC.

Kadota, Ryusho. 2012. *Shi no fuchi wo mita otoko Yoshida Masao to Fukushima Daiichi genpatsu no 500 nichi* [The man who saw the abyss of death: Yoshida Masao and the 500 days at Fukushima Dai-Ichi nuclear power plant]. Tokyo: PHP Kenkyujo.

Kan, Naoto. 2012. *Toden Fukushima Genpatsu Jiko: Souri Daijin toshite kangaeta koto* [The TEPCO Fukushima nuclear accident: What I thought as prime minister]. Tokyo: Gentosha.

Kimura, Hideaki. 2012. "Kantei no itsuka kan" [Five days in the prime minister's residence]. In *Purometeusu no wana: akasarenakatta fukushima genpatsu jiko no shinjitsu* [The trap of Prometheus: The truth about the Fukushima disaster], edited by *Asahi Shimbun* Special Reporting Group. Tokyo: Gakken.

Kurokawa, Kiyoshi. 2012a. "Message from the Chairman." In *The Official Report of the Fukushima Nuclear Accident Independent Investigation Commission*. Tokyo: National Diet of Japan. http://naiic.go.jp.

———. 2012b. *The Official Report of the Fukushima Nuclear Accident Independent Investigation Commission*. Tokyo: National Diet of Japan. http://naiic.go.jp.

Kushida, Kenji E. 2012. "Japan's Fukushima Nuclear Disaster: Narrative, Analysis, and Recommendations." Shorenstein APARC Working Paper Series (June). http://iis-db.stanford.edu/pubs/23762/2012Jun26_Fukushima Report_draft.pdf.

Lipscy, Phillip Y., Kenji E. Kushida, and Trevor Incerti. 2013. "The Fukushima Disaster and Japan's Nuclear Plant Vulnerability in Comparative Perspective." *Environmental Science & Technology* 47 (12): 6082–88.

METI (Ministry of Economy, Trade, and Industry). 2010. "The Strategic Energy Plan of Japan: Meeting Global Challenges and Securing Energy Futures." Revised June 2010. http://www.meti.go.jp/english/press/data/ pdf/20100618_08a.pdf.

Nihon Keizai Shimbun. 2011. "Noda naikaku hossoku—genpatsu saikadou susumeru, roukyuuka nara hairo, shinsetsu sezu" [Noda cabinet inaugurated—recommends restarting nuclear reactors, dismantling aged plants, halts building new plants]. September 3, 1.

———. 2012a. "Genpatsujiko chokugo, beikara osenchizu, monkashou to hoanin juumin hinan ni katsuyou sezu" [MEXT and NISA did not utilize the contamination map from the United States in the evacuation of residents]. June 19, 34.

———. 2012b. "Ōi Saikadō, Sansei ga Kahansū" [Majority support Ōi restart].
    June 13. http://www.nikkei.com/article/DGXNASFK12026_S2A610
    C1000000/

Nikkei Weekly. 2011. "Diet Begins Deliberations on Second Quake-Relief
    Budget." July 18. Accessed May 6, 2013. Lexis-Nexis Academic.

Ohmae, Kenichi. 2012. Genpatsu Saikadou "Saigo no Jouken": "Fukushima
    Daiichi" Jikokensou purojekuto saishuu houkokusho [The "final condi-
    tions" for restarting nuclear power plants: Final report of the "Fukushima
    Dai-Ichi" Accident Investigation Project]. Tokyo: Shogakukan.

Oshika, Yasuaki. 2012. Merutodaun: Dokyumento Fukushima daiichi
    genpatsu jiko [Meltdown: Documenting the Fukushima Dai-Ichi nuclear
    accident]. Tokyo: Kodansha.

Saito, Makoto. 2011. Genpatsu Kiki no Keizaigaku [The economics of the
    nuclear crisis]. Tokyo: Nihon Hyoron Sha.

Yomiuri Shimbun. 2011a. Boukoku no Saishou: Kantei Kinou Teishi no 180
    nichi [A ruined country's prime minister: 180 days of the prime minister's
    office paralysis]. Tokyo: Shinchosha.

———. 2011b. "Shushou ikou de kaisui chuunyuu chuudan" [Seawater injec-
    tion halted by prime minister's will]. June 21, 1.

———. 2012. "Bei teikyou no houshanou osen chizu monkashou hoanin
    katsuyou sezu" [MEXT/NISA did not use radiation map provided by the
    United States]. June 19, 2.

RECENT PUBLICATIONS OF THE
WALTER H. SHORENSTEIN ASIA-PACIFIC RESEARCH CENTER

BOOKS (distributed by the Brookings Institution Press)

Sang-Hun Choe, Gi-Wook Shin, and David Straub, eds. *Troubled Transition: North Korea's Politics, Economy and External Relations.* 2013.

Joon-Woo Park, Donald Keyser, and Gi-Wook Shin, eds. *Asia's Middle Powers? The Identity and Regional Policy of South Korea and Vietnam.* 2013.

Jang-Jip Choi. *Democracy after Democratization: The Korean Experience.* 2012.

Byung-Kook Kim, Eun Mee Kim, and Jean C. Oi, eds. *Adapt, Fragment, Transform: Corporate Restructuring and System Reform in South Korea.* 2012.

John Everard. *Only Beautiful, Please: A British Diplomat in North Korea.* 2012.

Dong-won Lim. *Peacemaker: Twenty Years of Inter-Korean Relations and the North Korean Nuclear Issue.* 2012.

Byung Kwan Kim, Gi-Wook Shin, and David Straub, eds. *Beyond North Korea: Future Challenges to South Korea's Security.* 2011.

Jean C. Oi, ed. *Going Private in China: The Politics of Corporate Restructuring and System Reform.* 2011.

Karen Eggleston and Shripad Tuljapurkar, eds. *Aging Asia: The Economic and Social Implications of Rapid Demographic Change in China, Japan and South Korea.* 2010.

Rafiq Dossani, Daniel C. Sneider, and Vikram Sood, eds. *Does South Asia Exist? Prospects for Regional Integration.* 2010.

Jean C. Oi, Scott Rozelle, and Xueguang Zhou. *Growing Pains: Tensions and Opportunity in China's Transition.* 2010.

Karen Eggleston, ed. *Prescribing Cultures and Pharmaceutical Policy in the Asia-Pacific.* 2009.

Donald A. L. Macintyre, Daniel C. Sneider, and Gi-Wook Shin, eds. *First Drafts of Korea: The U.S. Media and Perceptions of the Last Cold War Frontier.* 2009.

Steven Reed, Kenneth Mori McElwain, and Kay Shimizu, eds. *Political Change in Japan: Electoral Behavior, Party Realignment, and the Koizumi Reforms.* 2009.

Donald K. Emmerson. *Hard Choices: Security, Democracy, and Regionalism in Southeast Asia.* 2008.

Henry S. Rowen, Marguerite Gong Hancock, and William F. Miller, eds. *Greater China's Quest for Innovation.* 2008.

Gi-Wook Shin and Daniel C. Sneider, eds. *Cross Currents: Regionalism and Nationalism in Northeast Asia.* 2007.

Philip W Yun and Gi-Wook Shin, eds. *North Korea: 2005 and Beyond.* 2006.

STUDIES OF THE WALTER H. SHORENSTEIN
ASIA-PACIFIC RESEARCH CENTER (published with Stanford University Press)
Gene Park. *Spending Without Taxation: FILP and the Politics of Public Finance in Japan.* Stanford, CA: Stanford University Press, 2011.

Erik Martinez Kuhonta. *The Institutional Imperative: The Politics of Equitable Development in Southeast Asia.* Stanford, CA: Stanford University Press, 2011.

Yongshun Cai. *Collective Resistance in China: Why Popular Protests Succeed or Fail.* Stanford, CA: Stanford University Press, 2010.

Gi-Wook Shin. *One Alliance, Two Lenses: U.S.-Korea Relations in a New Era.* Stanford, CA: Stanford University Press, 2010.

Jean Oi and Nara Dillon, eds. *At the Crossroads of Empires: Middlemen, Social Networks, and State-building in Republican Shanghai.* Stanford, CA: Stanford University Press, 2007.

Henry S. Rowen, Marguerite Gong Hancock, and William F. Miller, eds. *Making IT: The Rise of Asia in High Tech.* Stanford, CA: Stanford University Press, 2006.

Gi-Wook Shin. *Ethnic Nationalism in Korea: Genealogy, Politics, and Legacy.* Stanford, CA: Stanford University Press, 2006.

Andrew Walder, Joseph Esherick, and Paul Pickowicz, eds. *The Chinese Cultural Revolution as History.* Stanford, CA: Stanford University Press, 2006.

Rafiq Dossani and Henry S. Rowen, eds. *Prospects for Peace in South Asia.* Stanford, CA: Stanford University Press, 2005.